Lecture Notes in Computer Science   12781

More information about this subseries at http://www.springer.com/series/7409

Marcelo M. Soares · Elizabeth Rosenzweig ·
Aaron Marcus (Eds.)

Design, User Experience, and Usability

Design for Contemporary Technological Environments

10th International Conference, DUXU 2021
Held as Part of the 23rd HCI International Conference, HCII 2021
Virtual Event, July 24–29, 2021
Proceedings, Part III

 Springer

Editors
Marcelo M. Soares
Hunan University, School of Design
Changsha, China

Department of Design
Federal University of Pernambuco
Recife, Brazil

Aaron Marcus
Aaron Marcus and Associates
Berkeley, CA, USA

Elizabeth Rosenzweig
World Usability Day and Rabb School
of Continuing Studies, Division of
Graduate Professional Studies
Brandeis University
Newton Center, MA, USA

ISSN 0302-9743   ISSN 1611-3349 (electronic)
Lecture Notes in Computer Science
ISBN 978-3-030-78226-9   ISBN 978-3-030-78227-6 (eBook)
https://doi.org/10.1007/978-3-030-78227-6

LNCS Sublibrary: SL3 – Information Systems and Applications, incl. Internet/Web, and HCI

This Springer imprint is published by the registered company Springer Nature Switzerland AG
The registered company address is: Gewerbestrasse 11, 6330 Cham, Switzerland

Foreword

Human-Computer Interaction (HCI) is acquiring an ever-increasing scientific and industrial importance, and having more impact on people's everyday life, as an ever-growing number of human activities are progressively moving from the physical to the digital world. This process, which has been ongoing for some time now, has been dramatically accelerated by the COVID-19 pandemic. The HCI International (HCII) conference series, held yearly, aims to respond to the compelling need to advance the exchange of knowledge and research and development efforts on the human aspects of design and use of computing systems.

The 23rd International Conference on Human-Computer Interaction, HCI International 2021 (HCII 2021), was planned to be held at the Washington Hilton Hotel, Washington DC, USA, during July 24–29, 2021. Due to the COVID-19 pandemic and with everyone's health and safety in mind, HCII 2021 was organized and run as a virtual conference. It incorporated the 21 thematic areas and affiliated conferences listed on the following page.

A total of 5222 individuals from academia, research institutes, industry, and governmental agencies from 81 countries submitted contributions, and 1276 papers and 241 posters were included in the proceedings to appear just before the start of the conference. The contributions thoroughly cover the entire field of HCI, addressing major advances in knowledge and effective use of computers in a variety of application areas. These papers provide academics, researchers, engineers, scientists, practitioners, and students with state-of-the-art information on the most recent advances in HCI. The volumes constituting the set of proceedings to appear before the start of the conference are listed in the following pages.

The HCI International (HCII) conference also offers the option of 'Late Breaking Work' which applies both for papers and posters, and the corresponding volume(s) of the proceedings will appear after the conference. Full papers will be included in the 'HCII 2021 - Late Breaking Papers' volumes of the proceedings to be published in the Springer LNCS series, while 'Poster Extended Abstracts' will be included as short research papers in the 'HCII 2021 - Late Breaking Posters' volumes to be published in the Springer CCIS series.

The present volume contains papers submitted and presented in the context of the 10th International Conference on Design, User Experience, and Usability (DUXU 2021), an affiliated conference to HCII 2021. I would like to thank the Co-chairs, Marcelo M. Soares, Elizabeth Rosenzweig, and Aaron Marcus, for their invaluable contribution to its organization and the preparation of the proceedings, as well as the members of the Program Board for their contributions and support. This year, the DUXU affiliated conference has focused on topics related to UX design and research methods and techniques, design education and practice, mobile UX, visual languages and information visualization, extended reality UX, and experience design across cultures, as well as UX design for inclusion and social development, health and well-being, and the creative industries.

I would also like to thank the Program Board Chairs and the members of the Program Boards of all thematic areas and affiliated conferences for their contribution towards the highest scientific quality and overall success of the HCI International 2021 conference.

This conference would not have been possible without the continuous and unwavering support and advice of Gavriel Salvendy, founder, General Chair Emeritus, and Scientific Advisor. For his outstanding efforts, I would like to express my appreciation to Abbas Moallem, Communications Chair and Editor of HCI International News.

July 2021   Constantine Stephanidis

HCI International 2021 Thematic Areas and Affiliated Conferences

Thematic Areas

- HCI: Human-Computer Interaction
- HIMI: Human Interface and the Management of Information

Affiliated Conferences

- EPCE: 18th International Conference on Engineering Psychology and Cognitive Ergonomics
- UAHCI: 15th International Conference on Universal Access in Human-Computer Interaction
- VAMR: 13th International Conference on Virtual, Augmented and Mixed Reality
- CCD: 13th International Conference on Cross-Cultural Design
- SCSM: 13th International Conference on Social Computing and Social Media
- AC: 15th International Conference on Augmented Cognition
- DHM: 12th International Conference on Digital Human Modeling and Applications in Health, Safety, Ergonomics and Risk Management
- DUXU: 10th International Conference on Design, User Experience, and Usability
- DAPI: 9th International Conference on Distributed, Ambient and Pervasive Interactions
- HCIBGO: 8th International Conference on HCI in Business, Government and Organizations
- LCT: 8th International Conference on Learning and Collaboration Technologies
- ITAP: 7th International Conference on Human Aspects of IT for the Aged Population
- HCI-CPT: 3rd International Conference on HCI for Cybersecurity, Privacy and Trust
- HCI-Games: 3rd International Conference on HCI in Games
- MobiTAS: 3rd International Conference on HCI in Mobility, Transport and Automotive Systems
- AIS: 3rd International Conference on Adaptive Instructional Systems
- C&C: 9th International Conference on Culture and Computing
- MOBILE: 2nd International Conference on Design, Operation and Evaluation of Mobile Communications
- AI-HCI: 2nd International Conference on Artificial Intelligence in HCI

List of Conference Proceedings Volumes Appearing Before the Conference

1. LNCS 12762, Human-Computer Interaction: Theory, Methods and Tools (Part I), edited by Masaaki Kurosu
2. LNCS 12763, Human-Computer Interaction: Interaction Techniques and Novel Applications (Part II), edited by Masaaki Kurosu
3. LNCS 12764, Human-Computer Interaction: Design and User Experience Case Studies (Part III), edited by Masaaki Kurosu
4. LNCS 12765, Human Interface and the Management of Information: Information Presentation and Visualization (Part I), edited by Sakae Yamamoto and Hirohiko Mori
5. LNCS 12766, Human Interface and the Management of Information: Information-rich and Intelligent Environments (Part II), edited by Sakae Yamamoto and Hirohiko Mori
6. LNAI 12767, Engineering Psychology and Cognitive Ergonomics, edited by Don Harris and Wen-Chin Li
7. LNCS 12768, Universal Access in Human-Computer Interaction: Design Methods and User Experience (Part I), edited by Margherita Antona and Constantine Stephanidis
8. LNCS 12769, Universal Access in Human-Computer Interaction: Access to Media, Learning and Assistive Environments (Part II), edited by Margherita Antona and Constantine Stephanidis
9. LNCS 12770, Virtual, Augmented and Mixed Reality, edited by Jessie Y. C. Chen and Gino Fragomeni
10. LNCS 12771, Cross-Cultural Design: Experience and Product Design Across Cultures (Part I), edited by P. L. Patrick Rau
11. LNCS 12772, Cross-Cultural Design: Applications in Arts, Learning, Well-being, and Social Development (Part II), edited by P. L. Patrick Rau
12. LNCS 12773, Cross-Cultural Design: Applications in Cultural Heritage, Tourism, Autonomous Vehicles, and Intelligent Agents (Part III), edited by P. L. Patrick Rau
13. LNCS 12774, Social Computing and Social Media: Experience Design and Social Network Analysis (Part I), edited by Gabriele Meiselwitz
14. LNCS 12775, Social Computing and Social Media: Applications in Marketing, Learning, and Health (Part II), edited by Gabriele Meiselwitz
15. LNAI 12776, Augmented Cognition, edited by Dylan D. Schmorrow and Cali M. Fidopiastis
16. LNCS 12777, Digital Human Modeling and Applications in Health, Safety, Ergonomics and Risk Management: Human Body, Motion and Behavior (Part I), edited by Vincent G. Duffy
17. LNCS 12778, Digital Human Modeling and Applications in Health, Safety, Ergonomics and Risk Management: AI, Product and Service (Part II), edited by Vincent G. Duffy

http://2021.hci.international/proceedings

10th International Conference on Design, User Experience, and Usability (DUXU 2021)

Program Board Chairs: **Marcelo M. Soares,** *Hunan University, China, and Federal University of Pernambuco, Brazil* **and Elizabeth Rosenzweig,** *World Usability Day and Brandeis University, USA* **and Aaron Marcus,** *Aaron Marcus and Associates, USA*

- Sisira Adikari, Australia
- Claire Ancient, UK
- Roger Ball, USA
- Eric Brangier, France
- Silvia de los Rios, Spain
- Marc Fabri, UK
- Ernesto Filgueiras, Portugal
- Josh A. Halstead, USA
- Chris Hass, USA
- Zhen Liu, China
- Wei Liu, China
- Martin Maguire, UK
- Judith Moldenhauer, USA
- Gunther Paul, Australia
- Francisco Rebelo, Portugal
- Christine Riedmann-Streitz, Germany
- Patricia Search, USA
- Dorothy Shamonsky, USA

The full list with the Program Board Chairs and the members of the Program Boards of all thematic areas and affiliated conferences is available online at:

http://www.hci.international/board-members-2021.php

HCI International 2022

The 24th International Conference on Human-Computer Interaction, HCI International 2022, will be held jointly with the affiliated conferences at the Gothia Towers Hotel and Swedish Exhibition & Congress Centre, Gothenburg, Sweden, June 26 – July 1, 2022. It will cover a broad spectrum of themes related to Human-Computer Interaction, including theoretical issues, methods, tools, processes, and case studies in HCI design, as well as novel interaction techniques, interfaces, and applications. The proceedings will be published by Springer. More information will be available on the conference website: http://2022.hci.international/:

General Chair
Prof. Constantine Stephanidis
University of Crete and ICS-FORTH
Heraklion, Crete, Greece
Email: general_chair@hcii2022.org

http://2022.hci.international/

Contents – Part III

DUXU for Extended Reality

DUXU for the Creative Industries

Usability and UX Studies

Mobile UX Research and Design

Hybrid Teaching Application and Exploration in the Mobile Media Era——Taking the "Interactive Animation" Course as an Example

Zhi Chen[✉] and Ming Cai

Beijing City University, No. 269 Bei si huan Zhong lu, Hai Dian District, Beijing, China

Abstract. In the era of mobile internet, the use of online and offline hybrid teaching methods can improve the effectiveness of teaching. The general trend of higher education is to combine traditional education with Internet education to meet the individualized learning demands of learners. Teachers should actively explore new models of education, and constantly introduce new concepts to guide the exploration of new teaching models. Online high-quality educational resources and learning processes bring learners a new learning experience, but due to monotonous presentation, lack of pertinence, insufficient online participation, and inability to meet personalized learning demands, it is difficult for learners to keep the state of deep learning. Based on the teaching practice of "Interactive Animation", this article analyzes the specific application strategies of the hybrid teaching model. Combining the concept of precision teaching, integrating teaching methods and teaching content, pursuing a hybrid teaching model that integrates online learning and traditional education, and applying data-driven hybrid teaching models to course practice.

Keywords: Interactive animation · Hybrid teaching · Dynamic learning data · Precision teaching

1 Introduction

The combination of curriculum theory and practice in animation majors, as an art major, has its own particularities. It is necessary to explore more attractive teaching methods to attract students, construct effective teaching methods, and be able to measure teaching effects. The "Interactive Animation" course is an optional Elective courses for freshmen. It is aimed at students who are interested in dynamic web pages and interactive animation and not requires their coding experience. The transition from basic design principles to create interactive animations themselves. The course also introduces the basic theories and design techniques of dynamic vision. It guides students to create content based on different topics. This course helps students to set up a knowledge system, combining online and offline teaching methods to establish a hybrid teaching system framework, and it uses UMOOC platform data to understand the status of students and teaching, completes the overall process of hybrid teaching.

© Springer Nature Switzerland AG 2021
M. M. Soares et al. (Eds.): HCII 2021, LNCS 12781, pp. 3–14, 2021.
https://doi.org/10.1007/978-3-030-78227-6_1

2 Background Introduction

2.1 Summary of Hybrid Teaching Method

Since 2012, benefiting from the speeding up of networks and popularization of terminals, online education in China has developed extremely rapidly. Online teaching has broken through the limits of time and space, and has made significant changes in curriculum, teaching, learning, and evaluation. However, in addition to the convenience of enjoying online courses, users also understand the shortcomings of online courses. MOOC has become the mainstream in the field of online education due to its diversified resources, ease of use of courses, and wide audiences. [1] However, MOOC faces the problems of "no prerequisites", "no scale limitation", "high registration rate, low accomplishment rate", and "indifferent teacher-student relationship". The students' basic knowledge is uneven, which damages students' confidence in learning. Some scholars believe that after the MOOC frenzy fades, SPOC, a hybrid teaching model that combines online education and offline physical teaching, may become a more popular teaching mode. [2] Zeng Mingxing pointed out that under the SPOC model, teachers can freely control the course progress according to their own preferences and particular demand of each student, They can select a small number of learners from the applicants to be included in SPOC course.

The essence of SPOC is to organically integrate high-quality MOOC course resources with classroom teaching, thereby flipping the teaching process, changing the teaching structure, and improving the quality of teaching. [3] Kang Yeqin believes that SPOC courses bring challenges to students that are not available in other classrooms, allowing teachers to return to campus again, return to small online classrooms, and become real course controllers. He Kekang analyzed the hybrid teaching mode of Flipping classroom. The teaching methods of Flipping Classroom have been reversed. Students watch videos and listen to explanations at home, freeing up time in class to complete homework or practice. Provide help for students in difficulties. Through the combing of domestic and international education reform methods, we can see that online and offline, the convergence of pre-class, in-class, and after-class phases is the trend of teaching reform. Li Fengqing explained the teaching design of the blended curriculum and conducted an indepth discussion on the three phases of teacher-student activities in the implementation of hybrid teaching. He proposed that hybrid teaching has many advantages like focusing on questions, promoting students' thinking ability and memory retention [4].

2.2 The Necessity of Face-to-Face Teaching

Some teachers use live stream lessons to complete online teaching, and this teaching method often has the disadvantages of a single organization, long teaching time, boring content, and low efficiency of teacher-student interaction. No matter Dingtalk, Rain Classroom, or UMOOC platform, the commonly used online teaching tools in Chinese universities are far less effective than face-to-face teaching by teachers and students in schools. There is no in-depth interaction between teachers and students during live teaching, and group cooperation between students is also a formality, and the teaching effect is greatly reduced. In addition, there are many interference factors in teaching, and curriculum management is inefficient. It is difficult for students to find a suitable environment for home study, sometimes they affected by other family members, network congestion, and insufficient hardware conditions. That has a negative impact on the perception of learning effectiveness and learning experience. The teachers have difficulties in classroom management and it is hard to achieve good teaching results.

With the enhancement of the subjectivity and independence of contemporary students' individual values, students' value orientations have shown diversified characteristics. The diversified value orientation reflects the progress of society, but there may also be a utilitarian tendency. The physical space of online teaching is uncertain. Students passively choose to study at home. Students who face electronic devices for a long time will inevitably only pursue the practicality and timeliness of learning skills and ignore the deep understanding of knowledge. Constructivism believes that the student learn knowledge is not imparted by teachers, but in a specific situation, with the help of teachers and classmates, using necessary learning resources, through meaning construction. Through the exchange and sharing of knowledge, students repeatedly stimulate, evaluate and revise each other, and gradually form new cognition. [5] if the students lack face-to-face communication, lack precepts and deeds from teachers, and lack socialized thinking collision, they will ignore basic theories and basic qualities, which may lead to deviations in personality and behavior.

2.3 Investigation on Platform Functions

The choice of teaching platform is an external factor affects students' enthusiasm for learning. A platform with monotonous functions and a cumbersome interface is bound to affect students' enthusiasm for learning. A fully functional platform brings a good learning experience. We made a survey of 65 animation students who have experienced 15 weeks of online platform teaching. The survey was conducted in the form of HTML5 WeChat form. The survey focused on the following two questions:

1. What functions do students expect the online teaching platform to provide?
2. Can the reminder and evaluation functions of the online platform improve the efficiency of learning?
3. What is the necessity of the "Communication Community" function of the online platform?

Among the valid answers received, 98% of students believe that the importance of platform storage functions (tutorial videos, live playback, note recording functions, etc.) is more important and above; 92.3% of students think the importance of platform evaluation functions (questionnaire surveys, quizzes, etc.) is more important and above; 87.3% of students believe that the importance of platform supervision functions (sign-in, course reminders, etc.) is more important and above, which shows that the platform has the above functions Can help students improve their learning efficiency. The survey also shows that the "Communication Community" function of the online platform is an effective supplement to live teaching and important space for students to complete exercises, answer questions, and consolidate knowledge. The teachers use the platform's announcements, forums, questionnaires, and one-to-one answer-function to feedback students' questions after class, and the records of discussions between teachers and students are also widely demanded by students. Within the duration of the course, a "Community exchange" system framework containing questions and feedback should be constructed (Fig. 1).

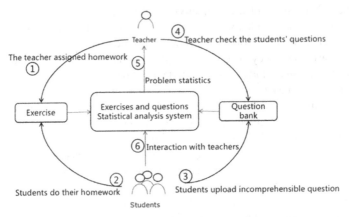

Fig. 1. "Community exchange" system framework

Teachers regularly post training program and design assignments online, and students are required to consciously complete them in time; assignments are allowed to be submitted multiple times to get the highest score until the score is satisfied. Students strengthen the knowledge they have learned in asking and solving problems again and again. The teachers can grasp the mastery of these students through the problem analysis system so that they can make appropriate adjustments in subsequent teaching.

2.4 The Concept of Precision Teaching

The Precision Teaching method [6] is derived from Skinner's behavioral learning theory, which advocates designing a measurement process to track learning performance and provide decision support. The development of precision teaching is relatively slow in the traditional teaching environment. The reasons are as follows: First, precision teaching ignores the individual attractiveness of a teacher and the personalized development of students. It obtains the characteristics of student behavior through data measurement. It is typical result-driven teaching. This teaching method lacks attention to the behavior process. Second, precision teaching is difficult to meet the talent training needs of design colleges and universities. There are many types of innovation and practical teaching courses in design colleges. The goal of teaching is not only knowledge points, but also emphasizes thinking methods and stimulating creativity. Some creative courses have the nature of inquiry and innovation, which are difficult to measure effectively. Third, before the popularization of information technology, the accurate measurement was carried out by paper and pen, which was inefficient. Today's data visualization technology can display measurement results more completely and intuitively. Just as Khan Academy provides personalized education to learners all over the world. Each student has his own assessment chart, uses the most advanced data analysis to identify learning progress and learning gaps, and recommends skills and knowledge to be learned in the next step. Use incentives and points to reward students for progress. Students will receive feedback on time instead of waiting until the exam to know their performance.

Case 1: Research conducted by Lei Yunhe—a member of the modern education center in Putuo District, Shanghai, China—believes that accurate information technology analysis can assist teaching decisions and is a feasible way to practice. [7] For instance, the histogram below the teaching video shows the pause and playback for students (Fig. 2). Where there are many pauses and playbacks, the knowledge points involved are accurately framed. Teachers can learn about the difficulties and confusions of students through the data records of pause and playback before class, so as to implement targeted adjustments in face-to-face classes. Therefore, it is very effective for academic prediction.

Fig. 2. Histogram of the number of video pauses

Case 2: Taking the reading and writing teaching content of the practical English course of Nanjing Communications Institute of Technology as an example, the course is based on the hybrid teaching exploration of the cloud class platform. The author collects student questionnaire survey data for the online learning part. The eight questions are divided into three dimensions: the completion of pre-class tasks, the completion of after-class tasks, and the analysis of learning behavior. The answer to each question has five levels ranging from "strongly agree" to "strongly disagree". Between 5 and 1, the students' responses can reflect their self-evaluation of online learning and their satisfaction to the courses [8].

As shown in Table 1, "Using online resources to expand learning" (M = 3.86), "Able to master the teaching content of micro-classes" (M = 3.85) and "Pause and playback videos to facilitate independent learning" (M = 3.94), three the average of each item is greater than 3, and the average of the other items is greater than 4. This shows that students are satisfied with their own learning state and can complete online learning tasks as required, especially pre-class learning tasks. Students can maintain a focused and concentrated attitude in the learning process.

Table 1. Mean value of students completing online learning.

Topic dimension	Item description	Mean
Completion of pre-class task	Watch the micro lesson	4.45
	Complete supporting exercises	4.02
	Complete other online activities	4.38
Completion of tasks after class	Review with online resources	4.13
	Use online resources to expand learning	3.86
	Stay focused on studying	4.05
Learning behavior analysis	Able to master the content of micro-course	3.85
	Will pause and play back the video to facilitate independent learning	3.94

3 Solutions to Hybrid Teaching

The content of the interactive animation course includes three parts: the integration of principles of animation and the concept of media; the introduction of software tools and code-free interactive technology; and the demonstration of interactive animation based on news works. Students need to understand the principles of animation in detail. These basic principles and techniques play a vital role in the aesthetics and style of the work. In terms of the mastery of software tools, students need to get used to using online tutorials to master the use of software tools. In terms of application, news-related works are an important field of interactive animation applications. Using group collaboration methods, students can use their respective advantages to jointly complete a work. On the basis of fully familiar with the teaching characteristics of the "Interactive Animation" course, the author mainly designs hybrid teaching from the following aspects: First, explain the principles of animation, digital image knowledge, and solve the problems that may be encountered in the use of tools. This part is done using short videos and online tutorials; the second is to share the latest interactive media works related to the course to students, which not only broadens students' horizons, but also urges students to create works that conform to design trends, and stimulate students' enthusiasm and innovation in learning thinking ability; The third is to combine the characteristics of the times and social needs, dig deep into the creativity and production skills of excellent works, and combine software skills within one's ability with creativity that meets social needs to complete interactive HTML5 media works.

Qualified teaching design includes three phases: course preparation, course operation, review and feedback. The design of each phase is essential.

1. In the pre-class preparation phase, teachers can upload the course content of the next lesson through the online teaching platform. These contents include explanation videos of corresponding knowledge points, explanation videos of the same knowledge points of other institutions, website addresses, and related electronic data. At

this phase, according to the students' foundation and characteristics, tasks of different difficulty are arranged, prompting students to preview and learn independently; after students accept the learning tasks, they can learn independently and complete related tasks.

2. At the phase of course operation, full attention is paid to the students' dominant position, and rigid "infusion" teaching is not carried out, and questions and assignments are appropriately based on classroom knowledge. Guide students to think deeply and give more time to students in face-to-face classrooms. Teachers and students can comment on homework together to inspire each other on how to improve and enrich the work, solve the problems and provide targeted guidance.

3. The review and feedback is also a key phase for testing teaching results. Teachers design effective questionnaires based on academic data. Students rely on the platform "Communication Community" to complete teacher questions, and teachers give timely feedback. In this process, teachers understand the difficulties and deficiencies encountered by students in their studies, and strengthen their explanations in a targeted manner to further consolidate their knowledge.

3.1 Helping Students to Construct a Knowledge System

For the "Interactive Animation" course, animation principles and design aesthetics are the foundation of creation. The course teaches students to recognize the principles of animation design so that students can be familiar with the relationship between pictures, actions, and time on a theoretical basis. In addition to teaching students basic theoretical knowledge, more attention is paid to the improvement of students' creativity and practical ability. In the hybrid teaching mode, students are allowed to discuss topics, art styles, and interactive technologies through the practical creation of specific projects, so as to enhance students' ability to solve practical problems.

Take the "70th Anniversary of PRC" as an example: the teaching goal is the mastery of image design and animation principles, the goal of skill is the use and effects of keyframe actions, interactive controls, and the goal of innovation is to construct attractive narrative methods.

3.2 Set up a Hybrid Teaching Framework

Traditional teaching provides more face-to-face communication, allowing students to become the protagonists of face-to-face classroom learning. At this time, the standard of curriculum criticism is no longer "systematic and reliable transfer of knowledge" but "face to the problem, reasonable and effective solution to the problem". Hybrid Teaching can effectively complement the shortcomings of single online learning and traditional classroom learning, support diversified teaching methods, and give full play to the guiding role of teachers [9] (Table 2).

Through the UMOOC platform, teachers can post topic discussions before class, and teachers can push different courseware, pictures, videos, and other learning resources to students, allowing students to conduct personalized learning. Students download relevant materials on the platform. The teacher guides the students to complete the task in groups, and finally, the teacher evaluates each group of students according to the task list and

Table 2. Hybrid teaching framework

		Teacher teaching content	Students learning activities
Self-study before class	UMOOC /Webchat	1. Uploading self-learning resources 2. Through interactive animation case URL 3. Set up pre-class thinking questions 4. Supervise student learning process	1. Log in to the UMOOC platform to complete the lecture 2. Participate in online interactive discussions 3. Reflect on the learning process
Study in class	Face-to-face teaching	1. Complete the explanation of the idea of the process of the media news case 2. Complete the explanation of the technical points of the production process 3. Set tasks, set up specific topics 4. Assist students to form groups	1. Complete the lecture, understand the key and difficult points 2. Exchange Q&A via online forums 3. Participate in group cooperation tasks, compile plans, collect materials, create creativity and production 4. Show results, mutual evaluation
Consolidate and expand learning after class	UMOOC /Webchat	1. Evaluation feedback homework 2. Comment on works and provide suggestions 3. Answer questions and guide extended learning 4. Reflect on the teaching process	1. Complete works, mutual evaluation 2. Watch the video repeatedly to consolidate knowledge 3. Learning to expend resources 4. Reflect on the learning process

classroom assessment standards. After class, the teacher uses the UMOOC platform to track the students' online time and the number of times the students have posted this topic, combined with pre-class homework, group scoring, and test scores, to give students a comprehensive learning evaluation of this unit. Focusing on the specific needs in the teaching process, the excellent curtain course platform connects the "content and the group of teachers and students" to meet the needs of the colleges and universities for the entire teaching process of "teaching operation, teaching management, examination evaluation, and effect evaluation".

3.3 Instant Communication and Group Collaboration

Group collaboration is a necessary quality for future career development, and interactive animation works often require multi-player collaboration. Therefore, it is necessary to use group collaboration to let students learn to manage planned tasks, deal with conflicts and contradictions, and learn to solve problems through communication. Teachers assume the role of facilitator and instructor of student learning and help the project run more efficiently. After the assignments were released in the sixth week, the 23 students in the class formed five groups of students to design their own assignments. Interactive animation works pay equal attention to art and technology and integrate various media forms such as text pictures, audio, and video, panoramic views, charts, animations, etc. It requires team members to perform their duties under a unified guiding ideology. These tasks include project management, collecting material, editing video and sound, writing copy, image processing, data visualization, and overcoming technical difficulties. According to different task propositions, students conduct creative selection and plan discussion to stimulate execution and interest in learning. Students are full of expectations and curiosity about the upcoming project. In the specific cooperation process, students may also use conventional social software to complete communication (Fig. 3). Group collaboration allows students to realize the atmosphere and culture of mutual cooperation and mutual support between themselves and other members. As shown in Fig. 4, students use social software to discuss whether the proportions and voices of the characters of their works are appropriate.

Fig. 3. Group collaboration to discuss creation details

Learning is a process of sharing wisdom. Each member ought to and have to be able to contribute to the realization of common goals. In this process, both teachers and students are equally essential participants in teaching. The teacher plays the role of guidance and feedback, provides necessary and effective support for each student, and guides students to essential concepts or theories during the exchange process. Team members can not only further reflect on and re-evaluate the already formed plan, but also work hard to defend their own opinions, and gain their own creative ability in the collision of views.

3.4 Collecting and Analyzing Dynamic Learning Data Through the Teaching Platform

In the current university Smart-campus system in China, the background data of academic situation mainly comes from student management and institutional operating data, such as educational administration management system, library management system, student management system, online teaching platform, online learning space, etc. The visualization of these data results is equivalent to making user portraits for students. Students' knowledge background, grades and performance, and effort level can be understood through user portraits. Curriculum operation data comes from real-time data generated during teaching operation. This is an important indicator of classroom teaching effect evaluation and the key to the accurate and personalized recommendation.

Through the online teaching platform to collect and analyze dynamic data in real-time, the classroom can only be judged qualitatively based on the teacher's experience in the classroom, to achieve a quantitative collection of classroom teaching information, instant feedback of teaching evaluation, and intelligent push to expand teaching resources. These functions are available on the UMOOC platform of Beijing City University, which can make statistics on teaching interaction. Which students are liked the most, what is the correct rate of the students in answering questions, how active are they participating in various learning activities online, and the classroom interaction data such as resource broadcasting, classroom assessment, questionnaire survey activities, topic discussions, etc. can be recorded and counted. Through these intuitive data, it can assist teachers to understand the learning situation in real-time and reflect the three-dimensional teaching interaction.

For art students, the time freedom of Hybrid Teaching is higher, and based on the knowledge points they have mastered, they can choose more abundant high-quality resources for learning to make improvement. For teachers, individualized education can be carried out through the collection and feedback of questions and evaluations on the platform. After the course is over, objective assignments can be submitted through the online platform, and data analysis can be performed in the background to calculate the overall knowledge of the class (Fig. 4). At the same time, teachers can also understand the individual learning situation of students based on statistical data and teach students in accordance with their aptitude.

The "Interactive Animation" Hybrid Teaching has been running for 10 weeks. From the perspective of the excellent rate of ordinary homework in teaching, it is much higher than before, this model has indeed achieved results. In addition, the platform can accurately check-in. Whether each video student is really learning and whether it is repeatedly

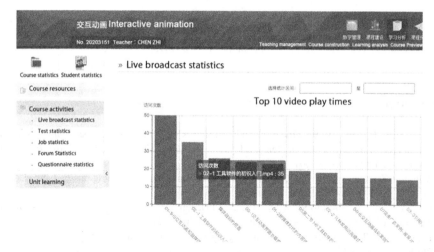

Fig. 4. "Interactive Animation" course video play times TOP10

watched, these data can be seen at a glance. In order to prevent students from unrealistically watching the video, a question will pop up during the video playback and require students to answer it. After the answer, the playback can continue. Hybrid Teaching also has a better supervision on students who do not submit homework on time.

4 Follow-Up Work and Outlook

In the era of mobile internet, teachers ought to make full use of Hybrid Teaching. This method not only needs to change the thinking of teachers and students but also needs to adjust the advantages of online and offline teaching in a targeted manner. This model is used in the teaching of the "Interactive Animation" course, the student's make-up test rate has dropped significantly, and the student's average score has improved significantly, indicating that this model has fully mobilized students' learning enthusiasm and achieved good teaching results. With the development of the times and the continuous advancement of science and technology, the integration and innovation of "Internet+education" has become a new topic. The technical means of precision teaching make the teacher's management of students' assignment convenient and efficient, forming a multi-dimensional curriculum evaluation system.

Acknowledgements. This research was supported by the Educational science research project of Beijing City University for program "Design enlightenment module - interactive animation" network course construction (project approval no. YJB20190735).

References

1. Hew, K.F., Cheung, W.S.: Students' and instructors' use of massive open online courses (MOOCs): Motivations and challenges. J. Educ. Res. Rev. **12**, 45–58 (2014). https://doi.org/10.1016/j.edurev.2014.05.001
2. Minxing, Z., et al.: From MOOC to SPOC: construction of a deep learning model. China Educ. Technol. **53**(11), 28–34 (2015)
3. Fox, A.: From MOOCs to SPOCs [EB/OL], 20 December 2013. http://cacm.acm.org/magazines/2013/12/169931-from-moocs-to-spocs/fulltext,2013-12-20
4. Fengqing, L.: Theoretical basis and teaching design of blended teaching. Mod. Educ. Technol. **26**(09), 18–24 (2016)
5. Changpin, H., Jiming, H.: Analysis of knowledge innovation service organization based on group interactive learning. Lib. Forum **29**(06), 54–57 (2009)
6. Lindsley, O.R.: Precision teaching: discoveries and effects. J. Appl. Behav. Anal. **1**, 51–57 (1992)
7. Yunhe, L., Zhiting, Z.: Accurate teaching decision based on pre learning data analysis. Chin. Electron. Educ. **06**, 27–35 (2016)
8. Danhui, H.: An empirical study of blended English teaching in higher vocational colleges based on cloud class platform. J. Ningbo Polytech. **24**(05), 32–39 (2020)
9. Jing, W., Zhuo, Y.: Design of hybrid teaching mode based on cloud classroom. Chin. Electron. Educ. **102**(04), 85–89 (2017)

Effects of Visual Cue Design and Gender Differences on Wayfinding Using Mobile Devices

Xiao Li$^{(\boxtimes)}$ ⓘ and Chien-Hsiung Chen ⓘ

Department of Design, National Taiwan University of Science and Technology,
Taipei City 10607, Taiwan
{d10410801,cchen}@mail.ntust.edu.tw

Abstract. The purpose of this study is to investigate the factors of visual cue and gender on users' wayfinding performance with mobile maps. The research variables were the visual cue designs (dot and border-line) and gender (males and females). Forty young adults participated in this study. This experiment is a 2 × 2 between-subjects design. All of the participants were invited to complete three wayfinding tasks. The NASA Task Load Index (NASA-TLX) questionnaire was also adopted. The results showed that different visual cue designs can affect users' wayfinding performance and reduce the perceived task load. When recognizing a route, the border-line visual cue exhibited better performance. Male and female participants perceived differences in the task workload aspect of temporal demand.

Keywords: Visual cue · Gender differences · Mobile device · User interface · Wayfinding

1 Introduction

Wayfinding happens in people's daily life. The term "wayfinding" was defined by Kevin Lynch [1] in 1960 as "the process of determining and following a path or route between an origin and destination." Typical wayfinding tasks include searching for landmarks, exploration, and route planning [2]. Researchers have also investigated several types of tasks, such as distinguishing order [3], route distance recognition, and route recognition [4], to test the various wayfinding scenarios.

With the rapid development of technologies, diverse types of information have become accessible from smart portable products, such as laptops, mobile phones, remote controls, wearable devices, etc. These products are accessible and portable, which has implications for wayfinding anywhere. With technology development, using the technology (e.g., peepholes) to obtain information for mobile wayfinding is not brand new in our current daily life [5, 6].

However, wayfinding with a mobile device often causes problems. It is difficult to immediately acquire information from large maps by using a mobile device. Thus, the limited mobile device screen size increases the difficulty of completing wayfinding [7]. To solve this problem, previous studies have designed visual cues to help users find the destination via a mobile map. Those visual cues appear in the screen's border region

© Springer Nature Switzerland AG 2021
M. M. Soares et al. (Eds.): HCII 2021, LNCS 12781, pp. 15–24, 2021.
https://doi.org/10.1007/978-3-030-78227-6_2

to help provide users with location awareness pertaining to the off-screen targets on a limited screen.

Many researchers have discussed the effect of gender differences in wayfinding and their workload [8] during the process of wayfinding. Gender differences appear to have a significant effect on the wayfinding strategy [9–11]. However, there has been limited research on gender differences as a variable in a peephole interface. Therefore, this study explored gender and different visual cues on users' wayfinding performance for mobile devices.

2   Method

In this study, a 2 × 2 between-subjects design was adopted, i.e., the dependent variables were "visual cue designs (dot and border-line)" and "gender (males and females)." The dependent variables were the participants' task performance and the scores obtained from the NASA-TLX questionnaire [12]. A total of three wayfinding tasks (i.e., Order distinguishing [3], Route distance recognition, and Route recognition [4]) were determined to test the participants' mobile wayfinding scenarios. The participants completed three tasks in each arranged set with the order and sequence effects controlled. The research model of this study is shown in Fig. 1.

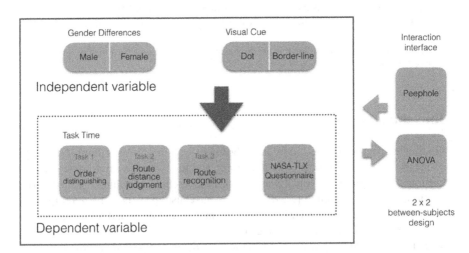

Fig. 1. Research model of this study.

2.1   Participants

A total of 13 males and 27 females in the range of 18 to 30 years old (mean = 21.98, SD = 1.510) were recruited to take part in the experiment by using the convenience sampling method. All participants had their own mobile devices, of whom 87.5% had more than two years' experience of using mobile devices for wayfinding, with 42.5% performing wayfinding for less than 10 min per week, 45.0% spending an average of 11–30 min per week, and 5.0% more than 30 min per week.

2.2 Materials and Apparatus

The experimental design in this study adopted the C++ language. The hardware comprised a Dell Venue 8 Pro with an 8-inch screen, 1200×800 pixels, and 189 dpi. A Creative Senz 3D depth camera was used to detect the screen of this experiment. In this

Fig. 2. The technical setup of this experiment.

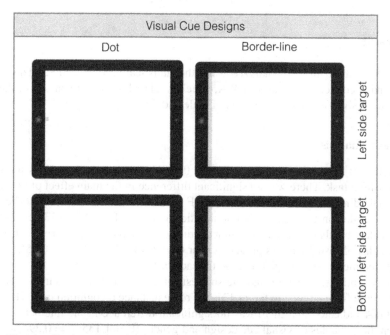

Fig. 3. The visualization of the visual cue designs (i.e., dot and border-line). Note: there are two distinct scenarios as the direction indicator. For example, the targets located on the left side of the display (shown in the top row), and the targets located on the bottom left side of the display (shown in the bottom row).

study, participants used the peephole as the interactive mode throughout the experiment, as shown in Fig. 2. A previous study [13] investigated the peephole which is formed by physically moving the screen of the device to the expected position in order to search for the off-screen targets in the experiment. Figure 3 shows the two types of visual cue designs in the experiment, the dot and the border-line, which provide a cue along the border region of the device screen to function as a wayfinding aid.

2.3 Experimental Procedure

The whole experiment was conducted in a laboratory. The 40 participants were randomly assigned to one of the visual cue groups by the method of randomized block design. First, the participants were provided with the mobile device and were informed of the experiment's purpose. Second, the tasks were explained and described to them. Third, after they operated with the mobile device for 5 min, the main session began. The participants completed the tasks, and their performance was recorded. Task 1 is the order distinguishing task. They were asked to search for the eight targets in ascending order. Task 2 is the route distance recognition task. They were asked to identify the shortest routes between the target and another target. Task 3 is the route recognition task. They were asked to plan a correct route between two targets. Third, after completing the tasks with one condition, the participants completed the unweighted version of the NASA-TLX questionnaire to assess their perceived task load.

3   Results

In this study, the data were analyzed using the statistical software, SPSS. The results were conducted from two-way ANOVA, which is related to the comparison of the two visual cue designs and the comparison of male and female participants.

3.1 Task Analysis

The first task: "Please find eight targets in the order of targets 1 to 8" is the order distinguishing task. There was no significant difference in the main effect of visual cue design regarding the task completion time ($F = 1.074$, $P = 0.307 > 0.05$). The main effect of gender on task time was not significant ($F = 0.114$, $P = 0.738 > 0.05$). It also revealed that there existed no significant difference in the interaction effect between the variables of visual cue design and gender ($F = 0.019$, $P = 0.892 > 0.05$). Table 1 presents the mean task completion time for each task.

The second task: "Please find the shortest route from target 3 to target 7 and the shortest route from target 7 to target 4" is the route distance recognition task. The result of ANOVA indicated that there was no significant difference in the interaction effect between the variables of visual cue design and gender ($F = 1.135$, $P = 0.294 > 0.05$). Besides, no significant difference was observed for these two main effects of visual cue design ($F = 1.845$, $P = 0.183 > 0.05$) and gender ($F = 2.310$, $P = 0.137 > 0.05$).

The third task: "Please find the route between targets 6 and 7 going through target 1" is a route recognition task. According to the statistical analysis results shown in Table 1,

Table 1. Descriptive statistics of task completion time.

		Task 1		Task 2		Task 3	
		M	SD	M	SD	M	SD
Gender	Male	74.22	18.43	63.50	21.83	30.50	11.35
	Female	71.95	26.22	75.76	27.13	31.80	10.95
Visual cue design	Dot	68.69	23.18	78.70	28.51	34.85	13.51
	Border-line	76.69	24.23	64.84	21.52	27.90	6.19

the main effect of the visual cue design on the task completion time was significant ($F = 4.170$, $P = 0.049 < 0.05$). A subsequent post hoc comparison shows that participants' task time of the border-line ($M = 27.90$, $SD = 6.19$) visual cue design is significantly shorter than that of the dot ($M = 34.85$, $SD = 13.51$) visual cue design. The main effects of gender ($F = 0.231$, $P = 0.633 > 0.05$) showed no significant difference. Also, Table 2 illustrates that there exists no significant difference in the interaction effect between the variables of response time and visual cue ($F = 0.093$, $P = 0.763 > 0.05$) regarding task time.

Table 2. The two-way ANOVA results of the third task.

Source	SS	df	MS	F	P	Post Hoc
Visual cue design	26.735	1	26.735	0.231	0.633	
Gender	481.634	1	481.634	4.170	0.049*	Border-line < Dot
Visual cue design * Gender	10.688	1	10.688	0.093	0.763	

*$P < 0.05$

3.2 NASA-TLX Questionnaire Analysis

The NASA-TLX questionnaire was administered to assess the participants' perceived weighted workload. Figure 4 illustrates the means for the six individual sub-scale ratings: mental demand (MD), physical demand (PD), temporal demand (TD), performance (PE), effort (EF), and frustration level (FL) pertinent to the means analysis and sub-scales workload ratings of the NASA-TLX. Each sub-scale score can range in the 1–100 interval.

The statistical results generated from the NASA-TLX indicated that there existed no significant difference in the interaction effect between the variables of visual cue design and gender regarding the aspects, i.e., physical demand ($F = 0.626$, $P = 0.434 > 0.05$), temporal demand ($F = 0.786$, $P = 0.381 > 0.05$), performance ($F = 0.002$, $P = 0.963 > 0.05$), effort ($F = 1.842$, $P = 0.183 > 0.05$), and frustration level ($F = 0.190$, $P = 0.665 > 0.05$).

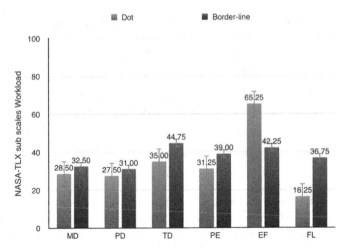

Fig. 4. The subjective workload assessment was measured using the NASA-Task Load Index.

Besides, Table 3 reveals that there exists a significant difference in the interaction effect between the variables of visual cue design and gender (F = 4.964, P = 0.032 < 0.05) regarding the mental demand aspect of NASA-TLX. The interaction diagram is illustrated in Fig. 5. Figure 5 indicates that the workload of a dot takes lower mental demand to complete the task for the male participants (M = 10.71, SD = 13.97) than the female participants (M = 38.08, SD = 23.14). On the contrary, regarding the border-line, the results obtained that the female participants (M = 30.36, SD = 21.26) rated lower mental demand than the male participants (M = 37.50, SD = 32.83).

Table 3. The two-way ANOVA results regarding the mental demand aspect of NASA-TLX.

Source	SS	df	MS	F	P	Post Hoc
Visual cue design	793.905	1	793.905	1.515	0.226	
Gender	892.905	1	892.905	1.704	0.200	
Visual cue design * Gender	2600.334	1	2600.334	4.964	0.032*	

*P < 0.05

Regarding the effort aspect of NASA-TLX, Table 4 indicates that the main effects of visual cue design showed a significant difference (F = 13.16, P = 0.001 < 0.05). Participants using the border-line (M = 42.25, SD = 17.13) visual cue exerted less effort than those using the dot (M = 65.25, SD = 25.10) visual cue. There was no significant difference in the interaction effect between the variables of gender and visual cue (F = 1.842, P = 0.183 > 0.05).

Also, regarding the frustration aspect of NASA-TLX, Table 5 obtains the main effects of visual cue design which showed a significant difference (F = 6.203, P = 0.018 < 0.05). Participants using the dot (M = 16.25, SD = 22.06) visual cue rated less frustration workload than those using the border-line (M = 36.75, SD = 28.25) visual cue. The

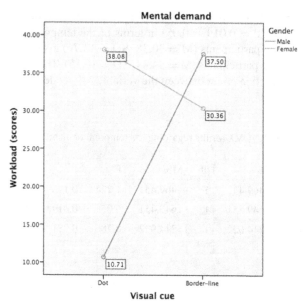

Fig. 5. The interaction diagram of visual cue design and gender in terms of the mental demand aspect of NASA-TLX.

Table 4. The two-way ANOVA results regarding the effort aspect of NASA-TLX.

Source	SS	df	MS	F	P	Post Hoc
Visual cue design	6099.714	1	6099.714	13.163	0.001	Border-line < Dot
Gender	4.514	1	4.514	0.010	0.992	
Visual cue design * Gender	853.714	1	853.714	1.842	0.183	

*P < 0.05

interaction effect between the variables of gender and visual cue (F = 0.190, P = 0.665 > 0.05) showed no significant difference.

Table 5. The two-way ANOVA results regarding the frustration level aspect of NASA-TLX.

Source	SS	df	MS	F	P	Post Hoc
Visual cue design	4182.938	1	4182.938	6.203	0.018*	Dot < Border-line
Gender	5.738	1	5.738	0.009	0.927	
Visual cue design * Gender	128.309	1	128.309	0.190	0.665	

*P < 0.05

In addition, Table 6 reveals that the main effects of gender showed a significant difference (F = 6.056, P = 0.019 < 0.05) in terms of the temporal demand aspect of NASA-TLX. The male participants (M = 30.38, SD = 13.76) assessed lower temporal demand than the female participants (M = 44.44, SD = 18.15). There was no significant difference in the interaction effect between the variables of gender and visual cue (F = 0.786, P = 0.381 > 0.05).

Table 6. The two-way ANOVA results regarding the temporal demand aspect of NASA-TLX.

Source	SS	df	MS	F	P	Post Hoc
Visual cue design	469.451	1	469.451	1.724	0.198	
Gender	1649.451	1	1649.451	6.056	0.019*	Males < Females
Visual cue design * Gender	214.022	1	214.022	0.786	0.381	

*P < 0.05

4 Discussion

Regarding the task performance in the route recognition task, the main effect results showed that the border-line gained better performance than the dot visual cue. In the route recognition task, the participants were asked to plan a correct route between two targets, which means there was not an exclusive answer to complete the task. Previous studies [7, 14] have proposed several visual cues, which provided accurate details for wayfinding, like the dot visual cue. The dot visual cue with an accurate direction for wayfinding might be a possible reason why the border-line performed better.

The main effect results indicated that there are significant differences with visual cue design in the effort and frustration aspects of NASA-TLX. The participants believed that they required more work with the dot visual cue when completing the wayfinding task than with the border-line visual cue. However, the participants assessed that they felt less frustrated when using the dot visual cue than the border-line visual cue to complete the wayfinding task. Besides, according to the results of the temporal aspect of NASA-TLX, the main effect results indicated that females felt more temporal demand than male participants.

The interaction between the visual cue design and gender exerts a significant effect on the mental aspect of NASA-TLX. The interaction results indicated that male participants assessed less mental demand when using the dot visual cue than the females felt. On the contrary, when adopting the border-line, it created higher mental demand for the male participants. A possible explanation for the generated results is that males and females adopt different wayfinding strategies [9, 15]. The males approach maps from a global perspective (allocentric/survey knowledge strategy), while females focus on local features (egocentric/landmarks). This might be the reason why males with the dot visual cue and females with the border-line visual cue felt that there was less mental workload.

5   Conclusions

In this study, we examined the effect of the dot and the border-line visual cue designs on the wayfinding performance and workload of male/female users. Several specific design guides can be applied to mobile wayfinding interfaces that employ visual cue designs to contribute to the wayfinding performance and subjective workload. The results of this study are summarized as follows:

1. For the task of route recognition, the border-line performed better than the dot on the peephole interface when using a mobile device.
2. In this study, participants assessed that using the border-line visual cue requires less effort, whereas using the dot visual cue reduces their frustration level.
3. Interacting with the peephole interface with a mobile device, male participants perceived lower temporal demand than females.
4. Male participants perceived a slight mental workload when adopting the dot visual cue. On the contrary, females assessed a higher mental workload. However, when using the border-line visual cue, female participants perceived a lower mental workload than males.

The visual cue design for mobile wayfinding can have exciting implications and commercial consequences. Designers can contribute to improving participants' wayfinding performance and can reduce their task workload.

References

1. Lynch, K.: The Image of the City. MIT press (1960)
2. Wiener, J.M., Büchner, S.J., Hölscher, C.: Taxonomy of human wayfinding tasks: a knowledge-based approach. Spat. Cogn. Comput. **9**, 152–165 (2009)
3. Araki, T., Komuro, T.: On-mouse projector: peephole interaction using a mouse with a mobile projector. Pervasive Mob. Comput. **50**, 124–136 (2018)
4. Burigat, S., Chittaro, L., Gabrielli, S.: Navigation techniques for small-screen devices: an evaluation on maps and web pages. Int. J. Hum Comput Stud. **66**, 78–97 (2008)
5. Kaufmann, B., Ahlström, D.: Studying spatial memory and map navigation performance on projector phones with peephole interaction. In: Proceedings of the SIGCHI Conference on Human Factors in Computing Systems, Paris, France, pp. 3173–3176. Association for Computing Machinery (2013)
6. Grubert, J., Pahud, M., Grasset, R., Schmalstieg, D., Seichter, H.: The utility of Magic Lens interfaces on handheld devices for touristic map navigation. Pervasive Mob. Comput. **18**, 88–103 (2015)
7. Burigat, S., Chittaro, L.: Visualizing references to off-screen content on mobile devices: a comparison of arrows, wedge, and overview+ detail. Interact. Comput. **23**, 156–166 (2011)
8. Henze, N., Boll, S.: Evaluation of an off-screen visualization for magic lens and dynamic peephole interfaces. In: Proceedings of the 12th International Conference on Human Computer Interaction with Mobile Devices and Services - MobileHCI 2010, Lisbon, Portugal, pp. 191–194. ACM (2010)
9. Bosco, A., Longoni, A.M., Vecchi, T.: Gender effects in spatial orientation: cognitive profiles and mental strategies. Appl. Cogn. Psychol. **18**, 519–532 (2004)

10. Chen, C.H., Chang, W.C., Chang, W.T.: Gender differences in relation to wayfinding strategies, navigational support design, and wayfinding task difficulty. J. Environ. Psychol. **29**, 220–226 (2009)
11. Lawton, C.A.: Gender, spatial abilities, and wayfinding. In: Chrisler, J., McCreary, D. (eds.) Handbook of Gender Research in Psychology, pp. 317–341. Springer, New York (2010). https://doi.org/10.1007/978-1-4419-1465-1_16
12. Hart, S.G., Staveland, L.E.: Development of NASA-TLX (Task Load Index): results of empirical and theoretical research. In: Hancock, P.A., Meshkati, N. (eds.) Advances in Psychology, North-Holland, vol. 52, pp. 139–183 (1988)
13. Chen, C.-H., Li, X.: Spatial knowledge acquisition with mobile maps: effects of map size on users' wayfinding performance with interactive interfaces. ISPRS Int. J. Geo Inf. **9**, 614 (2020)
14. Baudisch, P., Rosenholtz, R.: Halo: a technique for visualizing off-screen objects. In: Proceedings of the SIGCHI Conference on Human Factors in Computing Systems, Ft. Lauderdale, Florida, USA, pp. 481–488. Association for Computing Machinery (2003)
15. Lawton, C.A.: Gender differences in way-finding strategies - relationship to spatial ability and spatial anxiety. Sex Roles **30**, 765–779 (1994)

Can I Talk to Mickey Mouse Through My Phone? Children's Understanding of the Functions of Mobile Phones

Hui Li[1(✉)], Jacqueline D. Woolley[2], and Haoxue Yu[1]

[1] Central China Normal University, Wuhan, Hubei 430079, People's Republic of China
huilipsy@mail.ccnu.edu.cn, yhxxs@mails.ccnu.edu.cn
[2] The University of Texas at Austin, Austin, TX 78712, USA
woolley@austin.utexas.edu

Abstract. Mobile phones have become one of the most important and popular media in our daily life. With the progress of technology, the functions of mobile phones are becoming more and more diversified, and some of the new functions seem almost fantastical. As a result, the present study was conducted to examine children's and adults' beliefs about the functions of mobile phones. Forty 4-year-olds and thirty-seven adults made reality judgments about real and fantastical functions of mobile phone. Results indicated that 4-year-olds and adults judged fantastical events similarly, but children underestimated the reality of real functions of mobile phone. We also found that, unlike adults, children's beliefs about both the real and fantastical functions of mobile phones were significantly related with their experience of those mobile phone functions.

Keywords: Mobile phone · Function · Reality judgments · Events · Justification

1 Introduction

Mobile phones have arguably become the most important and popular media in our daily lives. With increasing technological advances, functions of mobile phones have become more and more diverse: they not only meet users' basic needs, such as phone calling and text messaging, but also sport various new and special uses, such as the ability to search for the name of a song according to the lyrics. Many of the tasks we have learned to perform on desktop computers, such as accessing social media, getting directions, and shopping, can now be performed on a phone. Some new mobile phone functions, such as moving one's head to perform commands, may even seem somewhat fantastical in nature.

The age of mobile phone users varies from very young children to the elderly [1]. The Pew Research Center's Spring 2018 Global Attitudes Survey found that cell phone ownership among American adults had reached 95% by February 2019 [2]. According to the latest report by Common Sense Media, the percentage of children aged 0–8 who have access to some type of "smart" mobile device at home (e.g., Smartphone, tablet) has jumped from 52% to 98% in the past nine years, and 83% children use a mobile

M. M. Soares et al. (Eds.): HCII 2021, LNCS 12781, pp. 25–36, 2021.
https://doi.org/10.1007/978-3-030-78227-6_3

device for some type of media activity [3]. Previous research also indicates that children as young as 2 are using smart phones or tablets and, by age 4, 97% have used a mobile phone [4].

There is limited research on what children understand about the functions of mobile phones and other electronic devices. Eisen and Lillard found that children as young as 4 easily recognized and identified both an iPhone and an iPad [5]. However, children were unaware of many of the functions of iPhones, specifically they seemed not to know that mobile phones can be used for work, for learning, for reading, and for watching shows or movies. One critical question that has not yet been explored is children's understanding of the fantasy-reality distinction as it pertains to mobile phone content and use. This is an area that is ripe for misconceptions of at least two sorts. First, children might be confused about the content of mobile phones, specifically, whether the objects depicted on them are really inside the device. Flavell et al. reported that when preschoolers viewed a video of a bottle of juice pouring on television, a number of 3-year-olds claimed that the juice would spill out [6]. Similarly, Goldstein and Bloom showed that, unlike adults, 3- and 4-year-old children appear to believe that actors acting or pretending to feel a certain emotion really do feel that (Fig. 1) emotion [7].

The second sort of misconception is the possibility for confusion about the functions of mobile phones. As with any new technology, understanding of the mechanism behind the technology is often lacking, even among adult users. This can sometimes generate a sense that a device has magical or special powers [8]. Research by Rosengren and Hickling has shown that parents, when faced with children's questions about how technological devices like garage door openers work, are often puzzled, because they lack an answer [9]. However, rather than admitting their ignorance, parents often simply tell their children that such devices are magic. Children have a rich belief system around magic [10–13] and hence, if told an object is magic might attribute various other magical properties to that object. Such beliefs about the magical nature of mobile phones might include the idea that one could use them to talk to fictional beings, like TV characters, or other fantastical entities. Related research with young children has shown that they are surprisingly likely to accept the possibility of various sorts of machines with apparently magical powers. DeLoache et al., for example, demonstrated that preschool-age children believe a machine could shrink to room to doll-house size [14], and Hood et al. revealed that children believe that a "duplication" device can produce replicas of live beings [15]. Given this, we expected that children might be more likely than adults to claim that fantastical functions of mobile phones were possible.

At the same time, however, research indicates that young children are often skeptical about the possibility of events that are uncommon or unusual. Shtulman and Carey presented 4-, 6-, and 8-year-olds with mundane (e.g., a boy eating ice cream), impossible (e.g., a boy eating lightning), and improbable (e.g., a boy drinking onion juice) events. Four-year-olds were particularly likely to claim that events that were unusual or unfamiliar were impossible [16]. Another study investigating children's understanding of the real versus fantastical nature of events in cartoons found that 4-year-olds often claimed that real televised events could not happen in real life [17]. This work, combined with the previous findings, suggests that children in our study might have a different understanding of the realistic versus fantastical capabilities of mobile phone functions from adults. Specifically, we expected that children might both judge more fantastical phone functions as possible and judge more real phone functions as impossible than adults.

2 Method

2.1 Participants

There were 77 participants: 40 4-year-olds ($M = 55.55$ months, $SD = 3.75$, range = 46–64; 22 girls) and 37 adults ($M = 224.16$ months, $SD = 12.98$, range = 192–252; 19 women). Four-year-olds were chosen because most previous research that suggests the presence of potential misconceptions has focused on this age group [6, 7, 17]. Participants were recruited from a preschool affiliated with a university in central China. All children were from Chinese middle-class families and were given a toy as thanks for their participation. The adults were undergraduate students who volunteered for the study in response to a flyer posted on a bulletin board in the department of psychology for either course credit or payment. All the experimental materials and procedures were approved by the Institutional Review Board of Central China Normal University. Undergraduates and parents of the children signed informed consent forms.

2.2 Materials and Procedure

Previous research indicates that children are competent at differentiating the real versus fantastical nature of events in still pictures; however, they are not as good at doing so when events are presented in videos [6, 18–20]. Thus, children and adults were randomly divided into two groups (picture vs. video) to explore this potential difference and were shown still pictures or videos on a computer. Videos were produced using available software packages and still pictures were created by using shots from the videos. Fantastical **events were defined as events that could not occur in the real world and were one of two types: either a real character communicating via mobile phone with a fantastical character (e.g.,** a boy calling his toy when he is traveling) **or a real character performing an impossible event with another real character (e.g.,** a girl giving her friend food through her phone; **see** Table 1). Participants were first asked to describe the events ("What can you see in the picture/video?") focusing on the function of the mobile phone shown in the picture or video (see Fig. 1). The purpose of the first question was to keep participants' attention. Regardless of their response, participants were told the correct answer after their response (e.g., "This picture/video shows a boy calling his toy when he is traveling"). After being told the correct answer, participants who gave the wrong description were asked to describe the event again. Next, participants were asked two questions: (1) whether they had seen the event in real life (e.g., "Have you ever seen a boy calling his toy when he is traveling?"), and (2) whether they thought the event was possible (e.g., "Do you think it is possible that a boy could call his toy when he is traveling?"). Finally, participants were asked to explain why they thought the event was or was not possible (e.g., "Why is it/is it not possible for a boy to call his toy when he is traveling?"). Based on both pilot data and a previous study conducted with 4-year-olds [17], it was assumed that children at this age understand the meaning of "possible". Twenty events were presented in the random order indicated by the numerals in Table 1.

2.3 Coding of Justifications

Three types of justifications were coded independently by both the first author and a research assistant, using the coding scheme used by Shtulman and Carey [16]. Factual justifications referenced facts about the world that would preclude an event's occurrence (e.g., "a boy calling his toy when he is traveling" is not possible because "his toy could not speak"). Hypothetical justifications referenced hypothetical events that could occur, or would occur, in place of the actual event under consideration (e.g., "A girl could give her friend food through her phone if she had magic"). Finally, redundant justifications provided no information beyond what was already mentioned in the description or what was already discernible from a participant's initial judgment (e.g., "It is not real" or "I don't know"). Of the 1520 justifications provided, two coders agreed on 1507 and inter-rater agreement was 99.15%. The disagreements were resolved through discussion.

Fig. 1. Materials showing a fantastic (left) and real (right) function

Table 1. List of events

Type of events	Descriptions
Real	1. A boy is calling his grandmother on the phone
	3. A man is looking for his way through GPS on the phone
	4. A boy is videoing with his grandfather through his phone
	6. A man is playing games on the phone
	9. A woman is listening to music on the phone
	11. A man is sending a message to his friend on the phone
	12. A woman is shopping online on the phone
	13. A girl is surfing the web on the phone
	16. A woman is taking a photo of herself with her phone
	19. A woman is using clock alarm to wake her up

(continued)

Table 1. (*continued*)

Type of events	Descriptions
Fantastical	2. A girl is giving her friend food through her phone
	5. A boy is calling his toy during his travel
	7. A girl is sharing what happened outside with her stuffed animal on the phone
	8. A girl is calling Mickey Mouse
	10. A boy is calling Confucius who lived thousands of years ago on the phone
	14. A boy is talking with his imaginary friend on the phone
	15. Mickey Mouse is talking with Hello Kitty on the phone
	17. A boy is talking to aliens on the phone
	18. A man is smelling his friend's food through the telephone
	20. A girl is talking to Happy Goat on the phone

3 Results

3.1 Event Descriptions

Participants described the events shown in the picture or video before they were asked about the reality status of each event. Adults gave a correct description of all twenty events. Children described 18.5 events correctly for the first time, and all events were given correct descriptions for the second time.

3.2 Event Experience

Figure 2 shows the number of events that participants reported as experienced for each age and media type. A repeated measures ANOVA with age (4-year-olds, adults) and media type (picture, video) as the between-participants variables and event type (real, fantastical) as the within-participants variable was conducted on experience judgments. There was a significant main effect of event type, $F(1, 73) = 580.44, p < 0.001, \eta_p^2 = 0.89$, and a main effect of age, $F(1, 73) = 23.40, p < 0.001, \eta_p^2 = 0.24$. These main effects were subsumed by a significant interaction between event type and age, $F(1, 73) = 37.77, p < 0.001, \eta_p^2 = 0.34$. Analysis of the simple effects of event type for each age group indicated that both adults ($M_{\text{Real}} = 9.38, SD_{\text{Real}} = 0.83; M_{\text{fantastical}} = 0.84, SD_{\text{fantastical}} = 1.21), F(1, 75) = 452.73, p < 0.001, \eta_p^2 = 0.86$ and 4-year-olds ($M_{\text{Real}} = 5.92, SD_{\text{Real}} = 2.97; M_{\text{fantastical}} = 0.88, SD_{\text{fantastical}} = 2.00$) claimed to have experienced more real events than fantastical ones, $F(1, 75) = 171.12, p < 0.001, \eta_p^2 = 0.70$. However, the magnitude of this difference was greater for adults. In addition, analysis of the simple effects of age for each event type indicated that 4-year-olds claimed to have experienced fewer real events than adults, $F(1, 75) = 45.20, p < 0.001, \eta_p^2 = 0.38$, whereas reports regarding fantastical events did not differ.

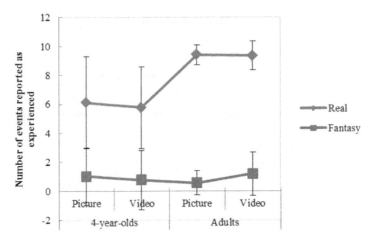

Fig. 2. Average number of events (out of 10) reported as experienced by each group.

3.3 Reality Status Judgments

Signal detection theory (SDT) was used for analysis. As in previous research (Li et al., 2015), we arranged children's responses into four categories: hit (real event as possible), miss (real event as impossible), false alarm (fantastical event as possible), and correct rejection (fantastical event as impossible). According to SDT, d' was calculated as an index of reality sensitivity ($d' = Z_{hit} - Z_{false\ alarm}$). Univariate ANOVA revealed a significant age difference for d', $F(1, 73) = 29.30$, $p < 0.001$, $\eta_p^2 = 0.29$; 4-year-olds' reality sensitivity was lower than that of adults ($M_{4\text{-year-olds}} = 2.46$, $SD_{4\text{-year-olds}} = 1.71$; $M_{adults} = 4.45$, $SD_{adults} = 1.48$).

The mean number of correct reality status judgments (out of 10) for each type of event at each age and media level is shown in Table 2. A repeated measures ANOVA with age (4-year-old, adults) and media type (picture, video) as the between-participants variables and event type (real, fantastical) as the within-participants variable was conducted on reality status judgments. There was a significant main effect of age, $F(1, 73) = 24.01$, $p < 0.001$, $\eta_p^2 = 0.25$, as well as a significant interaction between Event Type and Age, $F(1, 73) = 17.75$, $p < 0.001$, $\eta_p^2 = 0.02$. Analysis of the simple effects of event type for each age group indicated that 4-year-olds had better judgments of fantastical events than real ones ($M_{Real} = 0.69$, $SD_{Real} = 0.23$; $M_{fantastical} = 0.82$, $SD_{fantastical} = 0.24$), $F(1, 75) = 7.71$, $p < 0.01$, while adults showed the opposite pattern ($M_{Real} = 0.99$, $SD_{Real} = 0.04$; $M_{fantastical} = 0.82$, $SD_{fantastical} = 0.22$), $F(1, 75) = 11.04$, $p < 0.001$. In addition, analysis of the simple effects of age for each event type indicated that 4-year-olds had more incorrect judgments of real events than did adults, $F(1, 75) = 59.18$, $p < 0.001$, however the two age groups did not differ on the fantastical events. Finally, there were significant correlations between children's reported experience of both real ($r = 0.78$, $p < 0.001$) and fantastical ($r = 0.74$, $p < 0.001$) events and their reality judgments, which is consistent with previous research showing that children often appear to rely on their personal experience in making reality status judgments [17, 21–23]. For adults, there was only a significant correlation between their experiences of real events and their reality judgments ($r = 0.55, p < 0.001$).

Table 2. Mean number of correct reality status judgments (and standard deviations) for each event type by age and media level

	4-year-olds		Adults	
	Picture ($n = 19$)	Video ($n = 21$)	Picture ($n = 20$)	Video ($n = 17$)
Real	6.89 (2.51)	6.81 (2.25)	9.95 (0.22)	9.76 (0.56)
Fantastical	8.00 (2.40)	8.33 (2.50)	7.90 (2.49)	8.59 (1.70)

3.4 Justifications for Categorization Judgments

Three repeated measures ANOVAs with age (4-year-olds, adults) and media (picture, video) as the between-participants variables, and event type (real, fantastical) as the within-participants variable were conducted on the different types of justification (factual, hypothetical, or redundant); these data are shown in Fig. 3. With regard to factual justifications, there was a significant main effect of age, $F(1, 73) = 45.70, p < 0.001$, $\eta_p^2 = 0.39$, as well as a significant interaction between event type and age, $F(1, 73) = 20.64, p < 0.001, \eta_p^2 = 0.22$. Analysis of the simple effects of event type for each age group indicated that 4-year-olds used fewer factual justifications for judgments about real events than fantastical events ($M_{Real} = 4.13, SD_{Real} = 2.95$; $M_{fantastical} = 5.50$, $SD_{fantastical} = 3.20$), $F(1, 75) = 15.61, p < 0.001$, whereas adults used slightly more factual justifications for real events ($M_{Real} = 8.86, SD_{Real} = 1.70$; $M_{fantastical} = 7.92$, $SD_{fantastical} = 2.18$), $F(1, 75) = 6.84, p < 0.05$. In addition, analysis of the simple effects of age for each event type indicated that adults used more factual justifications than did 4-year-olds for judgments about both real events, $F(1, 75) = 73.16, p < 0.001$, and fantastical events, $F(1, 75) = 14.83, p < 0.001$. Thus, as in previous research on children's reality judgments of both still photos [16] and videos [17], factual justifications for mobile phone events increased with age. For hypothetical justifications, only a significant main effect of event type was found. Participants used more hypothetical justifications for fantastical events than for real events ($M_{Real} = 0.16, SD_{Real} = 0.43$; $M_{fantastical} = 1.09, SD_{fantastical} = 1.32$).

Finally, concerning redundant justifications, there was a significant main effect of event type, $F(1, 73) = 28.60, p < 0.001, \eta_p^2 = 0.28$, and a main effect of age, $F(1, 73) = 53.93, p < 0.001, \eta_p^2 = 0.43$, and a significant interaction between event type and age, $F(1, 73) = 19.52, p < 0.001, \eta_p^2 = 0.21$. Analysis of the simple effects of event type for each age group indicated that 4-year-olds used more redundant justifications for judgments about real events than fantastical events ($M_{Real} = 5.63, SD_{Real} = 2.78$; $M_{fantastical} = 3.53, SD_{fantastical} = 3.03$), $F(1, 75) = 50.91, p < 0.001$, but this was not the case for adults ($M_{Real} = 1.08, SD_{Real} = 1.61$; $M_{fantastical} = 0.86, SD_{fantastical} = 1.55$), $F(1, 75) = 0.05, p > 0.05$. In addition, analysis of the simple effects of age for each event type indicated that 4-year-olds used more redundant explanations than adults for both real events, $F(1, 75) = 75.52$, $p < 0.001$, and fantastical events, $F(1, 75) = 22.96$, $p < 0.001$), which is consistent with previous research [17].

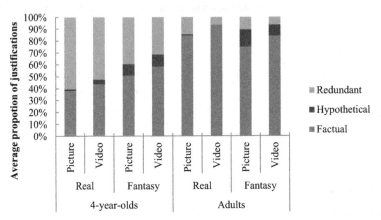

Fig. 3. Average proportion of justifications for categorization judgments by each level.

Results indicated that there were no significant differences between the picture and video groups. This may be because there was a brief description of each event before participants were asked for their experience and reality judgments. These descriptions might have played an important role in giving participants a clear understanding of the events regardless of which condition they were in. Further research should be conducted to compare children's perception of different types of media events without first providing descriptions of the events.

In summary, based on the nature of parent's explanations for technological devices [9], along with children's beliefs in magical properties of various sorts of machines [14, 15], we expected that children might accept as real various fantastical capacities of mobile phones. At the same time, we had mixed expectations regarding children's understanding of real functions. Based on reported increases in mobile phone use in children [3], it seemed possible that they would both be familiar with, and would judge as real, many of the real mobile phone functions at levels that were comparable to those of adults. At the same time, previous research had indicated a degree of skepticism about media content in young children [17], so it also seemed likely that they might judge many real mobile phone functions as impossible. Contrary to our first hypothesis, children performed as well as adults in judging the reality status of fantastical phone functions. Children's confusions, rather than being about the fantastical functions, seemed to center on the real functions of mobile phones, and their lack of experience with these functions appeared to play an important role.

4   Discussion

In recent years, mobile phones have become increasingly central to people's lives. We conducted this research to examine children's perception of possible and impossible functions of mobile phones. Results demonstrated that 4-year-old children, like adults, do not think that mobile phones have special powers. Yet children were less accepting of a range of real functions than were adults. Overall, we did not observe development in understanding the impossible nature of fantastical mobile phone events. Instead, we observed development in understanding of the real functions of mobile phones.

4.1 Fantastical Events

Previous research has shown that, by the age of 3, children have the ability to make the fantasy-reality distinction [24]. However, making this distinction continues to present challenges during the preschool years, as evidenced by children's beliefs in fantastical beings [25], their beliefs in magic [9, 10], and their judgments of the reality status of emotional fantastical events [18, 19]. Because children's ability to make the fantasy-reality distinction is still developing, and because mobile phone technology is not well understood by most users, we expected that children might exhibit belief in various fantastical properties of mobile phones. However, our findings indicated that 4-year-olds did not think mobile phones have special powers or fantastical functions. Thus our research identifies a new domain in which young children exhibit an ability to reason accurately about fantastical events. Our fantastical events were of two types: real people communicating with a not-real character, and real characters performing impossible events with other real characters, with most of our events of the former type. Because this study was somewhat exploratory, we did not include equal numbers of each event type, and so could not analyze whether children treated them differently. Future research should include more events of the latter type, to explore whether children have different levels of understanding of these two types of impossible events.

Children's justifications for the fantastical events suggested that, although they judged these events similarly to adults, the bases for their judgments may be differ-ent. For example, when asked why a boy could not use his phone to call his toy, most adults gave factual explanations, for example they explained that the toy was not alive and could not talk. Children were less likely to offer these sorts of factual justifications. In addition, children's reports of their experiences with fantastical events were significantly correlated with their reality status judgments about them, whereas those of adults were not. These finding are in line with previous research, which has suggested that children reason about the fantasy-reality distinction on the basis of their experiences, whereas adults reason on the basis of physical laws [16].

Li et al. also found that children may mainly rely on their own personal experiences when making judgments of event reality [23]. Some neuroimaging evidence supports the idea that children and adults might process fantastical events differently. Han et al. observed medial prefrontal cortex (mPFC) activity in adults and 10-year-old children while they viewed videos with humans in real-life situations and cartoon clips with non-human characters. The results indicated that children's mPFC was activated when watching both real and cartoon characters, whereas the mPFC of adults was only activated when watching real-life situations [26]. Li et al. found that prefrontal activation was higher in children than in adults when watching and judging the reality of events, especially in mPFC and rPFC [23]. In addition, some studies specifically explored prefrontal activations during the processing of fantastical events in young children, and functional near-infrared spectroscopy (fNIRS) data showed that viewing fantastical events performed by cartoon characters led to more activity in the dorsolateral prefrontal cortex in children aged 4–6 years relative to playing with them [27]. Moreover, children aged 4 to 6 who watched a video with multiple fantastical events had a higher concentration of oxygenated hemoglobin (Coxy-Hb) in PFC than children who watched a video with few fantastical events [28].

4.2 Real Events

Eisen and Lillard indicate that children and adults differ in their understanding of many of the functions of touchscreen devices, with adults showing a more complete understanding of the multifunctional capabilities of touchscreens [5]. Based on this finding, as well as findings of skepticism in children regarding other forms of media [17, 20], we expected that children in our studies would have a limited appreciation of the many things that phones could do. Indeed, relative to adults, 4-year-old children in the present study perceived real mobile phone events as less real. As with fantastical events, children's judgments of their experience with mobile phone events were also related to their reality status judgments for real events. Although this relationship was also present in adults, it was stronger in children, and suggests that experience may play a particularly important role in 4-year-olds' judgments. Cook and Sobel offer a similar proposal regarding 4-year-olds' judgments in their studies that unfamiliar machines were not real. They suggest that young children may have used their lack of experience with these machines to infer that they didn't exist [21]. Future studies should provide a broader range of real events, including ones that most adults might be unfamiliar with, to further assess the role of experience in reality status judgments of mobile phone events.

Overall, our research indicates that 4-year-old children are often skeptical of the reality status of real mobile phone events, and tend to categorize them as unreal. Previous studies have indicated that young children are often skeptical of the existence of characters and events in other forms of media, such as storybooks [29] and television [20]. Our finding that 4-year-olds were similarly skeptical about the real versus fantastical functions of mobile phones extends this pattern to a new type of media device. In addition, it appears that confusion regarding the role of experience may be at the root of their skepticism. This finding is consistent with a body of emerging findings showing that children are more skeptical about novel information than previously believed, and that the root of this skepticism may be an over-reliance on the role of experience [23, 30].

Acknowledgments. This research was funded by the Fundamental Research Funds for the Central Universities (CCNU20QN039).

References

1. Schüz, J.: Mobile phone use and exposures in children. Bioelectromagnetics **26**(S7), S45–S50 (2005)

2. Silver, L.: Smartphone ownership is growing rapidly around the world, but not always equally. https://www.pewresearch.org/. Accessed 25 Dec 2020
3. Rideout, V., Robb, M.B.: The common sense census: media use by kids age zero to eight, 2020. Common Sense Media (2020)
4. Radesky, J.S., Schumacher, J., Zuckerman, B.: Mobile and interactive media use by young children: the good, the bad, and the unknown. Pediatrics **135**(1), 1–3 (2015)
5. Eisen, S., Lillard, A.S.: Young children's thinking about touchscreens versus other media devices. In: Paper Presented at the Cognitive Development Society Meeting, Austin, TX (2015)
6. Flavell, J.H., Flavell, E.R., Green, F.L., Korfmacher, J.E.: Do young children think of television images as pictures or real objects? J. Broadcast. Electron. Media **34**(4), 399–419 (1990)
7. Goldstein, T.R., Bloom, P.: Characterizing characters: how children make sense of realistic acting. Cogn. Dev. **34**, 39–50 (2015)
8. Subbotsky, E.: Early rationality and magical thinking in preschoolers: space and time. Br. J. Dev. Psychol. **12**(1), 97–108 (1994)
9. Rosengren, K.S., Hickling, A.K.: Seeing is believing: children's explanations of commonplace, magical, and extraordinary transformations. Child Dev. **65**(6), 1605–1626 (1994)
10. Phelps, K.E., Woolley, J.D.: The form and function of young children's magical beliefs. Dev. Psychol. **30**(3), 385–394 (1994)
11. Subbotsky, E.V.: Foundations of the Mind: Children's Understanding of Reality. Harvard University Press, Cambridge (1993)
12. Rosengren, K.S., Johnson, C.N., Harris, P.L.: Imagining the Impossible: Magical, Scientific, and Religious Thinking in Children. Cambridge University Press, Cambridge (2000)
13. Subbotsky, E., Hysted, C., Jones, N.: Watching films with magical content facilitates creativity in children. Percept. Mot. Skills **111**(1), 261–277 (2010)
14. DeLoache, J.S., Miller, K.F., Rosengren, K.S.: The credible shrinking room: very young children's performance with symbolic and nonsymbolic relations. Psychol. Sci. **8**(4), 308–313 (1997)
15. Hood, B., Gjersoe, N.L., Bloom, P.: Do children think that duplicating the body also duplicates the mind? Cognition **125**(3), 466–474 (2012)
16. Shtulman, A., Carey, S.: Improbable or impossible? How children reason about the possibility of extraordinary events. Child Dev. **78**(3), 1015–1032 (2007)
17. Li, H., Boguszewski, K., Lillard, A.S.: Can that really happen? Children's knowledge about the reality status of fantastical events in television. J. Exp. Child Psychol. **139**, 99–114 (2015)
18. Carrick, N., Quas, J.A.: Effects of discrete emotions on young children's ability to discern fantasy and reality. Dev. Psychol. **42**(6), 1278–1288 (2006)
19. Samuels, A., Taylor, M.: Children's ability to distinguish fantasy events from real-life events. Br. J. Dev. Psychol. **12**(4), 417–427 (1994)
20. Wright, J.C., Huston, A.C., Reitz, A.L., Piemyat, S.: Young children's perceptions of television reality: determinants and developmental differences. Dev. Psychol. **30**(2), 229–239 (1994)
21. Cook, C., Sobel, D.M.: Children's beliefs about the fantasy/reality status of hypothesized machines. Dev. Sci. **14**(1), 1–8 (2011)
22. Woolley, J.D., Ma, L., Lopez-Mobilia, G.: Development of the use of conversational cues to assess reality status. J. Cogn. Dev. **12**(4), 537–555 (2011)
23. Li, H., Liu, T., Woolley, J.D., Zhang, P.: Reality status judgments of real and fantastical events in children's prefrontal cortex: an fNIRS study. Front. Hum. Neurosci. **13**, 444 (2019)
24. Woolley, J.D.: Thinking about fantasy: are children fundamentally different thinkers and believers from adults? Child Dev. **68**(6), 991–1011 (1997)
25. Woolley, J.D., Boerger, E.A., Markman, A.B.: A visit from the candy witch: factors influencing young children's belief in a novel fantastical being. Dev. Sci. **7**(4), 456–468 (2004)

26. Han, S., Jiang, Y., Humphreys, G.W.: Watching cartoons activates the medial prefrontal cortex in children. Chin. Sci. Bull. **52**(24), 3371–3375 (2007)
27. Li, H., Subrahmanyam, K., Bai, X., Xie, X., Liu, T.: Viewing fantastical events versus touching fantastical events: short-term effects on children's inhibitory control. Child Dev. **89**(1), 48–57 (2018)
28. Li, H., Hsueh, Y., Yu, H., Kitzmann, K.M.: Viewing fantastical events in animated television shows: Immediate effects on Chinese preschoolers' executive function. Front. Psychol. **11**, 3423 (2020)
29. Woolley, J.D., Cox, V.: Development of beliefs about storybook reality. Dev. Sci. **10**(5), 681–693 (2007)
30. Woolley, J.D., Ghossainy, M.E.: Revisiting the fantasy–reality distinction: children as naïve skeptics. Child Dev. **84**(5), 1496–1510 (2013)

Design Innovation of Intangible Cultural Heritage: Challenges on the Basis of Mobile Phone Culture

Xiangnuo Li[✉] and Ziyang Li

Beijing City University, No. 269 Bei si huan Zhong lu, Haidian District, Beijing, China

Abstract. Nowadays, the mobile phone culture derived from mobile media is infiltrating the daily study and life of college students in all dimensions. On the other hand, the traditional artistry and culture are gradually being marginalized. As the country pays more attention to the inheritance of "intangible cultural heritage" and introduces it as a topic into higher education, it is necessary to envisage how the intangible culture can adapt to the mode of communication in the era of digital media technology. Meanwhile, higher education workers are concerned over the issue that Chinese design has long lacked Chinese elements. Under such a context, this study will, starting with the concept of protection of intangible cultural heritage, propose that innovative designs are applied the protection and inheritance of intangible cultural heritage in the current digital media technology environment. And it will also analyze the interaction methods and characteristics of user-favorite innovative design products for excellent applications and superior "intangible culture heritage" in the era of digital media technology. Conclusion: in the era prevalent with information technology and digital art, the dissemination of intangible cultural heritage should adapt to the social development and make design innovations. The products oriented to inheritance and innovation of "intangible culture heritage" should fully take into consideration the user experience, the interestingness of interaction methods, and how to incorporate traditional Chinese elements, rather than simple arrangement and combination of such elements. The combination of traditional culture and digital art is not only an on-going trend, still with a lot of room for improvement, but will also inject new blood into social innovation.

Keywords: Creativity · Intangible cultural heritage · User-centered design

1 Introduction

Intangible cultural heritage (ICH) reflects cultural forms such as folk traditions, economic systems, religious beliefs, and politics and is imbued with national art, aesthetic taste, anthropology, sociology, aesthetics, history, and values. In the context of globalization, the protection of ICH has become the consensus of all countries in the world. In recent years, China has also attached increasing importance to the protection of ICH and rolled out a series of relevant policies. However, these policies have not achieved

© Springer Nature Switzerland AG 2021
M. M. Soares et al. (Eds.): HCII 2021, LNCS 12781, pp. 37–46, 2021.
https://doi.org/10.1007/978-3-030-78227-6_4

the expected publicity effects. Currently, with the burgeoning growth of mobile Internet technology and the application of mobile terminals, mobile devices represented by smartphones are becoming popular and various apps have enjoyed "explosive" growth. The mobile culture derived from mobile media is permeating the daily study and life of university students in an all-round way. It has become an important way of communication owing to its high prevalence and user viscosity. In this context, the dissemination of ICH is confronted with both opportunities and challenges. The author tries to use digital media devices to disseminate these distinctive regional cultures and bring in traditional Chinese elements rather than simply arrange and combine elements. It is hoped that this study can explore a new path for the protection and transmission of ICH.

2   Current Status of ICH Mobile Apps in China

By searching relevant keywords such as "ICH", "inheritance", and "cultural heritage" in China's Android app market and Apple app store, the author found that ICH apps cover a wide range of cultural industries, such as ICH protection projects, museums, tourism, traditional handicrafts, folklore, and folk art. Approximately over 40 apps are available for download in the Android app market and Apple app store. The 40 screened apps were classified into the following categories: education, entertainment, tool, consumption, social networking, reading, tourism, and life. The number of downloads from December 25, 2020 to January 23, 2021 was monitored on the "qimai" data network (Fig. 1). During the process of data monitoring, only 7 out of 40 apps were downloaded while the rest of the 33 apps were not downloaded at all. Among them, the most downloaded app was the "Shougongke" app with 4,425 downloads in the past month. Through this market survey, it can be seen that there is a wide range of ICH products on smartphones. Also, ICH keeps pace with the times and chooses to collaborate with smartphones to form the "smartphone plus ICH" model. However, this survey has also exposed the problems of ICH apps, namely the lack of a large number of users with rigid demand, low user viscosity, and fewer downloads.

ICH apps have a niche audience, so it is difficult for them to have the same large number of users as instant messaging, games, social networking, and news apps. Government departments, publishers, and cultural institutions are well aware of this, but still advocate the topic selection, planning, production, and distribution of such apps because such apps are uniquely positioned to protect and inherit ICH and realize social and cultural values. However, from the number of downloads, we can see the communication effects have not been well achieved. Therefore, the small audience group shall not be regarded as the reason to ignore user demand. In the process of the digital transformation of content, as designers of ICH apps, publishers and cultural institutions have habitually positioned ICH too high from the very beginning. However, they are not so familiar with the target audience, ignore user demand, and fail to accurately position such apps, and seldom comprehensively consider the visual interface, operation process, and user experience from the perspective of users, thus leading to the low dissemination efficiency, weak user viscosity, and awkward situation of most ICH apps ever since their inception [1].

The author surveyed the 40 ICH apps available in the market, discovering the following problems in the process of using such apps.

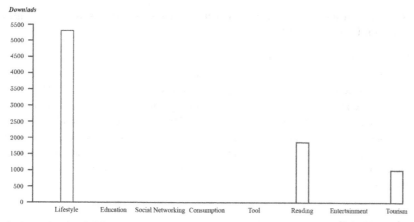

Fig. 1. Downloads of different categories of intangible cultural heritage apps from December 25, 2020 to January 23, 2021

2.1 Large Amount of Content Information but Few Diversified Messages

The ICH apps in the market cover all categories of information, but the introduction to each category is usually too superficial. They simply give users a rough idea of relevant rules and content such as the definition of ICH, the names of the inheritors, and the production process. There are very few channels available for users to probe deeper into details or extended information, so there is a lack of extensibility.

2.2 Lack of Variation and Diversity in Presentation Forms

Compared with other media, mobile apps are characterized by timeliness, convenience, interactivity, and content diversity. However, ICH apps mainly introduce content through photos, texts, and videos, which are not much different from the presentation forms on webpages [2]. The exclusive interactive advantage of apps has not been fully leveraged, so users will generate the feeling of fatigue and lose interest in using them.

2.3 No or Slow Update of Content and System

In terms of content, the vast majority of ICH apps have not been updated for a long time. Besides, the links for some of these apps cannot even be opened. Moreover, products do not have any reviews or sales in the shopping apps and some sellers are even unable to be contacted, so these apps are already products eliminated by the market. When it comes to the app system, almost all apps have not updated their systems for more than a year, which means that the companies have failed to observe the latest trends and innovate their apps. Therefore, ICH apps are gradually eliminated from the market in the fast trend of the whole mobile culture. Though there are a lot of ICH apps in app stores, few of them can be truly used.

2.4 ICH App Design Uses Traditional Chinese Elements but Simply Arranges and Combines These Elements

The design of all ICH-themed apps has Chinese characteristics. Chinese elements or ICH elements constitute the main style of interface design. Common elements in the visual effects of ICH apps include Chinese characters, ink painting, and ICH elements. However, few ICH apps can integrate modern design elements with traditional Chinese elements. The absence of redesign for traditional Chinese elements is merely tantamount to the simple arrangement and combination of traditional Chinese elements. Inadequate sense of design and detachment from modern design make users lose interest in ICH apps, especially young people. However, young people are the main target of publicity for ICH apps.

2.5 Diversified Design of the Main Interface and Monotonous Design of the Secondary Interface for ICH Apps

The design and content of the main interface of ICH apps are more diversified. However, when the secondary interface is opened, there is a lack of variety in design with less extended content and fewer design elements. The visual effects are only achieved through a stack of monotonous texts and graphics with little variation. This will easily generate a sense of fatigue among users, thus depriving them of their interest.

3 Design Strategy for ICH Apps Based on User Experience

The analysis of the current status of ICH apps in app stores has exposed quite a few problems in the design of these apps. The fundamental solution to these problems is to enhance the user experience of ICH apps. In his book entitled *The Design of Everyday Things*, Don Norman mentions that user-centered design is a key design method. "The essence of the UCD method is a type of design thinking, which ensures the correct estimation of user's feelings through effective methods and means, recognizes the real expectations and purposes of users, and truly achieves user-centeredness" [3]. The ultimate purpose of UCD is to improve user experience. Only by starting from user experience and emphasizing user-centeredness can we design an app with a high rate of dissemination and user viscosity. Hence, the author will propose the design strategy for ICH apps based on user demand.

Through research, it has been found that the model on the elements of user experience (See Fig. 2) proposed by Garrett in *The Elements of User experience* has been adopted by many scholars and design researchers. The model consists of the following five layers: strategy, scope, structure, skeleton, and surface. The strategy layer sets product objectives and user demand and proposes the objectives of product development; the scope layer conducts content demand analysis based on the objectives and user demand proposed in the strategy layer; the structure layer builds user experience through information architecture and interaction design; the skeleton layer determines the form and function of operation; the surface layer solves and remedies the perceptual presentation problem in the logical arrangement of the skeleton layer [4]. According to the five layers of user experience proposed by Garrett, targeting the above-mentioned problems found in the apps in the market through research, the author believes that it is necessary to study the design strategy for ICH apps from the following five aspects (See Fig. 3).

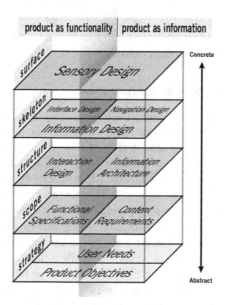

Fig. 2. Garrett user experience element model

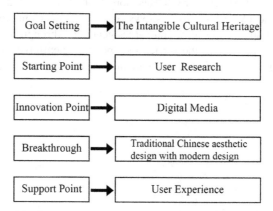

Fig. 3. Research on the design strategy of ICH apps

3.1 Setting the Objective of Inheriting ICH

ICH concerns a diverse range of areas. In the early stage of app incubation, it is crucial to determine a clear user group and product objective. As far as the age group is concerned, young people are the key target of dissemination in ICH inheritance. Only when young people understand, accept and enjoy ICH, can it stand the test of time and obtain enduring vitality. Thus, it has become the working priority of ICH inheritance to understand the user demand of young people. Taking ICH inheritance as the starting point, the author conducted a divergence analysis, listed out detailed product objectives, and nailed down the ultimate product objective list after sequencing and screening. Then, the author transformed the list of product objectives into specific and clear user behaviors, which can boost the achievement of product objectives [2].

3.2   Taking User Research as the Starting Point

The 5th batch of inheritors of national intangible cultural heritage in China consists of 1,082 people, including 107 inheritors aged above 80, 237 inheritors aged 70 to 79, 287 inheritors aged 60 to 69, 444 inheritors aged 40 to 59, and 7 inheritors aged below 40 with an average age of 63.29. In terms of age group, ICH inheritors are aging, so it becomes especially important to cultivate young inheritors. Among young people, university students are the main target of ICH inheritance because they have a good education, plenty of time, and strong learning capabilities. Hence, university students are regarded as the main target of this research. Altogether 21 university students were invited to get involved in the user research to sort out user demand. Figure 4 shows that text & graphics and videos are the most popular, while offline activities and tourism are worthy of attention. The combination of offline and online forms is indispensable for ICH. Figure 5 shows that most students download ICH apps to understand and appreciate ICH while only a minority of them want to probe deep into ICH culture and plan to learn ICH skills, so most users are just starting to become interested in ICH. Figure 6 shows that when combined with other forms, ICH is more popular among students, such as Two Dimensions, film and TV series, variety shows, and new media technology. The essence of the value of ICH apps is the spirit and values generated through the combination of culture which takes "people" as the carrier and "people" themselves. In the process of designing ICH apps, we should not ignore the preferences of user groups.

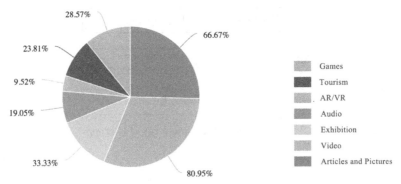

Fig. 4. 21 college students were investigated to understand the channels of intangible cultural heritage.

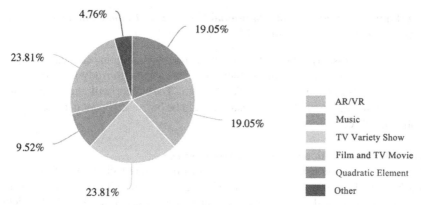

Fig. 5. According to the survey of 21 college students, if intangible cultural heritage app is combined with other forms, which form is more attractive.

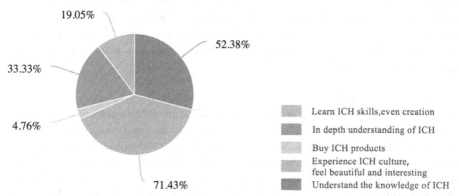

Fig. 6. According to the survey of 21 college students, what is their demand for the APP of intangible cultural heritage.

3.3 Taking the Combination with Digital Media Technology as the Innovation Point

As technology continues to evolve, digital media technologies such as video, VR, AR, and 360-degree virtual browsing have blurred the boundary between virtual and reality. Therefore, ICH apps can choose the appropriate digital media technology as the innovation point based on their theme to make ICH more authentic. The research shows that ICH apps that are combined with other forms are more popular among young people. The application of new media technology can generate unknown surprises, curiosity, and pleasure among people. Young people are easily receptive to and curious about new things. For this reason, the combination of ICH apps with new media technology exactly meets the needs of young people today. Thus, new media technology can be used to increase user viscosity.

3.4 Taking the Integration of Traditional Chinese Aesthetic Design with Modern Design as the Breakthrough of Visual Design

The visual effects displayed by ICH apps have distinctive traditional elements compared with other apps. Then, a pressing problem for such apps is to study how to integrate traditional Chinese elements with modern design. The author will elaborate on what elements among traditional Chinese aesthetics can be borrowed by modern design from the following three aspects.

Drawing Upon Traditional Chinese Layout Design
Since people wrote on bamboo slips in ancient times, they would write from the top to the bottom. In traditional Chinese paintings, we can usually see a red seal after the vertical text. A seal can balance the picture composition and enrich the picture effects in traditional Chinese painting. When applied to the interface design of ICH apps, the vertical seal layout can convey a strong, classical cultural atmosphere, echoing the theme of ICH [5]. The Chinese layout design also emphasizes blank-leaving, which is designed to highlight the qualities of simplicity, serenity, fun, elegance, and rules. Symmetrical design is also a traditional Chinese design approach. It makes the whole layout design look well-structured, dignified, and generous, thus effectively conveying the connotations of the theme.

Applying Traditional Colors
The five elements were used by ancient Chinese philosophers to describe the relationship between all things in the world. The color system is also inextricably linked to the five elements with red, yellow, blue, white, and black representing the five elements of fire, earth, wood, gold, and water, respectively. The colors of the five elements are directly related to the directions, corresponding to the east, west, north, south, and middle. Green Dragon, White Tiger, Vermilion Bird, Tortoise, and Yellow Dragon are the symbols of these direction colors, as is stated in the journal entitled *View Parametric Design's Influence on the Growing Trend of Visual Communication Design Major from the Perspective of Metric Design* by Chen Nan [6]. There are many examples of the application of the five-color system in China, such as the "five-color earth" in the Altar of Land and Grain in the Zhongshan Park of Tiananmen Square. This is a perfect example of the application of the five-color system. The five-color earth from the five directions of China is used to build the altar and the surrounding walls are designed with glazed tiles in four direction colors. In the Fuwa proposal designed by Chen Nan for the Beijing Olympic Games, the five Fuwas were designed with the five-element color system. He used the colors of five elements as the main colors and then used the inter-generated colors as adjacent and harmonizing colors. Moreover, he also obtained harmonizing colors by adding white and dull colors. The author believes that using the five elements as the main color system and then harmonizing it can be applied to the color operation

of ICH apps because it not only contains the accumulated traditional Chinese culture but also adds white and dull colors for harmonization to blend it with modern design.

Applying ICH Concrete Elements

In the interface design of ICH apps, concrete elements can be selected based on the chosen ICH theme. These elements may be integrated with navigation, frame, buttons, and app logo for creation. However, these elements should not be directly borrowed and applied but should be redesigned and reintegrated with modern design methods. For instance, the following two apps are designed in this way. One is a Beijing opera ICH app (See Fig. 7), which uses the design elements of traditional Beijing opera facial makeup. However, instead of directly borrowing the elements of facial makeup, it refines its graphics and colors. The other ICH app of Chengdu culture (See Fig. 8) directly borrows the elements of the ICH without any redesign. After looking at the two ICH apps, users can distinctly feel that the app with redesigned concrete elements is more consistent with the aesthetic preference of young people, and the image of the ICH is also more vivid without departing from ethnic characteristics. Hence, the application of ICH concrete elements should not be simply applied indiscriminately but should be redesigned based on the features of modern design.

Fig. 7. Beijing opera ICH app—Zui Yan   **Fig. 8.** Chengdu culture app–Interesting puzzle of Chengdu cultural heritage

3.5 Regarding User Experience as the Support Point

The popularity of smartphones has brought about a dazzling array of apps. In such a context, without market research and user demand analysis, ICH apps will certainly be eliminated by the market. Only by constantly analyzing user demand can we make users feel the user-friendliness of ICH apps, thus increasing user viscosity. When we take user experience as the supporting point and test user experience, we can verify whether products have reached the expected objectives, find out and change the design elements that affect user experience, optimize the design proposal, and enhance the user experience, thereby increasing user loyalty [7]. In this user-centered era, providing users with personalized and differentiated experiences will be the core competitiveness of ICH apps.

4 Conclusion

In the era of thriving information technology and digital art, the communication of ICH needs to adapt to social development and design innovation. This paper analyzes the current situation and shortcomings of ICH apps. It is proposed that we should adopt a design strategy that takes ICH inheritance as the design goal, user research as the starting point, digital media technology as the innovation point, and the integration of traditional Chinese aesthetic design with modern design as the breakthrough of visual design, and user experience as the supporting point. Though the survival status of ICH apps is not so optimistic, the combination of traditional culture with digital art is a growing trend that still enjoys a huge space for improvement. Meanwhile, the development of ICH apps will inject new blood into social innovation.

References

1. Lan, W.: 基于UCD视角的非物质文化遗产APP的痛点分析. View Publishing **09**, 60–62 (2017)
2. Xinxin, S.: 基于游戏化的非物质文化遗产APP设计策略研究. Beauty Times **01**, 84–86 (2020)
3. Jia, T.: Optimized design of JD User Experience based on UCD. Beijing Jiaotong University, Beijing (2014)
4. Garrett, J.J.: The Elements of User Experience: User- centered Design for Web and Beyond. Chain Machine Press, Beijing (2011)
5. Kun, T., Liu, Z., Lu, Y.: APP interface design in the context of inheriting and innovating "intangible cultural heritage." Pack. Eng. **36**(08), 60–63 (2015)
6. Nan, C.: View parametric design's influence on the growing trend of visual communication design major from the perspective of metric design. Creat. Des. **1**, 61–72 (2013)
7. Yi, D., Guo, F., Mingcai, H., Fengliang, S.: A review of user experience. Ind. Eng. Manag. **19**(4), 92–97 (2014)

The Influence of Icons on the Visual Search Performance of APP List Menu

Miao Liu and Shinan Yang[✉]

East China University of Science and Technology, Shanghai 200237, People's Republic of China

Abstract. In the current app list menu, in the face of a large number of list information, users need to quickly find the function to search. Designers make the page more beautiful by adding icons on the left side of the text message, and hope that this way can help users better search the text content. This study explored whether the existence of icon and the type of icon will affect the search speed, accuracy and cognitive resources utilization of the target in the list menu bar in the process of visual search. The experiment uses eye tracking method to simulate the process of users looking for the target function in app. There are three main variables in the experiment, including the number of items in the list, whether there is an icon, and the sign type of the icon. The search time, accuracy and eye movement data were recorded. The experimental results show that there are little difference between the text-only and icon-text on the reaction time and accuracy, but the presence of icons can affect the cognitive process; meaningless circle icons can make it easier for users to find the target; symbol signs and icon signs can make users understand the target more quickly. The research results provide theoretical guidance for the design of mobile phone interface and icon in human-computer interface, and help to improve the visual search speed of users and the user experience of human-computer interaction.

Keywords: Search performance · Icon · Menu

1 Introduction

Visual search is an essential cognitive process for people to obtain external information and then process it, which requires to find a specific stimulus in a certain stimulus background [1]. At present, with the rapid development of mobile information technology, digital interface has become an indispensable part of current life. As the task of interface task becomes more complex, the content of digital interface needs to present is also more and more diverse, users need to find the target in a large amount of information through vision [2]. With the rapid increase of the amount of information and the influx of a large amount of data into people's lives, how to better help users use the interface and improve the user experience needs more specifications for interface design [3]. A very common menu [4] form, list menu, which the menu content is presented in the form of a single column list from top to bottom and is often used in mobile app. Users need to find the target in this. With the use of icon has become a standard part of information interface

© Springer Nature Switzerland AG 2021
M. M. Soares et al. (Eds.): HCII 2021, LNCS 12781, pp. 47–65, 2021.
https://doi.org/10.1007/978-3-030-78227-6_5

design [4], this type of menu form has gradually evolved from the early pure text form to the icon text form, but so far, these two forms of menu options can be found (see Fig. 1). For usefulness of icon use in menu interfaces there have been some scholars who have made related studies and found that reaction times are shorter when there are icons than when only text is available [6], and that a list of 13 items, whether walking and sitting, on the menu is faster than when text icons are mixed [4].

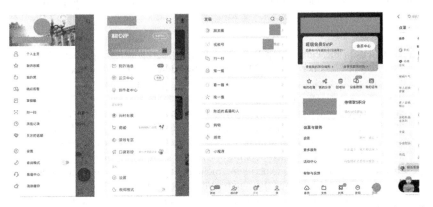

Fig. 1. The list menus in different apps. From left to right, are Sina Weibo, Netease cloud, wechat, baidu disk and meituan takeout. The first three have icons, and the second two have no or part of them.

Eye movement experiments are often used in visual search tasks, which can reflect the process of visual information processing. Through the analysis of eye movement data, the reasons behind the visual search results and the law of visual cognition can be further explored [7, 8]. For example, Xi and Wu [9] used eye movement experiment to study the search performance of icon matrix with different styles, and found that the linear style icon has the shortest fixation duration, faster cognitive process and easier recognition. In terms of the influence of icons on list menu, eye movement experiment has not been used to examine the influence of icons on cognitive factors, so this research used eye movement experiment to further explore the influence of icons on the cognitive process and search mode of list menu visual search.

The different existence of icons in terms of style, color, shape, semantic type, complexity has an impact on the search performance of icons [7, 10]. But most of the studies on icon features' search performance have focused on icons, and there are few related studies on visual search with icons containing accompanying text. At the same time, Chinese list menu nowadays, not only common image icons are used, but also some apps use Chinese character signs (see Fig. 2). Pierce's symbolic classification theory can help us to classify existing icons, in terms of classifying symbols into three categories: image, referent, and symbolic, and exploring whether different semantic types of icons have an effect on search performance on a list menu, as well as on the basis of observations that some list icons would adopt circles without any semantics as prefixing markers, so investigate this as a fourth type.

Based on previous studies, the contributions of this experiment are as follows:

Fig. 2. The icons of Yunbei Center (云贝中心) and Yuncun tickets (云村有票) use Chinese character ticket (票) and cloud (云)

- Behavioral data (response time and accuracy) and eye movement data (number of fixation points, average fixation time, first and continuous fixation time) after combination of different symbol types and words.
- Comparing eye movement data between plain text lists and text Icon lists after excluding the effect of changing list length

2   Related Work

2.1   Digital Interface and Visual Search

Visual search is a cognitive activity that almost everyone has ever done. With the popularity of electronic information technology, many experts begin to study the visual search on the digital interface. Smart phones bring the graphical interface to its extreme. All kinds of APPs attract users through eye-catching icons, which enrich the visual experience while providing a concise interface. With the advantage of over a thousand words, icons occupy a large part of the space and enrich the search performance research on icons. Wang et al. [10] summarized the influencing factors of icon's characteristics, including icon size, complexity, color, aesthetic appeal and icon style. For example, Xi and Wu [11] discovered that skeiomorphism style icons place a greater cognitive burden on users and take longer to search. While others found that, icon type classified according to semiological methods influenced both search performance and eye movement search patterns [7, 12].

In addition to the case of icon-only and text-only, icons with accompanying text have some differences in search performance compared with icon-only. Kacmar's [13] study, in which targets were sought by phrases, showed that icons were able to influence the search efficiency of the text menu and that the performance of the text-only group and icon-text groups was the optimal situation. While in Yao's [14] experiment was taken to find the target by icon, icon-only showed shorter reaction time than the form of icon-text. The above studies on the organizational form of stimulus and distractor items were generally in the form of a matrix grid, rather than as single columns; on the combination of icons and text. Differences in form can have an impact on search performance [15], so this must be studied separately.

The list menu is already presented in the early Windows interface as a pull menu, where the current mobile app receives screen size limits to be presented either as a side or as a whole screen menu. Aaltonen et al. [16] used eye movement to study the visual search mode of text-only pull-down menu as well as the eye movement data and revealed that different users would adopt different visual search modes. Two researchers [4, 6] both found the list menu in the form of a mixture of icons and words to be more effective for users. But Majrashi is more discussing the influence of icons on tabular menus in different states, walking and sitting, Muftah et al. So, whether the different types of icons themselves have an impact on the search performance of the tabulated menu needs further discussion.

2.2   Classification of Icons

As a sign, icon have the functions of simplifying the interaction steps, glorifying the layout of the interface, and improving the identification rate of users [17]. Lodding [5] separating icons into those that are characterization abstracted, and random. This classification begins with pictorial relationships between the icon and the referent, characterization is more of the expressed thing itself, whereas abstraction is a conceptual representation of the thing and, arbitrarily, an artificial deregulating the association between the thing and the symbol. Song [7] and Peng and Xue [12] both adopted Peirce's symbolic triad theory in semiology, which is the semantic angle within semiology to divide icons into icon, index, and symbol in their studies [18]. An icon sign reproduces the physical form of the thing itself, such as a bank card and the bank card icon; an index reproduces a thing logically, spatiotemporally, such as seeing the knife fork can be reminiscent of a restaurant; while a symbol has no sure logic with the thing itself. Most of these symbols are some of the less colloquial and artificially defined symbols, such as Chinese characters and its literal meaning, Red Cross and medical treatment, etc. Among their experiments were all found to differ in visual search performance and cognitive processes using icons of different semantics after applying Peirce's classification. For example, symbolic symbol cognition requires less allocation of visual attentional resources during the early identification process; target search efficiency is highest in which users initiate features with shape similarity in the feature-based reasoning visual search properties of icons.

For another perspective, icon perception by users, in a series of studies by McDougall et al., the importance of icon features was found to change dynamically as a function of the user's feelings, which included semantic distance, specificity, familiarity, icon complexity, and aesthetic attraction [19–21].

In the menu list present, there are figure icons and also character icons. In general, icons are widely used because of their inter-ethnic versatility, and the use of already symbolic Chinese characters icon to further dot the option of text is very interesting. For this phenomenon, it is most appropriate to use the angle one classification method, at the same time, Peirce's classification method has a more extensive history of application and research, so in this study, the symbols are divided into icon sign, index sign and symbol sign by using the Peirce sign trichotomy method, while adding the meaningless circle symbol as the fourth symbol type.

3 Method

3.1 Experimental Design

A two factor mixed level design was used for the experiments. Among them, based on Majrashi's [4] experiment dividing the menus into short menus of 7 items and medium menus of 13 items, it was found that among the short menus only the first operation would occur when text-only is better than icon-text condition, and on repetition the effect of the two was not significantly different, whereas in the experiment of Muftah et al. [6],when the list term is 5, a significant difference is already observed. So we put our focus on cases where the number of items is under 10, to explore whether the icon exactly promotes the search performance of the project. The list total number of items factor, level 3, is 4, 7 and 10 items, respectively. The other factor was icon type, which was divided into 4 levels, namely icon, index, symbol, and nonsense circle. As a control group without icons was set up for this experiment, the experimental material of the control group was consistent with the experimental group except for the absence of icons.

3.2 Pre Experiments and Materials

The icon for this experiment was mainly collected from the Iconfont website, which was owned by Amal, and influential factors such as affective effects, familiarity, and brand attributes were avoided in the icon picking [27, 28]. For the first time, a total of 74 common, brand-free attribute icon elements were taken, and 78 combinations of icons and text formation were made. To avoid an excessive gap in semantic association of icons and text that resulted in experimental error for participant due to their cognitive familiarity, all combinations of icons and text were tested for cognitive familiarity via the form of a web questionnaire. The questionnaire was in the form of a 5-level Likert scale. Due to the large number of icons and the feeling of fatigue easily caused by the participant being placed on them at random, all combinations of icons and words were placed into four questionnaires. Those older than 40 years and those who repeatedly completed the questionnaires were handled as invalid questionnaires. A total of 42 and 41 valid questionnaires were returned for the first questionnaire, 42 and 45 valid questionnaires were returned for the second and third questionnaires, respectively. Figure and word combinations with a score greater than or equal to 4 were calculated, from which 21 each of icon sign class, index sign class, symbol sign class and circle sign class word combinations were selected. All text items were at a minimum of 2 characters and a maximum of 4 characters in length. Four sets of combinations were picked out for each category, obtaining a total of 16 sets of target items (see Fig. 3), the others appeared as distractor. Charting text combinations as stimulus items will no longer appear as distractor.

All icons in the experiment are 30 × 30 px in size, all take linear icons and are colored black (#333333). To avoid interference from other factors, all the final screened

Icon	🐣	医生 (Doctor)	🗂	文件夹 (Folder)	🍔	美食 (Delicious food)	💄	化妆品 (Cosmetics)
Index	🛒	商城 (Mall)	📖	阅读 (Read)	☑	编辑 (Edit)	🔔	提醒 (Remind)
Symbol	¥	支付 (Pay)	⑱	招聘 (Recruit)	🏛	官方 (Official)	折	折扣商品 (Discount goods)
Circle	○	云朵 (Cloud)	○	打印 (Print)	○	热门 (Hot)	○	邮件 (Mail)

Fig. 3. Targeting items

icons were homogenized in this study. The final effect is shown in Fig. 4.Text aspects because all participant were native Chinese speakers, all accompanying text were Chinese characters. Font is in Android mobile phone common Chinese font Source Han Sans CN regular, and the font color is consistent with the icon color. To ensure clear visualization of the stimuli by all participant, font size was 20 px and text spacing was 30 px. Since Chinese characters are a kind of text read from left to right, all the words adopt left alignment. The icon is placed on the left side of the text. The distance between the center point of the icon and the left side of the text is calculated. The distance is required to be 35 px, as shown in the Fig. 5. The text part is aligned with the center of the background length, and the left end of the text exceeds the center line of the page by 20 px. No icon material is based on there being an icon material, with no alteration in terms of the text, and only the icon is removed.

Fig. 4. Processed distractor icons

The final material size is 1920 × 1080, the main background color is gray (#707070), in order to prevent visual fatigue caused by too white screen color. The width of the middle stimulus background is 300 px, which is pure white. In order to prevent the error caused by the location factor of the target item, each type of icon will have two positions above the center and two positions below the center. There are 48 icon materials and 48 non icon materials.

3.3 Experimental Equipment, Participants, and Procedures

The experimental used the SMI ETG 2W to record eye movements, the Begaze 3.7 was used for related data processing, and SPSS 20 was used for data analysis. Stimuli were presented by a notebook with a screen resolution of 1920 × 1080, 15.6 in. Content for experimental use was played back with WPS presentation.

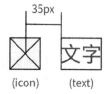

(icon)   (text)

Fig. 5. The part from the center of the icon to the left of the text is 35 px.

The experimental participant were all 24 students from Xuhui campus of East China University of technology, including 12 boys and 12 girls, all aged 18–30 years, with 6 boys and 6 girls as the blank control group and others as the experimental group. Participant all used smart phones and were familiar with the smart phone icon. All participant had normal corrected visual acuity, achromatopsia and weak colour, were right-handed, were trained before formal testing to ensure correct operation in formal experiments.

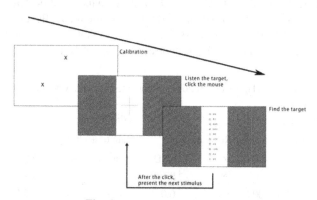

Fig. 6. Experimental procedure

Prior to formal commencement, participant were informed of the relevant precautions, and a calibration was performed where participants maintained head fixation at the time of testing. The formal testing process was as follows: 1) the participants first marked the cross on the screen and placed the mouse in the middle of the cross, 2) the investigator began reading the start word with the same start word and target text, clicked the mouse after being heard, and entered the next page, and 3) through the binocular search target, do not use the mouse until the target is not found, avoiding affecting eye movement data by mouse movement collection [17]; 4) after the target was found hold out and click; 5) then proceeded to the next cross, repeating the above step with every 10 material completed and a 10 s rest with eyes closed. (See Fig. 6) Each participant will view the 48 pieces of material, and in order to eliminate sequential effects and errors resulting from familiarity, the material is rendered in accordance with the order of the experimental material seen by each participant after random ordering.

4 Result

4.1 Rate of Accuracy and Reaction Time

The Rate of accuracy was obtained by manual recording of the video. The search time as the time from when the participants could clearly see the experimental material after clicking on the cross to the first 0.001s after the experimental material disappeared. The calculation of reaction time culled the data of participants selection error.

Between Group

In terms of accuracy, when the total number of items was 7, no one searched for errors. Through repeated measurement ANOVA, the results are shown in Table 3, whether there is interaction effect between the number of items and the icon ($F = 1.517$, $P = 0.221 > 0.05$, $\eta^2 = 0.012$); the main effect of the number of items is not significant ($F = 0.517$, $P = 0.597 > 0.05$, $\eta^2 = 0.004$), whether there is main effect of the icon is not significant ($F = 0.017$, $P = 0.897 > 0.05$, $\eta^2 < 0.001$).

In terms of reaction time, there was an interaction between number of items and icon ($F = 0.241$, $P = 0.786 > 0.05$, $\eta^2 = 0.002$); the main effect of item number was significant ($F = 109.843$, $P < 0.001$, $\eta^2 = 0.502$), and the main effect of icon was not significant ($F = 1.062$, $P = 0.304 > 0.05$, $\eta^2 = 0.005$) (Table 2). It can be seen from Table 1 that the reaction time of 4 is the shortest and that of 10 is the longest.

Table 1. Estimated marginal mean of reaction time and rate of accuracy between different quantity

Item quantity	Between group				Within group			
	Rate of accuracy		Reaction time		Rate of accuracy		Reaction time	
	Mean	STD error	Mean (sec)	STD error	Mean	STD error	Mean (sec)	STD error
4	0.990	0.009	1.250	0.036	0.995	0.003	1.246	0.044
7	1.000	0.009	1.526	0.035	1.000	0.003	1.486	0.042
10	0.987	0.009	1.956	0.033	1.000	0.003	1.942	0.041

Within Group

As shown in Table 3, repeated measurement variance showed that the icon type and item number had no interaction effect on the accuracy ($F = 1.000$, $P = 0.482 > 0.05$, $\eta^2 = 0.043$); the main effect of icon type was not significant ($F = 1.000$, $P = 0.371 > 0.05$, $\eta^2 = 0.022$); the item number had significant effect on the reaction time ($F = 1.000$, $P = 0.395 > 0.05$, $\eta^2 = 0.015$).

In terms of reaction time, there was no interaction effect between icon type and item number ($F = 1.236$, $P = 0.294 > 0.05$, $\eta^2 = 0.064$); the main effect of icon type was not significant ($F = 0.713$, $P = 0.546 > 0.05$, $\eta^2 = 0.019$); item number had significant effect on reaction time ($F = 70.323$, $P < 0.001$, $\eta^2 = 0.563$). It can be found from Table 1 that reaction time increased with the increase of item number when the project is 10, the most time is spent.

Table 2. Estimated marginal mean of reaction time, rate of accuracy

	Rate of accuracy		Reaction time	
	Mean	STD error	Mean (sec)	STD error
Condition(Text-only or icon-text)				
Text-only	0.992	0.008	1.598	0.029
Icon-text	0.993	0.007	1.557	0.027
Type of sign				
Icon	0.993	0.003	1.538	0.049
Index	1.000	0.003	1.610	0.050
Symbol	1.000	0.003	1.570	0.047
Circle	1.000	0.003	1.513	0.050

Table 3. ANOVA results of the reaction time and rate of accuracy

	Source	Rate of accuracy				Reaction time			
		df	F	P	η^2	df	F	P	η^2
Between group	Condition	1	0.017	0.897	< 0.001	1	1.062	0.304	0.005
	Quantity	2	0.517	0.597	0.004	2	109.843	< 0.001	0.502
	Quantity*condition	2	1.517	0.221	0.012	2	0.241	0.786	0.002
Within group	Type	3	1.000	0.395	0.022	3	0.713	0.546	0.019
	Quantity	2	1.000	0.371	0.015	2	70.323	< 0.001	0.563
	Type*quantity	6	1.000	0.428	0.043	6	1.236	0.294	0.064

4.2 Fixation Count and Average Fixation Duration

The fixation count refers to the number of all fixation points in the region of interest. The number of fixation points represents the number of information processed by users [7, 24, 25].

The average fixation time of fixation points refers to the average fixation time of each fixation point. The longer the fixation time is, the longer the visual processing process of the target item is, and the more processing resources are, which proves that the more complex information needs to be processed [12].

Between Group

Firstly, the fixation count and the average fixation time for the whole region of interest (including all text and icons) are analyzed. In Table 4, icon-text has more fixation count. Through repeated measurement ANOVA results (Table 5), the presence or absence of icon does have a significant impact on fixation count (F = 5.420, P = 0.021 < 0.05, η^2 = 0.025). The number of items had a significant effect on the number of fixation points (F = 64.571, P < 0.001, η^2 = 0.377). The larger the number of items, the more the fixation count (see Fig. 7). There was no interaction between the number of items and the presence or absence of icons (F = 0.461, P = 0.631 > 0.05, η^2 = 0.004).

Table 4. Estimated marginal mean of the total fixation count and average fixation duration between group

Condition (Text-only/icon-text)	Total fixation count		Average fixation duration (Including area of icon and text)		Average fixation duration (area of text)	
	Mean (ms)	STD error	Mean (ms)	STD error	Mean (ms)	STD error
Text-only	3.264	0.103	788.756	35.604	632.047	27.726
Icon-text	3.591	0.095	653.230	32.634	522.672	26.435

Table 5. ANOVA results of the fixation count and average fixation duration

	Source	Total fixation count				Average fixation duration			
		df	F	P	η^2	df	F	P	η^2
Between group	Condition	1	5.420	0.021	0.025	1	7.874	0.005	0.035
	quantity	2	64.571	<0.001	0.377	2	0.012	0.988	<0.001
	Quantity*condition	2	0.461	0.631	0.004	2	0.162	0.850	0.002
Within group	Type	3	2.411	0.071	0.064	3	1.224	0.305	0.033
	Quantity	2	43.991	<0.001	0.454	2	6.736	0.002	0.113
	Type*quantity	6	1.556	0.167	0.081	6	0.983	0.441	0.053

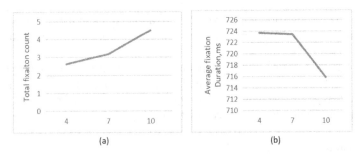

Fig. 7. Fixation count (a) and average fixation duration (b) of item quantity (Source: Writer)

In order to further understand whether the existence of icons has an impact on text retrieval performance, repeated measurement analysis of variance was conducted for the average fixation time in the text interest area (except icons) between the two groups. The results are shown in Table 6, whether there is interaction effect between the number of items and icons (F = 1.301, P = 0.275 > 0.05, η^2 = 0.012), and whether there is a contrast effect between icons Visual time had a significant effect (F = 8.152, P = 0.005 < 0.05, η^2 = 0.038). In the case of text-only, the fixation time is longer than that of icon-text, and the cognitive efficiency of text is improved.

Table 6. ANOVA results of the average fixation duration of area of text between group

Source	Average fixation duration			
	df	F	P	η^2
Condition	1	8.152	0.005	0.038
Quantity	2	3.386	0.036	0.032
Quantity*condition	2	1.301	0.275	0.012

Within Group

The main effect of icon type on the number of fixation points is not significant, but it has a weak effect (F = 2.411, P = 0.071 > 0.05, η^2 = 0.064), the main effect of item number is significant (F = 43.991, P < 0.001, η^2 = 0.454), and the interaction effect of icon type and item number is not significant (F = 1.556, P = 0.167 > 0.05, η^2 = 0.081). In the mean fixation time, the main effect of chart type was not significant (F = 1.224, P = 0.305 > 0.05, η^2 = 0.033), the main effect of item number was significant (F = 6.736, P = 0.002 < 0.05, η^2 = 0.113), and the interaction between icon type and item number was not significant (F = 0.983, P = 0.441 > 0.05, η^2 = 0.053) (See Table 5) (Table 7).

Table 7. Estimated marginal mean of the total fixation count and average fixation duration within group

	Total fixation count		Average fixation duration	
	Mean	STD error	Mean (ms)	STD error
Quantity				
4	2.730	0.167	571.872	33.349
7	3.278	0.154	619.849	31.612
10	4.734	0.151	461.433	30.872
Type of sign				
Icon	3.511	0.196	539.561	40.325
Index	3.837	0.181	552.425	37.105
Symbol	3.759	0.167	508.107	34.145
Circle	3.218	0.182	604.112	37.270

Since icon type has a weak influence on the number of annotated viewpoints, they were further paired compared, and the results are shown in Table 8. Of these, the circle has significantly fewer fixation points than the index and symbolic types, as shown in Fig. 8(a).

Table 8. Paired comparison results of the total fixation count of type within group

(I) type	(J) type	Mean difference	STD error	p
Icon	Index	−0.326	0.267	0.225
	Symbol	−0.248	0.258	0.337
	Circle	0.293	0.268	0.277
Index	Icon	0.326	0.267	0.225
	Symbol	0.078	0.246	0.752
	Circle	0.619	0.257	0.018
Symbol	Icon	0.248	0.258	0.337
	Index	−0.078	0.246	0.752
	Circle	0.541	0.247	0.030

4.3 First fixation Duration

The first fixation duration, which is the length of fixation at the first fixation point in a region of interest for a target, is the process of making the first preliminary identification of both the text and the icon and also reflects sensitivity to the difficulty of target processing [26, 27].

Between Group
AOI include target icons and text. After analyzing the data by repeated measures ANOVA, the results of Table 10, with and without icons, showed a significant effect on the first fixation time ($F = 7.854$, $P = 0.005 < 0.05$, $\eta^2 = 0.035$), the first fixation time with icon text was shorter than that with text only. There was no significant effect of the number of items on the first fixation time ($F = 0.012$, $P = 0.988 > 0.05$, $\eta^2 < 0.001$). There was also no interaction between the number of items and the list length ($F = 0.162$, $P = 0.850 > 0.05$, $\eta^2 = 0.002$).

Within Group
Within groups, Table 10 was obtained by repeated measures ANOVA, and the icon type and item number interaction effects were not significant ($F = 0.360$, $P = 0.903 > 0.05$, $\eta^2 = 0.020$), the icon type main effect was not significant ($F = 0.469$, $P = 0.704 > 0.05$, $\eta^2 = 0.013$), and the item number main effect was not significant ($F = 0.057$, $P = 0.945 > 0.05$, $\eta^2 = 0.001$).

Table 9. Estimated marginal mean of the first fixation duration and fixation time of type between group

	First fixation duration		Visual intake time	
	Mean (ms)	STD error	Mean (ms)	STD error
Condition (Text-only or icon-text)				
Text-only	788.756	35.604	960.531	33.371
Icon-text	653.230	32.634	981.493	30.731
Type of sign				
Icon	606.546	60.455	1034.688	52.883
Index	660.734	60.260	1020.782	52.712
Symbol	634.850	56.577	921.235	49.491
Circle	703.931	60.723	955.738	53.117

Table 10. ANOVA results of the first fixation duration and fixation time of type between group

	Source	First fixation duration				Visual intake time			
		df	F	P	η^2	df	F	P	η^2
Between group	Condition	1	7.854	0.005	0.035	1	0.214	0.644	0.001
	Quantity	2	0.012	0.988	< 0.001	2	0.796	0.452	0.007
	Quantity*condition	2	0.162	0.850	0.002	2	0.252	0.778	0.002
Within group	Type	3	0.469	0.704	0.013	3	1.095	0.355	0.030
	Quantity	2	0.057	0.945	0.001	2	0.520	0.596	0.010
	Quantity*type	6	0.360	0.903	0.020	6	0.887	0.507	0.047

Through the data presented in Table 9, the mean values of the first fixation time for the individual types of icons were smaller than the mean values from text only, although the gap between fixation times for the different types of icons was not large. So the different types of icon and text-only cases were further analyzed by repeated measures ANOVA followed by paired analysis to explore which types of icon had significantly less fixation time than the no icon cases. The results are shown in Table 11. Both the index and symbol icons had significantly less first fixation time than the no icon, as shown in Fig. 8(b).

4.4 Fixation Time

The longer the fixation time of the target, the more time it takes for the participants to identify the meaning of the target, or it can be said that the target item is harder to identify.

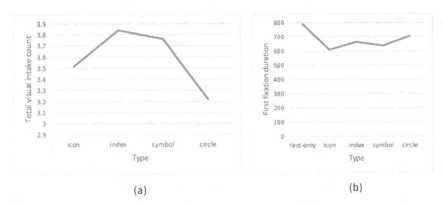

(a)   (b)

Fig. 8. (a)Total fixation count of different type within group. (b)First fixation duration of icon of different type and text-only. (Source: Writer)

Table 11. Paired comparison results of the first fixation duration between different type and text-only

(I) type	(J) type	Mean difference (I-J) (ms)	STD error	p
Text-only	Icon	182.210	76.597	0.018
	Index	128.022	76.405	0.095
	Symbol	153.906	72.804	0.036
	Circle	84.825	76.861	0.271

Icon with or without, item quantity and their interaction effect were all not significant effect on fixation duration. The type of icon, quantity of items and the their interaction effect had no significant effect on fixation duration. (See Table 10).

4.5 Heat Map and Eye Movement Contrail

The heat map reflects the concentration of fixation point, and the more concentrated the point of the heat map, the easier the participants is to find the target option, and the higher the search efficiency. When the number of items is 10, the heat map is most focused and the search efficiency is highest, but fewer people will notice the icon, when the icon is circle, when the quantity is 7, the heat map is more concentrated than the graph free hot spots, when the number of items is 7, the target icon is easier to find, and when the number of items is 4 Case, the heat map distributions of all icons are compared across the sets and no significant differences can be discerned. In addition, there were more participants in the icon region of the image icon to focus on regardless of the number of list items (Fig. 9).

Compared with the situation without icons, part of the participants took the way of not viewing icons when doing the lookup, while another part of the participants adopted

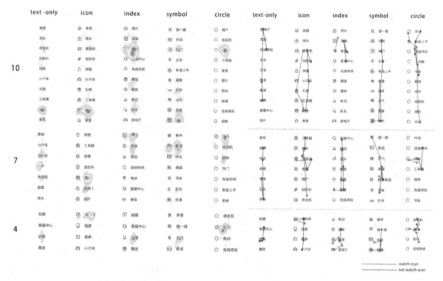

Fig. 9. The heat map and the eye movement contrail

the strategy of viewing icons after viewing the text, and this result was consistent with that in Fleetwood and Byrne [28]. But there is a very small number of participants who will reconfirm the text after viewing the icons. The pictures show the differences in the eye movement tracks between the participants who view icons and those who do not, where, the overall eye movement trajectory of the participants who view icons is more biased to the left, while for the participants who do not view icons, the overall trajectory and the status in plain text are similar, but will go slightly to the right.

5 Discussion

In this experiment, mainly investigated the presence of icons and whether the type of icons can have an effect on the app tabulated menu with an item number of 10 or less. Results showed that with the number of items on the list ranging from 4 to 10, the effects produced by icons did not change with the quantity of items on the list, and no interaction effects between the two were produced.

From the eye movement track, the presence of icons can only lead some people to pay attention to them. This and the individual's search habits were seen to have a great relationship by asking the participants. The reading habits of the tabular layout were more applicable to the reading mode of the text, so the participants tended to observe the text as the main body of the reading without reading and comprehension barriers in terms of words, and icons more often served an auxiliary purpose [29].

The correct rate of the search was more than 92% with and without icons, and this result was consistent with Majrashi's [4] sitting time short list experiment and Muftah et al.'s [6] control group experiment, which also proved the validity of this experiment in material selection. Search times with and without icons and different icon types did not differ significantly for item numbers less than and equal to 10. Two reasons for this result: 1) the initiation item takes the form of recitation of the text, and the content of the recitation and the text of the target item are consistent, leading people to pay more attention to the text than to the icon. 2) Participants will both look at the text, so the addition of icons rather increases the need for cognitive analysis and is more visuospatially complex, but because the icons are able to help the text understand to some extent, the time for the two offsets with each other. The results of the present study and those of Muftah et al. [6] are opposite, yielding results that may be explained by differences in language and participants age between the two or by differences in the arrangement of experimental designs.

The fixation counts reflects the amount of information processed by the participants. The bigger fixation counts, the more the participants pay attention to, which indicates the breadth of attention resources. Although the results show that the fixation count of the participants with icon is more, because in the case of icon, the participants who pay attention to the icon not only need to deal with the text information, but also need to deal with the content and meaning of the icon, so the attention resources will be more scattered, and the complexity of visual space will be increased [16]. The icon can promote the transmission of information through the visualization, which can indeed improve the efficiency of search.

Between icons of different symbol types, circles had the fewest fixation counts when combined with text, with mean values approaching those of pure text, or even less. Taken together, participants had fewer resources to process, were more efficient at retrieval and easier to find the target option.

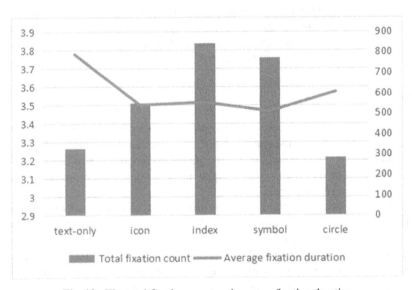

Fig. 10. The total fixation count and average fixation duration

The first fixation time with icons was shorter than that without, and lower for image and symbolic symbols (see Fig. 10). That is, with icons, participants would be faster to capture the meaning of the goal option, and icon and symbols would be more able to make participants cognitively feel the overall goal easy to recognize. This finding provides support for the partial App (e.g. the icon of 'Yuncun tickets') adoption of word type symbolic symbol icons.

There were icon groups that performed better on first fixation time, but both did not differ significantly on fixation duration, nor between the different types of icons, indicating that there was not a large difference in the amount of cognitive resource input between them, regardless of the type of icon.

 视频号

Fig. 11. The icon of video in Wechat

On the whole, icons will not have a great impact on the search performance of list menus with less than 10 lists, and the semantic types of icons will not have a great impact. This also provides some support for the use of icons that are not related to text content in some app lists on the market, such as the video Number icon and video Icon in wechat. The icon has no semantic relationship (see Fig. 11). In this study, affected by the epidemic, the selection range of educational background and age of the participants is narrow and the number is small. In the future research, more research will be carried out for users with different educational background and age background and different types of use scenarios.

6   Conclusion

1. The results show that for young users, the list style dishes with the item quantity less than 10 did not significantly differ in reaction time with or without icons, nor did different types of icons significantly affect search time.
2. In the case of having a specific search target, for a list with icons, only a part of the users will look at the icon, and a part of the users will not look at it.
3. To be able to reduce cognitive processing depth in the presence of icons, reducing attentional resources for early identification processes.
4. The use of a meaningless circle icon can help the user to concentrate more resources and process to a lighter depth, and the use of symbolic signs icon and image symbols can more allow the user to reduce the use of attentional resources in the early identification process and understand the meaning of the target earlier.
5. This study provides experimental support for the utilization of list menu part icons in the current human-computer interface to facilitate better visual search behaviors in the human-computer interface.

References

1. Yantao, R., Yuchang, H., Xue, S.: The saccades and its mechanism in the process of visual search. Adv. Psychol. Sci. **14**(003), 340–345 (2006). https://doi.org/10.3969/j.issn.1671-3710.2006.03.004

2. Miguel, P., Eckstein.: Visual search: a retrospective. J. Vis. **11**(5), 74–76 (2011)
3. Zhang, X., Chengqi, X., Zhangfan, S.: Analysis of icon complexity in human-computer interaction digital interface. Sheji. (19), 119–120 (2017). https://doi.org/10.3969/j.issn.1003-0069.2017.19.055
4. Majrashi, K.: Performance of mobile users with text-only and text-and-icon menus in seated and walking situations. Behav. Inf. Technol. (2020). https://doi.org/10.1080/0144929X.2020.1795257
5. Lodding, K.N.: Iconic interfacing. IEEE Comput. Graph. Appl. **3**(2), 11–20 (2006)
6. Muftah, M., Altaboli, A.: Investigating the Effect of Adding Visual Content to Textual Search Interfaces on Accessibility of Dyslexic Users. In: Antona, M., Stephanidis, C. (eds.) HCII 2020. LNCS, vol. 12188, pp. 289–299. Springer, Cham (2020). https://doi.org/10.1007/978-3-030-49282-3_20
7. Song, Z.: Research on Landmark Symbol Design of Mobile Navigation Map Based on Eye Movement Experiment. China University of Geosciences (2019)
8. Burmistrov, I., Zlokazova, T., Izmalkova, A., Leonova, A.: Flat Design vs Traditional Design: Comparative Experimental Study. In: Abascal, J., Barbosa, S., Fetter, M., Gross, T., Palanque, P., Winckler, M. (eds.) INTERACT 2015. LNCS, vol. 9297, pp. 106–114. Springer, Cham (2015). https://doi.org/10.1007/978-3-319-22668-2_10
9. Xi, T., Wu, X.: The influence of different style of icons on users' visual search in touch screen interface. In: International Conference on Applied Human Factors and Ergonomics (2018)
10. Wang, X., Li, H., Ma, S.: Research progress on factors affecting icon search performance. Packag. Eng. **42**(6), 206–211 (2021). https://doi.org/10.19554/j.cnki.1001-3563.2021.06.029
11. Tang, X.T., Yao, J., Hu, H.F.: Visual search experiment on text characteristics of vital signs monitor interface. Displays **62**, 101944 (2020)
12. Peng, N., Xue, C.: Experimental study on characteristics of icon searching based on feature inference. J. SE Univ. (Nat. Sci. Edn.) **47**, 703–709 (2017)
13. Charles, J.K., Jane, M.C.: Assessing the usability of icons in user interfaces. Behav. Inf. Technol. **10**(6), 443–457 (1991). https://doi.org/10.1080/01449299108924303
14. Yao, Y.: Effect of Icon Presentation and Complexity on Icon Search Efficiency. Sun Yat-sen University (2020)
15. Berget, G., Mulvey, F., Sandnes, F.E.: Is visual content in textual search interfaces beneficial to dyslexic users? Int. J. Hum. Comput. Stud. **92–93**, 17–29 (2016). https://doi.org/10.1016/j.ijhcs.2016.04.006
16. Aaltonen, A., Hyrskykari, A., Raiha, K.J.: 101 spots, or how do users read menus?, pp. 132–139 (1998)
17. Isherwood, S.: Graphics and semantics: the relationship between what is seen and what is meant in icon design. In: International Conference of Engineering Psychology and Cognitive Ergonomics, San Diego, CA, USA, pp.197–205 (2009). https://doi.org/10.1007/978-3-642-02728-4_21
18. Zhao, Y.: Semiotics Principles and Problems. Nanjing University Press (2011)
19. Isherwood, S.J., McDougall, S.J.P., Curry, M.B.: Icon identification in context: the changing role of icon characteristics with user experience. Hum. Factors **49**(3), 465–476 (2007). https://doi.org/10.1518/001872007X200102
20. McDougall, S., Isherwood, S.: What's in a name? The role of graphics, functions, and their interrelationships in icon identification. Behav. Res. Methods **41**, 325–336 (2009)
21. McDougall, S., Reppa, I., Kulik, J., Taylor, A.: What makes icons appealing? The role of processing fluency in predicting icon appeal in different task contexts. Appl. Ergon. **55**, 156–172 (2016). https://doi.org/10.1016/j.apergo.2016.02.006
22. Irwin, D.A., Knott, J.R., McAdam, D.W., et al.: Motivational determinants of the contingent negative variation. Electroencephalogr. Clin. Neurophysiol. **21**(6), 538–543 (2006)

23. Spruyt, A., Houwer, J.D., Hermans, D.: Modulation of automatic semantic priming by feature-specific attention allocation. J. Mem. Lang. **61**, 37–54 (2009). https://doi.org/10.1016/j.jml.2009.03.004

24. 安顺钰. Usability evaluation Research on mobile phone user interface base on eye tracking. Zhejiang University (2008)

25. Zelinsky, G.J., Sheinberg, D.L.: Eye movements during parallel-serial visual search. J. Exp. Psychol. Hum. Percept. Perform. **23**(1), 244–262 (1997). https://doi.org/10.1037//0096-1523.23.1.244

26. Wei, L., Chen, Y.: Cartography eye movements study and the experimental parameters analysis. Bull. Surveying Mapp. (10), 16–20 (2012)

27. Zhang, X., Wenling, Y.: Review of oculomotor measures in current reading research. Stud. Psychol. Behav. **4**(003), 236–240 (2006)

28. Fleetwood, M.D., Byrne, M.D.: Modeling icon search in ACT-R/PM. Cogn. Sys. Res. **3**(1), 25–33 (2002)

29. Shu, Y.: Research on Smartphone Icon Recognition Efficiency Based on Design Factors. Southwest Jiaotong University (2018)

Usability Assessment of the XiaoAi Touch Screen Speaker

Naixin Liu[✉], Shuyue Li, Wang Xiang, Yue Xu, Jiayu Zeng, and Marcelo M. Soares

School of Design, Hunan University, Hunan 410000, People's Republic of China

Abstract. With the development of modern economy and technology, people's living standards are constantly improving, and more intelligent products have come into people's vision. People's requirements for product availability are also increasing. This research is carried out with an intelligent speaker called Xiao MI XiaoAi touch screen speaker and the main and specific functions of it was measured through a series of tasks. And this experiment was described as a summary usability assessment. Through a variety of usability evaluation methods, the most troublesome part of Xiao Ai speakers was experimented to get and tried to give some solutions and new ideas. In addition, the participants were divided into three group of users in this experiment: novice, occasional and expert to ensure that the experimental results are authentic and credible.

Keywords: Usability · User · Product · Design · Intelligence speaker

1 Introduction

With the development of modern technology, the functions of the speakers have become ever more diverse. It can not only play music, but also set alarm clocks, provide recipes, play weather forecast, use as a calculator, etc. Sometimes it can also be used as a home wisdom center. In addition, the operation method of the product has become more and more complicated, from simple button adjustment to both touch screen control and voice control. From some perspectives, it has more usage scenarios such as remote control of smart appliances in the home or carry out orders while people are busy doing other things. It makes the lives more convenient, but for a speaker, with the increase of functions, its difficulty of use is gradually increasing. Through the usability research methods, some problems in the process of interacting with smart speakers were found, so that designers can solve these problems based on the research and provide users with a better experience.

2 Experiment Method

The study is based on the user experience measurement and usability metrics [1]. According to ISO [2] usability should be measured in three dimensions: effectiveness, efficiency and satisfaction. Jordan [3] claims that the definition of effectiveness refers to whether

M. M. Soares et al. (Eds.): HCII 2021, LNCS 12781, pp. 66–78, 2021.
https://doi.org/10.1007/978-3-030-78227-6_6

the user task is completed or not, and whether the task is completed is valid, Efficiency is defined as the refers to the amount of effort required to accomplish a goal, and Satisfaction refers to the level of comfort that the users feel when using a product and how acceptable the product is to users as a means of achieving their goals.

The main functions of the intelligence speaker were measured and identify whether the goal is combined well with the function, if not, the improvement proposal for reference to the participants' data will be putted forward.

2.1 Method

The Xiaomi's Xiaoai touch screen speakers (Fig. 1) were chosen because this touchscreen speakers are the future development trend of smart speakers. In addition, the functions of Xiaoai touchscreen speakers are relatively focused, with few influencing factors, which facilitates the advancement of experiments.

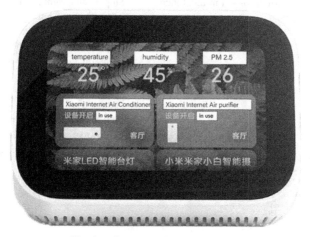

Fig. 1. Xiao Ai touch screen speaker

2.2 Participants

Eight participants were enrolled from Henan province and NingXia province, China. According to the methods from Jordan [3], Booth [4] and Leventhal and Barnes [5]. The participants were divided into three groups of users: novice (3), occasional (3), and expert (2). They were guided to finish the task by the task book. After that, they asked to fill the questionnaires. Subjective and the qualitative data based on the questionnaires were collected.

2.3 Task Analysis

Based on the speaker itself, there are three parts in its operation, including 1) getting prepared, 2) voice control, 3) touch screen control. Referring to the functions of the speaker, the detailed sub-tasks were set up. According to these sub-tasks, there are 4 tasks (Table 1):

Table 1. Experiment tasks

Task number	Mission details	Key operation
Task 1	Turn on the product	Step 1: connect the charging cable Step 2: wait for the speaker to turn on
Task 2	Make dumplings according to Xiao Ai's instructions	Step 1: "Xiao Ai" Step 2: "how to make dumplings?" Step 3: follow the instructions
Task 3	3–1:Play a piano piece through touch screen, 3–2:pause song through touch screen, 3–3: switch songs through touch screen	Step 1: click the screen (wake up XiaoAi) Step 2: click the "music" button Step 3: slide right and click the "classification" button Step 4: click the "light music" button Step 5: slide and find the "Classification of piano music" Step 6: click the "piano music" button Step 7: find the interface of the song being played Step 8: click the pause or toggle button
Task 4	4–1:Play Lin Junjie's song 'Mermaid' by voice control, 4–2:pause song by voice control, 4–3:switch songs by voice control	Step 1: "Xiao Ai" Step 2: "Play Lin Junjie's song 'Mermaid'" Step 3: "Pause" Step 4: "Next song"

2.4 Think Aloud

Think aloud method was used to let the user speak while thinking about what the user wants [3]. During the experiment, the user can say "I think the following should be done like this…". In this way, researchers can easily grasp which part of the user's attention, what he thinks, and what kind of operation is taken. This is a very effective evaluation method that can figure out why it leads to bad results.

Though this method we found that users felt confusing when they search the ideal songs by the touch screen because the classification instructions of the songs are not clear enough, and there is a lack of search bar. These shortcomings can lead to a poor user experience.

2.5 Questionnaire

In the experiment, the participants need to complete two kinds of questionnaires: the user information table questionnaire and the Likert scale [6].

User Information Table Questionnaire. The purpose of the questionnaire is to clarify the background of the participants, to guarantee whether they have ever used the smart speaker to divide them into appropriate group. Through the understanding of the basic information, the participants were split into three groups: novices, ordinary users, and expert users.

Likert Scale. The Likert scale was used to collect feedback from participants after completing each task. This scale is used to assess the user's satisfaction with product features.

We found that user satisfaction are mostly below average. Especially in using recipes and finding music by category.

2.6 Interview

In the experiment, after the participants finished the questionnaire, the users were interviewed. It was used two kinds of interview: Semi-structured and Unstructured interviews [7].

Semi-structured. The semi-structured interview is an exploratory interview used most often in the social sciences for qualitative research purposes or to gather clinical data. This interview was used after the users have finished the questionnaire and was based on the scores and ask the relevant question such as" What do you think can be done to improve the flow of music?".

Unstructured. Unstructured interview means Interview without any set format but in which the interviewer may have some key questions formulated in advance. Before experiment finished, the users were asked to open-ended questions, such as "Do you have any other ideas for this product".

Through the interview, we found new problems besides those mentioned before, such as users think it is inconvenient to connect wires.

2.7 Data Collection Process

We looked for 8 users, who were divided into three groups (novice, occasional, expert) by using experience.

Firstly, make sure the user is in an indoor environment without outside distractions. Secondly, the same model of Xiao mi Xiao AI touch screen speakers were used for experiments. Thirdly, ensure that each user's experimental materials and experimental procedures are completely consistent.

The user is given a task book with four tasks written on it. According to the lead tester's guidance, the user will complete the four tasks in turn. As users complete tasks, they are asked to speak out their thoughts. When each task is completed, users will be asked to fill out a Likert scale.We will also conduct some interviews based on users' ratings.

3 Analysis

On this study, the physical behavior and the subjective opinion tough think aloud and interview were collected as the qualitative data as well as the results of the Likert scale as quantitative data. The combination of qualitative and quantitative data were used to assess the usability of each task.

3.1 Qualitative Data

The qualitative data used in the research were "Think aloud" and "interview".

Think Aloud. The identified problems obtained in the Think aloud technique is shown in Table 2. The mentioned table shown that there are some problems with power supply, the pause of the voice broadcast, and some of the text and pictures can cause user's confusion according to the result.

Table 2. Think aloud data.

Number of people	2	5	4	2	1	6	4	2	4
Content	Tap the screen once to wake up	Want to add search function	Mistakenly thought that they can see the song operation page by clicking the icon of the song software while the song is playing	Unexpected speech recognition results	Misunderstood that the divider is the back button	Unnecessary content	Complex song classification	Click the icon to play the song directly instead of the song list	Text and picture issues
Picture	20:28								
Remarks	1 person: Misunderstood that it is the same as the mobile phone to slide to unlock			1 person: The content spoken is too simple and lacks qualifiers, resulting in other content being searched		2 people: unnecessary recommended content			1 person: the text is too long, the content is not displayed completely
	2 people: mistakenly believe that double-click to unlock			1 person: The song name is English, it is difficult to recognize English		2 people: text description should avoid modification			1 person: the text is too small
									2 people: text has nothing to do with pictures

In the process of the user completing the task, the user was encouraged to speak their inner thoughts while operating it again, and then the user's thoughts were summarized. One novice subject pointed out the following questions: don't know how to wake up the screen because it is different from the mobile phone's sliding unlock, it needs to click. He wanted to add search function because it's hard to find songs by category alone. He also said that supposed to see the song operation page by clicking the icon of the song software while the song is playing, but in fact he can't. He concludes that the speaker has difficulty in recognizing English correctly. One of the novices mistook a sidebar for a back button. A half of novice respondents answered that the song classification is complex they also said (how many) that they thought that when clicking in some icon or picture will make the song lists appear but in fact it will make the speaker play the song directly.

A majority of occasional respondents (2) said that the voice commands need to be as detailed as possible. All occasional respondents answered that some contents are unnecessary, such as Recommended songs and the very long text description.

All experts respondents answered that the text and picture issues make them feel difficult in finding out the song, such as text is too small, the content is not displayed completed and text has nothing to do with pictures.

High-frequency words from user answers were extracted in interview and found the following questions:

- Inconvenient to connect wires
- Recipes cannot be displayed in steps
- Song classification is too complicated
- The pictures of the song categories are not strongly related to the content
- No song search function.

Interview. After finishing the test, the testers were asked to fulfill the Questionnaire. According to the questionnaire, we asked some relevant questions such as: How do you like this function and how do you think it could be improved? The result of the interview is shown on Table 3, 4 and 5, respectively, for novice, occasional, and expert users.

Table 3. Result of the interview with novice users

	Novice1	Novice2	Novice3
Task1	That's OK	It would be better if he could swipe up to unlock it	It is very convenient
Task2	This function is kind of useless because it's hassle to bring it to the kitchen	It speaks too fast, and I can't follow the Instructions	I'd prefer it can give the instructions step by step
Task3	There's a lot of distracting information, it's hard to find the target information	The directory prompt is too complicated; it should be shorter	I don't understand its hierarchical logic
Task4	That's OK	I like to find songs this way	Very convenient

According to the interviewers, the main found problems were focused on instructions for recipes and using the touch screen to find songs. They recommended a more visual guide to find recipe and song classification for searching songs. Additionally, they recommended to optimize the display.

Table 4. Result of the interview with occasional users

	Occasional 1	Occasional 2	Occasional 3
Task1	I use voice wake-up more, but the touch screen is fine	That's OK	This is like waking up your phone, so it's easy to understand
Task2	I've never used this feature before, but it looks OK	I hope it can make the process more vivid	I'm good at cooking, so I don't need this feature
Task3	There's a lot of distracting information, it's hard to find the target information	I hardly ever use the screen to find songs, and from what I've just experienced, the category pages are confusing	I found the target information by accident. The interface is hard to understand
Task4	It's pretty good	This feature is very convenient to use, but sometimes it is not accurate	It's convenient

Table 5. Result of the interview with expert users

	Expert 1	Expert 2
Task1	That's good	——
Task2	I hope Xiao Ai can separate the steps so that the instructions can be more clear	That's OK
Task3	I don't quite understand the meaning of this function, and I don't think it's necessary to have it	I think it is necessary to add a touch search box
Task4	It's pretty good	In my previous use experience, I found that it can recognize Chinese more accurately, but can not recognize English

3.2 Quantitative Data

Quantitative data includes step and accurate to perform a task and self-report questionnaires. The sample was comprised by eight subjects including novice (3), occasional (3), and expert users (2).

Analysis of Step and Accuracy to Perform a Task. In order to measure user efficiency more objectively, we have taken time and number of steps into consideration. Because the operation time of some steps is extremely short, the measurement error is significant, so we choose to measure the number of steps the user completes the task operation.

Before carrying on the test, we conducted a pre-experiment. We measured the minimum steps required to complete each character and compared them with the actual steps of the user (Table 6).

Table 6. Number of steps of four tasks.

STATISTICAL TABLE OF THE NUMBER OF TIMES THE SCREEN IS PRESSED OR THE NUMBER OF VOICE COMMANDS ISSUED

	TASK1	TASK2	TASK3			TASK4		
novice01	1	1	70	5	8	1	1	1
novice02	1	1	25	8	12	1	1	1
novice03	1	1	56	6	4	1	1	1
occasional01	1	1	142 (Give up, mission failed)	2	2	1	1	1
occasional02	1	1	120	2	2	1	1	1
occasional03	1	1	104	2	33	4	1	1
expert01	1	1	19	2	2	1	1	1
expert02	1	1	70	2	2	1	1	1
Minimum number of steps	1	1	13	2	2	1	1	1

We believe that the greater the ratio of the user's actual operation steps to the minimum operation steps, the higher the efficiency of the use of this function.

Use Efficiency = the Minimum Operation Steps/The User's Actual Operation Steps. It can be shown from the table (Table 6), no matter what kind of user, the efficiency of task 3-1(Play a piano piece through touch screen) is the lowest. The usability of find the ideal song by touch screen is the most urgent need for improvement.

Questionnaires. The Likert scale was used to survey users (Table 7). In order to better compare the data, The Radar chart was drawn (Fig. 2). This gray line represents the user's neutral attitude. Some of the values are below this line, which means that these parts cannot satisfy the users.

Introduces Fig. 3. From the Fig. 3, it is obvious that the scores of task 2 and task 3 are lower than the average attitude. According to the Table 7. A large number of users (7) gave lower scores (less than three) to the effectiveness of task 3, which means it has the biggest usability problem.

The conclusions are that:

- User satisfaction and efficiency are mostly below average
- Even if connecting wires is easy to operate, users are still reluctant to connect wires
- The user is dissatisfied with the song list classification, and the song list classification is difficult to help the user to efficiently find the song

4 Findings

4.1 Preliminary Ideas

The quantitative data sheets illustrate that there are some problems in all the tasks. Firstly, this study pays attention to the subjective data to get to know about what prevents users

Table 7. Likert scale of four tasks

Number	Task1 I enjoy the process	Task2 I enjoy the process	Task3 I enjoy the process	Task4 I enjoy the process
1	4	3	1	5
2	5	2	1	4
3	5	3	2	5
4	3	4	1	5
5	4	3	1	4
6	5	2	3	3
7	5	3	2	4
8	4	1	2	5
Total	35	21	13	35

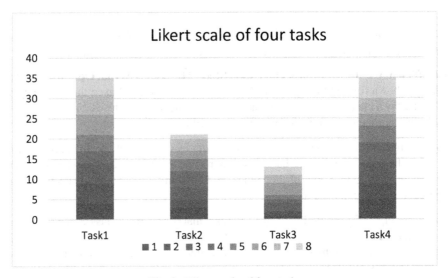

Fig. 2. Likert scale of four tasks

from using this product smoothly. Secondly, the study focused on recording and watching the video of the user operating the product carefully. Also it summarized the problem points into a list. Finally, this research carried out some user interview to get more detailed opinions related to the problem improvement, and the low fidelity pictures that shows the improvement of these problems under the guidance of opinions and suggestions.

4.2 Problems and Improvements

The participants of the study made the following suggestions:

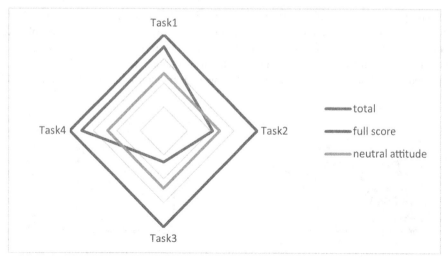

Fig. 3. User's attitude towards the task

Suggestion 1 – Improving Battery Performance. About 50% of the users emphasize the ease of mobility. The small size of the xiao ai speaker generally gives people a sense of mobility, but actually it has limited mobility because it must be connected to a power source.

The solution for this suggestion was set a build-in battery. According to Fig. 4, if it could have a built-in battery, it would not have to be plugged in all the time, When it's connected to a power source, it can recharge the built-in battery. When it isn't connected to a power source, it can work independently.

Fig. 4. The improvement of the power

Suggestion 2 - Visualize Song Classification. When carrying out the task of listening to the music, all of the users mentioned that the table of contents is confusing. It could be observed that the content of text is incomplete and the size of the character is too small, what's more, the pictures of the song list is not matching with the categories of songs.

This problem can be solved by changing the original pictures into new pictures which can show the specific song list. According to Fig. 5, this page is a catalog of songs played by different instruments. The original pictures that were less related to the instruments were replaced with more visual pictures of the instruments. The original long text was replaced by a short instrument name. In this way, users can find what they want more directly.

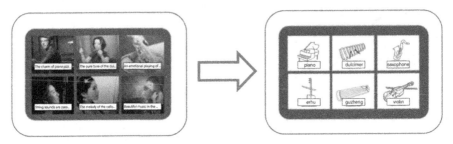

Fig. 5. The improvement of the music classification

Suggestion 3 - Broaden the Search Path. There is also a shortage of searching songs. When listening to the music, users can only find songs by speaking to Xiaoai, they cannot search by typing (Fig. 6). Once Xiaoai cannot successfully recognize the song title by voice, the user will not find the song he wants.

Therefore, it is significant to add the function of search, so that users can search songs by typing. It can be used as a supplement to voice search to further ensure that users can find what they are looking for.

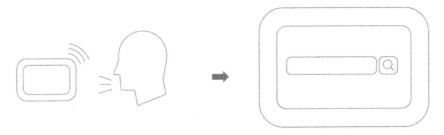

Fig. 6. The improvement of the search function

Suggestion 4 - Visualize the Prompt Steps. According to the interview, three users mentioned the necessity of visualization in recipe instructions. Take the dumpling making tutorial for example, there are seven steps to make dumplings. The steps are displayed in text on the same page, which makes it difficult for the users to read, and the audio broadcast doesn't stop between steps, so if users miss a step, they have to start all over again.

To solve this problem, the proposed solution was that each step is displayed on the screen with a corresponding picture (Fig. 7). In this way, users get information more intuitively, and follow the instructions step by step.

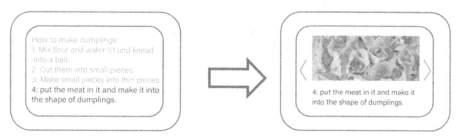

Fig. 7. The improvement of the recipe

5   Conclusion

The interactive interface and menu interface of song classification for Xiaoai touch screen speakers were improved and added a song search function based on user experimental data. Although many users point out that the speaker's touch screen makes the user experience better, but there are also a few users who believe that this screen is less useful. So, the combination of screen operation and voice operation is still to be explored. To a certain extent, the functions such as setting an alarm clock and playing music are overlapping. One thing needs to do is to find a place where the two functions complement each other, simplify complex operations, improve its usability, and enhance the user experience.

There are some limitations of this research: First, the number of tested users were small, and the probability of deviation was high. The results would be more convincing if the number of tested users bigger. Second, we experimented with only one type of touch-screen speaker which may lack universality.

In future, to ensure that the research is comprehensive and accurate. increase the number of testers three to five times which make the results more accurate. Increase the number of models of smart touch-screen speakers and do the same experiment to make sure the conclusions are more representative.

References

1. Tullis, T., William, A.: Measuring the User Experience: Collecting, Analyzing, and Presenting Usability Metrics, 2nd Ed. (2008)
2. ISO 9241-11:2018 (en). Ergonomics of human-system interaction — Part 11: Usability: Definitions and concepts. ISO Online Browsing Plataform (OBP) (2019). https://www.iso.org/obp/ui/#iso:std:iso:9241:-11:ed-2:v1:en, Accessed 8 September 2019
3. Jordan, P.W.: An introduction to usability. Taylor & Francis, London (1998). ISBN-13: 978-0748407620

4. Booth, P.: An Introduction to Human-Computer Interaction. Lawrence Erlbaur Associates Publishers, Hillsdale (1989)
5. Leventhal, L., Barnes, J.: Usability engineering: process, products & examples. Am. J. Psychol. **77**(1), 54–63 (2008)
6. Likert, R.: A technique for the measurement of attitudes. Arch. Psychol. **1932**(140), 1–55 (1932)
7. Welch, J., Patton, M.: Qualitative evaluation and research methods. Modern Lang. J. **76**(4), 543 (1992)

Insights and Lessons Learned from the Design, Development and Deployment of Pervasive Location-Based Mobile Systems "in the Wild"

Konstantinos Papangelis[1](✉), Alan Chamberlain[2], Nicolas LaLone[3], and Ting Cao[1]

[1] Rochester Institute of Technology, Rochester, NY 14623, USA
`kxpigm@rit.edu, tvcs@rit.edu`
[2] University of Nebraska at Omaha, Omaha, NE 68182, USA
`alan.chamberlain@nottingham.ac.uk`
[3] University of Nottingham, Nottingham NG7 2RD, UK
`nlalone@unomaha.edu`

Abstract. This paper, based on a reflective approach, presents several insights and lessons learned from the design, development, and deployment of a location-based social network and a location-based game. These are analyzed and discussed against the life-cycle of our studies, and range from engaging with the participants, to dealing with technical issues while on the field. Overall, the insights and lessons learned illustrate that one should be prepared and flexible enough to accommodate any issues as they arise in a professional manner considering not only the results of the study but also the participants and the researchers involved. The aim of this work to inform researchers and designers about some of the key challenges we encountered during our research into pervasive location-based mobile technologies in the wild.

Keywords: Lessons learned · Guidelines · Design · Development · Deployment · Location-based social networks · Location-based games · Mobile systems · in the wild

1 Introduction

Users' day-to-day life is the primarily focus of studies dealing with pervasive location-based mobile systems. These studies are often classified as in "the wild" [4, 7], and are challenging for both new and expert researchers, due to the amount of time that needs to be spent in the field, to both collect data and to engage with participants. In this paper, we present insights and lessons learned from designing, developing, deploying, and conducting 3 studies with two pervasive systems - a location based social-network (LBSN) called GeoMoments, and a location-based (LBG) game called CityConqueror.

© Springer Nature Switzerland AG 2021
M. M. Soares et al. (Eds.): HCII 2021, LNCS 12781, pp. 79–89, 2021.
https://doi.org/10.1007/978-3-030-78227-6_7

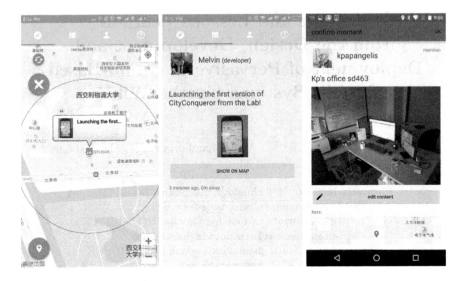

Fig. 1. Users can see and geo-tag pictorial and textual moments 500 m around them. The georestriction is indicated by the blue circle around them (left). The moments can be viewed in a map (left) or on a separate screen via a mobile device (center) or browser (right).

2   Systems and Studies

GeoMoments has been developed to help us explore the locative mobile social media phenomenon and view it through a social navigation and exploration lens. This is intended to provide us with a better understanding of vits influences and the ways in which we experience our surroundings. While there are several location-based social networks out there that let you access and look at the geo-tagged information they are not concerned about exploration, but rather about access to content – photographs, audio etc. In GeoMoments we deliberately restrict access to this content and enable the users to see only what is around 500m from their physical location. This is intended, and is used a feature that can enable us to further understand the ways in location-based social networks influence the creation and consumption of geographically based social information. See Figs. 1 through 4 screenshots of the various functions of GeoMoments.

CityConqueror was inspired by the board game 'Risk', in which a player conquers countries on a world map, deploys units to defend his countries and attacks countries owned by other players. In CityConqueror, players can conquer territories in their physical location, deploy units to defend their territories and attack territories of other players that lie in their physical proximity. When conquering a territory, the player can give it a name that is visible to other players, deploy units to defend the territory and hide a treasure in it. Territories are conquered and plotted on a map of the "real" urban terrain, showing the

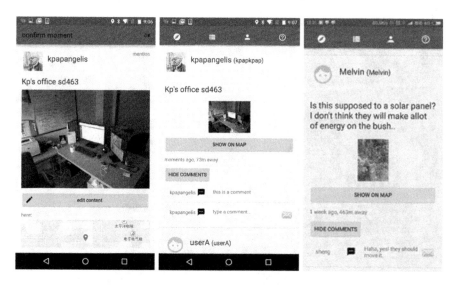

Fig. 2. Users can edit or delete their moments even if they are not physically near them (left). In addition, users can leave comment on other users' moments (center and right).

player's location. The map is covered by the "Fog of War", a mechanism used in other popular games dealing with territorial conquests (see right of Fig. 3).

A player can uncover the Fog of War to reveal more of the map by physically exploring the urban space. When a player has physically visited a space and thereby uncovered the Fog of War overlaying it, they are able to see enemy territories in this area, even after leaving it. To drive the exploration of the map and thereby the player's actual surroundings, the player can see glows (hotspots) in undiscovered spaces, indicating the location of enemy territories in the Fog of War. Territories generate resources over time which can be collected to buy units to defend their own territories or attack enemy territories. To conquer a new territory, players must first defeat all enemy territories in their range. If a player attacks an enemy territory and wins the fight, they have the chance to find the treasure hidden in the enemy territory. Searching for a treasure is a mini-game within the CityConqueror (see Fig. 4).

The player is given a compass that points in the direction of the treasure, the distance in meters to the treasure from the current location and three minutes' time to find the treasure. To find the treasure the player must move to the pointed location. Furthermore, a player can complete achievements that reward actions related to exploring their surroundings and success in the game such as conquering a certain number of territories, conquering territories with a large distance between them, defending territories or attacking others. The objectives of CityConqueror is to claim as many territories as possible to generate income and consequently to be able to defend territories against attacks from others and attack others to conquer their territories. Thus, the game experience of one

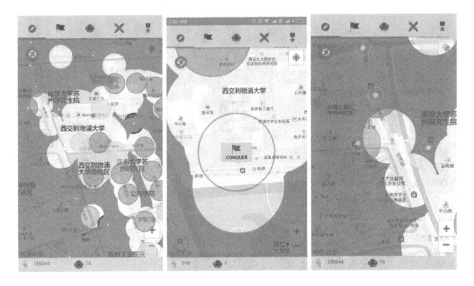

Fig. 3. Territories are plotted on the map (left). A player can conquer a territory in his location (center). Territories in the Fog of War are indicated with glows (right).

player is highly dependent on the actions and interactions of other players. In that way, we have implemented a salient social aspect in the game. See Fig. 2 for screenshots of the various functions of CityConqueror.

With GeoMoments and CityConquyeror we conducted three studies.

Studies 1 and 2 with GeoMoments too place over a 10-week period. The first study took place over a six-week period [2,3,12,13,17]. It aimed to explore the everyday usage of LBSN and involved 42 individuals with an average age of 31 years. The second study run over four weeks, and aimed at exploring the perception of self, space, place and LBSN usage. This second study involved 30 individuals with an average age of 28. Across the two studies the participants generated 985 textual and pictorial moments; 760 being pictorial moments and 225 being textual moments. In both studies, we interviewed the participants during the study, as well as conducting post-experience interviews.

For study 3, we conducted a study with CityConqueror aimed at exploring mobility and territoriality in LBGs [9,14,15]. 12 participants were randomly assigned to one of two teams in order to play CityConqueror over two weeks. The teams competed. The game had a team score mechanism, which was based on the resources collected and treasures found by the players. CityConqueror was played actively and had a high participant engagement level. After the subsequent testing and team play phases, each participant was interviewed to evaluate their experience of the game.

Based on our experiences with these studies, we present and discuss insights and lessons learned based on key challenges that we have successfully overcome with respect to the design, development, execution of the study, and data analysis. The goal of this work is to give researchers and designers a practical

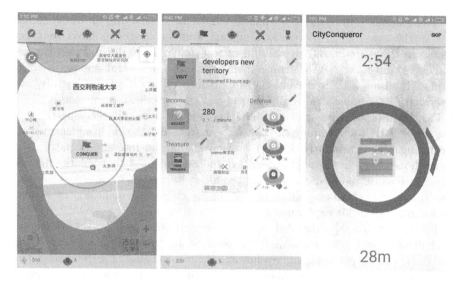

Fig. 4. To conquer a territory the player must first defeat all enemy territories in the range of the territory (the pink ring in the left screenshot). Over time, a territory generates resources (center). After winning a fight the player can try to find the treasure by getting to the indicated position within 3 min (right).

understanding of conducting studies within the LBSN and LBG domains, and to help and support practitioners to reflect on their own approaches and possibly apply the proposed solutions.

3   Related Work

Maps and play on maps are relatively new within the study of games. Playing on maps began after the Battle of Jena-Auerstedt wherein the Prussian military sought to use the techniques Napoleon had used against them (topographical mapping, disconnected command structures). The answer to this was a game called Kriegspiel [10]. The appearance of this game pushed not only military training, but the seeking of information hastened the formation of tools, mapping techniques, and ways to compute that information. After World War 2, this way of using maps as training were monetized and sold as self-contained games called war games. One of the games that embraced the features of war games was Dungeons and Dragons (D&D), a role-playing game wherein players take on the role of heroes and explore maps cooperatively as a party. D&D formed the basis of playing games with and on maps and this style of play was digitized as the first computers were made available to enthusiasts [10]. Since that time, role-playing games like Pokemon have embraced the style of play that sees players exploring maps [19,20]. LBGs are a new iteration of this style of game and formed the basis of our design [18].

There are several challenges when one embarks in studying mobile technologies in 'the wild'. Even though a significant number of studies have been conducted in the domain, only a handful of researchers have documented the key challenges and how they overcame them. For example, Barakovic and Skorin-Kapov [1] discussed extensively the importance of a well-planned study, and described as the most challenging aspects: i) the specification of methodology, ii) identification of dependent and independent variables, iii) choosing the user test subjects, iv) determining the testing scenarios and the environment; v) and the rating scales. Similarly, Earl [11] when examining interaction patterns of smartphone users 'in the wild', identified and documented that volatile file systems (such as un-mounting/mounting the file-system leads to data loss), energy constraints, third-party applications, nonlinear time, and malicious users were the main issues in his explorations.

Ferreira et al. [8] expanded upon these and discussed an additional set of challenges and considerations that need to be taken into account. These include: i) careful planning and evaluation of time and effort for the deployment of a research tool, ii) the number of participants, iii) non-biased participants (age/gender), iv) the amount of collected data, v) the representativeness of the data, the vi) need of conducting the study non-intrusively, and vii) a need of an introduction of a pilot/testing study before every deployment or study as there is a need for the users to become familiar with the application. This work aims to build upon and expand this body of work by presenting a set of key challenges we encountered during our studies with GeoMoments and CityConqueror, and how we overcame these challenges.

4   Methodology

Our approach for collecting the lessons learned involved a three-step process and was similar to [5,6,16]. Firstly, we collectively divided the analysis of these studies in four phases: design, development, and execution of the study and data analysis. Each author proposed a set of challenges that s/he encountered in each phase and felt that it was important. Secondly, we clustered the various proposals of the most important challenges that each author had independently prioritized relating to her/his own study. Thirdly agreed upon a common focus of the employed solutions and guidelines.

5   Findings

The understanding of smartphone users' experience is becoming vital in developing new mobile interaction concepts for LBSN and LBG. The successful approach for these experiments requires rigorous design, development, execution, and analysis of the collected results, in order for the important variables and their correlations and causalities to be captured, analyzed and understood. In this section, we draw upon our studies with GeoMoments and CityConqueror and aim to provide practical lessons learned on how to conduct user studies with LBSNs and LBGs. Our goal is to provide an overview on a set of challenges that we overcame in our studies, and to explain the solutions and guidelines we employed to the most critical challenges we identified.

5.1   Design Phase

Ethics and Consent Approval. This is one of the first considerations when designing a study. Depending the country and the institution where the study is conducted the rules and regulations may vary. Therefore, it is important to dedicate enough time for the approval as committees may ask to change the study method, hence, delaying the study, because of its late refactoring.

Pre-selection Process. The pre-selection process (or enrolment survey) should be open enough to involve as many participants as possible, designed in a way that explores the domain, and asks/discuss probable situations that the potential participants encounter daily.

Defining the Variables. This phase is very important and must be treated with caution very early in the design process because i) it defines the data and interpretations of the data throughout the study, ii) influences the ethics consent, iii) the procedure on how these variables are collected and IV) by consequence the outcome of the study.

Rewarding Participants. It is advised that the study participants receive an award if their participation requires a direct interaction (e.g. answering multiple questions in a day). In our studies the payment was a flat rate that got compounded depending how many times they would come back to answer questions throughout the study.

5.2   Development Phase

Device Issues. GeoMoments, and CityConqueror has been developed for Android OS. If issues with devices emerge during the study, they must be evaluated if a device specific solution is worthwhile, or exclude the device's users from participation in our study.

Collecting Smartphone Data. The frequency of data collection on the smartphone and the method to be used need to be chosen very carefully because they can influence the mobile application's performance, battery life, and data storage. As such only necessary data must be collected without jeopardizing the normal use of the participant's phone.

Testing. It is important to test the application in the lab as early as possible to find any technical issues that may compromise the study. This phase may span over several weeks before the lunch of the study depending on the complexity of the LBSN. We suggest that internal testers conduct scenario testing with different devices, and stress test the backend extensively.

Recruiting Participants. As GeoMoments and CityConqueror was developed for Android OS it was challenging to find enough participants ready to commit for 4 to 6 weeks of studies. This "recruiting" stage lasted several weeks and we had a lot of back and forth with several participants. The solution was to post advertisements in community forums, downplay the required continuous interaction with us throughout the study, and offer monetary compensation depending the number of interactions with us.

5.3   Execution Phase

Visualization of the Data. For the purpose of our study that it was important to show the participants the data we gathered from them through GeoMoments and CityConqueror during our weekly interactions with them. We experimented with a range of different visualizations and after a lot of 'trial and error' we created the following guidelines that we followed throughout our project: I) Avoid representation of geocoded traces and posts quantitatively as most participants are not able to understand them and they do not help in our discussions with them, II) Show only data related to the questions at hand. Don't show all their data to the participants at once as too much information will bias their overall behavior during the study and may change routines and related activities based on the results presented.

Participant Motivation. The participants must be kept motivated to fulfill the requirements of the study and provide unbiased data results. Motivation in our project came from monetary compensation, and a sense we conveyed to the participants that they were part of the project and helped us answer important research questions.

Privacy. Even though general rules should be described in the ethics consent there are a number of practical issues that should be taken into account. These include: i) if the study requires connecting participant' smartphone to a PC, disable any automatic download of personal information, ii) no overlapping interview schedule or involving third individuals outside of the study, not disclose other participants' opinion and experience to other participants (this includes not referring to other participants when giving examples during interviews), iii) offer the possibility to switch data logging off for a limited time when participants want extra privacy,

Performance Issues. Participants' phone performance issues may influence the final results of the study and the motivation of the participant. As such any complains regarding phone performance issues have to be investigated and addressed immediately.

Software Bugs and Related Behavior. In our studies we encountered a wide variety of Android OS devices that each created a wide array of bugs and weird behaviors. These ranged from high/low sampling frequency from the GPS, disturbing vibration, inconsistent logging etc. Our approach was to investigate and see if the bug can be easily, identified, replicated and solved fast while at the same time making sure that our solution did not create even more problems in the future.

5.4   Data Analysis Phase

Data Synchronization and Format. The format of the collected data should be well designed, so that post processing the data does not take too much extra effort. It is suggested that collation and synchronization of the data from various sources/databases etc. is an ongoing process through the study.

Analysis. Methodological issues and approaches aside, the data analysis process should be kept in digital format and kept separated per participant to lead to a faster data analysis. Themes, trends and directions as emerge from the data must be derived by at least 2 different coders and should be able to explain a particular set of situations when discussing and leveraging the study results.

Closing the Project. Closing the project involves a significant amount of challenging work. Extra care should be taken when addressing any finance issues, writing the final project reports, etc. However, admin work aside we suggest that one should confirm that the project has met all research objectives, and requirements from sponsor, customer, and stakeholder, verified that all deliverables have been delivered and accepted, and that the exit criteria have been met.

6   Conclusion

In this paper, we have touched upon a number of issues one may encounter and potential solutions one may employ when designing, developing, and deploying LBSN and LBG. The lessons learned relate to the lifecycles of the studies, and illustrate that when one should be prepared and flexible enough to accommodate any issues as they arise in a professional manner considering not only the results of the study but also the participants and the researchers involved. The goal of this work is not to provide specific solutions to any kind of challenge the researchers or practitioners may encounter, but to provide to researchers a practical view on conducting studies within the LBSN and LBG domains, and to help and support practitioners to reflect on their own approaches. As such future work should have a more formal approach. This is proposed to involve a systematic review of past projects from multiple authors, and focus on the development of a theoretical framework for conducting human subject studies in the wild.

Acknowledgements. This work was supported by the Engineering and Physical Sciences Research Council [grant number EP/T022493/1] Horizon: Trusted Data-Driven Products.

References

1. Baraković, S., Skorin-Kapov, L.: Survey and challenges of QoE management issues in wireless networks. J. Comput. Netw. Commun. **2013** (2013)
2. Chamberlain, A., Bødker, M., Hazzard, A., McGookin, D., Roure, D.D., Willcox, P., Papangelis, K.: Audio technology and mobile human computer interaction. Int. J. Mob. Human Comput. Interact. **9**(4), 25–40 (2017). https://doi.org/10.4018/ijmhci.2017100103
3. Chamberlain, A., Bødker, M., Papangelis, K.: Mapping media and meaning. In: Proceedings of the 12th International Audio Mostly Conference on Augmented and Participatory Sound and Music Experiences. ACM (2017). https://doi.org/10.1145/3123514.3123536
4. Chamberlain, A., Crabtree, A., Rodden, T., Jones, M., Rogers, Y.: Research in the wild: understanding 'in the wild' approaches to design and development. In: Proceedings of the Designing Interactive Systems Conference, pp. 795–796 (2012)
5. Corsar, D., et al.: Build an app and they will come? lessons learnt from trialling the ¡¿gettherebus¡/¿ app in rural communities. IET Intell. Transp. Syst. **12**, 194–201(7) (2018). https://digital-library.theiet.org/content/journals/10.1049/iet-its.2016.0216
6. Corsar, D., Edwards, P., Nelson, J., Papangelis, K.: Mobile phones, sensors & the crowd: Lessons learnt from development of a real-time travel information system. In: Proceedings of the The First International Conference on IoT in Urban Space. ICST (2014). https://doi.org/10.4108/icst.urb-iot.2014.257328
7. Crabtree, A., Chamberlin, A., Grinter, Jones, R., Rodden, M., Rogers, Y.: Introduction. In: Special Issue of "the Turn of the Wild" in Transactions of Computer-Human Interaction, vol. 20. ACM (2013)
8. Ferreira, D., Kostakos, V., Dey, A.K.: Lessons learned from large-scale user studies: using android market as a source of data. Int. J. Mob. Human Comput. Interact. (IJMHCI) **4**(3), 28–43 (2012)
9. Jones, C., Papangelis, K.: Reflective practice: lessons learnt by using board games as a design tool for location-based games. In: Kyriakidis, P., Hadjimitsis, D., Skarlatos, D., Mansourian, A. (eds.) AGILE 2019. LNGC, pp. 291–307. Springer, Cham (2020). https://doi.org/10.1007/978-3-030-14745-7_16
10. LaLone, N.: A tale of dungeons & dragons and the origins of the game platform. Analog Game Stud. **3**(6) (2019)
11. Oliver, E.: The challenges in large-scale smartphone user studies. In: Proceedings of the 2nd ACM International Workshop on Hot Topics in Planet-scale Measurement, pp. 1–5 (2010)

12. Papangelis, K., Chamberlain, A., Liang, H.N.: New directions for preserving intangible cultural heritage through the use of mobile technologies. In: Proceedings of the 18th International Conference on Human-Computer Interaction with Mobile Devices and Services Adjunct. ACM (2016). https://doi.org/10.1145/2957265.2962643
13. Papangelis, K., et al.: Performing the digital self. ACM Trans. Comput.-Human Interact. **27**(1), 1–26 (2020). https://doi.org/10.1145/3364997
14. Papangelis, K., Metzger, M., Sheng, Y., Liang, H.N., Chamberlain, A., Khan, V.J.: "get off my lawn!" starting to understand territoriality in location based mobile games. In: Proceedings of the 2017 CHI Conference Extended Abstracts on Human Factors in Computing Systems, pp. 1955–1961 (2017)
15. Papangelis, K., Metzger, M., Sheng, Y., Liang, H.N., Chamberlain, A., Cao, T.: Conquering the city. In: Proceedings of the ACM on Interactive, Mobile, Wearable and Ubiquitous Technologies, vol. 1, no. 3, pp. 1–24 (2017). https://doi.org/10.1145/3130955
16. Papangelis, K., Nelson, J.D., Sripada, S., Beecroft, M.: The effects of mobile real-time information on rural passengers. Transp. Plan. Technol. **39**(1), 97–114 (2015). https://doi.org/10.1080/03081060.2015.1108085
17. Papangelis, K., Sheng, Y., Liang, H.N., Chamberlain, A., Khan, V.J., Cao, T.: Unfolding the interplay of self-identity and expressions of territoriality in location-based social networks. In: Proceedings of the 2017 ACM International Joint Conference on Pervasive and Ubiquitous Computing and Proceedings of the 2017 ACM International Symposium on Wearable Computers. ACM (2017). https://doi.org/10.1145/3123024.3123081
18. Perkins, C.: Playful mapping: the potential of a ludic approach. In: International Cartographic Association Conference (2012)
19. Toups, Z.O., Lalone, N., Alharthi, S.A., Sharma, H.N., Webb, A.M.: Making maps available for play: analyzing the design of game cartography interfaces. ACM Trans. Comput.-Human Interact. (TOCHI) **26**(5), 1–43 (2019)
20. Toups, Z.O., LaLone, N., Spiel, K., Hamilton, B.: Paper to pixels: a chronicle of map interfaces in games. In: Proceedings of the 2020 ACM Designing Interactive Systems Conference, pp. 1433–1451 (2020)

Designing the Security Enhancement Features in the Future Headphone Experience

Fangli Song[✉] and Wei Wang

Georgia Institute of Technology, Atlanta, GA 30332, USA
Flsong1997@gatech.edu

Abstract. In recent years, headphones are becoming a more and more essential personal electronic device to carry cutting-edge consumer technology into everyday life. Hence, it's an urgent need to enhance security features on headphones. This study analyzed different techniques, technologies and applications to enhance security features in mainstream personal electronic devices, introducing a new taxonomy (Loss-Ownership-Data, LOD) of security features which is based on three categories: Loss Protection (LP), Ownership Protection (OP), Data Protection (DP). And it proposed ten concepts to enhance security features on headphones using this framework. An online user survey was conducted and the results and findings were discussed. This paper unified the general security design techniques into a framework which could be used to analyze and enhance security features in future personal electronic devices and it also proposed some possible solutions to enhance security features in headphone experience. Thirdly, it reported the user attitude, their acceptance, and expectation which can be used as a reference to related design practice.

Keywords: LOD security features · Headphone security · Security protection design

1 Introduction

The security enhancement features has become significantly important in personal electronic devices (PED) [1] which include but are not limited to mobile devices. It needs to be noticeable that while various security features on mainstream personal electronic devices are indispensable, protecting users' devices and personal data from stealing, there hasn't been such consideration on headphones so far. It's mostly because headphones are considered accessories to mobile phones or other personal devices.

However, the market of headphones expands rapidly, especially with the emergence of TWS (True Wireless Stereo) earphones in 2018. The global headphones market size was valued at USD 25.1 billion in 2019 and is expected to grow at a compound annual growth rate (CAGR) of 20.3% from 2020 to 2027 [2]. On the other hand, consumers are gradually shifting towards the purchase of more expensive headphones in pursuit of functions, style and fidelity [3]. These trends call for new feature possibilities such as integrating security enhancement features in future headphone experience which was generally neglected before.

M. M. Soares et al. (Eds.): HCII 2021, LNCS 12781, pp. 90–108, 2021.
https://doi.org/10.1007/978-3-030-78227-6_8

Existing research on headphone security mainly focus on securing wireless communication. In a survey conducted by Cisco in 2019 [4], 85% of users felt Bluetooth provided secure communications. However, Hassan et al. [5] discussed the security threats and weakness in Bluetooth communication and introduced some basic preventions such as remaining undiscoverable, securing headphone pairing, pair in short range etc. Beside the technical security issues, there is very little research on what features are appealing for consumers and how to design them from user experience perspective. Thus, future works need to be done to enhance headphone security in terms of securing pairing protocols and improving user experience.

This paper focused on how to introduce headphone security enhancement concepts based on a new taxonomy and what is the user attitude, their acceptance and expectation. The research structure is from enabling technology analysis to generate concepts, and then evaluating them with user survey to understand the design principles of security enhancement features in the future headphone. It is organized as follows: In Sect. 2, a new Loss-Ownership-Data (LOD) taxonomy of PEDs was proposed and elaborated in three categories, Loss Protection (LP), Ownership Protection (OP) and Data Protection (DP). Then, a case study of security design analysis in iPhone was introduced to let the readers better understand the taxonomy. In Sect. 3, ten possible security design concepts were generating by following the possibility of LOD taxonomy. And then in Sect. 4, an online user survey and the results were analyzed to derive the findings and design implications in Sect. 5.

2 Related Works and the Taxonomy

There is a lot of research made on personal electronic device security features already. Man and Kim-Kwang [6] focused on users' personal data privacy. They discussed how to prevent security threats targeted by cybercriminals, and offered insights on various threats, risks, issues, mitigations, and mobile device security strategies, as well as sections covering privacy, forensics, and individual versus organizational impacts. Kim et al. [7] presented a multimodal personal authentication approach that combines information obtained from face, teeth and voice to improve the performance of mobile device security. Stiakakis and Andronoudi [8] categorized mobile device security features into two main branches, device loss/theft and malware attacks in devices and applications and conducted a survey in terms of different users aiming to investigate their perceptions about the importance of security branches. Other works related either focus on lost/stolen prevention, identity authentication or mobile data protection. However, each of them has their own methodology and terminology. It calls a unified taxonomy to categorize and compare various security features among personal electronic devices. To present a new taxonomy of security features based on three categories, Loss Protection (LP), Ownership Protection (OP) and Data Protection (DP), this paper did a desktop research and reviewed more than 30 papers published from 2000 to 2020, analyzed their technical possibility to apply in security feature design in headphone, and finally cited 15 in total to construct the taxonomy, then explained it in a case study.

2.1 Loss Protection (LP)

Loss Protection is, by given the definition of, to prevent personal electronic devices from lost and stolen by employing accurate position tracking technology. From the enabling technology, it includes GPS-based and non-GPS-based techniques.

GPS-Based. The Global Positioning System (GPS), is a radio navigation system that allows land, sea and airborne users to determine their current exact location, velocity and time 24 h a day, in all weather conditions and anywhere in the world [9]. However, due to the limitations of GPS [10], the accuracy of GPS is influenced by various factors such as weather, obstacles, etc. In recent years, high sensitivity GPS chips have become widely employed due to their much better performance in underground and indoor circumstances. At the same time, assisted GPS could largely enhance GPS with mobile phone networks.

Non-GPS-Based. Due to the high cost and accuracy limitations of GPS so far, some non-GPS techniques have been developed and employed in indoor circumstances. The most commonly used technique is triangulation, which receives signals from three reference points to position target devices. Another important technique is fingerprinting which collects and stores the features of an environment before the closest location of the target object is estimated [11]. Among these techniques, a widely used technology is Bluetooth. Others are Wi-fi, WSN, RFID, Cellular and so on.

2.2 Ownership Protection (OP)

Ownership Protection is to proof the user's legitimate ownership to a particular personal electronic device, mainly includes biometric-based authentication, knowledge-based authentication and possession-based authentication.

Biometric-Based Authentication. Biometric-based authentication is the science of establishing the identity of a person using his/her anatomical and behavioral traits. Commonly used biometric traits include fingerprint, face, iris, hand geometry, voice, palmprint, handwritten signatures, and gait [12]. Current mainstream biometric techniques in personal electronic device to protect ownership are face recognition, fingerprint and voice recognition.

Face Recognition. The introduction of face recognition techniques can be traced back to the 1950s. Some of the earliest works include work on facial expression of emotions and others. The earliest practical models were concentrated on still image-based recognition. It then faced the problem to recognize 3-dimensional (3D) objects from 2-dimensional (2D) images [13]. To solve that, around 2000, more research started to concentrate on video-based recognition. As years pass, the great development in AI algorithms and machine learning technologies brings a new era to face recognition. Nowadays, face recognition is the most popular technique adopted by mobile phone companies due to its high accuracy and high speed. Of the total biometrics market, 14.7% are occupied by face identification technologies [14].

Fingerprint Recognition. Fingerprinting is the most mature technology and it occupies the majority of the biometric market. There are many fingerprint sensing methods including optical method, thermal method, ultrasonic method, RF method and the capacitive method [15]. Among them, the capacitive method is the most commonly adopted one. And optical fingerprint sensor is normally embedded under the display. Ultrasonic methods can provide 3D recognition, which has the highest accuracy. However, it needs complex manufacturer steps and the cost is the highest.

Voice Recognition. Voice recognition has been viewed as an auxiliary function apart from fingerprinting, face recognition and traditional passcode. It's often disturbed by noisy environment. One solution offered to reduce the negative consequences associated with noise-related errors is to implement a multimodal architecture [16]. This method combines voice recognition with other techniques but still does not fundamentally solve the problem. However, with the emergence of active noise cancellation (ANC) technology, it seems feasible to minimize the environmental noise. With this technology, voice recognition performance can be greatly improved.

Knowledge-Based Authentication. Knowledge-based authentication consists of unique passcodes and gestures which utilize the most convenient mechanisms.

Passcode. Passcodes are created by users and need to be memorized, also users could change them anytime they want. Passcodes can be entered on physical buttons (e.g., Laptop keyboard) or display (e.g., Phone, watch screen). A six-digits passcode has 1,000,000 possibilities of combination which is nearly impossible to break, not to mention passcodes consisting of digits and characters.

Gestures. Gesture is another version of passcode. By dragging fingers across the displayed pattern grid, usually within a 3x3 point matrix, users could create a unique pattern which also has numerous possibilities of combination. Usually, gestures are combined with passcodes to provide another option.

Possession-Based Authentication. Possession-based authentication makes use of a plug-in client device to fulfill identity authentication. For example, a USB token or a public key infrastructure into personal electronic devices. However, it's an uncommon ownership protection technique in personal electronic devices.

An alternative is Two step confirmation (Duo Two Factor Authentication) [17]. It is a mechanism that implements two techniques mentioned above and is therefore acknowledged more secure than traditional one factor authentication mechanism.

2.3 Data Protection (DP)

Data protection (DP) is to prevent personal data from stolen and attacked by breaking the link between data and the physical device. This approach is a combination of data Loss Protection (LP) and Ownership Protection (OP), which includes device-based protection and cloud-based protection.

Device-Based Protection. Since most of users' personal data is stored in their devices, protecting the devices' data become extremely important. When users' devices are lost or stolen and the ownership protection techniques of the device have been broken unfortunately, device-based protection could prevent the data leak. It consists of two techniques, device failure lock and additional data lock.

Device Failure Lock. This is a widely used method in personal electronic device security design. When users' devices are stolen, it's still technically possible to break the device lock with several attempts. Device failure lock will prevent this from happening. An example is, after 10 fail attempts to unlock the device, all data on this device will be eliminated and this device will be locked forever.

Additional Data Lock. Additional data lock means there's another lock mechanism before users gain access to their social and other Apps apart from the device lock. This could prevent someone from hacking into their account after the device lock is broken.

Cloud-Based Protection. Cloud-based protection consists of two general techniques, data backup and cloud storage. Both of them use the technology of cloud computing where a cloudlet of massive capacity [18] stores users' data. By storing users' data on the cloud, users can access and modify them anywhere and anytime. The difference between data backup and cloud storage is that data backup only copies data at a certain point in the past which is static. Correspondingly, cloud storage deals with dynamic data by saving data directly on the cloud. Additionally, to access their cloud base, users have to prove their ownership of these data. As a result, Ownership Protection (OP) techniques, are implemented to authenticate their identity.

Table 1 shows a comparison between the LOD security features in terms of security index, cost index and applicability index based on a five-point scale (from very low - very likely to be cracked to very high - very unlikely to be cracked). Security index represents how secure a feature is. Cost index represents the efforts and difficulties needed in manufacture. And applicability index represents the range to implement a feature. GPS-based, knowledge-based and cloud-based techniques have the highest index of applicability which could have a great potential in future personal electronic device security design.

2.4 Case Study: iPhone

The LOD security features were employed widely in personal electronic device such as the iPhone, which has the great potentials to apply in new headphone design. The case study here intends to explain the LOD technology in applications.

In terms of LP techniques, the iPhone is equipped with an accurate and high-cost GPS chip which can track position in real time. It has a powerful APP - Find my iPhone which was first released in 2010. In this APP, users can see the exact location of the lost device as long as its power is on. The lost iPhone can play a loud sound to stay noticeable. Also, some customized texts can show up on the display to let people know how to contact the owner once they pick up his/her phone.

Table 1. Comparison between the LOD security features in personal electronic device

LOD security features		Security	Cost	Applicability
Loss Protection (LP)	GPS-based	High	High	Very high
	Non-GPS-based	Very high	Very high	Low
Ownership Protection (OP)	Biometric-based	Very high	High	Median
	Knowledge-based	Median	Very low	Very high
	Possession-based	Very high	High	Low
Data Protection (DP)	Device-based	High	Very low	High
	Cloud-based	Median	High	Very high

The iPhone's OP techniques are a combination of Biometric-based authentications and knowledge-based authentications. The iPhone still keeps the passcode and iTouch identifications today, but it mostly focuses on the development of Face ID. However, it's only employed on iPhone X and later versions. Users' face information is encrypted and lives locked in their device, never backed up to the iCloud or anywhere else [19]. The unlock time for Face ID is 0.3s on the average which is three times faster than iTouch. However, Face ID also costs three times more than iTouch which is $60 per unit.

The iPhone has always been focusing on DP since iCloud was released in 2011. At that time, it was groundbreaking to personal electronic device storage solutions. Because it was way more convenient and secure, the future of cloud storage would be promising. The summary of iPhone's LOD features is shown in Fig. 1, which could be used as a framework to design security features into headphones.

Fig. 1. The LOD security features of iPhone

3 Headphone LOD Concept Design

This section explored the possibility of the framework of LOD taxonomy to apply to headphone concept design. In order to seek the greatest possibility, some techniques were adjusted and some new technologies were used. In total, ten possible concepts were generated by the first author himself.

3.1 LP Concepts

To implement LP techniques on headphones, an accurate position tracking system is needed. The easiest way is to integrate a compact GPS chip inside the skew. As was mentioned above, nowadays, some GPS chips are even smaller than a fingernail, which were designed to be implemented on any electronic devices. It's feasible to add such chips into headphones. There are two concepts, web-based GPS tracking and App-based GPS tracking.

Concept 1: Web-Based GPS Tracking. This concept proposes a dedicated website as is shown in Fig. 2. This website is linked to the database where everyone's headphone position data are stored. First user's login to this platform, then they enter the unique identification code of their headphones. Once the data transmission is done, they can see the real time position of their headphones.

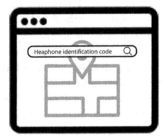

Fig. 2. Web-based GPS tracking

Concept 2: App-Based GPS Tracking. This concept requires the headphone manufacturers to provide a user-end app which can access the headphone's positioning database. Initially, users download this app on their device. Then they have to pair their headphones with the device using this app for the first time. Once the pairing is done, they can see the real time position data of their headphones through this app on this particular device. The pairing establishes a permanent relationship. Once the relationship is built, users can see the position data on this app as long as their headphones are turned on. The connection is broken only when users erase their headphones' information on the app manually. A brief introduction of this concept is shown in Fig. 3.

3.2 OP Concepts

The realization of Ownership Protection methods can be divided into two concepts. One is App-based OP techniques. Another one is making physical change to headphone appearance.

Concept 3: App-Based OP. App-based OP is similar to app-based GPS tracking which has been introduced above. Then both leverage the power of app, utilizing it as a bridge

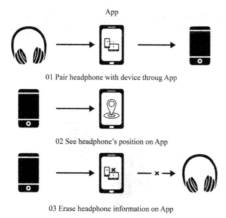

01 Pair headphone with device throug App

02 See headphone's position on App

03 Erase headphone information on App

Fig. 3. App-based GPS tracking

between headphones and device. First, users need to sign up or login to this app using their biometrics, passcode, gesture or plug-in devices. Then their information will be saved on the app, every time they pair their headphones to a new device, they must use this app to authenticate their ownership. And they don't need to repeat the process for devices they have connected before. A brief introduction is shown in Fig. 4.

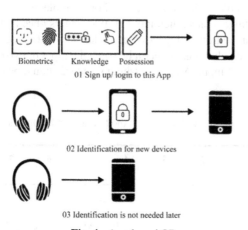

Biometrics   Knowledge   Possession
01 Sign up/ login to this App

02 Identification for new devices

03 Identification is not needed later

Fig. 4. App-based OP

Concept 4: Capacitive Fingerprint Sensor (Biometric-Based Concept). While face recognition is unrealistic on headphones, it's possible to employ fingerprinting on headphones. Since optical and ultrasonic techniques both have some shortcomings, a capacitive fingerprint sensor should be the optimal technique. The sensor can be placed on one side of a headphone. When first using the headphone, users enroll their fingerprints by placing the finger on the sensor and follow the instructions of the headphone. Then every time pairing the headphone with a device, they just have to place the finger on the sensor for authentication. A brief introduction is shown in Fig. 5.

Fig. 5. Headphone fingerprinting

Concept 5: Tap to Passcode (Knowledge-Based Concept). This technique consists of two concepts, using passcode and gestures to authenticate. Hiroyuyi Manabe and Masaaki Fukumoto introduced a novel way to add input functions to headphones without additional sensors [20, 21]. It detects the tap on headphones and transmits it into signal (input) and triggers different outputs. They used a plug-in device to connect a headphone to a device. Using their method, the tap can be coded as the input of different passcode digits. A coding example is shown in Table 2. For example, to input passcode "3549", first tap with three fingers once, then tap with two fingers once and three fingers once immediately, then tap with two fingers twice, at last tap with three fingers third times. There has to be a relatively longer interval between the input of two different digits than the interval in one-digit input. A distinguishing standard should be defined.

Table 2. A digit input method of taps on headphone

Digit	0	1	2	3	4	5	6	7	8	9
Tap Input	x2	x1	x1	x1	x2	x1 + x1	x2	x2 + x1	x1 + x2	x3

Concept 6: Gesture to Passcode. Utilizing gestures is another knowledge-based concept. Metzger introduced a contact-free method for gesture control on headphones [22].

He applied an infrared sensor to one side of a headphone. When users wave their fingers across the sensor, the sensor can detect how many fingers and how many times users waved. Using their method, users' gesture input signal can be transmitted into different passcode digits. Transmitting gestures into passcodes is similar to tap inputs on headphones. Users wave different numbers of fingers for different times to represent different digits. A coding example of this concept is shown in Table 3. For example, to input passcode "5820", users wave five fingers clockwise first, then wave four fingers clockwise and anticlockwise immediately, then wave two fingers clockwise, at last wave one finger clockwise and anticlockwise immediately. There has to be a relatively longer interval between the input of two different digits than the interval in one-digit input. A distinguishing standard should also be defined.

Table 3. A digital input method of gestures on headphone

Digit	0	1	2	3	4	5	6	7	8	9
Gesture input	↷ 👌 + ↶ ✋	↷ 👌	↷ 🤙	↷ 👌	↷ 🖐	↷ 🖐	↷ ✋ + ↶	↷ ✋ + ↶	↷ ✋ + ↶	↷ 🖐 + ↶

Concept 7: Simple Gesture Pattern. An example of a simplified gesture concept is shown in Fig. 6. For example, users first wave four fingers clockwise then anticlockwise, and wave two fingers clockwise after that. This could be recorded as a particular gesture pattern for the ownership authentication.

Fig. 6. A simple gesture pattern input method

Concept 8: Headphone Plug in (Possession-Based Concept). This concept requires an external device which can be plugged into a particular interface on a headphone. Every time when pairing the headphones, this device is needed for authentication. However, additional computing is needed. A brief introduction is shown in Fig. 7.

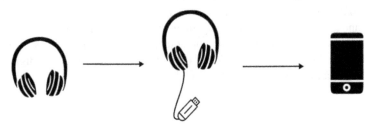

Fig. 7. Use a plug-in device for authentication

3.3 DP Concepts

Headphones have always been considered as an accessory to mainstream devices. Therefore, headphones are unable to produce and store users' personal data at the moment. If headphones become standalone, independent from mobile phones and others, users can actually use their headphones without pairing to any devices. Thus, users' music library, listening list, contacts and so on could be stored on headphones. However, some research is required in the future to evaluate its feasibility. To protect these data, generally, there are two concepts, adding a device lock and storing the data on the cloud.

Concept 9: Device Lock. A device lock can possibly be implemented on headphones. This concept is simple, after several times of failure in OP authentication, headphones will be locked for using and the data are eliminated. A simple example is shown in Fig. 8.

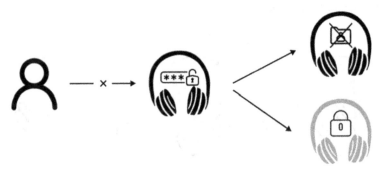

Fig. 8. An example of device lock

Concept 10: Cloud Data Storing. Headphone's data can be all stored on the cloud instead of inside the headphone. Hence, there is no need to make another backup of data. Based on this concept, users can access their data anytime from any devices with internet connection. A brief introduction is shown in Fig. 9.

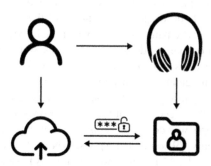

Fig. 9. Operation mode of cloud storage of headphone's data

Table 4 lists all feasible approaches to implement LOD techniques on headphones. A total of ten concepts have been introduced and discussed above. However, this section just gave a brief review and some future research needs to be done to examine the specific ways to carry out these concepts. Furthermore, to explore users' opinions, a user study was presented in the next section.

Table 4. Ten concepts to implement LOD techniques on headphones

Implementations		
Loss Protection (OP)	GPS-based	1 Web-based GPS tracking
		2 App-based GPS tracking
	Non-GPS-based	N/A
Ownership Protection (OP)	Biometric-based	3 App-based OP
	Knowledge-based	4 Capacitive fingerprint sensor
		5 Tap to passcode
		6 Gesture to passcode
		7 Simple gesture pattern
	Possession-based	8 Headphone plug in
Data Protection (DP)	Device-based	9 Device lock
	Cloud-based	10 Cloud data storing

4 User Survey

4.1 Summary

Approved by the Institutional Review Board (IRB) of Georgia Institute of Technology, protocol H20470, an online user survey was conducted to explore users' feedback. Participants were informed consent at the beginning of the survey. By voluntarily participating in this survey, participants' identity will remain confidential as no personal information, other than their age, gender and IP addresses, were be collected. This survey was divided into three sections and there were 15 questions in total. In the first section, basic information, age and gender of participants were given. The second section collected the information of participants' headphones using behaviors and their attitude and expectation of headphone security. In the last section, participants' acceptance on the ten introduced concepts was collected. This survey was published on Qualtrics and lasted for one week. Totally, 89 complete responses (N = 89) were collected at the end. The sex ratio is 1:1 (44 male, 44 female and 1 nonbinary). Most users (61.36%) were under 24 years old but no users were over 55 years old which generally match the major user group of headphones.

4.2 Results

Before the user survey, this paper made two hypotheses. Firstly, most participants will agree that headphones lack security protection features and need to be more secure. Secondly, LP and OP concepts will gain a better score than DP concepts.

Figure 10 shows participants' attitude and expectation on headphone security (N = 89). The horizontal axis represents the number of responses and the vertical axis represents users' extent of agreement (1 − strongly disagree, 7 − strongly agree). The answers distributions of both statements "There are no security protection features on headphones currently" and "Headphones need to be more secure in the future." are shown in the polylines with rectangle junctions (SD = 1.31, mean = 5.29) and triangular junctions (SD = 1.27, mean = 5.12) respectfully. It's noticeable at first sight that most participants agree with both statements to some extent. 64 (72%) participants somewhat agree, agree or strongly agree with the former statement, while 65 (73%) participants somewhat agree, agree or strongly agree with the latter statement. Besides, the two distributions are statistically very similar (Z = 0.89, p = 0.37). which indicates that participants who think headphones lack security protection features generally agree that headphones need to be more secure in the future.

$$Z = \frac{(\overline{X}_1 - \overline{X}_2)}{\sqrt{\sigma_{\overline{X}_1}^2 + \sigma_{\overline{X}_2}^2}}$$
$$\text{Where } \sigma_x = \sigma / \sqrt{n} \tag{1}$$

In the last section in the survey, participants were asked to what extent they agreed with this statement "This concept is very useful." based on a 7-point scale (1 − strongly disagree, 7 − strongly agree). Figure 11 shows participants' acceptance on ten concepts to enhance security features on headphones introduced in this paper (N = 89). The

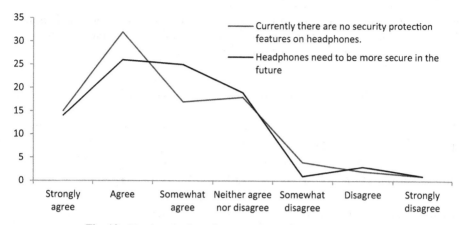

Fig. 10. User's attitude and expectation on headphone security

vertical axis represents the score and the horizontal axis represents the concepts. The mean scores of each concept and a threshold line are shown in the figure. Score above this threshold represents over 50% of participants think this concept is useful. And score below this threshold represents over 50% of participants think this concept is neither useful nor useless, or this concept is useless. The results show that LP concepts (concept one and two) were rated highest with concept two gained the highest score at 5.56. DP concepts (concept nine and ten) were rated just above the threshold. However, half of concepts in OP concepts (concepts five, six and eight) gained a score below the threshold with concepts eight gained the lowest score at 3.91. Overall, over half of users think that seven out of ten concepts are useful to enhance security features on headphones.

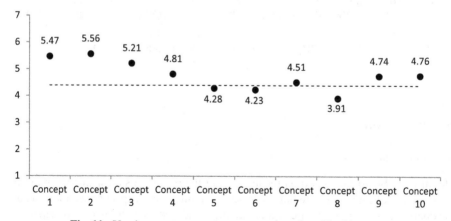

Fig. 11. User's acceptance on ten concepts introduced in this paper

Then, the results were analyzed accordingly based on different demographic groups. Table 5 shows the acceptance of users who often use a headphone (more than 3 times per day), (N = 30). More than half of them think that eight out of ten concepts are useful, including the concept No.5, the overall score of which is rated below the threshold. Besides, the mean scores of all concepts except the concept No.6 rated by them are higher than the overall score, while the score of the concept No.6 drops 0.06.

Table 5. Acceptance of users who often use a headphone

Concept	1	2	3	4	5	6	7	8	9	10
Useful	25 (83%)	25 (83%)	23 (77%)	19 (63%)	17 (56%)	13 (43%)	19 (63%)	14 (47%)	23 (77%)	21 (70%)
This group	5.67	5.67	5.5	4.97	4.63	4.17	4.9	4.1	5	5.13
Overall	5.47	5.56	5.21	4.81	4.28	4.23	4.51	3.91	4.74	4.76

The age might be another factor that influences rating. A comparison between acceptance of users below 24 years old (N = 53) and over 24 years old (N = 35) is shown in Table 6. This table shows how many of them think each concept is useful. It can be seen that users below 24 years old generally rate higher, while users over 24 years old think only six out of ten concepts are useful. It indicates that the younger users have a higher interest to accept LOD features in headphones.

Table 6. Comparison between acceptance of users from two age groups

Concept	1	2	3	4	5	6	7	8	9	10
<24	46 (87%)	49 (92%)	39 (74%)	34 (64%)	26 (49%)	22 (42%)	32 (60%)	20 (38%)	35 (66%)	32 (60%)
>24	25 (71%)	25 (71%)	25 (71%)	21 (60%)	15 (43%)	16 (46%)	16 (46%)	16 (46%)	23 (66%)	20 (57%)

5 Discussion

5.1 Findings

Headphone Security. Based on the analysis of the results, it's clear that the majority of users think headphones are not secure at the moment and expect to see more secure headphone design in the future, which confirms the first hypothesis of this paper and proves the necessity of implementing security protection features on headphones.

LP Concepts. In terms of the ten concepts based on LOD taxonomy introduced by this paper, over a half of users think seven of them are useful, which generally can be read as a positive attitude toward LOD features in headphone design. Among them, both

LP concepts gained very high scores which means users have the highest acceptance with these concepts. This phenomenon indicates users hope that headphones should be the same as mobile phones or tablets which have a GPS chip inside. There should be a greater chance to retrieve it after loss. The concept. "App-based GPS tracking" was rated a little higher (mean = 5.56) than "Web-based GPS tracking" (mean = 5.47). This is probably due to the mobility and convenience of phones, while the web is static with relatively poor compatibility.

OP Concepts. OP concepts, however, generally were not rated as high as expected, which is against the second hypothesis of this paper. Only "App-based OP", "headphone fingerprinting" and "simple gesture pattern" gained relatively good feedback while the other half were low-rated. Concept, "A plug-in device", indisputably, gained the lowest score. This might owe to the fact that such plug-in devices are commonly used to protect confidential documents instead of personal devices such as mobile phones or tablets. Users think there is no need to use this method to protect the headset, otherwise it will affect the using experience.

The concepts, "tap to passcode" (mean = 4.28) and "gesture to passcode" (mean = 4.23) didn't receive a high score. The reason might be that it's very time consuming to input a simple passcode and the coding is not easy to remember. What's more, when users are inputting the passcode, others around them are able to see their gestures. However, it's surprising to see that the concept of "simple gesture pattern" gained a higher score (mean = 4.51). This might indicate that users are more inclined to a much simpler and more convenient way to input a passcode than high confidentiality.

The concept of "headphone fingerprinting" gained a much higher score (mean = 4.81) mostly because it's fast and accurate to unlock also with high confidentiality. However, above them, "App-based OP" gained the highest score (mean = 5.21). It might because of the mobility and convenience of this concept. And most significantly, users have free choice on which unlock methods to use in the app on their mobile devices, face ID, fingerprinting, passcode or gesture.

DP Concepts. Against the second hypothesis, both DP concepts received relatively good and very similar scores. The score "cloud data storing" was slightly higher than "device lock". While at the moment, it's impossible to tell whether these concepts can be implemented, users already show high acceptance, which is also beyond the expectation of this paper.

Demographics. It should not be neglected that different demographic groups show different acceptance of the concepts. For example, users who often use headphones have much higher acceptance on almost all concepts which indicates that they are more willing to see these improvements on headphone security and are very likely to spend more money to purchase a more secure headphone in the future. However, they rated even lower on the concept No. 6, "Gesture to passcode", which indicates that complicated gesture interaction like this concept might not undergo further development. Besides, young users do have a higher acceptance of most of the concepts. It might due to the fact that young users use headphones more often and are more inclined to accept new technologies. It should also be noticed that the sample of young users is 20 more than that of older users. Theoretically, the result of a large sample size should be more accurate. So, the real acceptance of the older should be a little higher presumably.

5.2 Implications on Design

GPS Function on Headphones. As users show very high acceptance of the concepts to prevent headphones from losing, it's of great necessity to implement GPS function into headphones as soon as possible. As discussed above, it's both technically and usably feasible. While headphones with GPS function might be more expensive due to increased manufacturing costs, the opportunity in future market should be very broad.

Software-Assisted Techniques. Using software-assisted techniques to enhance security features on headphones has four advantages. Firstly, it doesn't involve any additional computing and structure change in headphone design. As a result, the cost would be very affordable. Secondly, it's easy to improve the software after it has been published by iterating and updating coding. Thirdly, abundant design opportunities lie in software design, including UI/UX and service design. Lastly, users have higher acceptance of this technique. Both app-based concepts gained high scores which indicates that users are more willing to use a convenient software on their personal devices anywhere and anytime to protect their headphones.

Trade-Offs. It's important to pay attention to the tradeoffs such as convenience versus confidentiality. Users are more willing to adopt a more convenient technique despite its relatively low confidentiality. As the simplified version of gesture to passcode gained a good score, it can be inferred that a simplified version of tap to passcode should also gain higher acceptance.

Headphones Could no Longer Just Be an Accessory. It is no doubt that headphones were considered a kind of accessories to mainstream personal electronic devices. However, as users show good acceptance to both DP concepts, with users' support, it's completely possible to develop standalone headphones which integrate cellular network, Wi-Fi module, Bluetooth, memory disk and so on in the future.

6 Conclusion

This paper first discussed the significance of implementing security features into headphones, then unified personal electronic device security design techniques by introducing a new taxonomy (Loss-Ownership-Data, LOD). The concepts presented in this paper explored the possibility of security features in future headphones. The evaluation result from the online user survey disclosed the design direction of future headphones design in security related features. From the result, it suggests that users show high acceptance of LP concepts and DP concepts, which could undergo further development. Meanwhile, users prefer simple and convenience features instead of complicated ones. Future design should consider user experience trade-offs from this study.

The limitation of this paper is that there is no in-depth exploration to each concept. For example, the form and technical design. According to the result of the user survey, most concepts could undergo further development. However, as discussed, many of them need to be modified and improved and it needs further exploration in future research. Besides, the user survey only lasted a short period through the internet which results in the small sample size and narrow demographics. The results could not be very accurate. As a result, a thorough and long-term user study needs to be conducted in the future.

References

1. Lando, A.M., Bazaco, M.C., Chen, Y.: Consumers' use of personal electronic devices in the kitchen. J. Food Prot. **81**(3), 437–443 (2018)
2. Grand view research. https://www.grandviewresearch.com/industry-analysis/earphone-and-headphone-market. Accessed 25 Oct 2020
3. Research and market. https://www.researchandmarkets.com/research/54mc23/earphones_and. Accessed 25 Oct 2020
4. Cisco's "Business Headsets" survey 2019. https://ebooks.cisco.com/story/business-headsets-key-to-workplace-ebook-us/page/4/1?ccid=cc001192&oid=ebkco020228. Accessed 12 Dec 2020
5. Hassan, S.S., Bibon, S.D., Hossain, M.S., Atiquzzaman, M.: Security threats in Bluetooth technology. Comput. Sec. **74**, 308–322 (2018)
6. Au, M.H., Choo, K.-K.R.: Mobile security and privacy. In: Mobile Security and Privacy, pp. 1–4 (2017)
7. Kim, D.-J., Chung, K.-W., Hong, K.-S.: Person authentication using face, teeth and voice modalities for mobile device security. IEEE Trans. Consum. Electron. **56**(4), 2678–2685 (2010). https://doi.org/10.1109/TCE.2010.5681156
8. Stiakakis, E., Georgiadis, C.K., Andronoudi, A.: Users' perceptions about mobile security breaches. IseB **14**(4), 857–882 (2015). https://doi.org/10.1007/s10257-015-0302-7
9. Janowski, Bednarczyk, M.: Considerations on indoor navigation based on cheap mobile devices. In: 2016 Baltic Geodetic Congress (BGC Geomatics), Gdansk, pp. 78–84 (2016)
10. Zandbergen, P.A., Barbeau, S.J.: Positional accuracy of assisted GPS data from high-sensitivity GPS-enabled mobile phones. J. Navig. **64**(3), 381–399 (2011)
11. Tariq, Z.B., Cheema, D.M., Kamran, M.Z., Naqvi, I.H.: Non-GPS positioning systems: a survey. ACM Comput. Surv. **50**(4), 34 (2017)
12. Jain, A.K., Nandakumar, K., Nagar, A.: Biometric template security. EURASIP J. Adv. Signal Process. **2008**, 17 (2018)
13. Zhao, W., Chellappa, R., Phillips, P.J., Rosenfeld, A.: Face recognition: a literature survey. ACM Comput. Surv. **35**(4), 399–458 (2003)
14. Syryamkim, V.I., Kuznetsov, D.N., Kuznetsova, A.S.: Biometric identification. In: IOP Conference Series: Materials Science and Engineering. II International Conference "Cognitive Robotics", 22–25, Tomsk, Russian Federation, vol. 363 (2017)
15. Hassan, H., Kim, H.-W.: CMOS capacitive fingerprint sensor based on differential sensing circuit with noise cancellation. Sensors **18**(7), 2020 (2018)
16. Simon, S.J., Paper, D.: User acceptance of voice recognition technology: an empirical extension of the technology acceptance model. J. Organ. End User Comput. (JOEUC) **19**(1), 24–50 (2007)
17. Schneier, B.: Two-factor authentication: too little, too late. Commun. ACM **48**(4), 136 (2005)

18. Elazhary, H.: Internet of Things (IoT), mobile cloud, cloudlet, mobile IoT, IoT cloud, fog, mobile edge, and edge emerging computing paradigms: disambiguation and research directions. J. Netw. Comput. Appl. **128**, 105–140 (2019)

19. Nest Audio. https://www.cnet.com/how-to/iphones-face-id-problems-tricks-tips/. Accessed 02 Nov 2020

20. Manabe, H., Fukumoto, M.: Headphone taps: a simple technique to add input function to regular headphones. In: Proceedings of the 14th International Conference on Human-Computer Interaction with Mobile Devices and Services Companion (MobileHCI 2012), pp. 177–180. Association for Computing Machinery, New York (2012)

21. Manabe, H., Fukumoto, M.: Tap control for headphones without sensors. In: Proceedings of the 24th Annual ACM Symposium on User Interface Software and Technology (UIST 2011), pp. 309–314. Association for Computing Machinery. New York (2011)

22. Metzger, C., Anderson, M., Starner, T.: FreeDigiter, a contact-free device for gesture control. In: Proceedings of the IEEE International Symposium on Wearable Computing (ISWC 2004), Arlington, USA, pp. 18–21 (2004)

Usability Assessment of the OSMO Pocket Mini Sports Video Camera and Improvement Plan

Chengzhi Zhang[(✉)], Yawen Cong, Jiaqian Long, Xinyang Wang, Marcelo M. Soares, and Jiayu Zeng

School of Design, Hunan University, Hunan 410000, People's Republic of China

Abstract. The video camera have gained its popularity over the years with the increasing popularity of taking vlog and other videos to record life. So it is necessary to conduct a usability study on video cameras. The most widely-accepted product on the market is Go-Pro, however, DJI OSMO Pocket Mini has also conquered a great market share due to its' unique design and function. This research included a detailed usability assessment on the OSMO Pocket Mini to explore what problems users encounter while using the product and accordingly, the possible solutions and improvement plans. These findings provide insights to designers and engineers.

Keywords: Video camera · Usability assessment · Solutions · Design

1 Introduction

With the development of technology, the use of camera products has gained popularity over the years. The usability of the product is of high importance while considering purchasing the video camera product. OSMO Pocket Mini Sports Video Camera has distinguished itself out of the market for its small size that can fit into the pocket and its unique way of holding: using one hand to grab the vertical stick and move it around all the time to record the video. While the sales of the OSMO Pocket is only next to GoPro and Insta360 among the big brands, according to Kushniruk, Andre W., et al., the improper use of a handheld electronic may cause a lot of trouble [1].

This research explored what are the possible improvement of the OSMO Pocket and draw improvement plans for better usability.

Since the OSMO Pocket has one touchscreen embedded in it. The research included not only the physical product but also the interaction on the touchscreen.

2 Methodology

The research contains both quantitative and qualitative methods to explore usability. It used four methods to conduct the research and the usability testing. Interview, questionnaire with feature checklists [2, 3], think-aloud protocol [4, 5], and focus group [6].

The research did not adopt Nielsen, Jakob's usability heuristics [7, 8] since this method requires the participation of several experts and involves complicated interfaces.

© Springer Nature Switzerland AG 2021
M. M. Soares et al. (Eds.): HCII 2021, LNCS 12781, pp. 109–117, 2021.
https://doi.org/10.1007/978-3-030-78227-6_9

2.1 Interview

The interview consists of the steps as follows: Firstly, preparing the interview outline, contacting the participants, and choosing a suitable interview time. Secondly, starting the interview and recording the screen. During the quarantine, the remote meeting software was adopted to conduct the interview. Finally, gathering the recording and analyze the results before concluding [Appendix. A].

2.2 Questionnaire with Feature Checklist

The questionnaires are used to find out: the users' age, the frequency of using the product, the learning cost, the usability, and the user's satisfaction level with the product. Twelve users were hired in total, all of whom had experienced the product before. They are expert users and intermittent users. None of them are novices.

The distributed questionnaires were as indicated in the picture (Fig. 1), the authors viewed the survey results and analyzed before drawing conclusions. The feature checklist was included in the questionnaire, to find out what function the user has used before and what function he or she uses the most.

The feature checklist listed all the main features of the product. The authors designed the questions before distributing them to the participants along with the questionnaire. The final step is analyzing the results and to conclude.

2.3 Think Aloud Protocol

The purpose of conducting the Think Aloud Protocol is to understand the learnability and the task match, whether the feedback is appropriate, and the user's satisfaction level towards the product. Three novice users were hired for the test (Fig. 2).

Firstly, the researchers handed the product to the users and observed their behaviors. Then the researchers asked them to talk about what they think in each step and recorded the whole operation process. At last, they analyzed the video and drew conclusions.

2.4 Focus Group

The purpose of the focus group is to understand the learnability and users' experiences and relating feelings towards the product as well as their satisfaction level.

In total, there are four people including the novice user, the intermittent user, the expert user, and the researcher.

3   Results

3.1 Interview

Most people use the OSMO pocket to record their life. Most usage scenarios are during outdoor activities, like during travel. According to four users interviewed, it is relatively easy to learn and understand how to operate. Besides, the battery durability is ideal. Users can hold it for a long time without feeling uncomfortable since the ergonomics of

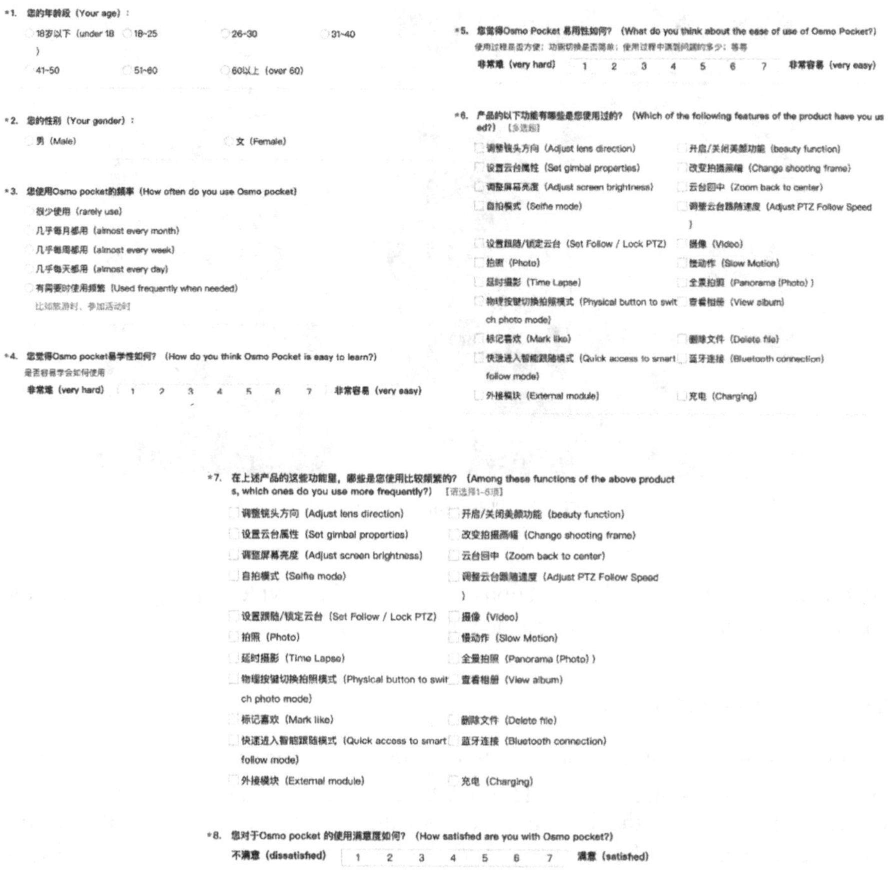
*1. 您的年龄段（Your age）：
18岁以下（under 18） 18~25 26~30 31~40
41~50 51~60 60以上（over 60）

*2. 您的性别（Your gender）：
男（Male） 女（Female）

*3. 您使用Osmo pocket的频率（How often do you use Osmo pocket）
很少使用（rarely use）
几乎每月都用（almost every month）
几乎每周都用（almost every week）
几乎每天都用（almost every day）
有需要时使用频繁（Used frequently when needed）
比如旅游时、参加活动时

*4. 您觉得Osmo pocket易学性如何？（How do you think Osmo Pocket is easy to learn?）
是否容易学会如何使用
非常难（very hard） 1 2 3 4 5 6 7 非常容易（very easy）

*5. 您觉得Osmo Pocket 易用性如何？（What do you think about the ease of use of Osmo Pocket?）
使用过程是否方便；功能切换是否简单；使用过程中遇到问题的多少；等等
非常难（very hard） 1 2 3 4 5 6 7 非常容易（very easy）

*6. 产品的以下功能有哪些是您使用过的？（Which of the following features of the product have you used?）【多选题】
调整镜头方向（Adjust lens direction）
开启/关闭美颜功能（beauty function）
设置云台属性（Set gimbal properties）
改变拍摄画幅（Change shooting frame）
调整屏幕亮度（Adjust screen brightness）
云台回中（Zoom back to center）
自拍模式（Selfie mode）
调整云台跟随速度（Adjust PTZ Follow Speed）
设置跟随/锁定云台（Set Follow / Lock PTZ）
摄像（Video）
拍照（Photo）
慢动作（Slow Motion）
延时摄影（Time Lapse）
全景拍照（Panorama (Photo)）
物理按键切换拍照模式（Physical button to switch photo mode）
查看相册（View album）
标记喜欢（Mark like）
删除文件（Delete file）
快速进入智能跟随模式（Quick access to smart follow mode）
蓝牙连接（Bluetooth connection）
外接模块（External module）
充电（Charging）

*7. 在上述产品的这些功能里，哪些是您使用比较频繁的？（Among these functions of the above products, which ones do you use more frequently?）【请选择1-6项】
调整镜头方向（Adjust lens direction）
开启/关闭美颜功能（beauty function）
设置云台属性（Set gimbal properties）
改变拍摄画幅（Change shooting frame）
调整屏幕亮度（Adjust screen brightness）
云台回中（Zoom back to center）
自拍模式（Selfie mode）
调整云台跟随速度（Adjust PTZ Follow Speed）
设置跟随/锁定云台（Set Follow / Lock PTZ）
摄像（Video）
拍照（Photo）
慢动作（Slow Motion）
延时摄影（Time Lapse）
全景拍照（Panorama (Photo)）
物理按键切换拍照模式（Physical button to switch photo mode）
查看相册（View album）
标记喜欢（Mark like）
删除文件（Delete file）
快速进入智能跟随模式（Quick access to smart follow mode）
蓝牙连接（Bluetooth connection）
外接模块（External module）
充电（Charging）

*8. 您对于Osmo pocket 的使用满意度如何？（How satisfied are you with Osmo pocket?）
不满意（dissatisfied） 1 2 3 4 5 6 7 满意（satisfied）

Fig. 1. Questionnaire with feature checklist

the design is great. The screen is too small, though, making the operations inconvenient. The inconvenience of adjusting the angle of the lens poses trouble to the users. Fewer physical buttons and insufficient control make it a little hard to manipulate. The shortcuts can be easily forgotten after a long time of not using them.

3.2 Questionnaire with Feature Checklist

Among the 12 samples, the users are mostly young people aged 18–25, consisting of 91.67% of the interviewee's body. The frequency of using the product is rather high during travel or activities. The users generally think that the OSMO Pocket is easy to operate (5.5 Point Avg. on a 1–7 Point Scale.) and the satisfaction with the product is high (5.5 Point Avg. on a 1–7 Point Scale).

For the checklist, it can be seen that nearly all the main features have been used by more than two participants. Adjusting the lens direction and video recording function has been used by all the interviewees (12 out of 12 interviewees, 100%). One user hasn't used the photo-taking function, though most of them (11 out of 12) have used both

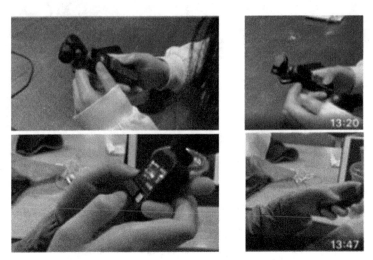

Fig. 2. Think aloud protocol

video taking and photo-taking functions. In all functions, video-taking, adjusting the lens direction, and taking photos are the top three (Fig. 3).

3.3 Think Aloud Protocol

The research found that the power button is not obvious enough and the icon hasn't indicated clear enough that it's a power button. The screen is too small, making it inconvenient to use. For the first-time user, they think the screen is only for display but not a touchscreen due to the small size. A lot of functions on the screen only have display icons without any description text, making the meaning not clear for the users.

Finally, the users tried to pry open the external module instead of slide-open it as it was designed (Fig. 4).

3.4 Focus Group

The conclusions include: the purpose of each physical button is hard to understand but easy to be forgotten. The buttons are not clearly labeled enough, novice users may regard the recording button as an on/off button. After using it for some time, the device heats up where the handle and the camera join together. Moreover, how the gimbal rotation of the lens works is difficult to understand. The slider structure of the external module always fails to slide out, as well. Finally, the users may touch the screen by accident, causing misuses.

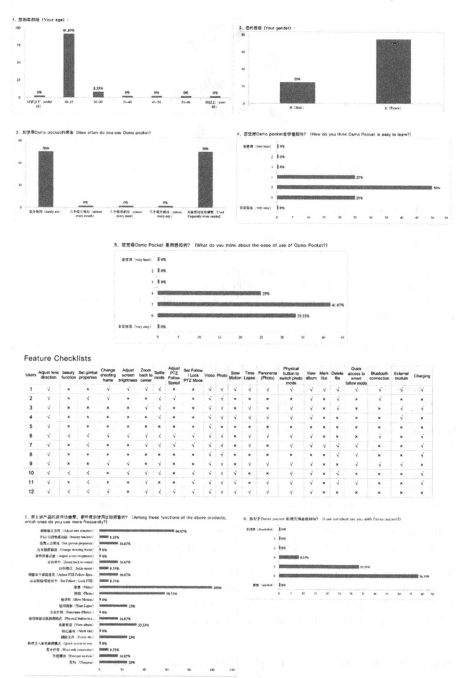

Fig. 3. Questionnaire with feature checklist survey results

Fig. 4. The user trying to pry open the external module

4 Findings and Improvement Plan

These are the findings according to the research:

1. The screen is too small, which have limited the ways of interaction using the fingers.
2. Too few physical buttons has limited the sense of control.
3. The unique power button makes it hard to understand for the first-time user.
4. The indication on the screen is not obvious enough, making it hard to understand.

Accordingly, this research raised the following recommendations as illustrated in the picture below: (Fig. 5).

Improvement 1: Adjusting the screen size to make it easy to handle.
By enlarging the screen size, the buttons can be hit more precisely by the user.

Improvement 2: Adding the physical button on the right of the screen for lens direction, and the scrolling wheel for lens zoom in and out effect.

Improvement 3: Adding photo-taking/video recording/off switch button. To replace the original obscure on/off button, adding the physical switch button on the left of the screen to switch between the three statuses: Off, Video-recording, and Photo-taking.

Improvement 4: Adding the slide-to-open sticker. By adding the sticker, the newbie will know that the external module is to slice open instead of prying open.

Improvement 5: Reforming the user interface while in the recording. The improvement plan added a prompt of the menu at the bottom of the screen to indicate the right entrance for the menu. Besides, the thumbnail of the former picture was placed at the bottom-left, indicating the entrance for the album. A camera icon indicated the conversion of camera type.

Improvement 6: Adding the text explaining the meaning of each icon. In the former version, there isn't text for explaining the icon's meaning. Though the reason may be to satisfy the international market, we added the text for clearer indication. Moreover, the difference between the on/off status of a single icon is for clearer indication. There will be a temporal pop-up window when close or open the PRO function.

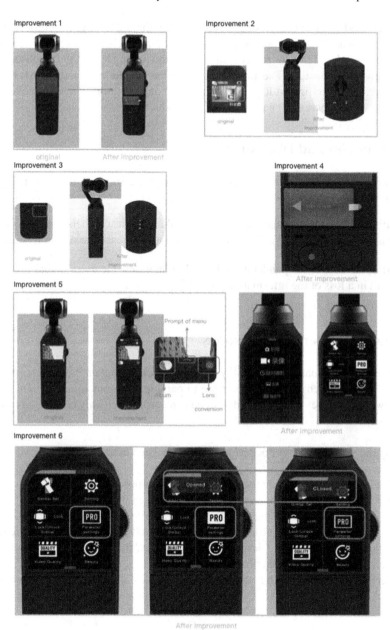

Fig. 5. Improvement plan, before and after

5   Conclusions

Although OSMO Pocket is one of the most popular video cameras. The research still found these limitations of the OSMO Pocket after conducting the experiments. No matter how much market share one product has conquered, there is always room for improvement. This research raised a detailed improvement plan, including increasing the space of the touchscreen, adding more physical buttons, and relying less on the touchscreen for human-product interaction. The improvement plan has also added an icon with text on the touchscreen for better indication and reformed the on/off button. These improvements, if adopted, would increase the usability of the product.

6   Limitations and Discussion

There are some limitations in our experiments though we've tried our best for the most fairest results:

Limitation 1. The sample and the users we hired are the researchers' aquitances, who are not a random sample from the users' pool. It may influence the research result.

Limitation 2. Due to the pandemic, it is hard to interview the users in real life, which may result in a loss of the information we get.

Appendix. A-Interview Questions

We are currently evaluating the usability of the DJI Pocket Lingyun PTZ camera product. Thank you very much for taking the time to participate in our interview. During the interview, all dialogues will be recorded, and the recording will only be used for research purposes.

1. Why did you buy Osmo Pocket? (If it has only been used and not purchased: what in specific do you use?).
2. What is your most frequent usage scenario and purpose?
3. What is your approximate frequency of use, or when will it be used?
4. How long do you usually use each time?
5. Please think about the first time you use it, do you have any doubts or inconvenience about some operations and designs of Osmo Pocket? (hope the user can describe the situation and feelings of the first use).
6. After you are familiar with it, do you feel any inconvenience of using Osmo Pocket?

References

1. Kushniruk, A.W., Triola, M.M., Borycki, E.M., Stein, B., Kannry, J.L.: Technology induced error and usability: the relationship between usability problems and prescription errors when using a handheld application. Int. J. Med. Inform. **74**(7–8), 519–526 (2005). https://doi.org/10.1016/j.ijmedinf.2005.01.003
2. Kuniavsky, M.: Observing the User Experience: A Practitioner's Guide to User Research. Elsevier, Amsterdam (2003)

3. Wilson, C.: Interview Techniques for UX Practitioners: A User-Centered Design Method. Newnes (2013)
4. Van Den Haak, M., De Jong, M., Schellens, P.J.: Retrospective vs. concurrent think-aloud protocols: testing the usability of an online library catalogue. Behav. Inform. Technol. **22**(5), 339–351 (2003)
5. Fonteyn, M.E., Kuipers, B., Grobe, S.J.: A description of think aloud method and protocol analysis. Qual. Health Res. **3**(4), 430–441 (1993)
6. Eysenbach, G., Köhler, C.: How do consumers search for and appraise health information on the world wide web? Qualitative study using focus groups, usability tests, and in-depth interviews. BMJ **324**(7337), 573–577 (2002)
7. Leventhal, L., Barnes, J.: Usability Engineering: Process, Products and Examples. Prentice-Hall Inc., Hoboken (2007)
8. Nielsen, J.: Ten usability heuristics (2005)
9. Cooper, A., et al.: About Face: The Essentials of Interaction Design. Wiley, Hoboken (2014)
10. Han, S.H., Yun, M.H., Kwahk, J., Hong, S.W.: Usability of consumer electronic products. Int. J. Ind. Ergon. **28**(3–4), 143–151 (2001). https://doi.org/10.1016/S0169-8141(01)00025-7

The Design of a Mobile App to Promote Young People's Digital Financial Literacy

Yi Zhang[✉]

University of Gothenburg, Gothenburg, Sweden

Abstract. With the popularity of Digital Financial Services (DFS), it is urgent and prudent to equip people with necessary knowledge and increased awareness to achieve financial well-being. This study, as a first step, employed the Design Thinking Methodology to design a mobile app for young people's digital financial literacy promotion. In the content design, it covers the fundamentals of DFS, awareness of potential DFS risks, and practical strategies for making informed DFS decisions. These content components work together to enable young people to make critical judgments on the state-of-the-art DFS offerings. In the delivery design, it implements digital nudges in an effort to reduce cognitive load and sustain user engagement. The nudging strategies include: 1) facilitator nudges to keep learning chunks small and easy-to-understand; 2) spark nudges to enhance users' learning motivation; 3) signal nudges to navigate the entire learning journey; 4) inquiry nudges to provide the scaffoldings anywhere anytime.

Keywords: Digital financial literacy · Digital nudging · Mobile learning

1 Introduction

Digitalization is the greatest transformational force in this era. As technology innovation progresses, Digital Financial Services (DFS), which incorporates any financial operation using digital technology, has been a global upward trend (G20 2017; OECD 2018; WorldBank 2020). Conventional Financial Institutions and start-ups are increasingly tapping into this innovation landscape. Accordingly, "the financial marketplace is much more complex for the average consumers. Consumers have more opportunities to manage their finances, but increased complexity makes them more vulnerable to financial fraud and more prone to unwise financial decisions" (IOSCO & OECD 2018, p. 16).

It is the lack of sufficient information and knowledge about DFS that make people exhibit vulnerability to potential DFS risks (G20 2017). For this reason, digital financial literacy learning has been positioned as an essential ingredient to fill in people's knowledge gaps and prepare for their lifelong financial well-being (G20 2017; IOSCO & OECD 2018).

Meanwhile, there has been a general consensus on using digital tools to deliver digital financial literacy learning, given that most DFS are delivered through digital means (e.g., mobile phones). In particular, mobile phones might be a promising alternative due to their high penetration rate. According to the latest Ericsson Mobility Report (Ericsson

M. M. Soares et al. (Eds.): HCII 2021, LNCS 12781, pp. 118–136, 2021.
https://doi.org/10.1007/978-3-030-78227-6_10

2020), "the number of smartphone use is forecast to reach 7.5 billion in 2025". The increased access to smartphones would make mobile apps an attractive medium for delivering digital financial literacy learning and facilitate seamless learning support.

Yet the efforts made in designing such learning are still at an early stage. The currently available learning materials fail to present DFS information in an accessible and salient manner (G20 2017). The vast majority of them are filled with jargon, resulting in consumers being overwhelmed by the sophisticated DFS features. Especially for young people who have been targeted by many Fintech companies, this issue might cause more concerns. Young generations tend to make quick judgments without fully understanding the terms and conditions, due to their low tolerance to redundant and complicated information. As a result, they are "more easily fall prey to personal bias such as overconfidence in their own digital capabilities to manage DFS risks" (G20 2017, p. 42).

Against this backdrop, this paper proposes the design of a mobile app to promote young people's digital financial literacy. Specifically, it focuses on a set of content design and delivery design strategies. The app serves as an educational tool to equip users with the fundamentals of DFS and actionable guidance about DFS safe use. With these bits of knowledge, the underprivileged consumers would ultimately improve their competence to question financial offerings too good to be true, and take actions to change their status quo.

2   Research Questions

- RQ1: What knowledge do young people need to promote their digital financial literacy? What are the potential content design strategies to fill in the knowledge gaps?
- RQ2: What key concerns should be considered when designing a mobile app to promote young people's digital financial literacy? What are the potential delivery strategies to address these concerns?

3   Theoretical Background

3.1   The Affordances of Mobile Learning

The growing penetration of smartphones has led to the popularity of mobile learning. As noted in the latest statistics, apps for educational purposes experienced an increase in usage of 20%, as well as a net new user growth of 8% (Ericsson 2020). We have witnessed an increased awareness of mobile learning. It offers a ubiquitous learning environment where people exploit mobile technologies to support learning activities anywhere, anytime (Brown & Mbati 2015; Kukulska-Hulme and Traxler 2019; Martin and Ertzberger 2013; Sharples et al. 2005).

Furthermore, mobile learning is personalized and informal (Kukulska-Hulme and Traxler 2019; Martin and Ertzberger 2013; Sharples et al. 2005; Yau and Joy 2007). It is personalized in the sense that mobile learning empowers learners to engage in their own learning, from their own settings, and by their own preferences (Kukulska-Hulme and Traxler 2019; Yau and Joy 2007). Meanwhile, it is informal in the sense that learners move from topic to topic, devoting time and efforts to small learning chunks, rather than following a defined curriculum (Martin and Ertzberger 2013).

As Koole and Ally (2006, p. 6) put it, "the major advantages of mobile learning include greater access to appropriate and timely information, reduced cognitive load during learning tasks, and increased interaction with systems and other people". Keeping this in mind, we would be more likely to exploit the affordances of mobile learning to design fit-for-purpose educational tools.

3.2 Mobile Learning Design Approach: Digital Nudges

In a ubiquitous learning environment, people come across a wealth of information, along with distractions and mind wandering. As a result, their ability to process the information might be hindered, increasing stress and anxiety to make sound decisions. As Palalas (2018, p. 19) pointed out, "Cognitive load, which has been identified as a key issue in successful instructional design, is yet another aspect that is impacted by the content, delivery, and setting of mobile learning". Moreover, the financial marketplace is rather complicated for the average consumers, due to the evolving technology and sophisticated products (G20 2017; OECD 2019). This adds an extra layer of complexity for people's working memory capacity, which means people can only "hold in mind, attend, or maintain a small amount of information in a rapidly accessible state at one time" (Cowan 2016, p. 1). As such, designers need to figure out a set of effective strategies to promote users' learning and engagement in mobile settings.

With this regard, the notion of "digital nudging" (Weinmann et al. 2016, p. 433) sheds light on our exploration. It refers to "the use of user-interface design elements to guide people's behavior in digital choice environments" (Weinmann et al. 2016, p. 433). The key message it conveys is that how the information is presented can exert a subtle influence on the outcomes. Even simple modification would nudge users into behaving in particular ways. Hence, Caraban et al. (2019) summarized 23 mechanisms of digital nudging, and further clustered them into three overall categories: facilitator nudges, spark nudges, and signal nudges. Facilitator nudges apply the rule of thumb to present the information in a simple and straightforward way, so that people can efficiently tackle the complexity; Spark nudges are designed to incorporate the motivational elements in the digital environment; Signal nudges aim to provide the ongoing reinforcements for user engagement, such as feedback, just-in-time promotes, etc.

4 Methodology

4.1 Research Approach: Design Thinking

This study applied the Design Thinking (DT) Methodology to design the mobile app. "It draws from the designers' toolkit to integrates the needs of people, the possibilities of technology, and the requirements of success" (IDEO 2020). This methodology provides us a systematic view to come up with a tailored mobile learning solution to promote young people's digital financial literacy. Within the DT framework, designers could capture users' learning needs, generate a broad set of design ideas, and flesh out ideas through rapid prototyping in order to test users' acceptances.

4.2   Research Design

The design adopted the five-phases process of DT (Stanford 2010), including empathy (data collection based on user research), defining (data synthesis to frame the problem statements), ideation (generating design ideas), prototyping (developing a tangible solution), and testing (with potential users). Table 1 outlines the overall research design.

Table 1. The overall research design

Phase 1 Empathize	Phase 2 Define	Phase 3 Ideate	Phase 4 Prototype	Phase 5 Test

Phases	Empathize	Define	Ideate	Prototype	Test
Description	data collection based on user research	data synthesis to frame the problem statements	suggest ideas for solving the problem	develop tangible and experienceable representations of the ideas	test with the potential users
Methods	Questionnaire	Content analysis	Card sorting	Prototyping	Questionnaire; Think-aloud sessions
Output	User survey results	Persona; Problem Statements	Idea board	High-fidelity Prototype	User Testing Results

5   Design Procedures

5.1   Phase 1: Empathize

Empathy plays a critical role in "keeping designers from falling into a common design pitfall-designing for oneself" (Luchs et al. 2016, p. 27). It requires capturing the key attributes of intended users, so that we could identify their needs and unfulfilled requirements. Therefore, a user research was conducted in the initial phase. The variables relating to digital financial literacy learning were transferred into an online survey.

The Description of the Participants. In the initial user research, 38 participants were recruited through convenience sampling and snowball sampling. Most of them were young adults between the ages of 20 and 35, using DFS on a regular basis (see Fig. 1 and Table 2). However, they still feel puzzled when dealing with sophisticated DFS products, such as blockchain, cryptocurrencies, P2P lending, and crowdfunding (see Table 3).

Beyond that, "risk is a basic element of decision making in most financial context" (Estelami 2009, p. 15). DFS is no exception. As Fig. 2 suggested, the participants lack the competencies mitigating the potential risks of personal cybersecurity and information asymmetry. For instance, they are not well aware of how to protect their digital keys and digital wallets. They usually don't fully understand the terms and conditions before committing to a specific DFS.

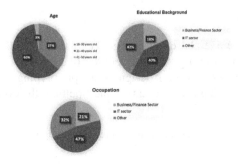

Fig. 1. The demographic information of the participants (N = 38)

Table 2. DFS experience of the participants

Variable	Items	Percentage
Digital Finance service Usage	use digital finance services very often	94.74%
	prefer traditional financial services	5.26%
	have no experience in investing	23.68%
Investing Experience	make the investments with the aid of brokers/investment advisors	28.95%
	make the investments on their own	47.37%

Table 3. DFS knowledge gaps of the participants

DFS Jargon	Easy	Either Easy or Difficult	Difficult
Mobile Banking	81.58%	15.79%	2.63%
Digital Wallet	71.43%	20.00%	8.57%
Blockchain	14.71%	44.12%	41.18%
Cryptocurrencies	35.29%	38.24%	26.47%
P2P lending	50.00%	38.24%	11.76%
Crowdfunding	58.82%	23.53%	17.65%

The Learning Requirements of the Participants. The survey was also used for collecting data about user learning needs. First, it showed that the participants prefer to cram learning into the interstice of daily lives. 57% of them were willing to devote 15–30 min/day to digital financial literacy learning (see Fig. 3). It is also noted that a subset of the participants (31%) was not interested in the learning. Among them, 58.3% make investments on their own. This is consistent with the findings in financial literacy research. The scholars asserted that seasoned investors are more likely to fall into the trap of overconfidence, which would further lead to inaccurate awareness of risks and risky financial behaviors (Drew and Cross 2013; Shen 2014).

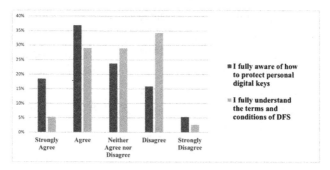

Fig. 2. The participants' DFS risk awareness

Second, it revealed that the participants considered the factors such as infographics, plain and simple language, and small chunks of information facilitating them to understand DFS concepts better (see Table 4). In terms of the content, they displayed more interest and motivation to learn the mechanism and potential risks of DFS (see Table 5).

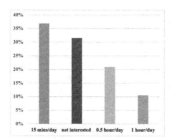

Fig. 3. The time for digital financial literacy learning

Table 4. The factors facilitating learning

Favorable Factors	MOST IMPORTANT	IMPORTANT	LESS IMPORTANT	LEAST IMPORTANT
Pictures illustrated the definitions	51.43%	28.57%	14.29%	5.71%
Plain and simple language	26.47%	26.47%	17.65%	29.41%
Small-chunk of information	15.63%	21.88%	34.38%	28.13%
Others' experience	10.00%	20.00%	36.67%	33.33%

Table 5. The content requirements

Learning Content	MOST IMPORTANT	IMPORTANT	LESS IMPORTANT	LEAST IMPORTANT
Mechanism (how it works)	62.86%	8.57%	8.57%	20.00%
Potential benefits	21.88%	31.25%	28.13%	18.75%
Potential risks	15.63%	46.88%	31.25%	6.25%
Consumer protection regulations	8.57%	11.43%	31.43%	48.57%

5.2   Phase 2: Define

In this phase, it involves synthesizing the scattered data into powerful insights and guiding design efforts forward (Stanford 2010). Yet "it is all too easy to see only the surface problems and never dig deeper to address the real issues" (Norman 2013, p. 218). Therefore, I took a step-by-step approach to define the problem statements. First, the persona of intended users was portrayed (see Fig. 4). After that, the problem statements were framed in order to address the RIGHT challenge (see Fig. 4).

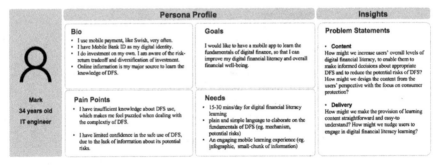

Fig. 4. The persona and problem statements

5.3   Phase 3: Ideate

Ideation calls for divergent thinking based on persona and problem statements. A list of "How-might-we…" responses was generated in the light of literature and subject matter experts' suggestions (Instructional design/Finance). In this case, that is to generate ideas in terms of the content design and delivery design of the app. Figure 5 presented an idea board of collective insights, including the data in user research, the suggestions from subject matter experts, and the design ideas of the author.

5.4   Phase 4: Prototype

In this phase, a high-fidelity prototype was created as a tangible solution. The aim was to simulate the possible user experience so that users would be able to envision the final product and give meaningful feedback.

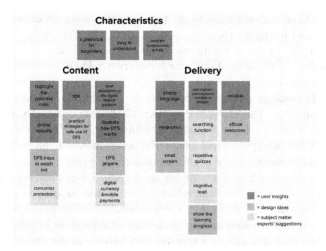

Fig. 5. The idea board of the project

Content: The Information Architecture of the App. The app strives to enable users to make the most of DFS while keeping them in 'safe' use. It appears to be a meaningful yet challenging task, since currently available DFS information remains scattered and fragmented. Therefore, it calls for a systematic view to structure the intended content coverage. In this case, the Digital Finance Cube (Gomber et al. 2017) was adopted, which provides a solid framework to navigate through the DFS field. Drawing on this model, I modified the three dimensions by linking to the portmanteau of FINTECH (see Fig. 6): fin-part (DFS dimension), tech-part (Technology dimension) and Subsections.

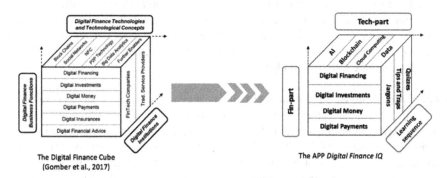

Fig. 6. The content framework of the app

- **Fin-part (DFS dimension)** covers the fundamentals of DFS. Among them, the basics of digital money and digital payments are particularly highlighted. The rationale behind this is that young people, who perceive digital money as a fast track to wealth, tend to expose themselves at the heart of cryptocurrency fever (Clatworthy 2018).

On the other hand, digital payments are popular with young generations, due to its convenience and flexibility (Koenig-Lewis et al. 2015). Yet when it comes to the relevant cybersecurity issues, young consumers exhibit substantial vulnerability. After learning the basics, the desired outcome for users would be an appropriate attitude towards DFS.

- **Tech-part (Technology dimension)** includes the concepts of AI, Blockchain, Cloud Computing, and Data. This is inspired by HKU (2020)'s study which summarized the driving forces allowing DFS to flourish can be known as ABCD technologies (i.e. AI, Blockchain, Cloud computing and Data). The acronym ABCD gives learners a hint to understand and memorize the sophisticated technology terms.
- **Subsections** outline the learning sequences in the app. Specifically, the learning journey starts with the *jargon* section, which serves as the building blocks of digital financial literacy learning. After that, learners would level up to the *Tips and Traps* section. With a better understanding of the DFS tactics, people would be able to undertake their own research on a specific DFS before committing to it, as well as to question offerings too good to be true. Finally, the *quiz* section quickly checks learners' learning outcomes.

Based on the above content framework, the information architecture of the app was fleshed out (see Fig. 7). It not only presents an overall structure of the app, but also navigates a potential user experience. As can be seen, the learning content is made up of 8 learning units, including 4 units of DFS financial concepts (i.e. Fin-part) and 4 units of DFS technology concepts (i.e. Tech-part). Each unit serves as a micro-learning chunk, explicitly explaining *jargon, tips and traps,* and finally ending up with *quizzes.*

Delivery: The Digital Nudges of the App. To design an engaging mobile learning experience, the app employed the notion of *Digital Nudging* (Weinmann et al. 2016). It is eagerly adopted in UX design, which suggested that subtle changes in digital choice architecture can "alter people's behaviors in predictable ways" (Thaler and Sunstein 2009). Its application to this work involved design effective strategies that sustain user engagement in the entire mobile learning experience. Inspired by Caraban et al. (2019)'s idea, I designed the following nudges into the app.

- **Facilitator Nudges.** "The complexity of financial services may enable providers to introduce additional information to the consumers' decision environment, some of which may be non-diagnostic and thereby exhaust consumers' short-term memory capacity" (Estelami 2009, p. 279). Consequently, people appear to think that DFS are complicated concepts that require more time and effort to digest. Especially young generations crave for being fast learners (Thompson 2013), resulting in low tolerance to redundant information and complicated explanation. Thus, facilitator nudges were implemented in the delivery design, aiming to reduce users' cognitive load in their mobile learning. Specifically, the design efforts involved keeping information short and small-chunked, sorting jargon by their relevance, using infographics, and underlining keywords (see Fig. 8). By doing so, learners would be able to anchor to the essential attributes and ultimately arrive at optimal learning outcomes.

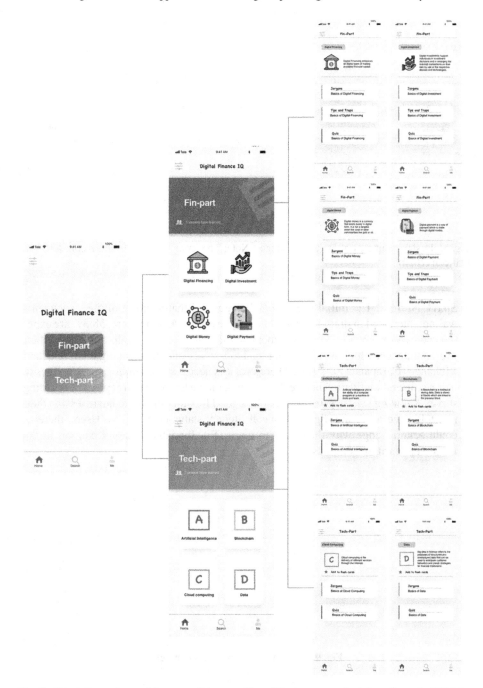

Fig. 7. The information architecture of the app. Note: The icons are cited from Freepik (2020a), Justicon (2020), SBTS2018 (2020).

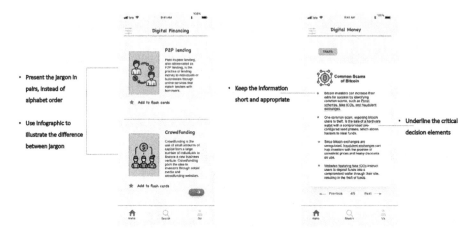

Fig. 8. Design examples of facilitator nudges. Note: The icons are cited from Freepik (2020b), FlatIcon (2020).

- **Spark Nudges.** The initial user research suggested that a subset of the respondents was not interested in digital financial literacy learning. Among them, 58.3% are experienced investors who make investments on their own. This might attribute to their overconfidence, which would further lead to a status-quo bias making them reluctant to change (Caraban et al. 2019). Therefore, it is necessary to employ spark nudges to increase users' motivation before they embark on the learning journey. An onboarding survey *Knowing yourself Better* might be a good fit, nudging users into assessing their risk tolerance level and digital financial literacy status (see Fig. 9). Users, thereby, could acknowledge why they need to learn DFS fundamentals and commit to the follow-up learning activities.

Fig. 9. Design examples of spark nudges

- **Signal Nudges.** "Mobile learners have to be able to self-regulate their ubiquitous learning habits, and pay attention to learning tasks consistently and mindfully" (Palalas 2018, p. 172). As such, a set of signal nudges were employed alongside the learning journey (see Fig. 10). They constitute a key thread of tasks to sustain higher levels of user engagement. The learning journey starts with an onboarding test to assess their

DFS risk perceptions and then goes through knowledge sections (i.e., *jargon, tips and traps*) and quiz section. The signal nudges as self-regulation learning reminders, keeping users informed of their learning progress.

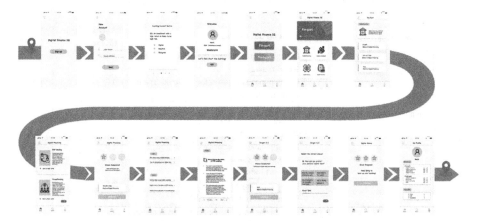

Fig. 10. Design examples of signal nudges

5.5 Phase 5: Test

The primary task in this phase is to collect user feedback on the prototype. To achieve this, I conducted a user satisfaction questionnaire and three think-aloud sessions. The testing results were analyzed and lead to further iterations.

User Satisfaction Questionnaire. 10 young adults were recruited through convenience sampling to respond to the user satisfaction questionnaire. They answered the questions by selecting a rating from a 1–5 scale, with 1 being the lowest rating and 5 being the highest. The measurement was driven by questions about how they perceived the usefulness/ease of use/ease of learning/satisfaction of the app. Table 6 revealed that the participants were satisfied with the app usability in general. 60% of them would download the app to learn DFS fundamentals. In particular, the delivery design (i.e., ease of use, and ease of learning) was viewed as the most favored aspect. The mean rating on a 1–5 scale for the metrics *ease of use* was 4.3, followed by the mean for *ease of learning* (4.25). These reflected the effectiveness of digital nudges incorporated into the app. With the facilitator nudges, the participants perceived that the app elaborated on the DFS knowledge in an easy-to-understand way; the text was easily readable; the app presented the relevance of different DFS concepts in a systematic way. Similarly, the participants assessed that the user flow was easy to follow and offered clear navigation through a set of signal nudges.

Yet there was still some room for improvements regarding the content design. The participants perceived that the app failed to help them balance the risks and rewards of DFS to some degree. This indicated that more efforts are needed to emphasize both the pros and cons of DFS. With knowing both sides very well, users would be able to make their critical judgments on DFS offerings.

Table 6. The results of the user satisfaction questionnaire

Categories	Metrics	Items on questionnaire	Average score (Mean)
Content	Usefulness	This app helps me learn the fundamentals of digital finance.	4.1
		This app makes it easier for me to understand the digital finance jargon.	4.2
		This app makes it easier for me to balance the risk and reward of digital finance services/products.	3.5
		This app makes it easier for me to mitigate the risks associated with digital finance services/products.	4.0
Delivery	Ease of use	This app is easy to use.	4.5
		The app text is easily readable.	4.4
		The app has an effective layout, organization, and grouping.	4.1
	Ease of learning	This app explains the digital finance concepts and features in a simple and easy-to-understand way.	4.3
		This app helps me understand how different digital finance concepts relate to each other.	4.2
Overall	Satisfaction	This app is visually pleasing.	4.3
		I would download the app to learn the digital finance foundations.	3.9

At the end of the questionnaire, two open-ended questions were asked to collect suggestions for improvements. A significant subset of the participants suggested that the app needs to improve the search function, considering that *"people tend to use the search tab/search bar as a shortcut to access the information they need in the app"*. Additionally, the participants recommended that the future version could incorporate more user interactions, for instance, *"users can ask or add comments when they have problems in understanding the specific concepts"*, *"the app could encourage user-generated content, allowing users to share their own experience briefly"*.

Think-Aloud Sessions. For each think-aloud session, one participant was asked to describe what he/she was thinking and doing out loud (the "think aloud" technique) while interacting with the app. A set of benchmark tasks were designed as vehicles for driving evaluation (Hartson and Pyla 2019) (Table 7).

It revealed that the app's favorable features included: 1) the onboarding test to assess their risk tolerance; 2) the approaches to organizing the content; 3) the quick quizzes after learning; 4) the flashcards for learning DFS jargon. Yet they perceived that the search function was less satisfactory, since it failed to provide ready-to-hand access to the information they inquire. Additionally, the participants proposed some recommendations

Table 7. The results of the think-aloud sessions

	Task 1	Task 2	Task 3	Task 4	Task 5	Task 6
	Before	During			After	
	Sign up	Learn the DFS jargon	Learn the Tips & Traps	Take a quiz	Review the user profile	Try out the search function
Task Description	The participants were asked to: • sign up a new account • take the onboarding test to assess their risk tolerance	The participants were asked to: • pick a unit of DFS jargon to learn • add the jargon to the flashcards	The participants were asked to: • pick a unit of DFS tips and traps to learn	The participants were asked to: • take a corresponding quiz after learning a specific DFS unit	The participants were asked to: • go into the Me subpage and review the design	The participants were asked to: • go into the Search subpage and review the design
User Satisfaction	Participant 1: ☺ Participant 2: ☺ Participant 3: ☺	Participant 1: ☺ Participant 2: ☺ Participant 3: ☹	Participant 1: ☺ Participant 2: ☺ Participant 3: ☺	Participant 1: ☺ Participant 2: ☺ Participant 3: ☺	Participant 1: ☹ Participant 2: ☺ Participant 3: ☺	Participant 1: ☺ Participant 2: ☺ Participant 3: ☹
User Comments	Participant 3: "The onboarding test is a good idea! It helps me clarify the motivation why I need this APP. And i would suggest that you could personalize the learning content based on each user's risk tolerance level."	Participant 2: "I like the way you organize the jargon, like Bitcoin and Ethereum are grouped together. These two are the leading ones in digital currencies." Participant 3: "In the digital investment part, the jargon are quite limited. The basic terms of investment, such as equity, yield, and asset, are not included."	Participant 1: "These tips are really helpful! Now I know that I could evalute an ICO project by checking out its whitepaper. Maybe I had a sterotype about digital money before, hahaha." "But i think the part about Facebook Libra might not be a fair point. Even though it was challenged by the U.S. government, we still can see the value in it. It would be better if you mention both pros and cons, and then let the users to make the judgments "	Participant 1: Quiz on Digital money Time to complete: 28 sec Accurancy:100% Participant 2: Quiz on Digital money Time to complete: 35 sec Accurancy:100% Participant 3: Quiz on Digital Investment Time to complete: 15 sec Accuracy:100%	Participant 1: "The feature of Flashcard is really thoughtful! It would be easy for me to check in and review the jargon I am not familiar with whenever I feel like to. So, I would suggest having the flashcards in a sperate section. The current version is a little bit crowded. "	Participant 3: "The search function could be strengthened in the next version, since I assume this app works as a quick-guide or a cheatsheet of digital finance. Here is a user case. If people have something that they are unfamiliar with, they just need to check in your app and get the answers by using the search function. This would be a quite efficient way to learn. They can learn whatever they need at the moment they need.

to enhance the content, such as supplementing additional investing jargon, summarizing a pros and cons list, etc.

5.6 Iteration

Design Thinking Methodology is an iterative process, rather than a linear one. This suggests that testing is not the final step. As designers, we need to evolve the design ideas based on the inputs from user testing. The following outlines the ideas for iteration. In content design, the issue concerning the right amount of content was prioritized. The next iteration could insert external links (e.g. YouTube links) as supplementary reading for users. Meanwhile, the interactive feature would be added in the app, allowing users to tag for likes and leave comments on relevant learning content. In delivery design, the search function needs further modification. A potential solution could be specifying the search scope into jargon, tips, and traps. That way, users would be able to narrow down the search scope and obtain the DFS information they inquire about at any given moment.

6 Discussion

6.1 Content Design Strategies

To formulate the content design strategies, we need to address the research question *What knowledge do young people need to promote their digital financial literacy? What are the potential content design strategies to fill in the knowledge gaps?* This requires us to summarize and synthesize the findings from an on-going line of inquiry. The efforts involved generating insights from user empathy and revisiting the user content requirements through prototype testing.

The Knowledge Gaps in Digital Financial Literacy. As the initial user research showed, the participants have insufficient knowledge about DFS. More precisely, that is the lack of the fundamentals of DFS, such as commonly used jargon and underlying mechanisms. Consequently, consumers are left in a passive position where they have to make decisions without fully understanding the terms and conditions of the DFS they received.

Beyond that, "risk is a basic element of decision making in most financial context" (Estelami 2009, p. 15). DFS is no exception. Key risks may arise in many forms, such as cybercrime, online fraud, phishing scams, digital profiling, and data theft, etc., (G20 2017; OECD 2019). Yet young people haven't been equipped with the competencies mitigating such potential risks. As the user survey showed, the participants lack the knowledge and skills to protect their digital keys, digital wallets, and other access information relating to DFS against fraud or theft. This is in line with the findings of IFC (2019). They claimed that one factor holding back users is the lack of actionable guidance to help them evaluate the DFS risks. Therefore, beyond the fundamentals of DFS, users also should be well aware of possible DFS risks and a set of practical strategies to prevent themselves from being defrauded.

A Content Framework to Fill in the Knowledge Gaps. To fill in these knowledge gaps, it is necessary to offer users a systematic view pursuing DFS knowledge. This work applied the Digital Finance Cube Framework (Gomber et al. 2017) to develop the intended content coverage. DFS concepts were categorized into three dimensions, namely *fin-part (DFS dimension), tech-part (Technology dimension),* and *learning sequences (i.e., Jargon, Tips and Traps, Quizzes).* The effectiveness of this content framework has been demonstrated by the testing results. Moreover, the provision of *tips and traps* was perceived as a good value proposition, helping users mitigate the risks associated with DFS effectively and efficiently.

Reflections on the Content Design Strategies. Meanwhile, the testing results suggested the prototype failed to help the participants balance the risks and rewards of DFS to some degree. This indicated that the benefits of DFS was a missing part in the current content coverage. Without knowing both the pros and cons, it is difficult for users to make critical judgments on the products delivered by DFS providers.

The above unexpected result also raised the issue about the right amount of content. To tackle it, we need to consider more options to design content coverage in accordance with users' requirements. First of all, designers have to deal with "the apparent contradiction of having to both increase and decrease content" (Garrison 2017, p. 72). In this case, the content could be increased by providing external links that may elaborate on important DFS concepts or including supplementary material; and decreased by focusing on the essential DFS knowledge and skills. This is an art form where we exploit mobile learning affordances to hit the sweet spot where learners feel comfortable with the amount of content. Another approach is to pull in user-generated content. The focus is to "help learners contribute as well as consume mobile content" (Kukulska-Hulme and Traxler 2019, p. 193). Content development is not a big-bang effort. Instead, we would be better off taking an incremental approach to building up the breadth and width of content coverage. More options and considerations would be tested out by users.

6.2 Delivery Design Strategies

To formulate the delivery design strategies, we need to address the research question *what key concerns should be considered when designing a mobile app to promote young people's digital financial literacy? What are the potential delivery strategies to address these concerns?*

Key Concerns: Cognitive Overload and Continuous User Engagement. Cognitive overload has been claimed as a central issue of mobile learning (Palalas 2018). DFS puts an extra layer of complexity on people's cognitive processes, given that most DFS are sophisticated and multi-dimensional. People always have confusion about "what they understand to be offered and what is actually being offered by DFS providers" (G20 2017, p. 38). Hence, "the ruthless management of cognitive load" (Dirksen 2016, p. 167) has become a top priority in the context of digital financial literacy promotion.

What's more, young generations crave for being fast learners and thereby prefer to cram learning into the interstice of daily lives. They have multiple tasks and distractions that compete for their attention, especially in mobile settings. This brings up another key concern, continuous user engagement, which requires a set of strategies keeping users engaged alongside the entire learning journey.

Applying Digital Nudges to Address the Key Concerns. As a pilot study, this paper adopted the notion of "digital nudges" (Weinmann et al. 2016, p. 433) in an effort to address the above key concerns. Three nudging strategies were proposed: facilitator nudges, spark nudges, and signal nudges. They gently steer users towards "developing a habit of lifelong learning to improve their digital financial literacy and financial well-being" (OECD 2016, p. 26).

- **Facilitator nudges: keep learning chunks small and easy-to-understand.** This study employed the components such as infographic, plain and simple language, and small-chunked information to mitigate the concerns of cognitive overload. They act as facilitator nudges to simplify the tasks and ease the learning-curve (Caraban et al. 2019). The core is to tackle the following two limitations: 1) the limitations of short-term memory capacity. "The number of items that the short-term memory system can hold at any one point of time is seven, and the length of time for which the information is available has been determined to be about 10 s" (Estelami 2009, p. 275). To overcome this limitation, a potential strategy is framing the information short and easy-to-understand. That way, learners would be able to anchor the most salient aspect of the content and expand their effective working memory capacity (Estelami 2009; OECD 2019). 2) the limitations of display capacity in mobile settings. The small screens of mobile phones make it difficult to show large chunks of information. As such, it is common to split learning content into small chunks (Elias 2011; Hug and Friesen 2009; Koole and Ally 2006). The desired outcome would be nudging users to dig into DFS knowledge bit by bit.
- **Spark nudges: enhance learning motivation.** Spark nudges fit for the scenario where users lack the motivation to pursue the behavior (Caraban et al. 2019). In this case, an onboarding test was implemented as spark nudges at the very beginning. The rationale

is that a subset of the participants displayed limited interests in digital financial literacy learning. 58.% of them make investments on their own. It was overconfidence that induced people's status-quo bias, making them resist upgrading their DFS knowledge. Thus, it is necessary to apply spark nudges to steer users in a way that they have the motivation to learn the fundamentals of DFS. Ultimately, young generations would be less likely to "fall prey to personal biases such as overconfidence in their own digital capabilities to manage DFS risks" G20 (2017, p. 42). More options for spark nudges could be further explored, yet the motivational trait is at the core.

- **Signal nudges: navigate the learning journey.** The primary aim of signal nudges is to sustain user engagement. As Palalas (2018, p. 19) argued, "with mobile learners being able to squeeze in learning in-between other daily activities, they face contesting demands on their attention and their brain". Especially for young adults, more multi-tasks and distractions in mobile settings compete for their attention at a given moment. This situation calls for signal nudges working as self-regulation reminders, which not only inform them of learning progress, but also provide immediate feedback on the tasks they have completed.

Reflections on the Delivery Design Strategies. The testing results also indicated that self-scaffolding was a compelling need of young people, yet the current version of the app didn't fulfill this need. The way young generations receive information and acquire knowledge has been transformed by ubiquitous technologies (Monem 2015). They highly rely on the search function as just-in-time learning support to "provide scaffolding WHEN and WHERE learners need it" (Martin and Ertzberger 2013, p. 78). Especially, the information available in the DFS domain is so scattered and fragmented that they have to spend much time searching for the relevant knowledge. It therefore would be appealing to them to get ready-to-hand access to certain knowledge when they are struggling with DFS tasks. These are the "teachable moments" proposed by OECD (2019), which means users are provided useful DFS knowledge when it is most needed. At such moments, learners are more likely to interact with learning content in an attentive manner and process information effectively (Palalas 2018). In this sense, a robust search capability would be an inquiry nudge to make the design engaging at delivering content, as well as effective at enhancing user learning.

7 Conclusion

This study explores the design of a mobile app to promote young people's digital financial literacy. Through the design efforts, the study found that young people have knowledge gaps in DFS fundamentals and risk awareness. To fill in these gaps, the provision of DFS content involves elaboration on jargon, actionable guidance, as well as risks and rewards. In the delivery design, digital nudges can be implemented to mitigate the key concerns of cognitive overload and continuous user engagement. A set of nudging strategies were proposed: 1) exploit facilitator nudges to keep learning chunks small and easy-to-understand; 2) incorporate spark nudges to enhance users' learning motivation; 3) embody signal nudges to navigate the learning journey; 4) add inquiry nudges to provide the scaffolding anywhere anytime.

As a first step towards the design for digital financial literacy promotion, this paper specifically focuses on the approaches in mobile settings. More digital environments could be explored in future research. Furthermore, it might be a meaningful task to empirically investigate the effectiveness of different digital nudges in such environments. The interactions of user experience can be collected and analyzed as valuable data to achieve this goal. It is also worth mentioning that ethical aspects should be considered carefully as well, if we capture users' digital footprint as raw data to speculate how different digital nudges are played out.

References

Brown, H., Mbati, S.: Mobile learning: moving past the myths and embracing the opportunities. Int. Rev. Res. Open Distrib. Learn. **16**(2), 115–135 (2015)

Caraban, A., Karapanos, E., Gonçalves, D., Campos, P.: 23 ways to nudge: a review of technology-mediated nudging in human-computer interaction. Paper presented at the Conference on Human Factors in Computing Systems (2019)

Clatworthy, B.: Young people put too many eggs in the cryptobasket. The Times (2018). https://www.thetimes.co.uk/article/young-people-put-too-many-eggs-in-thecryptobasket-ppsn95gzp

Cowan, N.: Working Memory Capacity, Classic Routledge, Milton Park (2016)

Dirksen, J.: Design for How People Learn. New Riders, Berkeley (2016)

Drew, J., Cross, C.: Fraud and its PREY: conceptualising social engineering tactics and its impact on financial literacy outcomes. J. Financ. Serv. Maket. **18**(3), 188–198 (2013)

Elias, T.: Universal instructional design principles for mobile learning. Int. Rev. Res. Open Distance Learn. **12**(2), 144–153 (2011)

Ericsson: Ericsson Mobility Report, June 2020 (2020). https://www.ericsson.com/en/mobility-report/reports/june-2020

Estelami, H.: Cognitive drivers of suboptimal financial decisions: implications for financial literacy campaigns. J. Financ. Serv. Market. **13**(4), 273–283 (2009)

FlatIcons (Producer) (2020). P2p. https://www.flaticon.com/free-icon/p2p_2133101

Freepik (Producer). Crowdfunding (2020a). https://www.flaticon.com/free-icon/crowdfunding_2418475

Freepik (Producer). Online payment (2020b). https://www.flaticon.com/premium-icon/online-payment_1532715

G20. Ensuring financial education and consumer protection for all in the digital age (2017). https://www.oecd.org/finance/g20-oecd-report-on-ensuring-financial-education-and-consumer-protection-for-all-in-the-digital-age.htm

Garrison, D.: E-Learning in the 21st Century: A Community of Inquiry Framework for Research and Practice. Routledge, Milton Park (2017)

Gomber, P., Koch, J.-A., Siering, M.: Digital finance and FinTech: current research and future research directions. J. Bus. Econ. **87**(5), 537–580 (2017). https://doi.org/10.1007/s11573-017-0852-x

Guest, R., Brimble, M.: Financial literacy 101. Policy J. Public Policy Ideas **34**, 3–7 (2018)

Hartson, R., Pyla, P.: The UX Book: Agile UX Design for a Quality User Experience. Morgan Kaufmann Publications, San Francisco (2019)

HKU. Introduction of Fintech (2020). https://www.edx.org/course/introduction-to-fintech

Hug, T., Friesen, N.: Outline of a microlearning agenda. eLearning Papers, vol. 16, pp. 1–13 (2009)

IDEO. IDEO Design Thinking (2020). https://designthinking.ideo.com/

IFC. The Case for Responsible Investing in Digital Financial Services (2019). www.ifc.org/thoughtleadership

IOSCO & OECD. The Application of Behavioural Insights to Financial Literacy and Investor Education Programmes and Initiatives (2018). http://www.oecd.org/finance/The-Application-of-Behavioural-Insights-to-Financial-Literacy-and-Investor-Education-Programmes-and-Ini tiatives.pdf

Justicon (Producer). Bitcoin (2020). https://www.flaticon.com/premium-icon/bitcoin_968773

Koenig-Lewis, N., Marquet, M., Palmer, A., Zhao, A.: Enjoyment and social influence: predicting mobile payment adoption. Serv. Ind. J. **35**(10), 537–554 (2015)

Koole, M., Ally, M.: Framework for the rational analysis of mobile education (FRAME) model: revising the ABCs of educational practices. Paper presented at the International Conference on Networking, International Conference on Systems and International Conference on Mobile Communications and Learning Technologies (2006)

Kukulska-Hulme, A., Traxler, J.: Design principles for learning with mobile devices. In: Beetham, H., Sharpe, R. (eds.) Rethinking Pedagogy for a Digital Age. Routledge, Milton Park (2019)

Luchs, M., Swan, S., Griffin, A.: Design Thinking: New Product Development Essentials from the PDMA. Wiley, Hoboken (2016)

Martin, F., Ertzberger, J.: Here and now mobile learning: an experimental study on the use of mobile technology. Comput. Educ. **68**, 76–86 (2013)

Monem, R.: Metacognition and self-scaffolding in MMORPGs: case study of an adolescent male gamer. Qual. Rep. **20**(4), 454–465 (2015)

Norman, D.: The Design of Eeveryday Things. Perseus Book Group, New York (2013)

OECD. G20/OECD INFE Core competencies framework on fi nancial literacy for adults (2016). https://www.oecd.org/daf/fin/financial-education/Core-Competencies-Framework-Adults.pdf

OECD. G20/OECD INFE Policy Guidance on Digitalisation and Financial Literacy (2018). http://www.oecd.org/g20/G20-OECD-INFE-Policy-Guidance-Digitalisation-and-Fin ancial-Literacy.pdf

OECD. Smarter Financial Education: Key lessons from behavioural insights for financial literacy initiatives (2019). http://www.oecd.org/financial/education/smarter-financial-education-behavi oural-insights.pdf

Palalas, A.: Mindfulness in mobile and ubiquitous learning: harnessing the power of attention. In: Yu, S., Ally, M., Tsinakos, A. (eds.) Mobile and Ubiquitous Learning. PRRE, pp. 19–44. Springer, Singapore (2018). https://doi.org/10.1007/978-981-10-6144-8_2

SBTS2018 (Producer). Cash (2020). https://www.flaticon.com/premium-icon/cash_1770392

Sharples, M., Taylor, J., Vavoula, G.: Towards a Theory of Mobile Learning (2005). https://www.oecd.org/education/ceri/38360564.pdf

Shen, N.: Consumer rationality/irrationality and financial literacy in the credit card market: implications from an integrative review. J. Financ. Serv. Market. **19**(1), 29–42 (2014)

Stanford, I. o. D. a. An Introduction to Design Thinking Process Guide (2010). https://dschool-old.stanford.edu/sandbox/groups/designresources/wiki/36873/attachments/74b3d/ModeGu ideBOOTCAMP2010L.pdf

Thaler, R., Sunstein, C.: Nudge: Improving Decisions About Health, Wealth, and Happiness. Penguin Books, New York (2009)

Thompson, P.: The digital natives as learners: technology use patterns and approaches to learning. Comput. Educ. **65**, 12–33 (2013)

Ultimatearm (Producer). Risk (2020). https://www.flaticon.com/free-icon/risk_2422787

Weinmann, M., Schneider, C., Brocke, J.V.: Digital nudging: guiding judgment and decision-making in digital choice environments. Bus. Inf. Syst. Eng. **58**, 433–436 (2016)

WorldBank: Digital Financial Services (2020). http://pubdocs.worldbank.org/en/230281588169 110691/Digital-Financial-Services.pdf

Yau, J., Joy, M.: A context-aware and adaptive learning schedule framework for supporting learners' daily routines. In: Second International Conference on Systems (ICONS 2007), pp. 31–31 (2007)

DUXU for Extended Reality

User Experience in Augmented Reality: A Holistic Evaluation of a Prototype for Assembly Instructions

Zackarias Alenljung[✉] and Jessica Lindblom

University of Skövde, Box 408, 54128 Skövde, Sweden
zaca1483@student.liu.se

Abstract. Industries are under development with new upcoming tools that will further streamline the work of operators, not least in assembly. Assembly instructions are usually visualized by traditional paper or data bases. A new way of showing instruction is provided by augmented reality (AR). The focus of this paper is the user experience (UX) of AR based instructions for assembly. In order to study the UX in AR an evaluation matrix and an AR prototype has been developed and evaluated in a UX test, where data regarding both hedonic and pragmatic qualities was collected. The UX test yielded a result of three out of nine sub-goals completed while six did not. There was a general low degree of cognitive load while assembling but not low enough. However, there are promising results for AR based instructions, though the technology still needs improvement and more testing is also necessary. The assembly scenario for this study was somewhat simple and could be one reason why this study generated ambiguous results.

Keywords: User experience · Augmented reality · Evaluation · Assembly instructions

1 Introduction

A shift in the industries is currently taking place, which some refer to as a new industrial revolution, also known as Industry 4.0 [1–5]. The driving force for this development is due to the fact that today's digital tools and enabling technologies such as Internet of Things (IoT), Augmented Reality (AR), Virtual Reality (VR), and Human-Robot Collaboration (HRC) are becoming increasingly "smarter". They are being able to be connected to each other and provide additional support in the industrial domain [1]. Manufacturing systems are becoming more modular and efficient where products themselves to a larger extent are able to control their own manufacturing process [1]. For the manufacturing industry, the intended benefits of this revolution is expected to result in shorter development periods, individualization on demand for the customers, decentralization, flexibility, and resource efficiency [4]. A consequence of this revolution is a shift in working environments throughout all aspects of the manufacturing industry towards increasingly advanced digital workspaces.

A central issue of Industry 4.0's digital workspace is the development with respect to Operator 4.0 [5, 6]. Operator 4.0 refers to smart and skilled operators of the future,

© Springer Nature Switzerland AG 2021
M. M. Soares et al. (Eds.): HCII 2021, LNCS 12781, pp. 139–157, 2021.
https://doi.org/10.1007/978-3-030-78227-6_11

who are assisted by various kinds of enabling technologies that provide sustainable physical and cognitive support, allowing operators to achieve and develop a high degree of cognitive, collaborative, and innovative knowledge and skills - without compromising safety, competitiveness and productivity [6]. A key area that is affected by the progress of Industry 4.0 is assembly, specifically manual assembly [7]. As pointed out by Danielsson [8], among others, operators in Industry 4.0 will need better access to various kinds of assembly information and this particular information has to be regularly updated so that the operators have access to the correct assembly instructions 'here and now'. Given the increased amount of customization on demand, the operators have to handle more frequently occurring updates of assembly tasks. Hence, it is an increasing demand on their assembly flexibility. Therefore, are assembly instructions a prominent application area of AR technology, and whereas some assembly stations are currently equipped with digital instructions, paper-based instructions are still the dominating format. If these instructions instead would be digitalized and displayed in mobile AR technology, this could result in a significant improvement when compared to the present procedure of printing and distributing paper-based instructions to every work station [8]. AR technology has been proposed as a way to digitalize information for operators and increase their efficiency [9]. Briefly stated, AR is characterized as the superimposition of digital information (usually a virtual image) on a scene in the real world to enhance the user's experience [10]. It has been acknowledged that operators using AR are able to more freely move around in their work environment and manipulate digital objects naturally. They can see digital information and digital object dynamically in the real world in their field of vision (FOV) [8, 10, 11]. To summarize, these expected benefits have made AR one of the most promising enabling technologies to facilitate manual assembly processes in manufacturing [8, 9].

However, for a long time there has been a rather winding road for AR to find its place in the manufacturing context, due to several constraints such as ergonomics, operator training, and the reliability of the proposed AR solutions [8, 12, 13]. However, there has been a shift recently, and currently there are several examples of AR solutions implemented for operators in manufacturing assembly contexts [14]. Many studies emphasize the benefits of using AR technology to improve assembly tasks for operator 4.0 in industry, e.g., decreasing cognitive load [15–17], reducing the time on assembly tasks [14, 18, 19], and increasing accuracy on performed manual assembly tasks [9, 20–22]. Although there are several intended benefits, the AR technology is yet only used to a limited extent in manual assembly [8, 23]. Several studies have identified that AR has several limitations in complex assembly processes: time-consuming authoring processes, integration with enterprise data, and the design of so-called intuitive interfaces [9]. Danielsson [8] presents some knowledge gaps of AR for assembly operators, such as real-time tracking for industrial scenarios, poor hardware maturity, and an identified need to integrate AR technology with other interactive systems. Indeed, the AR technology is still in its infancy, and not yet ready to be fully implemented. Conventional methods for assembly instructions, such as using paper-based instructions, are still better than using AR instructions during certain conditions [24].

Thus, there are many benefits of AR technology, however, primarily are concerned with the application and human performance of AR. Few have investigated the potential effects on the actual operator's experience of using AR technology in assembly tasks. As pointed out by Schuster et al. [11], the user perspective often falls by the wayside, even though it is a key aspect of the dissemination of new technologies in the digital workplace and society at large [25]. Schuster et al. [11] have taken a promising step in this direction by examine the acceptance of AR in assembly scenarios by a model-based approach for acceptance evaluation. The outcome of their empirical study is two-fold. Their synthesized acceptance model appears to be resilient, and the AR is accepted by the participants that assembled a toy truck at a workstation.

The present study follows in the footsteps of Schuster et al. [11] by taking a user-centered perspective. However, it seems that no study yet has evaluated user experience (UX) of AR instructions during an assembly task, which can provide new insights about how AR technology should be developed to enhance the operators' experience and streamline their work. Grundgeiger et al. [26] argue that considering and improving UX is one of the fundamental aims of the ISO standards on human factors and human-computer interaction. Grundgeiger et al. [26] address several reasons why UX should be considered when interacting with technology in the workplace. Interaction *per se* is an ongoing experience, implying that interaction with technology always has an associated UX, which is ubiquitously present whether or not it is explicitly addressed by researchers or designers. The UX does not only occur during interaction, but also the time before and after usage [27]. Moreover, it is not enough to ensure pragmatic qualities, e.g., error reduction, effective performance, and reduced cognitive load when humans are interacting with AR technology in the workplace. Much more emphasis needs to be focused on hedonic qualities, e.g., satisfying humans' motives and psychological needs, including expectations, emotions, and wellbeing [28]. Neglecting various aspects of UX may cause poor interaction design and decreased interaction quality, which in turn may have a negative impact on acceptance of AR technology.

The aim of the study presented in this paper is to gain a deeper understanding of the possibilities of implementing AR-based instructions in manual assembly from a UX perspective, with the goal of maintaining productivity and quality as well as reducing the amount of errors and decreasing cognitive load on the operators. In this context, the goal was to evaluate different pragmatic and hedonic aspects of the UX when using AR-based instructions in a manual assembly scenario. In order to achieve this goal, the following objectives were stated:

- Design an AR prototype to display assembly instructions in an assembly scenario.
- Develop an UX evaluation framework for AR technology use in manual assembly tasks.
- Conduct a rigorous UX testing with participants who have prior experience of manual assembly with paper-based instructions.

The remainder of this paper is structured as follows. Next, in Sect. 2, the method for the UX evaluation is described, and then, in Sect. 3, the obtained results are presented. The paper ends with a discussion in Sect. 4and some concluding remarks in Sect. 5.

2 Method

To investigate and analyze the UX of AR instructions in manual assembly, an empirical UX evaluation was selected as the method approach [27]. To be more precise, a formative UX evaluation was conducted in the form of a rigorous UX testing on an AR prototype that displayed assembly instructions on a pedal car. It was revealed that no UX evaluation framework for AR exists in the literature, so there was an identified need to develop such as framework for conducting a holistic UX evaluation of AR instructions in manual assembly that included pragmatic and hedonic qualities.

2.1 UX Evaluation Framework

In order to evaluate the UX of the AR instructions, six UX goals were identified and formulated [27]. The hedonic UX goals were: perceived cognitive load, emotional state, intuition, and immersion. The two pragmatic UX goals were: time-on task (efficiency), and number of errors. These UX goals were inspired by addressed aspects in the UX, AR, and assembly instructions literature. The motivations for the baseline and expected levels for the hedonic UX goals were based on previous studies of AR. For the UX testing, the following data collection techniques were used: observation, questionnaires, and semi-structured interview. To provide a systematic overview of the UX testing, an evaluation matrix was created (see Table 1). The evaluation matrix visualizes the UX goals and descriptions of them, the metrics, the data collection techniques, and predefined baseline and maximal levels. The baseline and maximum levels for the pragmatic UX goals such as time-on-task were estimations from a perfectly completed assembly run by the first author. The baseline level was set to one (1) total error, and zero (0) for max level.

Table 1. The developed UX testing matrix.

UX-GOALS		DATA COLLECTION TECHNIQUES	METRIC	BASELINE	MAX LEVEL
Cognitive Load	The Operator should not feel an increased cognitive load when assembling with AR-glasses	Likert scale	Quant	8	1/20
Emotional State	The Operator's emotion for assembling with AR pre-, during and post-assembly	Survey	Quant	"Somewhat interested"	"Very interested"
		Observation	Qual	"Less satisfied"	"Satisfied"
		Interview	Qual	"Slightly above expectations"	"Above expectations"
Intuition	The Interaction with the AR technology should feel natural	Observation	Qual	"Somewhat natural interactions"	"Natural instructions"
		Interview	Qual	"Clear instructions"	"Clear instructions"
Immersion	The User's immersion in the AR technology and the assembly	Observation	Qual	"Good focus on the task"	"High focus on the task"
Time	The Operator should complete the assembly within a reasonable time	Observation	Quant	4 minutes	2.30 minutes
Number of Errors	The Assembly should be completed without errors	Observation	Quant	1	0

Observations were conducted by the first author to study how the participants moved and behaved while wearing the AR glasses. The observation was video-recorded by a video-camera as well as by the AR glasses to get access to the participants' perspective (that was not viewable for the observer).

Three different questionnaires were used, a pre-test questionnaire, a post-run questionnaire, and a post-test questionnaire. The pre-test questionnaire was based on Papadimitriou's [29] pre-questionnaire regarding UX in VR. The pre-questionnaire intended to collect participant information, e.g., demographic data, information of previous experience with AR technology, and their interest in AR. For assessing the participants' perceived cognitive load, the NASA TLX questionnaire was applied. NASA TLX refers to Task Load Index and it is a well-established and reliable way to measure cognitive load [30], and has previously been used in studies of AR instructions [24]. Finally, qualitative data were collected by open-ended interview questions, which were inspired by Alenljung's et al. [31] post-test interview to summarize the participants' experiences and insights after conducting the assembly scenario.

2.2 Participants

Due to the Covid-19 restrictions, the intended primary user group of professional operators working in assembly were not available to participate. Instead, the recruited participants were teachers in Engineering from a high school with a specialization in industrial processes and technology. Five participants (3 males, 2 females) were recruited. All of them had previous experience of manual assembly, which was a key criterion for participating in the UX evaluation.

2.3 Materials

A pair of Epson Moverio BT-350 smart glasses was used (see Fig. 1). They are based on OLED technology that projects the image into the glasses, which offers more colorful images. The glasses have adjustable frames that fit most head shapes. It should also be enough space for ordinary glasses to be combined with them. Other specifications are that the glasses support a field of view of approximately 23° and can project at a distance of 5–20 m.

Fig. 1. A person wearing the Epson BT-350 smart glasses (photo by the first author).

The software was developed in Unity with Maxst's engine which provided a basic tool set of different kinds of features for AR. One of the features were AR projections on QR codes that the AR glasses read and then projects the desired object onto the code.

The assembly object was a pedal car (see Fig. 2). The pedal car had a few items that should be assembled, some of them being more complex to assemble correctly than others. The assembly instructions consisted of AR projection onto QR-codes. The assembly process was divided into four steps. These steps were chosen because of level of simplicity, where the participants should manage to assemble these items with the information provided through the AR glasses. The items that the participants should assemble were: both front wheels, the seat, and the handbrake.

Fig. 2. The pedal car (all photos by the first author).

The physical objects that were used in the assembly instructions were modelled and put into the software. The next step was to place the QR codes on strategic locations near the steps of the assembly process. The assembly process included a total of seven QR codes that were placed onto the pedal car, and there were two QR codes for each tire, one for the seat, and two for the handbrake (see Fig. 3).

Fig. 3. The five items that should be assembled and the QR codes placed at the correct spots.

A task-based scenario was designed so the participants should be able to perceive that they were located in an assembly context, and served to introduce the tasks to be performed in the UX testing. The participants had to perform four tasks, which could be performed in any order. The first and second tasks were to assemble the right and left front wheels respectively. These tasks required four items in the following order: tire, metal washer, screw nut, and a socket wrench used to tighten the screw nut (see Fig. 4).

Step 1. Look at the QR code   Step 2. Assemble the tire   Step 3. Screw on the parts

Fig. 4. The assembly of the he right and left front tires.

The third task was the assembly of the seat (Fig. 5). This task required only one item, the seat, but the participants had to place the seat in the correct place since there were several holes available to adjust the position of the seat. The correct assembly occurred when the seat was directed forward and placed in the third hole closest to the steering wheel.

Step 1. Look at the QR code   Step 2. Place the seat in the
                                                      third hole

Fig. 5. The assembly of the seat

The final task was to assemble the handbrake in the rear of the pedal car (see Fig. 6). This task consisted of five parts that were assembled in the following order: handbrake washer, plastic washer, plastic washer, small iron washer and finally a nut.

The following images show the AR instructions from the participant's perspective. These images are from the video recordings of the assembly scenario. The AR instructions for the wheel assembly are displayed in Fig. 7 where the participants could view what parts that were involved and how these should be assembled.

Figure 8 depicts the AR instruction for the seat assembly, and unfortunately this one became a bit "buggy" that resulted in the seat was flattering around in the AR glasses.

Step 1. Look at the QR codes   Step 2. Place and screw on
the parts

Fig. 6. The assembly of the handbrake.

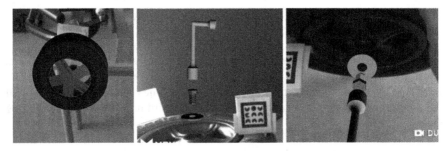

Fig. 7. The AR instructions for the wheel assembly.

Fig. 8. The AR instruction for the seat assembly.

This could have a negative impact on the user's perception to grasp the details where the seat should be placed.

The last AR instruction was for the handbrake assembly (see Fig. 9). This step could be a bit tricky to perform correctly, because the user needed to take a close look inwards behind the QR code to detect a little hole that the handbrake should be put into. This particular operation was difficult to represent accurately in the AR instruction and could therefore be challenging to perceive by the user.

Fig. 9. The AR instructions for the handbrake assembly.

As depicted in Fig. 9, it is possible to perceive both QR codes at the same time, which can be beneficial for the assembly operation. It was expected that if the users were able to look at these QR codes simultaneously, it would be easier to grasp that they belonged together that in turn could make it easier to accomplish the operation successfully. This assembly included more items and was therefore considered to have an increased level of difficulty.

2.4 Procedure

A pilot test was conducted before the UX testing with one participant who matched the participant profile. The pilot test did not reveal any crucial problems and hence the UX testing could proceed as planned, after small adjustment. An insight gained from the pilot study was that the AR instructions could sometimes be hard to remember once the participant had seen them, so it was decided to put the QR codes on the workbench where the pedal car was placed.

In order to avoid first-encounter effects, the participant run the scenario twice, i.e., referred to as one round. Before each UX testing round, all materials must be in place to conduct the UX testing in a smooth way. Therefore, a checklist was created which specified what needed to be prepared and ready for each run. The most important aspect was that the AR glasses would operate normally and were fully charged. The software for the AR glasses should be running and all the items of the pedal car should be disassembled and situated in the correct place. The pre-questionnaire and scenario should be presented on the computer screen, and lastly the TLX questionnaires were in place and the AR glasses were ready to record. A shorter manuscript checklist of what should be presented to each participant, for example about the aim of the study and the ethical aspects were prepared. An assistant that conducted the video-recordings was also present, so the evaluator could focus on counting key reactions and the number of errors.

The UX testing took place at the Interaction lab facilities at the University of Skövde, and the assembly room was spacious, offering enough room for the participants to walk around the pedal car. The pedal car was placed in the center of the room and next to it the workbench with associated items and tools.

When each participant entered the room, they received information of the purpose of the study and about their ethical rights. The participant started the UX test by answering the pre-questionnaire. Then the assembly scenario was presented on a computer that the participant were asked to read through. When he/she finished reading the scenario, the evaluator asked whether the scenario and the including tasks was understandable. If the answer was yes, the evaluator handed over the AR glasses and started the video recording. Field notes were taken during the assembly tasks with a focus on erroneous assemblies and behavioral reactions. When the participant had completed the first assembly run, they handed over the AR glasses and filed in the TLX questionnaire. In the meantime, the pedal car was disassembled and the items and tools were put back on the workbench. After finishing the questionnaire, he/she received the AR glasses and was asked to assemble the pedal car once again. When the participant completed the second assembly run, they handed over the AR glasses and filled in the TLX questionnaire a second time. Finally, the interview that consisted of three open-ended questions were asked to summarize his/her experience and reflections. The interviews were audio recorded to facilitate data collection and analysis, and to avoid missing any key statements. Each session lasted for approximately twenty minutes.

3   Results

3.1   Pre-questionnaire

The analysis of the questionnaires confirmed that the participants had worked with paper-based instructions in their previous professions as operators in assembly. Two of them had no prior knowledge or experience of AR, while the remaining three had minimal knowledge to some familiarity of AR. All participants expressed an interest in AR, where one replied that he was very interested. The areas of interest were spread among the participants where one expressed that he/she were interested in "information presentation and design" another answered "in industry and the car industry in particular", or "future areas of use". One of the participants had previous experience with AR glasses. Three out of the five participants currently wore glasses, and no one had any physical or cognitive impairment that could impact the outcome of the UX testing.

3.2   Pragmatic Qualities

Time was measured by the time-on-task that the participants used to assemble the items on the pedal car. In the first round, none of the participants managed to assemble the items on the pedal car in the scenario under 4 min. The fastest time measured was 4 min and 53 s. The longest time measured was 9 min and 10 s. However, during the second session, all participants managed to assemble the pedal car in less than 4 min, where the fastest assembly time was measured to 2 min and 31 s, and the longest one was measured to 3 min and 37 s. The mean assembly time in the first round was calculated to 7 min and 28 s, and the mean time for the second round was calculated to 3 min and 23 s.

Number of errors was measured by observations of the participants during the first and second rounds. In total, the obtained results show small differences between the first and second rounds, where eight (8) incorrect assemblies were noticed during the first round and seven (7) noticed during the second round. The mean value for the number of errors in the first round is calculated to 1.6, and in the second round to 1.4. To sum, the UX goal time achieved the baseline level (4.0 min) but did not reach the desired max level (2:30 min). The UX goal number of errors did neither reach the baseline level (1 error) nor the max level (zero error).

3.3   Hedonic Qualities

Cognitive load was measured with the TLX questionnaire, in which the participants' replies were summed based on the 20-point score index. An index of 20 is referred to high cognitive load, and an index of 1 is referred to as low [30] +. By calculating the mean value of the subjective ratings of all participants on the NASA TLX questionnaire, it was possible to obtain an indication of how the participants in general perceived their cognitive load during the first and second rounds. First, the mean value for each participant was calculated, and then for all participants in each round. The result from the first round has a mean value of 8.6 on the NASA TLX index scale. The highest mean value for an individual was 11.8 and the lowest mean value is 1.8. In the first round, the standard deviation was calculated to 4.03. The results from the second round had a mean value of 6.6 on the NASA TLX index scale. The highest obtained mean value for an individual was 10.8 and the lowest mean value was 1. In the second round, the standard deviation was calculated to 4 (see Fig. 10). To sum, the UX goal "cognitive load" achieved the baseline level (8/20 on the index scale) in the second round, but did not reach the desired max level (1/20 on the index scale).

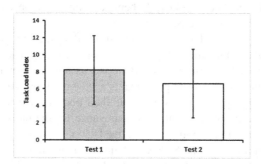

Fig. 10. Mean values and standard deviation for each participant's experienced cognitive load in the first round (left) and the second round (right) based on the index scale of NASA TLX.

Emotional state was assessed through qualitative inquiries such as observation and interview. The video and audio recordings enabled the evaluator to afterwards assess the participants' behavior during the assembly. Subsequently, events and aspects that could affect their emotional state during assembly were analyzed by looking at aspects during the assembly tasks that could be experienced as irritating or frustrating for the participants. The collected data were analyzed by noticing and marking significant steps during the assembly that seemed to have a positive or negative impact on the participants. Accordingly, all key markings were summarized to obtain an accurate overview of the various aspects that could have affected the participant's emotions. The identified factors that could affect the participant's emotions were as follows.

First, the two female participants showed constant problems with their hair getting in the way of the glasses. It was revealed that this was not only perceived as annoying when the hair came in front of their eyes, but became even worse when the hair ended up in front of the camera of the AR glasses. As a consequence, technical problems occurred in reading the QR codes and subsequently correctly projecting the instructions.

Second, this is aligned to the next identified factor that could affect emotions, which was the difficulty to view the instructions on several occasions. Sometimes, the instructions "jumped" in and out of the picture, which was a problem all participants but one experienced: "*It was kind of difficult to see the tools, like, it just blinked*". Some participants talked out load, uttering how they perceived the recurring problems when items were not visible or the instructions were blinking, which are expressed in the following quotes "*Now I do not see which tool I should use*" and "*Something blinked there, but it did not show up again*". These quotes were interpreted as referring to annoyance that could have a negative impact on the participants' emotions, especially if this problem occurred in more stressful situations than the testing environment.

Third, another identified factor that could affect the participants' emotional state was that all participants needed to either crouch and/or bend over during assembly which could be perceived as unnatural or unnecessary movement from a physical ergonomics perspective. Most of the placement of the QR on the pedal car were intended to avoid the participants from having to crouch down to see the instructions. Moreover, this problem could also be caused by the AR technology's limitation of how the AR glasses must be directed towards the QR codes in order to be able to accurately project the instructions. As a result, the participants had to crouch, bend, and turn their heads to be able to see the instructions at several occasions.

Fourth, the last identified factor that seemed to affect the participants' emotional state was that the AR application stopped working at two occasions for two of the participants. The cause for these unplanned stops was not completely sorted out, but a plausible explanation was that the participants accidentally pressed the home button on the AR glasses' touchpad that was placed in their pockets. This could definitely be perceived as a serious problem resulting in annoyance for the participant who had to restart the application again, resulting in negative UX.

The subjective ratings from the NASA TLX questionnaire indicated a variety of frustration levels among the participants. The obtained result from the first round has a mean value of 7.8 on the NASA TLX index scale. For the first round, the standard deviation was calculated to 5.26. The results from the second round have a mean value of 6.8 on the NASA TLX index scale. The highest mean value for an individual participant was 10.8 and the lowest was 1. For the second round, the standard deviation was calculated to 5.27 (see Fig. 11).

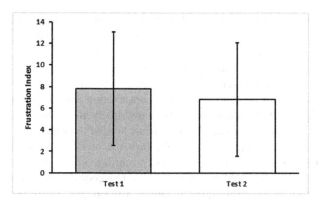

Fig. 11. Mean values and standard deviation for each participant's experienced frustration in the first round (left) and the second round (right) based on the index scale of NASA TLX.

As illustrated in Fig. 11, the experience of frustration among the participants differs slightly more in the first round than in the second. A possible explanation is that most participants encountered more assembly problems in the first round than in the second. Hence, the participants' emotional states during the first round seemed to range from predominantly frustrating to less frustrating, whereas the emotional states during the second round seemed to range from neutral to less frustrating. Three of the participants conducted a more flawless and smooth assembly during the second round, while the other two participants encountered more problems with the AR technology.

The analysis of the post-test interviews revealed some additional insights of the participants' attitudes towards AR technology. All participants expressed a positive attitude towards the use of AR glasses during assembly, although one participant was more skeptical than the others: "*it was good, I think, it… once you saw what it was, it was easy to see what I needed, but only if I saw it and it would stay there*". However, there was a consensus among the participants that the AR concept was considered beneficial and a bit exciting, but that the current AR technology did not work so well. Some quotes from the participants go as follows:"*Uhm, fun, new, exciting, but also a little unclear because they were not completely perfec*t", and "*Exciting, a little future thinking, you get, you do not have to read what to take but you see it in the glasses. To put it bluntly, it's a little cool*". In other words, in general there was a positive attitude towards AR-based assembly instructions, but due to the fact that the AR instructions could be unclear and that the technology was not completely error-free, some negative experience of assembly in AR occurred. However, the participants realized the potential of AR-based instructions. The overall assessment of the participants' opinions, the UX goal of attitudes was "slightly above expectations", since all participants believed that it serves as viable technology for instructions, but it needs to be improved. To sum, the UX goal "emotional state" achieved one out of three baselines that were set for pre-, during, and post-assembly. The emotional state of pre-assembly was stated as "somewhat interested" and max level were "very interested" at pre-assembly, and the result shows that it was assessed as "somewhat interested", i.e., it reached the baseline level, and was only assessed initially. The emotional state of the participants were assessed as "less frustrated" during the first round and "neutral" during the second. This means that none of the rounds achieved the set baseline level. The emotional state for post-assembly, i.e., the participants' attitudes afterwards, was assessed as "somewhat above expectations" which means that it reached the baseline level (assessed in the second round only).

Intuition refers to how natural the interaction with the AR glasses was experienced. It was assessed through qualitative inquiries, observation and interview, focusing on how the participants interacted with the AR-based instructions and how they handled the QR codes. It was revealed that all participants needed to crouch and tried to adjust their head position to be able to perceive the instructions. The QR codes were placed so the participants could stand in normal body postures to see an instruction. However, all participants had some problems of seeing the QR codes, although one stood out. This participant encountered more problems than the others, and needed more time to grasp each instruction. Moreover, another problem was the difficulty to determine the precise distance they should keep when looking at the AR-based instructions. An additional identified problem was the need for most participants to hold the AR glasses when looking down on the QR codes. This behavior could be considered unnatural interaction because one of the purposes of using AR glasses is to free their hands, and not that the users must hold them. Otherwise, a smart phone could be used to project the AR instructions. Another problem was the QR codes that were placed on the tires. The intention was that the participants would initially assemble the tires on the car, and then look at the QR code to receive the remaining instructions. Instead, the participants directly picked up the tires from the workbench and looked closely at them before assembly. As a result, the actual distance was not optimal for some of the participants to accurately display the AR-based instructions. The optimal distance to read the AR-based instructions properly was to place the QR codes at an arm's length. Before figuring out the proper distance, some participants seemed to be a bit puzzled. Hence, the general impression was that most participants quickly understood how to read the QR codes, and managed to assemble the pedal car rather fast with few errors. They rapidly acted by their own, and all of them managed to complete the assembly tasks without any major difficulties. They received minimal instructions from the evaluator at the beginning of the UX test, e.g., "look at the QR codes to get the instructions". To conclude, the participants' behavior could be summarized as "somewhat natural interactions", since the overall impression was that the interaction with the AR glasses worked rather smoothly. This assessment is strengthened by the fact that all participants performed better and with less remarks in the second round, which indicates an increase in learning how to use the AR glasses properly or that the assembly tasks were too trivial.

The analysis of the interview data revealed that the perceived clarity of the instructions varied among the participants, although no single factor could be identified why they occasionally were considered unclear. The participants who considered the instructions were clear expressed that it was hard to make an assembly mistake, because the digital visualizations represented where the items should be placed. The participant who made the largest number of assembly errors considered that the instructions were very unclear, arguing that "*it [the instruction] provides support, but at the same time it is a bit misleading, I think or... I got thoughtful here because I think I get different instructions for the front tires on how to assemble them and I think there will be parts left over that I feel should be assembled. I did not feel that I saw in the instruction that I would assemble both tires*". This quote is aligned with another participant's thoughts, expressing that a clear assembly order was lacking. The participant expressed a worry of doing a so-called dependent error, in which one mistake leads to another mistake, uttering "*what is the order? Where do I start? Should I just... like, I am damaged from production when it is step by step by step. Then I got a little confused, what I would, I thought if I do it in the wrong order then maybe it will end up wrong*". Several expressed that they would have assembled the car differently if using paper-based or computer-based instructions. They expressed that they had preferred to bring several items for each assembly step, such as the wheels, instead of bringing the related items repeatedly. Accordingly, this raises the question whether the instructions themselves are unclear or that there is lack of overview of the entire assembly sequence, which usually is presented in paper-based instructions. It is hard to determine to what extent the assembly instructions were unclear given how trivial the assembly tasks were in comparison to an assembly in manufacturing. To summarize, the UX goal "intuition" included naturalness of the interaction and clearness of instructions. The natural interaction part was assessed to achieve beyond the set baseline level in both rounds, where the second round was assessed to achieve the set maximal level. The clarity of the instructions was assessed as "somewhat unclear instructions", given that the AR-based instructions used for the trivial assembly tasks resulted in some repeated errors that probably were due to misleading instructions. This means that this part did not reach the baseline level.

Immersion refers to what extent the participants' experienced immersion while using the AR glasses. Four of the five participants experienced the assembly differed compared to using paper-based instructions, while the one who did not agree expressed that assembly is assembly, the end result will still be the same. However, the other four participants said that they found paper-based instructions as being easier to grasp the whole assembly sequence, enabling several operations simultaneously. One expressed that the assembly process was perceived as being less frustrating when using paper-based instruction. The earlier identified factors, e.g., that 1) the AR glasses were perceived bulky and a bit heavy, 2) the need to hold them in place when looking down at the QR codes, 3) the female participants with longer hair needed to move their hair away from their faces, 4) the sometimes "jumpy" and vague instructions, resulted in the conclusion that the AR glasses could be considered to have a negative impact on the experienced immersion since the need to shift the focus of attention to handling these factors severely disturbed the experience of immersion. In addition, these factors may also cause an increased cognitive load. To sum, the UX goal "immersion" was assessed as "somewhat difficult to focus on the task" for the first round, and for the second, it was assessed as "good focus on the task". The baseline level for this sub-goal was "good focus on the task" and maximal level "high focus on the task". Hence, the baseline level was only achieved during the second round.

3.4 Summarized Results from the UX Testing

The assessments of the six UX goals are summarized in the UX evaluation matrix below (see Table 2). The results show a mixture of reached and unreached UX goals. As a whole, the prototype for AR-based assembly instructions is not considered to meet the requirements to the extent as expected based on the decided UX goals. In most cases the participants performed much better in the second round, and even though could fail to meet the requirement in the first round while it was met in the second round. The results of the UX goals were as a majority not met. Only three out of nine indicators was achieved at least at baseline level. The other seven that did not reach a baseline level were either ambiguous, which means they reached a baseline level for one of the rounds or that they failed both. In order to achieve an approved UX testing based on the evaluation matrix, all the UX goals had to be achieved (see Table 2).

Table 2 The results from the user experience test in the evaluation matrix.

	UX-GOALS	BASELINE	MAX LEVEL	ROUND 1	ROUND 2	GOAL ACHIEVED
Cognitive Load	The Operator should not feel an increased cognitive load when assembling with AR-glasses	8	1/20	8.6	6.6	NO
Emotional State	The Operator's emotion for assembling with AR pre-, during and post-assembly	"Somewhat interested"	"Very interested"	"Somewhat interested"	N/A	YES
		"Less satisfied"	"Satisfied"	"Less frustrated"	"Neutral"	NO
		"Somewhat above expectations"	"Above expectations"	"Somewhat above expectations"	N/A	YES
Intuition	The interaction with the AR technology should feel natural	"Somewhat natural interactions"	"Natural instructions"	"Somewhat natural interactions"	"Natural interactions"	YES
		"Clear instructions"	"Clear instructions"	"Somewhat unclear instructions"	N/A	NO
Immersion	The User's immersion in the AR technology and the assembly	"Good focus on the task"	"High focus on the task"	"Slight difficulty to focus on the task"	"Good focus on the task"	NO
Time	The Operator should complete the assembly within a reasonable time	4 minutes	2.30 minutes	7.28 minutes	3.23 minutes	NO
Number of Errors	The Assembly should be completed without errors	1	0	1.6	1.4	NO

The identified UX problems have different impact in terms of scope and severity [27]. Some of the local problems were dazzling images when the AR projection did not function properly, the need to hold the glasses when looking down, preventing them from falling off, and getting longer hair away from the face. Although several of them are rather severe, some of them are cheap and easily handled by providing a strap around the head to keep the glasses in place, and pulling the hair backwards via a ponytail or using hairpins. The UX problem with global scope and high severity is the clarity of the instructions including sharper projections. The most prioritized task is to improve the instructions, because having unclear instructions will negatively affect any kind of assembly by impeding the progress of the operator. The second prioritized UX problem is the placement of QR codes and how the items will be displayed in the projected images. Although this particular aspect was considered beforehand, the participants still needed to bend and crouch to properly project the instructions. Less severe and perhaps more local UX problems are related to the physical ergonomics of the headset. It should be lighter to wear or at least not as front heavy, which would be a more severe problem during longer periods of usage. If these suggested modifications would be realized, the overall UX would be more positive.

4   Discussion

The objectives of the study was to create an AR prototype and evaluate it in an assembly scenario, to develop an UX evaluation matrix that includes both hedonic and pragmatic aspects, and to conduct a UX test with participants that has prior assembly experience. The aim was to gain a deeper understanding of the possibilities of implementing AR-based instructions in manual assembly from a UX perspective, with the goal of maintaining productivity and quality as well as reducing the amount of errors and decreasing cognitive load on the operators. The outcome was systematically summarized in the UX evaluation matrix, which revealed that only three of nine indicators of the six UX goals achieved the stated levels. As the evaluation matrix exposed there are shortcomings in the AR technology that does not meet both the hedonic and pragmatic expectations which result in negative UX. The main contribution is the developed UX evaluation framework that includes both pragmatic and hedonic qualities of UX for AR-based assembly. The framework lays a foundation for including UX aspect when designing AR-based instructions for assembly.

The study has several limitations. The assembly scenario was rather trivial. The AR-based instructions were not that complicated, but still resulting in minor assembly errors and unreached UX goals. The instructions should have been more structured so the participants had received a step-wise guidance. Some methodological limitations were that the recruited participants were not currently working in manufacturing although having past work experience. The limited number of participants is another limitation, although it is stated in the UX literature that 5–7 participants should be sufficient for identifying relevant UX problems [27]. The original idea was to encourage the participants think aloud during assembly to facilitate the data collection and analysis of their perceptions and experiences during assembly, but this was not explicitly stated to all participants.

Several aspects have been identified that should be elaborated in future work. The developed UX evaluation matrix for AR-based assembly should be tested in a larger set of studies as well as be used by other researchers, and subsequently modified. Moreover, there is a need to evaluate more complex assembly scenarios with improved instructions. The obtained results from this evaluation show ambiguous outcomes, which probably originated from unclear instructions or a too simple assembly scenario. Future work should further investigate and analyze these UX goals more thoroughly.

Other issues that have emerged are in which kinds of assembly tasks and domains can gain from implementing AR-based. One of the suggested advantages with AR-based instructions is the ability to customize them for each operator's needs, but given the technical maturity level this does not seem to be possible in the nearest future. Future studies should also include long-term UX evaluations of AR-based, with more complex instructions that varies frequently depending of what item that should be assembled. The major identified research challenge appears to be: what particular kinds of assembly tasks are suitable for using AR-based instructions?

5   Concluding Remarks

To the best our knowledge, this research is the first study to evaluate the UX of AR-based instructions in manual assembly that includes pragmatic and hedonic qualities. Thus, this study is a first step towards improving AR-based instructions through a holistic UX approach. The developed AR prototype failed to meet the UX goals requirements, proving more studies needs to be conducted in order to fully develop and make AR-based instruction for the industrial market. The participants had a general positive attitude towards AR-based instructions for assembly, which is a good first step when implementing new technique in the workplace. To conclude, we want to enhance the positive UX of interacting with AR-based instructions. By this way of working, we hopefully contribute the operator 4.0 of the factories of the future, promoting a positive UX at work.

References

1. Lasi, H., Fettke, P., Kemper, H.-G., Feld, T., Hoffmann, M.: Industry 4.0. Bus. Inf. Syst. Eng. **6**(4), 239–242 (2014). https://doi.org/10.1007/s12599-014-0334-4
2. Stock, T., Seliger, G.: Opportunities of sustainable manufacturing in industry 4.0. Procedia CIRP **40**, 536–541 (2016)
3. Lee, J., Bagheri, B., Kao, H.A.: A cyber-physical systems architecture for industry 4.0-based manufacturing systems. Manuf. Lett. **3**, 18–23 (2015)
4. Kagermann, H., Helbig, J., Hellinger, A., Wahlster, W.: Recommendations for implementing the strategic initiative INDUSTRIE 4.0: securing the future of German manufacturing industry. Final report of the Industrie 4.0 Working Group. Forschungsunion (2013)
5. Mattsson, S., Fast-Berglund, Å., Li, D., Thorvald, P.: Forming a cognitive automation strategy for Operator 4.0 in complex assembly. Comput. Ind. Eng. **139**, 105360 (2018)
6. Romero, D., Bernus, P., Noran, O., Stahre, J., Fast-Berglund, Åsa.: The operator 4.0: human cyber-physical systems & adaptive automation towards human-automation symbiosis work systems. In: Nääs, I., et al. (eds.) APMS 2016. IAICT, vol. 488, pp. 677–686. Springer, Cham (2016). https://doi.org/10.1007/978-3-319-51133-7_80
7. Paelke, V.: Augmented reality in the smart factory: supporting workers in an industry 4.0. environment. In: Proceedings of the 2014 IEEE Emerging Technology and Factory Automation (ETFA), pp. 1–4. IEEE (2014)
8. Danielsson, O., Holm, M., Syberfeldt, A.: Augmented reality smart glasses in industrial assembly: current status and future challenges. J. Ind. Inf. Integr. **20**, 10 (2020)
9. Wang, X., Ong, S.K., Nee, A.Y.C.: A comprehensive survey of augmented reality assembly research. Adv. Manuf. **4**(1), 1–22 (2016). https://doi.org/10.1007/s40436-015-0131-4
10. Drouot, M., Le Bigot, N., Bolloc'h, J., Bricard, E., de Bougrenet, J.L., Nourrit, V.: The visual impact of augmented reality during an assembly task. Displays **66**, 101987 (2021)
11. Schuster, F., Engelmann, B., Sponholz, U., Schmitt, J., Institute Digital Engineering: Human acceptance evaluation of AR-assisted assembly scenarios. J. Manuf. Syst. (2021, in press). https://doi.org/10.1016/j.jmsy.2020.12.012
12. Syberfeldt, A., Danielsson, O., Gustavsson, P.: Augmented reality smart glasses in the smart factory: product evaluation guidelines and review of available products. IEEE Access **5**, 9118–9130 (2017)
13. Syberfeldt, A., Danielsson, O., Holm, M., Wang, L.: Visual assembling guidance using augmented reality. Procedia Manuf. **1**, 98–109 (2015)
14. Serván, J., Mas, F., Menéndez, J.L., Ríos, J.: Using augmented reality in AIRBUS A400M shop floor assembly work instructions. In: AIP Conference Proceedings, vol. 1431, no. 1, pp. 633–640. American Institute of Physics (2012)
15. De Crescenzio, F., Fantini, M., Persiani, F., Di Stefano, L., Azzari, P., Salti, S.: Augmented reality for aircraft maintenance training and operations support. IEEE Comput. Graph. Appl. **31**(1), 96–101 (2010)
16. Funk, M., Kosch, T., Greenwald, S.W., Schmidt, A.: A benchmark for interactive augmented reality instructions for assembly tasks. In: Proceedings of the 14th International Conference on Mobile and Ubiquitous Multimedia, pp. 253–257 (2015)

17. Zolotová, I., Papcun, P., Kajáti, E., Miškuf, M., Mocnej, J.: Smart and cognitive solutions for Operator 4.0: laboratory H-CPPS case studies. Comput. Ind. Eng. **139**, 105471 (2020)
18. Friedrich, W., Jahn, D., Schmidt, L.: ARVIKA-augmented reality for development, production and service. In: ISMAR, vol. 2, pp. 3–4 (2002)
19. Weaver, K.A., Baumann, H., Starner, T., Iben, H., Lawo, M.: An empirical task analysis of warehouse order picking using head-mounted displays. In: Proceedings of the SIGCHI Conference on Human Factors in Computing Systems, pp. 1695–1704 (2010)
20. Baird, K.M., Barfield, W.: Evaluating the effectiveness of augmented reality displays for a manual assembly task. Virtual Reality **4**(4), 250–259 (1999)
21. Tang, A., Owen, C., Biocca, F., Mou, W.: Comparative effectiveness of augmented reality in object assembly. In: Proceedings of the SIGCHI Conference on Human Factors in Computing Systems, pp. 73–80 (2003)
22. Tatić, D., Tešić, B.: The application of augmented reality technologies for the improvement of occupational safety in an industrial environment. Comput. Ind. **85**, 1–10 (2017)
23. Campbell, M., Kelly, S., Lang, J., Immerman, D.: The State of Industrial Augmented Reality 2019. PTC, White Paper (2019)
24. Blattgerste, J., Strenge, B., Renner, P., Pfeiffer, T., Essig, K.: Comparing conventional and augmented reality instructions for manual assembly tasks. In: Proceedings of the 10th International Conference on Pervasive Technologies Related to Assistive Environments, pp. 75–82 (2017)
25. Stephanidis, C., et al.: Seven HCI grand challenges. Int. J. Hum.-Comput. Interact. **35**(14), 1229–1269 (2019)
26. Grundgeiger, T., Hurtienne, J., Happel, O.: Why and how to approach user experience in safety-critical domains: the example of health care. Hum. Factors J. Hum. Factors Ergon. Soc. (2020, in press). https://doi.org/10.1177/0018720819887575
27. Hartson, H., Pyla, P.: The UX Book: Process and Guidelines for Ensuring a Quality User Experience. Elsevier, Amsterdam (2018)
28. Lindblom, J., Kolbeinsson, A., Thorvald, P.: Narrowing the gap of cognitive and physical ergonomics in DHM through embodied tool use. In: Hanson, L., Högberg, D., Brolin, E. (eds.) DHM2020: Proceedings of the 6th International Digital Human Modeling Symposium. Advances in Transdisciplinary Engineering, vol. 11, pp. 311–322. IOS Press, Amsterdam (2020)
29. Papadimitriou, D.G.: User experience evaluation in virtual reality. Master thesis, Tampere University (2019)
30. Hart, S.G.: NASA-task load index (NASA-TLX); 20 years later. In: Proceedings of the Human Factors and Ergonomics Society Annual Meeting, vol. 50, no. 9, pp. 904–908. Sage CA, Los Angeles (2006)
31. Alenljung, B., Andreasson, R., Lowe, R., Billing, E., Lindblom, J.: Conveying emotions by touch to the Nao Robot: a user experience perspective. Multimodal Technol. Interact. **2**(4), 82 (2018)

Virtual Reality and Ergonomics: Making the Immersive Experience

Janaina Ferreira Cavalcanti[1]([⊠]), Fernanda Carolina Armando Duarte[2,3,4],
Rodrigo Crissiuma Figueiredo Ayabe[2], and Anderson Gonçalves Barbosa da Silva[2]

[1] Universitat Politècnica de València, 46022 Valencia, Spain
jaferca@doctor.upv.es
[2] Universidade Estadual Paulista Júlio de Mesquita Filho,
Barra Funda, São Paulo 01140-070, Brasil
[3] Universidade Anhembi Morumbi, Morumbi, São Paulo 04705-000, Brasil
[4] Faculdade Impacta de Tecnologia, Bom Retiro, São Paulo 01133-000, Brasil

Abstract. The hardware requirements of Virtual Reality (VR) environments are more affordable each day. Users can be immersed in virtual environments by different technologies but the most affordable immersive technology with enough feature is Head-mounted display (HMD), a visual display that is more or less rigidly attached to the head. Devices like HTC Vive and Oculus Rift allow creating VR experience with reduced budget and high levels of interaction.

The human experience is a multisensory process, which shifts according to changes in perception and individual experiences. Ergonomics emerges as an indispensable discipline for human interaction with the new technologies providing high usability (efficiency, learnability and satisfaction), proper functionality (easy navigation, easy interface condition) and achieving the most varied possible ends of them. To supply which aspects provides a better experience, recent research addressing technical and structural issues of technological devices will be considered, taking into account the immersion variables and the user's comfort. It will be shown that since of the hand-held stereoscope by David Brewster among of the years, there is an incessant search for the creation of what is not presented, sharpening our imagination, capturing our attention and providing new interactions. Also, since the Renaissance technology has become an essential element in the perception of the gazer thanks to the development of optical devices and techniques for representing the perspective.

This synthesis of current research will be helpful to VR Researchers, developers, designers, entrepreneurs, managers, marketers and users to select the appropriate features and hardware for each VR experience abstract should summarize the contents of the paper in short terms, i.e. 150–250 words.

Keywords: Virtual reality · Immersive design · Virtual reality devices · Ergonomics · Human-computer interaction

1 Introduction

Computing is present in our lives in a ubiquitous and pervasive way. Discreet, almost imperceptible immersions build interactions between people and technologies. mobile

© Springer Nature Switzerland AG 2021
M. M. Soares et al. (Eds.): HCII 2021, LNCS 12781, pp. 158–170, 2021.
https://doi.org/10.1007/978-3-030-78227-6_12

devices, motion detectors, smartphones, watches which make readings of position, altitude, location and even angulation for mapping the individual in the relationship between his body, space and some digital system are example. And in this way algorithms with machine learning, can count steps or even turn on lighting, air conditioning and music, in an environment with "internet of things".

In spite of this, we are not clearly aware of their presence or participation, as they seem to be part of the material reality, when mixing the physical and electronic environments, leaving the boundaries between the material and the digital little blurred. In contrast, Virtual Reality, through HMD's, is able to insert the individual in a simulated, real, but immaterial environment [1], inside the computer with a clear perception of immersion, which allows us to be involved from the imbued sense, isolated from external means. In this way, we immerse ourselves in the virtual experience, of this space through an interaction of the observer with the image.

Consider the greatest challenge of VR the adverse health effects of Virtual system and their causes can be presented in a multitude of ways. The VR sickness consists in any sickness caused by using Virtual Reality (motion and non-motion- challenges).

According to Silva the term cybersickness is recently applied to define a condition that has been identified for decades [2]. And in this theme, we highlight several vocables such as: "Simulator Sickness" (when resulting from shortcomings of the simulation), "Virtual Reality Sickness" (including any sickness caused by using VR, irrespective of the specific cause of that sickness) and "Motion Sickness" (motion-induced sickness). The literature reports that "discomfort" manifests itself from different symptoms, the most evident being nausea, spatial disorientation, visual tiredness, headaches, dizziness and, even more adverse effects such as vomiting, among others [3–6], and others authors present in our bibliographic).

In this paper we adopted the cybersickness definition of a physiological discomfort resulting from immersion in a computer-generated virtual word (motion sickness). But we thought important mention that some references just consider in that term the motion sickness.

Over time researchers, tools technological advances and ergonomics solutions are implemented in an attempt to reduce these adverse reactions as much as possible. We will explore them over the next sections.

2   Evolution of HMD

According to Crary mainly in the 19th century, the observer's optical experience was radically abstracted and reconstructed, based on the use of technologies for producing "realistic" effects and strongly dependent on the subjective view [7]. This movement changed a tradition thought developed since the rediscovery of the obscure chamber in the 17th and 18th centuries, which intended to suppress the subjectivity of vision, transposing the physical world to representation in the most objective way possible. In this way, optical experiments like the stereoscope can be understood as the way in which they are inserted in a much larger set of events [8]. This perception is in line with the development of the devices that culminate in contemporary HMDs, considering that the meaning of "realism" needs to be reconsidered in this context.

Charles Wheastone, English scientist, in 1838 presented the first know concept of a stereoscope, an instrument capable of emulating three-dimensional vision by displacing the point of view of photographs (or illustrations) using prims, lenses and mirrors. In his publication, he describes the phenomenon of perspective taking into account the average physical distance between the eyes, proposing different projections of an object. Finds proved the existence of a difference in the projection of the images captured by each eye related in relation to the distance from the object to the observer. The experiment emulated this disparity using mirrors angled 45o to reflect images into the eyes from the left and right side. The study was important once this concept was largely used in three-dimensional simulation trough planes and the binocular apparatus. Brewster developed one simplified device without mirrors [9]. The pair of images was loaded frontally with two glasses spaced apart in a wooden casing, in an arrangement similar to the current smartphone dedicated to visualizing virtual reality. The lenticular stereoscope was noted for the portability and small size, starting the popularization of the device and development of an industry around the creation of images compatible with the device. In 18569, an even lighter and cheaper device was created by Oliver Wendell Holmes, consisting of two prismatic lenses and an image holder, made of wood and accessible even for children. Holmes envisioned a growing "realism" that sought the "solidy of surfaces" through the use of the stereoscope and the correct manipulation of lights and shadows in the most diverse supports that photography has offered until then. He also proposed the creation of libraries that contain images of places relevant to the consultation of the general public. In the 20th century, William Gruber developed a method for printing stereo photographs on Kodak flexible films and, with Harol Graves, founded the View Master Company in 1939. The company was responsible for developing a first device based on a small circular card stock containing seven stereo images, and a viewer that exchanged images with a lever. The "C" model, developed in 1946 already made of plastic, allowed the loading of new images, a fundamental reason why it was used by the American army to train its navy and army forces during the Second War.

In the 1960s, the pioneer computer scientist Ivan Sutherland developed several devices that aimed to facilitate user interaction with computer systems. Sutherland's premise was to make simulates representations accessible to the nonprofessional public by increasing immersion though familiar gestures. Working with his students, he created the first virtual reality system designated as "The Ultimate Display" and the first modern HMD that used electronics screens and rendered images for each eye, in addition to sensors that captured the observer's movement by reintroducing data into a computer [10]. This system was widely used for military purposes, being developed to assist fighter aircraft pilots in targeting and killing. In fact, the development of this type of equipment led the evolution of technology in the following decades, also for training. This device was mounted on the pilot's helmet, giving rise to the term "Helmet-Mounted Display" [11], and this wasn't not necessarily binocular. The use of semi-reflective acrylic to superimpose the image of the physical world with a compact monitor gave rise to "Thirdy Eye for Space Explorer", creation of Hughes Aircraft Company in 1962. It is as precursor arrangement that years later would be the augmented reality device like Google Glass, in 2013 [12].

The advancement in computational processing has enabled increasingly realistic simulations at lower costs. The production of miniaturized screens, with more definition and more energy efficient, allowed other segments to develop their own applications in virtual reality. In virtual games sector, cheaper products created by manufacture like Sony and Sega in the 1990s provoke the interest of domestic consumers, culminating in the line of current HMDs, like HTC Vive and Oculus Rift, both in 2016. For medical purpose, the use of this devices for training and remote surgeries became possible, in addition to greater precision in viewing diagnostic tests. Production engineering and architecture can emulate and present complex designs to their customers using virtual and augmented reality based on CAD drawings. And the aircrafts and drones pilots are able to view the images generated by the airplane on the ground at a relatively low cost.

With the advent of more powerful smartphones and with acceleration and motion sensors, it became possible to emulate HMDs at an extremely low cost using supports such as Google Cardboard and its derivatives. The popularization of development platforms combined with internet high-speed connections allows remote access to cloud processing and complex applications on external servers. These facilities draw an ubiquitous future towards the popularization of HMDs as viable alternatives to the visualization of these simulation.

3   Measuring Cybersickness

Some of the cybersickness symptoms are usually temporary and limit their occurrence immediately after or during periods of immersion in virtual environments, which would similarly happen in situations present in our daily lives, such as motion sickness when we travel in a means of transport that we are not in used to getting around. We can take as an example a ship ride, which causes its passengers more sensitive or unfamiliar with a condition named "tide", which consists of a kind of malaise provoked by the sensation of moving at a speed a means different from we are used to it. Or even, when we expose ourselves to these situations more often, our organism adapts and, little by little, these symptoms are attenuated or even disappear completely. In the case of cybersickness, something similar happens, as some of its effects can be mitigates or eliminates through continuous contact with Virtual Reality technologies, as highlighted by Silva [2]: "Studies indicate that 30% to 80% of the population may be susceptible to these effects (REBENITSCH; OWEN, 2016) and, despite the physiological symptoms of Simulator Sickness decrease with continuous exposure (REASON, 1978) and do not cause know permanent sequelae (REBENITSCH; OWEN, 2016), they can be a problem for the health area, considering the increased availability of these devices on a larger scale for risk groups such as children, adolescents and the elderly."

However, even though we can identify similarities between the physiological discomfort already known in our daily lives and cybersickness, we understand that there are still many aspects to be studied in more depth on this topic, about which we have no parallels, once we have never had contact with such technologies advanced as those that make up the current devices. In addition, we realized that despite being a phenomenon that has been famously for decades, it starts to acquire new aspects as technological improvements belonging to different areas of knowledge become accessible and popular. Therefore, in order to study the theme in depth, we resort to texts formulated by researchers from different field of knowledge that approach this theme through different perspectives (computer science, communication, design, psychopathology and psychology, engineering, mathematics and economics). [2–5, 13].

In all the texts examined, the main causes pointed of for cybersickness happen are related to the mismatch between the information sent to the brain by the vestibular system in the inner ear and other sensory information received by other senses, especially the vision. According to Silva [2] the vestibular system is responsible for transmitting information regarding "head movements in space, acceleration and posture". Thus, it is understandable that an immersion in virtual reality can propose displacement that will not be performed in the concrete world, so a user's vision and hearing would inform his brain that he would be flying over an area, and that his physical body could meet at rest, sitting in a chair, then this dissociation would cause confusion in your nervous system, activating signs that something is not right. This description corresponds to the premises of a theory known as Sensory Rearrangement Theory (SRT), proposed by Reason & Brand in 1975, which Silva claims to be the most accepted by researchers who are dedicated to this subject today.

We still have to consider the structure of the devices used for immersion in VR, which can be related to the design of the HMDs and their physical characteristics (weight distribution, required posture, and others which we will elucidate with more details in next section) as well as those related to the configurations of the associated software.

Other factors that also influence are: the type of equipment used for immersion, for example, the type of visualization system (VR glasses versus CAVE system), the graphic characteristics of the VR environment, the size and weight of hardware (e.g. VR glasses), or the field of view that allows the display device; they all seem to have a great influence on the appearance of the symptoms of cybersickness. [5].

Nevertheless, it is important to note that some researchers call attention to any symptoms reports by people who experience immersive experiences, which are not necessarily associated with cybersickness, but are the product of anxiety [5] and other conditions that may be present at the time of the experiment, such as Stimmung and mood. Suetu [3] related this term with the ambience of the scene and the mood of the individual at the moment, respectively. These elements can also frustrate the expectations of the nervous system and cause some degree of weirdness.

To finish this topic, we just need to comment on the ways to measure the level of cybersickness caused by an immersive experience. We will highlight below the three main verified solutions verified in our bibliographic references:

Simulator Sickness Questionary (SSQ)
Formulated in 1993 by Lane Kennedy, the questionnaire describes 16 symptoms classified into three main areas: nausea, oculomotor problems (visual tiredness, difficulty in focusing, among others) and Disorientation (vertigo, dizziness, etc.). It serves so that volunteers from an immersive experience can assign a degree of intensity that varies from 1 to 4 the symptoms during the experience.

Postural Instability Assessment
This assessment is linked to a theory, which according to Silva [2] has been gaining strength in recent years. The Postural Instability Theory states that the effects of cybersickness area actually caused by the reason that the individual who participates in an

immersive experience cannot maintain a posture aligned with the horizon for a long time.

Analysis of Physiological Data

In this analysis, physiological data such as heart rate and brain activity of individuals are monitored while they undergo immersion experiences. Electroencephalography equipment (EEGs) such as neural helmets and other sensors are used.

According to Silva [2], none of these methods alone can encompass all variables related to cybersickness and neither accurately recognized the data important to their cause, so it is recommended that these methodologies be used together to obtain more reliable data.

4   VR Sickness and Ergonomics.

In 1995 the Nintendo Virtual Boy console, which could only be accessed when connected to a support that should be placed on some surface like a table, forcing the user to remain bent, and even if he was sitting still became a very uncomfortable position. However, this very inadequate solution by the company occurred because its professionals tried to limit the user's, movements, inspired by a situation that occurred with competitor SEGA, who two years earlier had given up on launching its VR device prototype because it consider in an official note that this equipment could cause users to be injured during use due to the high degree of realism of the equipment.

The fact described above serves to illustrate the importance in better understand the interaction human-machine, and consider this elements, the physical issues involved with the use of VR devices and the anthropometry in order to optimize this relation.

An immersive VR system consists of a VR head-mounted display device, a head and/or body tracking system, interaction devices and processing subsystem. For this paper we focus on HMD once it enables users to move their heads, legs and arms, but in some cases, inappropriate match of them with human body, turns the experience a little poor.

Guna et al. (2020) [14], investigating about Virtual Reality Sickness and the different technologies divided current VR system into four categories: (i) high-performance VR untethered solutions (Oculus Rift CV1, HTC Vive and open source OVSR), (ii) stand-alone VR untethered solutions (Oculus Go, for example), (iii) mobile VR (the most popular, Google Daydream and Samsung GearVr systems),and (iv) gaming VR solutions (as SonyPSVR). They consider 3 different generations of Oculus Rift and Samsung Gear displaying a neutral and an action video. Results of the SSQ Questionnaire showed that for neutral contents Samsung Gear presented more discomfort. On the other hand, Oculus Rift results more inconvenience for action content.

The continued exposure to bright lights very close to the eyes which can stress this system when performed for a long time, is an important point to consider as highlighted by Suetu: "It is curious to think about the disparity of sensations that a person can feel, being inside a crowed bus, but visually connected such a large and luxurious space. In general, this is an interesting experience for a few minutes, after that the glasses start to bother and the eyes hurt, as an effect for proximity of the smartphone screen to the eyes (in more advanced system such as Oculus Rift, Quest or HTC VIVE, that discomfort is reduced)." [3]. This efforts the importance of the distance from the lens to the eyes.

The weight of worn/held equipment is pointed out as a possible cause of physical fatigue. But, in reason of the weights of HMDs have decreased [15], it is more important to consider the distance from the center of equipment's mass to the center of the head's mass. Willemsen [16] reinforces that if the HMD mass is not centered, then the neck must exert extra torque to offset gravity. Therefore, think about the postural position during the virtual experiment is quite important. This concern was taken into account in 2019 by Microsoft, when presenting the second version of the HoloLens mixed reality glasses. The distribution of the components in the glasses was adjusted so that their weight could be more comfortably balanced to minimize the postural problems reported by users in the previous version, which concentrated all the weight of the device on its front.

Fig. 1. Omnidirectional electric treadmill

Also, Jerald [15] defined headset fit as how well an HMD fits a user's head and how comfortable it feels. The contacts point between the device and head used to result in pressure uncomfortable points on the skin, and even, sometimes can cause headache. Removable solutions incorporating the biomechanical properties of the human face, help to distributes the force of the HMD contact regions onto most robust areas of the face resulting in maximum comfort and secure connection.

Other point to consider is the injury risks. One of them is the physical trauma resulting from a real-world physical object (cables, for example). This is the reason for sitting is preferred as standing. But, once again the sitting position hurts the freedom of movement characteristic provided by the HMD. A commonly used solution is hanging the wires from the ceiling and, if possible, use wireless system. Other example are the injury risks caused by imbalance. In the immersive games industry, it is possible to observe a system that have bars to support the movement of players. This is so that users have security while they are immersed, in the face of adopting postures they are not used to, as walking looking down. The omnidirectional treadmills are equipped with proximity sensory or, even, as Suetu [3] describes a kind of walker "for adults, who can read a range of movements, without risks for those who use it, because it is stuck to the device all time" (Fig. 1).

The hygiene become a more important factor with the COVID-19. Wiping down the system with alcohol can be helpful, but not enough. The porous material difficult to remove biological agents. A good solution for this question is the removable-from-the HMD solutions for face VR. Firstly, thought by Eric Greenbaum [15] are easily found today.

5 Immersion and Motion Sickness

Our idea of reality is formed by what is captured by our senses, constantly stimulated by sensory information, supplied by the environment and presented to the organism, which reacts with self-regulation and organizes itself with actions, essential to human survival, also in relationship with the world and with the other [17].The reality, as Cézanne presented in his brushstrokes, which expressed the minutiae of light, begins with the photons, which are used by our brain, arising from each blink of our eyes, our first instruments optical, the trigger a process of imagination, "which transform light residues into worlds of forms in space, in the understanding mechanism" of what surrounds us, in this assumption, reality is not necessarily what is outside, in the external environment, but what is conceived in our mind.

Therefore, Virtual Reality, although composed of code created digitally, according to Lévy [4], is as real as the material world, Thus, even without having its own consistency of matter, since it does not have the need to be tangible so that existence is true and has the capacity to provoke reaction in our body. It is perceived by our brain, which in this way is self-regulating.

5.1 Multissensory as Immediate and Intuitive Knowledge

According Dalgalarrondo [17], multisensory are phenomena generated by physical, chemical or biological stimuli originating outside or inside the organism (DALGALAR-RONDO, 2019, p. 105). They produce changes in organs, which supply the sensory system with specific information related to tactile, visual, auditory, olfactory, gustatory, labyrinthine and proprioceptive discriminations. This are the sensitivities of the organs, such as legs and arms, for the cognitive supply of spatial location, body balance aids and kinesthetic.

Sensations are the set of information collected from the environment, by the senses in relation to our body. They are passive, with no awareness of action. The reception of stimuli is done as an instinctive reaction, of the inputs of stimulus by the special and general receptors, which are directly related to the neuroepithelium, responsible for the various sensitivities of the sense organs, such as sight, hearing and balance, taste and smell. Perception, in turn, is a comparative process between the repertoire and the experience. Perception is active, it is the awareness of the sensory stimulus, to recognize events environments and objects. It is part of the learning process, as the brain builds bridges between stored, active and individual, due to these sensory experiences in perception [17].

This recognition of the world and self-regulation, which the mind does efficiently and adaptively, comes from the constant mappings produced in the brain, both for the "analog" material environment and for the immersive digital. This is done through the multisensory channels spread throughout our body, which supply the Central Nervous System, with the necessary information, so that we know the world around us. In this way it makes possible for us to locate and recognizes objects, measure distance, balance the body, as well as activate the members. Proprioceptive are divided into kinesthetics that regulate the various bodily movements, such as the kinetic postural sense (the segmented position of the body), balance, baresthesia (sensibility for weight or pressure) and a Pallesthesia (sensibility to vibrations).

Based on this knowledge, the development of Virtual Reality environments, conceived the concept of LOD (level of detail) in the development of 3D games. The variation of representations in graphics objects in the distance relationship of the observer-interactor, the alignment of the development techniques of interface/usability design (UI/UX), with our body LOD, or body memory, allow to project the reaction of the environment to user movement, viewing angle, gravity and other information from the physical world, In this way, a successful experience is feasible, that is, it allows the perception of "immersion" without the sensation of Motion sickness.

5.2 *Cybersickness* – Perceptual Inconsistency of Presence and Non- Presence

The human experience is essentially a multisensory process, with changes according to changes in perception and individual experiences. The experience of an architectural environment involves these nuances derives from the ambience with a place. In this way, a set of information is generated and stored in our memory (mental and body), forming our visual and imagery repertoire. Our Perception is conceived through the activation of the memories of precious empirical experiences, combined with new sensitive information with the imagination. From this complex process, our mind conceives the notions of presence, in the construction of reality.

The Immersion in the environment to promote multisensory stimuli is named by Jon Charles Coe [4] as "Immersive Design". Studies in this field have deepened understanding of the mechanism used by the brain, with body memory, combined with its mental visual repertoire. Omer Shapira, senior engineer at Nvidia, puts it as a basis for developers of VR systems to improve LOD concepts, to make the multisensory stimuli produced, as close as possible to those perceived in material reality. This process makes the immersion credibility on the part of our brain possible, generating the perception of "presence".

The concept of "presence" in immersive environments, presents itself as a state of consciousness, which is a psychological perception of being there, present in the virtual

[18]. Due to its subjectivity, it is difficult to measure, which is why Lombard e Ditton [19] refer to it as a "perceptual illusion of non-mediation".

Baudrillard [20] points out that as not in the excess of reality, on the contrary in its collapse, in vertigo, is that immersion is found. The narrative also. Presents itself as a promoter of the "perception of immersion", added to the production of the "mise in scéne", with objects modeled in detail in 3D, lighting and minute effects that are increasingly realistic, believable [21].

Therefore, to understand this process, it is necessary to understand its mechanism of action. The mind and the brain are not the same "organ" and have different functions, in what would be the body/mind duality. The body is subject to the laws of physics, which are then responsible for bodily information of the "senses" (literal and denotative). Mental perception (figurative and connotative), in its abstractions, throughts and imagination, to interpret the tacit world, is not subject to the same rule of volume, weight or gravity of the material.

Between these two processes, tacit objective and the subjective concept, the adaptation of the subject takes place "immerse" in a virtual environment. At first there is the adaptation, marked by a "strangeness" in the case of comparing what we see or know of the physical world, it is presented in digital. It generates a state of "disbelief" due to the vertigo of the moment, a type of halophytic disorientation [17] that prevents delivery to the new visual narrative, which has not yet been established in this hiatus of time, which we can call space (time) between "presence and non-presence". We are not dealing here with adapting and learning the interface of the new system, but with the location of the individual in space and in his "body awareness" of the moment.

In this inconsistency of experiences between the information received by the eye and what the body is feeling, Cybersickness occurs. It can cause discomfort with vertigo and nausea, similar to "labyrinthitis" because it affects the Vestibular system (responsible for balance), being more common the comparison to "motion sickness", which happens when the body makes an unusual movement, for. Example, when we are trying to write a message on a cell phone in a moving car. In this case the senses alternately map the external physical and internal scenarios, on the device's display, in this alternation of the point of interest at different speeds, the brain tries to adapt, causing the unwanted symptoms, already described. On the other hand, the opposite of motion sickness occurs when the body's sense read a situation, while another type of conflicting information is beings provided through the stereoscopic images of the HMDs. This fact results in a dichotomy between visual, vestibular and proprioception systems, in the difficulty in situating "body awareness" in virtual immersion environments (HEETER, 1992), staying between "presence and non-presence, until that suspension of disbelief occurs. While this does not happen, the brain identifies inconsistency between messages, as a problem, tries to correct it by adjusting the system, but causes discomfort, which in the symptomatic alert causing the so-called Motionsickness. This phenomenon has already occurred with airplane pilots, in trainng with flight simulators, even extending the symptoms for up to 12th after the experience.

This relationship with space and its division of time – the present and the real- is conceived in a specific and physical area that Dalgalarrondo [17] points out as the main cerebral region, the so called "posterior medial orbital-frontal cortex". There, the "reality filtering" is done. Therefore, reality has a construction process in our brain, which is related to living in space, and which is a sense of presence [4]. Thus, Motion or Cybersickness may have as part of its mechanism of action, "dysfunction" or "noise" in the communication between the construction of reality and living in space, as a comparative perception.

6   Reducing Adverse Effects

In the manuals of devices dedicated to the reproduction of virtual reality, there are topics dedicated to guiding users and content producers on the configuration of the main parameters, including those related to reducing the effects of cybersickness, are the so called good practices.

Such parameters take into account the comfort and safety of users when enjoying an immersion. As each device has very particular characteristics and structures according to the resources that can be made available, therefore, there is no "universal manual" that can be followed. However, the website of the company Oculus VRm the developer of sophisticated HMDs such as Oculus Rift and Oculus Quest, has a section aimed at (https://developer.oculus.com/) in which the features and the most important resources for the production of content, which helps to reduce the effects of cybersickness. One of the main issues pointed out in the mitigation of this problem is the latency time, or system update time, which should give the user the feeling that their physical actions are synchronous to what happens in the virtual environment. Still other properties help to reinforce this sensation to alleviate the symptoms of cybersickness as mentioned by NUNES, TREVISAN, SANTOS NUNES et al. [6]: "In order to do not cause discomfort and to guarantee the user's presence condition, the latency time should be low (<20 ms). Currently, Virtual Reality devices already offer a response time of less than 10 ms.

To achieve a low response time, some of the approaches used are:

1. Use the Timewarp/Reprojection technique;
2. Decrease the update time of all pixel;
3. Increase the update rate;
4. GPU buffering optimization;
5. Prediction of the user's head movement."

Here is possible to observe that in this list all related practices refer to the reinforcement of the synchronous response to the user's actions and expectations. It is important to note, that we do not have the resolution of the images as the main item, something highlighted by Silva [2] in his experiments when he affirms that this is not such a significant item for the production of symptoms, reinforcing that "the lack of Positional Tracking and low refresh rate" are much more related to this issues. Later in this same text, the autor states that it is very important to coordinate the values referring to the angular acceleration of the user and the angular acceleration of the avatar, where the first value corresponds to the "maximum angular value acceleration that the user can develop by turning the head" and the second is the "maximum value of angular accelerations that the virtual avatar can develop by turning the head". Both values are associated with the device's gyroscope.

These concepts are intrinsically linked to the feeling of presence and performance in the virtual environment; Thus, it is very important to understand how the individual feels represented by his avatar within the immersive experience. Thus, in addition to the avatar's ability to turn the head as synchronously as possible, it is also important that there is a through adjustment in relation to the POV (point of view) -height from the viewer's point of view and also from FOV (field of view) – open of the field of view. As described by Nunes, Trevisan, Santos Nunes et. & tal [6], "the lower observer's point of view, the faster the changes seen in the terrestrial plane of the virtual environment and in the user's visual field" ("field of view - FOV"), creating an intense flow of images". This means that we will have a situation here that is not natural for human and can cause uncomfortable symptoms even when they occur in the physical world, it is a circumstance that can be compared to the feeling of discomfort that occurs when climbing stairs looking at the steps". In the most sophisticated devices, the adjustments of several configurations necessary to reduce cybersickness are already foreseen by its creators, however, in simpler systems, based on smartphones, it is still very difficult to have access to all the necessary resources, as this depends on the technology each device and not necessarily the HMD.

At the end of this topic, we only need to comment on the issue of cybersickness measurement tests already explored earlier in this paper, Many of these tests are carried out with "neutral" content, that is, without a structured narrative, which is not the reality of a usual narrative immersion, which can be a game, a fiction film or even documentary content, which will require different forms of interaction form users who participate in this experience, Thus, some contents can cause some degree of discomfort as they will provoke the users' emotions and many of these symptoms, such as sweating, or acceleration of the heart rhythm, may be caused by this reason, In this way, we warn that the analysis of the data and the necessary adjustments to prevent users from having uncomfortable feelings above what was expected by the producers of the content must be carried out taking into account these changes caused by immersive narratives. Preferably, through the evaluation of a multidisciplinary team, so that broader scenario is formed, facilitating the resolution of possible problem that the user my face during the immersive experience.

7   Conclusion and Future Works

In this paper we review the appreciate de VR sickness and how this topic has and have been approach along the decades. It is clear from the research reviewed that a lot was already done in this aspect, as reduce equipment weight, produce support systems and others. But also, that a lot of improvements still should be done.

Our research has found that an important attention should be taken with the synchronous response between user's actions and expectation. It is also clear the importance of correct communication between the physical reality and the comparative perception.

This work should be used to help direct VR workers in developed a better virtual reality experience. And further researchers could be done in order to make sure that the constant technological advances are well used.

References

1. Lévy, P.: As tecnologias da inteligência: o futuro do pensamento na era da informática. Editora 34, Rio de Janeiro (1993)
2. da Silva, V.B.: Uma abordagem para análise e monitoramento de simulator sickness em ambientes de realidade virtual. Dissertação, São Paulo (2016)
3. Suetu, C.: Mundos imersíveis:presença, interação e stimmung no ambiente virtual. Ph.D. Tesis, São Paulo (2019)
4. Ayabe, R.C.F.: Design imersivo: realidade em perspectiva. Dissertação, São Paulo (2020)
5. Quintana, P., Bourchard, S., Cárdenas-López, G.: Efectos secundarios negativos de la inmesión con realidad virtual en poblaciónes clínicas que padecen ansieda. In: Revista de Psicopatología y Psicología Clínica (2014)
6. Nunes, T., Santos, N., et al.: Avaliação. In: Tori, R., Hounsell. INTRODUÇÃO A REALIDADE VIRTUAL AUMENTADA. SBC, Porto Alegre (2018)
7. Crary, J.: Técnicas do observador- visão e modernidade no sec.XIX. Contraponto, São Paulo (2012)
8. Wheatstone, C.: Contributions to the physiology of vision. Philos. Trans. R. Soc. London **128**, 371–394 (1838)
9. Stafford, B.M., et al.: Devices of Wonder: from the World in a Box to Images on a Screen. Getty Publications, Los Angeles (2001)
10. Sutherland, I.E.: A head-mounted three dimensional display. In: Proceedings of the Fall Joint Computer Conference, pp. 757–764 Association for Computing Machinery, New York (1968)
11. Belt, R., Kelley, J., Lewandowski, R.J.: Evolution of helmet-mounted display requirements and Honeywell HMD/HMS system, vol. 3362, pp. 373–384 (1998)
12. Meinel, C., Sack, H.: Historical overview. In: Digital Communication, pp. 17–88. Springer, Heidelberg (2014). https://doi.org/10.1007/978-3-642-54331-9_2
13. Tori, R.: Introdução a realidade virtual e aumentsda. Hounsell, Porto Alegre (2018)
14. Guna, J., et al.: Virtual reality sickness and challenges behind different technology and content settings. Mobile Netw. Appl. **25**(4), 1436–1445 (2019). https://doi.org/10.1007/s11036-019-01373-w
15. Jerald, J.: The VR Book: Human-Centered Design for Virtual Reality, 1st edn. ACM Books, Illinois (2016)
16. Willwmsen, P., Colton, M.B., Creem-Regehr, S.H., Thompson, W.B.: The effects of head-mounted display mechanical properties and field of view on distance judgments in virtual environments. ACM Trans. Appñied Percept. (2009). https://doi.org/10.1145/1498700.1498702.177
17. Dalgalarrondo, P.: Psicopatologia e semiologia dos transtornos mentais. Artmed, Porto Alegre (2019)
18. Slater, M., Wilbur, S.: A framework for immersive virtual environments. Presence Teleoperators Virtual Environ. **6**(6), 603–616 (1997)
19. Lombard, M., Ditton, T.: At the heart of it all: the concept of presence. J. Comput.-Mediated Commun. **3**, 1–24 (1997)
20. Baudrilland, J.: A arte da desaparição. Ed.UFRJ, Rio de Janeiro (1997)
21. Murray, J.: Hamlet on the Holodeck: The Future of Narrative in Cyberspace. MIT Press, Cambridge (1998)

ExperienceDNA

A Framework to Conduct and Analyse User Tests in VR Using the Wizard-of-Oz Methodology

Jamil Joundi[1]([📧])(ID), Klaas Bombeke[1](ID), Niels Van Kets[2](ID), Wouter Durnez[1](ID),
Jonas De Bruyne[1](ID), Glenn Van Wallendael[2](ID), Peter Lambert[2](ID),
Jelle Saldien[1](ID), and Lieven De Marez[1](ID)

[1] imec-mict-UGent, Department of Communication Sciences, Ghent University,
Miriam Makebaplein 1, 9000 Gent, Belgium
jamil.joundi@ugent.be
[2] imec-IDLab-UGent, Department of Electronics and Information Systems,
Ghent University, Technologiepark-Zwijnaarde 126, 9052 Zwijnaarde, Belgium

Abstract. It is often challenging to measure participants' reactions during user tests where a Wizard-of-Oz (WoZ) method is applied. This method is applied by the observers to validate functionalities of concepts that are difficult to build. In this study, a new technique is developed using virtual reality (VR) to improve the measurement of the participant's reactions during such a test. In this system, called ExperienceDNA, VR user tests can be monitored and controlled through a desktop interface. In addition, physiological trackers (eye tracking and heart rate monitoring) are used to measure what the participant is looking at and to gauge their preferences. Moreover, the use of VR allows for quick adaptations to the virtual environment the participant is confronted with. In this way, highly versatile tests can be conducted while minimising the initial setup effort. Our approach has been validated by performing a pilot test on a predefined use case. The qualitative feedback collected from analysing batches of data from the pilot test is presented in the results section. In conclusion, this paper covers the development, description and evaluation of the ExperienceDNA framework, as well as some ideas for future improvements to this framework.

Keywords: Virtual reality · User testing · Design review · Virtual training · WoZ testing

1 Introduction

In an ever-digitizing society, we face a new wave of smart products and services [20]. Interfaces are shifting, and the key differentiator is the end user's experience. However, in this smart and ubiquitous technological environment, experiences are increasingly determined by a complex interplay of interactions

M. M. Soares et al. (Eds.): HCII 2021, LNCS 12781, pp. 171–186, 2021.
https://doi.org/10.1007/978-3-030-78227-6_13

people are not always aware of [22]. People not only interact with each other and technological objects anymore, but also with a broad diversity of content, contexts and platforms [25]. This interplay applies to many aspects of our lives: smart cities tell us how to optimize energy consumption, smart cars guide us to avoid traffic jams while playing our favorite music, smart homes reduce our heating bill by learning our habits, and smart factories help reduce the cognitive workload on their operators [24]. Interestingly, this shift from manifest to latent interactions, where interactions between human and computer become less prominent, has also led to new theoretical frameworks in the fields of product design, human-computer interactions and quality of experience research. Geerts and colleagues [5], for example, proposed an integrated Quality of Experience (QoE) framework consisting of four main components: the user, the (ICT) product, the use process and the context. These components can be measured distinctively in order to bring subtle aspects of QoE to the surface that could otherwise be overlooked. The more recent Human-Computer-Context Interaction (HCCI) framework of Van Hove and colleagues [25] defined the experience on five relevant interaction levels instead of using distinct components. These interaction levels include user-object, user-user, user-content, user-platform and user-context interactions, all of which should be considered during every stage of the user research or new product development processes to optimize the user experience. One of the advantages of this theoretical framework is that interactions can occur in two directions: user-object interactions, for example, can be about the user manipulating an object (e.g. switching on the vacuum cleaner), but also about the object having an effect on the user (e.g. an alarm informs the user that the cleaner got stuck).

However, in order to shape and guide a truly user-centric design process for these future smart products, we do not only need new theoretical frameworks, but also new methodologies and tools to disentangle this complexity of interactions. Doing so will allow us to isolate, simulate and assess the impact of each single determinant of the end-user's experience. In this sense, we like to think of user experiences as strands of DNA. One strand of this 'experience DNA' represents an ideal scenario, where users interact with the product or service exactly as the creators envisioned it. Another strand shows how the experience actually unfolds. In a perfect world, both strands bind perfectly. In untested products, however, things tend to be slightly different. QoE is often not what is expected, and it is difficult to pinpoint where things went wrong [10]. Perhaps the product is not as intuitive as we hoped, leading to some unwanted confusion about its 'smartness'. Possibly, end users do not interface with the product at the right time, in the appropriately 'smart' way. Hence, our objective was to build a concrete framework or methodology to detect these 'genetic malfunctions' – points of pain in the experience – in an early stage of the design process, allowing us to redesign the solution, and create the best possible experience.

When conceptualizing our ExperienceDNA framework, three main requirements were identified. First, our framework requires a highly immersive product-testing experience, allowing researchers to seamlessly simulate various contextual factors. Second, researchers should be able to steer the interactions happening during this experience. Third, and finally, our framework demands the capability to objectively capture all occurring interactions, as well as measure the cognitive-affective state and behavior of the test subjects.

In order to meet the first requirement – the capability to simulate immersive experiences and contexts – we turned to virtual reality (VR). Although it would also be possible to make product testing experiences more immersive without VR (e.g. putting furniture in a video dome or using augmented reality glasses), we believe that VR, at this point in time, has several advantages over other options. The accessibility of VR technology has increased in recent years, not only in terms of hardware costs (i.e., the HMD and supporting computer with appropriate GPU), but also in terms of software, with 3D software platforms (e.g. Unity) inviting non-experts to create VR environments themselves. The accessibility of such 3D engines is further complemented by the availability of vast libraries containing pre-made assets (e.g. [8,14]) giving users access to realistic models with minimal design efforts. To maximize the valorization potential of our tool and methodology, cost and accessibility (and relatedly, scalability) need to be considered, as such factors weigh heavily on a company's decision to adopt such a solution. Indeed, advanced prototyping is inherently risky given the costs associated with developing a first functional, real-world product, particularly when the core concepts are futuristic or unproven. As such, using VR as a testing platform yields a second advantage: the possibility to simulate products and their intended functionalities, regardless of their (potentially very low) technological readiness level (TRL). A final advantage of using VR to create immersive product testing experiences relates to another requirement described below. The latest generations of VR HMDs are progressively equipped with built-in sensors (e.g. eyetracking, facial expression recognition) that can be used to obtain objective measurements of the test subjects while they are engaged in the experience. Nevertheless, using VR during the product design [4,6,19] or automotive prototyping process [13] is not new. However, in these cases VR was mainly used as a visualisation tool (for products such as car interiors, shoes and accessories) but was not integrated as a tool facilitating the possible HCCI interactions.

Next to the capability to simulate experiences in immersive contexts, our approach requires the ability to give the researcher control over the interactions happening during the experience. Doing so not only makes it possible to evaluate all would-be functionalities of product, but also allows designers to simulate suboptimal use circumstances. This way, the product is effectively subjected to a virtual *stress test*, which may lead to the identification of previously hidden points-of-pain. This second requirement led us to a specific methodology in innovation research, the Wizard-of-Oz (WoZ) test protocol. When applying the WoZ methodology, users interact with an interface or system as if it were functional, even though its actions and responses are prompted by the researcher rather than the system itself. In other words, the researcher is pulling the strings, whereas the user thinks the system is automatically reacting to his or her actions [3,11,28].

The benefits of using a WoZ protocol include a shorter development time, less resources and more freedom in conducting the user test since adaptations of the test can be materialised very quickly.

A third requirement was the ability to measure all possible interactions in an objective way, along with cognitive-affective and behavioral markers of the user during these interactions. Traditionally, product design and QoE research heavily rely on self-report methods: through focus groups, think-aloud protocols and post-hoc interviews, users can communicate their thoughts and experiences in detail with the designer. In addition, standardized questionnaires can be used before and after the test, such as the System Usability Scale [1], AttrakDiff [7] questionnaire or the Unified theory of acceptance and use of technology scale (UTAUT) [30]. However, although subjective reporting will always be very important during product design and user experience research, user responses might be clouded by various biases [18]. For example, the social desirability bias – i.e., the human tendency to give socially desirable responses instead of responses that are reflective of true feelings [23] – can be a significant problem.

The approach described in this paper combines VR technology, WoZ test protocols and an objective measurement strategy in a single tool in order to benefit to both the product development and user research domains, especially in the early stages of the (mostly IoT) product development process. The technical details of our tool are described in the next section.

2   Framework Overview

ExperienceDNA represents a research framework that makes it possible to create immersive experiences for product testing, control the interactions between users and their surroundings, and collect a wide range of fine-grained sensor data, allowing researchers to map the entire user experience. In the following sections, this system is described in greater detail. This section is structured in line with the requirements mentioned earlier. Figure 1 presents the reader with an overview of the ExperienceDNA framework's key components.

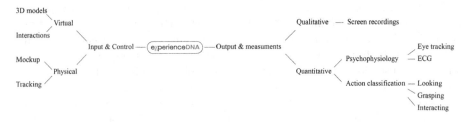

Fig. 1. Overview of the ExperienceDNA framework.

2.1 Creating a Highly Immersive Product Testing Experience

ExperienceDNA is developed in Unity (version 2019.1.14f1), allowing researchers to both customize the visual aspect of their test setup (room, objects, materials, lighting) and the procedural aspect (animated events or prerecorded actions).

When tackling a new use case, the researchers first design the corresponding VR environment. A VR scene can be designed from scratch (3d modeling), imported from asset stores (e.g. a surgery room, surveillance control room, classroom, etc.), or built using a combination of custom models and pre-made assets. In some cases, 3D scanning techniques can be used to create digital copies of existing environments or objects.

Next, the researchers determine which of these static assets need to be made interactable, so users are able to experience the affordances of an object (e.g. a tablet or Alexa speaker). This is achieved using custom 'behavioral' scripts, which are appended to the assets in Unity. Apart from simulating interactive functionalities, these scripts (the backend of our framework) also allow researchers to manipulate the flow of the user testing through our dashboard (the researcher-friendly frontend), which is described in the next section.

Fig. 2. The multi-functional wizard-of-Oz dashboard allows researchers to trigger actions and monitor the data in real-time.

2.2 Controlling the Product Testing Experience and Initiation of Interactions

Researchers interface with the ExperienceDNA framework through a visual dashboard (Fig. 2), which is composed of three sections. First, the wizard – i.e. the researcher who is at the helm of the WoZ protocol – can manipulate the experiment in real-time by pressing scene control or general control buttons.

Second, the dashboard offers a real-time window on the data streams as the experiment proceeds. Presenting this live data view also helps the wizard to assure that all measurement channels are actively recording. In addition, and more importantly, it allows the wizard to monitor and compare the interaction data (looking at objects, grasping object and interacting with objects) with the real-time physiological data of the participant (see Sect. 2.3). This gives the wizard a first, momentaneous indication of the participant's response to certain triggers.

Third and finally, the wizard can monitor what the participant sees through the headset, as the HMD's video feed is forwarded to the dashboard (Fig. 3). Several visual overlays are added to this 'wizard view', such as a dot representing the participants gaze (as measured by the built-in eye tracker), a heatmap function highlighting the objects that received the most eye contact, and the possibility to shift into the position of one of several static scene cameras rather than monitoring the user's point of view.

Fig. 3. Image of the wizard view with gaze tracking toggled on (left) and a third person view showing the avatar (right)

2.3   Objective Measurement of Interactions, Cognitive-Affective States, and User Behavior

The ExperienceDNA framework facilitates both qualitative and quantitative QoE evaluations. To accommodate qualitative research efforts, researchers and designers can rely on screen recordings – capturing both the subject's PoV and static perspectives from cameras placed in the scene. Quantitative measures consist of two main categories: psychophysiological measures and behavioral measures (actions).

Our use of a fully immersive virtual environment facilitates the capture of user actions to a great extent. ExperienceDNA is able to register various types of interaction, such as 'looking at' (using the built-in eye tracker), 'grasping' or 'interacting' (using the handheld controllers and positional trackers). Every interaction is timestamped, allowing researchers to explore reaction times or durations. These events can then be analyzed in combination with physiological data, providing researchers with insights into the affective characteristics of the user's experience.

In the present iteration of ExperienceDNA, both heart rate (HR) monitoring and eye-tracking measures have been implemented[1]. The former allows researchers to analyze heart rate (HR) and heart rate variability (HRV). HRV has been associated with emotional valence (i.e., affective quality: positive or negative), whereas HR has been shown to reflect arousal (i.e., physical intensity of responses to emotional stimuli) [9,12,17]. The current setup uses the affordable Polar H7 heart rate monitor, though other, more high end sensors can easily be integrated.

Eye tracking, apart from its aforementioned use in determining what users look *at*, also yields a measure for pupil dilation (associated with emotional arousal and cognitive effort [2,21]) and eye openness (a marker for drowsiness [16]). In addition, these raw data streams can be used to determine blink rate, which has also been identified as a marker of cognitive load [15,29]).

Once a session is concluded, ExperienceDNA saves all the recorded data (i.e. behavioral and psychophysiological data) in a .csv and .json format for post-hoc processing. In addition, aggregated output is generated, such as the durations and counts of *looking*, *grasping* and *interacting* events for each category of the human-computer-context interactions (user-to-object, user-to-user, user-to-platform, user-to-content and user-to-context). Psychophysiological data is stored in separate files, albeit with synchronized timestamps to facilitate post-processing.

3   Applied Use Case

In order to evaluate the core principles of the ExperienceDNA framework, an inaugural 'test flight' was conducted. In a series of pilot tests, the aim was to qualitatively validate the effectiveness of the framework, as well as the ease of implementation. To this effect, a cooking experience was created in which users need to cook a dish (i.e. bacon and eggs) following a recipe that was presented on a tablet next to the stove. This scenario was derived from a previous project on 'smart kitchen appliances', involving a tablet-based cooking assistant. The recipe was chosen to amount for a distinct , though limited, set of interactions to be implemented and evaluated in the pilot test. In the scene, the wizard could initiate certain events, such as letting a phone ring to distract the user from the main task.

First, a Unity scene was designed in which users were able to perform the necessary actions (e.g. pour water from a faucet, heat it on a stove and boil eggs). Simultaneously, automated instructions were implemented on the virtual

---

[1] In further iterations of this framework, we foresee the integration of brain signals using an electroencephalography (EEG) headset.

tablet, which presented users with the steps they needed to complete during the cooking task. In a second trial, this smart tablet was interchanged with a smart speaker – instructions were now presented verbally, and users were able to use voice commands to interact with the speaker. The intent of both trials was to evaluate the user experience of both the auditive and visual assisted cooking process.

The virtual environment was modelled after a real-life kitchen setting, which had already been used in the context of physical user testing (the "Homelab"). A true-to-life 3D model of the space was created using the 3D modelling software 'Rhino'. This model was then imported in Unity, where materials (e.g., textures) and assets (e.g., furniture and cooking items) were added. The process of creating environments and assets can be further sped up using 3D scans or pre-existing models.

In a second phase, all potential interactions were implemented in the scene. Using the WoZ prefabs, custom scripts were linked to the interactive 3D models. For instance, sound was linked to the phone asset, the bacon's model was made to change appearance based on the cooking time (raw, cooked, and burnt), realistic physics were assigned to the cooking assets (i.e., gravity, interaction with the controllers for grasping actions, collisions). Additionally, the scripts for logging physiological data were attached to the project. At the time of writing, this phase remains most time consuming, however there are many opportunities that will be pursued in the near future to further streamline the process (e.g. optimization of the code, cultivating a library a standardized objects types and behaviors, etc.).

In a last phase, and in order to deliver a high degree of realism to the participant, the visual quality of the scene was increased. This process involved placing extra lights and reflection probes to mimic real world lighting conditions. Furthermore, a more realistic shadow was achieved by creating baked light-maps that capture light bouncing of walls and objects in the scene. This phase is recommended if visual (photo)realism is deemed important for the test.

3.1   Setup

In order to have an objective evaluation of our framework, a professional design researcher (female, 26) was recruited to test the 'Wizard' functionalities of the system. In addition, an experienced user researcher (male, 28) to participated as a test user. Their feedback was gathered in order to optimise the virtual reality aspect of the experience as well as to enhance the usability of the ExperienceDNA dashboard. Both the design researcher and participant were accustomed to the use of VR.

The test was conducted in the Ghent University Art and Science Interaction Lab [26]. This lab is a state-of-the-art research facility able to effectively bring, analyze and test experiences and interactions in virtual or augmented contexts. The test (Fig. 4) was conducted using a high-end rendering machine equipped with a VR-ready graphics card (NVIDIA RTX 2080Ti), which was connected to an untethered HTC Vive Pro Eye headset. This setup delivered optimal free roaming capabilities, allowing the user to walk freely in a $\approx 10 \times 10$ m area. The user's position was tracked using six HTC Vive 2.0 base stations. In addition, the user was fitted with a Polar H7 in order to monitor HR and HRV.

As specified earlier, the ExperienceDNA framework was designed in Unity. A custom (java)script was used to log heart rate data from the polar H7 monitor, and steam it in real time towards the Unity framework.

Since the focus of this first pilot test was to evaluate the overall ExperienceDNA framework (including the dashboard), the interactions are performed with the HTC Vive controllers. However, future iterations of ExperienceDNA will accommodate the use of (virtually tracked) real-life objects and haptic gloves. This makes haptic interactions, such as tapping on a tablet for example, more realistic.

3.2   Procedure

Our evaluation followed a think-aloud protocol [27] to detect usability problems during the VR user test. After the VR portion of the test, a semi-structured interview was conducted with the wizard, containing general and qualitative questions inspired by usability frameworks such as the System Usability Scale (SUS) [1], Unified Theory of Acceptance and Use of Technology (UTAUT) [30]. Twelve questions from the SUS and 17 questions from the UTAUT framework were used to assess usability, confidence, performance expectancy, effort expectancy and behavioural intention towards the tested dashboard. Although these questions could be used in every experiment performed with the ExperienceDNA system, their goal was mainly to get deeper insight in usability problems when using the dashboard during this pilot test. Typical questions of the UTAUT framework are: "Does the use of this dashboard allow you to conduct experiments faster?", "Are you confident using this dashboard?", "Would people be willing to learn how to use this dashboard?", "Would this system be used in the future and by whom?". Important questions related to usability are:"Do you think the system is easy to use?", "Do you think you will need technical support when using this system?", "Do you think that the functionalities of this system are well integrated?". In order to collect more specific feedback, the wizard (i.e. the researcher) was asked how they evaluated their interactions with the three main features of the dashboard. These specific questions were oriented towards using the 'Wizard View', 'Scene controls' and data visualisation. In another interview, a QoE (Quality of experience) [31] assessment was done with the (VR) participant and semi structured interview followed to evaluate his experience and his tasks in VR. This pilot study was videotaped and comments were recorded and annotated for a more complete and unbiased overview of the responses from wizard and participant.

Fig. 4. The setup during pilot test with the wizard (right) and the participant (left).

3.3 Results

This section sheds light on the usability of the ExperienceDNA framework from two vantage points: that of a participant (taking part in the immersive experience), and that of a researcher (the wizard at the helm of the experience flow). The results of two semi-structured interviews are restructured in paragraphs highlighting both the framework's merits, as well as its current points of pain.

Subjective Experience of the Wizard. The following subsection elucidates the wizard his general impression and the feedback on three specific functionalities of the system: the wizard view, scene controls and experiment data. In a final paragraph we included some future improvements suggested by the wizard.

General Impression. The wizard complimented the system's ease of use and the integration of different functionalities. She also commented that chances to conduct a good test increase because this system is easy for a single person to operate.

"This system increases my productivity, because it is much more realistic than building a quick 'wizard of test' yourself. You don't have to rebuild everything from scratch."

The VR setting of the framework was considered to be a versatile choice, mainly since it can be used to conduct the same experiment repeatedly even with slightly different interaction and context settings. The VR dashboard not only indicates whether people will use the tested product as envisioned but also delivers insight whether they engage in a positive experience regarding the tested product. "This system would be very useful for assessing whether people like to use something. It takes less time to find out that people don't like something because you don't have to build the thing first."

The used ExperienceDNA framework was perceived as especially interesting for evaluating new envisioned concepts as well as for testing bigger projects (such as escape games, public spaces, smart device interactions). Tests in these domains are generally difficult to recreate in a conventional wizard of Oz test.

Even though the system was perceived as easy to use, three functionality problems were detected during the pilot test. First, some functionalities remained unnoticed during the first-time use (e.g. a button for switching from the 'tablet interaction mode' to the 'voice assistant interaction mode'). Another functional problem that remained was anticipating behavior of the participant.In that case, the wizard could respond erroneous resulting in unnatural interactions during a user test (e.g. when the wizard reacts too late or not at all). In a final remark, the cost of the VR setup and limited knowledge of programming appeared to limit the chance of adoption of this kind of system by test designers.

Specific Functionalities. Next, the wizard commented on the 'wizard view'. Several features made it interesting for real-time evaluations. Even though it remains impossible to read body language just as in real life, it allowed the wizard to follow the participant and his gaze in the virtual space. The secondary camera facilitated the overview and showed objects that are out of the field of view of the participant.

The wizard liked the integration of the scene control and general control buttons. This section functioned well, although user friendliness could still be increased. Buttons could be easier to read if button text were accompanied by icons. The wizard commented that she was eager to learn how to create her own buttons to trigger actions in future experiments. If possible, coding should be avoided and drag-and-drop functionality or a library of prefabricated components should help wizards to implement control buttons in future projects.

The 'live' interaction data can be useful for probing and real-time interpretations. Behavior can be triggered to draw live conclusions. The data generated in the experiment could be useful for post analysis of large samples. First, you can see in the data when something in the experiment went wrong. For example, the wizard can identify if text was hard to read for certain participants (mistakes or exceptionally long gaze times can be found in the data). Second, you can test if one scenario outperforms another. You could even see if data collection went wrong in an experiment by doing certain queries comparing different types of data streams. "You can analyze this data both horizontally as vertically, you can check if the user's eyes dilate when something explodes or you can check the sequences that people make (are they looking at the tablet after looking at the cooking pot). This is interesting to analyze what participants their next step will be."

Future Improvements. Two impactful improvements to the system were proposed. First, the system could be improved if the wizard is able to experience the same auditory stimuli as the participant at all times. Another useful adaptation would be a shadow mode where the wizard can prepare interactions before activating them for the participant. In the current version of the framework, the wizard and participant see the same scene at all times. Asynchronous interactions could alleviate the load of the wizard during the user test.

Subjective Experience of the Participant. The semi-structured interview used questions from the QoE framework combined with in-depth questions to probe for a general impression of the participant. The answers of this semi-structured interview are restructured in paragraphs highlighting the positive and negative aspects of the experience. This subsection is finalised with a paragraph discussing future improvements suggested by the participant.

General Feedback. During the interview afterwards, the participant indicated that the tasks in VR were sufficiently developed to do a comparative assessment between the functionalities of the tablet interface and the voice assistant. Regarding the quality of experience, the participant commented that he felt immersed in the VR world. The participant also mentioned that the adaptation to the virtual environment occurred naturally. The participant was willing to wear all peripherals needed for the test (wireless HMD, battery, heart rate sensor). The use of wireless peripherals in this test allowed for optimal freedom of movement for the participant. The participant did not notice that there was a 'wizard' controlling his actions. Afterwards it became clear to him that most interactions he had performed (e.g. filling a pot with water, baking bacon on the stove, controlling the tablet) were triggered by the 'wizard'.

The participant expressed his confusion regarding the interaction with some of the virtual objects. Specifically, actions that were not implemented in the kitchen were cutting vegetables and using the oven. This perceived lack of definition could be due to the open ended nature of Wizard of Oz tests. By displaying interactive and static objects in the same way, the participant assumed that all objects in the scene could be interacted with. Another discrepancy with real life was the timing of steps or tasks to be performed. For example, filling the pot with water goes instantly. The participant warns for a blind spot in the research due to not incorporating some realistic aspects, water flow, sunlight reflections. However, for the evaluation of the steps presented by the tablet this did not cause a problem, since the focus is on the smart interfaces. Apart from content related problems the VR test produced problems with visual focus, nausea and a small headache. This was caused mainly due to a bad calibration of distance between the lenses inside the headset. Being mentioned earlier in the paper, using hand-held controllers can contribute to a lack of realism or even cause interaction issues in a virtual environment. This indicates that user testing could benefit from more natural interaction modalities including haptic feedback. Consequently, confusion about controller input to interaction mapping could be minimised. The participant remarked that this discrepancy could be a bigger issue with persons who are less accustomed to testing new technologies. "It's in the details, interactions should be very detailed. Pressing buttons takes away from the naturalness of the interactions. Consequently, choices have to be made by the wizard which action he allows are performed well to move on with the experience."

Future Improvements. Making the interaction with controllers less ambiguous can improve the experience of the participant in VR. Furthermore, some usability issues could be resolved using a better onboarding strategy. For instance, a tutorial where the participant presses all controller buttons before the observations can start.

3.4   Comments on Findings

Reflection on Evaluation of the Wizard. When reflecting back on this first evaluation, it becomes clear that first time users are able to assess the functionality of the tool. Also, two usability issues were identified towards audio playback and option for an asynchronous workflow where the wizard can prepare future actions instead of working in real-time. When confronted with the logged output after the VR user test took place, both the participant and wizard reacted with the intention of using this data for comparing interactions and different scenarios. Further steps towards making it easier for the researchers to create interactions themselves using ready made modules will be important. Notwithstanding the prepared interactions on the dashboard were used successfully, the wizard indicated being interested in adding interactions to the scene controls menu herself.

Reflection on Evaluation of the Participant. Besides the evaluation of the wizard, the reaction of the participant towards this system was mostly positive. Some remarks were made regarding clarity about the distinction between interactive and static objects in the scene and a lack of realism during interactions. The comments indicate that onboarding is a crucial factor when introducing participants to VR experiments.

4   Discussion

In this paper, we presented the ExperienceDNA framework as an easy-to-use WoZ user testing tool in virtual reality with a strong emphasis on the capture of objective data. It aims to address three requirements: the framework facilitates the use of immersive environments (contexts), grants WoZ-style control to researchers and designers who use it, and aids in the capture of various behavioral and psychophysiological data streams. In doing so, we contend that the ExperienceDNA framework represents an overall useful methodology for testing products, services and systems, though it may be particularly suited to evaluate concepts and ideas that are difficult to test in real life. An example of such hard-to-prototype systems are so-called 'smart' systems, typically involving one or more IoT devices. Given the cost associated with developing a fully functional prototype, modelling these products and services in a VR simulation is budget- and cost-efficient, as virtual models can function in a 'black box' fashion: unlike the functionalities offered by a device, only the outcome needs to be modelled.

We believe that our framework has several other advantages over other traditional user testing methodologies. Where current user testing demands physical space, objects and people, VR user testing is possible in a virtual space – that can be modelled to represent any context – with virtual objects and people. This results in a faster workflow, a smaller development cost and an overall increase in versatility. The automatic logging of HCCI events, as well as psychophysiological markers allows researchers and designers to not only monitor the experience as it unfolds, but also helps them to analyze specific events post-hoc. Since interactions are automatically registered in the virtual world, these events can easily be synced with the behavioral (HCCI) and psychophysiological data streams. Finally, the virtual nature of our framework allows researchers to capture and replay experiences from the user's PoV, as well as from any number of (virtual) camera angles – a highly cumbersome and convoluted feat to be achieved in real-life user testing settings.

The modular structure of the ExperienceDNA framework allows us to gradually increase and improve functionalities. First, we will improve the current usability for the researcher designing a product testing experience.

From a more technical perspective, we will first make it possible for users to also physically touch objects while performing a VR user test. This new implementation will make the use of controllers in VR obsolete since we will use wireless gloves with a kit to make mock-up objects (cardboard, foam or 3d printed) interactive. This kit (named 'reality blocks') of tangible buttons, connectors and wireless trackers will allow the wizard to build a physical WoZ test where the functionality and looks can be assessed in VR. The implementation of tangibles has two main advantages: the augmentation of realism enhances the experience for the user. It also results in deeper qualitative feedback.

Secondly, we will implement multiplayer interaction, which will be interesting to test multi-person experiences where, for example, an actor is involved to play along with the scenario. It can also be used to test a scenario with multiple test users at the same time.

Finally, with regard to the objective measurements, EEG will be added. EEG allows the wizard to have more accurate physiological data and better assessments can be done towards cognitive load and the emotional state of the participants.

In sum, we believe that the proposed system is a great step forward for interactive user testing of smart systems. This paper describes and validates the different aspects of a system for performing live VR user tests using the 'Wizard of Oz' method. This early validation was done through a pilot test of a smart kitchen use case.

References

1. Bangor, A., Kortum, P.T., Miller, J.T.: An empirical evaluation of the system usability scale. Intl. J. Hum.-Comput. Interact. **24**(6), 574–594 (2008)
2. Bradley, M.B., Miccoli, L.M., Escrig, M.A., Lang, P.J.: The pupil as a measure of emotional arousal and automatic activation. Psychophysiol. **45**(4), 602 (2008). https://doi.org/10.1111/j.1469-8986.2008.00654
3. Dahlbäck, N., Jönsson, A., Ahrenberg, L.: Wizard of Oz studies – why and how. Knowledge-Based Systems. **6**(4), 258–266 (1993). https://doi.org/10.1016/0950-7051(93)90017-N. http://www.sciencedirect.com/science/article/pii/095070519390017N. Special Issue: Intelligent User Interfaces
4. Exner, K., Stark, R.: Validation of product-service systems in virtual reality. Procedia CIRP **30**, 96–101 (2015)
5. Geerts, D., et al.: Linking an integrated framework with appropriate methods for measuring QoE. In: 2010 Second International Workshop on Quality of Multimedia Experience (QoMEX), pp. 158–163. IEEE (2010)
6. Gengnagel, C., Nagy, E., Stark, R. (eds.): Rethink! Prototyping. Springer, Cham (2016). https://doi.org/10.1007/978-3-319-24439-6
7. Hassenzahl, M., Burmester, M., Koller, F.: Attrakdiff: Ein fragebogen zur messung wahrgenommener hedonischer und pragmatischer qualität. In: Szwillus, G., Ziegler, J. (eds.) Mensch & Computer 2003, pp. 187–196. Springer, Stuttgart (2003). https://doi.org/10.1007/978-3-322-80058-9_19
8. Inc., A.: Mixamo - animate 3D characters for games, film, and more (2021). https://www.mixamo.com/ (2021)
9. Kim, H.G., Cheon, E.J., Bai, D.S., Lee, Y.H., Koo, B.H.: Stress and heart rate variability: a meta-analysis and review of the literature. Psychiatry Invest. **15**(3), 235 (2018)
10. Kirkevold, M., Bergland, A.: The quality of qualitative data: issues to consider when interviewing participants who have difficulties providing detailed accounts of their experiences. Int. J. Qual. Stud. Health Well-being **2**(2), 68–75 (2007). https://doi.org/10.1080/17482620701259273
11. Klemmer, S.R., Sinha, A.K., Chen, J., Landay, J.A., Aboobaker, N., Wang, A.: Suede: a wizard of Oz prototyping tool for speech user interfaces. In: Proceedings of the 13th Annual ACM Symposium on User Interface Software and Technology, pp. 1–10 (2000)
12. Lane, R.D., McRae, K., Reiman, E.M., Chen, K., Ahern, G.L., Thayer, J.F.: Neural correlates of heart rate variability during emotion. Neuroimage **44**(1), 213–222 (2009)
13. Lawson, G., Salanitri, D., Waterfield, B.: Future directions for the development of virtual reality within an automotive manufacturer. Appl. Ergon. **53**, 323–330 (2016)
14. LLC, M.: Turbosquid - 3D models for professionals (2021). https://www.turbosquid.com/ (2021)
15. Magliacano, A., Fiorenza, S., Estraneo, A., Trojano, L.: Eye blink rate increases as a function of cognitive load during an auditory oddball paradigm. Neurosci. Lett. **736**, 135293 (2020). https://doi.org/10.1016/j.neulet.2020.135293. http://www.sciencedirect.com/science/article/pii/S0304394020305632
16. Mandal, B., Li, L., Wang, G.S., Lin, J.: Towards detection of bus driver fatigue based on robust visual analysis of eye state. IEEE Trans. Intell. Transport. Syst. **18**(3), 545–557 (2017). https://doi.org/10.1109/TITS.2016.2582900

17. Nardelli, M., Valenza, G., Greco, A., Lanata, A., Scilingo, E.P.: Recognizing emotions induced by affective sounds through heart rate variability. IEEE Trans. Affect. Comput. **6**(4), 385–394 (2015)
18. Noble, H., Smith, J.: Issues of validity and reliability in qualitative research. Evid.-based Nurs. **18**(2), 34–35 (2015)
19. Ottosson, S.: Virtual reality in the product development process. J. Eng. Des. **13**(2), 159–172 (2002)
20. Pardo, C., Ivens, B.S., Pagani, M.: Are products striking back? The rise of smart products in business markets. Ind. Mark. Manage. **90**, 205–220 (2020). https://doi.org/10.1016/j.indmarman.2020.06.011. http://www.sciencedirect.com/science/article/pii/S001985011930330X
21. Piquado, T., Isaacowitz, D., Wingfield, A.: Pupillometry as a measure of cognitive effort in younger and older adults. Psychophysiol. **47**(3), 560–569 (2010). https://doi.org/10.1111/j.1469-8986.2009.00947.x
22. Rahman, L.F., Ozcelebi, T., Lukkien, J.: Understanding IoT systems: a life cycle approach. Procedia Comput. Sci. **130**, 1057–1062 (2018). https://doi.org/10.1016/j.procs.2018.04.148. http://www.sciencedirect.com/science/article/pii/S1877050918305106. In: 9th International Conference on Ambient Systems, Networks and Technologies (ANT 2018)/The 8th International Conference on Sustainable Energy Information Technology (SEIT-2018)/Affiliated Workshops
23. Steenkamp, J.B.E., De Jong, M.G., Baumgartner, H.: Socially desirable response tendencies in survey research. J. Mark. Res. **47**(2), 199–214 (2010)
24. Van Acker, B.B., Parmentier, D.D., Vlerick, P., Saldien, J.: Understanding mental workload: from a clarifying concept analysis toward an implementable framework. Cogn. Technol. Work **20**(3), 351–365 (2018)
25. Van Hove, S., et al.: Human-computer interaction to human-computer-context interaction: towards a conceptual framework for conducting user studies for shifting interfaces. In: Marcus, A., Wang, W. (eds.) DUXU 2018. LNCS, vol. 10918, pp. 277–293. Springer, Cham (2018). https://doi.org/10.1007/978-3-319-91797-9_20
26. Van Kets, N., et al.: Art and science interaction lab - a highly flexible and modular interaction science research facility. arXiv open-access archive 2101.11691 (2021). https://arxiv.org/abs/2101.11691
27. Van Someren, M., Barnard, Y., Sandberg, J.: The Think Aloud Method: A Practical Approach to Modelling Cognitive. AcademicPress, London (1994)
28. Wang, P., Sibi, S., Mok, B., Ju, W.: Marionette: enabling on-road wizard-of-Oz autonomous driving studies. In: Proceedings of the 2017 ACM/IEEE International Conference on Human-Robot Interaction, pp. 234–243 (2017)
29. van der Wel, P., van Steenbergen, H.: Pupil dilation as an index of effort in cognitive control tasks: a review. Psychon. Bull. Rev. **25**(6), 2005–2015 (2018)
30. Williams, M.D., Rana, N.P., Dwivedi, Y.K.: The unified theory of acceptance and use of technology (UTAUT): a literature review. J. Enterp. Inf. Manage. **28**(3), 443–488 (2015)
31. Zheleva, A., Durnez, W., Bombeke, K., Van Wallendael, G., De Marez, L.: Seeing is believing: the effect of video quality on quality of experience in virtual reality. In: 2020 Twelfth International Conference on Quality of Multimedia Experience (QoMEX), pp. 1–4. IEEE (2020)

A Study on VR Training of Baseball Athletes

Jack A. Kincaid⬥, Fengchen Gong, Tianjie Jia, Hong Z. Tan$^{(\boxtimes)}$⬥,
Casey Kohr, and Gary Bertoline

Purdue University, West Lafayette, IN 47906, USA
{kincaid3,gongf,tjia,hongtan,ckohr,bertolig}@purdue.edu

Abstract. As virtual reality (VR) technologies continue to mature and with VR headsets becoming widely available on the consumer market, more people are using VR for gaming, entertainment and skill training. It is inevitable that VR simulations have permeated sports training as a tool to enhance athletic performance. The present study is part of an ongoing program at Purdue University where short VR modules are routinely used by the coaching and sports medicine staff to train baseball players. For the present study, three VR simulations were developed to train a player's ability to recognize ball colors, type of ball trajectories, and strike vs. ball. Twenty-four baseball players took part in the study where half served as the control group and the other half received 12 sessions of VR training. The participants also completed two tasks before and after the main experiment. Although no significant difference was found between the pre- and post-tests, the participants did respond positively to a survey and found the VR training fun and useful for training their eyes. Future work will continue to assess the efficacy of VR training with Purdue baseball team players.

Keywords: VR sports training · Athletic training · User study

1 Introduction

Virtual reality (VR) is becoming an accessible tool for a wide array of applications. Sports teams are uniquely positioned to take advantage of VR technology. With VR, training can take place at any time, in any environment, regardless of physical limitations. Additionally, virtual simulations can be designed efficiently with a variety of open-source assets and software applications. Even complex simulations, such as those that attempt to elicit natural responses such as fear, can now be developed for training purposes using primarily commercially available VR technology [5]. Baseball is one sport where VR is particularly well suited due to the limited motion necessary to simulate a batter's experience. Specific apparatus and experiments have been developed to relate baseball performance with VR [11,19]. Previous studies have used VR training to improve athletic skills directly [20] and there is plenty of evidence that VR training is effective

© Springer Nature Switzerland AG 2021
M. M. Soares et al. (Eds.): HCII 2021, LNCS 12781, pp. 187–204, 2021.
https://doi.org/10.1007/978-3-030-78227-6_14

Fig. 1. A Purdue baseball player in a VR session. The player's view is projected on a monitor for the experimenter to keep track of his progress.

on real-world skill development [9]. We have developed a number of VR tasks to train different aspects of necessary baseball batting skills (see Fig. 1). The goal of the present study is to ascertain whether VR training will carry over to the players' performance during the regular season. Due to the COVID-19 pandemic, however, we were unable to collect season statistics as we had planned. We therefore report the study itself in this paper.

The present study focused on using VR as a tool to improve the recognition and reaction skills of Purdue baseball athletes. It was the second study in an ongoing research and development program to develop a suite of baseball-related training modules to supplement the baseball training program at Purdue University. It was unique in that the program was driven by the needs as identified by the Purdue baseball coaching and sports medicine staff, provided an excellent learning and research opportunity for undergraduate electrical and computer engineering majors, and had been incorporated into the daily activities of Purdue baseball athletes. There were many challenges in working with real athletes in a user study, especially given their busy training schedule. However, this was the only way to assess the efficacy of VR technology in real-world applications.

The rest of this article is organized as follows. We first present a literature review of virtual reality for training in general and its efficacy in sports training in particular. We then provide an overview of the tasks performed by the athletes during the study. The methods used in our study are presented next. This is followed by the results and a discussion and concluding section.

2   Literature Review

Virtual reality devices are becoming increasingly commonplace as the amount of potential applications increases. A variety of industries including sports, medicine, and entertainment have all begun to utilize VR for skill training and immersive experiences. Virtual reality has been proven to be an effective training tool in the medical industry. In one study by Seymour et al. (2002), 16 surgical residents were divided into two groups. The VR group received 10 sessions of VR surgical training each lasting one hour, in addition to standard training. The control group only received the standard training. The study concluded that while there was no initial significant difference between the groups, the control group was on average six times more likely to make an error than the VR group after the VR training [18]. Sewell et al. (2007) indicated a potential benefit of VR training on a surgical drilling task aimed at penetrating the temporal bone without damaging the structure behind it [17]. In a series of studies by Baillie et al., a visuohaptic simulation for bovine rectal palpation was shown to be effective at training veterinary students, and later successfully incorporated into an undergraduate curriculum for both training and assessment [2,3]. In the medical industry, VR training was utilized in therapy applications with one method designed for the rehabilitation of phantom limb pain [12]. In the construction industry, it has been shown that VR training was more effective at capturing a trainee's attention over other training methods such as lectures [16]. At the Virtual Reality Training Lab in NASA's Johnson Space Center, astronauts received VR training for a variety of tasks that would otherwise be difficult to conduct on Earth [8].

For reasons similar to astronaut training on Earth, VR training is also an attractive alternative and supplement to sports training as it allows for focus on sub-skills (e.g., hand-eye coordination), maintenance during inclement weather, and customization for injuries. Baseball, basketball, American football, rugby, and rowing have all experimented with athlete training using VR [4,10,15,19,20], as it provides a unique opportunity to model complex situations that are difficult or costly to replicate in the real world. Athletes of many sports, such as baseball, basketball and football, rely heavily on their perception of a moving ball in order to perform well. Any method to improve their perceptual capability and decision making is always desirable. Tsai et al. (2019) demonstrated that the use of VR training resulted in a faster decision time in basketball players [20]. Software designed by Huang et al. (2015) for American football allowed football coaches to efficiently create plays and demonstrate them to their teams in VR. The VR software was tested with a short 3-day user evaluation. A 30% overall score improvement was shown between assessments on Day 1 and Day 3 [10].

Baseball coaches are perhaps the earliest and most enthusiastic adopters of VR technologies in athlete training, which is the focus of the present study. Promising evidence has been reported that supports the effectiveness of virtual environments in replacing standard baseball training environments [11]. VR simulations for baseball applications have previously been developed to assist athletes during their standard training. A notable VR baseball training method was discussed by Takahashi et al. (2019) and was designed around maximizing ease of use and providing user feedback [19]. The system operated by simulating a virtual environment where the participant could swing at a virtual baseball. The system tracked the participant's body position in 3D coordinates and provided swing timing feedback [19]. In another study by Isogawa et al. (2018), the effectiveness of the virtual environment was demonstrated where three skilled baseball players tested a variety of environments, including both virtual and real environments. Each participant's objective was to react to both fastballs and curveballs. No statistical differences were found in either pitch type for swing duration between the real and virtual environments, indicating that VR may be a suitable replacement for real baseball training environments [11]. Evidence of learning transfer from VR training to baseball fields has been presented by Gray (2017) in a study that involved 80 high school baseball athletes [9]. Four groups of 20 participants each were formed, with three training groups and one control group that only completed regular high school practices. All groups continued their standard high school training activities. Of the three training groups, the first group completed adaptive training in a virtual environment that adjusted task difficultly to match the participants' abilities, the second group completed additional non-adaptive training in the virtual environment, and the third group completed additional real environment batting practice sessions. The training sessions lasted 45 min each and occurred twice a week for six weeks. The adaptive VR training group achieved the greatest improvement. There was also a significantly higher batting performance for the adaptive training group during the following season with a higher proportion of participants advancing in baseball after high school [9]. Overall, this study demonstrated clearly the ability of virtual environments to complement standard baseball training activities.

Many factors influence the effectiveness of VR training outcomes, including access to athlete participants, study duration, participant motivation, and technological limitations. For example, Adolf et al. (2019) utilized VR to simulate a juggling training environment with beginning juggler participants separated into a VR group and a control group [1]. At the end of the study, the participants in the VR group reported having more fun and higher motivation to continue learning. However, there was no significant performance difference between the two groups in their juggling skill [1]. Zaal and Bootsma (2011) discussed several VR studies designed to train participants to catch fly balls (baseballs hit high and far into the outfield). They described the challenges encountered during these studies that were centered on technological limitations such as lack of haptic feedback or a reduced visual field of view [21].

3   Overview of Tasks

All participants were tested at the beginning of the study (pre-test) and at the end of the study (post-test). The pre- and post-test consisted of two tasks: identification of pitch and ball/strike type using a GameSense software, and ball color call-out using a pitching machine. Scores of the two tasks from the pre-test and post-test were compared to assess any improvement in performance. During the main experiment, all participants engaged in typical fall training activities. One half of the participants completed additional VR training sessions, while the other half served as the control group. The tasks for the pre- and post-test, main experiment, and VR training were selected and developed with input from the Purdue baseball coaching and sports medicine staff. This section provides an overview of all the tasks conducted during the study.

3.1   Pre- and Post-Test Tasks

One of the tasks used in the pre-test and post-test is a tablet-based pitch recognition software developed by GameSense Sports (https://gamesensesports.com/).

Fig. 2. A participant completing the GameSense task

The same test was utilized for all participants. During the test, the participant was shown a series of video recordings from professional baseball pitchers. The participant's task was to determine the type of pitch and whether it was a ball or a strike (see Fig. 2). The difficulty of the GameSense task was adjusted by how much of the video clip was shown to the user (e.g., showing only the first third of the video clip made the task harder). Shorter clips required the participant to predict the pitch type from the pitcher's initial movements, the initial ball path and the initial spin rather than relying on such information over the entire trajectory of the pitched ball. The efficacy of GameSense as a training tool has been demonstrated by a positive correlation between the video-occlusion exercises and baseball statistics [13]. The method, based on occlusion and anticipation, was previously used to confirm the difference in predictive ability between experienced and novice baseball athletes [6].

The other task used in the pre- and post-test was a pitching machine test where the participant identified colored dots on baseballs that were inserted into a pitching machine. The task was setup as if the participant was in a batting practice session, where a coach would stand behind the pitching machine to feed in baseballs (see Fig. 3). Black cloths were hung over the protective nets in front of the pitching machine as visual shields. An additional, smaller cloth was hung right above the pitching machine (not shown) to prevent the participant from seeing the ball being fed into the machine. The participant, i.e., the batter, stood at a home plate approximately 60 ft and 6 in. from the pitching machine (same as a pitching mound) and was ready with a bat. Prior to the test, the participant was shown four baseballs each having two same-colored dots in red, green, blue and black, respectively. Pilot tests were conducted with an injured baseball athlete who was not in the study to determine an appropriate speed for the pitches thrown by the pitching machine. Seventy mph was deemed an acceptable pitch speed as it was neither too easy nor too difficult. During the

Fig. 3. Scenes from the pitching machine task: A participant in ready stance (left), and a sports medicine staff feeding balls to the pitching machine (right).

pitching machine test, the participant was asked to be in a batting stance. The participant was instructed not to follow the baseball with his eyes after it passed him, and not to swing. He was to call out the color of the dots on the baseball as it passed him. A total of 20 pitches were thrown for the participant.

3.2 Fall Season Training Activities

During the main experiment, all participants took part in the fall season training. The activities included Stretching, Open Field (free form hitting and fielding work), Agility Stations (agility ladders, hurdle jumping, hip mobility, and pilates), Arm Care (therapy bands and partner stretching), Throwing, Base Running, Individual Defense by Position, Team Defense, Batting Practice, Weights and Conditioning after Practice.

3.3 Virtual Reality Training Tasks

Half of the participants were randomly selected to take part in virtual reality training, in addition to their fall season training. This section covers the VR simulation environment and the three VR tasks that were iteratively developed with close collaboration between the Purdue baseball coaching and sports medicine staff and Purdue engineering students.

Simulation Environment. The VR simulations focused primarily on visual recognition of ball color, pitch and strike. The simulation utilized the Unity3D Game Engine as the primary software component. There were three simulated tasks, referred to as "Call Color", "Call Pitch", and "Call Strike." A tutorial was designed to introduce the participants to VR and the three tasks. The primary model presented in the scene was a pitcher in a baseball stadium. Additional models included the baseballs and a black wall behind the pitcher to simulate the "Batter's Eye" of a baseball field.

Table 1. Range of parameters that define the four pitch types

Pitch Type	Start Velocity ($\mathbf{V}$)	Start Spin ($\mathbf{S}$)	Start Position ($\mathbf{P}$)
Fastball	$V_x \in [0.3, 1.0]$	$S_x \in [2000.0, 2100.0]$	$P_x = -0.3$
	$V_y \in [-1.55, -1.25]$	$S_y = 0.0$	$P_y \in [2.25, 2.35]$
	$V_z \in [-38.0, -42.0]$	$S_z = 0.0$	$P_z = 18.5$
Curveball	$V_x \in [-2.0, -2.1]$	$S_x = 1000.0$	$P_x = -0.3$
	$V_y \in [0.7, 0.9]$	$S_y = -3000.0$	$P_y \in [2.25, 2.35]$
	$V_z \in [-33.0, -35.0]$	$S_z = 0.0$	$P_z = 18.8$
Slider	$V_x \in [-3.0, -3.5]$	$S_x \in [1050.0, 1150.0]$	$P_x = -0.3$
	$V_y \in [0.35, 0.7]$	$S_y \in [-4500.0, -4700.0]$	$P_y \in [2.25, 2.35]$
	$V_z \in [-33.0, -35.0]$	$S_z = 0.0$	$P_z = 18.5$
Changeup	$V_x \in [0.5, 1.0]$	$S_x \in [1700.0, 1800.0]$	$P_x = -0.3$
	$V_y \in [-0.7, -0.4]$	$S_y = 0.0$	$P_y \in [2.25, 2.35]$
	$V_z \in [-36.0, -38.0]$	$S_z = 0.0$	$P_z = 18.5$

The virtual ball's trajectory was generated by Unity3D's physics engine based on three vectors: start velocity, start spin, and start position. The parameter ranges of the three vectors (see Table 1) define the four pitch types: changeup, curveball, fastball, and slider. Variations within a pitch type was realized by randomly selecting parameter values within their respective ranges.

For Task 1 ("Call Color"), the pitch type was set to fastballs only and the color with which the ball flashed was randomly selected with equal *a priori* probabilities among six alternatives. For Task 2 ("Call Pitch") and Task 3 ("Call Strike"), the type of pitch thrown on each trial was randomly selected. The same two force vectors, the Magnus force due to the ball's rotation and the gravity force calculated from the ball's mass, were applied regardless of pitch type. Other natural forces, such as air resistance, were not modeled. The velocity and spin of the ball were continuously updated via Unity's rigid body component. They were then used to determine the Magnus force applied to the ball. This rendering method, along with the change in start position, resulted in the different pitch types. The force vectors on the ball were updated every 0.02 s, or equivalently at 50 times per second.

Overall, the VR simulation was designed to train the participant's ability to recognize specific details regarding the virtual baseball's color and trajectory. Focus was placed primarily on the experience rather than realism, as judged by the Purdue baseball coaching and sports medicine staff. The goal was to provide a training tool that could be used by athletes any time, anywhere, rain or shine, to improve their pitch recognition and reaction skills.

Task 1: "Call Color". In this task, a virtual baseball was thrown towards the participant by a virtual pitcher. During the first third of the ball's path, the baseball flashed in one of six colors for a short period of time: blue, green,

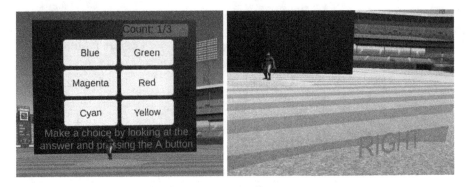

Fig. 4. Screenshots of "Call Color" Task: The response screen for color section (left) and the feedback screen after each response (right).

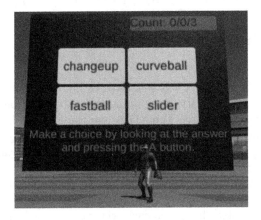

Fig. 5. The response selection screen in the "Call Pitch" Task

magenta, red, cyan, or yellow. Only fastballs were used in this task. The participant indicated the perceived color of the ball by selecting the corresponding response area shown on the black wall behind the pitcher (see the left image in Fig. 4). Trial-by-trial correct-answer feedback was provided (see the right image in Fig. 4). If the response was correct, the next pitch would start after a short pause. If the response was incorrect, the pitch was replayed before a new pitch was thrown. This process continued until 10 trials had been completed.

Task 2: "Call Pitch". The "Call Pitch" task was utilized to train the participant's ability to identify pitch type in the virtual environment. Four types of pitches were modeled: changeup, curveball, fastball, and slider. After each pitch was thrown, the participant responded by selecting the perceived pitch type from the four choices shown on the black wall (see Fig. 5). Similar to the "Call Color" task, trial-by-trial correct-answer feedback was provided and a total of 10 randomly-selected pitches were thrown.

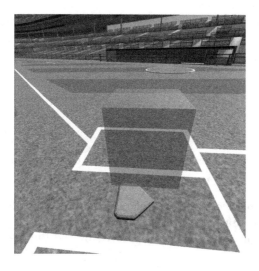

Fig. 6. The strike zone in the "Call Strike" Task

Task 3: "Call Strike". The final task trained the participant's ability to judge whether a pitch thrown was a strike or a ball. After each pitch, the participant was prompted to respond whether the pitch had passed through the simulated strike zone (see Fig. 6) or it had missed and was a ball. The participant indicated "strike" or "ball" by pressing the right or left trigger on a hand controller, respectively. The strike zone was shown to the participant before the first pitch and after each incorrect response. As was the case with the other two tasks, if the response was incorrect, the same pitch was shown again with the strike zone visible and the ball's flight path illuminated with a brightly colored trail. Again, a total of 10 balls were thrown for this task.

4 Methods

Now that we have explained the tasks performed by the participants in the present study, this section presents the methods including participants, equipment, procedures and data analysis.

4.1 Participants

The study was conducted with the athletes of the Purdue Boilermakers varsity baseball team. Twenty-five participants (males, age range 18–22 years old) were recruited and one dropped out after pre-test. The participants included infielders, outfielders, and catchers. As will be explained later, the remaining 24 participants were randomly assigned to a control group and a VR group, each consisting of 12 participants. Both groups completed the pre-test tasks, fall training activities, and post-test tasks. The VR group took some time out of

Fig. 7. Diamond Training Series baseballs (image from www.sportsadvantage.com)

their fall training to receive VR training 2–3 times per week for 3–4 weeks for a total of 12 sessions. Each session lasted for 15–20 min. Each participant signed an informed consent form that was approved by the Purdue Institute Review Board.

4.2   Equipment

Pitching Machine. A HomePlate Premier Hand Fed Pitching Machine by Sports Tutor was utilized in the pre- and post-test tasks. The pitching machine is capable of throwing 9 different pitch types at a velocity ranging between 40 and 90 mph. The exit height of the ball above the ground is approximately 56 in..

Baseballs with Color Dots. Diamond Training Series baseballs with colored dots (see Fig. 7; sourced from Sports Advantage) were used with the pitching machine. Each baseball had two same-colored dots that were approximately 1-inch in diameter. There were four color variations: red, green, blue and black.

Oculus Quest. The Oculus Quest headset was selected because it operates without any tether and allowed the participants to move around in a more realistic manner (see Fig. 8). The headset contains two 1600×1440 OLED displays controlled by a Qualcomm Snapdragon 835 chipset that allows the displays to run at 72 frames per second [14]. The participants interacted with the virtual environment through the use of two wireless hand controllers. Responses were received wirelessly by the headset through the use of the controller's buttons and triggers. The VR simulations were developed first on a PC and then stored in the Quest headset. Data were collected for each trial and stored on the Oculus Quest headset temporarily. At the end of each day, the data were backed up and stored on the PC. The relevant data collected included participant's ID, a trial-by-trial record of stimulus and response pairs for each task ("Call Color," "Call Pitch," "Call Strike"), and time stamps for the start and end of each trial during the VR sessions.

Fig. 8. Oculus Quest headset with controllers (image from www.amazon.com)

4.3 Procedures

The study took place in three phases: pre-test, main experiment, and post-test. It was conducted from Oct. 21st to Dec. 3rd, 2019 (see Fig. 9). This section describes the procedures of the entire study.

Fig. 9. VR baseball study timeline (Fall 2019)

Pre-Test. All participants performed the GameSense task first, followed by the pitching machine task. The GameSense test was conducted with the participant seated at a table, wearing headphones to block surrounding sound, and interacting with an iPad (Apple Inc.). The participant completed a short tutorial first, followed by the GameSense test. The test presented the participant with 56 pitches from 4 different pitchers. Two sets of 24 occluded pitches each and one set of 8 non-occluded pitches were shown. The occlusion difficulty was either one-sixth or one-third of the ball's entire trajectory. At the end of the test, the participant's performance was displayed as a score out of 1000. The scores for all participants were recorded and analyzed. The GameSense task took around 5 min to complete for each participant.

During the pitching machine test, a Purdue sports medicine staff member stood behind the pitching machine to feed the balls with color dots into the machine. A researcher stood next to the feeder and had a full view of the participant as well. Before each trial, the feeder raised his hand above the curtain covering the pitching machine to signal the participant to get ready. A ball with colored dots was randomly picked from a container and shown to the researcher while being hidden from the participant. The researcher recorded the ball color on a pre-printed form. The feeder fed the ball into the pitching machine, and the participant called out a response as the ball passed him. The response was recorded by the researcher. No correct-answer feedback was provided to the participant. After the ball passed the participant, it was collected in a net and occluded from view with a black cloth. When a total of 20 balls had been fed into the pitching machine, the researcher informed the feeder to stop the session. A percent-correct score was computed by dividing the number of correctly-recognized balls by the total number of 20 balls. The average time taken to complete the pitching machine task was 5–10 min per participant.

After all 24 participants had completed both the GameSense and pitching machine tasks, their scores from the two tasks were combined to obtain weighted total scores as described in Sect. 4.4. The participants were then equally divided into a control group and a VR group, as follows. The participants were first rank-ordered by their weighted total scores. The two highest-scoring participants were randomly assigned to the control and VR groups, respectively. The next two best performing participants were randomly assigned to the two groups, etc., until all 24 participants had been assigned to either the control or the VR group. It follows that each group had 12 participants. This procedure ensured that the two groups of participants had similar skill levels according to their pre-test performance.

Main Experiment. All 24 participants took part in the same baseball training activities as part of their fall season training. The 12 participants in the VR group took 15–20 min out of their daily training to conduct VR training tasks when their schedule allowed. Each participant in the VR group was able to complete 12 VR sessions. The 12 days were not necessarily consecutive and not all participants completed the VR sessions on the same 12 days. Before the first VR session, each participant familiarized himself with the Oculus Quest headset and the controllers. A 3-min tutorial in the virtual reality environment walked the participant through each step of the three tasks. For each VR session, the participant started with the scene of a baseball stadium with a pitcher standing at the center in a location referred to as the pitching mound. Each participant completed all three VR tasks in one session. One of the researchers monitored the participant's progress via live casting from the Oculus Quest headset to a mobile phone or a television screen (see Fig. 10). Trial-by-trial stimulus-response data were logged.

Post-Test. After the main experiment, all participants completed the Game-Sense and pitching machine tasks again in a post-test. The same procedure was followed in the pre- and post-tests.

Fig. 10. Research assistant and participant during VR training

4.4 Data Analysis

After the pre-test, the scores from the GameSense and pitching machine color identification tasks were normalized and combined, as follows. For each participant, the GameSense score (GS_{raw}) was first normalized to obtain (1), where min and max indicate the minimum and maximum scores among the 24 participants. Likewise, the ball-color identification score using the pitching machine (PM_{raw}) was also normalized to obtain (2). A weighted total score was then computed as (3). The GameSense score had a higher weight than the color identification score as the former used video clips of recorded ball trajectories from real pitchers and its efficacy had been validated earlier.

$$GS_{norm} = (GS_{raw} - min)/(max - min) \tag{1}$$

$$PM_{norm} = (PM_{raw} - min)/(max - min) \tag{2}$$

$$Score = 0.6 * GS_{norm} + 0.4 * PM_{norm} \tag{3}$$

After the main experiment was completed, the data from the pre-test and post-test were averaged over the 12 participants in the control and VR groups. An analysis of variance (ANOVA) was conducted to compare performance from the pre-test and post-test and between the control and VR groups. For the VR group, the percent-correct scores for each of the 12 sessions were averaged across the 12 participants, to examine possible learning effects for each of the three VR tasks.

5 Results

The participants' performance before and after the main experiment can be compared for the two tasks of GameSense and pitching machine testing. Figure 11 shows the GameSense scores (left panel) from pre-test and post-test for the two groups of participants. At a first glance, it appears that the control group

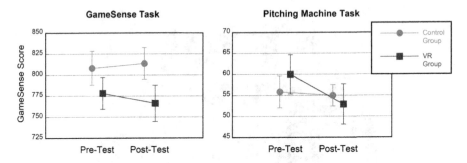

Fig. 11. Mean pre- and post-test scores for GameSense (left) and pitching machine ball-color recognition (right). The data for the control and VR groups are slightly offset from each other for clarity. Error bars indicate standard errors.

started at a higher level than the VR group at pre-test (808.3) and improved slightly at post-test (813.8). The VR group shows a slight decrease in performance score from pre-test (778.3) to post-test (766.3). However, a two-way analysis of variance (ANOVA) with factors test (pre, post) and group (control, VR) shows that test type did not have a significant effect on the GameSense scores [$F(1,1)=0.03$, $p=0.866$], but group type was borderline significant [$F(1,1)=3.86$, $p=0.056$]. Note that there were significant between-participant differences in the GameSense scores during both pre- and post-tests. This is reflected in the large standard errors in the left panel of Fig. 11 and the borderline difference between the two groups even though care was taken to split the participants with similar pre-test scores into different groups. Based on these results, we conclude that neither group improved significantly from pre- to post-test in the GameSense task.

The results were similar for the color recognition task using the pitching machine. As seen from the right panel of Fig. 11, the percent-correct scores for the control group started at a lower level than the VR group at pre-test (55.8%) and remained roughly the same at post-test (55.0%). The VR group shows a drop in percent-correct score from pre-test (60.0%) to post-test (52.9%). However, similar to the GameSense scores, an ANOVA with factors test and group failed to show either factor to be significant [test: $F(1,1)=0.97$, $p=0.330$; group: $F(1,1)=0.07$, $p=0.797$]. There were again large between-participant differences as seen in the large standard errors. We therefore concluded that the pitching machine ball-color recognition performance did not improve significantly from pre-test to post-test for either the control group or the VR group.

The VR group's performance on the "Call Color," "Call Pitch," and "Call Strike" tasks are summarized in Fig. 12. Shown are the average percent-correct scores by the order of VR sessions. It can be observed that the participants in the VR group were very good at the simulated "Call Color" and "Call Pitch" tasks in VR, and performed well on the "Call Strike" task as well. The percent-correct scores for the three VR tasks did not change much over the course of the 12 VR sessions.

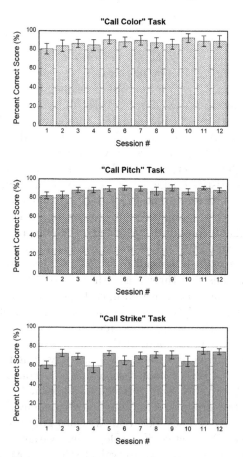

Fig. 12. Percent-correct scores for the "Call Color," "Call Pitch," and "Call Strike" tasks, averaged over the 12 participants in the VR group. Error bars indicate standard errors.

After the study was completed, the participants in the VR group were asked to fill out a survey on aspects such as simulation realism, effectiveness, and entertainment value. The responses were generally positive. The percentages of positive responses on the effectiveness of each VR task as a training tool were 66%, 91%, and 91% for the "Call Color", "Call Pitch", and "Call Strike" tasks, respectively. When asked to describe the overall experience, all participants responded positively with descriptions such as "Very good experience and helped me train my eyes...," "Helped my eyes and focus," "Loved every second," and "...felt like I got better as time went on."

6   Discussion

We have presented a study on the efficacy of VR training for college baseball athletes during the Fall 2019 training season. A total of 24 baseball players participated in the study. The VR modules developed for the present study have since been incorporated into the Purdue baseball team's routine practice. Our results do not show a statistically significant improvement from pre- to post-tests. This was expected due to the relatively short period of time during which we had access to the student athletes for VR training (12 VR sessions, approx. 10 min per session per participant). We had planned to track the participants and collect season statistics during their regular season in Spring 2020 as other studies have done [7]. However the COVID-19 pandemic cut the Spring 2020 season short and we were unable to complete our data collection.

Isogawa et al. (2018) provided evidence to the effectiveness of virtual reality environments in simulating a real world baseball environment in their study conducted with three skilled baseball participants. Each participant attempted to swing at a virtual baseball thrown as either a fastball or curveball. The participant's swing duration was measured in each environment. No significant differences were found between the real and virtual environments. This result was taken as evidence that the participants were able to judge the accuracy of the ball's trajectory in similar manners in the virtual and real environments [11]. Gray (2017) utilized virtual environments in a study designed to evaluate their effectiveness in training high school baseball players. Four groups, one control group and three test groups, were formed. In additional to standard practice activities, the first test group had an adaptive virtual environment, the second conducted non-adaptive VR sessions, and the third group completed additional real environment batting practice. Eight dependent variables, such as number of strikes correctly identified, were used to evaluate the improvement of each group. The results of the study indicated the adaptive VR group improved the most with a significant increase in 7 of the 8 dependent variables. A five year follow-up study was conducted with the study participants. The adaptive VR group had more than twice the number of participants play at least one full season at a level higher than high school when compared with the other groups [9]. Compared to these studies, our study has yet to track performance of Purdue baseball players in their future regular seasons in order to observe any positive changes in their performance in baseball fields using the metrics proposed by Gray (2017).

The long-term goal of our ongoing project is to provide Purdue baseball coaching and sports medicine staff with state-of-the-art VR simulations aimed at improving the overall performance of baseball players. As such, we will continue to assess the effectiveness of VR training with Purdue baseball players to gain a better understanding of when and how VR modules contribute to performance enhancement in the baseball field. The data collected in this study and the continued use of the VR modules by the Purdue baseball team will open the door for potential long-term benefits of VR training in the years to come.

Acknowledgements. The authors thank Taylor Morton for scheduling the athlete participants throughout the study, Emily Sagstetter and Caylie Jones for their assistance with running the study, and Matthew Boyle and Henry Fortenbaugh for compiling the results and running statistical analysis. We would also like to thank Dr. Peter Fadde for providing us access to the GameSense software used in the pre-test and post-test, processing and sharing the results, and insightful discussion throughout the development of the study.

References

1. Adolf, J., Kán, P., Outram, B., Kaufmann, H., Doležal, J., Lhotská, L.: Juggling in VR: Advantages of immersive virtual reality in juggling learning. In: 25th ACM Symposium on Virtual Reality Software and Technology (2019). https://doi.org/10.1145/3359996.3364246

2. Baillie, S., Crossan, A., Brewster, S., Mellor, D., Reid, S.: Validation of a bovine rectal palpation simulator for training veterinary students. Stud. Health Technol. Inf. **111**, 33–6 (2005)

3. Baillie, S., Mellor, D., Brewster, S., Reid, S.: Integrating a bovine rectal palpation simulator into an undergraduate veterinary curriculum. J. Vet. Med. Educ. **32**, 79–85 (2005). https://doi.org/10.3138/jvme.32.1.79

4. Bideau, B., Kulpa, R., Vignais, N., Brault, S., Multon, F.: Using virtual reality to analyze sports performance. IEEE Comput. Graphics Appl. **30**(2), 14–21 (2009). https://doi.org/10.1109/mcg.2009.134

5. Chardonnet, J.R., Loreto, C.D., Ryard, J., Housseau, A.: A virtual reality simulator to detect acrophobia in work-at-height situations. In: 2018 IEEE Conference on Virtual Reality and 3D User Interfaces (2018). https://doi.org/10.1109/vr.2018.8446395

6. Christopher, G.M., Müller, S.: Transfer of expert visual anticipation to a similar domain. Q. J. Exp. Psychol. **67**(1), 186–196 (2014). https://doi.org/10.1080/17470218.2013.798003

7. Clark, J., Ellis, J., Bench, J., Khoury, J., Graman, P.: High-performance vision training improves batting statistics for university of cincinnati baseball players. PloS one **7**, e29109 (2012). https://doi.org/10.1371/journal.pone.0029109

8. Garcia, A.D., Schlueter, J., Paddock, E.: Training astronauts using hardware-in-the-loop simulations and virtual reality. In: AIAA Scitech 2020 Forum (2020). https://doi.org/10.2514/6.2020-0167

9. Gray, R.: Transfer of training from virtual to real baseball batting. Front. Psychol. **8** (2017). https://doi.org/10.3389/fpsyg.2017.02183

10. Huang, Y., Churches, L., Reilly, B.: A case study on virtual reality american football training. In: Proceedings of the 2015 Virtual Reality International Conference on ZZZ - VRIC 2015 (2015). https://doi.org/10.1145/2806173.2806178

11. Isogawa, M., Mikami, D., Fukuda, T., Saijo, N., Takahashi, K., Kimata, H., Kashino, M.: What can VR systems tell sports players? reaction-based analysis of baseball batters in virtual and real worlds. In: 2018 IEEE Conference on Virtual Reality and 3D User Interfaces (2018). https://doi.org/10.1109/vr.2018.8446073

12. Molla, E., Boulic, R.: A two-arm coordination model for phantom limb pain rehabilitation. In: Proceedings of the 19th ACM Symposium on Virtual Reality Software and Technology - VRST 2013 (2013). https://doi.org/10.1145/2503713.2503739

13. Morris-Binelli, K., Müller, S., Fadde, P.: Use of pitcher game footage to measure visual anticipation and its relationship to baseball batting statistics. J. Motor Learn. Dev. **6**(2), 197–208 (2018). https://doi.org/10.1123/jmld.2017-0015

14. Pruett, C.: Down the rabbit hole with oculus quest: The hardware + software (2019). https://developer.oculus.com/blog/down-the-rabbit-hole-w-oculus-quest-the-hardware-software/?locale=en_US

15. Rauter, G., et al.: Transfer of complex skill learning from virtual to real rowing. PLoS ONE **8**(12) (2013). https://doi.org/10.1371/journal.pone.0082145

16. Sacks, R., Perlman, A., Barak, R.: Construction safety training using immersive virtual reality. Constr. Manag. Econ. **31**(9), 1005–1017 (2013). https://doi.org/10.1080/01446193.2013.828844

17. Sewell, C., Blevins, N.H., Peddamatham, S., Tan, H.Z.: The effect of virtual haptic training on real surgical drilling proficiency. In: Second Joint EuroHaptics Conference and Symposium on Haptic Interfaces for Virtual Environment and Teleoperator Systems (WHC 2007), pp. 601–603 (2007). https://doi.org/10.1109/whc.2007.111

18. Seymour, N.E., et al.: Virtual reality training improves operating room performance. Ann. Surg. **236**(4), 458–464 (2002). https://doi.org/10.1097/00000658-200210000-00008

19. Takahashi, K., Mikami, D., Isogawa, M., Kusachi, Y., Saijo, N.: Vr-based batter training system with motion sensing and performance visualization. In: 2019 IEEE Conference on Virtual Reality and 3D User Interfaces (2019). https://doi.org/10.1109/vr.2019.8798005

20. Tsai, W.L., Su, L.W., Ko, T.Y., Yang, C.T., Hu, M.C.: Improve the decision-making skill of basketball players by an action-aware vr training system. In: 2019 IEEE Conference on Virtual Reality and 3D User Interfaces (2019). https://doi.org/10.1109/vr.2019.8798309

21. Zaal, F.T.J.M., Bootsma, R.J.: Virtual reality as a tool for the study of perception-action: the case of running to catch fly balls. Pres. Teleoper. Virt. Environ. **20**(1), 93–103 (2011). https://doi.org/10.1162/pres_a_00037

Augmented Reality Enhanced Traditional Paper Book Reading Experience Design: A Case for University Library

Peixuan Li and Zhen Liu[✉]

School of Design, South China University of Technology,
Guangzhou 510006, People's Republic of China
liuzjames@scut.edu.cn

Abstract. Paper-based books in university libraries are important learning materials for university students, but there are some drawbacks in traditional reading methods, and it is necessary to utilize scientific and technological means to solve the pain points of users, i.e. the students. With the development of information technology, augmented reality (AR) technology has gradually penetrated into all areas of the students' lives. The fusion of AR technology and traditional paper books brings a potential new approach of reading and a sense of experience. At present, the application of AR technology in library is mainly for book navigation and book protection. AR technology has also appeared in some children's books, but most of the books are still in the traditional way of reading. Therefore, this research aims to implement AR technology with traditional reading methods, optimize the reading experience of paper books, and enhance the interactivity and interest of paper book reading. This article selects university students in the library of South China University of Technology for the case study. Firstly, it finds the application method of AR technology in the library through the literature, and then observes and interviews the students to summarize the pain points and design opportunities from traditional reading. Based on AR technology, this paper designed a social reading application with a human-oriented design concept, thereby optimizing the reading experience of paper books for library.

Keywords: Augmented reality · Reading experience · University library · Paper books

1 Introduction

Augmented reality is a technology that tracks and locates the position and angle of camera images in real time, and adds corresponding images, audio, video, and 3D models. The goal of this technology is to realize the interaction between the virtual world and the real world on the screen. In recent years, augmented reality technology has also been applied in publishing and education industries. The intuitive way of reading experience can increase learners' interest in reading, stimulate interest in learning, strengthen knowledge understanding, and consolidate knowledge [1].

© Springer Nature Switzerland AG 2021
M. M. Soares et al. (Eds.): HCII 2021, LNCS 12781, pp. 205–217, 2021.
https://doi.org/10.1007/978-3-030-78227-6_15

Paper books in university libraries are academic resources that the students often come into contact with. But in the process of reading paper books, it can be found that this traditional way of reading has many pain points that need to be resolved. The development of AR technology has brought new development to traditional reading methods. At present, the application of AR technology in libraries mainly includes library navigation, personalized reading guidance services, comprehensive development and integration of resources, and intelligent arrangement of books. Meredith has studied how to use AR technology to improve the services of children's libraries, and believes that the integrated indoor positioning system can meet the indoor navigation needs of young readers [2]. Zhou of the China Academy of Art and others have implemented a book navigation system based on AR technology for the library of the school [3]. Zeng of Beijing University of Posts and Telecommunications has applied AR technology to develop a personalized service platform for the library of the school, recommending books that may be of interest to readers [4]. AR technology can also assist researchers in learning special collections of ancient books in the library and research. While enhancing readers' interest in reading, it is better to preserve and utilize precious documents and improve the utilization rate of collection resources, which is conducive to sustainable development [5]. The application of AR technology in the field of children's book publishing mainly combines paper publications with virtual scenes depicted in books through computers or handheld terminal devices, so that children can experience the virtual scenes in the books, or with the virtual characters in the books, of which reading experience can greatly enhance children's reading interest [6].

In this paper, by studying the process of university students borrowing books in the library, to get design opportunities, and design a paper book social APP based on AR technology to optimize the reading experience of the students in the library. This research expands the application scenarios of AR technology in libraries, and also explores the method of embedding AR technology with traditional reading methods.

2   Method

The study selects students from South China University of Technology as the case study sample, adopts the human-oriented design concept and refers to the double-diamond model to observe the real needs of users in the library reading process, and optimize the user's experience when reading paper books. In the exploratory stage, it aims to observe the user's behavior in the real scene, and analyze the user's needs and potential design opportunities through the empathy map, which is followed by conducting user interviews with target users, and getting deeper needs of users through interviews. In the definition stage, the pain points of users are summarized, and the breakthrough points of the design are obtained by referring to relevant research results. In the conception stage, the design opportunity points are transformed into functional architecture, and the priority of functions is evaluated. In the implementation phase, a low-fidelity prototype is made for user testing, and user suggestions are summarized.

2.1 User Observation

In order to find the real user needs, it is necessary to observe the real scene of the user. The place of observation is the library of South China University of Technology. Observation shows that there are five steps in the process of college students borrowing books in the library (see Fig. 1). The first step in borrowing books in the library is to search for the target book on the library website, and then write down the index number or location information of the target book. The second step is to find the target book on the shelf according to the index number. The third step is to put the book on the borrowing machine and record the borrowing information. The fourth step is to read a book and take notes. The last step is to return the book.

In the whole process, the book index navigation and book borrowing and returning are assisted by intelligent systems. However, the reading of books is still a traditional reading mode, and there are some pain points in the reading process of paper books. Reading in the paper library is a key part of the library experience, so the design focus is on this part. In the process of users reading paper books, we found that the current library book information query only has a web portal, and there is no mobile client. The ownership of paper books is the library, so users cannot write on the books. In the process of reading books, users will use mobile phones or computers to query related materials, and will take pictures to save key content.

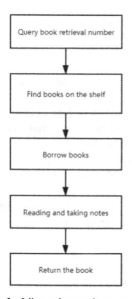

Fig. 1. Library borrowing process.

2.2 User Interview

A total of 10 participants were recruited for user interviews, including 5 undergraduates and 5 postgraduates, all of whom were from the School of Design, South China University of Technology. The interview questions are listed in Table 1. According to user interviews, the information obtained is summarized and generalized answers are found.

Table 1. The main questions mentioned in the interview.

No.	Questions
1	How often do you go to the library?
2	How many books do you borrow in one semester?
3	Have you used AR books?
4	How to solve the problems you encounter while reading?
5	How do you learn about the books you want to read?
6	In which way do you take notes while reading?
7	Do you prefer paper books or e-books?
8	Will you share a book you like with others? How to share?
9	Do you pay attention to book reviews?
10	In the process of reading the paper version of the book, what makes you feel bad about the experience?

After user interviews, we got the following conclusions:

- The frequency of going to the library and the number of books borrowed vary greatly among individuals. Normally, when college students start a new course, they will go to the library to borrow related books.
- When a user encounters a problem in reading a book, he will first look for the answer from the Internet, and if the problem is not solved, he will seek help from classmates and teachers.
- Most users will look for basic information and book reviews of target books from the Internet, followed by recommendations from classmates and teachers. Book reviews are useful for reference.
- Although the price of e-books is low and easy to use, it is more comfortable to read paper books and more focused.
- Most users will keep reading notes on their mobile phones or iPads, and take photos of key content.
- When users encounter good books that are inspiring, they are willing to share with others, usually through chatting with friends or sharing on social media.
- Most users know AR books, but few people actually come into contact with them.
- Some website addresses and complex proper nouns in the paper version of the book, users need to manually input in the search website, which is a pain point in reading the paper version of the book.

2.3 Empathy Map

According to the observation results, the following empathy map is obtained (see Fig. 2). The empathy diagram explains the deep motivation behind the user's behavior, choice, and decision, so that we can discover his true needs, because some motivations are difficult to perceive or users are inconvenient to express directly, and it is more difficult to insight. Empathy maps can help us resonate with users and open up ideas.

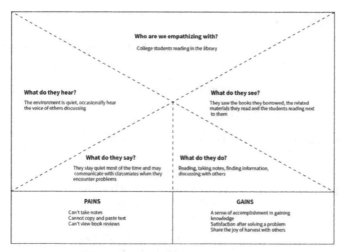

Fig. 2. Empathy map.

2.4 Personas

Based on the above analysis, the target user role is established, and the product target can be better positioned through the user role (see Fig. 3).

Fig. 3. The persona.

3   Problem Definition

3.1   How Might We Brainstorm

- How might we make the reading experience of paper books in the library better?
- How might we allow paper readers to communicate with previous readers?
- How might we recommend more suitable paper books to college students?

3.2   User Requirements

According to the above analysis, the user requirements listed in Table 2 are obtained.

Table 2. The user needs.

Type	Needs
Book recommendation	Get the latest book information Recommend books that suit you Popular books recommendation
Book reading	View book reviews, write book reviews Query the difficulties in books Take notes
Book sharing	Share your book reviews and reading experience Communicate with like-minded people Start a topic or question to communicate with others

3.3   Experience Objectives

According to the above analysis of user needs, and based on existing technical means. Design a paper book reading experience application based on AR technology. The application is for college students. Users can query the latest book information and popular book recommendations on the application. Users can use AR technology to see book reviews left by people who have borrowed books before. Users can also leave book reviews or questions, and interact with other users. If users want to take notes or search for complex proper nouns in the book, they can scan to generate text or keyword links. After reading the book, users can leave their thoughts and experiences in the interactive community to communicate with others.

4 Solutions

4.1 Product Definition

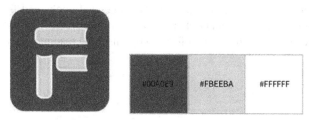

Fig. 4. The APP logo design. (Color figure online)

The name of the application is "fun-read", which allows college students to have a better reading experience in the library. The main functions of the app include recommending popular books in the library, browsing book reviews left by others, book scanning, and social functions.

Good-looking visual design and efficient interaction design have an important impact on user experience. Because the application target group is college students, the overall design style is relatively simple and fresh. The graphic of the LOGO is "F" composed of the silhouettes of three books, symbolizing that "Fun" corresponds to the name of the application (see Fig. 4). The color matching adopts blue and yellow as the main tones, giving people a lively and bright feeling.

4.2 Software Architecture

After the user's needs are refined, the following software structure diagram is obtained, as shown in Fig. 5.

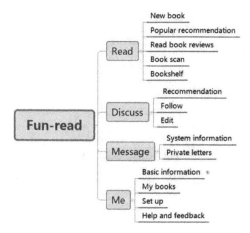

Fig. 5. The software architecture.

4.3 Task Flow

The task flow chart clearly shows the user's use process, which has important reference value for the interface design (see Fig. 6).The task of the user is mainly divided into the target book and the non-target book. If the user does not have a target book, then after entering the application, the user can view recommended books and find books they like. If users already have a target book, they can view book reviews or use the scanning function to take notes or generate text links to optimize the reading experience.

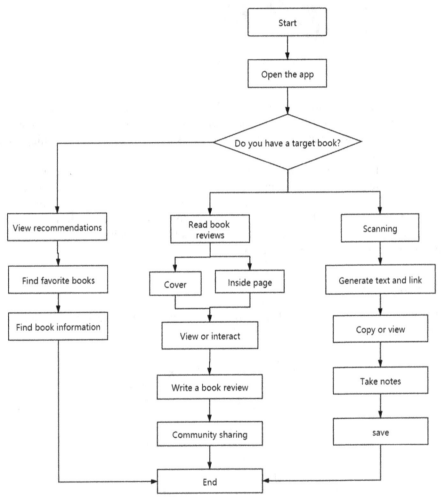

Fig. 6. The task flow.

4.4 Low-Fidelity Model Display

The homepage can provide users with the latest library information and a list of popular books (see Fig. 7). This information can help users better target the books they want to read. An important function in the homepage is AR to view book reviews of paper books. Book reviews are left by people who have borrowed the book before. Users can interact with people who have previously commented. In this way, the human resources of the university can be fully mobilized. Another important function in the homepage is to scan books. The current paper version of the book cannot copy a target text. Using this scanning function, users can quickly copy the text of a paper book. Important keywords or URLs can also directly generate links to facilitate users to take notes and find information.

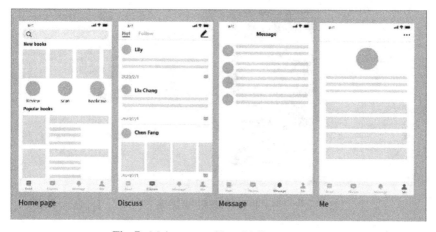

Fig. 7. Main pages of low fidelity prototype.

"Discuss" is a community for readers to interact. Users can post comments on books that the community has read. If users have any questions during the reading process, they can ask questions in the community. Users who see the question can reply to the question. In addition to sharing book reviews and questions in the community, users can also share their favorite books or reading notes. The role of the community is to exchange ideas, to find resonance between different views and to meet interesting classmates.

"Message" is used to receive system notifications and private messages sent by other users in the community. Here, users can communicate with each other in depth. The information is arranged according to the time received, and users can choose to reply according to their needs.

"Me" is the self-management center of this application, it will display basic user information. Check the number of users followed, who has followed, and which books have been read. There is also a setting function in this section, which is used to set the usage habits and personalized interface of the entire APP. Feedback and help are also in this interface, allowing users to ask for help when they encounter problems.

4.5 Usage Flow

User Scenario 1: Read Book Reviews. On the homepage, users can see popular books and new books in the library, and users can select books of interest to borrow. An important function on the homepage is Ar to read book reviews (see Fig. 8). This function can scan the cover of a book, and then a book review will pop up. Book reviews move on the screen like a bullet screen. When the user is reading the inner pages of a book, this function can also be used. The blue dots indicate the number of comments left by others. Users can view comments after clicking, and can interact with other users.

Fig. 8. The process of reading book reviews.

User Scenario 2: Scan Book. Another important function in the home page is to scan books (see Fig. 9). After the user enters this function, first enter the camera interface. After taking a photo, the screen will display the scanned text information. The text can be copied and recognized, the keywords in the article will generate links, and the user can directly click the keywords to search. At the same time, the scanning function is also a tool for taking notes. After the photo is recognized, you can use the pen or text box tool to record. The user can save the picture later.

User Scenario 3: Community Interaction. Users can share reading notes and experiences with other users after entering the "Discuss" (see Fig. 10). If users have questions, they can also ask questions in "Discuss". When users encounter comments that they are interested in, they can click on the avatars of other users to follow and communicate with them.

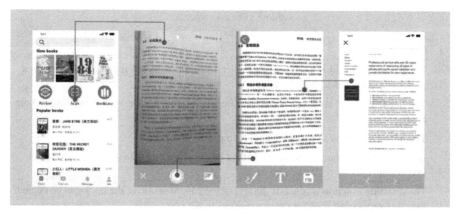

Fig. 9. The process of scanning books.

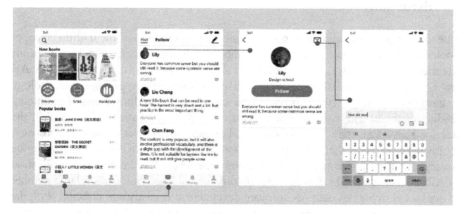

Fig. 10. The process of community communication.

4.6   Usability Test

In the user test, ten participants were recruited. Let ten participants complete three tasks in the app, and then collect feedback from users to get directions for improvement (see Table 3). The three tasks are: 1. Find a book you like in the popular book recommendation. 2. The user AR read book reviews function to view book reviews. 3. Use the scan function, copy the text and click the relevant link. User comments provide reference for software iteration.

Table 3. User comments.

No.	Comments
1	There is no book I like in the popular books. If the software can recommend books in a personalized way, then it feels better
2	The function of AR book reviews is very interesting, and book reviews have inspired me a lot
3	The book reviews on the cover are confusing
4	Book reviews written for each book should be classified and managed so that you can find your own book reviews more easily
5	The scanning function is great. If the text of the paper version of the book can be copied, then it is very convenient for me to make electronic notes
6	It is more convenient if the scanned image can be cut automatically

5   Discussions

Due to the rapid development of network information technology, the traditional paper book market will inevitably be impacted. Embedding scientific and technological means to enrich the traditional reading experience is a development trend of the paper books. AR technology can associate the real world with the virtual world. Applying AR technology to traditional reading methods is one of the ways to solve the limitations of traditional reading methods. The current application of AR in the education field is still in the development stage, and related products and research are not yet mature. The research in this paper expands the usage scenarios for the application of AR technology in the library, and also optimizes the user's reading experience. But the practical application of AR technology in libraries also has its difficulties. The library has a large number of books and rich types, and AR software development is costly and difficult. With the increase of the database, the higher the hardware requirements of the software function increase. However, with the continuous development of science and technology, the application of AR technology in the education field has great potential. In the future, with the development and popularization of AR technology and the advancement of hardware equipment, this research will have greater development potential and more application scenarios.

6   Conclusions

This article discusses the application scenarios of user AR technology in a university library. The smart library is an important part of the smart campus. The integration of new technology into the library is the future development direction of the library. Although traditional paper books have been impacted by the e-book market, paper books still have their application scenarios. The paper books in the library are also indispensable educational resources. At present, AR technology has penetrated into the education field. The addition of AR technology has changed the way of reading traditional books, and the intervention of multimedia devices has enhanced users' sense of immersion and interest. However, at present, AR technology is mostly used in children's books, through which the pictures in the paper version of the book can be stereoscopic or video can be watched. In the application of the library, there are mainly scenes such as user book navigation and intelligent recommendation. This research uses literature review and user research to find the real pain points of users, and uses new technology to try to improve the pain points encountered by users in the process of reading traditional books. The output of the research is an application that can assist users in reading. Users can view book reviews left by other people in paper books in the application, and can also scan the text in paper books to be recognized. Better record information and search information. The application not only improves the user's reading experience of paper books, but also expands the user's social connection with book review exchange and social functions. This research provides reference for the construction and development of library reading experience in the future.

Acknowledgements. The authors wish to thank all the people who provided their time and efforts for the investigation. This research is supported by "South China University of Technology Central University Basic Scientific Research Operating Expenses Subsidy, project approval no. XYZD201928, (x2sjC2191370)".

References

1. Liao, Y.: Application research of augmented reality (AR) technology in libraries. Inf. Doc. Serv. **01**, 62–66 (2017)
2. Meredith, T.: Using augmented reality tools to enhance children's library services. Technol. Knowl. Learn. **20**(1), 71–77 (2015)
3. Zhou, W., Chen, L., Song, J.: Library navigation department based on augmented reality technology systematic research. J. Syst. Simul. **4**, 810–815 (2015)
4. Zeng, X.: Application Research of Augmented Reality Technology in Library Personalized Service Platform. Beijing University of Posts and Telecommunications, Beijing (2013)
5. Feng, J., Guo, W.: The application and significance of AR technology in university libraries. Inner Mongolia Sci. Technol. Econ. (12), 74–75+85 (2016).
6. Han, L.: Application analysis of AR technology in children's book publishing. Media Forum **3**(10), 94–95 (2020)
7. Bacca Acosta, J.L., Baldiris Navarro, S.M., Fabregat Gesa, R., Graf, S.: Augmented reality trends in education: a systematic review of research and applications. J. Educ. Technol. Soc. **17**(4), 133–149 (2014)
8. Oyelude, A.A.: Virtual reality (VR) and augmented reality (AR) in libraries and museums. Libr. Hi Tech News **35**, 1–4 (2018)
9. Romli, R., Razali, A.F., Ghazali, N.H., Hanin, N.A., Ibrahim, S.Z.: Mobile augmented reality (AR) marker-based for indoor library navigation. IOP Conf. Ser. Mater. Sci. Eng. **767**(1), 012062 (2020)

Potential Integration of Virtual Reality and Sound for University Student Experience Therapy

Zhen Liu and Zhanhong Su(✉)

South China University of Technology, Guangzhou 510006, People's Republic of China

Abstract. Social Anxiety Disorder (SAD) is currently common among young-sters all over the globe. Technological development that creates virtual environment and environmental factors are possible causes besides the traditional cognition of SAD. Different types of therapy have been applied to mitigating or even curing SAD, some use advanced technologies like virtual reality, while others are quite conventional, such as music therapy that has been applied decades ago. Based on the findings of different types of previous study on SAD and its corresponding therapies, the study investigated the basic evidence of SAD and self-cognition of university students. To further develop the concept of possible application of music therapy to modern technology, the musical knowledge and preference were also parts of the investigation. Participants were 15 university students from different regions of China. A questionnaire that is comprised of 9 questions was filled. The questions included basic family composition (number of siblings), some representational questions about SAD extracted from Liebowitz Social Anxiety Scale (LSAS), self-cognition of the ability to judge conversational emotions, and how well they are trained in music and their preference for specific types of music. The questions are generally based on previous studies, which demonstrate the inner connection between relevant separate concepts including music, vocal conversation, exposure and happiness recognition. Specifically we studied those who considered themselves to lack the ability of emotional recognition. The majority of them grew up with no or only one sibling. They tended to work in relatively spacious and empty places without surveillance; meanwhile most of them have low initiative to speak in public when unnecessary. From the musical perspective, most of them have not been trained with musical theory or just have a superficial understanding, which according to previous study, might result in inability in happiness recognition in vocal conversation, which consequently result in SAD.

Keywords: Virtual Reality · Sound Therapy · Social Anxiety Disorder · University student · Experience therapy · Emotion recognition

1 Introduction

Social anxiety disorder (SAD) is one of the most common psychiatric disorders and many patients with SAD are refractory to pharmacotherapy [1]. SAD often co-occurs with other

© Springer Nature Switzerland AG 2021
M. M. Soares et al. (Eds.): HCII 2021, LNCS 12781, pp. 218–232, 2021.
https://doi.org/10.1007/978-3-030-78227-6_16

psychiatric conditions such as additional mood disorders, substance use disorders, and is significantly associated with suicidal ideation. Despite its frequency and severity, only between one third and half of people with SAD seek treatment. This may be linked to the nature of the disorder itself, as people with SAD avoid healthcare services like they would avoid any other social interaction. Factors like the feeling of getting embarrassed and fear of what others might think have been found to prevent patients with SAD from seeking treatment [2]. Simultaneously, even though the treatment is received, the positive effects end soon after the end of the treatment [3]. Additionally, further barriers exist in regards to accessing treatment such as the lack of skilled therapists, lack of evidence-based treatments and long waiting lists [4].

Social anxiety symptoms are very common among adolescents and adults, and their onset typically occurs during early and middle adolescence. Adolescents' vulnerability to social anxiety is enhanced by age-related tasks—identity construction, redefinition of social roles and body image changes—which normally provoke major concerns about the self [5]. These tasks indicate that even adolescents are possibly the most vulnerable group to SAD, people of other identities and age groups, such as university students or the graduates that have just started their career in the society, may also be potential patients of SAD. The corresponding symptoms can undermine the self-adjustment and the quality of peer communication, and consequently negatively influence mental well-being.

Since the pharmacotherapy do not help address this issue effectively, researcher have made attempts to approach psychiatric or cognitive treatments. Just like many other kinds of mental diseases associated with certain scenes, such as the phobia caused by experiencing rape or murder, SAD is frequently treated with exposure therapy, including conventional In Vivo Exposure Therapy (IVET) and Virtual Reality Exposure Therapy (VRET). Superficially speaking, such exposure related to SAD refers to the virtual or tangible exposure of patients to specific situations where social contact is frequent and required, and the key to addressing the issue is to correctly shape their cognition of the normal communication, which might be considered excessively aggressive and harmful [6].

Simultaneously, sound/music-related therapy was applied, but rather rarely, to the treatment of SAD. Previously music was mainly applied to curing different forms of depression, yet several studies were carried out by means of music in terms of SAD, based on theories that were formulated in more previous studies. Such therapies are related to cognitive and/or behavioral therapeutic knowledge.

2 Literature Review

2.1 Preface

As mentioned before, Social Anxiety Disorder (SAD) is a global mental healthcare issue despite the regional factors. Researches and consequent solutions have commenced in different parts of the world, the methods and forms of which are associated with knowledge about cognitive science, and music.

So far, relevant researchers, along with psychologists and scientists, have made attempts to address SAD utilizing various conventional or advanced methods, such as Virtual Reality Exposure Therapy (VRET), Musical Therapy (MT) focusing on emotional recognition and/or cognitive-behavioral therapy (CBT).

This review aims to summarize the previous study and therapies around SAD, in terms of studied group, research methods and forms and contents of therapies. Further development of concepts and assumptions of new forms of therapies will be stated in latter parts of the paper.

2.2 Virtual Reality Exposure Therapy and in Vivo Exposure Therapy

As other mental issues related to certain types of scenes or environments, SAD has been treated by means of exposure therapy. For SAD, such exposure basically refers to surrounding the patients with certain densities of people in given environments that mostly resemble those in which their social communication takes place.

Virtual Reality (VR) has been applied to exposure therapy in numbers of previous studies. Similar to in vivo exposure therapy (IVET), Virtual Reality Exposure Therapy (VRET) is often integrated with CBT. Compared to IVET, VRET has apparent advantages [7]:

1. While providing environments that are similar to those in real life, the situational factors of virtual environments are more controllable, such as the density of the people and the reaction and interaction involved.
2. While presenting the scenarios to the patients, they can still stay in the room with safety and comfort.
3. VRET has better flexibility of the presenting the situations. Thus, it is possible to show the patients with more crowded and even exaggerated situations, to further demonstrate that the interpersonal interaction can be harmless.
4. Even knowing that the situation is virtual, patients' bodies and minds react as if it is real. It is easier to face such situation in VR than in real life, while still maintaining relevant reactions.
5. VR sessions required less time than in vivo sessions, which brings more flexibility and lower costs.

However, previous researches indicate that VRET has shown similar efficacy as IVET [8, 9]. They were both proved to be more effective than each other in different period post-intervention. Additionally, there was no significant difference in efficacy between intervention methods that combined VRET with psychotherapy and VRET-only methods [1].

Such efficacy is not theoretical but real-life. After receiving treatment based on VRET, some patients showed less fear of social communication according to follow-up, and even took occupations that required public speaking, such as teacher [7].

2.3 Music Therapy for SAD

Sound and music have been applied to the treatment for various mental diseases in different forms. For SAD, most previous studies tend to focus on the environment and thus, seek for appropriate approaches by means of exposure. The number of sound-related therapies for SAD is quite limited.

In the last century it has been proved that there is similarity between music and speech in terms of emotion recognition [11, 12]. Speech and music share similar components, such as dynamics, pitch, timbre and rhythm, as well as overlapping parts of the brain, which process speech and music patterns. Such resemblance between speech and music is particularly obvious in rhythmic and melodic patterns, which play a significant role regarding these two modes of expressions [10].

Such theories had been proved with scientific approaches, but had not been applied to relevant research around therapy for mental diseases like SAD. Based on that, a study was carried out in Tel Aviv University, Israel, aiming to train the ability of emotion recognition, particularly happiness recognition, by means of music [10]. The researchers formulated hypotheses, that the SAD patient shows less accuracy in happiness recognition and more accuracy in fear recognition, compared to the healthy controls (HC), and that after music-based training, the accuracy of happiness recognition of the trained can transcend that of the untrained and reach the same level as the HC.

The results basically correspond with the hypotheses. However, it is interesting that the trained SAD patients even revealed less accuracy of fear recognition compared to the HC. It is controversial whether such a phenomenon is positive as the elimination of fear helps the patients with interpersonal communication or negative as the bias from the accuracy of HC will be abnormal and harmful to correct recognition of emotions in real life.

In another study, music was applied as reward in the form of Gaze-Contingent Therapy [13]. Patients were asked to stare at matrices comprised of disgusting faces and neutral faces with eye-tracking calibration. For the patients in the experimental group, when they stared at the neutral faces, the music piece that they have selected beforehand was played as a kind of reward. Conversely, when the disgusting faces were stared at, the music stopped. As for the control group, the music was played throughout the experiment.

The pre-treatment, post-treatment and follow-up, based on clinical measures like LSAS and self-report, all showed that this specific kind of music therapy had remarkable efficacy to most patients that received the treatment.

Both of the therapies worked with music as a crucial element. Compared to the therapy mentioned as treatment on emotion recognition, this therapy utilized human face expressions as visual means, and music was familiar to the patients and not analyzed.

2.4 Summary

Virtual Reality has been applied to the treatment for SAD for a long time in various forms, while music/sound therapies have rarely been used to address this troublesome global mental issue.

The majority of relevant therapies are associated with cognition, some with behavior. Exposure therapies emphasize the significance of environment, while the limited music therapies focus on facial expression and speech, which are possibly the two most important elements of interpersonal communication.

These two kinds of therapies focus on different aspects of the difficulties that the SAD patients face. If the integration of different aspects can be realized, perhaps a higher level of efficacy can be reached.

3 Objective

3.1 Construction of Mental Model of SAD Patients as University Students

As mentioned before, adolescents and even older university students are vulnerable to SAD, which can be more harmful to them than to other age groups of people. As teacher and student in university, it is convenient for studying local university students, who might be just preparing for their social careers.

This group of Chinese students grew up in a special period. When they were born, China's one-child policy had not yet been abolished, which means most grew up with no siblings; they grew up in 21st century, surrounded by advanced electronic devices that create virtual worlds that separate them from the real one. Under such circumstances, it is significant to study the mental model of the current university students to further conclude the possible difference or additional features compared to previous subjects.

3.2 Research for Potential Integration of VR and Sound Therapy

VRET focuses on the phobia-related environments, while sound/music therapy focuses on the ways in which information is received, by not only audible, but also visual means. There may be possibilities to integrate these two dimensions of cognition, and apply them together to a new therapy that maybe, through further tests, proved to show more efficacy than the therapies applied to the treatment of SAD before.

4 Method

4.1 Questionnaire Formulation

To study the potential group of SAD patients in universities, a questionnaire was made for primary investigation. It aims to conclude the relevant backgrounds and preferences of the potential patients, and consequently deduct and summarize a primary mental model of this specific group of patients.

The questionnaire should firstly ask the participants to judge their potential symptoms of SAD. In order not to reveal any indication of SAD, this specific question was not extracted from the Liebowitz Social Anxiety Scale (LSAS). Instead, based on the correlation of emotion recognition and SAD, it asks to participants to judge their own competence of emotion recognition.

As mentioned before, this study aims to seek for potential integration of environment and visual/audio perception. Therefore, the participants' preferences for working environment and music type were included.

Accordingly, the questions are:

1. The age (group) of participant;

2. The number of siblings;
3. The actual/ideal population density of working environment;
4. The difference of working efficiency, alone and under surveillance;
5. Self-judgement of the competence of emotion recognition;
6. Preference for music type;
7. Level of received music training.

The questionnaire was designed, formulated online. It was then published in social media applications where the whole process goes more conveniently and efficiently.

4.2 Questionnaire Results

15 people filled the questionnaire. Even though their precise identities and occupations were not asked in the questionnaire, judging from the group to which the questionnaire was accessible and participants' age groups according to their answers, they were all university students.

Among the 15 participants, nine of them considered themselves to lack the competence of emotion recognition (four considered themselves mildly lacking), as shown in Fig. 1.

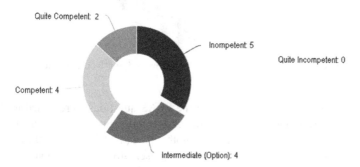

Fig. 1. Self-judgement of competence of emotion recognition.

To specifically study these potential patients of SAD, we extracted the corresponding answers of theirs.

Among these nine potential patients, only three (33.3%) had no sibling, which indicates that there can probably be no correlation between SAD and the family composition (number of siblings).

As for the environmental preference, six (66.7%) of them preferred to work or study with nobody around, and two (22.2%) chose to work in spacious environment where there are only a few people around, as shown in Fig. 2.

Accordingly, as they were asked about the influence of others' surveillance on the efficiency of studying/working, five (55.5%) considered such surveillance to be considerately negative to the efficiency, while another two (22.2%) considered such influence negative but slight. The rest two (22.2%) believed such situations could help them work slightly more efficiently, as shown in Fig. 3.

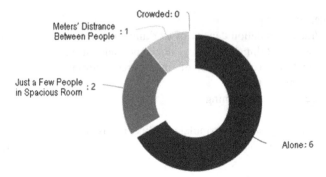

Fig. 2. Preference for environment of studying/working.

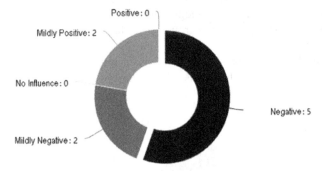

Fig. 3. Influence of others' surveillance on studying/working efficiency.

Also, a question analogous to one of the LSAS questions were added to the questionnaire, asking whether the participants tend to represent a team to speak in public. Four (44.4%) preferred not to do this, and another four (44.4%) selected the intermediate option. Only one (11.1%) tended to speak as representative, which probably verifies the previous judgement for potential SAD patients, as shown in Fig. 4.

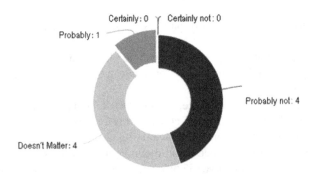

Fig. 4. Probability for speaking in public representing a team.

As for musical preference, these nine potential patients were partial to mild styles instead of extreme ones. Six (66.6%) preferred lyric music with mild positive emotions, while the rest three (33.3%) preferred music with mild sorrow.

Concerning the level of received music training, only one (11.1%) had proficient command of professional musical theories and terms. The rest had only superficial understanding of the theories, and even three (33.3%) had barely received musical training, as shown in Fig. 5.

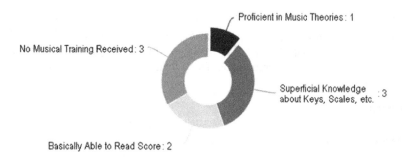

Proficient in Music Theories : 1

No Musical Training Received : 3

Superficial Knowledge
about Keys, Scales, etc. : 3

Basically Able to Read Score : 2

Fig. 5. Level of received musical training.

In summary, the potential SAD patients showed preferences for relatively empty spaces and mild styles of music. Whether having siblings or not probably do not influence the ability of emotion recognition, which reveals symptoms of SAD, and the lack of musical training is possibly a reason that explains the lack of such ability.

4.3 Interview

To further study the detailed preferences, three online interviews were carried out. The interviewees, after confirmation, were all university students around us and in the group of the studied nine. This deeper interview was mainly about more precise details about preference for the environments and excavating further factors of their choices, to help us formulate an explicit and in-depth mental model.

During the interview, apart from the population density of the environment, we aimed to discover detailed visual factors around their preference. Two evident factors can be the hue and decoration style. Therefore, we showed the interviewees two pictures that are different in these two ways and asked for their perspectives, as shown in Fig. 6.

All the three interviewees prefer the atmosphere created by the warm hue in the first picture, even though two of them believe there should be less decorations or furniture there. The rest one said that if the second room could be given the same warm light as the first one does, he would have chosen the second. All of them expressed the point that the decorations/furniture style is not an important factor.

In summary, the warm hue shows less aggression, in the atmosphere of which they would feel more comfortable to interact with others. The room should not contain too much decoration or furniture, otherwise the space can be severely compressed, bringing the aggressive atmosphere back.

Fig. 6. Different environments displayed in the Interview using pictures from the internet.

As for the question about public speaking, they showed more or less fear. They tended to consider silence as disapproval, and the reactions that is usually seen as normal ones, such as carelessness, is considered aggressive to them.

5   Results

5.1   Mental Model

The mental model for developing the VR experience therapy has been developed as below:

1) The SAD patients as university students believe that they lack the competence to correctly recognize people's emotion during social communication, which to some extent, eliminate their confidence to interact with others in social occasions.
2) When giving a speech, these patients may consider normal reaction of others harmful and aggressive. Consequently, even though the speech is good enough, they still doubt themselves.
3) They prefer to interact with other people in a warm atmosphere, which indicates less aggression. The room should not be crowded with people or decorations.
4) They wish to receive instant positive feedback from the listeners. Silence may indicate disapproval to them even though in most occasions, it does not.

5.2   Primary Integration and Testable Prototype

Based on the mental model, it is feasible to integrate the VR exposure with music instruction. With VR as the form of the therapy, the experience of the patients can also be interactive. However, such exposure here, according to their communication-phobia and the wish to receive positive feedback, may not be real people in the scene with vivid speech and expressions. The gadgets or utensils in the scene, can be made interactive, sending instant feedback to the patients.

With such assumption, the music can also be applied in two ways. Apart from conventional instructions about the music composition which can also take place in virtual environments, the music can be created by the patients themselves. Once they create new sound, corresponding sound or segments of music can be instantly played as feedback. Even without a real human's figure in the scene, an invisible man exists and sends positive feedback. Using Unity 3D and C# as programming language, a testable prototype has been constructed. The environment was basically a wood cabin with warm lights inside. Surplus furniture has been removed. The utensils such as bowls, cups and pots were kept, embedding the musical feedback, as shown in Fig. 7 and Fig. 8.

Fig. 7. Exterior of the VR scene.

Fig. 8. Interior of VR scene.

The visual and audio feedbacks both exist. When a pot is stared at, a gyration animation is played, with the figure of the pot emphasized with a different color, using different Shaders of the Unity 3D engine, as shown in Fig. 9.

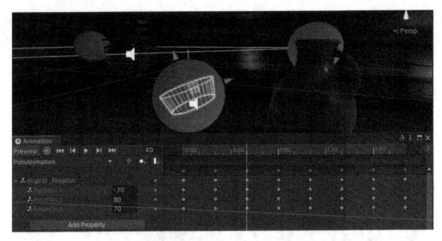

Fig. 9. Feedback: utensil gyration

In the primary experiment we chose the primary notes as the medium. When the animation is triggered, the corresponding major chord of the specific note is played as feedback, as shown in Fig. 10.

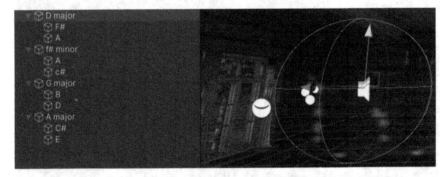

Fig. 10. Feedback: broken chords

The broken chords can be played in certain rhythms, if possible, simulating the speech with happy emotion. Such effect can be realized with the inner function of C#, stopping the processing for certain lengths of time, as shown in Fig. 11.

The conventional music instruction is taken beside a piano. We used the music of Mozart, which demonstrates purer musicality and usually exhilaration. Music visualization is the primary method that we use for instruction, as shown in Fig. 12.

```
int mode = (int)Random.Range(0, 3);
//Setting different rhythms of broken chords
switch (mode)
{
    case 0:
        Thread.Sleep(500);
        chord[0].GetComponent<AudioSource>().Play();
        Thread.Sleep(500);
        chord[1].GetComponent<AudioSource>().Play();
        Thread.Sleep(500);
        chord[0].GetComponent<AudioSource>().Play();
        break;
    case 1:
        Thread.Sleep(500);
        chord[2].GetComponent<AudioSource>().Play();
        Thread.Sleep(500);
        chord[1].GetComponent<AudioSource>().Play();
        Thread.Sleep(250);
        chord[0].GetComponent<AudioSource>().Play();
        Thread.Sleep(250);
        chord[2].GetComponent<AudioSource>().Play();
        ...
}
```

Fig. 11. Coding of feedback musical rhythm

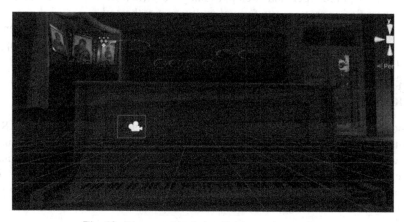

Fig. 12. Piano: musical visualization as instruction

6   Discussion

6.1   Accordance with Previous Studies

From such perspective, the research can be considered as verification of previous findings. Parts of the results have shown accordance with those of previous studies. For
instance, one of the factors that causes SAD is the fear of the listeners' disapproval and
aggressive behavior or expressions. The selected nine subjects were mostly repelling to

public speaking as representative (question extracted from LSAS), which correspond with the theory of the correlation between emotion recognition and SAD.

6.2 Unexpected Results

Parts of the results are beyond our expectation. For instance, initially we considered as this generation grew up with the one-child policy in China, whether having siblings or not might be a potential factor of SAD, or at least there should be correlation. However, the data we collected did not support such correlation.

The expected the result that probably most participants would show rejection against the surveillance, considering it as distraction. However, nearly a half chose the intermediate option, and even two of them considered it helpful to increasing working efficiency. This urged to modify the concept of surveillance and the context of working, and extend the topic to the existence of others and context of staying.

7   Conclusion

7.1   Objective

This study aims to specifically study the potential SAD patients as university students, carry out in-depth research and attempt to integrate Virtual Reality with sound/music-related therapies, to create a new form of multi-sensory therapy.

To achieve this, the research should gather typical university students of the generation, and through the in-depth research, to formulate a primary mental model to support further development of the therapy system.

7.2   Results

The most important result is the mental model formulated according to the potential SAD patients. This specific group of university students have rarely been specifically studied in the context of both SAD and corresponding therapies. The mental model formulated is a key to understanding this group of people, and the prototype indicates a possible way to integrate VR and Sound Therapy, offering a pleasurable experience during the treatment.

7.3   Significance

The mental healthcare of the youngsters is a major one among all healthcare topics, particularly in the rapidly developing society. This study focuses on the university students who are on the way to starting social life. The integration and prototype are just possible primary experiments. Hopefully the mental model can help other researchers understand this group and implement different therapy systems.

7.4 Limitation

This study findings obtained for a limited number of 15 university students for the primary study to spot on the phenomenon. Due to limited research facility and resource, further professional cognitive scientists or musicians can be involved to enhance the study. The prototype is merely a primary approach to addressing SAD in the context of university student patients. Whether it can be applied to the treatment for other SAD patients still need to be further studied.

7.5 Prospect

Currently the application was built for Android Devices, which means the VR environment is only accessible with VR glasses such as Google Cardboard. In the future a more advanced and specialized VR platform can be further applied, such as Oculus or HTC VIVE, etc. In that way the whole system can be integrated with more types of interaction.

Acknowledgements. The authors wish to thank all the people who provided their time and efforts for the investigation. This research was funded by Guangdong Province Education Science Planning Project, "Research on Youth Psychological/Mind Models and Art Therapy Strategies: Taking Greater Bay Area University as an Example", grant number 2019GXJK196.

References

1. Horigome, T., et al.: Virtual reality exposure therapy for social anxiety disorder: a systematic review and meta-analysis. Psychol. Med. **50**(15), 1–11 (2020)
2. Lars, C., et al.: STUDY PROTOCOL: EXPOSURE IN VIRTUAL REALITY FOR SOCIAL ANXIETY DISORDER - a randomized controlled superiority trial comparing cognitive behavioral therapy with virtual reality based exposure to cognitive behavioral therapy with in vivo exposure. BMC Psychiatry (2019). https://doi.org/10.1186/s12888-020-2453-4
3. Bruno, H.: Virtual reality exposure therapy for social phobia. THÈSE NO 3351 (2005)
4. Andersson, G., Carlbring, P.: Social phobia social anxiety disorder. In: Draper, C., O'Donohue, W. (eds.) Stepped Care and e-Health. Springer, New York (2011). https://doi.org/10.1007/978-1-4419-6510-3_6
5. Dora, B., Antonia, L., Roberto, B., Emma, B., Fiorenzo, L.: Social anxiety and peer communication quality during adolescence: the interaction of social avoidance, empathic concern and perspective taking. Child Youth Care Forum **49**, 853–876 (2020). Springer Science + Business Media, LLC 2012
6. Mishkind, M.C., Norr, A.M., Katz, A.C., Reger, G.M.: Review of virtual reality treatment in psychiatry: evidence versus current diffusion and use. Curr. Psychiatry Rep. **19**(11), 80 (2017)
7. Francisco, J., et al.: Virtual reality treatment for public speaking anxiety in students. Advancements and results in personalized medicine. J. Pers. Med. **10**, 14 (2020)
8. Chesham, R.K., Malouff, J.M., Schutte, N.S.: Meta-analysis of the efficacy of virtual reality exposure therapy for social anxiety. Behav. Chang. **35**(3), 152–166 (2018)
9. Carl, E., et al.: Virtual reality exposure therapy for anxiety and related disorders: a meta-analysis of randomized controlled trials. J. Anxiety Disord. **61**, 27–36 (2019)

10. Ehud, B., Ronit, A., Iulian, I.: The effect of training with music on happiness recognition. J. Psychopathol. Behav. Assess. **34**, 458–466 (2012). Springer Science + Business Media, LLC 2012
11. Scherer, K.R.: Expression of emotion in voice and music. J. Voice **3**, 235–248 (1995)
12. Juslin, P.N., Laukka, P.: Communication of emotions in vocal expression and music performance: different channels, same code? Psychol. Bull. **129**, 770–814 (2003)
13. Lazarov, A., Pine, D.S., Bar-Haim, Y.: Gaze-contingent music reward therapy for social anxiety disorder: a randomized controlled trial. Am J. Psychiatry. **174**, 649–656 (2017)

Practical Use of Edutainment Systems for Science Museums with XR Technology

Hiroshi Suzuki[1]([⊠]) and Naoki Tubuku[2]

[1] Kanagawa Institute of Technology, Shimooguno 1030, Atsugi, Kanagawa, Japan
hsuzuki@ic.kanagawa-it.ac.jp
[2] Trigger Device Inc., Ogaki, Gifu, Japan
tnaoki@triggerdevice.com

Abstract. In recent years, various services using XR technology have been developing within commercial and public institutions, including the entertainment industry, to use technology to provide children with enjoyable experiences. Science museums, however, cannot rely simply on entertainment value, as they need to combine entertainment with content that contains educational themes. Educational XR systems generally involve the use of a smartphone or tablet terminal used to capture footage of markers or objects, after which moving images and/or 3D-models are shown on the terminal display. Through observing and interacting with this content, children can deepen their understanding of a given theme or idea. While such systems provide new and exciting opportunities for the activities that can be offered to children, implementing and operating them requires significant costs for science museums. In addition, as for the types of experiences that the XR system can provide, these can be difficult to understand without concrete experience, which can tend to lead into more passive use of the system such as simply observing content. In this paper, in order to offer solutions to these problems, we introduce XR+Crafting content that combines XR technology with creative activities. Through its use of XR technology, the XR+Crafting system proposed in this paper can not only reduce implementation and operation costs, but can also shift the relationship between children and the technology into one that is more active. This paper will also introduce an example of an interactive XR system that incorporates creative activities for children that can be used as content by science museums using XR technology. Building on these suggestions for practical use, we will provide guidelines for the implementation, design, and operation of XR technology at science museums using the XR+Crafting system.

Keywords: Science museum · AR · MR · Workshop

1 Introduction

Through various activities involving making things themselves, children are able to demonstrate their subjective self-expression while developing sensibilities as human beings such as how to observe and think deeply about things that go beyond simple pleasure and enjoyment [1]. It is generally accepted that computers provide novel and

© Springer Nature Switzerland AG 2021
M. M. Soares et al. (Eds.): HCII 2021, LNCS 12781, pp. 233–244, 2021.
https://doi.org/10.1007/978-3-030-78227-6_17

exciting opportunities for children's activities [2], which has resulted in the development of many different systems that encourage children to construct things themselves [3–5].

On the other Hand, In recent years, various services using XR technology have been developing within commercial and public institutions, including the entertainment industry, to use technology to provide children with enjoyable experiences. This is especially true at science museums, where the development of XR systems has been active incorporated width exhibits and themes. Some systems deploy markers via installing them on exhibits [6, 7], while others use head-mounted displays [8, 9]. There are also systems that use exhibits as checkpoints for stamp rallies that include these features [10, 11] and apps that transform places outside science museums into science museums [12, 13]. It has been reported in research results that educational effects are improved when systems such as those mentioned above attract interest and enthusiasm to themes and topics [14].

However, not many science museums are able to effectively implement such systems, likely due to the high costs of implementation and operation. Many systems using XR technology require relatively expensive equipment for each visitor engaged in the experience, such as individual PC or tablet terminals. One possible way around this is through the type of marker AR technology now used widely in society, making it possible for parents to install an app on their smartphones, for example, but even with this adaptation, not all children will be able to experience the system. Costs will also be further increased in cases where the content is an original creation by a science museum. While this is not limited to science museums, it is true that when considering the implementation of a system using original XR technology, the order will generally be placed with a typical XR production company, in which case a budget requirement of several tens of thousands of dollars is not uncommon. This decision between the content and the budget is a bit of a double-edged sword as well, because creating unique XR content involves spending a lot of money, but a small budget allocation will likely lead to very bland and mundane generalized content. Even if a museum does introduce this type of generalized content, it can be difficult to promote its increased usage to visitors, creating a risk that the system will not be well-used.

2 Motivation

In terms of operations following XR system implementation, staff members at science museums must be directly trained so that they can operate the system without difficulty. While most simple XR systems require no more than downloading and installing the app from the App Store, detailed explanations may be required regarding how to use the app or what can be done with the app, as well as how to deal with problems if the system stops working. It is also necessary to check whether there are any problems with the terminals and to check the mechanisms installed in the exhibits so that the system can continue to operate smoothly. As the number of terminals increase, the management costs of such maintenance also increase.

It is true that some science museums with large budgets may be able to overcome these challenges and implement their own systems or, in the case of commercial facilities focused largely on entertainment, these costs can be borne by customers. However, for science museums run as public facilities, charging high participation fees for activities and experiences flies in the face of their most fundamental and intrinsic policies.

Therefore, As one of the solutions to these problems, we propose XR+Crafting Contents, which combines XR technology with children's creative activities. In this paper, we introduce three XR contents that we have implemented in our science museum.

With these systems, children can be exposed to scientific topics through creative activities. In addition, the cost of the materials needed for the creative activities is low, and there is no need to install special applications on smartphones or other devices.

3   Case 1: Corotama System

3.1   Introduction of "Corotama System"

Mayutama is a children's toy that evolved from imomushi-korokoro, one of the mechanically-operated karakuri children's toys of Japan's Edo period. Since it is low-cost, safe and easy for anyone to make, it is still frequently chosen by science museums as a focus on hands-on events for children. Because *Mayutama* make strange movements when rolled, it is a lot of fun for children to roll them on slopes. At the *Mayutama* Handicraft Workshop Experience, participants (children) made *Mayutama* using colored paper or aluminum foil, then rolled their finished *Mayutama* through a course prepared by the science museum. We then developed a dedicated "Corotama System" of multiple proximity sensors installed to enable interactive productions according to the *Mayutama's* rolling trajectory. With such a dedicated course built with a partition acting as a wall, an interactive course could be set up via the installation of screens.

3.2   Corotama System: Overview

In order to use this system, children begin by making their own *Mayutama*. *Mayutama* can be made simply via putting marbles into a cylinder of aluminum foil, sealing it, placing the aluminum foil into a container, and shaking it vigorously up and down. While this is a very simple production process, the rhythm at which the container is shaken and the sound of the marbles hitting the container are very unique each time. The aluminum foil is formed within the container into an egg-like shape by the pounding of the marbles. Using the system, the rolling position and speed of the *Mayutama* are picked up by sensors, which then project a CG animation of these factors onto the background so that they children can see how their *Mayutama* rolls through enjoying the animation that displays this.

For this system, eight sensors are arranged along one lane, with 4 lanes arranged in order from the top down, making it possible therefore for sensors to generate 32 data points in one course. A USB camera was also installed at the start of the course to provide a variety of interactions such as switching the animation that is displayed and changing the tone at which it is played. The color of the *Mayutama* is detected using the image acquired by the USB camera, which is then used as a parameter to change the tone reproduced in the animation depending on color differences. We also devised a mechanism to change the inclination of the lane so that different tones would flow out according to changes in the rolling speed of the *Mayutama*. Figure 1 s shows the installation of the system implemented at the Science Museum. For the sensor lane, 32 QTR-1RC photo-reflective modules are used as sensors to detect the *Mayutama*. When id is given from 0–31 from the top and each sensor responds, the audio reproduction module produces a different tone. This tone is one that can be recognized as a song when sensors 0–31 respond in order. The image recognition/audio playback module sends the id from the sensors, the *Mayutama* color information obtained via image recognition, and tilt information from the lane to the animation playback module. The animation playback module then plays the animation at a predetermined sensor position based on the information it has received. As a result, sound and animation are reproduced right at the position where the *Mayutama* passes the sensor.

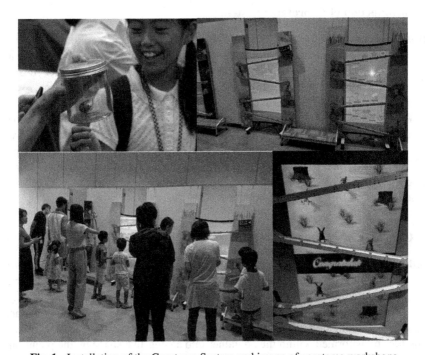

Fig. 1. Installation of the Corotama System and image of corotama workshops

3.3 The Creative Workshops Using the Corotama System

The creative workshops using this system were held at Science Hills Komatsu on August 24–25 in 2019. The first workshop involved free participation with no limits on participants. In the Free Workshop Experience, all visitors to the special exhibition room of our chosen venue Science Hills Komatsu were targeted for participation, There was no need to make reservations for the experience, and children were free to make their own *Mayutama* and play with the Corotama System at the event site. nor were there any restrictions based on factors such as age or capacity, making it easy for all to participate.

The average time spent at the experience was approximately 20 min per individual. In total, approximately 600 individuals made *Mayutama* and experienced the system within the time allotted.

3.4 Findings from Use of the Corotama System

Figure 1 shows images of the workshop that made use of the Corotama System. The focus of this workshop, *Mayutama*, is an easy object for anyone to create simply through a process of shaking the materials. The act of shaking also helped to appeal to the physicality of the participants. There was no age limit imposed on participation, so everyone from small children up to adults could be involved simultaneously. Many children made more than one *Mayutama*, meaning that they were probably very actively engaged in the activity if they were willing to go through making *Mayutama* multiple times. The animation displayed by the Corotama System was highly appreciated, with many children experiencing all prepared courses. It was possible to operate this system at low cost because cheap items (marbles and aluminum foil) were sufficient. Since the system operates automatically, a large number of staff members were not required to run the workshop, making it possible to have several staff members assisting participants with making *Mayutama*. Overall, we think that this system and the content used proved that even small children can become involved in the active making of objects.

4 Case 2: Kuru-Kuru Disc Tops

4.1 Introduction of "Kuru-Kuru Disc Tops"

Spinning tops have been common toys throughout history in many corners of the globe. In Japan, they are widely recognized as traditional Japanese toys dating back to the Edo period, evolving through the generations into the various popular forms such as the kyokugei-goma (performance tops), sakadachi-goma (revere standing tops), be-goma (flat coin-like tops) and others. Tops have a structure so simple that even very young children can make them. When constructing a top at home, one common material that can be used is a CD, which results in a top that turns quickly and accurately. Using CDs not only makes it easier to make tops that turn well, but they can be made more attractive through decoration using stickers or marker pens. From a more scientific perspective, the developers have created a "Koma scouter" that involves placing a colored nut onto the CD top in order to measure the degree of its rotation. Using the Koma scouter, each top produced by children can have its degree of rotation measured as a score, making it possible to utilize each top's parameters such as color, balance of the center of gravity, and value of the moment of inertia.

4.2 The Concept Behind This Content

Using the position of the nut placed on the CD, the Koma scouter created by we can measure the CD's center of gravity and moment of inertia, then present this as a score based on the top's degree of rotation. Through utilizing the Koma scouter in this way, characteristics of each to such as its degree of rotation and number of colors can be stored in the database. By using this detailed data gathered from each top stored in the database to create interactive content, displays relating to each top can be shown in multiple layers where the top spins. In other words, it is possible to present individual displays based on each different spinning, generating different production display. This workshop can be roughly divided into these three activities: 1. using an original top kit to create an original spinning top; 2. measuring the characteristics of a spinning top using a Koma scouter; 3. playing with spinning tops on an interactive stage.

Interactive Top Stage

The interactive top stage is a space where children can play with their original spinning tops. A display is placed on the floor of the spinning top stage and by spinning tops on this display, Animation effects of each spinning top are displayed interactively. The table possesses a QR code reader for selecting tops spinning on the table at the time, a USB camera for recognizing position and a color code of each rotating top, a top detection program that analyzes images from the USB camera, and a production program that displays animations based on detected XY coordinates and the parameters of each top.

4.3   The Creative Workshops Using the Kuru-Kuru Disc Tops System

The workshop "Kuru-kuru Disc Tops—Make and Play!" was held during summer vacation from August 10–18 in 2019 at the Toshiba Science Museum. The children who participated first received their original top creation kits at the reception desk, then created their own original tops with inspiration provided by the sample in the creation corner. Next, the top's scores were measured using the Koma scouter. Finally, participants played with the tops they had made by spinning them on the interactive top table.

For this event, we prepared three Koma scouters to measure scores of the tops as well as four interactive top tables. Figure 2 shows the children experiencing these activities. On the interactive top tables, animations can be clearly seen around the tops. Since each table was different, many children played at different tables. There were also children who played with two different tops. At the same time and even children who turned their tops upside down and spinning, there playing was something unexpected.

4.4   Findings from Use of "Kuru-Kuru Disc"

The method of making tops was only briefly explained at the reception of the event, but the experiencers were not confused, and children and adults created their own original tops. By presenting the spinning ability of tops to the experiencers with a "Koma scouter", it was seen that they enjoyed comparing the good and bad of tops created with family and friends who experienced. So, We Thought that having an objectively easy-to-understand index had the effect of activating communication between experienced people through crafting.

In aspect of science education, children are to listen to explanations from staff about how to improve the score and how a top can measure the spinning ability of a top, and to actually recreate the top many times based on those advices. By those activities were touched on the scientific elements of tops such as the moment of inertia and the moment

Fig. 2. Kuru-kuru Disc Tops workshop

of inertia. The staff of the science museum in charge of the event suggested that if this system could be used as a teaching tool in a lecture-style science class on the theme of the top, the mechanism of the rotation of the top could be conveyed in an easy-to-understand manner.

5   Case 3: SUMO SONIC

5.1   Introduction of "SUMO SONIC"

"SUMO SONIC" is the creative-based edutainment content that based on paper sumo wrestling. The way of playing traditional paper sumo wrestling are like a sumo wrestling by players tapping the stage with hands and making vibrations and pushing out each other paper sumo wrestlers from stage. However, in the "SUMO SONIC", players not generating vibrations by tapping the sumo stage by hand, but converts players voice as vibration by voice processing. Attempts to move the object by using vibration are deployed in various science toys. It is also made to extend how to playing by utilizing advanced technologies paper sumo wrestling.

5.2   The Concept Behind This Content

In this content, Children create their own original paper wrestlers. The child then wrestles with the paper sumo wrestling using voice vibration. Children can choose the wrestler they want to make from several paper wrestler templates. They can then color the template and assemble it easily. Paper Wrestlers are characterized by the fact that they do not require expensive materials, and can be made with familiar tools such as scissors, cutters, glue, and marker pens.

The top of the paper wrestlers established the AR marker, at the top of the arena to play the paper sumo to install a USB camera and projector. By recognizing the AR marker by utilizing this USB camera, it is possible to obtain position information of each paper wrestler. When the system can recognize the positions of the two paper wrestlers, it can project CG animation staging on the stage as the sumo match unfolds. The advantage of projection is that it can be easily changed to other themes. For example, by changing the template of a sumo wrestler to an object with a different theme, such as an animal, insect, or robot, a CG animation appropriate for each theme can be projected on the stage.

In the conventional paper sumo, first of all, put a wrestler of paper on top of the playing field made of cardboard, then players play by hitting the playing field by hand. On the other hand, in the present content, by shouting to a microphone, you can play a paper sumo wrestling by converting a wave of the voice to the vibration. This systems merit is able to play not only normal users but also the user who older people or cannot freely controlling for the hand by handicaps. Also, we thought, this system is very attractive for children. We use the players voice and the voice volume of the spectrum, as an element of effect animation. As a result, the generated animation that to work with paper sumo, system can have provided effective animation that linked with a game situation. Experience user of this system, it is necessary to issue a positively voice. The voice of the players, is believed to function as a means to invite another children to this content.

Fig. 3. SUMO SONIC workshop

5.3 The Creative Workshops Using SUMO SONIC System

We have to evaluate the effectiveness of this system, exhibited this system to the workshop event, was actually investigated the reaction of the children. The purpose of the experiment is to investigate whether the paper sumo imparted with paper sumo wrestling and AR by voice is accepted how the children. Was exhibited at the Fukushima Prefecture, Fukushima City workshop carnival in Fukushima 2017 was carried out in "facility KomuKomu to nurture the dream of a child." on March 8 and March 9, 2017. We used SUMO SONIC system of two in the same event. Also, we made a content as utilizing the AR technology. Content is of the "robot battle". Figure 3 shows the workshop and the paper wrestlers created by the children.

5.4 Findings from Use of the SUMO SONIC System

The children were free to use their creativity to create their own paper wrestlers. In the voice-activated paper sumo match, all the children were very loud. The match was very heated, and the children repeatedly played the game. From the interviews with the children after the experience, we learned that the main motivation for them to experience SUMMO SONIC was the loud voices of other players. This was in line with what we had expected when we designed this system. It was also the first time for most of the children to experience paper sumo by voice, and we found that they found paper sumo by voice more enjoyable than regular paper sumo. The use of AR was very well received, and seemed to make the SUMMO SONIC experience an extraordinary event. As for the science education aspect, many children wondered why the stage vibrated with their voices. This approach of using paper sumo to relate voice and vibration was thought to be very effective in getting the children interested in sound and vibration.

6 Edutainment Design Using XR+Crafting

As the three cases introduced in this paper suggest amidst the rapid progress and spread of XR technology, introducing XR technology within hands-on workshops at science museums has the potential to entice children to engage actively in creating real materials. The following is a summary of the common elements between the experiencer and the operator in implementing the three systems.

6.1 Experiencer Side

The following three elements are common to the experiencer side.

- The ability to participate at a low cost
- The inclusion of creative activities.
- There is no limit to the number of participants or their age.

The three systems discussed in this paper allow users to experience the XR system without the need for equipment such as smartphones or tablet devices. While each system created contains elements of entertainment, all were informed by scientific principles and ideas, which children seemed able to experience through their experiential engagement when creating original items and observing them in action. In addition, the interaction of the experience is structured in such a way that the experiencer does not need to learn to use the system, such as drawing pictures or doing crafts. Thus, it is important that there are few requirements for system participation. By incorporating manufacturing into the experience, children can become emotionally involved in their own work, transforming their experience of the XR content into a special experience. We thought that this is the element that allows children to actively participate in the system. More importantly, there is no limit to the number of people who can experience the content, nor to their age, allowing family and friends to participate in the content at the same time. Although learning is sometimes perceived as a formal and rigid image, with school education as the representative, some believe that informal experiences that include play that induce spontaneous behavior are important to elicit children's intellectual curiosity and interest in science [15]. It is said that the communication that arises from sharing experiences with parents, friends, and siblings is a factor that draws out interest and fascination in learning [16, 17]. From this point of view, XR+Crafting is characterized by the inclusion of the above three elements on the part of the experiencer.

6.2   Science Museum Side

XR+Crafting contents have the following three points in common for Science Museum side.

- No cost for installation
- Does not place a heavy burden on the operating staff
- Incorporating universal scientific themes

Table 1. The scientific elements and necessary materials of XR+Crafting

Content name	Scientific topic	Required materials
Corotama system	Friction, center of gravity	Aluminum foil, marbles
Kuru-kuru discs tops	Inertia, center of gravity	CDs, nuts
Sumo Sonic	Sound and vibration	Paper cups, cardboard

The three systems discussed in this paper are packaged and do not require a large installation cost for any of them. Furthermore, it can be set up in a science museum without any special knowledge or skills, and can be easily taken down after the event period. In addition, the system is designed in such a way that it requires very little training for the operating staff on how to use and operate the system. The activity of the experiencer is to create a work of art and to experience the system using that work of art. Since the interaction between the user and the system is simple, there are no complicated procedures or system requirements. This leads to a low cost of education on the part of the staff.

Each system incorporates a universal science theme. By using these "manufacturing experiences" as an introduction to science education and moving on to more detailed knowledge programs, we believe that they can be applied more effectively in science education. For example, with SUMO SONIC, it is thought that deeper understanding of the relationship between the functions of sound and vibration can occur through conducting it as a systematic workshop informed by specialized knowledge of sound. The universal science elements of the three contents and the materials required for the experiencers are shown in Table 1. The materials for each content can be obtained for less than 30 yen per person. This low cost of participation is an important factor for the management.

7 Summary

In this paper, we introduced XR+Crafting contents, which combines XR technology with creative activities, as an alternative to the conventional XR system that requires a lot of cost for installation and operation for science museums. The XR+Crafting contents, as a system using XR technology, can not only reduce installation and operation costs, but also change the relationship between children and technology into an active one. In addition, from the XR + Crafting contents we introduced, we presented three common elements for both the experiencer and the operator sides. By designing an XR system that meets these requirements and introducing it into a science museum, we can lead children to "making things" with an active attitude at a low cost of installation and operation. In the future, we would like to evaluate the educational effects of XR+Crafting by designing an educational program that conveys scientific themes in depth, using this system as an entrance to science education, and implementing it in many science museums.

References

1. Anna, C.: Creativity and Early Years Education: A lifewide foundation. Continuum. 1st edition, UK (2002)
2. Roschelle, J.M., Pea, R.D., Hoadley, C.M., Gordin, D.N., Means, B.M.: Changing how and what children learn in school with computer-based technologies. Child. Comput. Technol. **10**(2), 76–101 (2000)
3. Golsteijn, C., Hoven, E., Frohlich, D., Sellen, A.: Hybrid crafting: towards an integrated practice of crafting with physical and digital components. Pers. Ubiq. Comput. **18**(3), 593–611 (2013). https://doi.org/10.1007/s00779-013-0684-9
4. Igarashi, Y., Igarashi, T.: Designing plush toys with a computer. Commun. ACM **52**, 81–88 (2009)
5. Suzuki, H., Sato, H., Hayami, H.: Fight our shadow robot. In: ACM SIGGRAPH 2013 Studio Talk, Article No. 15. ACM (2013)
6. Silva, M., Assaf, R., Pollini, D., Morais, D.G., Teixeira, L.: The apprentice gaze - AR experience on serralves museum. In: ARTECH 2019 Proceedings of the 9th International Conference on Digital and Interactive, Article No. 93, pp. 1–4. ACM (2019)

7. Woods, E., Billinghurst, M.K., Looser, J., Aldridge, G., Brown, D.: Augmenting the science centre and museum experience. In: GRAPHITE 2004: Proceedings of the 2nd International Conference on Computer Graphics and Interactive Techniques in Australasia and South East Asia, pp. 230–236. ACM (2004).
8. Bone-hall. https://naturalhistory.si.edu/exhibits/bone-hall, Accessed 10 Feb 2021
9. Hunsucker, A.J., Baumgartner, E., McClinton, K.: Evaluating an AR-based museum experience. Interactions **25**(4), 66–68 (2018)
10. Zhang, S., Zhao, W., Wang, J., Luo, H., Feng, X., Peng, J.: Mixed-reality museum tourism framework based on HMD and fisheye camera. In: VRCAI 2016: Proceedings of the 15th ACM SIGGRAPH Conference on Virtual-Reality Continuum and Its Applications in Industry, vol. 1, pp 47–50. ACM (2016)
11. Alvermann, J.: Mobile media in the museum space: the example of the neanderthal museum's app "neanderthal+". In: UbiComp 2016: Proceedings of the 2016 ACM International Joint Conference on Pervasive and Ubiquitous Computing, pp. 1509–1512. ACM (2016)
12. Ceipidor, U.B., Medaglia, C.M., Perrone, A., Marsico, M.D.: A museum mobile game for children using QR-codes. In: IDC 2009: Proceedings of the 8th International Conference on Interaction Design and Children, pp. 282–283. ACM (2009)
13. AR TOUR OCEAN. https://www.arappli.com, Accessed 10 Feb 2021
14. Sharples, M., Corlett, D.: The design and implementation of a mobile learning resource. Pers. Ubiq. Comput. **6**(3), 220–234 (2002)
15. Radu, I.: Augmented reality in education: a meta-review and cross-media analysis. Pers. Ubiq. Comput. **18**(6), 1533–1543 (2014). https://doi.org/10.1007/s00779-013-0747-y
16. Roussou, M.: Learning by doing and learning through play: an exploration of interactivity in virtual environments for children. Comput. Entertain. **2**(1), 1–10 (2004)
17. Ahn, J., Clegg, T.L., Yip, J., et al.: Science everywhere: designing public, tangible displays to connect youth learning across settings. In: Proceedings IDC 2018, pp. 1–12. ACM (2019)

Immersive and Interactive Digital Stage Design Based on Computer Automatic Virtual Environment and Performance Experience Innovation

Chen Wang[✉]

South China University of Technology, Guangzhou 510006, China

Abstract. In recent years, it has been the forefront of the performing arts industry and academic research to integrate VR into the physical space of stage, so that the audience can get sensory immersive and interactive experience in the scene of mutual creation between the factual and the imaginary. This study combines the principle of Computer Automatic Virtual Environment (CAVE), a kind of immersive VR systems with theater stage space and develops an immersive interactive digital performance stage (VR-CAVE stage) that can be viewed by the audience with naked eyes, then applies it to the design and construction of an experimental small theater. Through the first experimental drama performance of the theater, it can be seen that the integration of immersive VR helps the stage to realize the new performance effect of four-dimensional space, the body represent and drive the scene, and deep immersion. Finally, the application prospect and development direction are pointed out.

Keywords: CAVE · Drama stage · Immersive interaction

1 Introduction

1.1 VR and Drama Stage

Throughout the history of dramatic art, it can be seen that every important change in its ideology, expression form and creation method is closely related to the new technology adopted at that time. Although the drama stage design styles are varied in different regions and periods, there are also relatively consistent and lofty artistic goals that are constantly pursued, that is, the synthesis of space, time and action. This synthesis was even regarded by Josef Svoboda, the famous stage artist, as the culmination of the development of stage design. In order to achieve this goal, the three-dimensional scenery system, flexible machinery, changing light projection…Each stage attempted to use the most advanced techniques of that time. In the digital information age, the application of Virtual Reality (VR) and other new media technologies can provide innovative solutions for the drama stage to continue to explore and realize this artistic goal, and also bring new formal language even innovative ideas to the drama.

M. M. Soares et al. (Eds.): HCII 2021, LNCS 12781, pp. 245–255, 2021.
https://doi.org/10.1007/978-3-030-78227-6_18

1.2 Multiple Ways of Integrating VR into Drama Stage

VR takes computer technology as the core, combined with related technology to generate digital environment that is highly approximate real environment in some aspects such as see, hear, and touch. With the help of necessary equipment, users can interact with objects in the digital environment, so as to generate feelings and experiences corresponding to the real environment in person. At present, the perceptual experience of VR users is mainly realized in two ways: Head-Mounted Display (HMD) or large fully immersive and semi-immersive projection systems, such as CAVE and Dome [1]. The former is equivalent to watching a desktop display, which is essentially a 2D window into a 3D world, while the latter provides the user with an actual perception in a 3D model or model environment. The combination of these two ways and dramatic art can give rise to three different forms of performance watching. Firstly, construct a completely virtual scene to interpret the drama content; Secondly, after recording the real theater performance, the audience on or off the scene can watch it by wearing video perspective HDM in the way of live or recorded broadcasting. Thirdly, computer-generated virtual elements are mixed into the real theater stage to varying degrees. For example, virtual images are projected on the screen or physical objects as stage setting, virtual actors or props. The audience is present at the same time to watch together with naked eyes or through optical perspective HMD. The last approach is often seen as an attempt to integrate Augmented Reality (AR) or Mixed Reality (MR) into the theatrical stage, as it is usually represented by covering virtual digital images on the physical stage.

1.3 Theoretical Model of Immersive and Interactive VR Drama Stage

Computer Automatic Virtual Environment (CAVE) is a kind of room-style visual collaborative environment based on multi-channel synchronization technology, three-dimensional space correction algorithm and stereo display technology [2]. In theory, the system can provide a six-sided cube projection display space of the same room size for multiple participants (Fig. 1). All participants at the same time totally are immersed in a virtual simulation environment, surrounded by a 3D stereo projection panoramic image. With the help of the corresponding VR interaction equipment (such as data gloves, position tracker, force feedback device, etc.), participants get an immersive high-resolution stereo audio-visual image and six-degree-of-freedom interaction experience. There are mainly two kinds of user participation experience in CAVE: firstly, naked eye viewing, through motion-sensing camera to realize human interaction with the virtual environment; Secondly, people can interact with the virtual environment by using stereoscopic glasses and handheld devices. Although the latter provides a greater sense of immersion for participants, the former approach is more comfortable and natural for users who don't need to wear a device and is suitable for multiple participants to be present at the same time. By combining the CAVE of the first experience mode with the 3D physical stage of the theater, a kind of immersive interactive digital performance stage, referred to as VR-CAVE stage, can be designed and developed for naked eye viewing by the audience.

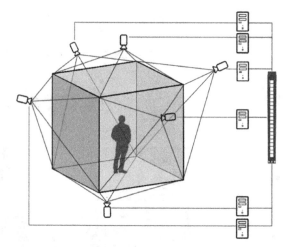

Fig.1. VR-CAVE system

Panorama is the total of all the surroundings observed by the observer at a relatively fixed position. On the stage, the virtual environment in which the drama takes place, namely the virtual world scene in which the actors are placed, can be regarded as a hemispherical or globular virtual panorama with the actors as the center of the circle. The length, width and height 3D space interfaces of the stage are respectively corresponding to the CAVE projection interface and the digital panoramic scene is presented as a whole. Actors are not only in the drama scene surrounded by digital panorama, but also can use body movements to drive the scene to produce visual real-time change or overall transformation. Actors can freely roam in the scene, the scene changes in real time with actor's movement, and the audience can watch the performance with naked eyes and feel immersed. As the audience facing side of the stage must be opened under normal circumstances, the five faces of the semi-enclosed CAVE correspond to the back, top, side and ground of the stage respectively. Theoretically, it is also possible to match the whole enclosed CAVE with the whole indoor space of the theater, so that both actors and audience are surrounded by the panoramic drama scene and interact with it in real time (Fig. 2).

2 Realization of VR-CAVE Stage Theory Model

2.1 Technical Architecture of VR-CAVE Stage Implementation Scheme

VR-CAVE stage has been applied in the design and construction of "Robot Performance Digital Small Theater" (hereinafter referred to as "Small Theater") in Harbin Institute of Technology (Shenzhen). In 2018, the experimental drama "The Bean Sprout that Came to Shenzhen" was created, rehearsed and premiered in it. The drama tells the story of the protagonist, "Bean Sprout", who travels thousands of miles to Shenzhen to find his mother with the help of various robot friends. This is a multi-time closely combined,

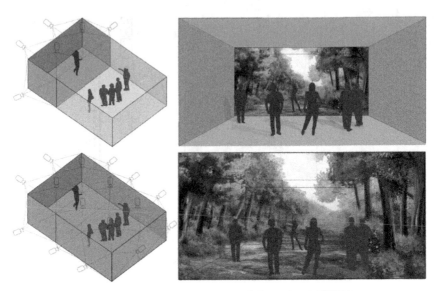

Fig.2. Application of semi-enclosed and fully enclosed CAVE in stage.

no round, interactive stage robot drama performance work. The work combines VR, human-computer interaction and other new technologies to assist the performance of real people and bionic robots. The aim is to try the crossover integration of modern drama stage performance and technological products, and to express the realistic and surreal scenes overlapping to promote the development of the plot in a meaningful artistic perspective. The Small Theater transforms an amphitheater with an area of about 300 m^2 inside a university teaching building. It is mainly divided into three interlinked areas: the performance stage, the auditorium and the operator control (Fig. 3).

Considering the actual limitations of indoor space size, top lighting, projection and other factors, and the demands of actors' performances and scenes in the script, the theoretical model of VR-CAVE stage was adjusted and further developed in the implementation scheme. The whole stage technical framework is mainly divided into three modules: panoramic production, scene control and scene presentation. The three modules cooperate with each other to form a system. As shown in (Fig. 4). Firstly, the high-resolution panoramic video scene is produced by panoramic camera shooting or 3D animation, then loaded into the Unity3D engine and presented as a whole in the three-dimensional stage setting. Secondly, action information of actors is captured by Kinect motion sensor camera, transmitted to Unity3D and transformed into interactive commands to drive the panoramic video scene in the setting system, the virtual actors, scenery or props in the holographic screen, and make them interact in real time. Finally, a host is used as a terminal operation platform to centrally control the play or switch of projected materials in the stereoscopic setting system of the stage.

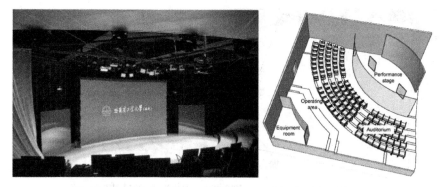

Fig. 3. The interior of the small theater and its functional layout

2.2   Implementation of VR-CAVE Stage

Three-Dimensional Stage Setting System. The stage setting system consists of an arc screen as the background, two holographic screens as the middle scene, a ground and a veil as the foreground. The virtual setting images in front, middle and rear are super-imposed with the real actors to form a multi-level, strong sense of spatial depth and three-dimensional stage setting effect (Fig. 4).

Background Stage. Projection arc screen with strong sense of enclosure serves as the stage background. In order to avoid the mutual interference between actors, props and the front projection light, the arc screen is back projected by several high-lumen short-throw projectors installed in the rear attached platform. The hardware graphics fusion device integrates the projected images, which is controlled by a high-performance graphics processing workstation.

Mid-Stage. The middle position is the core area for actors to perform their actions. The setting factors include the horizontal stage floor and the movable transparent holographic screen on the vertical floor.

The floor scenery of the stage performance area and part of the audience area is projected by multiple projectors above the stage and integrated into a whole through software, which is controlled by a computer host. Two groups of projections are projected from the upper part of the stage from two different angles and completely coincide with each other on the ground, so as to eliminate the phenomenon that actors, props and other entities block the projection light and thus reduce the image of the ground. Two groups of projections were projected from the upper part of the stage with two different angles and completely overlapped on the ground, so that actors, props and other entities will not block the projected light. The combination of the horizontal stage floor projection and the vertical background arc screen projection is the key to present the dramatic panoramic video scene. The junction of the arc screen and the ground needs special structural design and fine construction to ensure that the gap between the ground, the skirting and the arc screen is reduced as far as possible. In addition, the floor of the stage and the audience area adopts the optimized washable rigid material, making it

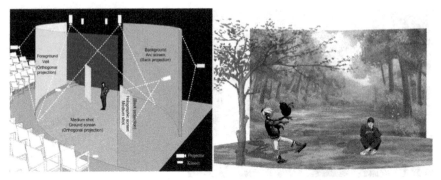

Fig. 4. Stage setting system and its superimposed effect

not only dirt-resistant and durable, but also able to undertake the top projection with high brightness and high definition. Based on the background image of the arc screen, the difference of graphics, brightness and color of the ground projection is adjusted by the fusion software to make them consistent with the image of the arc screen, so as to achieve seamless integration of the two parts.

In addition to the ground scenery, the stage also includes two transparent holographic screens, which are rotated to the corresponding positions by mechanical derrick during the performance. Two projectors under the control of a computer host project holographic video materials respectively to represent actors, scenery or props in a virtual way.

Foreground Stage. The foreground screen is located between the performance stage area and the audience area, and the transparent veil is used as the projection material. Multiple projectors under the control of a single computer host project and integrate the picture through fusion software to present the close shot effect of the drama scene. Due to the gap of the veil itself, the light projection effect of the front and back is completely different. When the light is cast from the front, it appears as it really is, a completely opaque image or color of its own. When the objects behind the screen are under light and the front of the screen is in a state of no light, the veil becomes transparent, and the audience can see the actors, scenery and props behind the screen through the veil.

Stage Panoramic Video Scene Production. Panoramic video is a VR technology with low cost, high visual performance. According to the plot needs of the script, the real scene that meets the needs of the drama scene is selected, then the 360° panoramic camera is used to shoot the scene from multiple angles, and the panoramic video is produced through the synthesis software and saved in the form of a stream file. For the scenes that are difficult to find or not realistic, we use Maya, 3DMax and other three-dimensional computer software to model, and then edit and synthesize in the video post-processing software. Furthermore, we conduct color correction, special effects, stereo sound effects and other processing, to create three-dimensional simulation of a panoramic video scene. The shooting and production of panoramic video scenes need to pay attention to three "consistency": Firstly, the scene is consistent with the audience's perspective; Secondly, the scene is presented in the same dimension as the actors on the stage. Thirdly, the lighting in the scene is the same as the lighting on the stage. Panoramic video scenes are loaded into Unity3D and presented in a three-dimensional way through projection in the semi-enclosed stage space composed of the arc screen of the stage background and the ground of the mid-scene. Button identification is made for each panoramic video scene whose configuration information is scenes.xml, which is sequentially placed on the main interface of Unity3D. Operators can click the button to play in turn according to the round.

Stage Setting Interactive Control. In order to make the actors feel free during the performance and not affect the costume requirements of the actors, they tend to choose the non-wearable and wireless connection motion capture equipment, so Kinect motion sensing camera is selected in the realization scheme. In order to enhance the robustness of motion recognition, multiple fused and calibrated Kinect are installed above and on both sides of the stage to provide point cloud, so as to identify specific body movements of actors more sensitively and accurately. By using the plug-in of Unity3D called Kinect Wrapper. Unity package, we can put the human bone node information accessed by Kinect into the Unity3D. According to the pre-set instruction library, Unity3D triggers the corresponding image change in the same scene or the switch between different scenes with a specific action.

Stage Setting System Control. In the LAN connection, we select a host as terminal control operation platform of the whole stage setting system, each part of the setting projection control host is connected to it through the LAN, by its unified control. The front, middle and rear stage setting can be controlled as a whole or can be transformed into a single panel display device to be controlled separately to meet the needs of different stage performance scenes.

3   Implementation Effect of VR-CAVE Stage

Compared with other VR theater viewing methods, VR-CAVE stage is more comfortable and natural way for audience and actors because they don't need to wear devices. It is suitable for many people to be present at the same time. It also continues the core feature of the drama, simultaneous presence and real-time communication between actors and audience. Through the performances of the experimental drama premiere in small theater and observations and interviews to the director, actors and audience after rehearsals and show, it can be seen that VR -CAVE stage express technical advantages of VR, "3I"-- Imagination, Interactivity, and Immersion. VR-CAVE stage promotes the theater stage to realize the integration of space, time and actions in a unique way, bringing audio-visual effects and deeply immersive viewing experience that are different from the past to the audience, which is embodied in the following three aspects.

3.1   The Four-Dimensional Space

It is the drama space that truly achieves the synthesis of space and time, namely the four-dimensional space. Although digital images have gradually replaced the traditional perspective painting setting in the current drama stage, most of them follow the perspective painting method of two-dimensional representation of three-dimensional. As a result, no matter how three-dimensional the visual effect is, it is actually difficult to be compatible with three-dimensional and real actors due to its two-dimensional and virtual attributes. Every time the actors approached the setting, the three-dimensional illusion created by the two-dimensional perspective immediately weakened or even disappeared. Therefore, the actors' performance was forced to the shallow part of the stage, and the far-reaching part became the performance forbidden area. VR-CAVE stage integrates digital panoramic video with the stage space interface, especially long neglected stage floors with actual physical depth are activated. The stage floors, as a horizontal set and integrated with the vertical set, displays three-dimensional, dynamic and interactive digital panoramic video as a whole, enabling actors to perform in the three-dimensional space, and achieving the space-time feeling of the roles in the scene. The imagination advantage of VR can freely construct a broad and imaginable environment, so that the drama scene can be extended in the small theater's stage with limited space and equipment. (Figure 5) shows a series of three-dimensional rendering effect of panoramic video scenes of drama on the stage.

3.2 Body Represent and Drive the Scene

Actors' actions contain space and time, and the stage space needs to follow the actors' actions and coordinate with the drama. In the past, restricted by the technical conditions, the changes of the scene and the coordination of actors' actions and sounds needed to be rehearsed repeatedly in advance to match the effect. During the performance, the backstage personnel played according to the preset process, and the actors cooperated with actions set by the rehearsal to ensure the performance effect. Or, the actors fully arouse the imagination of the audience through the hypothetical means of performing actions and other symbolic hints, such as the performance feature of the body represent and drive the scene in traditional Chinese drama. The interactivity strength of VR emphasizes the operational degree of objects in the virtual environment and the natural degree of getting feedback from the environment. In the VR-CAVE stage, actors and audience realize real-time and active visual and auditory interaction with digital scenes, virtual actors or props through their own body movements, so that actors can grasp the performance rhythm more autonomously. For example, the actors' splashing and washing actions stimulate ripples and water sounds on the water surface. Likewise, the actor left footprints while walking on the beach. What's more, the actor imitates the gesture of pressing the elevator button to trigger the panoramic video playback, which looks like the actual lift in the elevator. At present, the performance of non-wearable and wireless transmission motion capture devices such as Kinect motion-sensing camera needs to be improved. At present and in the future, the field of human-computer interaction technology is constantly exploring the use of human gestures, behaviors and movements to achieve more direct and natural interactive technical means and devices. This technological development trend helps actors more freely integrate physical vitality into virtual drama scenes.

Fig. 5. A series of three-dimensional rendering effect of panoramic video scenes of drama on the stage.

3.3 Deep Immersion

Immersion -- making people feel like they are present rather than absent. The theatrical stage and theater itself are illusionary Spaces that can be immersed in for the purpose of temporarily separating actors and audiences from the real world and entering the virtual theatrical environment. The immersion of VR makes users seem to be completely in the virtual environment and enhance the realistic experience of active participation by perceiving and manipulating various objects in the VR world. The panoramic video scenes of drama presented on the stage of VR-CAVE and even in the interior of the theater can cover all the visual fields of actors and audiences, thus generating the potential feeling of being separated from the outside world and immersed in the theater space and time. If panoramas are designed to create a high level of immersion and presence (an "immersive" emotional cue), these emotions can be further enhanced by interaction with a "living" environment in "reality" [3]. The scene of multi-channel surround sound is accompanied by visual interaction. As shown in (Fig. 5), the sound effects such as ripple of water, robot dialogue, wave beating on the shore, elevator motor and other sound effects recorded on the spot or combined in the post-production play a key auxiliary role in creating a sense of presence and immersion during the performance and emphasize the visual impression. Both the audience and the actors can be involved in the interaction with the scene. The "fourth wall" between the actors and the audience is broken, and the audience is transformed from mere spectators into empathetic experiencers and even participants of the plot, which further enhances the subjective feeling of immersive experience.

4 Application Prospect of VR-CAVE Stage

VR-CAVE stage is one of the ways for VR to integrate into physical theater and live performance. In the past, limited by venue area, equipment and facilities and other material conditions, small theatres could not meet the needs of complex scenes and props. VR-CAVE stage can help small theaters break through the material limitations in this respect and adapt to the plays with complex plot content and frequent changes of location and time, thus lowering the threshold for theater appreciation and enabling it to enter various public Spaces such as campus and community. VR-CAVE stage itself has the technical characteristics of modularity and unlimited extension, which can provide digital, integrated and interactive panoramic scene solutions for drama stages and theaters of different scales. The functional characteristics of VR-CAVE stage also enable it to be used in a variety of complex functions besides as a performance place, so that the space utilization rate of the theater can be greatly improved. For example, with the feature of fusion of people and scenes, the speaker can play through gesture control software when the small theater is used as a lecture hall. Or as a multimedia classroom, teachers and students can realize embodied cognitive situational teaching by being in a three-dimensional scene and interaction. With the popularity of 5G network, the stage can not only realize the same stage in different places for drama performance, but also realize multi-party remote immersive conference and lecture, virtual live broadcast and other functions.

5 Conclusion

Drama in different periods has always absorbed the cultural and scientific achievements provided by the era, thus reflecting different forms. With the improvement of computer, display, motion capture and other technical equipment surrounding VR, and the reduction of cost and maintenance, the exploration and application of VR and its derivative AR and MR on the drama stage will continue to heat up, and the creation means and realization effect will also be constantly enriched and optimized. Through the combination of multi-channel perception and dynamic monitoring, human-computer interaction, physiological or psychological data sensing and other cutting-edge technologies to achieve visual, auditory, touch, smell and other multi-channel, multi-sensory immersive and interactive performance experience, is becoming the leading development direction of the performing arts industry and related research. This will not only influence the form of drama in the form language, but also promote the development of the drama form of "immersive and interactive drama", or bring about a change in the more fundamental relationship form of "time, space and action" for the drama art.

Acknowledgements. This paper is supported by Youth Fund Project of Humanities and Social Science, Ministry of Education of the people republic of China (17YJC760087).

References

1. Aukstakalnis, S.: Practical Augmented Reality: A Guide to the Technologies, Applications, and Human Factors for AR and VR, 1st edn. Addison-Wesley Professional, Boston (2016)
2. Nan, X., Zhang, Z., Zhang, N., Guo, F., He, Y., Guan, L.: V design: a CAVE-based virtual design environment using hand interactions. J. Multimodal User Interfaces **8**(4), 367–379 (2014). https://doi.org/10.1007/s12193-014-0168-x
3. Grau, O.: Virtual Art: From Illusion to Immersion, 1st edn. The MIT Press, Cambridge (2004)

Research on Virtual Reality for Intelligent Sculpting Teaching Experience of Printmaking Art in Primary and Secondary Schools

Ke Zhang and Lan Lin[✉]

School of Design, South China University of Technology,
Guangzhou 510006, People's Republic of China

Abstract. This paper introduces that when VR technology and printmaking are applied to art education in ordinary primary and secondary schools, students' contact with emerging technologies would help expand the learning thinking and enthusiasm, and would also help students' learning and relieve teachers' teaching pressure. Nowadays, printmaking, as a major part of art, also occupies an important position in art teaching in primary and secondary schools. Traditional printmaking teaching cannot be separated from the existence of the laboratory. The laboratory is the foundation of printmaking art whether it is woodcut printmaking, silk screen printmaking, copperplate printmaking or lithography. However, according to the investigation, it is found that the current printmaking laboratories in primary and secondary schools are not fully equipped, and some art teachers are not majoring in printmaking, which makes our teenagers and children know little about the art of printmaking. Therefore, VR smart print teaching research based on Unity3D is particularly important, which brings fresh blood to the art education industry. In view of the lack of professional printmaking laboratories and the lack of professional printmaking teachers in primary and secondary schools in China, this paper takes printmaking teaching as the research object, and writes corresponding C# scripts as the technical support based on Unity3d game engine and 3Dmax as the relevant software support. During this period, LIDAR lenses in iPad2020pro and the app "3D Scanner" are used to scan local real scenes. The construction of virtual scenes is enhanced by transforming the model into some virtual scenes. Students use VR helmets and sensing handles to simulate the teaching state of virtual prints. This paper covers my research objectives, research contents and lists some computer C# scripts when I used Unity3d to simulate student experiments in printmaking laboratory.

Keywords: Teaching experience · Printmaking art · Primary and secondary schools

1 Introduction

On October 13, 2020, the Central Committee of the Communist Party of China (CPC) and the State Council issued the General Plan for Deepening Education Evaluation Reform

© Springer Nature Switzerland AG 2021
M. M. Soares et al. (Eds.): HCII 2021, LNCS 12781, pp. 256–267, 2021.
https://doi.org/10.1007/978-3-030-78227-6_19

in a New Era, which pointed out the improvement of aesthetic education evaluation. The General Plan incorporates elementary and middle school students' study of music, art, calligraphy, and other art courses, as well as their participation in school-organized art practice activities, into academic requirements, intending to promote students' formation of an artistic hobby, enhancing their artistic literacy, and comprehensively improving their ability to feel, express, appreciate and create beauty. The program intends to explore the inclusion of art subjects in the secondary school examination reform pilot, promote colleges and universities to include public art courses and art practice in the talent training program, and implement a credit management system in the teaching process, and only students can graduate after completing the required credits. The document fully and effectively shows that the art education business in China should receive more attention, and art educators should bring a different educational experience as well as better curriculum results to students by combining scientific methods.

Today's society can also be regarded as an intelligent society, and in the context of 5G technology, virtual reality technology has become one of the most popular technologies. As a product of this modern information era, VR has a good sense of immersion and experience can bring people a different experience. In recent years, VR technology has been widely used in various aspects of medical, military, education, and games and has been fully recognized. China's Ministry of Education released the "Thirteenth Five-Year Plan for Education Informatization" in 2016, mentioning that "education informatization is ushering in a major historical development opportunity, and efforts are being made to expand the coverage of high-quality educational resources by means of informatization." Therefore, in the general environment of education informatization, the development of Unity3D-based VR education programs has also received wide attention from the education community.

Chinese printmaking has long occupied an important position in Chinese art. The unique "knife sense" and "wood sense" of Chinese printmaking have made it an independent artistic value in the history of Chinese culture and art. Nowadays, as a major part of art studies, printmaking occupies an important position in the art teaching of primary and secondary schools. For the traditional teaching of printmaking, the presence of a laboratory is indispensable. Whether it is wood-block prints, screenprints, copper prints, or lithographs, the laboratory is the foundation of printmaking art. However, according to the survey results, primary and secondary schools are not well-equipped with printmaking laboratories, and some of the art teachers do not specialize in printmaking, which makes our young children not know much about the traditional art of printmaking. Given this, Unity3d-based VR wisdom printmaking teaching research is particularly important, which is also expected to inject fresh blood into the modern art education industry [1].

On September 06, 2020, a new exploration of Guangdong's "Strengthening Teacher Quality Project" in the new era was featured in a ten-year special report on the National Training Program released by the Ministry of Education [2]. It shows that during this year's epidemic, all Guangdong teachers' workshops developed online courses and conducted online guidance for primary and secondary schools in the province, leading the development of school education in special times. This initiative also fully affirms the necessity of combining virtual reality technology in printmaking teaching. In this special period and special situation, the development of printmaking teaching platform based on unity3D technology also has a more important teaching value and significance. Through the virtual simulation printmaking teaching system, students can not only truly experience the combination of art and technology but also have more latitude of creative experience.

2 Method

In this study, I used the methods of literature survey and comparative study. By searching the keywords about virtual reality and experimental research from the Internet, 49 academic journals, 81 dissertations, and 6 conferences were retrieved. And the disciplines involved include computer software and computing, educational theory and educational management, architectural science and engineering, automation technology, art calligraphy sculpture and photography, medical education, and medical fringe, respectively. Among them, the virtual reality research papers on fine arts only accounted for two, accounting for a relatively small number.

A total of 1189 documents were retrieved by searching the theme "Virtual reality and Art", and the time span was "2010–2020" search keyword "Virtual reality and Art". Of these, 11 are about virtual reality technology and art education. By analyzing the contents of the literature, we can get the present situation of the development of virtual reality technology, the efficiency of the space sense of art education, the development of the game of art education, and the feasibility of the application of virtual reality technology in art education. This provides a good research premise and background for my research object, Virtual reality Technology and printmaking Teaching.

3 Literature Review

3.1 Current Status of Domestic and International Research

Thanks to the development of today's scientific information technology, virtual reality technology has received" technical support and a favorable development environment. The combination of derivation with teaching has received wide attention from scholars at home and abroad. In the Action Plan for Education Informatization 2.0 proposed in 2018, it is also mentioned that "information technology and intelligent technology should be integrated into the whole process of education to promote improved teaching, optimized management, and enhanced performance."

But even so, virtual technology in China is still a marginal discipline at the crossroads of many disciplines, and the pool of professional talents is far less developed than in foreign countries. Besides, the direction of focus is also different at home and abroad. In comparison, domestic research on virtual reality and educational learning are not as deep as foreign virtual learning research, so there are still many aspects and excellent projects that can be learned from foreign research. In the next section, I will review the relevant research at home and abroad in terms of cases and data.

3.2 A Review of Relevant Domestic Research

At present, most of the domestic content for the combination of virtual reality technology remains focused on pedagogy, accounting for 76.11%, followed by library, intelligence and literature, and computer application science, respectively, accounting for 10.72% and 5.51%, respectively.

The keywords "virtual reality" and "printmaking" yielded a total of three papers, of which only one, "Analysis of a Virtual Printmaking Studio Based on Mobile Terminals," was more in line with the topic of this study. The remaining two papers are almost not related to the field of virtual reality technology. Regarding the actual development cases of virtual reality and art, the platforms I checked were bilibili and the official unity platform. The areas involved are VR painting through the use of Google's virtual reality software or other artistic creations. Few of them are related to the field of printmaking and printmaking teaching board. I found a project called "VR Virtual Interaction with Foshan Woodblock Prints" that provides an example of how this research could be implemented. However, the project is mainly a game experience. It does not involve the professional printmaking lab section, but more of an introduction to the development and culture of woodblock printmaking to the audience.

The "Foshan Wooden Board Year Painting VR Virtual Interactive" presents a first-person perspective into the wooden board year painting game by using 3d modeling to build the virtual game world and adds knowledge-based game levels to learn the knowledge of wooden board year painting in the process of passing. Figure 1 and Fig. 2 are the screenshots of the game interface in this virtual interactive game.

Fig. 1. New Year picture virtual game into the interface

3.3 Literature Review of Relevant Foreign Studies

A survey of foreign research was conducted by searching the keywords Virtual reality and experimental research in CALIS foreign language journals to obtain 162012 articles, of which 41973 articles were published in the decade from 2011 to 2021. By reviewing the keywords and abstracts of the literature, the general characteristics of foreign

Fig. 2. New Year picture virtual game asking interface

research directions are education research-oriented, cross-disciplinary and interdisciplinary research nature is more obvious, and the articles published in 2016 and 2017 increased faster.

However, among the title information, Woodcut only retrieved 15 articles according to the include search criteria of Virtual reality and printmaking, and these 15 articles were published before 2007, providing little research value.

So virtual research on printmaking labs is still generally low, but there are still more cases about traditional labs and labs in other disciplines involved. We learned about VR virtual interaction labs abroad by reviewing an interview titled "Interview with the Founder of Stanford University's VR Interaction Lab: How Virtual Reality Affects Reality." In an interview with Jeremy Bailenson, founder of the VR Interaction Lab at Stanford University, he argues that the VR industry is now maturing and can be applied to new scenarios, including environmental conservation and heritage preservation and the treatment of PTSD.

One of the studies was an environmental study on the Italian island of Ischia, which was based on ecosystem data from the island of Ischia and made into a VR-ready video. The video demonstrates the impact of CO_2 on the ecosystem and shows what the ocean will look like in 50 years. They took the 7-min video to high schools and universities to test it and set up a permanent experience at the San Jose Museum of Technology to raise awareness of how climate change will affect us all.

3.4 Visual Analysis of Domestic and International Virtual Learning Research Hotspots

Research hotspots are articles discussing their topical issues with a high number of studies and intrinsic relationships within a certain period of time. By reviewing the literature, the word frequency distribution of the keywords of virtual learning research literature included in domestic and foreign core journals can be obtained in Table 1 [3].

Table 1. Word frequency distribution of keywords of virtual learning research literature included in core journals at home and abroad

No.	Keywords	Frequency	Centrality	No.	Keywords	Frequency	Centrality
1	Virtual learning communities	135	0.44	11	Learners	8	0
2	Virtual learning environments	38	0.25	12	Virtual learning teams	8	0
3	Virtual reality	35	0.14	13	Deep learning	7	0
4	Social network Analysis	20	0.05	14	College library	7	0.04
5	Virtual learning	18	0.06	15	Virtual environment	6	0
6	Learning environments	15	0.17	16	Teacher professional development	6	0.03
7	Influencing factors	11	0.07	17	Knowledge building	6	0
8	Virtual communities	9	0.07	18	Learning activities	5	0
9	Virtual reality technology	9	0	19	Online education	5	0
10	Distance education	9	0	20	e-learning	8	0.17

4 Virtual Reality and Printmaking

4.1 Exploring the Integration Path of Virtual Reality Technology and Printmaking Teaching

Compared with traditional printmaking lab teaching, the addition of virtual reality technology breaks conventional thinking and brings students and classrooms a more technological experience. At the same time, it can also enable primary and secondary schools that are not equipped with experimental equipment for print-making machines to allow students to understand the principles and process of printmaking better. We will use the unity3d system platform to build an interactive virtual platform for the printmaking lab based on the total system design of U3D, which can be put into practical use. This study will be conducted after the students enter the printmaking lab to learn the safety instructions and the initial system of tool placement in the printmaking lab, and then perform the professional simulation. The study of virtual printmaking in the printmaking lab will involve the use of handle sense to start, engrave, color, align, and dry virtual prints, as well as the c# programming of a series of actions and the creation of the corresponding model rendering.

In the virtual unity engine, it is necessary to add rigid body physics components to all objects and to add matching scripts for the corresponding actions. For example, scripts for picking up objects, scripts for carving objects, and virtual mechanics changes of wooden boards when they are carved with a printmaking knife in hand. The corresponding programming work was also written as part of this study. In the preliminary stage, the printmaking machine's virtual model is created by using 3Dmax, and the model is rendered. Importing local models and writing independent scripts for physical operation. In the middle and later stages, the proposed problem is to transform the physical buttons of the PC side of the original project induction into the physical buttons of the VR remote control handle and the export of virtual reality.

4.2   The Basis of Work for This Study

Hardware configuration iPad2020pro in the LIDAR lens and "3D Scanner" app to carry out local realistic scene scanning by modifying the conversion to part of the virtual scene. As well as through the VR handle and headset (HTC VIVE, Occulus, etc.) operation using the script ChTrack.cs and Move.cs to achieve. ChTrack.cs script is used to sense the movement of the x, y, z-axis on the helmet and export the value. move.cs script is used to control the position change of the main camera, using deright. ChTrack.cs when the transform component of this script information to obtain the direction of movement, so as to achieve the helmet rotation control experience in the virtual reality world to move the direction, and the use of the handle keys to achieving the purpose of walking back and forth, as well as the corresponding virtual screen button to provide some knowledge of the question and answer options.

4.3   The C# Script Used in This Study

At present, the research is in the preliminary stage of progress, the c# script written is not completely comprehensive. I have researched the script is listed below.

When clicking any button unity system backend engine can detect the button as well as the mouse.

// Update is called once per frame.

```
void Update()
{
//
if ( Input.GetKey (KeyCode.A))
{
Debug.Log (" GetKey:A ");
}
if ( Input.GetKeyUp (KeyCode.A))
{
Debug.Log (" GetKeyUp:AUp ");
}
if ( Input.GetKeyDown (KeyCode.A))
{
Debug.Log ("G etKeyDown:ADown ");
}
if ( Input.GetMouseButton (0))
{
Debug.Log ("MouseLeft");
}
if ( Input.GetMouseButtonUp (0))
{
Debug.Log ("MouseLeft Up");
}
if ( Input.GetMouseButtonDown (0))
{
Debug.Log ("MouseLeft Down");
}
```

Code 2 has been implemented to move the code, detect the transform component in the script, and combine with the world coordinate axis to move.

```
void Update() {
if( Input.GetKey (KeyCode.W))
{
m_ Transfrom.Translate (Vector3.forward * 0.1f,  Space.World );
}
if ( Input.GetKey (KeyCode.S))
{
m_ Transfrom.Translate (Vector3.back * 0.1f,  Space.World );
}
if ( Input.GetKey (KeyCode.A))
{
m_ Transfrom.Translate (Vector3.left * 0.1f,  Space.World );
}
if ( Input.GetKey (KeyCode.D))
{
m_ Transfrom.Translate (Vector3.right * 0.1f,  Space.World );
}
```

Code 3 has been implemented to add rigid body components to the object to achieve the corresponding physical effects.

```
void Start()
{
m_ Rigidbody= gameObject.GetComponent <Rigidbody>();
m_ Transform= gameObject.GetComponent <Transform>();
}
```

Code 4 has been implemented to detect whether students have entered the classroom,

```
{
// Start is called before the first frame update
void OnTriggerEnter(Collider coll)
{
Debug.Log ("Student Enter" + coll.gameObject.name );
}
void OnTriggerExit(Collider coll)
{
Debug.Log ("Student Exit" + coll.gameObject.name );
}
void OnTriggerStay(Collider coll)
{
Debug.Log ("Student Stay" + coll.gameObject.name );
}
}
```

Code 5 has been implemented to add a sensor to the door. The premise of this code is to create a sensor for the classroom door. When the sensor senses "student", the door can be opened.

```
private Door m_ Door;
void Start()
{
m_ Door= GameObject.Find ("doorparent").GetComponent<Door>();
}
// Update is called once per frame
void Update()
{
}
void OnTriggerEnter(Collider coll)
{
if ( coll.gameObject.name  == "Student")
{
//open
m_ Door.OpenDoor ();
}
}
void OnTriggerExit(Collider coll)
{
if ( coll.gameObject.name  == "Student")
{
//close
m_ Door.CloseDoor ();
}
}
```

After that, more diverse action research will be needed. For example, when students enter the printmaking classroom, they can carve on the wood with a hand-held engraving knife, pick up the roller by hand to ink the wood, cover the paper on the wood, and shake the engraving machine to print the picture.

5 Discussion

By combing the research papers on virtual reality technology and printmaking collected in the WOS core database and the core journal of China Zhiwang from 2010 to 2020, it is found that the study heat of virtual reality technology at home and abroad is not reduced, and the trend of steady growth is maintained. However, the research on virtual reality technology and printmaking has converged at home and abroad, and the amount of writing is not much. Foreign studies attach more importance to virtual learning environment and technical support. At home and abroad also from different perspectives to demonstrate the importance of virtual learning. However, it is found that domestic research still has great room for improvement and reference.

In the field of research, the scope of domestic research is relatively narrow, the exploration of virtual reality technology and printmaking mostly stays at the theoretical level, and there is no output of more content. Foreign countries attach great importance to the application of interdisciplinary methods, the interdisciplinary nature is more prominent, and good at using 3 D scanning technology to capture imaging, which also makes virtual learning research have a more solid theoretical and technical foundation. In terms of research methods, the domestic research on virtual reality technology between printmaking is slightly inadequate. Domestic research is mostly theoretical analysis, experimental research and empirical application research results are less, foreign research pays more attention to the practical application of research, in-depth and meticulous quantitative research more.

From the perspective of research, there are many researches on virtual learning in macro and meso level in our country. The research often pays attention to virtual learning from the macro perspective of learning environment construction, the relationship between virtual community environment and community members, the teaching and application of virtual reality technology and print-making, and is used to trying to establish universal theory. There is still a lack of in-depth exploration on the internal structure characteristics, factor analysis and learning process mechanism of virtual learning. Foreign scholars tend to choose relatively micro problems, analyze them from many angles, and the research perspective is closer to the learning process itself, so as to improve the pertinence of the research problems, the depth of theoretical development and the effectiveness of practical guidance.

In the research frontier, the deep learning of virtual reality technology and printmaking research will be the frontier of foreign research, and will pay more attention to the landing and practical nature of specific projects. With the vertical approach of information technology to promote the modernization of education, virtual learning at the micro level is expected to become the focus of domestic research and further combine with the learning process. The continuous updating iteration of information technology also puts forward new proposition and innovation space for virtual learning research in China. In the future, we need to pay attention to the following aspects:

First, pay attention to the integration of disciplines. The educational application of virtual reality technology involves the integration of many disciplines. The future research should be more devoted to the cooperative research of many disciplines. On the basis of consolidating the existing research of virtual reality technology and printmaking, Give full play to the research role of computer science in the field of virtual display technology and printmaking, and construct a multi-disciplinary virtual learning research theory system.

Second, in the process of virtual reality technology and printmaking research, we should not discuss the feasibility and necessity of the project too theoretically, but rather start to do it to perfect the feasibility of the project. Make a landing project rather than a shell project.

Third, refine the virtual reality technology and printmaking learning related research topics. The research of virtual learning should be gradually excavated from the aspects of virtual learning community, virtual learning environment and virtual reality macro level to strengthen the research on the internal elements and cognitive processing mechanism of virtual printmaking learning. Such as paying attention to the influence mechanism of learning process elements and learners' cognitive and non-cognitive characteristics in virtual learning environment. At the same time, we should pay attention to the research of virtual learning evaluation, pay attention to the scientific evaluation of virtual learning experience and teaching effect, and develop a scientific and reasonable evaluation system.

In summary, I sum up as follows: the combination of virtual reality technology and printmaking is a feasible development direction of modern printmaking education. After studying the development situation at home and abroad, we should combine multidisciplinary research to effectively carry out the progress of the project.

6   Conclusion

Combining virtual reality technology with printmaking teaching not only enables students to understand the process of printmaking more clearly but also motivates them to learn. Besides, it also means that our art teaching will usher in a new technological breakthrough. This research is using unity3d, visual studio, 3DMax, and other technologies to initially build a virtual classroom simulation system, which is expected to provide students with a virtual simulation of an experimental printmaking platform. The research is not yet finished, and I will continue to write the relevant C# scripts and build the corresponding models to provide students with a more realistic scenario experience.

Acknowledgements. This research is supported by "South China University of Technology Central University Basic Scientific Research Operating Expenses Subsidy (project appeoval no.x2sj/D2190390)".

References

1. Li, X., Sun, Y., Liu, M., Xi, X., Ji, Z.: The reform of the experimental content system of virtual reality teaching materials. Electron. World **18**, 50–51 (2020)
2. Zhao, B.: Strategy research on the effectiveness of the implementation of the national training program. Chin. J. Multimed. Netw. Teach. **12**, 206–208 (2020)
3. Chen, L., Lin, W.: A visual comparative analysis of the progress of virtual learning research at home and abroad. J. Guangzhou Radio Telev. Univ. **20**(04), 6–13 (2020)

A Experimental Study of the Cognitive Load of In-vehicle Multiscreen Connected HUD

Yancong Zhu[✉], Yuchen Jing, Ming Jiang, Ziwei Zhang, Dawei Wang, and Wei Liu

Faculty of Psychology, Beijing Normal University, Beijing 100875, People's Republic of China
{yancong.zhu,wei.liu}@bnu.edu.cn, {yuchen.jing,202028061033,
ziwei.zhang,202028061014}@mail.bnu.edu.cn

Abstract. The large variety of information that a driver must interpret while driving has caused an increasing number of screens to appear inside vehicles, making heads-up display (HUD) multiscreen interconnections more applicable inside cars. However, human cognitive resources are limited, and too much information can easily lead to distraction. Whether HUD multiscreen interconnections can effectively reduce driver distraction is still controversial. This study investigated the information and road conditions that drivers must be alerted. Based on the types of information and scenarios obtained from a study of users, a simulated driving experiment was used to measure drivers' response times and cognitive loads when viewing driving-assistance information to complete a driving task. The study aimed to verify whether a HUD could help the driver respond more quickly and use fewer cognitive resources when driving-assistance information was shown separately from the central screen. Experimental results show that HUDs can effectively reduce a driver's cognitive load compared having information displayed on only a central screen. Additionally, HUDs can improve a driver's reaction time when displaying all types of driving assistance information. This study compared drivers' reaction times and cognitive loads when using HUDs and central control screens that display the same and different types of information. We also analysed the distribution of information displayed between screens in a multiscreen car. Results show that when the type of content between the car screens is the same, there is no significant difference in the driver's reaction time compared to the reaction time associated with the HUD alone. This study also provides ideas and suggestions for the future development of HUD-based multiscreen interconnections.

Keywords: HUD · Multi-screen · Cognitive load

1 Introduction

With an increasing amount of information being displayed in vehicles, traditional in-vehicle interactive interfaces, such as the centre console screen, can no longer display all information relevant to a driver. Thus, an increasing number of screens are appearing in the vehicles' interiors to display this increasing amount and variety of information.

© Springer Nature Switzerland AG 2021
M. M. Soares et al. (Eds.): HCII 2021, LNCS 12781, pp. 268–285, 2021.
https://doi.org/10.1007/978-3-030-78227-6_20

Navigation, multimedia, and other standard in-vehicle multimedia functions began to be included on different car screens to enhance drivers' experiences [1].

Compared to other information display screens in vehicles, such as the dashboard and the central display, heads-up displays (HUDs) have been widely used in car cabin interiors [2]. Early on, HUDs were only used to present information like vehicle speed and engine RPM (Revolutions Per Minute). The amount of information was relatively homogeneous, and the display accuracy was low. With increasing computing power and network in vehicles, the type of information presented on HUDs has become increasingly abundant and varied. In addition to necessary driving information, HUDs on the market are also used for vehicle navigation, communication information, multimedia information, etc. [3] A HUD is a display area located closest to the centre of the driver's field of view when the driver is in a normal driving position. The information contained in this area is often important to driving. In a related study that used experimental psychophysical methods, HUDs were shown to reduce vehicle crashes by 25% [4]. In a simulated driving experiment, drivers felt a greater sense of subjective safety and comfort when viewing emergency alerts shown on HUDs compared to other screens in the vehicle [1].

However, due to the marked overlap between the display area of the head-up display system and the driver's field of view of the road, certain studies have raised concerns about the interference of HUDs with the driver's field of view [5]. The virtual image projected by the HUD in the driver's field of view may interfere with the driver's perception of the real driving environment due to its cluttered information and large projection area, resulting in more severe cognitive load and distraction [5]. HUDs' role in reducing driver distraction compared to other screens has not yet been clarified.

Currently, HUDs' interface information architecture in the market typically uses a "narrow and deep" column with time to reduce the total amount of information shown in a single interface and highlight important driver-assistance information. However, this HUD information category is more limited and overlaps with information shown on the vehicle's dashboard. In-vehicle voice interaction applications that are not fully mature are typically cumbersome for users to manually operate when they must find or switch to other types of information. Most in-car HUDs on the market today, regardless of how they are organized, are used as interfaces for displaying driver-assistance information, including vehicle speed, engine RPM, fuel consumption, and other information that is similar to the instrument panel display [6]. However, with the complex information displayed by a multiscreen interconnection in a car, only proper management and arrangement of information distribution and division of work among the car's screens can effectively improve the driver's experience [7].

This study investigates the driver's performance and cognitive load when the HUD and other information displays in the vehicle simultaneously display driver-assistance information. We investigate the appropriate type of information to be shown by a HUD in a multiscreen in-vehicle information environment and the distribution of information between different screens.

2 Related Work

With the development of multiscreen interactive technology, various screens are commonly used in driving situations: dashboard, centre, interior mirror, cell phone and HUD. Based on IGRS, DLAN, and other protocols, multiple screens in a car can be connected via an in-vehicle wireless network to integrate information to transmit, share, control, and display different types of multimedia contents on different in-vehicle multimedia displays. The development of multiscreen connectivity allows people to operate and access information between screens in different car areas at any time [6].

However, the multiscreen in-vehicle navigation environment provides drivers with a multisource, dynamic, and complex information environment while increasing driver's task complexity and safety risks [8]. Screens at different locations in the vehicle can distract the driver when presenting information, thus increasing the driver's cognitive load in perceiving and reacting to driving-assistance information. With autonomous driving not yet being widespread, a multiscreen information environment can easily lead to distracted driving. Secondary tasks requiring visual channel involvement had the most significant effect on normal driving behaviour (Guan et al., 2019). Many screens in the car in different areas for the driver may be move drivers' eyes away from the road, thus causing the driver to lose sight of road conditions and endangering the safety of the driver, the vehicle's occupants and others near the vehicle. However, the pursuit of complexity is the embodiment of human demand for product functionality and sensual experience [9]. In today's driving environment, which is already filled with a rich variety of ideations, we cannot ask drivers to focus only on information relevant to driving. The use of cell phones while driving affects drivers' situational awareness and can significantly increase the frequency of driving violations [10]. Regardless of the level of difficulty in using cell phones for secondary behaviours, cell phones significantly affect drivers' ability to drive safely [11]. Therefore, how to reasonably filter relevant information and distribute this information in each information display area in this multisource information environment has become an important issue to improve driving experience and safety.

HUDs have been widely used in car cabin interior to reduce driver distraction from roads while viewing various information [2]. HUDs are now widely used in automobiles for driving assistance and safety information [6]. Compared to other information displays in cars, such as the dashboard and the centre display, HUDs project all types of driving assistance information onto the windshield or a separate transparent piece of glass in front of the driver. HUDs improve driving safety by reducing distractions caused by the driver's eyes being diverted from viewing information. Its principal function is to help the driver see critical information when needed without looking away from the road, reducing the frequency with which the driver must look down at the dashboard or centre display. HUDs also reduce the discomfort and delay caused by ignoring rapid changes in road conditions while looking down from and then back up at the road, which requires changes in eye focus between the near instruments and the distant road. Avoiding disruption of attention and loss of situational awareness is paramount to maintain safety. A lack of situational awareness or inadequate situational awareness has been identified as a significant factor in human-error incidents. Situational awareness is critical when executing any dynamic and problematic task, including driving in heavy traffic [12].

Situational awareness involves identifying relevant environmental stimuli or cues, integrating that information, forming a mental model of the current situation, and using it to predict what is likely to occur next [12, 13]. When driving, drivers must recognize relevant information (e.g., distance to other vehicles, the relative speed between vehicles) in rapidly changing road conditions and be prepared to react to possible events to avoid accidents [14]. The implementation of situational awareness relies on driver perception, pattern recognition [13], attention and working memory, and long-term memory [15]. Therefore, cognitive interference that burdens the driver's attention or memory load may hurt situational awareness.

Thus, with the development of connected cars and in-car multimedia systems, drivers can view and process more types of information while driving, and the emergence of more kinds of information requires more screen space in cars. The trend of multiple screens in the cabin of a car yields a richer and more convenient driving experience to the driver, quickly causing the driver's attention to switch back and forth between different pieces of information on each screen, increasing the complexity of driving and causing additional cognitive load. At a time when autonomous driving is not yet widespread, certain vehicles already have assisted driving features, such as lane-maintaining systems. Drivers still must stay aware of road conditions at all times and provide timely feedback for unexpected road conditions. HUDs were transplanted from the cockpit of an airplane to the driver's seat of a car as a safety assistance system to reduce driver distraction, in addition to verifying that the HUD can display relevant driver assistance information. This study also investigates the division of labour among the screens in a car when the HUD displays information along with other screens in the car, such as the centre console screen, in terms of driver response and cognitive load. Additionally, due to the layout and partitioning of the human-machine interface in a car, each screen does not always present the same information simultaneously. Thus, we investigate whether the display of different information between screens causes additional interference with the driver's normal behaviour.

3 Experiment

Based on previous research and trends in the field of in-vehicle multimedia (HMI), this study proposes the following research questions for the HUD interface in the context of in-vehicle multiscreen interaction.

Question 1: What are the most common types of driver assistance information viewed by drivers in the vehicle and the driving scenarios corresponding to these information types?

Question 2: When there are multiple information display areas in the vehicle, can a HUD display driver assistance information more effectively than a centre console screen, which is the most commonly used information display area in vehicles today, to improve the efficiency of accurate information reading and improve driving safety?

Question 3: In the context of a multiscreen interconnection, when a HUD and centre console screen display different types of information for driving assistance, will they interfere with the driver's reaction time to make a given response to changing road conditions, and when the same information is shown concurrently, will the information redundancy interfere with the driver's reaction?

For question 1, we conducted online questionnaires and user interviews to determine the common information and corresponding scenarios in assisted driving. For questions 2 and 3, based on the findings from question 1, we evaluated the advantages and disadvantages of a HUD for displaying different types of driver assistance information by measuring the effectiveness of the driver's access to driver assistance information from different information display areas (HUD on the centre console screen) and explored the organization of information between different screens in the case of a multiscreen interconnection.

Because a real driving situation is more complex, and there are more unexpected traffic situations, it is impossible to control the influence of irrelevant variables on the experimental results. It is also difficult to ensure the repeatability of the experimental results. Without ensuring that the experimental materials can reduce driver distraction and ensure driving safety, driving experiments under real road conditions can easily endanger the lives of the subjects and others; thus, the experimental environment of this study is a laboratory simulated driving environment.

3.1 Cognitive Load Assessment Methods and Materials in the Driving Task

The RSME scale was used to assess the cognitive load of the driver while answering the phone and driving, which was used as a dimension to measure the driver's driving performance and the effect of using the phone to answer the phone during normal driving.

The primary methods for measuring cognitive load are subjective evaluation measures, behavioural performance measures, and physiological indicator measures. Among these, subjective evaluation is simple but yields results that are too subjective with large between-observer differences. Behavioural performance measurement can quantify indicators and determine load characterization indicators; however, the task setting is more difficult. Physiological indicator measurement can monitor the driver's attentional load in real time; however, the use of the instrument affects normal driving behaviour and is affected by the environment.

The construct of cognitive load is too complex to be accurately measured by a single measurement method; thus, it is more accurate to combine multiple methods to measure cognitive load than to use any one type of method. Many experiments on cognitive load have used the RSME subjective rating scale in conjunction with measures of heart rate, blink frequency, and blood pressure. However, in vehicle driving situations, where a road condition is independent of its corresponding driver assistance information, measuring the cognitive load of the driver for the entire driving trip may confound the cognitive load of the specific road condition with the act of viewing and responding to the corresponding driver assistance information. Physiological indicators are not applicable to the specific experimental task of measuring the driver's response to a specific road condition and the corresponding driver assistance information; thus, this study chose to combine behavioural performance measures with subjective psychological load scale evaluations to measure the driver's performance and cognitive load on the task of viewing and responding to a particular type of driver assistance information.

To more accurately compare drivers' efficiency in reading driver assistance information from different information display areas and to assess whether drivers can ensure safe driving when reading valid information, we used drivers' behavioural data when completing a specific driving task as a measure of task performance and set the experimental task with drivers viewing different driver assistance information as different scenarios, maintaining the singularity of the user receiving driving assistance information and road information within the same scenario as much as possible, thus reducing the influence of irrelevant variables on the experimental results. Because each driving scenario in this study only required the driver to complete the basic task of slowing down or changing lanes and considering that the driver could still complete the basic driving tasks involved in this study with a high rate of completion, even when performing secondary behaviours in the visual or auditory channels concurrently, this study no longer included the rate of completing driving tasks when characterizing performance. However, the rate of completion was measured using the in-vehicle information display area (centre console screen, HUD, or centre console screen and HUD) that was displayed a specific driver assistance message until the driver makes the corresponding correct response as a measure of the driver's task performance in completing that driving task. The shorter the time from the appearance of the information to the correct response, the more effective the information presentation method is.

The Rating Scale Mental Effort (RSME) scale was used as a tool to measure the cognitive load perceived by the driver while driving. After completing each set of driving tasks, the drivers completed an RSME scale to subjectively evaluate the cognitive load they exerted during the task.

3.2 Driving Simulation Experiment

The experimental program used in the driving simulation experiment is written in Unity version 5.6.1 f1. The program records the time required from the appearance of the assisted driving information to the user's correct key response, and the operating vehicle will move based on the correct response after the user makes the correct key response. The driving simulation experiment uses a computer display to present a simulated driving situation, and the user operates the vehicle using the four arrow keys "↑", "↓", " ←" and " →" on the QWERTY standard keyboard to respond to different types of assisted driving information and road conditions. To test path navigation, emergency message reminders, such as "pedestrians ahead but speed is not reduced", "people or obstacles in the visual blind spot", and "emergency reminders ahead") were displayed. The user's reaction to the corresponding driving operations when three types of information – route navigation, emergency information (e.g., alerts for pedestrians ahead but speed not reduced, people or obstacles in the visual blind spot, and emergencies on the road ahead), and nonemergency information (e.g., information on road conditions ahead, speed limit information and speed camera information) – are shown on the HUD, the centre console screen, or both the HUD and the centre console screen, where operations such as avoiding road obstacles, slowing down and controlling vehicle turns may exist.

The presentation of driving assistance information in this study can be divided into four types: 1) the HUD displays driving assistance information alone; 2) the centre console screen displays driving assistance information alone; 3) the HUD and centre console screen display the same type of driving assistance information concurrently; and 4) the HUD and centre console screen display different driving assistance information concurrently. The first three types of driving assistance information display methods cover all three types of scenarios; however, in the fourth type of display method (i.e., the HUD and centre console screen display different types of driving assistance information concurrently), this study takes the driver's correct response to emergency information alerts as the judgement criterion rather than the response to normal route navigation information to clarify whether the driver subjects reacted correctly. In the test scenario with this type of display, the driver drives into a situation where there is an emergency on the road ahead, and the HUD and centre console screen will display different types of driving assistance information, with the HUD displaying emergency information alerts and the centre console screen displaying route navigation information.

In this study, guidance at the exit of the highway ramp is used as the test scenario for route navigation information presentation; road closure in front of the left side is used as the test scenario for emergency information presentation; and a speed camera in front is used as the test scenario for nonemergency information presentation.

Fig. 1. Simulated driving experiment screen

The scene model used in the experimental procedure was modelled with reference to driving simulation games such as "Forza Horizon 4" and "Need for Speed 17", and the driver's view in the experiment was similar to that of a real driver sitting in a normal position in the driver's seat and looking straight ahead. As shown in Fig. 1, the left side of the subject's field of view in the experiment includes the complete rear-view mirror, and the HUD is located in the middle of the driver's field of view, which is the area most easily covered by the driver's vision in normal driving. The centre console screen is on the lower right side of the driver's field of view, and the driver's field of view can cover the entire centre console screen.

To mitigate the practice effect on the same driving task in the same scenario when the same information is presented in different ways, this driving simulation experiment uses a mixture of within- and between-subject designs. Different driving scenarios are designed for within-subjects: the same subject will drive the vehicle in the driving simulation experiment through three scenarios (highway ramp exit in front, road closure in front and road closure in front). In the same driving scenario, different driving information presentation methods (HUD system alone; centre console screen alone; HUD and centre console screen showing the same information concurrently; HUD and centre console screen showing different information concurrently) were designed between subjects to avoid subjects' familiarity with the same scenario. The experiment was designed to avoid shortening the reaction time of the driving task and reducing the cognitive load of subjective perception due to familiarity with the same road scenario, which would affect the accuracy of the experimental data. Experimental scenarios were grouped as shown in Table 1.

Table 1. Description of laboratory scenarios and subject groups

	Control group	Subject group1	Subject group2	Subject group2
Scenario 1 The vehicle is driving normally, the left lane of the road ahead is closed, the vehicle needs to change lanes to the right	1-a: Centre screen displays the sign of changing lanes to the right, and the time from when the icon appears to when the subject clicks " →" is measured	1-b: HUD displays the sign of changing lanes to the right, and the time from when the icon appears to when the subject clicks " →" is measured	1-c: Centre screen and HUD displays the sign of changing lanes to the right, and the time from when the icon appears to when the subject clicks " →" is measured	1-d: HUD displays the sign of changing lanes to the right. At the same time Centre screen displays straight navigation prompt and the time from when the icon appears to when the subject clicks " →" is measured
Scenario 2 The vehicle is driving normally, the speed limit sign appears on the road ahead, and the vehicle needs to slow down	2-a: Centre screen displays the speed limit sign, and the time from when the icon appears to when the subject clicks "↓" is measured	2-b:HUD displays the speed limit sign,, and the time from when the icon appears to when the subject clicks " →" is measured	2-c:Centre screen and HUD displays the speed limit sign, and the time from when the icon appears to when the subject clicks " →" is measured	
Scenario 3 The vehicle is driving normally, a ramp appears on the right side of the road ahead, and the vehicle needs to turn right	3-a: Centre screen displays the icon of turning right after 100 m and the time from when the icon appears to when the subject clicks " →" is measured	3-b:HUD displays the icon of turning right after 100 m and the time from when the icon appears to when the subject clicks " →" is measured	3-c:Centre screen and HUD displays the icon of turning right after 100 m and the time from when the icon appears to when the subject clicks " →" is measured	

A Dell Inspiron Turbo laptop computer with a 15.6-inch screen and a resolution of 1920 × 720 pixels was used in the experiment, which was conducted in a closed laboratory with white overhead lighting and white walls on all sides; the brightness of the computer screen was kept constant. Study subjects arrived at the laboratory at the appointed time and filled in basic information, including their age, gender and driving age, and read the informed consent form before being brought to the laptop computer for testing. The subject sat in front of the computer with his eyes approximately 35 cm from the computer screen, and a video demonstration of the experiment was played on the computer screen to familiarize the subject with the first-person driving perspective of the test situation.

Concurrently, the subject read out the experimental instructions, telling the subject to look straight ahead like a normal driver with the right hand on the keyboard's arrow keys. The subjects read the following:

'Please use the "↑", "↓", " ←" and " →" keys on the keyboard to respond to the assisted driving information by slowing down, turning left or right at the first time when the information appears. If the HUD is different from the information shown on the centre screen, please only respond to the red emergency message. '

After watching the scenario and having no objection to the experimental instructions, the subject can click the button on the right side of the screen to start the experiment. After entering the first driving scenario, the vehicle will be driven forward for 6 s, and the driving assistance message will appear in the HUD area or the centre screen area. After the message appears, the programme timer begins to count the time from the appearance of the driver assistance message to the time when the subject responds with the correct button. After the subject responds with the correct keystroke, the driver assistance message disappears from the corresponding display area, and the vehicle steers or slows down with the user's operation, as shown in Fig. 2.

Then, the driving scenario ends, the program goes to a black screen, and the next driving scenario begins after 3 s. The control group, experimental group 1 and experimental group 2 all contained three scenarios, while experimental group 3 had only one scenario. After subjects completed all scenarios, the program jumped back to the start screen. At this point, the subject was brought to a side table to fill out the RSME scale, which evaluates the effort required to read the driving assistance information and respond to keystrokes in the previously completed driving task. When the subject completes the RSME scale, the experiment is completed.

4   Analysis and Results

4.1   Subjects and Response Time Analysis

In this experiment, 40 subjects from Beijing Normal University were recruited, and the number of males and females was similar (male N = 19, female N = 21). The subjects' age range was 20–27 years (Mean = 23.67, sD = 1.526), and the subjects had some driving experience with a minimum of 1 year and a maximum of 7 years (Mean = 2.73, sD = 1.569). The mean driving experience of male subjects was 2.89 years, sD = 1.663, and the mean driving experience of female subjects was 2.57 years, sD = 1.502; the difference in driving experience between genders was not significant based on

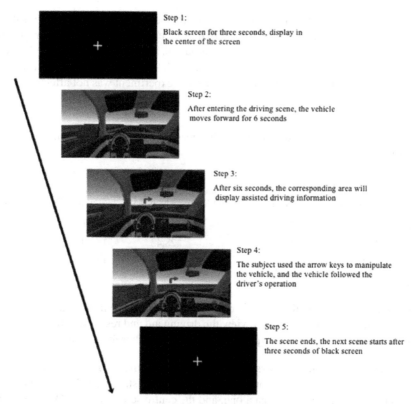

Step 1:

Black screen for three seconds, display in the center of the screen

Step 2:

After entering the driving scene, the vehicle moves forward for 6 seconds

Step 3:

After six seconds, the corresponding area will display assisted driving information

Step 4:

The subject used the arrow keys to manipulate the vehicle, and the vehicle followed the driver's operation

Step 5:

The scene ends, the next scene starts after three seconds of black screen

Fig. 2. Simulated driving experiment process (Take scenario 3-b as an example)

independent samples t-test, $l(38) = 0.646$, $p = 0.522$. All subjects had normal or corrected visual acuity. The subjects were grouped into four groups in the formal experiment, and 40 subjects were randomly assigned to the corresponding subject groups. In this study, a mixed intrasubject and intersubject design was used: different driving scenarios were designed within subjects, and the same subject would drive the vehicle through three scenarios in the driving simulation experiment, while different ways of presenting driving information in the same driving scenario were designed between subjects. Ten trials were conducted for each subject ($N = 100$). To clarify whether the effects of driving age on reaction time and RSME scores differed between subject groups, a two-factor multivariate analysis of variance (ANOVA) was conducted on driving age and group and showed that the interaction between the subject group and driving age was not significant, $F(20, 160) = 1.466$, $p = 0.10$. There was thus no significant difference between the groups. Therefore, the grouping of subjects in this experiment effectively avoided any possible effect on the experimental results due to the difference in driving age between the experimental groups. However, driving age did have a significant effect on subjects' reaction time scores ($p = 0.001$) and RSME scale scores ($p = 0.006$).

As shown in Table 2, males' mean reaction time was marginally higher than that of females in the simulated driving experiment. A one-way ANOVA was conducted on the reaction time data and RSME scale scores between male and female subjects in each scenario. Conversely, females exerted more effort than males on average when identifying and using driving assistance information, and the difference in RSME scale scores by gender was only marginally significant, $F(1, 98) = 2.848, p = 0.095$. Therefore, the subjects' performance in the simulated driving experiment was not affected by their gender.

Table 2. Means and standard deviations of driver reaction time and RSME scale scores during the driving task $(N = 100)$

	Reaction time		RSME scale	
	Mean (M)	Standard Deviation (SD)	Mean (M)	Standard Deviation (SD)
Subjects	1.13	0.56	31.04	15.31
Male	1.17	0.61	28.43	15.40
Female	1.09	0.51	33.55	14.94

These results indicate that there is no significant difference in the amount of time it takes for male and female drivers to view the driving aid and respond to it; however, the cognitive load required for this type of driving task is higher for female drivers.

Each Screen in the Car Displays Separate Assisted Driving Information

In this experiment, there were four types of driving assistance displays, in which the centre screen alone, the HUD area alone, and the centre screen and HUD area simultaneously displaying the same information were used in three driving scenarios; these types of displays corresponded to three types of driving assistance information: emergency alert information, nonemergency alert information and route navigation information. However, because the experimental design only required the subjects to respond to the emergency messages as a priority when they saw different contents in the two display areas, this way of displaying different information on the centre screen and the HUD area concurrently was only used in the first driving scenario where there was an emergency on the road; this method was not used in the other scenarios to avoid confusing the subjects. There were 10 data sets in this experiment; however, because the study does not discuss the driver's response performance and cognitive load between driving scenarios, the study does not compare the subjective assessment of cognitive load with the subject's response time performance across scenarios. Because this experiment focused on comparing the performance of the subjects in different display modes, an independent samples t-test was used to compare the performance of the subjects between the two groups; the subjective ratings of the response times and cognitive loads of the subjects to view and respond to the corresponding actions in the different display modes of the driver assistance information within each scene are shown in Table 3.

To compare the effectiveness of using a HUD to display driver assistance information in a vehicle with multiple information display areas compared to only using the centre console screen, which is commonly used to display driver assistance information in current in-car systems and to improve the driver's ability to accurately read the

Table. 3 Driver reaction time and RSME scale scores for different scenarios and displays (N = 100)

		Reaction time		RSME scale	
		Mean (M)	Standard Deviation (SD)	Mean (M)	Standard Deviation (SD)
Scenario 1	Centre screen	1.14	0.28	34.30	10.75
	HUD	0.79	0.29	20.50	9.49
	Same information	1.03	0.89	36.70	19.18
	Different information	1.49	0.69	35.90	17.86
Scenario 2	Centre screen	1.48	0.57	34.30	10.75
	HUD	0.90	0.34	20.50	9.49
	Same information	1.24	0.59	36.70	19.18
Scenario 3	Centre screen	1.46	0.44	34.30	10.75
	HUD	0.81	0.21	20.50	9.49
	Same information	0.89	0.45	36.70	19.18

information and improve driving safety, this study compared the use of only the centre console screen with the use of only the HUD area to display driver assistance information in different scenarios. This study compared whether using only the centre console screen and only the HUD area for driver assistance information significantly affected driver performance and cognitive load in different scenarios. There was a significant difference between the reaction time scores and the subjective cognitive load scores of the subjects in the same driving scenario when comparing the centre console screen and the HUD. Due to the between-subjects design, an independent samples t-test was used to compare the differences in reaction time and cognitive load between the two display modes.

4.2 Scenario Conclusion

First, this study compared the reaction time scores and the self-rated RSME scores of the participants in Scenario 1, where an emergency alert was required for left-hand road closure when the centre screen was used to display the emergency alert type of driver assistance message with the HUD. As shown in Fig. 3a, the reaction time when viewing the HUD to display the emergency alert was significantly lower than when using the centre screen to view the driver assistance messages ($l(18) = 2.714$, $p = 0.01^*$). Using a

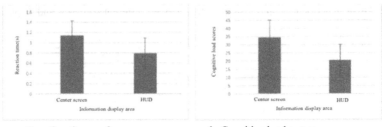

a. Reaction time performance   b. Cognitive load scores

Fig. 3. Scenario 1: HUD and centre screen display information on test scores

HUD to display emergency information can significantly reduce drivers' reaction time to road emergencies and help drivers respond more quickly and safely than when only the centre console screen is used.

Additionally, given the short duration of the individual driving tasks, the first three groups of subjects completed all three scenarios before completing the RSME scale, a subjective measure of the amount of effort put into the driving task. As shown in Fig. 3b, the cognitive load on the driver to view the information and respond to the corresponding driving actions was significantly below the cognitive load on the driver to view the centre screen and respond to the driving actions when the HUD area was used to display three types of driving aids: emergency information, nonemergency information, and route navigation information, $l(18) = 2.394$, $p = 0.007^*$. Using an HUD to display driving assistance information in a driving situation requires fewer cognitive resources, allowing the driver to allocate more of his or her limited cognitive resources to road conditions, such as distance to the vehicle in front and pedestrians on the road, increasing the driver's awareness of road conditions and improving driving safety.

In scenario 2, where nonemergency information was presented (i.e., slow down in response to a speed limit alert ahead), the subjects performed better with the HUD as the assisted driving information display area, and the time for the subjects to view the HUD-shown deceleration alert and respond by pressing the "↓" button was significantly lower than the time to view the centre screen-shown deceleration information and respond, $l(18) = 2.774$, $p = 0.013^*$. The time to view the deceleration alert message shown by the HUD and press the "↓" button to respond was significantly lower than that to view the deceleration message shown on the centre screen and respond, $l(18) = 2.774$, $p = 0.013^*$. A HUD can reduce the driver's reaction time when it is used to display nonemergency information, such as speed limit alerts ahead.

4.3   HUD Screen and Centre Console Screen Display the Same Information Concurrently

In Scenario 1, as shown in Fig. 4a, the average response time of the user in the scenario where the HUD. The centre screen simultaneously displays the same driving assistance information is higher than that of the HUD alone; however, there is no significant difference in the response time of the two display methods in terms of the user's ability to view the information and execute a corresponding driving response, $t(18) = 0.797$, p =

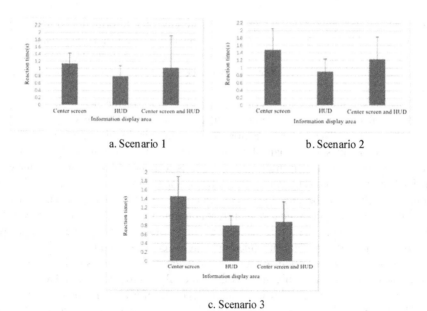

a. Scenario 1   b. Scenario 2

c. Scenario 3

Fig. 4. Subjects' response time performance in three information display arrangements in Scenarios 1–3

0.436. Additionally, compared to the centre screen alone, the average response time of users viewing the HUD and the centre screen together was marginally lower; however, the difference was still not significant, $t(18) = 0.385$, $p = 0.705$. When emergency alerts were shown in both the HUD and centre screen, the driver's reaction speed to view the information and make corresponding driving actions was marginally higher than when the HUD alone displayed the information and marginally lower than when the centre screen alone shown the information; however, the difference did not reach a statistically significant level.

In Scenario 2, where the driver is asked to respond to a nonemergency message such as a speed alert, the driver's response time is the shortest when the HUD alone displays the driving assistance message, as shown in Fig. 4b. The second shortest response time occurs when both the HUD and the centre screen display the message concurrently, and when the centre screen is the only display area, the driver's reaction time is the longest. However, with speed-alert messages, the difference in response time between the HUD alone and the centre screen alone was not significant, $t(18) = 1.586$, $p = 0.13$. The difference in response time between the two areas with the same message and the centre screen alone was also not significant, $t(18) = 0.93$, $p = 0.93$. Therefore, the efficiency of displaying speed alert information on the HUD and the centre screen concurrently was not better than that of displaying the same information on the HUD alone and both areas concurrently.

In Scenario 3, where the driver must turn right into the ramp based on the route guidance information, as shown in Fig. 4c, the driver's reaction time is marginally higher when the HUD and the centre screen display the route guidance information simultaneously than when the HUD is shown alone; however, the difference is not significant.

The average response time of the driver with the same information shown in both areas was significantly lower than that of the centre screen alone, $t(18) = 2.873$, $p = 0.01*$.

Thus, the simultaneous display of the same information on the in-vehicle HUD screen and the centre console screen did not significantly contribute to the driver's performance in the driving task. The driver's reaction time was marginally higher when viewing the information on both screens than when the HUD screen was used alone. In particular, in the case of route navigation information, subjects responded significantly faster when the HUD alone showed route navigation information than when both areas were shown simultaneously, likely because the associated cognitive load was significantly lower. In the simultaneous-display scenario, their reaction time were only marginally lower than the reaction time when the centre screen was shown alone; however, the difference was not significant, and it was accompanied by a higher cognitive load.

Because it is easy to confuse the subjects when different types of information are shown on multiple screens, this study required the subjects to prioritize and respond only to emergency alerts when receiving different types of information concurrently.

The driver's reaction time to emergency alerts was higher in the scenario where the HUD and centre console screen showed different information concurrently than in the scenario where the HUD screen and the centre console screen were shown alone. The difference between the HUD screen and the HUD screen alone was significant, and the driver's average reaction time was higher in the scenario where the HUD screen and the centre console screen were shown alone; however, the difference was not significant.

When comparing the influence of the three display modes on the cognitive load of drivers to complete normal driving tasks, this study found that the cognitive load required to recognize and respond to emergency alerts was higher in the case of different information shown in the two areas than in the case of emergency alert information shown on the HUD and the centre screen alone. There was also a significant difference between the cognitive load of the driver in the case of different information shown in the two areas and the HUD alone; however, the difference was not statistically significant in the case of the centre screen display alone.

There was no significant difference in the response time between the HUD alone and the two areas displaying the same information concurrently. In the case of the centre screen alone, the reaction time of the subjects was higher than that of these two display modes. Among the three display modes, the HUD alone helped the driver make a faster response with less cognitive effort, while the use of two display areas to present the driving assistance information concurrently did not shorten the driver's response time and resulted in a greater cognitive load on the driver. The use of two display areas to simultaneously present driver assistance information does not reduce driver reaction time and results in greater cognitive load on the driver. Additionally, displaying different types of driver assistance information on the HUD and the centre screen can increase the driver's reaction time and require more cognitive effort to read the assistance information and perform driving actions than if the HUD or the centre screen were shown separately.

5 Discussion

Screens in different areas of a car tend to distract a driver and increase the driver's cognitive load during information presentation. In a car, the layout of each screen must be more reasonably distributed; otherwise, information will easily distract the driver. Particularly when multiple screens are shown concurrently in a car, the driver's attention will have to switch back and forth, yielding additional cognitive load, particularly when route navigation information is shown concurrently; the reaction time for the driver to view the information and make corresponding driving response will thus increase.

Additionally, because the experimental paradigm of Veltman (2002) was used to test the cognitive load of pilots during flight tasks, the first three groups of subjects completed all three scenarios before completing the RSME scale, which is a subjective measure of the amount of effort put into the driving task, given the short duration of the individual driving tasks. In the first three groups, subjects completed all three scenarios and then filled out the RSME scale, subjectively measuring their effort in the driving task; thus, the subjects put in significantly less effort to view and respond to the nonemergency information shown by the HUD than to view the assisted driving information shown on the centre console. However, if we could accurately measure the effort required to perform driving actions in the same scenario with different displays, we could more accurately compare the cognitive load of different driver assistance messages in subsequent studies. Second, the driving simulation experiment in this study remains based on a laptop computer and requires subjects to respond via a keyboard in a simulated driving scenario; this can enhance the generalizability of the research content by making the experimental results more realistic without endangering traffic safety.

To control the size of the experimental study and better control irrelevant variables, this experiment empirically demonstrates that the driving behaviour in the simulated driving scenario can help reduce the driver's reaction time and cognitive load compared to the centre screen, which is the most widely used information display area in the car at this stage. Using the HUD alone to display driving assistance information can further reduce the driver's reaction time and cognitive load compared to the multiscreen display. Therefore, based on this experiment, the subsequent application of a HUD in a vehicle can focus on the information architecture and interface layout of the HUD as a separate display area for different types of driver assistance information to achieve a more convenient and safe driving experience without affecting the driver's normal vision. It is also possible to compare the efficiency of a HUD with that of a cell phone screen or the instrument panel when displaying different types of driver assistance information.

6 Conclusion

In this study, we measured drivers' performances when reading and responding to information from different information display areas in a car while driving to compare whether a HUD can reduce a driver's cognitive load of reading information compared to other screens in the car and help the driver respond to road conditions more quickly. By comparing the results when only a HUD displayed information to those when multiple screens displayed information concurrently, we investigated how to achieve reasonable information distribution among the screens in a multiscreen interconnection scenario and identified the most efficient display method to help drivers read and interpret driving assistance information more easily and quickly, and reduce distraction. Experimental results show that a HUD is more helpful to drivers' viewing of driving information than other screens.

Based on the results of this study, HUDs can effectively help drivers respond to road conditions more quickly and require fewer cognitive resources when displaying driving assistance information. It is possible to further compare the effects of different information organization methods of HUDs on driving performance and cognitive load to more carefully establish the optimal arrangement of displaying driving assistance information using HUDs.

Acknowledgements. We thank HMI lab in Beijing Normal University, who provide the context of our simulation. Moreover, thank all the participants for their contribution.

References

1. Tan, J., Xu, S.H.: Multi-screen interactive experience of car navigation based on Internet of Vehicles. Packag. Eng. **38**(20), 17–22 (2017)
2. Caudell, T.P., Mizell, D.W.: Augmented reality: an application of heads-up display technology to manual manufacturing processes. In: Hawaii International Conference on System Sciences, vol. 2, pp. 659–669. IEEE (1992)
3. Zhan, J.: Information architecture and visual design of vehicle HUD interface. J. Shandong Inst. Arts Des. **2**, 41–46 (2014)
4. Hibberd, D.L., Jamson, S.L., Carsten, O.M.: Managing in-vehicle distractions: evidence from the psychological refractory period paradigm. In: Proceedings of the 2nd International Conference on Automotive User Interfaces and Interactive Vehicular Applications, pp. 4–11 (2010)
5. Smith, M., Streeter, J., Burnett, G., Gabbard, J.L.: Visual search tasks: the effects of head-up displays on driving and task performance. In: Proceedings of the 7th International Conference on Automotive User Interfaces and Interactive Vehicular Applications, pp. 80–87 (2015)
6. Wang, J.M., Luo, W.D., Cao, B., Jia, L., Ma, X.Q.: Human-machine interface design of vehicle HUD. Autom. Instrum. **36**(7), 85–87 (2015)
7. Haeuslschmid, R., Pfleging, B., Alt, F.: A design space to support the development of windshield applications for the car. In: 2016 CHI Conference, pp. 5076–5091. ACM (2016)
8. Ji, X.F., Lian, C.X., Feng, C., Guo, F.X.: Research on the measurement method of driver's cognitive load based on multi-source information. China Saf. Sci. J. **25**(12), 34–39 (2015)
9. Norman, D.A.: Emotional Design: Why We Love (or Hate) Everyday Things. Basic Civitas Books (2004)
10. Beede, K.E., Kass, S.J.: Engrossed in conversation: the impact of cell phones on simulated driving performance. Accid. Anal. Prev. **38**(2), 415–421 (2006)
11. Rakauskas, M.E., Gugerty, L.J., Ward, N.J.: Effects of naturalistic cell phone conversations on driving performance. J. Saf. Res. **35**(4), 453–464 (2004)
12. Endsley, M.R.: Predictive utility of an objective measure of situation awareness. In: Proceedings of the Human Factors Society Annual Meeting, vol. 34, no. 1, pp. 41–45. SAGE Publications, Sage, Los Angeles (October 1990)
13. Kass, S.J., Herschler, D.A., Companion, M.A.: Training situational awareness through pattern recognition in a battlefield environment. Mil. Psychol. **3**(2), 105–112 (1991)

14. Kass, S.J., Cole, K.S., Stanny, C.J.: Effects of distraction and experience on situation awareness and simulated driving. Transport. Res. F Traffic Psychol. Behav. **10**(4), 321–329 (2007)
15. Endsley, M.R.: Measurement of situation awareness in dynamic systems. Hum. Factors **37**(1), 65–84 (1995)
16. Martins, M.M., Santos, C.P., Frizera-Neto, A., Ceres, R.: Assistive mobility devices focusing on smart walkers: classification and review. Robot. Auton. Syst. **60**(4), 548–562 (2012)
17. Kim, D.H., Lee, H.: Effects of user experience on user resistance to change to the voice user interface of an in vehicle infotainment system: implications for platform and standards competition. Int. J. Inf. Manage. **36**(4), 653–667 (2016)
18. Cycil, C., Perry, M., Laurier, E.: Designing for frustration and disputes in the family car. Int. J. Mob. Hum. Comput. Interact. **6**(2), 46–60 (2014)
19. Liu, H.: Method of physical education informationization requirement analysis. J. Beijing Sport Univ. **4**, 80–84 (2016)
20. Kumar, S., Dolev, E., Pecht, M.: Parameter selection for health monitoring of electronic products. Microelectron. Reliab. **50**(2), 161–168 (2010)
21. Mozaffarian, D., et al.: Executive summary: heart disease and stroke statistics—2015 update: a report from the American Heart Association. Circulation **131**(4), 434–441 (2015)
22. Tbatou, S., Ramrami, A., Tabii, Y.: Security of communications in connected cars Modeling and safety assessment. In: Proceedings of the 2nd International Conference on Big Data, Cloud and Applications, p. 56. ACM (March 2017)
23. Kaiwartya, O., et al.: Internet of vehicles: Motivation, layered architecture, network model, challenges, and future aspects. IEEE Access **4**, 5356–5373 (2016)
24. Sun, J., Wu, Z.: An integrated simulation platform for connected vehicle system experiments. Res. Explor. Lab. **33**(2), 75–78 (2014)
25. Liu, He, Li: J. Hubei Univ. Econ. (Humanit. Soc. Sci.) **12**(3), 81–82 (2015)

DUXU for the Creative Industries

Interfacing with the Macromedium: The Web 4.0 and the Digital Media Converging into a Medium of All Media

Herlander Elias[✉]

University of Beira Interior and LabCom, CB 6201-001 Covilhã, Portugal
`http://www.herlanderelias.com`

Abstract. This text displays a unifying theory on digital media. Its focus is on the Web 4.0 and terminal digital devices we use to be online. In our present time we are interfacing with a new medium, a medium of all media. We call it the "macromedium". Following the trend of convergence, the new macromedium encompasses all apps, websites, social media and terminals, like the computers and the smartphones and tablets.

When speaking of results, one has to highlight three specific characteristics of the macromedium. First, the macromedium has a large scale in size, because it is both all the hardware and all the software we use to interface with data (websites, apps, devices, cloud storage, search engines, servers); second, the macromedium because it records everything we do, it transforms the Web 4.0 and the digital devices we use, like the smartphone, into history-media. All our digital trails, keystrokes and searches, purchases and connection events become recorded, an indelible record; third, the macromedium is so powerful and all-encompassing that in the near future different file types will not matter, as any device or system will be able to read any format. As long as it is on the macromedium, it will be like flipping the switch to have electricity on. Last, but not least, the macromedium favors access to data in a different way. For the first time in history, all generations have access to the same news, the same sources, the same entertainment and regardless of their age, location, social class and political views. Convergence is taking place, on a technological level, but also on a social level. Younger crowds and the elderly have access to the same information, the same space, what once would be called "cyberspace", "virtual domain". At least in the northern hemisphere, the macromedium is coherent.

Keywords: Interfacing · Digital media · Macromedium

1 Introduction: An Always Online World

In this context we witness that this superspace of digital media becomes a synonym for digital media with peculiar emphasis on the online world. We could say that today the Web and the digital devices we use are blending in so that the User Experience (UX) becomes more uniform and simplified, thanks to the "unimedia" phenomenon (Lunenfeld 2011). In this sense, all that worries the current user-consumer is the data,

© Springer Nature Switzerland AG 2021
M. M. Soares et al. (Eds.): HCII 2021, LNCS 12781, pp. 289–302, 2021.
https://doi.org/10.1007/978-3-030-78227-6_21

different file formats shall disappear or become readable by any digital device. This is in itself a revolution in the age of Web 4.0, the time in which the macro scale of the Web and digital media and its continuum formula are something we cannot deny or flee from. It means that the macromedium is not the "cyberspace" of the past, or the social networks that came after 2004. We are using a digital connection to a space of information, entertainment and brands that brings a new form of interfacing based on time (going backwards, going forth), rather than being based on the space metaphor or the desktop, which lasted for a few decades.

The new fact and motto are that the Internet is the stage for every kind of media consultation, file sharing, uploads and downloads. The Internet is a library and is a stage for acting, file exchange, archiving data, a stage and a laboratory for role-playing (Turkle 2011). This medium, which now is maturing, is the medium for all media; it is, actually, the first "macromedium", a medium that gathers all the applications, all kinds of media's files, platforms and services. In its basics the macromedium is the Internet converging with digital media (the hardware and the software) of every type. Kelly calls this event-medium the "technium" (2010). He means that the "digital", or the "online" will become representative of all things becoming technological on a civilization scale.

What has been making the macromedium as overwhelming as the days go by is the fact that being a medium in the present age means it is dedicated to all generations (Rushkoff 2013). The Internet is the medium of all media, it is the medium devoted to all ages. One thing to be considered is that the people of different ages converge into the Internet, and we are all simultaneously online even more aligned with the macromedium that encompasses, spreads (Jenkins 2013) and informs. For this reason, the Internet is macro for being gigantic and it is a medium because it follows the actual trend that everything attaches to it regardless of its format. All the contents and provisions develop themselves around a medium that unifies them all, and each user approaches it. We are also considering that the younger people from the Generation Z and from the Generation Alpha (even younger) spend a lot of time online (McCrindle and Wolfinger 2011; Kerckhove 2010). Regarding the new generations, what one can say is that the only thing that remain is the Internet, e.g., the macromedium, and this medium self-configures itself. In a very close future, we will be "human addendums" (McLuhan 1994a, b) of a content, service and communication vicious machine wired forever to terminals and the thriving of this macromedium is such that words like offline do not make any sense anymore (Manovich 2001; Kelly 2010). This way, the macromedium will have an impact way bigger than the computer. What is happening is the Web 4.0 computation's experience. This is, beyond question, the age of the smart network linked with people and smart machines. For the first time in the digital history, we are forehanded by a machine of the machines which controls the digital, the space that once was iconic designated as "cyberspace" (Gibson in Neale 2000). We gave up making choices. Moreover, this is a machine that makes those choices for us (Mattelart 2000). Furthermore, what some people consider as a regression is truly a remarkable progress, thanks to Artificial Intelligence, Machine Learning and Smart Assistants. We have before us a macromedium, which perceives, consults, anticipates, guides and manages the information for ourselves. All the borders are highlighted since the simplified digital understands us and arranges each user's life

(Simanowski 2018). We are piloting our devices to log into the macromedium, we feel mesmerized by the scale of information produced on a daily basis.

Without differences between being online and being offline (Kelly 2010), the thing is that we are even more synchronized with the macromedium that allures us with its proposals, products and services (Armano 2009). In the age of the unifying multimedia medium (Lunenfeld 2011), what is happening is that we are more consigned to the condition of user-consumers (Gibson 2010). The Internet macromedium is a result of the Information Society plus the Capitalist Society (Castells apud Bell 2007). Hereupon, what remains is a new instance that does not have a center (if it ever had), in order to have a tendency to make us interact and interface only with a constellation of data, considering that the bluntest phenomenon is the unimedia and we are facing an unstoppable convergence (Jenkins 2006). The macromedium is a medium that allows the corporations to better-know our profile. One thing that changed was the software, too. There is no more ultimate software. Instead, there is always a "bug" to be solved (Kelly 2010; Lunenfeld 2011; Rushkoff 2013). We are in an era of unifying and convergence; such thing means that what is left is not the product but the experience. According to this, we feel formatted to act legally with a macromedium of the originals. The copies ended, so did the piracy. Or most of it. What remains is the user experience that we have, through terminals, to the information that is somewhere in the medium that contains-it-all and attracts everybody (Simanowski 2018). It is not by any chance that what endures people is the experience, the union and the convergence. These concepts have already been worked on by the corporate culture and the capital society. By met-up with the Internet 4.0, Capitalist Society inoculate the Information Society with its codes and, thus, thriving a model of interaction with the digital that leaves no choices to the user except to test and use it. In this macromedium age, nothing belongs to anyone. What we do have is access to a huge agglutinative medium, which contains the data of each age of the humanity (Srnicek 2017). This is a revolution. The huge quantity of information available nowadays proves that the user-consumers abdicated of their privacy to gain access to specific applications, products and services. The digital, or the so-called macromedium, works like a space that is transmedia, hypermedia and unifying, in which machines manage our data in order to have everything working better and linked with more machines. At the same time that even more information becomes available on the Internet, it turns into an even more privatized and functional space only if the users subscribe themselves (Smith and Telang 2016). The free-to-use Internet ended, so did the free contents. Together we are a legion in the macromedium where the compulsory future imposed for us is to consume things. In the future many people will be befuddled when they think that a pre-history, a remote phase existed on the Internet, in which amateurs set the consulted data because now everything is branded (Berardi 2011). The macromedium seduces us to adhere to new mediums and proposals (Karen Armstrong apud Castanheira 2012). The big difference in the present is that this network recognizes us, it knows what we do and what we are going to do. We are becoming as predictable as the 80's videogame characters (Frissen et al. 2015). Somewhere in the macromedium there is a brand that has access to our data and decided that it knows how to convince us to join the novelties. We have stopped being surprised by the proposals. We do not possess antibodies; thus, we are defenseless towards the macromedium. This enormous medium contains data within data and sub-media that we even are not aware of, but they surely know who we are. In addition, what makes all this fascinating is the fact that to the younger generations the Internet is healthy, normal, functional and cool. The positive side is that in the present any person with a smartphone can do many things (Jenkins 2013). Like now, that we are all terminal users as we use unfinished devices, the Internet connection becomes more prominent, mandatory, technical and systematically necessary. The digital equipment only makes sense when connected to the macromedium to take part into a big data constellation (Gibson 2010), which is the Web 4.0, meaning to have the power of the world-culture in the grasp of the hands. The Macromedium begins with our contribution, our login, on a micro scale, the smartphone, for instance.

2 Inside the Macromedium

Over the last decades, the all-encompassing medium was made with few gadgets and expansions. It is, in fact, the result of many media, brands, platforms and protocols, which culminate in the smartphone like a portal to the world's culture. The access that a user-consumer got today is a simplified and privileged one. The experience that unified and formed the unimedia (Lunenfeld 2011) is due to the fact the macromedium has become more seductive and reduced. We have ascended to the Internet macromedium by using our smartphones and in there we stay, consuming, being reformatted by the codes of this medium. We are the product and the message. Everything in this Internet is a fake flux because we make so many things and so many different ones that we are in a practically frozen mode, focusing on ourselves, as we returned the final product of the digital handing over our information to the macromedium (Simanowski 2018). This massive and dynamic medium has its own structure, a super-structure (Kelly 2010). Once inside the macromedium everything is turned into a constellation, we consult strings of data from files of even more data. We are archivists and collectors. We want to be in a bigger and polymorphic network, and as we can recall it all began with smartphones and their software, the apps, and then, we became sluggish and we chose the super-apps— they are the last bricks in the data constellation of the macromedium, they are unifying software pieces. Inside that, the user-consumer makes everything without leaving the app, always inside and always online (Smith and Telang 2016). The today's individual has on the Internet a way to become proficient. Now it is impossible to be outside. It is unnatural to be outside the macromedium. For what reason should we be out? The normal attitude is being inside, wired, updated and synchronized, apparently informed. Nowadays, nobody uses the computer to be online, the smartphone is the ultimate portal and access gateway to the real through the virtual macromedium (Rushkoff 2013). The smartphone became the primary device to pilot our way online.

Nowadays, the problem of the digital lies in its dimension and it is there that all the assistance and aid mechanisms come in so that we can check what is online. There is too much available information in our present time (Rushkoff 2013). These territories do not have some measurable charts, because they are dynamic and volatile. Yet, they transform themselves into fake fluxes. We tend to use only one app, only one brand, only one ecosystem and by doing this we become prisoners from nexus (Baudrillard 2010). We are overcome by the related paradigm—we are more connected and yet, we are more disabled due to the immersion of existing information. What caught us is the information and consumerism, creativity and novelty, knowledge and culture, technology and science, but the consumption is where we all find ourselves more frequently. There were moments in which the world was bigger than the Internet, then there was a second stage of this medium, which had as many spaces as the Internet; during the third stage, a unimedia process happened (Lunenfeld 2011), and in the actual Web 4.0, we have more Internet than the world. The macromedium became "worldlier" than the world itself, and it is now a separate world, unifier and demanding of our attention. "A medium in which everything is digital and uncomplicated", that was a goal to be reached some decades ago, but it is now that we truly reached to a phase where the macromedium is only one thing that we access to. Moreover, we are eager of information and we learn online with other people from a constellation. We are always in social mode and interlinked, we are interested in many different things (and even more interested in the good sense), we are adults and curious, we are proficient citizens of this new digital republic where every vote count, and we all have spectators. In this Web 4.0 phase, the experience we have got from the digital changed our habits. We do not know how to do anything offline. To possess offline devices has become suspect for many people. According to the mainstream opinion, the normal thing is being inside the wired social information flow in the macromedium platforms (Srnicek 2017). In addition, despite everything fits inside this medium, every user-consumer has its own unique and unified experiences, and no one sees or logs into something like any other person. The data constellations are of such magnitude that every path to be followed is countless, be it in a search engine, app or in a social network. It seems like we are more interlinked to one another, but on the other hand we are more distant from each other (Turkle 2011). There is only a link inside the macromedium. Outside the macromedium, there is only loneliness, fragmentation and alienation. Inside it, everything makes sense. We cannot be off because we are governed by some sort of mandatory fate. Being linked to the Internet has turned into a necessary priority. There is a neo-bourgeois horror of emptiness. In general, all people want to have everything and to be connected with everyone. We need guidance in this "pseudo digital desert" disguised as a cosmopolitan city. It is already common to be used to the commercial noise of the network, and that we do not stand the loneliness and the emptiness, we have difficulty in being alone with ourselves.

The main question that stands up is the fact that we are incapable of returning to a world without any mediation (Gibson in Neale 2000), media and announcements, games and brands, promotions and systems, software and platforms. One of the macromedium characteristics is the way it makes us feel like citizens of the world-flux. However, instead, it is capturing our attention and holds us by showing us mostly entertaining content. This new macromedium is as a comfort space, a playful data zone of learning and consumption (Baudrillard 2010). And when before there were elites and masses, now we all become elites and masses, spectators and producers. We are all Influencers now, both actors and audience of each other.

3   The Eternal Age

We are constantly bombarded with news about products, science spreads new feats and technology overcomes itself every two months. Everything changes, but at the very same time as we have a unified experience of the split landscape, what is happening is that it does not have the same time concept. The future is not so distant, and the past is not, too. It is a kind of an eternal present (Rushkoff 2013). We look back and forward always in a privileged position of a present so viciously eager about novelties. Following this we can find everything on Google or on YouTube (Gibson 2010). The macromedium leads us to a better way. It is impossible to surpass this system. In this moment of eternal novelty provided by the Web 4.0 the social changes and no longer these come from the outside but from the inside. Moreover, as we naively agree to give away our data on behalf of the macromedium proficiency, what is up is that this medium becomes even more agile, smarter and convenient. It scores on everything; it guides and corrects us. It jeopardizes our freedom of suggestions and rules. It is no more the man leading the machine. It is the machine leading the man, the addendum of its digital terminal (McLuhan 1994a, b). In addition, like in the twentieth century that the massification conquered the society of masses and the mass media, in this twentieth-first century the datafication is prevailing. Our data are the fuel to the new macromedium.

There were many paradigms: one was about the screen (Manovich 2001), after that there was another one about the window, and after that the one about the portal followed by the one about the network, and now the constellation seems to be likely in a society unplugged from the reality but pretty efficient in the digital relationships. In the new space, the concept of "macro" is apparent everywhere (Gibson et al. 2010). Every digital thing has a super-structure behind its curtains. It is so true that our relationship with the time is also a link towards the great archives of the real past. The unified experience sorts out for us the problem that all is excessive and what should get on is having a simple relationship with the digital. What we feel is due to the fact that everything seems to be always available online, either things in the present or things from the past. The eternal descendant from the digital now feeds up from the past. The more the macromedium knows about who we are and what we do, the better it anticipates our choices, and we do not need to leave the place because we are gifted with news and novelties according to our profile (Curtis 2011). We are always in line in this "always", imprisoned by "happiness machines" (Ibid). In the new macromedium, the space we attend is a semi-public space. We either are on the streets, or in our house, or, also, in the workplace. We are always wired and that, which is initially fascinating, ends up being somewhat scary, as time goes by. We are always working and always entertained. It seems like a contradiction, but it, indeed, is not. However, it is worth mention one thing: all the macromedium is a corporative space (Jenkins 2006).

The reader may question where the revolution resides. Well, it resides in the fact of having a consciousness ourselves, that the changes from the Internet mutated the society, which means, every one of us at all time. "Time" is our interface to move forward or backwards in the macromedium. This way we won't miss anything that occurs in the reality or in the digital files, too. We can always go back whenever we want. The error was eliminated from the system. The error is now rare. For all this, the data constellations we have the opportunity to look into are simultaneously playful and corporative (Rushkoff 2013). This new space is out of the control with those who seek the rarest things of all, because everybody has, see and buy the same things. Due to these reasons, the "non-mainstream" people are endangered. There is a lack of total connection and original connection on us. Again, we are being massified in some sort of new eternal digital that encompasses and embraces it all. We search in order to find something "truly" new that belongs to our time, since the macromedium lets us borrow things from the past and the glimpses from the future that previous generations had about the potential of our present.

4 Pilots of a New Environment

A heritage that comes from a digital culture since always is the idea that we could control our future and somehow, we could use the "cyber" media to be linked with the "cyberspace". Well, a few decades later we do that with our smartphones when we connect to the macromedium. The facilitated interaction present in these days helps us a lot in the daily life. There are no longer borders between online and offline, as well as the separation between leisure and work. Besides that, it is also true that now everything works with the apps and with "smart labels", icons and tags that allows us to interact quickly with the digital and with our friends and colleagues. Each user-consumer has his own community, and it tends to become a trend, which gets bigger. Now, instead of a vertical hierarchy, what rules is a horizontal heterarchy—we are tag manipulators, and we leap from link to link. For us everything is a matter of tag management actively in a smart environment, which comprehends, knows and guides us all. What changed in the last decades was the notion that exists a "seamless computing experience", and here Apple, Google, Facebook, WeChat and Microsoft have been following their roles to increase the integration with the smart environment and the super-apps in the macromedium, which is now widespread. Still, we cannot forget that to interact with this Web 4.0 means to interact with an overgrown medium of "enhancements", because we are augmented (Kerckhove 2010), expanded, connected and understood by a unifying digital medium, which is composed by a massive number of sub-pieces.

The Internet was a "scrolling medium" owing to the fact of its history of sequential media, something that came from with the Gutenbergian typography (McLuhan 1977a), the industrial revolution's assembly line (McLuhan 1977b). However, little by little, since 1990 we started being molded into pilots for smart environments. In 2007, when the smartphones expanded the market with the release of the Apple iPhone, everything changed. Suddenly the macromedium established itself observing the growing market of mobile devices for the user-consumers. Due to that, the first digital native contents emerge. In other words, not those digitized into the network, but contents directly done in the digital. This procedure started the network age (Postman 1994), which evolves into the cloud with the Web 2.0, the social networks and everything that progressively vanquished the blogs and brought forth the vlogues of the YouTube channels (Rodgers and Thorson 2012).

For people with radical views, we always were pilots of the reality even when we just read books. Nevertheless, it is the expansion of the macromedium that makes this clearer, namely with the assumption that there is no such things like a possible map, a real cartography for the digital (Baudrillard 2010), since everything changes in seconds. We are pilots sailing between waves of contents, screens and data constellations (Gibson 2010). What we can add is that there is something "arch-o-logical" in the macromedium, because it is as if everything is centered in a circular structure, a monolithic space with massive protection. Therefore, it is our digital space, a space mostly tried through smartphones where we are always totally exposed, many times by our own fault as it happens in Facebook and on Instagram, in which a person observes herself and self-controls through media, wishing to look good. The problem is that we are increasingly becoming more isolated, which is a paradox if we have in mind the social technologies we use (Turkle 2011). Moreover, this happens regardless of age and generation (McCrindle and Wolfinger 2011). Any person is a pilot in the way he or she enters the macromedium and ignores the surrounding reality. Now there is only portals or gateways accessing (apps and smartphones) to the huge medium that looks like a "big brother". Corporations ruling the whole system was predicted in cyberpunk science fiction (Gibson 2010). From our keyboard to the servers, we are in the medium interacting and piloting. There has never been so much access to information as now. In this moment, only those who do not want "to be in" are those who do not access it.

The Web 4.0 "killed" the computer; what remained were the tablets and the smartphones as favorite terminals access chosen by the user-consumers. Furthermore, what "killed" the Web 3.0 was the cloud. This generation of user-consumers has before themselves the macromedium, the biggest and most sophisticated access medium to the digital ever established by the man, an inestimable file archive. There is only one problem, which is that our interactions are basically public, because everything we do leaves a digital footprint (Carr 2008). What we do is a double-edged space synchronized with the network, and what prevailed was an "anarchic exploration" mentioned by Sherry Turkle. As of now, we learn how to deal with the digital with other user-consumers. No one knows more than any people do together. After all, we are people, authors, producers, editors and crowd at the same time. The difference is that in this age we also learn with the machines. We are a hybrid society (Bolton 2007).

The new currency is data. There is no doubt about that. In order to take advantage of this macromedium we need to understand that if something is integrated in the digital is because it was previously digitized, or it is a digital native content. This way, it is possible for every user-consumer to find something online due to the fact that conditions to occur the "findability" are created. For those who search, they always find something. Once more, we are all pilots, and we are all users and consumers. We are the ones who notice that the macromedium is the medium of all generations. There is also another factor to be considered: "search-capital". Knowing how to search for relevant information is of a great importance, so is to know how to be found online. Whoever knows the system's rules have more advantages. For some reason, it is called of "macro" and "medium". In a single place, we find everything and everyone, after all those are its greatest virtues. It was thought that disruption would come from outside, but in fact came from the inside, from the medium of all mediums, from the macromedium which is popularly and commonly called by Web 4.0. This is the greatest artificial memory ever been created in the history of humanity. Everything we do and could eventually do is predicted in the system. This hyper-medium is only comparable to cities in construction in the civilization that we know—it is one of the men's most remarkable machines and systems (McLuhan 1994a, b; Manovich 2001; Postman 1994).

The great dilemma is that despite people having more culture and information, it does not mean that the macromedium eradicates ignorance. Ignorance persists in a digital society because books provide the sure foundation for the development of all technologies and sciences, the book is the king and only a few people read books and study. The same occurs with Spotify, but after all the radios still play music. The macromedium is not a substitute medium; it is a medium where everything is found. It is a place of rendezvous, and not a replacement. The mass society ended but the mass media still exists. Nevertheless, the macromedium imposes itself, like technology in general (Kelly 2010). The macromedium is the outcome and the continuum of previous separate media.

5   Relationships and Spaces

In the macromedium space, we can make the following discrimination: connections are not relations (Turkle 2011). They both are very distinctive situations. What binds us is different from the relationships we keep. We feel more connected by "social media", but relationships that prevail depend on the classical social engineering, this means talking and interacting with people. Once in the macromedium what we have before us is basically a way to interact, to interface and work. What gradually increases is the expansive datafication (Simanowski 2018; Rushkoff 2013). All the digital spaces and apps gather data about us, and in this way, there is a lot information travelling around. We are as nomads in the digital desert except that in this desert there are many oases composed by brands that allure us with products and services all the time. In the present time, everything has a branding system (Armano 2009; Curtis 2011; Jhally 1995), and brands proliferate themselves, each one of them with its own unique identity and codes. We are a society of information, entertainment, and brands. In addition, everyone and everything fights for our attention. In this macromedium space, we are always patrolling as if we were on a war. We need to be careful about what we publish, say, show and register because we are always wired, and we do not have enough time to check all the items we post. There is no such thing as outskirts. We are always inside the medium of all mediums, in the space of all spaces, once called as "cyberspace".

To thrive in this society, we need to think-system, and when doing it culture, data and friendships are essential. Another thing we cannot escape from is the fact that products end but processes take place (Kelly 2010). This digital legacy implies the notion that everything updates and subscribes is becoming more normal. The property notion is in disuse. The idea comes from the software that is always unfinished and requires constant updates. In the current days, we do not possess things, but we are "obtaining" and "knowing" if we pay for such. In this society, the real spaces are mixing themselves with the digital spaces. What is not on the digital will get there soon. Nothing can stop the capitalist macromedium that merges the capital with information. We gave up owning things, instead we own services, and it is all a joint of relations, something intangible (Jhally 1995).

We are all using a "commitment device". We are only connected to what and to whom we consider interesting for us. There is a switch or icon to turn on or turn off (Carr 2008), but deep inside it, even when switched off the macromedium still operates in a stealthily way. The digital is not an option (Jenkins 2006), is a condition and that implies that we no longer have the option to leave, turn it off or disrupt from it. It is not possible to us to not participate. Also, that is why the word "computer" seems so outdated, because what we have before us is daily computation everywhere. There are no more connections and naïf relationships. Everything in the info-capitalist age has a reason to be. We live in an era of intangibilities, of processes and relationships (Kelly 2010). People no longer possess things, they subscribe services, and user-consumers seek for connector-events, something that boosts them and connects to more things, culture, consumption and the people (Jenkins 2013). We are information hunters in the macromedium's age. It is stronger than we are. In a mcluhanesque way, we can say that this digital medium that all encompasses is a medium that enhances, extends and continues us. Each one of us with his own unique story expands his narrative in the macro-narrative of the macromedium. It is impossible to say no to this allurement. Moreover, when we talk of a space, a place, we all are referring to media, to the digital space that embraces us, this multidimensional, enticing and shinning medium. We turned into tribes and market niches, neo-segments of thinkers and brands of the new age. We live in total synchrony with the media, since no one talks about formats. Formats do not matter. Any device opens any kind of file. What worries us are the relationships, which are getting more difficult to synchronize with us because we have been spending too much time of our lives in the digital.

Let us be realistic, the computer never was just a computer. The computer always was the network. From the computer to the macromedium some nanoseconds passed, and we suffer from this speed of the Information and Communication Technologies (ICTs). The digital spaces establish themselves, but the relationships are unstable because the human and anthropological social architecture was not planned to be mechanized or even electrified. We have been living and interacting according to the locals, cultures, and needs from each people. It was like this, before. Now it is not. What fact changed everything? The fact that now we all have media, or we all are crowds in a global scale. We all are brand personalities obsessed with new fashionable devices. We are a twentieth first century meta-society. At this moment, half a dozen of corporations is mastering everything we do and know everything about us. Apparently, we are in the age of the "you", but in fact, it seems like we live in soviet age of the "we". Remember, "big brother is watching us" (Curtis 2011).

There are no longer borders. It is all one planetary macromedium space; so, the concept of "devices" is diminishing. The remaining device is the one and only the macromedium itself. It is with it that we are wired. No one ever switches off from his terminal, the smartphone. The medium is not media; the medium is the mind (Kerckhove 2010). The macromedium is a neural device. It anticipates us, guides us and informs us. Thanks to that, the things can be found in a beta status (Lunenfeld 2011). We are in contact with a medium that demands constantly reconnection; this is the new sacred space, the new cathedral to where we look into. Whoever has more means, capital and resources wins the mediatic war that is the interaction with the macromedium where everyone is nowadays.

Once again, it is necessary to system-think in post-device and post-relation age. The computing experience changed drastically. Now we are all actors in a network, we behold narratives, and we are the heroes of the system. Our power is nomadic, because we are always moving. We are bound in the nexus of this network (Baudrillard 2010).

6 Images and Codes

Flusser told us that "Despite the text being image's metacode, some images will turn into text metacode" (1985, 7). When we are in the Web 4.0 surrounded by information, we see that there is an amalgam. Images allow us to search and interpret texts, and the same is valid the other way around. We are a meta-media society, as suggested by Manovich (2001). This society consumes trillions of images and videos per seconds. According to Postman "(…) the technopolitan remains still in the belief that the world's most need is information" (1994, 60). One thing that is not lacking in the macromedium is information that is only traceable because meta-data exists, which means information about information. We are all cyberpunk technopolitans. That is why Postman is right when saying that for a man with a computer everything seems to be computer's data (1994, 20).

The macromedium that surrounds us with screens, smartphones, smart TVs, tablets and laptops is something that keeps evolving since the cloud. Our data are remotely saved. As time passes, our data are becoming further away from us. What is happening is that the Web 4.0 has become a transmedia portrait, something fluid, commercial, irreverent, but also something predictable and abstract. Gibson develops the most important idea about the cyberspace, the idea of "macro-form" (2010). This way, the interaction model is the one of constellation since the beginning of the Virtual Reality in the 80's. What we consult in the digital spaces are the network "nodes", a fast cluster, an agglomerate of intermittent novelties. For those more casual "social media" users, everything is just a fake flux. Seems like the more we make "scroll", the more we are standing still in the same place, because the images change, but the codes are still the same. This society, according to Bauman, is confessional. Everyone shares his or her whole lives in the social network. Beyond this, as Barry Wellman would say, suddenly "the person has become a portal" ([2001] (cit. In Jeroen Timmermans apud Frissen et al 2015, 281). This is visible in the Facebook and Instagram user-consumer's cases. There is a mural and a timeline. We post everything in there. What is saving the experience from this kind of media is the fact that user-consumers publish their content creatively; this is also the case on YouTube, except that this creativity is a rebellion act (Joel Mokyr Apud Florida 2011, 19). The impact and the roles in the social network on the Arab Spring is a well-known example of this.

What turns the macromedium so peculiar is the fact that it can be considered as an "augmented environment" (Turkle 2011, 143). What is published has its own codes and extends our mind (Kerckhove 2010): what we think, how we are and what is our vision, on a specific moment, about the life, liquid, if we summon Bauman. In order to understand thus humanity's phase, not only as "Antropocenic" (the age of man), but also as "Mediacenic" (the age of media), we must know what have been expanding in the last five centuries with Gutenberg, and in the last ten years with the smartphones. We watch more movies, we read more news, and we publish and edit more contents. We have more media surrounding us hence we can speak of macromedium. Nowadays, the way to exist with so many social media require a little dose of "creative citizenship" (Koslow in Rodgers and Thorson 2012, 194). Presently, all of us have is entitled to have our 15 min of fame as said by Andy Warhol in the 80's, plus, now everyone has branding and a YouTube Channel. William Gibson said that "this is really happening.

We are inside … something, right here, right now… And it is out of control" (in Neale 2000). Now, what one can verify, even those who did believe in the end of the TV, is that the screens have multiplied—from computers to tablets and smartphones. Maybe that is why Gibson believed that we would be nothing else but "screen creatures" (2010, 155).

7 Conclusion and What Is Coming Next

Nicholas Carr assures that "data are the twentieth first century's dynamo". There is no doubt about that. The problem is that the designated digital masses are always linked to what Jhally names as fake "images systems" (1995, 189). The advertising and marketing images fit in this system. There is a whole communication emporium that makes the macromedium so efficient. The more apps and channels we use, the closer we are from the brands. Mentioned in another context, Phillip Kendrick Dick said that "the empire was never over". It seems that Karen Armstrong makes herself known in the documentary movie "The Time and The Mode" (Castanheira 2012), by saying "The empire is a fierce thing. It exists to dominate, plunder and conquer (…)". The brands' online role is to do this very same thing but focus mainly to ransack our data. By convenience we abide our privacy in exchange for using the apps. In order to be user-consumers, we gave up of our space. If in Mattelart we know that there are "monocultural borders" (2000, 156), in the macromedium age we are a little bit beyond this stage, we are in a new age of a single macro-culture because we all resort to the very same media in most parts of the globe.

   In the 90's, Alvin Toffler spoke of a "multi-channel society" (1991, 372). Not only we turned into that, but also, we made even worse, we turned into a multi-channel society inside of a macro-system. All of our actions are already predicted in the system. There is no escape. We are the network prisoners, or of the nexus, as said by Baudrillard (2010, 37). Spooked by the fact that the "cyberspace" is "mainstream" since the 90's, William Gibson says that macromedium which we experience nowadays, is a hallucinatory space, consensual, and among other things, it deals with a "space" notion more than concretely being just some sort of space (2010, 43). The one thing that is for sure is that no one seems to have the notion of what really is the cyberspace, but everyone is there and meets there. There is no greater example than the social networks. To Eric McLuhan, what astonishes him in the digital media nowadays is the fact that the individual is a system, "a legion" (cit. in Kerckhove 2010 LOC 255–397). Note that for Kerckhove the actual generation of "hyper-kids" has as its main characteristic the fact they are always online. (2010, LOC 73–397). On one hand this feeds the social networks and the entire macromedium which is the Web 4.0, on the other hand it increases the information entropy with the capital. We live in times in which everything seems to be ruled by a management system led by number and goals (Curtis 2011).

   It seems unavoidable that user-consumers turn into celebrities in neo-segments of the market. Armano truly believes that what we have today are "brandividuals" (2009, 5). In the same path, Lipovetsky and Serroy (2010) discusses that brands turned the individuals into an expansion of it, of its corporative speech. In what concerns the macromedium, we are not wrong, it is indeed a corporative, technical, agile and branded space. The positive side is that there is even more a monoculture in a worldwide scale, some sort of "young global culture" (Bolton et al. in Bolton et al. [Ed.], 2007, vii). And everywhere the younger generation are experts when dealing with the digital and the new media, well, with what Bell calls of "gibsonian datascape" (2007, 24), the digital data landscape, which seems more like to be a magnanimous and great medium: the macromedium. Who would say that from the "post-narrative world chaos" (Rushkoff 2013, Chapter 1, 63/64–564, paragraph 62), would bloom a unifying and simplifying medium? We passed from mass media to unimedia. And it was abrupt. There was an event of connection by "nodal points" and behold, nothing will be the same as ever before (Kackman et al. 2011, 10).

References

Armano, D.: When personal and corporate 2.0 brands collide. In: Digital Marketing: Personal and Corporate Web 2.0 Brands, Digital Next Column. Advertising Age, US, 23 February 2009. http://adage.com/article/digitalnext/digital-marketing-personal-corporate-Web-2-0-brands/134800/. Accessed 18 May 2014

Baudrillard, J.: The agony of power [2007]. Intervention series, n°6. Semiotext(e), Los Angeles (2010)

Bell, D.: Cyberculture Theorists: Manuel Castells and Donna Haraway. Routledge, New York (2007)

Berardi, F.: After the Future. AK Press, Oakland (2011)

Bolton, C., et al. (eds.): Robot Ghosts and wired Dreams - Japanese Science Fiction from Origins to Anime. University of Minnesota Press, Minneapolis (2007)

Carr, N.: The Big Switch - Rewiring the World, from Edison to Google. W.W. Norton & Company, New York (2008)

Castanheira, G.: O Tempo e o Modo [The Time and The Mode], Episode 3 – Karen Armstrong. In: RTP TV Documentaries, Pop, Filmes, Portugal, 14 June 2012

Curtis, A.: All Watched Over by Machines of Loving Grace - Episode 1. Love and Power. BBC, UK (2011)

Florida, R.: The Rise of the Creative Class [revisited] [orig.2011]. Basic Books/Perseus, New York (2012)

Flusser, V.: Filosofia da caixa preta [Black Box Philosophy]. Hucitec, San Paulo (1985)

Frissen, V., Lammes, S., Lange, M.D., Mul, J.D., Raessens, J. (eds.): Playful Identities - The Ludification of Digital Media Cultures. Amsterdam University Press, Amsterdam (2015)

Gibson, W.: Zero History. G.P. Putnam's Sons, New York. Apple iBook Store ebook version (2010). Accessed 1 May 2015

Jenkins, H.: Spreadable Media. New York University Press, New York (2013)

Jenkins, H.: Convergence Culture. New York University Press, New York (2006)

Jhally, S.: Os códigos da publicidade - o feiticismo e a economia política do significado na sociedade de consumo [the codes of advertising - fetishism and the political economy of meaning in the consumer society, 1987]. Edições Asa, Porto (1995)

Kackman, M., et al.: Flow TV: Television in the Age of Media Convergence. Routledge, New York (2011)

Kelly, K.: What Technology Wants. Viking, New York (2010)

de Kerckhove, D.: The Augmented Mind. 40 K Books, Milano, Italy (2010). (Kindle version). Amazon.com (2014). www.40kbooks.com. Accessed 1 Mar 2020

Lunenfeld, P.: The Secret War Between Downloading & Uploading. Tales of the Computer as Culture Machine. MIT Press, Cambridge (2011)

Manovich, L.: The Language of New Media. MIT Press, Cambridge (2001)

Mattelart, A.: A Globalização da comunicação [la mondialisation de la communication (1996)]. EDUSC - Editora da Universidade do Sagrado Coração, San Paulo, SP, Brazil (2000)

McCrindle, M., Wolfinger, E.: The ABC of XYZ [2009]. UNSW Press, Australia (2011)

McLuhan, M.: Understanding Media: The Extensions of Man [1964]. MIT Press, Massachusetts (1994)

McLuhan, M.: The playboy interview [March, 1969]. In: Playboy Magazine, US (1994b). www.digitallantern.net/mcluhan/mcluhanplayboy.htm. Accessed 3 Mar 2015

McLuhan, M.: La galaxie de gutenbergue, vol. 1. Gallimard Paris, France (1977a)

McLuhan, M.: La galaxie de gutenbergue, vol. 2. Gallimard Paris, France (1977b)

Neale, M.: No Maps for These Territories - William Gibson. Neale, M., US (2000)

Postman, N.: Tecnopolia - quando a cultura se rende à tecnologia [1992]. Difusão Cultural, Lisbon, Portugal (1994)

Rodgers, S., Thorson, E. (eds.): Advertising Theory. Routledge, New York (2012)

Rushkoff, D.: Present Shock - When Everything Happen Now. Current - Penguin Books, US (Apple iBook Store ebook version) (2013). Accessed 1 May 2013

Simanowski, R.: Facebook Society: Losing Ourselves in Sharing Ourselves. Columbia University Press, New York (2018)

Smith, M.D., Telang, R.: Streaming, Sharing, Stealing. Big Data and the Future of Entertainment. MIT Press, Cambridge (2016)

Srnicek, N.: Platform Capitalism. Polity Press, Cambridge (2017)

Toffler, A.: Os Novos Poderes [Powershift, 1990]. Livros do Brasil, Lisbon (1991)

Turkle, S.: Reclaiming Conversation – The Power of Talk in a Digital Age. Penguin Press, New York (2015)

Turkle, S.: Alone Together – Why Expect More from Technology and Less from Each Other. Basic Books, New York (2011)

Ustundag, A., Cevikcan, E. (eds.): Industry 4.0: Managing the Digital Transformation. Springer, Birmingham (2018). https://doi.org/10.1007/978-3-319-57870-5

Watson, R.: Future Minds. How the Digital Age is Changing Our Minds, Why this Matters and What We Can Do About It. Nicholas Brealey Publishing, Boston (2010)

Wilhelm, A.: Digital Nation: Toward an Inclusive Information Society. The MIT Press, Cambridge (2004)

Spheroids as Playful Audiovisual Interface on Tabletop Display

Yuma Ikawa[1] and Akihiro Matsuura[2(✉)]

[1] AlphaTheta Corporation, 4-4-5 Minatomirai, Nishi-ku, Yokohama, Japan
yuma.ikawa@pioneerdj.com
[2] Tokyo Denki University, Ishizaka, Hatoyama-machi, Hiki, Saitama, Japan
matsu@rd.dendai.ac.jp

Abstract. This paper presents a playful interactive system in which players manipulate solids of revolution called spheroids on tabletop display to create audiovisual expressions and make corresponding performance. Spheroids allow four basic movements based on spinning and rolling, whose geometric and physical parameters such as the contact area, its centroid, the (angular) velocity, and the curvature of locus are recognized from the data of the sensor sheet at the display based on electromagnetic induction. These parameters are effectively used for generating audiovisual expressions in real-time that match the movements. We developed an audiovisual content that integrates these functionalities and enables players to create their own expressions by manipulating a set of spheroids.

Keywords: Spheroids · Spinning · Rolling · Audiovisual · Interface · Musical instrument · Performance

1 Introduction

Simple 3D objects have been successfully used as tools and equipments in various situations and fields such as in daily life, engineering, manufacturing, play, sports, music, and so forth. Computer interfaces can be also regarded as such objects in the first place, but because of their digital nature, physical actions for input can be reduced to, for example, just minimally hitting a keyboard for command-line input. The concept of "direct manipulation" [1], in contrast to such command-line input, values the immediacy and the haptic quality in fostering physical engagement with an object, in which a manipulated object can be either physical or abstract. A more direct physical manipulation of objects is used for accessing digital information in the seminal paper [2] under the concept of Tangible Bits. Their Tangible Media Group at MIT has presented a number of systems in which physical objects, surfaces, and spaces are used as tangible user interfaces. The systems and installations of musicBottles [3], which uses glass bottles with cork lids for initializing and controlling music, and PingPongPlus [4], which enables digitally-augmented cooperative ping pong play, should be some of the initial systems that embody the concept.

© Springer Nature Switzerland AG 2021
M. M. Soares et al. (Eds.): HCII 2021, LNCS 12781, pp. 303–314, 2021.
https://doi.org/10.1007/978-3-030-78227-6_22

As for musical instruments, there are also novel digital tangible instruments [5–9], with which players can make sound and/or visual by manipulating physical objects, mainly on a table. However, types of movements and manipulation are rather limited to well-known ones, so it is of interest what kinds of new objects and movements we can use for audiovisual expressions.

There is also another viewpoint of "playfulness" of manipulation, which should be important especially in the fields such as entertainment, play, sports, and art. Manipulations of balls such as throwing, bouncing, rolling, and spinning, for example, should be playful themselves and help players to engage in the related activities. There are researches that use playful manipulation of objects as basis and further augment the activities by device and network technologies and audiovisual effects [4, 10–13].

In this paper, we focus on manipulating the geometric object called the *spheroid*, which is the symmetric round type of an ellipsoid and has a unique physical property of smoothly spinning and rolling on a flat surface in a variety of ways. We utilize it as playful interface manipulated on tabletop display for creating audiovisual expressions and for making corresponding performance. In the developed system, the spinning and rolling movements are accurately recognized through the geometric and physical parameters such as the contact area, its centroid, the (angular) velocity, and the curvature of locus, all of which are extracted from the sensor data at the display based on electromagnetic induction. The values of these parameters are also used for creating audiovisual effects that match the movements. After developing the basic system, we created an audiovisual content with emphasis on the unique musical functionalities of creating rhythms, their loops, and sound effects. We show demonstration of creating and performing original audiovisual expressions.

This paper is organized as follows. In Sect. 2, the object spheroid and its basic movements are introduced. In Sect. 3, the overview of the system we devised is given. In Sect. 4, the detail of the geometric and physical parameters extracted from the sensor data is explained and then in Sect. 5, we show how to use the parameters for audiovisual expressions and also demonstrate them in the actual performance. After making discussion on the system and the content in Sect. 6, concluding remarks are given in Sect. 7.

2 A Spheroid and Its Basic Movements

A spheroid is a special type of an ellipsoid that is obtained by rotating an ellipse along one of its axes. Different from a general ellipsoid with three distinct radii, two of the three radii of a spheroid are the same. This makes a spheroid possible to be manipulated on a surface in various ways and use it as a novel interface. More concretely, a spheroid has two types of rolling movements: (a) one is rolling with the longer side of the body laid horizontally, which we call Horizontal Roll; and (b) the other is rolling with the sectional ellipse to remain standing perpendicular to the surface, which we call Vertical Roll. These movements are shown in the first row of Fig. 1. Furthermore, a spheroid has two types of spinning movements: (c) one is spinning horizontally to the surface, which we call Horizontal Spin; and (d) the other is spinning vertically, which we call Vertical Spin. These movements are shown in the second row of Fig. 1. Since all of these four movements have their own ways of manipulation and physical properties, we utilize them for creating a new interactive system and content.

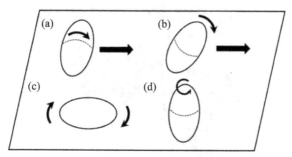

Fig. 1. Basic movements of spheroids: (a) Horizontal Roll; (b) Vertical Roll; (c) Horizontal Spin; and (d) Vertical Spin.

3 System Description

In this section, we describe the technical detail of the interactive system that uses spheroids on tabletop display. Figure 2 illustrates the overview of the system. It consists of a flat sensor sheet on which a white screen is set, spheroids manipulated on the display, a computer, and a projection system with a projector and a sputtering mirror. The sensor sheet we use is the product LL sensor [14] shown in Fig. 3(a), which is based on electromagnetic induction that reacts to metal and is specially laminated. The size of the sheet is 60 × 60 [cm] and the coefficients of electromagnetic induction are obtained at each cell of size 1 × 1 [cm], with values ranging from 0 to $2^{16} - 1 = 65,535$. The matrix data of the coefficients are sent to the computer with frequency of 100 [Hz]. When material made of aluminum or copper touches the sheet, the values of around 19,000–21,000 are obtained. At the computer, the matrix data are first utilized for extracting basic geometric and physical parameters of the spheroid on the display such as the contact area, its centroid, the velocity, the angular velocity, and the curvature of locus. Then, they are used for recognizing the four types of movements of the spheroid and for generating audiovisual expressions.

We designed and fabricated spheroids of various sizes using PLA and nylon resins. Some of the fabricated objects of sizes (diameter, height) = (6, 12), (6.75, 13.5), and (5, 15) [cm] are shown in Fig. 3(b). They are all covered with aluminum tape.

4 Detecting the Movement of Spheroids

In this section, we first describe the geometric and physical parameters of a spheroid and the methods to extract them. Then, we show how to recognize each of the four basic movements of the spheroid.

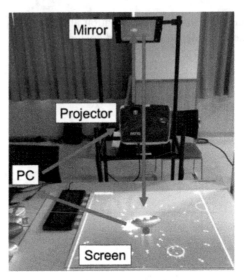

Fig. 2. System overview.

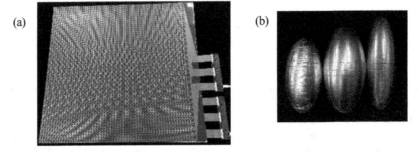

Fig. 3. (a) The sensor sheet based on electromagnetic induction; (b) Spheroids of three sizes.

4.1 Extraction of Geometric and Physical Parameters

The physical parameters such as contact area on the display, the centroid, the (angular) velocity, and curvature of locus are obtained respectively as follows.

The *contact area* of a spheroid is defined to be the number of cells with coefficients of values more than 2,000 as shown in Fig. 4. It is almost constant at Horizontal Roll and Horizontal Spin, while at Vertical Roll, it oscillates between the value in the vertical (smallest) case and the value in the horizontal (largest) case. At Vertical Spin, the contact area is the smallest in the beginning and it gradually increases as the body of the spheroid tilts. The *centroid* of the contact area is used as the point location of the spheroid. Its x- and y-coordinates are obtained by computing the weighted sum of the coordinates with the values of coefficients of electromagnetic induction over the cells of the contact area. The *velocity* of the spheroid is represented by the velocity of the centroid. The *angular velocity* of the spheroid is computed as the velocity of the angle of the unit vector of the longer diameter shown in Fig. 5, which is obtained by the method of least squares of the representative points of the cells in the contact area. The direction of rotation is obtained by computing the exterior product of the two unit direction vectors of the neighboring time frames. The angular velocity plays an important role at Horizontal Spin.

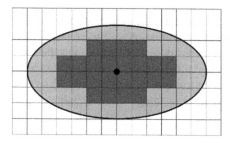

Fig. 4. The contact area of the spheroid and its centroid.

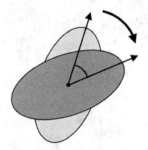

Fig. 5. Detecting the angle between the unit direction vectors of two neighboring time frames.

At all of the four basic movements, the locus of the centroid gives viewers main impression on the movement. So, we detect the information related to the *curvature of locus* and utilize them for audiovisual expressions. We first consider the set of vectors that connect two centroids of contact area for neighboring time frames and represent the curvature of locus at each time frame by the angle between the vectors. Then, when the angle is close to zero, so is the curvature and results locally in a straight line, while when the angle is large, so is the curvature and results in a steep curve.

4.2 Recognition of the Four Basic Movements

The four basic movements of a spheroid are recognized using the afore-mentioned geometric and physical parameters. The outline of the method is described below.

First we observe that at horizontal movements (roll and spin), the initial contact area is close to the maximum because the spheroid is laid horizontally to the surface, while it is close to the minimum at vertical movements because the spheroid initially stands vertically. So, horizontal and vertical movements are distinguished by the contact area in the initial time frames. Furthermore, Horizontal Roll and Spin can be distinguished on the velocity and the angular velocity in the initial time frames as follows. At Horizontal

Roll, the spheroid has a velocity of some amount and has a rather small angular velocity that oscillates, while at Horizontal Spin, the velocity is almost zero and the angular velocity is quite large in the beginning and is locally almost unchanged (or gradually decreasing). Therefore, they can be stably distinguished. Finally, Vertical Roll and Spin are distinguished on the contact area and the angle related to the curvature in the initial time frames as follows. At Vertical Roll, the contact area rapidly initially increases since the spheroid is laid down and furthermore, the angle of the vectors connecting two neighboring centroids remains almost zero since the spheroid rolls straightly, while at Vertical Spin, the contact area initially does not change much but the angle of the two vectors of the connected centroids changes drastically. Therefore, they can be also stably distinguished. Finally, we show an image of manipulating two spheroids simultaneously in Fig. 6.

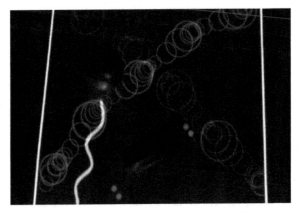

Fig. 6. Simultaneous manipulation of two spheroids in different movements.

5   Audiovisual Expressions

5.1   Basic Audiovisual Expressions

As our general strategy for audiovisual expressions, we assign minimal types of effects suitable to the movements. For visual effects, we use the simple ones such as the small circles for the centroid and the locus, circles or ripples around the centroid, and lines or end points for the long diameter of the spheroid. For sound effects, we correspond the volume and pitch to the parameters such as the contact area, the (angular) velocity, and the curvature. The actual correspondence and demonstration will be described in the next section for each of the movements.

(1) Horizontal Roll

Since Horizontal Roll is characterized by the velocity of a spheroid and the curvature of locus, given sound sources that we created beforehand, we assign the volume proportional to the velocity and also oscillate the pitch according to the curvature. The image on the display is shown in Fig. 7.

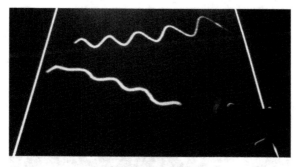

Fig. 7. Horizontal Roll.

(2) Vertical Roll

Vertical Roll is characterized by the contact area and the velocity, so we assign the volume and pitch proportional to the velocity and the contact area, respectively. The image on the display is shown in Fig. 8.

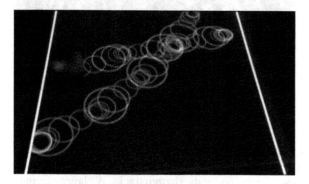

Fig. 8. Vertical Roll.

(3) Horizontal Spin

Horizontal Spin is characterized by the angular velocity, so we assign the volume and pitch proportional to it. The image on the display is shown in Fig. 9.

(4) Vertical Spin

Vertical Spin is characterized by the velocity, curvature, and the angular velocity, so this time we assigned the volume and pitch proportional to the velocity and the curvature, respectively. We note that the angular velocity is not used this time because the shape of the contact area is a mere circle in the beginning and the sensor data cannot tell the revolution of the spheroid itself. The image on the display is shown in Fig. 10.

5.2 Integrated Audiovisual Content for Performance

We developed an audiovisual content with emphasis on interactive sound generation and performance. The system was developed using Unity 2017.1.0f3 with C#. The graphical

Fig. 9. Horizontal Spin.

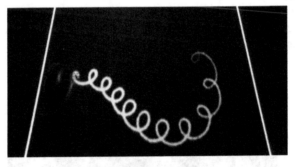

Fig. 10. Vertical Spin.

interface on the display consists of two regions: one is the region for rhythm tracks and the other is the region for free manipulation. The detail is written below.

Figure 11 shows the region for the rhythm tracks. A player executes Horizontal Spin in one of the three squares with desired speed, which results in the line segments to rotate in the circles like a radar chart. Different types of drum sounds such as bass drum, snare drum, and high-hat are assigned to each of the squares. Then, a player plots several points anywhere in the circles with desired contact area, which are used for generating drum sound when the line segments hit them. The farther a point is plotted from the center, the higher the sound pitch is defined to be, and the larger the contact area is, so is the sound volume. Figure 12 shows the remaining region on the display mainly used for freely manipulating several spheroids (we have tried three of them at a time). In this figure, Vertical Spin with an explosion-like visual effect is demonstrated. We have confirmed that two spheroids can be stably manipulated in different types of movements in a coordinated way to make audiovisual play and performance.

Figure 13 shows a screenshot of the demonstration of our audiovisual performance in which two spheroids are manipulated. In the performance, the basic speed of the rhythm tracks is first determined by executing Horizontal Spin. Then, points with various sizes are freely plotted in the circles, which make the original rhythm tracks to start. A pair of spheroids are then rolled and spun in the lower region synchronously to the background rhythms to make aurally and visually appealing expressions. In the figure,

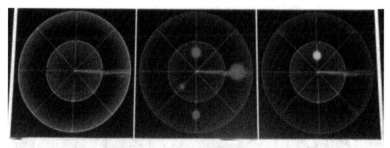

Fig. 11. The region for rhythm tracks controlled by Horizontal Spin.

Fig. 12. The free region in which Vertical Spin is performed with explosive effect. (Color figure online)

almost symmetric lines which consist of blue circles are drawn by Vertical Rolls using the pair of spheroids asynchronously with a little time lag, making tones with pitch oscillating according to the contact area. The purple curve segment at the right-bottom is drawn by Horizontal Roll, making tones with pitch oscillating according to the curvature. At the bottom, red (or rather orange) points are drawn along the long side of the spheroids when Horizontal Spin is employed. At the last portion of the performance, after executing Vertical Spin in the free region with the explosive effect shown in Fig. 12, the performance is finalized by gradually slowing down the rhythm with Horizontal Spins in the upper region and by finally cutting it out.

6 Discussion

In this study, we have used spheroids as interface that enables players to make audiovisual expressions and performance. Here, we discuss the results and potential of the spheroids as audiovisual instruments, system performance of the developed system, and the potential for live performance.

First, on the possibility of spheroids as audiovisual instruments, we confirmed through actual fabrication and manipulation that they can be handled and controlled rather easily. To be more concrete, Horizontal Spin and Vertical Roll among the basic

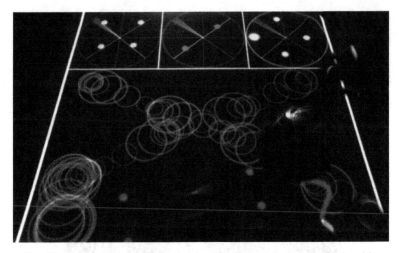

Fig. 13. Screenshot of an audiovisual performance using a pair of spheroids.

movements can be quickly learned because the moment of inertia lets the spheroids continue spinning/rolling stably as they are, which helps us manipulate them and make basic rhythms as we desire. Horizontal Roll and Vertical Spin, on the other hand, require some more trials, say, tens of trials, for skillful manipulation because spheroids tend to shake during Horizontal Roll and tend to decline by energy dissipation at Vertical Spin. But still, they can be learned for reasonable and appreciable manipulation. And once they are learned, at least two spheroids can be fairly controlled simultaneously (although it is a bit tricky to manipulate three of them). The uniquely tangible and dynamic aspect of spheroid interface with the audiovisual augmentation has also made the manipulation playful and entertaining for both players and audience, which should help the play and performance engaging and attractive. This implies that the spheroid interface is applied to a broader range of entertainment including gaming, (e-)sports, and media arts.

On the system performance of our system, it achieves real-time sound and visual generation, owing to the performance of the sensor sheets running in 100 [Hz] and also owing to the algorithms we developed for extracting the geometric and physical parameters. These features enable the interactive play and performance not only by a single player but also by several players. On the other hand, the system has prepared at present a limited number of audio and visual effects, so we need to prepare for a richer set of effects for allowing a variety of creations and performances.

Finally, in the viewpoint of artistic expressions, we have confirmed that we can create and make aurally and visually appealing performance with the unique style of rolling and spinning spheroids. So, we expect our system and the way of expressions are promising for both creation and live performance of audiovisual expressions. As for the variations of expressions, they should be further verified with a richer set of effects and an easy-to-use editing tool.

7 Concluding Remarks

We developed an interactive system for creating audiovisual expressions and making performance using spheroids manipulated on tabletop display and showed demonstration. The manipulation is unique, playful, rather easy, and can be applied to make one's own audiovisual expressions. As future work, we are aiming at improving and evolving the system on the issues discussed in Sect. 6 for a broader range of expressions and applications.

References

1. Shneiderman, B.: Direct manipulation: a step beyond programming languages. IEEE Comput. **16**(8), 57–69 (1983)
2. Ishii, H., Ullmer, B.: Tangible bits: towards seamless interfaces between people, bits and atoms. In: Proceedings of SIGCHI Conference on Human Factors in Computing Systems (CHI 1997), pp. 234–241. ACM Press (1997)
3. Ishii, H., et al.: musicBottles. In: Conference Abstracts and Applications of SIGGRAPH '99, Emerging Technologies, p. 174. ACM Press (1999)
4. Ishii, H., Wisneski, C., Orbanes, J., Chun, B., Paradiso, J.: PingPongPlus: design of an athletic-tangible interface for computer-supported cooperative play. In: Proceedings of the SIGCHI Conference on Human Factors in Computing Systems (CHI 1999), pp. 394–401. ACM Press (1999)
5. Patten, J., Recht, B., Ishii, H.: Audiopad: a tag-based interface for musical performance. In: Proceedings of the 2002 Conference on New Interfaces for Musical Expression (NIME 2002), pp. 1–6 (2002)
6. Dunn, H.N., Nakano, H., Gibson, J.: Block jam: a tangible interface for interactive music. In: Proceedings of the 2003 Conference on New Interfaces for Musical Expression (NIME 2003), pp. 170–177 (2003)
7. Jordà, S., Geiger, G., Alonso, M., Kaltenbrunner, M.: The reacTable: exploring the synergy between live music performance and tabletop tangible interfaces. In: Proceedings of the 1st International Conference on Tangible and Embedded Interaction (TEI 2007), pp. 139–146. ACM Press (2007)
8. Levin, G.: The table is the score: an augmented-reality interface for real-time, tangible, spectrographic performance. In: Proceedings of the International Computer Music Conference, 4 pages (2006)
9. Schiettecatte, B., Vanderdonckt, J.: AudioCubes: a distributed cube tangible interface based on interaction range for sound design. In: Proceedings of the 2nd International Conference on Tangible and Embedded Interaction (TEI 2008), pp. 3–10. ACM Press (2008)
10. Sato, T., Matoba, Y., Koike, H.: InteractiveTop: an entertainment system that enhances the experience of playing with tops. In: ACM SIGGRAPH 2011 Emerging Technologies (2011). Article no. 8
11. Kodama, S., Sato, T., Koike, H.: Smart ball and a new dynamic form of entertainment. In: Nijholt, A. (ed.) Playful User Interfaces. GMSE, pp. 141–160. Springer, Singapore (2014). https://doi.org/10.1007/978-981-4560-96-2_7
12. Matsuura, A., Matsukawa, T., Ohshima, H., Kurihara, H., Oriono H.: Stick'n roll: a playful stick interface for curved display. In: Proceedings of the 2015 Virtual Reality International Conference (VRIC 2015) (2015). Article no. 20

13. Nishino, T., Matsuura, A.: Magic bounce: playful interaction on superelastic display. In: 2020 IEEE Conference on Virtual Reality and 3D User Interfaces Abstracts and Workshops (VRW), pp. 680–681 (2020)
14. LL sensor. https://www.llsensor.com/. Accessed 10 Feb 2021. (in Japanese)

Path of Protecting Intellectual Property Rights on Fashion Design

Jia Liu[1,2,3]($\boxtimes$) ⓘ and Wenjing Li[4] ⓘ

[1] Nanjing University of Science and Technology,
200 Xiaolingwei, Nanjing 210094, Jiangsu, China
lyuuka@aliyun.com
[2] Jiangsu Research Center for Intellectual Property Development,
200 Xiaolingwei, Nanjing 210094, Jiangsu, China
[3] Jiangsu Copyright Research Center, 200 Xiaolingwei, Nanjing 210094, Jiangsu, China
[4] Beijing City University, 269 Beisihuan Zhonglu, Beijing 100083, China

Abstract. Fashion has become an important carrier of aesthetics in the eyes of modern people and fashion design has also become an important factor affecting the development of the fashion industry. With the increasing problems of intellectual property infringement of fashion design, it has correspondingly become an important topic as how to protect the Intellectual Property rights of fashion design. There are generally four paths of Intellectual Property protection for fashion designs: Copyright, Design Patent Right, Trademark Right and Anti-Unfair Competition Law Protection. The path of protecting copyright of fashion designs is the most comprehensive, but it has higher requirements for originality and aesthetics of fashion designs. The condition for protection by Design Patents is that the aesthetic nature of the fashion design shall be distinguished from the fashion functionality. The condition for protection under Trademark Law is that the achievement of distinctiveness in fashion design. The conditions for protection under the law against Unfair Competition are that the fashion product causes certain impact and that the fashion design leads to confusion; Each of the four protection paths has its own strengths and weaknesses. The fashion design in China is still in a mature stage of development, and a comprehensive protection path shall be adopted, which is characterized by the copyright protection as the main focus with the Design Patent Rights, Trademark Rights and Anti-Unfair Competition Law protection as complementary.

Keywords: Fashion design · Intellectual Property protection · Trade dress · Design Patent

1 Intellectual Property Issues in Fashion Design

Fashion design is a general term for a comprehensive design, which belongs to the category of arts and crafts, and is an artistic expression combining practicality and artistry. Fashion design art, as a carrier of the dressing function of people, has not only

M. M. Soares et al. (Eds.): HCII 2021, LNCS 12781, pp. 315–325, 2021.
https://doi.org/10.1007/978-3-030-78227-6_23

the commonality of general applied art, but also its own uniqueness in design content and form as well as artistic expression.

The earliest practical case in China that focused on the Intellectual Property Rights of fashion design was the "First Case of Chinese Fashion Design Copyright" in 1999- "The Fashion Copyright Infringement Dispute between Hu Sansan and Qiu Haisuo". Especially since China's accession to the World Trade Organization in 2001, the Intellectual Property Rights of fashion designs have received increasing attention. In recent years, with the establishment of the fashion design industry, the rise of fashion design and a large number of fashion design brands, the problem of Intellectual Property infringement of fashion design has also become increasingly salient.

Judging from the types of infringement, the problems of Intellectual Property Rights of fashion design mainly include copying or counterfeiting fashion design, confusing or taking advantage of famous fashion design brands, etc. In the type of copying or counterfeiting fashion design, the main manifestations include the highly similar designs of fashion pattern, fashion graphics and the overall style of fashion, which not only causes losses to the intellectual creation and economic gains of fashion designers, but also disturbs the order of the fashion design market; Confusion or taking advantage of famous fashion design brands mainly include the high degree of similarity in brand logo design, brand packaging design, brand publicity design, etc.

In response to this, there have been more and more calls for the necessity of Intellectual Property protection for fashion design, and so are the discussions and theoretical studies about the specific path of Intellectual Property protection for fashion design. The existing researches mainly hold two viewpoints: one is that the copyright of fashion design should be protected by multiple paths, for example, both Hao Min [1] and Jin Yin [2] believed that fashion design can be protected by multiple and comprehensive Intellectual Property Rights such as Copyright, Patent Right and Trademark Right; The other view is that fashion design is more suitable for adopting the separate protecting path. For instance, it is considered that the multiple Intellectual Property protection modes are more suitable for developed countries where the fashion design industry has become very mature, while there are still less well-known brands in fashion design industry in China. Therefore, it is necessary to adopt the separate protection mode with clear division between Copyright Law and Patent Law as appropriate. Generally speaking, among the existing research, there have been some research results on Intellectual Property Rights of fashion design, but relatively speaking; the systematic and targeted research results are still insufficient. Therefore, in this paper, it is intended to analyze the necessity of Intellectual Property protection of fashion design from a systematic perspective and to explore the optimal path of Intellectual Property protection.

2   Necessity of Protecting Intellectual Property Rights on Fashion Design in China

2.1   Fashion Designs Are Eligible for Intellectual Property Protection

First, fashion design is immaterial. Different from physical fashion, fashion design is the crystallization of fashion styles, patterns, overall styles, etc. It is essentially the artistic expression form of designers. It is widely believed in the Intellectual Property circle that the substantive characteristic of Intellectual Property is that the object is immaterial, that is, the object of Intellectual Property protection is the immaterial intellectual achievements carried on the material carrier [3, 4]. The immaterial nature of fashion design is consistent with the characteristics of the object of Intellectual Property protection.

Second, fashion design is creative. The process of fashion design can be divided into five steps, including: triggering inspiration; Looking for design concepts; Confirming design concepts; Design development; Extract and integrate all the analytical results for the final design. In this process, the fashion designers are required to constantly look at different fashion elements and integrate the design elements to innovate or even create new ones. The vitality and essence of fashion design lies in aesthetics and innovation, which conform to the creative character of the Intellectual Property object.

2.2 Protection of Intellectual Property Rights for Fashion Design Is a Demand for the Development of the Fashion Industry

According to relevant data and industry research reports [5], since 2014, China's fashion industry has been above 20 billion pieces, and in 2015 and 2016, the output was more than 30 billion pieces. In 2019, enterprises above designated size of China's fashion industry completed fashion production of 24.472 billion pieces. In 2020, under the impact of COVID-19 epidemic, enterprises above designated scale of the fashion industry completed a cumulative output of about 21.09 billion pieces. See the chart below for details (Fig. 1).

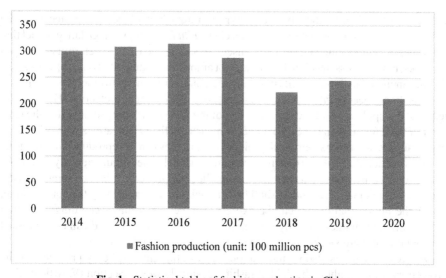

Fig. 1. Statistical table of fashion production in China

In recent years, young consumers have gradually become the main force of the fashion industry, and consumer philosophy has also been on the rational trend. With the steady growth of the high-end and low-end consumer markets of the fashion industry, the intermediate markets are on the gradual decrease, and such development trend is also fully consistent with the trend of fashion production in the statistical chart in the past three years.

With the development of the fashion industry, China's fashion industry has transformed into a fashion consumption trend of culture, fashion, branding and image, which are all dependent on fashion design. The personalization and fashion factors of fashion design are also gradually becoming the important factors in consumers' choice of fashion. It can be said that fashion design plays a vital role in the development of the fashion industry. However, disputes over Intellectual Property infringement of fashion designs are gradually increasing. It is imperative to strengthen the protection of Intellectual Property rights of fashion design, but the actual implementation is obstructed by loads of difficulties in fashion design [6].

3   Comparison of Intellectual Property Protection Paths for Fashion Design

An overview of the situations in both China and abroad, the existing Intellectual Property protection paths for fashion design are mainly four categories, namely the path of Copyright protection, the path of Patent protection, the path of Trademark protection and the path of Anti-Unfair Competition Law protection.

3.1   Path of Copyright Protection

It is not specified under the Chinese Copyright Law which objects are protected in the field of fashion design. Article 3 of China's *Copyright Law* adopts a legislative model that combines "exemplifying clause" and "miscellaneous provisions" to determine the types of works; nevertheless, fashion designs are not among the enumerated types of works, nor are they included in the exemplifying clause as a matter of course. In other words, fashion designs do not necessarily fall under the category of Copyright protection. However, in terms of the application of the law, Article 3 of the *Copyright Law* provides that the term "works" as referred to in the *Copyright Law* means intellectual creations with originality in the literary, artistic or scientific domain, insofar as they can be reproduced in a tangible form. It is generally accepted that three conditions shall be met simultaneously for a work to be protected by Copyright: first, it is an intellectual production in the literary, artistic and scientific domain. Second, it shall be original, i.e. it is created by the author alone; Third, the intellectual output can be expressed in certain forms. Accordingly, fashion designs that are characterized by originality, high aesthetic value and can be expressed in a certain form are works and can be protected by *Copyright law*.

At present, there is also no international convention that explicitly provides for the protection of Copyright in the field of fashion design, however, Section IV, Article 25(2) of the *TRIPs Agreement* requires member states shall choose either industrial design law or Copyright Law for the protection of textile designs. Although *Berne Convention* and *WCT* do not directly address the protection of "fashion designs" in their texts, they require member states to protect Works of Applied Art in their domestic legislation, and fashion designs can be protected under *copyright law* as Works of Applied Art. Although China's *Copyright Law* does not directly provide for Works of Applied Art, as a member of *Berne Convention* and *WCT*, Works of Applied Art shall be protected.

Thus, from a practical point of view, fashion designs with originality and high aesthetic value that comply with the law can be protected by the *Copyright law* as Art Works, Graphic Works, Model Works and Applied Art Works respectively in the different stages of fashion production. However, it is worth discussion as how fashion designs can be protected by *Copyright law*.

On the one hand, the originality of fashion design is reflected in the aesthetic value of tailoring, color matching, pattern design, etc. It is not easy when conducting the determination of originality and the similarity of two works in the comparison course of Copyright infringement. In the 1999 case of "the Fashion Copyright Infringement Dispute between Hu Sansan and Qiu Haisuo" [7], in which the plaintiff and the defendant were student and teacher, and the plaintiff argued that the defendant's award-winning fashion design *Story of Spring* had copied her design, thus suing to the court for copyright infringement. After the first and the second instance, the court held that the fashion design consisted of design elements, artistic shapes, craft structure and color matching, and was both practical and artistic, and shall be protected by *Copyright law* as works of applied art. Although the court affirmed that the fashion design can be a work, the court of first and second instance held that the overall expression of the fashion works of the plaintiff and defendant were different and so are their expression of emotions and thus did not constitute an infringement.

On the other hand, it can be found from the practical cases that *Copyright Law* requires a high level of aesthetics in fashion design. *Copyright law* does not protect creativity and colors or styles that are not original, and therefore it would be difficult to defend the rights when some of the popular simple and elegant fashion designs on the market are copied. In the lawsuit case between "HERAS Company and Dream Swallow Company" [8], the court of second instance held that the generic elements used by the plaintiff in the fashion design did not constitute original expression and could not be protected by *Copyright law*, otherwise it would lead to the tremendous monopoly of the design elements of the fashion, thus resulting in an imbalance of rights. In order to reflect the originality, the creative inspiration and individuality of the fashion designer shall be expressed artistically with a more aesthetic value through the combination of artistic modelling and color fabric.

3.2   Path of Patent Right Protection

In the context of textile design protection, *WTO* has suggested that "fashion" designs can easily be protected by invoking the industrial design protection methods [9]. Article 2 of China's *Patent Law* stipulates that "The term "design" refers to any new design of a product's shape, pattern or a combination thereof, as well as the combination of the color and the shape or pattern of a product, which creates an aesthetic feeling and is fit for industrial application". If the fashion design is to pass appearance design protection, the following three conditions must be met:

First, fashion design is the novelty of the overall or partial shapes, patterns, colors and the combinations thereof. Based on their own aesthetics, fashion designers create fashion design results that are both aesthetic and practical by using aesthetic knowledge and the comprehensive application of colors, lines, and design elements, and fashion designs should be distinctly different from existing designs or design features and combinations on the market.

Second, the fashion design can be applied in industry, for example, it can be applied to mass production of fashion. Fashion design is not only a conceptual design but should be used for realization of mass production insofar as the current conditions such as fashion materials, fashion production technology and so on are available. The designed fashion shall be able to fulfill the practical function of wearing.

Third, fashion design shall have its aesthetic value. Although it is in the category of a patent, the technical requirements of appearance design are not high, and the focus is on the aesthetic "appearance design", which is not recognized as a patent in many countries, and the examination criteria for design applications in China are not strict either. The aesthetic value of fashion design should be based on public acceptance.

Fashion designs can be protected by the appearance design system, but an important condition for appearance Design Patent protection is that the aesthetic nature of the design must be separated from its functionality. In other words, for fashion design, it should be aesthetically pleasing, which must be separated from the wearing function of fashion; if the tailoring and overall design of the fashion is necessary for the wearing function as a fashion, then it cannot be protected by the appearance design. However, most aesthetic designs of fashion are so integrated with functional utility that they can hardly be identified as aesthetic as required by the appearance design. In addition, fashion design enjoys a more highlighted timeliness than other designs. It is not so complicated in terms of the design application process, but it takes about six months from application to authorization. However, fashion is a seasonal commodity, and by the time a design is obtained, the fashion will be out of fashion.

3.3 Path of Trademark Protection

Fashion designs are generally not directly protected by *Trademark Rights Law*, which can protect Trademarks for fashion products but not fashion designs per se. This is because the function of Trademarks is to distinguish between different product providers and to enable consumers to be clearly aware of the origin of commodities. However, the possibility of fashion designs being protected by *Trademark Law* still exists. According to Article 9 of the *Trademark Law* in China, a distinctive trademark is indispensable in order to register and obtain protection under *Trademark Law*. If the fashion design itself obtains distinctiveness in design appearance because of its strong recognition, then it can also be protected by registering the Trademark. In addition, according to Article 11 of the *Trademark Law*, the aesthetic nature of the Trademark should also be separated from the functionality of the commodity, that is, if the fashionable aesthetic appearance of the fashion design cannot be separated from the function of the fashion such as covering and keeping warm, it is also not possible to apply for a registered Trademark for protection. This is the same requirement for Design Patent protection, where the fashion design should have a non-functional aesthetic nature.

The path to Trademark protection for fashion designs has been relatively lenient internationally. For example, the United States has been protecting the fashion design industry through *Trademark Law*, namely, by defining that fashion designs are protected through trade dress. Today, China is also beginning to move towards granting *Trademark Law* protection for designs. For example, the fashion shoes of the French luxury footwear brand Christian Louboutin are characterized by a "uniform color of red soles", and many celebrities wear the shoes of that brand, thus forming a certain social awareness and public influence. Generally, the relevant public will deem the shoes of that brand the same as the "red-soled high heels" (hereinafter referred to as "red-soled high heels"). It is exactly because of this, shoes of this brand were granted an international trademark registration for the distinctive feature "red color (Pantone 18.1663TP) used on the sole". However, in 2010, the application for territorial extended protection of the trademark for "red-soled high heels" in China was hindered when the Trademark Office rejected the application, considering that it lacked distinctiveness in terms of distinctive feature of the shoes –"red soles", thus rejecting the application. After the review, the first and the second instance court litigation, the Higher People's Court of Beijing Municipality made a final judgment at the end of 2018 [10], finding that "red for shoe soles (Pantone 18.1663TP)" belongs to a single color trademark with a limited location of use and can be protected, which means that China has for the first time protected a single color with a limited position, thus providing a very important path for the protection of Trademark Rights for fashion designs. Elements such as a single color of a fashion design are not protected by Intellectual Property Rights, but if such a single element gains distinctiveness in a designated position, it can be protected through *Trademark Rights Law*. In this case, it poses a very high requirement in terms of the recognition and visibility level of the fashion design in society, and if the public does not form a wide recognition on the design elements used in the designated position of the fashion, then it cannot be protected by *Trademark Rights Law* either, and may not be practical for a fashion design that has just been put on the market (Fig. 2).

Fig. 2. "Red-soled high heels" G1031242 trademark pattern (Color figure online)

3.4   Path of Anti-Unfair Competition Protection

It is most prone to have copying and free-riding problems in fashion design. Although it is still quite rare for people to mention the protection of the Intellectual Property rights of fashion designs through the perspective of *Anti-Unfair Competition*. However, the *Anti-Unfair Competition Law*, which protects the order of market competition, can effectively regulate the copying, counterfeiting and free-riding in fashion designs on the market. According to Article 6 of the *Anti-Unfair Competition Law* in China, it can be considered as unfair competition if there is an unauthorized use of a logo that is identical or similar to the decoration of another person's goods with a certain influence, or if there is a confusing act that is sufficient to lead people to believe that it is another person's goods or that there is a specific connection with another person.

Fashion design includes the design of fashion decoration itself and fashion packaging, and the unauthorized use of fashion decoration design shall be deemed as copying or counterfeiting fashion design. The decoration of fashion packaging is an important factor for the public to identify and choose from different fashion. Therefore, the unauthorized use of fashion packaging decoration not only damages the intellectual achievements of fashion designers, but also causes confusion to consumers, which can be regarded as Unfair Competition and shall be regulated. However, the prerequisite of identifying such confusion is that the logo of the goods needs to have "some influence" in the market, namely the fashion design should have "some influence" on the public.

4   Choice of Path of Protecting Intellectual Property Rights on Fashion Design in China

The past two decades have witnessed great changes taken place in China's fashion design. From the early years when fashion was only used to meet the basic function of covering up body and keeping warm, to the present situation that it has become an important carrier for modern people to meet aesthetic needs. Besides fashion quality, fashion design has become one of the most important factors affecting sales in the fashion market. However, as a later starter, and also due to the lack of design innovation abilities, China's fashion design is not yet fully mature. Moreover, the market competition pressures, and copying have seriously damaged the initiative of original designers and affected the development of the fashion industry.

From the discussion in the previous parts, it can be seen that there are many Intellectual Property protection paths in fashion design. Nevertheless, each protection path has its own applicable conditions and restrictions. The specific comparison is as shown in the following figure (Table 1).

By comprehensive comparison, the four Intellectual Property protection paths of fashion design have their own advantages and disadvantages. Therefore, China should adopt a comprehensive and diversified path of the Intellectual Property protection for fashion design. Among them, the Copyright protection path has the advantages of the simplest procedure, the shortest time cost and the most comprehensive protection scope, which is most suitable for the Intellectual Property protection of the fashion design in China, especially seasonal fashion design. However, in case there is a dispute over Copyright infringement of fashion design, and when identifying Copyright infringement, both the creative and aesthetic requirements of fashion design are relatively high, so it is difficult to directly identify as an infringement.

For example, in 2019, Shenzhen designer ROARINGWILD could not help but complained on the Internet that the latest fashion of HLAJEANS, a fast fashion brand under HLA, copied several of his original fashion designs [11] in 2018 (Figs. 3, 4 and 5).

Table 1. Comparison of intellectual property protection condition

	Applicable conditions	Restricted conditions
Copyright	Originality and aesthetics	High requirements for aesthetics
Design patent	Aesthetics	Differentiation between aesthetics and function
Trademark right	Distinctiveness	High requirements of distinctiveness, differentiation between aesthetics and function
Anti-Unfair competition	Constitute "confusion"	Have some influence in society

ROARINGWILD SS2018   HLA JEANS SS2019

Fig. 3. Comparison of two styles of fashion design (1)

It can be seen from the comparison diagram that from the overall visual effect, the fashion designs of the two companies are indeed very similar by integrating the design factors such as color matching, tailoring characteristics, overall fashion type and fashion materials in fashion design. In addition, Shenzhen designers' fashion was sold on the market earlier than HLA, which can basically be considered as copying in fashion design. However, although the original fashion designs of ROARINGWILD would be recognized by the relevant public as fashionable fashion, it is difficult to be recognized by the court in terms of originality and aesthetics of Copyright protection. The fashion of Shenzhen ROARINGWILD is characterized by color combination, logo of large letters and fashion tailoring. Although these designs would leave a fashionable impression to people, and they are also sought after by the fashion industry; however, on the one hand, these designs cannot highlight the originality of designers as the design elements such as T-shirt stripes and dark green are the public primary colors of fashion design. On the other hand, it is debatable whether the large neckline design of these fashionable fashion designs constitutes the aesthetics in the *Copyright Law*. Therefore, in this case, it is more

ROARINGWILD SS2018   HLA JEANS SS2019

Fig. 4. Comparison of two styles of fashion design (2)

ROARINGWILD SS2018   HLA JEANS SS2019

Fig. 5. Comparison of two styles of fashion design (3)

suitable to adopt protection through appearance design or Anti-Unfair Competition. Due to the strong seasonality of fashion design, the application time for appearance design may be too long. However, if such fashion design is recognized by the relevant public, it can also be protected through Anti-Unfair Competition, which may be more effective.

In conclusion, a comprehensive protection path shall be adopted for the fashion design in China, which is characterized by the Copyright protection as the main focus with the Design Patent Rights, Trademark Rights and Anti-Unfair Competition Law protection as complementary. That is, under the condition that fashion design can be recognized as a work, it will be protected by Copyright, otherwise it will be subject to the application for appearance design or Trademark protection according to the characteristics of fashion design, or if the fashion has certain influence in society, it can be protected under *Anti-Unfair Competition Law* (Fig. 6).

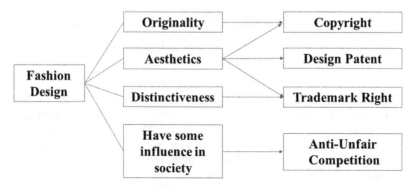

Fig. 6. Model of Intellectual Property protection on fashion design

Acknowledgements. This paper is the phased research result of the National Social Science Fund Project titled "Copyright Authorization Mode in All-Media Era" (Project No: 19CXW040).

References

1. Min, H.: Analysis of intellectual property protection modes related to fashion design. Intellect. Prop. **9**, 33–36 (2019)
2. Yin, J.: Intellectual property protection of fashion design. Silk **10**, 56–57 (2019)
3. Yang, L.: Basic Theory of Intellectual Property(I). China Social Science Press, Beijing (2013)
4. Qian, W.: A Course of Intellectual Property Law, 6th edn. China Renmin University Press, Beijing (2019)
5. Zhiyan.org. https://www.cir.cn/Pdf/FangZhiFuZhuang/22/ResearchofChina'sClothingIndust ryMarket_1686722.pdf. Accessed 5 Feb 2021
6. Bo, Y.: http://data.chinaxwcb.com/epaper2017/epaper/d6651/d5b/201712/83664.html. Accessed 5 Feb 2021
7. Higher People's Court of Beijing Municipality (2001). No. 18 Civil Judgment
8. Higher People's Court of Hebei Province (2007). No. 16 Civil Judgment
9. Zheng, Z., Xue, R.: WTO Accession and Intellectual Property Protection. China Foreign Economic and Trade Press (2000)
10. Higher People's Court of Beijing Municipality (2018). No. 2631 Administrative Judgment
11. ROARINGWILD Official. https://mp.weixin.qq.com/s/lYrD79G9ITDGkwNCJSnlnQ. Accessed 5 Feb 2021

Digital Fashion Communication: An Explorative Study of Fashion Newsletters

Tekila Harley Nobile[(⊠)] [iD] and Lorenzo Cantoni [iD]

USI - Università della Svizzera italiana, Lugano, Switzerland
{tekila.harley.nobile,lorenzo.cantoni}@usi.ch

Abstract. The retail sector is experiencing a time of change due to technological advances; also consumer habits are changing. This process of change has been accelerated by the Covid-19 pandemic, which is impacting individuals' daily lives. Digitalization is not only impacting consumers' shopping habits but also the communication between brands and consumers.

This study focuses on email marketing, in specific fashion brands' newsletters. The top 50 apparel brands according to the 2020 brand finance are utilized as a sample. It emerges that most brands have a newsletter, showing that it is still an important and widely utilized form of communication.

Then, it analyses the messages utilized to drive individuals' subscription. Three main themes are identified, cognitive, emotional and financial. Moreover, the information collected for the subscription process is registered. This allows to gain an insight into the personal information collected. Subsequently, it conducts a benchmark of the confirmation emails received. In total thirty-four confirmation emails are analysed, both the subject lines and the content. Interestingly, low levels of explicit personalization are found within the analysed messages.

Overall, this study shows the relevancy of newsletters and provides suggestions for future research.

Keywords: Fashion communication · Email marketing · Newsletters · Personalization

1 Introduction

Digitalisation is having a significant impact on society and businesses. Due to digital advances, the retail sector is undergoing a time of change, which is resulting in new opportunities and challenges. Also, consumer habits and desires are changing within the omnichannel environment. Consumers desire avant-garde interactions with brands and are willing to experiment more, leaving behind their favourite brands for new experiences. Hence, fashion firms are searching for new ways to integrate digital and physical experiences to better meet consumers' desires [1, 2].

The Covid19 pandemic is accelerating such transformation, forcing fashion brands to embrace digital advances and consumer changing habits [3]. To provide a full digital experience, brands are looking at innovations such as social shopping, gamification and

© Springer Nature Switzerland AG 2021
M. M. Soares et al. (Eds.): HCII 2021, LNCS 12781, pp. 326–339, 2021.
https://doi.org/10.1007/978-3-030-78227-6_24

personalisation. Moreover, in a time of pandemic and forced distancing regulations, the inaccessibility of physical stores is being addressed by technologies such as virtual and augmented reality to find original ways to integrate the human touch within the online experience and engage shoppers.

Now more than ever, agility is essential for successful marketing [4]. In such context and competitive market, developing and maintaining a relationship with shoppers on a regular basis is crucial for the success of a brand. Retailers have a vast choice of innovative communication tools to reach consumers, yet traditional tools such as emails are still widely utilized. The number of email users globally is expected to increase to 4.48 billion in 2024 from 3.9 billion of 2019 and the number of emails sent daily is forecast to grow to 347 billion [5].

Companies have long utilized emails to connect with consumers and create an asynchronous conversation. Email marketing has been widely adopted as it enables to reach a wide audience at a relatively low cost, and to engage consumers [6]. Despite its advantages, developing an email strategy/campaign can be challenging, as many elements should be carefully developed, from the content, the format and the design.

During the Covid19 pandemic the use of emails has intensified; firms have been utilizing emails to connect with their consumers and send comfort messages during the time of crisis to develop a sentiment of empathy [7]. However, this risks in resulting in a vast number of unsolicited emails in an individual's inbox and creating a sense of frustration and unsatisfaction [7]. The issue of information overload in the digital context is not a new phenomenon, hence developing effective and efficient forms of communication is essential [6].

As the online fashion sector continues to grow, it is crucial to understand the development of the digital communication strategies adopted by fashion retailers [8]. This study aims to gain an insight into fashion retailers' email communication strategy by analysing some of their pull and push elements. In particular, for the pull strategy, it analyses the *stimuli* or calls to action in the form of messages utilized to invite individuals to subscribe to their newsletter. For the push strategy, it analyses the content of the emails sent by the brands as a confirmation for the successful subscription. The top 50 apparel brands ranked by brand value in 2020 are utilized as a sample for this study [9].

2 Literature Review

2.1 Email Marketing

Developing and maintaining relationships with consumers has become increasingly important for firms in such a competitive retail environment. Hence, firms are implementing customer relationship management strategies aimed at managing existing and potential customers [10]. Various elements contribute to building a customer-oriented strategy; amongst them the literature shows the benefits of an active communication strategy [11]. Firms can utilize different kinds of media to communicate, engage, and build a relationship with consumers through a mixture of "paid", "owned" and "earned" media [12]. This research focuses on a type of "owned media", namely email marketing. Moreover, firms can utilize pull and push communication strategies. Pull marketing communication implies that consumers have control over the messages they receive [13], thus email marketing can be considered a pull marketing strategy when consumers have control over the messages they receive by actively deciding to which newsletters they wish to subscribe to. However, following the subscription, email marketing can be considered a push form of communication, as individuals do not have full control over the messages received.

As stated by Pavlov et al. [14, p. 1193] "email is part of a complex social system", hence it requires in-depth research. Moreover, to our knowledge, limited research has been conducted on fashion newsletters, hence the fashion field has been selected for this study.

Email marketing represents an important tool for a firm's digital strategy. It involves sending advertising messages with email accounts to either specific user accounts or mass messaging [15, 16]. A way to classify emails is to differentiate between spam and permission-based emails. In contrast to spam emails, permission-based email marketing requires an individual to opt-in and allow marketers to send them advertising content. As individuals do not expect emails from brands to which they have not provided consent through subscription, they usually perceive negatively spam emails [16]. This study when discussing email marketing refers to permission-based email marketing. In particular, it focuses on newsletters, which involve establishing an ongoing dialogue with consumers.

Due to its extensive use, email marketing is sometimes considered as an "old" form of communication compared to more recent forms such as social media. Yet, it is adopted for multiple purposes due to the advantages it offers retailers [11, 17]. It enables to deliver information to a large audience at a relatively low cost and create an asynchronous conversation between the firm and the individual [18]. Additionally, it represents a tool for consumer empowerment through consumer ubiquity, as individuals can access the information anywhere and anytime and they can share the information with other consumers without the involvement of the firm. The opt-in feature to obtain permission before sending a newsletter also enables to empower individuals [19]. By exploiting technology advances, email marketing can be utilized to increase interactivity, for example by embedding alternative forms of content such as videos, and drive traffic to the firm's website and other channels [16, 17]. Moreover, the opening of email messages and all further activities on them (e.g.: clicking on a link and eventually buying a product) can be fully traced, yielding to a rich information about addressees' interests and practices.

However, due to information overload, sending the newsletter to the recipient is not sufficient, as it is challenging to gain consumers' attention and reach the desired results. To overcome this challenge, firms are introducing strategies such as A/B testing to check which are the most effective messages, or personalised content, in order to create a better appeal for each recipient [14].

Despite its advantages, creating a successful newsletter campaign can be demanding [20]. The different aspects of a newsletter design are shown to be important for newsletters' effectiveness and consumer responses. The content in itself is not sufficient to attract consumers' attention [20]. Other elements contribute to its effectiveness, such as the location of the content. For example, the position and the number of links are shown to be crucial for consumer click-through rate, with links positioned at the left of a newsletter to be more effective than those positioned at the right and those at the top to be more effective than those at the bottom [20]. Thus, both psychological aspects and visual elements of a newsletter should be taken into consideration for optimal design, as they all contribute to information processing [18, 20].

2.1.1 Newsletter Personalisation

Emails risk of being perceived as invasive and intrusive. Additionally, navigating the vast amount of information can be overwhelming for individuals. Hence, firms are increasingly looking at personalisation in order to attract consumers' attention and provide relevant information facilitated by technology advances [21, 22].

Personalising a communication for an individual involves sending messages tailored to his/her characteristics or preferences [22]. To do so, different types of information can be utilized, such as an individual's personal information and/or product information [23]. Personal information is generally collected by retailers though pull marketing strategies. Whereas, in emails, product personalisation involves sending emails with products that match consumers' preferences. Such types of product-based emails can be explicit or implicit. The former type makes explicitly clear to the individual the reason for which he/she is receiving the suggestion, the latter type does not disclose the match between the product and the preferences, hence the individual might not be aware of the personalisation which has taken place [24].

Research has focused on the effects of personalised greetings. It is suggested that individuals are more likely to engage with emails which include an individual's personal information, such as the name. Addressing an individual by name compared to a generic version, has provided positive evaluations by individuals [23]. For example, emails with the individual's name in the subject line in the context of charitable donations purposes had higher open rates and higher donations compared to emails with a name mismatch [25]. However, negative effects have also been identified for personalised greetings. Such negative responses have been found to be moderated by familiarity with a firm. Whereas, consumers are shown to respond positively to implicit product personalisation. Hence, it is suggested that privacy concerns may be the reason for the negative responses [24]. Similarly, Munz [25] suggests that recent studies have more positive results compared to older studies because individuals are less concerned with privacy issues. Also, justification, which involves explaining the use of personal information for the offer suggested and perceived utility from the consumer, has been suggested to mitigate an individual's reactance to the personalised messages in emails [22].

Firms can utilize different personalisation strategies. In Human Computer Interaction studies, they are distinguished in implicit and explicit profiling methods. The explicit approach elicits the information directly from the individual, for instance through a questionnaire. Hence, individuals are generally aware how the information provided influences their interaction with the company. Whereas, implicit personalisation is based on an individual's responses to the firm's persuasive attempts. In such case, the individual might not be aware of the personalisation and how the information is utilized [26]. This study solely focuses on explicit personalisation. It analyses if and to what extent fashion apparel brands collect individuals' personal information during the subscription process and if it is utilized as part of the email confirming the subscription.

3 Methodology

A benchmark analysis has been conducted to analyse the content of the newsletters and compare them. The benchmark technique was developed to identify the industry practices that lead to the best performances. The goal of identifying the best practices is that a firm can then implement them in their own business [27, 28]. The benchmark technique has also been applied to evaluate online channels and understand the dynamics of a specific sector. For example, it has been utilized to analyse the website of a specific organization in order to measure it against other websites and identify its strengths and weaknesses [28].

The benchmark technique was applied to fashion newsletters in order to gain an insight into such practice. The top 50 apparel brands from the brand finance directory 2020 were utilized as a sample for this study. The subsequent section provides details regarding the process followed.

Firstly, their websites were checked for the presence of a newsletter. When present, the messages utilized by the brands to motivate individuals to subscribe were registered. A quantitative analysis of such messages was conducted through a word frequency count performed with the tool Nvivo. Then, two researchers, a male and a female, subscribed to the newsletters. When possible, during the subscription process, the sex was chosen accordingly. A grid was developed to classify the information collected by the brands from the subscription process. Finally, the emails confirming the subscription were collected and analysed. An analysis of the content of the subject lines was conducted with Nvivo. Then, a table was developed to classify the contents. The table included the indicators to describe the type of contents identified. It was developed through an iterative process. Each newsletter was analysed one at the time to find the indicators that enabled to classify all the contents; whenever a new indicator was identified, it was retrospectively searched for in the newsletters already analysed.

Such process also enabled to identify whether the explicit personalised information as the salutation or the name provided while subscribing was present in the newsletter. Moreover, the involvement of two researchers allowed to compare the messages received. In terms of messages, it also allowed to identify any differences in the contents depending on the personal information provided, for example the sex.

4 Results

The results are presented in three main sections: firstly, the strategies in the form of messages utilized to drive individuals to subscribe to the newsletters; secondly, the information collected by the brands during the subscription process; lastly, the content of the confirmation emails received following the subscription.

4.1 Strategies Utilized to Get Subscriptions

Forty-six of the fifty apparel brands selected for this study have a newsletter.

Only four – Next, Chow Tai Fook, Anta, and Primark – do not have a traditional newsletter. However, this does not exclude their presence online through other online channels or a different approach to email marketing. The brand Next provides the possibility to create an account, which involves the collection of personal information and the option to opt-out from receiving by email sale and other information relating to Next Group. Chow Tai Fook has a "Club newsletter". However, it is not necessary to sign-up to it in order to view it, as there is an archive of all the newsletters accessible to everyone on the website in the membership programme section. Whereas, Anta, which includes a portfolio of brands, does not have its own newsletter, yet this does not exclude that the brands part of the portfolio have a newsletter. Finally, a newsletter system was not identified on the website of Primark, which, due to its main audiences, might have decided to focus on social media channels.

From the sample of the forty-six apparel brands which offer a newsletter, it emerges that fashion brands utilize different ways to invite individuals to subscribe. Nine of the forty-six brands utilize pop-ups on their website to invite individuals to sign-up. Whereas, the others provide the option without pushing the individual, who can subscribe when navigating the website.

The most frequent words identified in the motivation messages are "newsletter" (19), followed by "get" (17), "sign (up)" (17) and "subscribe" (14). Some of these brands limit the message to such essential information. Whereas, other brands add information to highlight the positive implications that could derive from subscribing with words such as "latest" (11), "updates" (11), "first" (10), "exclusive" (9) and so on.

4.2 Data Collected to Subscribe

This section focuses on the data collected by the brands when subscribing to the newsletter other than the email address.

Table 1 shows the information that the brands either collect or do not collect.

Table 1. Information to subscribe

Information collected	Yes	No
Gender	23	23
Name	11	35
Surname	10	36
Country/postal code	10	36
Type of products	5	41
Date of birth	4	42
Captcha	4	42

The most frequent type of information brands ask for regards the gender. This type of information is collected by asking the title or the sex. These were checked for mutually exclusiveness; those brands which collect information regarding sex do not ask individuals for their title and vice versa. As from these types of information the brands collect similar knowledge regarding the individual, in this analysis all are grouped under "gender". Then, it emerges that brands are interested in the individuals' name and surname and information regarding the location in the form of country or postal code. Fewer brands collect individuals' preferences regarding the type of product they wish to receive, their date of birth, and use captcha to verify the subscriber is human. Moreover, an interesting case to highlight is that of the brand Rolex, which has the option "Please send me a copy as well". This option allows to subscribe not only yourself, but also someone else.

4.3   Confirmation Message

This section provides the results from the analysis of the confirmation emails received post-subscription. A total of thirty-four brands sent a confirmation email. Although the subscription to the newsletters was conducted in English, three confirmation emails were received in other languages, French or Italian. When possible, the contents of the emails received by the two researchers from the same brand were compared. For the brands for which only one email was received for analysis, this single newsletter was considered as part of the sample.

4.3.1   Subject Lines

Nvivo was utilized to find the most frequent words within the subject lines of the newsletters, then words in French and Italian with the same meaning were added to the count manually (Table 2). From this set of data, the most frequent message is a general "welcome" message. Other brands send a similar message by highlighting a sense of belonging to the brand community "You're in" or "You're On the Squad". The second most frequent word is "subscription", followed by "newsletter", and "confirmation". In the subject line, no personal identifiable information provided during the subscription is present.

Table 2. Subject lines word frequency

Word	Count
Welcome	15
Subscription – Iscrizione Inscription	11
Newsletter	10
Confirmation	4

4.3.2   Newsletter Content

From the analysis of the newsletters' contents, eleven themes are identified. The first theme identified is that of double-opt in. Three brands sent an email requiring a double opt-in, action to be taken by clicking on a link/button. As most brands do not utilize the double-opt in option, the first newsletter received is that of an introductory email to the brand's mailing list.

Of the thirty-four messages, nine have opening greetings. This theme classified as opening regard messages, includes the salutation messages utilized to introduce the newsletter, such as "Dear Valued Dior Client", "Dear Customer", "Dear newsletter subscriber", and a French greeting "Bonjour". Of these greetings, four were personalised in different forms as follows:

- "Dear Mr/Ms. name and surname": from a brand that collected title, name and surname
- "Dear name and surname": from a brand that collected title, name and surname
- "Dear surname": from a brand that collected title, name and surname
- "Dear name": from a brand that collected name

A theme connected to this one is the closing regard messages, which includes a closing salutation identified in ten emails, such as "Sincerely, Your OMEGA Team" and "With love, Pandora".

A total of thirty-one of the thirty-four emails include an introduction message to the brand newsletter. This message can take different forms: an explicit confirmation message of the successful subscription, welcome messages and/or thank you messages. The presence of these messages is not mutually exclusive.

Only three brands include an explicit confirmation of the successful subscription, which explicitly mentions the subscription such as "You're subscribed" or the more elaborated "Congratulations! You have successfully subscribed to receive our emails".

Twenty brands utilized explicit welcome messages to introduce the individual to the brand, such as "We're delighted to welcome you" and "We're happy you are here". Only one brand addressed the welcome by name.

Moreover, nineteen brands show their gratitude by thanking the individual for joining the newsletter "Thank you for choosing to be a part of the Valentino universe."

Five brands also insert their brand mission in the newsletter, for example "WHO WE ARE Calvin Klein stands for self-expression. From our iconic worn-to-be-seen underwear to our effortlessly evocative denim".

Another theme includes the type of messages the individual can expect to receive. The brands provide details regarding the type of content they will be sending and the benefits they will receive, such as online exclusives, pre-launches, latest collections, events, exclusive offers and many more.

Then, a theme classified as personalisation. This theme does not include the personalisation conducted by the brand, rather the invitation from the brand to provide personal information "Tell us more about yourself" and to create a personal account "Personalise your shopping experience by registering in My Account. You will be able to save your favourite items, addresses and card details, and verify the status of your orders and returns at any time".

Another theme identified is that of the discount code/gift/benefit provided the brand. These are the advantages that brands promise the individuals in order to motivate them to sign up.

Finally, a theme classified as "other" includes all those messages provided by brands to stay in touch, such as "discover more" messages, social media accounts, contact information, legal and privacy information, and unsubscription. Brands offer individuals the possibility to unsubscribe from the newsletter to stop the communication flow and in some cases they also provide the chance to modify the communication flow by selecting some personalised preferences.

5 Discussion

The advancement of digital technologies is enabling the development of sophisticated communication tools. Hence, firms have many communication outlets to reach consumers, yet it can be challenging to gain individuals' attention, which is divided across many channels [29].

This research focused on newsletters. Although, email marketing has been considered as an "old" form of communication, the study shows that traditional newsletters remain an important tool to reach consumers, as the majority of the fashion brands from the study sample have a newsletter. It is also important to specify that the few brands without a traditional newsletter have an online presence.

Firstly, this study examined the messages utilized to drive individuals to subscribe to their newsletter. While in general the overall driver is having a personal and unique relation with the brand, becoming known by it and familiar with it, provided motivations can be grouped in three major themes: cognitive, emotional and financial, as presented in Table 3.

Table 3. Main drivers to subscribe

Themes	Drivers/reasons why
Cognitive	*Completeness*: know everything should be known *Currency*: know before others (*vs.* FOMO)
Emotional	*Exclusiveness*: get a relation others cannot get *Discovery*: enjoy discovering the unexpected
Financial	*Pay less*: get discounts or receive special conditions/promotions

The cognitive theme refers to the factual positive implications that individuals will benefit from subscribing to the newsletter. Individuals can expect to receive "updates" (11) and "news" (10), stressing the timing aspect by being the "first" (10) to receive the information from the brand. Some brands do not specify which kind of updates, whereas others provide further details "Sign up for email updates on the latest Burberry collections, campaigns and videos." Firms appeal to consumers' fear of missing out (FOMO), a widely utilized tactic to stimulate an individual to action [30], in this case subscribing to the newsletter.

Then, some brands utilize emotional motivations. This is reflected in different terms adopted in the messages by the brands. Some stress the benefit of receiving something "exclusive" (9) and "special" (7), and the sense of discovery ("discover", 4). Brands utilize messages to elicit emotions [29]. These terms can be considered as an attempt to create a connection with the individual. In such a competitive retail market, developing a relationship with customers is essential [2].

Lastly, a financial theme is identified. This emerges from terms such as "offers" (6) "Sign up for emails to get special news and offers from the Nike family of brands."

Secondly, the study focused on the information collected by the brands for the subscription process. Brands collect mainly personal details such as gender, name, surname, country, and date of birth. In terms of preferences they only collect information regarding the type or category of products the individual is interested in receiving. Overall, it emerges that brands are not interested in collecting many types of information other than basic personal details. That might be due to several reasons. Among them: lowering the threshold to subscription (the more you ask, the higher the risk that a person leaves the subscription process), reducing legal obligations, not knowing (yet) how to use such data.

Thirdly, newsletters are considered to be easy to personalise [14]. Hence, this study analysed the content of the thirty-four emails received by the brands for confirming the subscription. Interestingly, not all the brands that collect some kind of personal details include them in the conformation newsletter. The gender is not utilized to tailor the content for the recipient and not all the brands that collect the name and/or surname include it in the communication. Although the newsletters do not present a high level of explicit tailoring, brands appear to be interested in personalisation as a frequent theme identified in the welcome newsletters is the invitation to provide further personal information and an invitation to create a personal account.

Moreover, the contents of the newsletters show a clear connection with the cognitive, emotional and financial themes identified in the motivational messages to drive subscription: the cognitive theme is identified in the information regarding what the subscriber can expect to receive; the emotional theme is reflected in salutation, the welcome, and thank you messages as they are arguably used to create a connection with the individual; the financial theme revealed by the discount code and gift information. These types of contents are in line with the literature findings, according to which emails are considered less intrusive when they offer value to the individual by providing product information, entertainment or some kind of financial reward [16].

6   Limitations and Future Research

This study provides an insight in the newsletter subscription practices adopted by apparel brands from the messages utilized to drive consumers' subscription process to the confirmation email. Results add to the understanding of online interactions between companies and their stakeholders, and can inform better practices by communication managers.

The results should however be considered also with their limitations. Firstly, the sample size is limited to 50 apparel brands, hence expanding it could provide further insights. Moreover, the images and the emojis are not considered in the analysis. Future research could include such information. Furthermore, not all personal information could be analysed, such as the use of the date of birth as the birthday dates inserted occur subsequent to the data collection for this study. Also, only explicit information was considered. Thus, further research could focus on the use of both explicit and implicit personalisation strategies within fashion brands' newsletters. Online behavioural insights will be fundamental for the e-commerce growth of fashion brands [31], thus research on individuals' online behaviour and the way in which such information can be utilized for personalisation and its effectiveness could provide valuable insights to firms' communication strategies.

Annex

	Brands
1	Nike
2	GUCCI
3	Adidas
4	Louis Vuitton
5	Cartier
6	ZARA
7	H&M
8	Chanel
9	UNIQLO
10	Hermes
11	Rolex
12	Dior
13	COACH
14	Tiffany & Co.
15	Chow Tai Fook
16	Victoria's Secret
17	Burberry
18	Anta
19	Ralph Lauren
20	Prada
21	Ray-Ban
22	The North Face
23	Levi's
24	Omega
25	Armani
26	Under Armour
27	Bulgari
28	Old Navy

(*continued*)

(continued)

	Brands
29	Moncler
30	Puma
31	Michael Kors
32	Saint Laurent
33	Primark/Penney's
34	NEXT
35	Tommy Hilfiger
36	Calvin Klein
37	Skechers
38	Hugo Boss
39	TAG Heuer
40	New Balance
41	Pandora
42	Bottega Veneta
43	Swatch
44	Bershka
45	Gap
46	Gilda
47	Converse
48	Valentino
49	Salvatore Ferragamo
50	American Eagle Outfitters

Source: Apparel 50 2020 Ranking. https://brandirectory.com/rankings/apparel/table

References

1. Bray, J., De Silva, K.M., Dragouni, M., Douglas, J.: Thinking inside the box: an empirical exploration of subscription retailing. J. Retail. Consum. Serv. **58** (2021). https://doi.org/10.1016/j.jretconser.2020.102333
2. Alexander, B. Blazquez Cano, M.B.: Store of the future: towards a (re)invention and (re)imagination of physical store space in an omnichannel context. J. Retail. Consum. Serv. **55** (2020). https://doi.org/10.1016/j.jretconser.2019.101913
3. BoF and Verizon Media: At Verizon Media, Making Extended Reality Technology Accessible (2020). https://www.businessoffashion.com/articles/technology/at-verizon-media-making-extended-reality-technology-accessible?utm_source=MyBoF&utm_medium=email&utm_campaign=follow_mvp&utm_content=1289850
4. Lewnes, A.: Commentary: the future of marketing is Agile. J. Market. **85**(1), 64–67 (2021). https://doi.org/10.1177/0022242920972022

5. Clement, J.: Number of e-mail users worldwide (2020) 2017–2024. https://www.statista.com/statistics/255080/number-of-e-mail-users-worldwide/
6. Deligiannis, A., Argyriou, C., Kourtesis, D.: Predicting the optimal date and time to send personalized marketing messages to repeat buyers. Int. J. Adv. Comput. Sci. Appl. 11 (2020). https://doi.org/10.14569/IJACSA.2020.0110413
7. Winet, K., Winet, R.L.: We're here for you: the unsolicited covid-19 Email. J. Bus. Tech. Commun. 35(1), 134–139 (2021). https://doi.org/10.1177/1050651920959192
8. Cantoni, L., Cominelli, F., Kalbaska, N., Ornati, M., Sádaba, T., SanMiguel, P.: Fashion communication research: a way ahead. Stud. Commun. Sci. 20(1), 121–125 (2020). https://doi.org/10.24434/j.scoms.2020.01.011
9. Apparel 50 2020 Ranking. https://brandirectory.com/rankings/apparel/table
10. Rahimi, R.: Customer relationship management (people, process and technology) and organisational culture in hotels: Which traits matter?". Int. J. Contemp. Hosp. Manage. 29(5), 1380–1402 (2017). https://doi.org/10.1108/IJCHM-10-2015-0617
11. Merisavo, M., Raulas, M.: The impact of email marketing on brand loyalty. J. Prod. Brand Manage. 13(7), 498–505 (2004). https://doi.org/10.1108/10610420410568435
12. Lovett, M.J., Staelin, R.: The role of paid, earned, and owned media in building entertainment brands: reminding, informing, and enhancing enjoyment. Market. Sci. 35(1), 142–157 (2016). https://doi.org/10.1287/mksc.2015.0961
13. Watson, C., McCarthy, J., Rowley, J.: Consumer attitudes towards mobile marketing in the smart phone era. Int. J. Inf. Manage. 33(5), 840–849 (2013). https://doi.org/10.1016/j.ijinfomgt.2013.06.004
14. Pavlov, O., Melville, N., Plice, R.K.: Toward a sustainable email marketing infrastructure. J. Bus. Res. 61, 1191–1199 (2008). https://doi.org/10.1016/j.jbusres.2007.11.010
15. Conceição, A., Gama, J.: Main factors driving the open rate of email marketing campaign. International Conference on Discovery Science (2019). https://link.springer.com/chapter/10.1007/978-3-030-33778-0_12
16. Chang, H., Rizal, H., Amin, H.: The determinants of consumer behavior towards email advertisement. Internet Res. 23(3), 316–337 (2013). https://doi.org/10.1108/10662241311331754
17. Tran, G.A., Strutton, D.: Comparing email and SNS users: Investigating e-servicescape, customer reviews, trust, loyalty and E-WOM. J. Retail. Consum. Serv. 53, (2020). https://doi.org/10.1016/j.jretconser.2019.03.009
18. Kumar A.: An empirical examination of the effects of design elements of email newsletters on consumers' email responses and their purchase. J. Retail. Consum. Serv. 13 (2021)
19. Hartemo, M.: Email marketing in the era of the empowered consumer. J. Res. Interact. Mark. 10, 212–230 (2016). https://doi.org/10.1108/JRIM-06-2015-0040
20. Kumar, A., Salo, J.: Effects of link placements in email newsletters on their click-through rate. J. Market. Commun. 24(5), 535–548 (2018). https://doi.org/10.1080/13527266.2016.1147485
21. Nobile, T.H., Kalbaksa, N.: An Exploration of Personalization in Digital Communication. Insights in Fashion Springer. HCI in Business, Government and Organizations. HCII 2020. Lecture Notes in Computer Science (2020). https://link.springer.com/chapter/10.1007/978-3-030-50341-3_35
22. White, T.B., Zahay, D.L., Thorbjørnsen, H., Shavitt, S.: Getting too personal: reactance to highly personalized email solicitations. Mark. Lett. 19(1), 39–50 (2008). https://doi.org/10.1007/s11002-007-9027-9
23. Walrave, M., Poels, K., Antheunis, M.L., Van den Broeck, E., van Noort, G.: Like or dislike? Adolescents' responses to personalized social network site advertising. J. Mark. Commun. 24, 599–616 (2016). https://doi.org/10.1080/13527266.2016.1182938

24. Wattal, S., Telang, R., Mukhopadhyay, T., Boatwright, P.: What's in a "Name"? Impact of use of customer information in e-mail advertisements. Inf. Syst. Res. **23**(3), 679–697 (2012). https://doi.org/10.1287/isre.1110.0384
25. Munz, K.P., Jung, M.H., Alter, A.L.: Name similarity encourages generosity: a field experiment in email personalization. Mark. Sci. **39**, 1071–1091 (2020). https://doi.org/10.1287/mksc.2019.1220
26. Kaptein, M., Markopoulos, P., deRuyter, B., Aarts, E.: Personalizing persuasive technologies: explicit and implicit personalization using persuasion profiles. Int. J. Hum Comput Stud. **77**, 38–51 (2015). https://doi.org/10.1016/j.ijhcs.2015.01.004
27. Madsen, D.Ø., Slåtten, K., Johanson, D.: The emergence and evolution of benchmarking: a management fashion perspective. Benchmark.: Int. J. **24**(3), 775–805 (2017). https://doi.org/10.1108/BIJ-05-2016-0077
28. Hassan, S., Li, F.: Evaluating the usability and content usefulness of web sites: a benchmarking. J. Electr. Comm. Organ. **3**(2), 46–67 (2005). https://doi.org/10.4018/jeco.2005040104
29. Batra, R., Keller, K.L.: Integrating marketing communications: new findings, new lessons, and new ideas. J. Mark.: AMA/MSI Spec. Issue **80**, 122–145 (2016). https://doi.org/10.1509/jm.15.0419
30. Hodkinson, C.: 'Fear of Missing Out' (FOMO) marketing appeals: a conceptual model. J. Mark. Commun. **20**(2), 65–88 (2016). http://dx.doi.org/10.1080/13527266.2016.1234504
31. BoF & McKinsey Company: The state of fashion 2021. http://cdn.businessoffashion.com/reports/The_State_of_Fashion_2021.pdf

COVID-19 Outbreak and Fashion Communication Strategies on Instagram: A Content Analysis

Alice Noris[✉] (iD) and Lorenzo Cantoni (iD)

USI – Università della Svizzera italiana, Lugano, Switzerland
{alice.noris,lorenzo.cantoni}@usi.ch

Abstract. The COVID-19 outbreak took place end of 2019 in Wuhan city in China, and since then, it has spread across the world. The virus has not only impacted the health of millions of citizens, since, in such a globalized and interconnected system, it has also impacted on human being's daily life and activities. In this context, the volatility of the global economy has led many companies to modify and readapt their communication and marketing strategies and the fashion sector has not been exempted from these changes aimed at further engaging customers and at encouraging sales on e-commerce platforms.

The present paper aims to provide an overview of the communication strategies on Instagram by fashion companies during an exogenous crisis, such as the first Covid19 wave, in a period that goes from January until end of May 2020.

The research seeks to determine if and when the selected companies reacted on their Instagram accounts to the first wave of the pandemic, and which were the contents and the topics proposed across the considered period.

The goal of the research is to present the state of the art of digital fashion contents offered during a period of crisis such as a global pandemic, where many fashion companies have decided to change their marketing and communication strategies to rebalance their usual conversational Instagram "tone of voice" with the needs and feelings of their stakeholders. It also aims to set the ground for further academic discussions on issues related to human computer interaction limits and potentials, when it comes to establishing alternative communication and marketing strategies during crises, such as the Covid19.

Keywords: Covid19 · Digital fashion · Fashion companies · Fashion communication · Instagram

1 Introduction

The COVID-19 outbreak took place end of December 2019 in Wuhan city in China [1], since then, the pandemic has spread across the world reaching, as in the week from 9th to 16th November 2020, 3'977'223 confirmed cases and 59'699 deaths [2]. But Covid19 spread has not only affected the health and the wellbeing of millions of people, its impact goes beyond its morbidity and mortality, since, in such an internationalized and interconnected planet, it has also deeply affected people's lives and habits across the whole

© Springer Nature Switzerland AG 2021
M. M. Soares et al. (Eds.): HCII 2021, LNCS 12781, pp. 340–355, 2021.
https://doi.org/10.1007/978-3-030-78227-6_25

world. According to Fernandes [3], the global economy and all the financial markets have experienced a fall due to the Covid19 pandemic and also due to the restrictive measures taken to reduce the spread of the virus, such as business interruptions, shutdowns and lockdowns. Furthermore, the volatility of the global economy has touched levels similar or even higher to the 2008/2009 financial crisis [4]. The pandemic, due to this uncertainty of economies, caused by the (potential) loss of jobs, by the stops of production and of the supply and distribution chains, has led many companies to modify and readapt their communication and marketing strategies to better meet people new situation and needs. Fashion companies have not been exempted from the impact of the pandemic, and according to McKinsey report [5], to survive Covid19, fashion executives and business leaders had to reinvent and still are trying to re-image the industry. Public health concerns have led many governments across the world to adapt social distancing measures and to require the closure of non-essential retail activities, such as also fashion. After the closure, many fashion companies pivoted their activities online and have started a series of social campaigns to fundraise for local and international communities and to help people across the world to survive the pandemic [6]. They also have put in place new business strategies, in order to further engage customers and to encourage sales on e-commerce platforms and on retail, despite the critical and delicate situation [7].

Such social distancing measures and lockdowns have underlined the increasing importance of well-designed social media strategies across the whole fashion value chain and have emphasized the inconsistency and narrowness of standardized human computer interaction (HCI) strategies, when it comes to face unexpected situations or events such as the current pandemic [8, 9].

During the Covid19 first wave, fashion companies on social media platforms showed different reactions to the spread of the pandemic, both in terms of timing and of contents provided. Some companies did not react immediately – be it due to an explicit decision or to a lack of preparedness – others, instead, decided to respond by proposing new contents to better attune with their customers, by showing to their audiences higher levels of empathy and closeness.

The present paper aims to provide a first preliminary overview of the communication put in place by fashion companies across a period that goes from the spread of the pandemic on January, until May 2020. In order to provide this overview, the research seeks to determine (i) if and (ii) when the selected sample of fashion companies reacted on their Instagram accounts to the first wave of the pandemic; and (iii) which are the contents and the topics proposed across the whole considered period.

The first part of the analysis has been dedicated to determining if fashion companies adapted their Instagram communication during the first wave of Covid19 pandemic and, if yes, their timing. The following part of the study, developed through a content analysis, aims to determine which have been the main topics proposed on Instagram by fashion companies during the period that goes from the first Coronavirus related post on each company Instagram profile (if any) until May 31, 2020.

The aim of the study is to investigate the state of the art of the digital communication strategies adopted by fashion brands during a period of global crisis. It seeks also to lay the foundation for further academic exchanges and reflections on aspects connected with human computer interaction limits and potentials, when it comes to set and propose alternative communication and marketing solutions in contingency and disruptive situations, such as the Covid19 one, that forced societies and communities to extensively and deeply reorganize people's lives and habits.

2 Literature Review

Human Computer Interaction (HCI) activities, broadly concerned with the design of instruments and tools that support and assist not only computer-mediated interactions between human and computers but also computer mediated interactions that occur among groups and individuals, especially after the birth of internet [10, 11] have more and more often an impact on people's and companies' everyday activities and habits. Among technologies that have most widely spread across the world by exploiting the intertwining between HCI and internet there are social media, which have been able to exploit the spread of the internet and through the years have incorporated some HCI principles [12, 13].

Despite such an increasing interest in social media studies from a technical and informatics point of view, still little academic research has been done on how companies should interact with these tools in order to increase marketing and communication performances [14].

Social media platforms offer a wide range of opportunities to companies through reduced costs, the enhancement of brand awareness and the increase of sale incomes [10]. According to recent studies, Social networks have become one of the most popular digital activities across the whole world and in 2020 over 3.6 billion people were using these platforms, a number which is expected to grow up to 4.12 billion by 2023 [15]. Through social media platforms, companies do not only promote their products through advertising campaigns, but they also use them as valuable sources to know more about customers' preferences and opinions [16].

However, while social networks are perceived as a valuable tool for marketing and communication activities, many questions still remain open concerning the most effective techniques for companies to present their contents and to communicate with their audiences in such an interactive, intimate as well as public, colloquial domain [17]. Furthermore, by using social media (blogs, social networks and online communities), consumers not only have discussions, share opinions and thoughts but also determine and reconsider which items are significant for them also in terms of brands relationships [18]. Brands in such environment have become facilitators of these social interactions by contributing to make all the stakeholders not external to their activities on these platforms, and making them active participants to the co-creation of the brand image and reputation, and of its economic value [18].

Moreover, social media popularity is increasingly growing, and managers are called to strike the right balance in order to define a coherent and cohesive online presence and to present the adequate "tone of voice" to their audiences [17]. Some experts argue that brands should utilize a more human tone of voice on social networks [17], others suggest that companies that succeed in social media are those which have maximized their abilities to tailor contents, language and tone according to whether the audience is a consumer, a prospect, supporter or a detractor, and others expects brands to adopt a traditional corporate communication style [19].

2.1 Crisis Communication

The value of a properly designed social media communication has been also emphasized by crises, that companies are constantly called to face in such an interconnected digital environment [20]. According to Dubrowski [21] a company crisis can be described as a short-term, unsought, adverse and critical situation within a company, which could be derived from both endogenous and exogenous variables, and which can put at risk the existence and the development of the company itself.

From a communication perspective within the fashion environment, a crisis can impact the whole company life cycle. The Rana Plaza and the Bravo Textile case as well as the Dolce & Gabbana's Chopsticks Backlash, the Gucci blackface sweater and the H&M's 'coolest monkey' jumper, are just some examples of endogenous crisis, which have involved fashion companies and that have demonstrated that this sector is not exempt from such crises, which not only impact business and production, but also communication strategies [22, 23]. Each of these companies was, in fact, called to face these crises also from a digital point of view by preparing *ad-hoc* social media strategies, in order to reduce the loss of credibility and to address criticisms [22, 23]. Also, exogenous crises, although not directly depending on fashion companies' choices, deeply impact on the communication strategies of the brands themselves, especially when it comes to a not fully "controlled" media [24]. In 2020, social media strategies have been, in fact, disrupted by the spread of Covid19 pandemic, which has had a strong impact on people social lives, including their time and practices on social media themselves [25]. To face such situation, many fashion brands had to rethink and adapt their communication and marketing strategies to keep engaging their audiences.

3 Research Design

To develop the present research, a content analysis has been performed, since according to the literature it allows an in-depth analysis and a detailed focus on social, cultural, environmental aspects of fashion on social media platforms [26]. Instagram has been identified as the preferred platform to analyze Coronavirus related contents provided by fashion brands, since, from one side, it is placed at the sixth place among the most popular social networks as for July 2020, considering the number of active users [27], and on the other, this platform is a highly visual medium, and it is among the preferred social media platforms by fashion brands, since it easily allows them to present their contents and products [28].

The content analysis has been realized considering the first 25 strongest retail brands (in US dollars) out of 500, listed by brandirectory.com [29], who evaluated retail brands according to the following criteria: overall brand value, marketing investment, familiarity, loyalty, staff satisfaction, and corporate reputation (see Table 1). The 25 brands represent 10 different countries: China, France, Germany, Italy, Japan, Spain, Sweden,

Switzerland, UK, USA and 6 different typologies of fashion retail businesses: Casual, Jewelry, Luxury, Sportswear, Underwear and Watches.

Three main research questions have been defined:

- Did fashion brands considered the pandemic within their contents provided on Instagram during the first Coronavirus wave?
- If yes, when have fashion companies started to keep into consideration the pandemic within their Instagram contents?
- Which kind of Covid19 related content did fashion companies provided?

4 Methodology

The study has been performed using a qualitative content analysis as research methodology, and only textual contents have been considered both on the captions and on the images, when available.

The analysis has been performed from December 5th to December 12th, 2020, and it collects all the posts published on Instagram by each selected fashion brand starting from the first Covid19 directly or not directly related post up to May 31st, 2020. A total of 1'758 Instagram posts has been collected (in the two cases in which no Covid related posts were found, no post has been included in the analysis).

In order to investigate the main contents related to Covid19 published by fashion brands the following research protocol has been designed. To analyze posts the English language has been used, which is the language mainly used by fashion brands in their Instagram communication strategies. When English was not available the coders have translated each post in English. The first part of the analysis was aimed to detect whether and when fashion brands posted the first content related to Coronavirus.

In order to measure the preparedness of each company, the simple indication of the date in which the first Covid19-related post has been published, has not appeared as a convincing solution. In fact, the Coronavirus crisis has affected different countries in different ways and times. In order to take this into account, several approaches have been considered. Using data people tested positive, or about death cases, or about lockdowns or other political decisions seemed to be problematic, because the comparability of such data across different countries appeared very limited. In the end, the Google Trend tool has been used.

This tool provides the frequency of searches of given keywords according to selected timeframes and geographical areas. It does not provide actual numbers of queries performed on Google, but it indicates when the highest number has occurred, giving it the standard value of 100, and plots the relative values of researches for other periods. The peak day for the "Coronavirus" Google searches, within the studied period and in the countries where the studied companies are headquartered, has been used as the reference point. It has been assumed as a proxy to indicate people awareness of the issue and interest in it. In fact, similar search data have powered the Google Flue Trends service, which since 2008 has provided a quite likely proxy to the actual flue prevalence in the USA and in other countries. In 2013, however, it appeared biased and not precise, because people started to search for flu-related keywords even without being directly affected:

social interest and concerns related with flue biased health-related measures [30, 31] up to the point that the service was eventually closed in 2015. However, for the goal of this research, such search-related measure appears to be relevant and unbiased: we might assume that in the peak day communication teams within the studied companies could not ignore the Coronavirus issue and should have been aware of its major relevance for their audiences.

Once determined whether Covid19 has found a place among Instagram posts by fashion brands during the first pandemic wave, and when, a content analysis has been performed.

First, Covid related posts (#880) have been distinguished into two different categories: "Directly Covid Related" (DCR) and "Non-Directly Covid Related" (NDCR). DCR posts (#612) are those posts where the reference to the pandemic is explicit, while NDCR posts (#268) are those posts where it was possible to see a reference to Covid but could also have been written in a non-Covid situation. For instance, posts suggesting make-up tutorials at home: they could refer to people confined at home because of lockdowns but could have been proposed also as general make-up recommendations in a non-pandemic situation.

The remaining "Non Covid Related" (NCR) are those posts (#878) that make no reference at all to the pandemic.

Then, to analyze the different typologies of posts, a codebook has been designed with a mixed, both top-down and bottom-up approach, to ensure thematic saturation. Although it was possible, in some cases, to identify within a post more than one topic, it has been decided to assign each post to only a category, the one that appeared dominant in the post itself. Table 2 presents such codes.

5 Results and Discussion

Hereafter, results are presented and discussed according to the three research questions.

5.1 Did Fashion Brands Consider the Pandemic Within Their Contents Provided on Instagram During the First Coronavirus Wave?

In relation with the first research question, which was aimed to understand whether fashion brands considered the pandemic within their contents provided on Instagram during the first Coronavirus wave, it is possible to state that 23 brands out of 25 (directly or indirectly) mentioned the pandemic situation within their posts. Two companies – Omega and Rolex, headquartered in Switzerland – never covered the pandemic in their posts, most probably to stay consistent with an image of timelessness and of strength, which is able to overcome all obstacles.

5.2 If Yes, When Have Fashion Companies Started to Keep into Consideration the Pandemic Within Their Instagram Contents?

Concerning the second research question, aimed to understand when fashion companies started to consider Coronavirus in their Instagram posts, Table 1 offers an overview on the analyzed items.

Table 1. Analyzed companies, ordered by headquarters' country.

	Country	Google Trends peak day (GTP)	Day of the first Covid-related Post (FCP)	Days between GTP & FCP	Total # of posts	Total # of Covid-related posts
Anta	China	25.01.2020	13.04.2020	79	33	13
Chow Tai Fook			09.03.2020	44	27	5
Cartier	France	15.03.2020	04.04.2020	20	36	15
Chanel			29.03.2020	14	95	49
Dior			20.03.2020	5	174	92
Hermes			24.04.2020	40	32	7
Louis Vuitton			20.03.2020	5	83	74
Adidas	Germany	22.03.2020	18.03.2020	-4	32	30
Armani	Italy	23.02.2020	16.03.2020	22	128	14
Gucci			24.03.2020	30	157	95
Prada			11.04.2020	48	68	8
Ray-Ban			27.04.2020	64	24	15
Uniqlo	Japan	25.03.2020	27.03.2020	2	42	23
Zara	Spain	12.03.2020	01.04.2020	20	63	6
H&M	Sweden	12.03.2020	18.03.2020	6	92	72
Omega	Switzerland	13.03.2020	–	–	–	–
Rolex			–	–	–	–
Burberry	UK	16.03.2020	28.03.2020	12	113	47
Coach	USA	15.03.2020	17.03.2020	2	116	62
Levi's			17.03.2020	2	131	70
Nike			15.03.2020	0	5	3
Ralph Lauren			18.03.2020	3	70	46
The North Face			17.03.2020	2	52	36
Tiffany			18.03.2020	3	90	39
Victoria's Secret			17.03.2020	2	95	59
Total					*1'758*	*880*
Average		*8.03.2020**	*25.03.2020*	*18.3*		

*While 8.03.2020 is the average of the dates listed in the table, 16.03.2020 it the peak day for the "Coronavirus" keyword at the global level, in the period 01.01/31-05-2020

Comparing the temporal reaction of the first Covid19 related post for each brand with the corresponding Google Trend peak date for each headquarter country, it is possible to observe that 12 brands (Adidas, Coach, Dior, H&M, Levi's, Louis Vuitton, Nike, Ralph Lauren, The North Face, Tiffany, Uniqlo and Victoria's Secret) adapted their communication strategy to the pandemic within maximum 10 days or even earlier than the Google Trend Search peak; 4 brands (Burberry, Chanel, Cartier and Zara) took between 11 and 20 days to adapt their contents to the Covid19 situation. Two brands (Armani and Gucci) took between 21 and 30 days to mention the pandemic for the first time within their Instagram accounts; while one brand (Hermes) mentioned Covid19 between 31 and 40 days after the Google trend peak of its country. Two brands (Chow Thai Fook and Prada) mentioned the Covid19 situation between 41 and 50 days after each Country related Google Trend peak date. Finally, two brands (Anta and Ray Ban) took more than 51 days to refer to the pandemic.

Results show that among the countries that host 2 or more headquarters of the considered brands, USA brands are the ones that reacted more promptly, taking on average 2 days to react to the pandemic. French brands took nearly 17 days to mention the pandemic while the Italian ones took nearly 41 days to consider it and the Chinese ones 62 days. Concerning the German, Japan, Spanish, Swedish and UK brands they took respectively, −4, 2, 20, 6, 12 days to react to the pandemic.

We could assume, however, that many international brands preferred to consider the international environment more than their national one, which is consistent with the use of English language also by those headquartered in countries where it is not the national language. From this perspective, which assumes March 16th, 2020 as the global Google Trends peak for Coronavirus, it can be noted that USA brands are, once again, the ones that reacted more promptly, taking on average 1 day to react to the pandemic. Chinese brands took nearly 11 days to mention the pandemic, while the French ones took nearly 16 days to consider it, and the Italian ones 19 days on average. Concerning the German, Japan, Spanish, Swedish and UK brands, they took respectively 2, 11, 16, 2, 12 days to react to the pandemic. A special caveat needs to be done about Chinese brands: Google usages are not representative of China because of censorship, for the same reason making a reference to the pandemic might have been a problem for those companies.

5.3   Which Kind of Covid19 Related Content Did Fashion Companies Provide?

As for the last research question, aimed to understand which kind of Covid19 related contents fashion companies provided on Instagram to communicate with their audience during the first wave of pandemic, results are summarized in Table 2.

Due to the fact that both DCR and NDCR posts could be referred to the Pandemic, and in many cases NDCR acquired a fuller meaning due to such a context (hence they were quite likely interpreted as such by their audiences), all their codes have been eventually combined. Doing so, a thematic classification of the topics according to four main categories has emerged: "Active Reaction to Pandemic", "Brand Reputation & Image", "Closeness to the Audience" and "Marketing" (Fig. 1).

Table 2. Codebook for DCR, NDCR and NCR posts. Categories are listed according to the frequency of Covid related posts (if not applicable, according to the overall number of posts).

Code	Description	DCR + NDCR	DCR	NDCR	NCR	Tot. #
Activities	Proposal of activities to entertain audience	260	189	71	56	316
Product advertisement	Advertisement of products or services with or without reference to the pandemic and its consequences	119	42	77	457	576
Brand representation & storytelling	Contents related to the storytelling of the brand both with a reference or without to Covid19	89	41	48	118	207
Empathy & closeness	Messages of closeness, empathy in relation to the pandemic	75	72	3		75
Positive vibes	Messages of hope, happiness and good wishes	67	60	7		67
Stay in contact	Direct questions or imperatives utilized by fashion brands to involve and engage audience	58	33	25	10	68
Stay at home	Expressions that relate to the life at home	56	53	3		56
Aid initiatives	Voluntary offers of help from brands to overcome the pandemic	40	40			40
Closing/Opening information	Information relating to the closure/opening of the stores	24	21	3		24

(continued)

Table 2. (*continued*)

Code	Description	*DCR + NDCR*	DCR	NDCR	NCR	Tot. #
Festivities & Events	Reference to the celebrations of festivities and events both Covid19 or non Covid19 related (ex. Earth Day, Mother's Day, Anniversaries, Birthdays, etc.)	22	11	11	83	105
Press	Information about the brand presence on the press	12	3	9	56	68
Health & Safety	Messages related to the importance of keeping people safe by adopting measures and by sharing information	11	10	1		11
Patriotism	Expressions related to the motherland	7	4	3		7
Thankful to collaborators	Expressions of gratefulness to all the employees that where engaged during the pandemic	7	7			7
(New) Projects & collaborations	Presentation of projects and collaborations with other entities, brands or stars	6	3	3	38	44
Togetherness	Expressions related to the possibility to overcome the pandemic together	6	5	1		6
Daily life	References to the daily activities that have changed due to Coronavirus	5	4	1		5

(*continued*)

Table 2. (*continued*)

Code	Description	*DCR + NDCR*	DCR	NDCR	NCR	Tot. #
Thankful to heroes	Expressions of gratefulness to all the people that work against the pandemic	*5*	5			5
Contact	Brands remind their audience that their webpages/social media accounts are actives to assist customers	*3*	1	2		3
Home working	Expressions used to highlight the condition related to the home working	*3*	3			3
Initiatives for Women	Support for gender equality, women empowerment with reference or not to pandemic	*3*	3		2	5
Logistic	Technical information related to product purchase and delivery	*1*	1			1
Sustainability	Information related to the development of sustainable products and to the promotion of sustainable initiatives	*1*	1		34	35
Black Lives Matter	Support to the movement Black Lives Matter and to activities against racism				7	7
Tips	Recommendations related to the use of products and to the possible activities to do with them				6	6

(*continued*)

Table 2. (*continued*)

Code	Description	DCR + NDCR	DCR	NDCR	NCR	Tot. #
Personalization	Information related to the possibility to personalize products				5	5
In memory of…	Remembrance of dead people				4	4
Made In…	Expressions related the idea and to the concept of "Made In"				1	1
Reviews	Request to provide reviews to the products				1	1

The category "Active Reaction to Pandemic", according to the present classification, encompasses all those contents provided by fashion companies that relate to concrete reactions to fight or to help people during Coronavirus pandemic, through activities proposed to the followers to entertain them, to advise them about the health and safety current regulations, through aid initiatives in order to provide money/materials/support to hospitals, associations and to women empowerment, and through the sharing of useful information for customers such as the closure or opening of physical shops due to Covid19, logistic and contact information to support the purchase and the delivery of products through their online platforms such as e-commerce and social media.

The category "Brand Reputation & Image" includes instead all those codes, whose main aim is to promote a positive image of the company during the pandemic in front of its stakeholders. It encompasses codes that refer to the brand history, storytelling and general representation. It also encompasses the launch or the promotions of new projects and collaborations, of sustainable activities and products, with the aim to further strengthen the image and the reputation of the brands. The category also includes the press representation of the brand and the interviews proposed on media, such as fashion magazines (Marie Claire, Harper's Bazar, Vogue, etc.).

The category "Closeness to the Audience" encompasses all those codes that relate to expressions of closeness to brand's audience, referring both to internal and external stakeholders, through the sharing of messages of hope, empathy, love, happiness, togetherness, patriotism and through a communication made of direct questions to further engage the followers. Furthermore, it includes the code related to festivities and events, through which companies share their closeness and celebrate anniversaries and festivities such as Easter, the Mother's Day, the Earth Day etc. This category also encompasses codes that share gratitude towards all those people that with their work and efforts have been engaged with the fight against Covid19, both within fashion companies, such as employees working to produce masks and medical gowns and outside fashion companies, such as all the medical and first aid staff engaged to save lives.

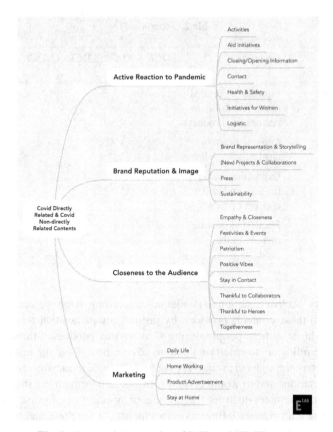

Fig. 1. Four main categories of DCR and NDCR posts.

The last category, which has been named "Marketing", refers to all those codes, that promote marketing strategies referring more or less directly to the pandemic. It includes posts that cover products, making reference to daily life, that has changed due to Covid19, and all the posts which are referred to product/service promotion, referring to the home working condition and to the necessity of staying and being at home. Finally, the present category includes the code called "Product Advertisement", that encompasses all those posts of product advertisement, which generally refer to some aspects of the pandemic such as the fact of being in quarantine, the lack of direct human relations, the lack of nature within people's life, and of outdoor sport activities.

6 Conclusions, Limitations, and Further Work

The objectives of the paper were to propose a first analysis in order to understand whether, when and through which contents, fashion brands have adapted their online communication strategy to face a situation of exogenous crisis such as the Coronavirus pandemic.

Despite the importance recognized to the digital communication within the fashion environment both from academics and practitioners [32], and to the fact that social media popularity is growing, and that practitioners are called to determine the right balance to promote a proper online presence and to present the adequate brand "tone of voice" [17] not all the companies analyzed have adapted their contents and their communication strategies to the Covid19.

The content analysis has revealed that during the first wave of the pandemic out of 1'758 analyzed posts, 880 were referred to Covid19. Although the global Google Trend peak of the search of the word "Coronavirus" is on March 16, 2020 the average date according to each first Covid related post publication is March 25, and on average, companies took nearly 18 days to post the first Covid related content. Furthermore, data show that less than half brands (12) reacted to the pandemic within 10 days from the Google Search Peak for each related country, 2 brands never reacted and 11 took between 19 and 79 days to mention it.

The paper shows the limits and the challenges that HCI still needs to face when it comes to face unexpected situations such as a global pandemic, which not only has increased the use of digital tools, but it has also changed the attitude of the stakeholders towards them.

Furthermore, the research shows that among the companies that have decided to adapt their contents addressing the topic of the pandemic, most of them emphasized the sense of closeness and empathy with their stakeholders.

The present paper has also some limitations: at first instance the research only considers 25 fashion companies, more extensive researches are needed to enlarge the sample. Moreover, the present study considers 10 countries, and the sample taken into account mainly refers to luxury brands, therefore, further studies are needed in order to amplify both the sample of countries and the typology of companies.

From a social media studies perspective, the analysis only considers one social media, Instagram, and therefore more extensive researches are required also on other platforms; in addition, the research does not consider for the content analysis visual elements of the Instagram posts, such as videos and images, unless containing textual elements.

In conclusion, further studies are required to also consider the direct experience of marketing and communication managers, who have worked within fashion brands, during the first pandemic wave, in order to analyze more in depth how the communication strategies have been developed and reorganized, and to further investigate whether some companies have purposely decided not to talk about the pandemic or to consider the first pandemic wave only at the end of it.

Other more in-depth researches could also be performed within the context of exogenous crisis communication within the fashion domain, also considering the audience reactions to each social media strategy adopted by the fashion brands.

References

1. Archived: WHO Timeline - COVID-19. https://www.who.int/news/item/27-04-2020-who-timeline—covid-19
2. COVID-19 Weekly Epidemiological Update. https://www.who.int/emergencies/diseases/novel-coronavirus-2019/situation-reports/

3. Fernandes, N.: Economic Effects of Coronavirus Outbreak (COVID-19) on the World Economy: IESE Business School Working Paper No. WP-1240-E (2020). Available at SSRN: https://ssrn.com/abstract=3557504 or http://dx.doi.org/10.2139/ssrn.3557504

4. IMF Warns Coronavirus Will Hurt Global Economy 'Way Worse' Than 2008 Financial Crisis. https://www.forbes.com/sites/sergeiklebnikov/2020/04/03/imf-warns-coronavirus-will-hurt-global-economy-way-worse-than-2008-financial-crisis/

5. The State of Fashion 2020. https://www.mckinsey.com/industries/retail/our-insights/state-of-fashion

6. Brydges, T., Hanlon, M.: Garment worker rights and the fashion industry's response to COVID-19. Dialogues Hum. Geogr. **10**, 195–198 (2020). https://doi.org/10.1177/2043820620933851

7. "Coronavirus" - Google Trends. https://trends.google.it/trends/explore?q=coronavirus

8. Six Tips For Using Social Media To Grow Your Business During The Pandemic. https://www.forbes.com/sites/forbesagencycouncil/2020/08/12/six-tips-for-using-social-media-to-grow-your-business-during-the-pandemic/?sh=1301ea8f7a22

9. Refocus Your Social Media Efforts During The Pandemic. https://www.sciencedirect.com/science/article/pii/S0895435620306521

10. Dwivedi, Y.K., et al.: Setting the future of digital and social media marketing research: perspectives and research propositions. Int. J. Inf. Manag. 102168 (2020). https://doi.org/10.1016/j.ijinfomgt.2020.102168

11. Van House, N.A.: Feminist HCI meets facebook: Performativity and social networking sites. Interact. Comput. **23**, 422–429 (2011). https://doi.org/10.1016/j.intcom.2011.03.003

12. Du Preez, M.: Blogging and other social media: exploiting the technology and protecting the enterprise. By Alex Newson with Deryck Houghton and Justin Patten. Farnham: Gower Publishing, 2010. 184 pp. £60.00 hard cover ISBN 9780566087899. Aust. Libr. J. **60**, 260–261 (2011). https://doi.org/10.1080/00049670.2011.10722624

13. McCarthy, J.: Bridging the gaps between HCI and social media. Interactions **18**, 15–18 (2011). https://doi.org/10.1145/1925820.1925825

14. Killian, G., McManus, K.: A marketing communications approach for the digital era: managerial guidelines for social media integration. Bus. Horiz. **58**, 539–549 (2015). https://doi.org/10.1016/j.bushor.2015.05.006

15. Number of social network users worldwide from 2017 to 2025. https://www.statista.com/statistics/278414/number-of-worldwide-social-network-users/

16. Bellavista, P., Foschini, L., Ghiselli, N.: Analysis of growth strategies in social media: the instagram use case. In: 2019 IEEE 24th International Workshop on Computer Aided Modeling and Design of Communication Links and Networks (CAMAD), pp. 1–7. IEEE, Limassol, Cyprus (2019). https://doi.org/10.1109/CAMAD.2019.8858439

17. Barcelos, R.H., Dantas, D.C., Sénécal, S.: Watch your tone: how a brand's tone of voice on social media influences consumer responses. J. Interact. Mark. **41**, 60–80 (2018). https://doi.org/10.1016/j.intmar.2017.10.001

18. Mandelli, A., Cantoni, L.: Social media impact on corporate reputation: proposing a new methodological approach. Cuadernos.info. 61–74 (2010). https://doi.org/10.7764/cdi.27.23

19. Ramsay, M.: Social media etiquette: a guide and checklist to the benefits and perils of social marketing. J. Database Mark. Cust. Strategy Manag. **17**, 257–261 (2010). https://doi.org/10.1057/dbm.2010.24

20. Vignal Lambret, C., Barki, E.: Social media crisis management: Aligning corporate response strategies with stakeholders' emotions online. J. Contingencies Crisis Manag. **26**, 295–305 (2018). https://doi.org/10.1111/1468-5973.12198

21. Dubrovski, D.: Peculiarities of managing a company in crisis. Total Qual. Manag. Bus. Excell. **15**, 1199–1207 (2004). https://doi.org/10.1080/1478336042000255578

22. Sádaba, T., SanMiguel, P., Gargoles, P.: Communication crisis in fashion: from the rana plaza tragedy to the bravo Tekstil factory crisis. In: Kalbaska, N., Sádaba, T., Cominelli, F., Cantoni, L. (eds.) Fashion Communication in the Digital Age, pp. 259–275. Springer International Publishing, Cham (2019). https://doi.org/10.1007/978-3-030-15436-3_24
23. Courting controversy: from H&M's 'coolest monkey' to Gucci's blackface jumper. https://www.theguardian.com/fashion/2019/feb/08/courting-controversy-from-hms-coolest-monkey-to-guccis-blackface-jumper
24. Fashion's digital transformation: Now or never. https://www.mckinsey.com/industries/retail/our-insights/fashions-digital-transformation-now-or-never
25. Koosha Z., Farahbakhsh, R., Crespi, N., Tyson, G.: A First Instagram Dataset on COVID-19 (2020). https://doi.org/10.13140/RG.2.2.13968.15364
26. Acuti, D., Mazzoli, V., Donvito, R., Chan, P.: An instagram content analysis for city branding in London and Florence. J. Glob. Fash. Mark. **9**, 185–204 (2018). https://doi.org/10.1080/20932685.2018.1463859
27. Global social networks ranked by number of users 2020. https://www.statista.com/statistics/272014/global-social-networks-ranked-by-number-of-users/
28. Kusumasondjaja, S.: Exploring the role of visual aesthetics and presentation modality in luxury fashion brand communication on Instagram. J. Fash. Mark. Manag. Int. J. **24**, 15–31 (2019). https://doi.org/10.1108/JFMM-02-2019-0019
29. Apparel 50 2020 Ranking. https://brandirectory.com/rankings/apparel/table
30. Lazer, D., Kennedy, R., King, G., Vespignani, A.: The parable of google flu: traps in big data analysis. Science **343**, 1203–1205 (2014). https://doi.org/10.1126/science.1248506
31. When Google got flu wrong US outbreak foxes a leading web-based method for tracking seasonal flu. https://www.nature.com/news/when-google-got-flu-wrong-1.12413
32. Noris, A., Nobile, T., Kalbaska, N., Cantoni, L.: Digital fashion: a systematic literature review. A perspective on marketing and communication. J. Glob. Fash. Mark. (2020). https://doi.org/10.1080/20932685.2020.1835522

Online Communication Design Within Fashion Curricula

Anna Picco-Schwendener[✉], Tekila Harley Nobile, and Tetteng Gaduel Thaloka

Università della Svizzera italiana, 6900 Lugano, Switzerland
anna.picco.schwendener@usi.ch

Abstract. The Covid19 pandemic has highly impacted on the education system. This paper presents the case of the Online Communication Design course of Università della Svizzera italiana. It focuses on the challenges and opportunities of adapting a traditional course to a hybrid and then to a fully online course. The research advances the literature on fashion education by discussing the relevance of the updated curricula for fashion students. Moorever, from the analysis of the course outcome, the research suggests practices that positively contributed to reaching the goals of the course and could be adopted in structuring and developing future courses.

Keywords: Online Communication Design · Online teaching · Digital fashion · Fashion curricula · Kanga

1 Introduction

Research on higher education is attracting the interest of scholars. Students should be equipped with the relevant skills to enter the challenging and competitive job market. Yet, education curricula are often outdated and fail to meet the requirements needed by the industries, leading to a gap between the education system and the job market (Morley and Jamil 2021).

The Covid19 pandemic is strongly impacting the education system worldwide as the traditional face-to-face teaching is being replaced by hybrid or online learning, which requires to deeply rethink the traditional instructional design.

This study addresses the topic through the case of the course Online Communication Design (OCD) taught at Università della Svizzera italiana (USI) as part of the curriculum of the Master of Science in Digital Fashion Communication.

Fashion students should be prepared to enter a difficult job market as employment opportunities will remain unstable until the Covid19 pandemic stabilizes (Milner 2020). Hence, addressing the topic of fashion curricula appears to be relevant as the fashion industry is undergoing a period of transformation due to technological advances. Moreover, the digitalization process of the fashion industry is being highly accelerated by the pandemic. The restrictions such as limited travel and social distancing are impacting the way in which the industry operates and such changes are expected to remain post

M. M. Soares et al. (Eds.): HCII 2021, LNCS 12781, pp. 356–370, 2021.
https://doi.org/10.1007/978-3-030-78227-6_26

Covid19, thus the fashion industry should be ready to embrace the new ways of operating and it requires employees with the relevant skills.

This paper is structured as follows: firstly, the theories of the OCD course and the instructional design aspects relevant for the design of the course are introduced; secondly, the course goals, structure, and group work project are presented, finally, the challenges and the opportunities identified from adapting the course to a fully online course are discussed, including the skills developed by the students relevant to their future career in the fashion industry.

2 Literature Review

This literature is structured as follows: firstly, it introduces the main theories and concepts used in the OCD course - role of communication, Online Communication Model, UX Wheel and User Requirements with Lego (URL) methodology - secondly it provides an overview of teaching instructional design aspects that were useful for the design of such a course for fashion curricula and with a combination of in-presence and online teaching methods.

2.1 Online Communication Design (OCD)

The Role of Communication. OCD wants to approach the design process from a communication point of view. It considers websites, apps and other softwares not only as a technical artefact, created by technicians, programmers or software designers, or as objects of visual design created by graphic designers, but first of all as a medium through which to communicate and to convey or share information, ideas and feelings successfully (Cantoni and Tardini 2006; Van Der Geest 2001).

Communication comes from the Latin word 'communis' which means 'common' and highlights the importance of creating a common understanding through the exchange and sharing of information (Lunenburg 2010). Various models have been developed, especially in the field of linguistics to explain the role of communication. Jackobson (1960) for example highlights six fundamental aspects of communication that are inter-related: there is always an addresser, also called sender, who conveys a message to the addressee or receiver. To be understood the message needs a context and code (e.g. a language) that are at least partially shared by the addresser and the addressee. Finally, a "contact, a physical channel and psychological connection between the addresser and the addressee, enabling both of them to enter and stay in communication" (Jackobson 1960, p. 3) is needed. Such channels might be "a phone call, an e-mail message, a face-to face communication, or a written report" (Lunenburg 2010, p. 2) but also a website, an app or social media. According to Rigotti and Cigada (2004) communication has to be considered as an event which produces a change in the addressee. It should be seen as an invitation to get involved by informing, making happy, requesting an answer, or soliciting an action.

These communication aspects remain true also in an online environment: a website is a channel through which an addresser, usually the manager or owner of a website wants to convey a message to an addressee, usually called user or audience of the website (Cantoni and Tardini 2006). The online environment allows for a vast variety of different communication types. As Cantoni and Tardini (2006) indicate "it is possible to have spoken conversations as well as written interactions; one-to-one communications as well as one-to-many or even many-to-many ones; it is possible to publish written texts with images and audio and video as well; it is possible to communicate in real time or to send messages that will be read later; it is possible to send and share documents of all kinds; and so on" (Cantoni and Tardini 2006, p. 43).

Even though websites, apps and social media are certainly technology-centered arte-facts, they should also "be framed as communication media" (Tardini and Catoni 2015, p. 134). To do so the Online Communication Model (OCM) developed by Cantoni and Tardini (2006, 2010, 2015), offers a comprehensive framework and the URL a well-fitting methodology, while the UX Wheel complements them with a user experience perspective on design.

Online Communication Model (OCM). The OCM offers a framework which facilitates the management of communication assets and which helps to understand what is needed to manage communication assets. It is structured around four pillars and a fifth element: the content and services, the accessibility tools, the people managing the resources and the people accessing the resources; the fifth element is represented by the context and the information competitors (Tardini and Cantoni 2015). Within the design process this framework is generally applied in reverse order (reverse design) starting from the 5th element.

A website or an app always has to be considered within a given context, the so-called semiosphere, in order to acquire a specific meaning and value of what it is and of what it is not. It is placed in a market with competitors. This is particularly relevant for the online environment where all other players are just one click away. Thus, a competitive advantage often lasts only for a few hours. Furthermore, in the online environment, both direct and indirect competitors should be considered.

Pillar IV is about the audience, the users of the website or the app. It is of fundamental importance to clearly define the primary and eventually secondary audience and identify their needs and expectations. There are many different methods to learn about user needs ranging from surveys to interviews and focus groups and to observational techniques.

Pillar III involves identifying all those people who are involved in the management of the website or app. This includes those having the initial idea, those who design, code, test, maintain, promote, evaluate and eventually those who interact with the users. Each role has to be clearly defined and adequate resources allocated in a way that the editorial management of the website/app can be sustainable for the organization.

Pillar II solicits designers to consider everything that is actually needed to make the contents and the services (Pillar I) available to the intended audience. This means for example reflecting about the most suitable hardware, needed software, Internet con-nectivity and publication outlets. In this step it is particularly important to consider accessibility issues by disabled, badly equipped or less-skilled people.

Finally Pillar I focuses on the contents and services of a website. Possible services might be buying, voting, interacting, gambling, booking, making appointments, paying taxes, etc. while contents are texts, images, videos, sounds, colors, layout etc. Email is an example of both content and service. The content simply says "our email address is xxx".

This short text however is also an implicit declaration of a service meaning that if you send an email, there will be someone responsible for reading and possibly answering it. Particular attention has to be paid to information quality and its five main evaluation criteria: accuracy, authority, objectivity, currency and coverage (Tate and Alexander 1999). Just as important is the service quality, which should help to bridge the distance between the user and the service provider. It includes all the conditions of the service, providing detailed information about the steps in a process (e.g. completed steps, next steps to be done, how to cancel a process) and guaranteeing that the offered services work. Additionally, aspects of localization have to be considered in order to guarantee the adequacy of contents to users from a cultural point of view. This might include translations, date format, currencies, measures and sizes, rules and laws, historical, cultural, religious, and seasonal elements.

The OCM framework considers communication and its design is a process and suggests that it is important to design the whole process and not only the final artefact. This is particularly important because often the operational costs of a good website or app are much higher than the production costs. Hence, management, promotion and evaluation through the definition of key performance indicators (KPIs) are important aspects to be considered.

UX Wheel. User Experience (UX) is another discipline that approaches design in a holistic and user-centered way and attributes importance to communication aspects. According to Norman and Nielsen (n.d.), the inventors of the term UX, it "encompasses all aspects of the en-user's interaction with the company, its services, and its products". Functionality, esthetics and emotions all play an important role. In fact, Norman and Nielsen (n.d.) suggest that products need to be simple, elegant and "a joy to own, and a joy to use". To achieve a high-quality user experience, it is important that several disciplines like "engineering, marketing, graphical and industrial design, and interface design" are all directly involved in the design process (Norman and Nielsen n.d.). The UX design process should "create products that provide meaningful and relevant experiences to users" by designing "the entire process of acquiring and integrating the product, including aspects of branding, design, usability and function" (Interaction Design Foundation n.d.).

The UX Wheel proposed by Hartson and Pyla (2012) is a lifecycle template of the design process which guides designers through the entire design process. It serves as a checklist and shows designers where they currently are in the design process and what they should follow. It offers a shared concept of what should be done and "externalizes the state of development for observation, measurement, analysis and control" (Hartson and Pyla 2021, p. 49) and facilitates communication among different project roles.

The UX Wheel is composed of various activities and sub-activities, methods and techniques. The four main activities, which succeed each other in a circular process are: analyze (understand the context, work domain and user needs), design (create conceptual design and define interactions and the look and feel), implement (produce design alternatives as prototypes) and evaluate (verify and refine the design and make sure that the design meets the needs of the users). Each of these four activities has various sub-activities. You always have three transition possibilities: 1) move forward to the next activity; 2) iterate some more within the current activity; 3) move back to a previous activity. Budget and time might be stronger criteria to move on or remain on an activity and it is not necessary to go through all activities and sub-activities.

The UX wheel with its iterations is inspired by a quote of the Danish poet Piet Hein (1992) saying that "The road to wisdom? Well, it's plain and simple to express: Err and err and err again but less and less and less." (Hein 1992). It suggests that during the design process it has to be possible to continuously adapt and correct a product so that it can really meet the needs of the users and that it is important to plan time for such iterations right from the beginning. In fact, often the lifecycle of a product never really ends. The moment a first version is published, newer versions are already tested.

User Requirements with Lego (URL). URL is a methodology to elicit user requirements for online communication applications (Cantoni et al. 2011). It is a specific application of Lego Serious Play (LSP) (Association of Master Trainers in the Lego Serious Play Method 2019), that has been developed to allow innovation to emerge within companies. LSP favors the sharing of ideas, the engagement in discussion and the elaboration of shared solutions and suggests that everyone within a company can actively contribute to this process of innovation generation. Participants of a Lego session use Lego bricks to build models that express their thoughts and ideas. Having to model an idea with their hands and bricks actually helps people to develop ideas, thoughts and solutions explicitly by giving them a shape. The building activity and the involvement of manuality support reflections and give space to creativity. Lego bricks are ideal for this as they are simple to use, known by most people, have different colors and shapes, can be built into simple and complex forms, and are used in many different cultures. Thus, URL is a specific application of LSP.

According to Cantoni et al. (2011) "URL helps in finding communicative requirements that usually do not emerge with other methodologies" (p. 13). It is thus complementary to other, more traditional methods such as interviews or focus groups. When building a company website, different stakeholders should be involved and have the possibility to express their needs and ideas. URL proposes a "structure sequence of timed individual and collaborative activities led by a facilitator" (p. 14) in which people with different roles can participate and allows to define a shared and agreed vision of how a website should look like.

The advantages of URL are that it is playful and fun, it fosters innovation, it is a powerful methodology and stimulates communication and teamwork. It might be limited by its costs (in time and money), the incompleteness of emerging requirements and the fear to try something different.

An URL workshop is conducted by facilitators, who is an URL expert and possibly not part of the stakeholder group. She/he designs the workshop goals with the customer, introduces the method, assigns the building challenges, structures the various phases of the workshop and manages time. Generally, a workshop lasts between three and four hours and should take place in a room with two big tables. The ideal size of a workshop group is between 7–12 people.

The URL workshop is composed of several activities structured into three phases: challenge, build, share. During the sharing phase each participant explains his/her model to the group and assigns a single key word to the model. The workshop starts with some warm-up activities like building the highest tower or a dream holiday. The following activities are closely related to the OCM and its pillars: 1) build their own role (pillar III), 2) build a model of a relevant user of the website (pillar IV) and 3) build the most relevant or important content or functionality of the website (pillar I and II). After activity 2 and 3, so-called landscapes are created in which participants position the individually created models according to a shared narrative. This activity allows for collaborative thinking and team alignment. In a next activity the participants connect role models with content models and user models with content models. This highlights which elements of the planned website are more central and which ones peripheral. After this, a final completeness check is done.

2.2   Instructional Design

The instructional design process has been widely researched. Generally, it is described as a problem-solving process, following a series of steps, namely analysis, design, development, implementation and evaluation (ADDIE model). It has been recognized that the process is not always linear (Visscher-Voerman and Gustafson 2004). This is especially true in the current education system, which can involve various types of teaching methods and learning. The learning process can take place face-to-face, online and through blended learning.

Technology has long been identified as an enabler for the student learning experience. Many institutions utilize Learning Management Systems (LMS) such as Moodle or Blackboard to manage the course content and activities. These platforms have mainly been utilized to share the course material and lecture slides with students. However, they offer other features for learning activities, such as forums to facilitate the online communication, which have not been widely utilized (Nadiyaha and Faaizaha 2015). Technologies are increasingly being used not only as an instrument to provide students the knowledge but also as a tool to develop soft skills. Hence, they are increasingly being integrated within the students' learning experience.

The Covid19 had and is still having a big impact on education, requiring a major reassessment of pedagogical practices as the pandemic forced major changes by disrupting the traditional delivery of face-to-face interactions. However, the pandemic has also brought some opportunities as it accelerated innovation within the education system. This has required identifying alternative solutions to adapt to the situation (Brammer et al. 2020). One of the advantages brought by the pandemic is the adoption of online tools such as Zoom or Teams for communication (Brammer et al. 2020). Technology-enhance learning is defined as "the process of utilising information and communication technologies to support teaching and learning" (Bolton and Emery 2020, p. 343).

Blended learning involves integrating different types of learning and activities. It has been widely utilized to complement face-to-face teaching with online learning, increase the number of students thanks to its flexibility, and improve the communication with students (Cheung and Hew 2011).

As stated by Chaeruman et al. (2020) blended learning is not limited to the integration of traditional face-to-face learning and online learning as "the ultimate goal of blended learning is combining the most appropriate learning technologies and activities both in synchronous or asynchronous learning settings to create optimum learning experiences" (p. 176). In order to develop a good course with blended learning it is useful to have an instructional design system as a model to follow. The model developed by Chaeruman et al. (2020) involves four main interrelated steps: determining the objectives of the course, structuring the content, developing the learning activities, and designing the synchronous and asynchronous activities. Synchronous learning is characterized by the timing element as it occurs at the same time and it can happen in the same place or in different places. Whereas asynchronous learning can happen at any time and any place and it can be self-directed or collaborative.

Interaction is a major challenge for blended learning. The interactions can be learner-instructor, learner-learner, and learner-content interaction. Moreover, in the online context learner-interface interaction is also important due to the technology mediated type of learning (Su et al. 2005; Chaeruman et al. 2020).

Learning is not an isolated occurrence, it is the result of many factors. Students need to develop long-life skills which will enable them to meet the industry requirements and adapt to the changing needs and responsibilities. This kind of learning, which refers to learning that is context-bound, culture-oriented and applied practice, has been defined as real world learning. In practice work-based learning involves the application of the knowledge acquired (Morley et al. 2021). To do so, learning pedagogies that go beyond traditional learning should be implemented (Brindley and Sims 2020). A way to integrate such learning is through a project, which refers to the creation of a final product. The value of developing a project for students is not the end product itself, it is the learning journey they need to go through. Hence, it requires high quality mentoring or coaching from industry professionals (Hanney 2020).

Carefully designed assessments are important in order to measure learning. The assessment chosen should be relevant and beneficial for the students. These can be both formal and informal. Important is the role of feedback given to the student for the best performance. For example, this can take place though group meetings or one-to-one support. Moreover, introducing the peer assessment to the students from the very beginning gives them the opportunity to reflect and improve on their performance by using it as a formative assessment tool (Archer et al. 2021).

Teaching in Fashion. The fashion industry is being impacted by Information and Communication Technologies (ICTs) (Kalbaska and Cantoni 2017). As a result, the industry requires employees who have relevant skills and who are able to work in the challenging, demanding and competitive fashion market.

It is important that students start developing the appropriate skills at university. Hence, fashion students' learning process should be managed by taking into consideration such context (Marques and Moschatou 2017). This is to be achieved through the development of curricula designed to respond to the market needs.

The term curriculum is utilized within the education system as an umbrella term to include the teaching methods, approaches, resources and strategies (Jamil et al. 2021).

While developing the learning activities for a fashion communication curriculum within higher education it should be considered that it requires a medium to long term approach. It should not be based on the current fashion trends, rather it should provide students with critical and reflective tools (Cantoni et al. 2020). Research on the skills needed by employees in digital fashion (Kalbaska and Cantoni 2017; Ronchetti et al. 2020). Online communication skills have been identified amongst the top skills. Hence, this study shows the relevancy of OCD and the skills students can develop by taking this course.

The subsequent section introduces the OCD course and its relevance within a fashion curriculum.

3 The OCD Course

3.1 Course Context

The OCD course has been part of MSc in Digital Fashion Communication first year students since 2018. The course is also an elective course for students from masters in other majors such as Media Management, Marketing, and Tourism, an asset to the course due to the multidisciplinary approach.

Due to the Covid19 pandemic, the structure and the content of the course for the class of 2020 was adapted to the situation. At the time when the course was being designed, it was possible to give lessons in attendance while respecting social distancing regulations. Hence, in line with the regulations of USI, the course was organized to be 50% in class and 50% online, by alternating a week in a class and a week online as there were not enough rooms with a sufficient capacity. The classes in presence were recorded and shared on the iCorsi platform in order to guarantee access to the material for students that could not reach campus.

As of October 28, 2020, the Federal Government announced that no lessons could be conducted in person in order to contain the pandemic. In such context, online synchronous and asynchronous online classes were alternated. The online synchronous lectures, which were also recorded, were conducted via Microsoft Teams and covered the relevant theory.

3.2 Course Goals and Challenges

As future managers, students will be required to successfully interact with ICTs experts, to design and evaluate ICT projects and to manage available ICT assets in the most effective and efficient way.

The course focuses on the phase before a technical artefact is produced, that is on the analysis of (information-) competitors, the analysis of needs and goals and the design of new solutions, up to the production of a prototype. It thus stays at a relatively high and conceptual level if compared to a design course addressed to informatics students, who will go much more in detail and continue up to the implementation of the artefact.

Part of the challenges of an online communication course is that it requires students to be creative and to think out-of-the-box. There are various principles and some rules, yet often there is no single correct solution, and it is only possible to compare different solutions and rank them. Also, instructors often do not know "the" right solution, but they can suggest changes and have to challenge the students to continuously improve their designs. Students have to be able to provide good and compelling arguments in favor of their design decisions, but they also have to be aware that the users are always king.

Design is not something you can just learn from theory but requires a lot of practice. Design thinking can be trained by observing day-to-day objects and asking oneself why the object is like it is and the reasons behind certain design decisions.

3.3   Course Structure

An important aspect of the course is to illustrate all theoretical aspects with a lot of examples from real life in order to show students what works and what does not. This is a fundamental aspect of the course as through many very concrete examples the students master theoretical concepts and can see how they are applied in and linked to real life. Because of the very practical orientation of the course, this is very important. The aim of the course is that students understand how to apply the theories rather than memorize all the content. Therefore, the course included a mixture of theoretical and practical classes.

In presence classes were designed to cover the theory and the fundamentals of the course; whereas the online weeks were structured to allow students to apply the theory through tasks and activities aimed at implementing the group project of the course. For each online week, students had to prepare specific outputs related to the course project. The course project involved the development of an app or a website for Kanga, a popular garment from East Africa with strong communication meaning (Ressler 2012). The tasks were designed to help students apply the theory and the tutoring sessions to support students in the course project. The main theoretical aspects covered are: definition of design, OCM, design process and reverse design, UX Wheel, URL, Contextual Inquiry, Personas and Prototyping.

Tutoring sessions were organized with each group to allow the students to present their outputs and receive feedback from the course director, the assistant, and also the intern of USI UNESCO Chair, who grew up in Kenia and could offer local expertise on the topic.

Moreover, two guest speakers were invited to the course. The aim was to show students the applicability of the course contents. The first guest speaker discussed the importance of user experience in digital settings and provided real company scenarios. Whereas the other guest speaker presented an example of how instructional design and prototyping was utilized for designing a new website.

An interesting example is represented by the Lego Serious Play session, which had to be adapted to distant learning and was conducted on MS Teams. Some students had access to their own Lego Bricks at home, whereas those that did not have them utilized online brick building tools and then shared the models created with their group members through a group Jamboard. Each group of students was assigned a facilitator.

The evaluation was conducted fully online. The project was evaluated based on a recorded video presentation. The objective of the presentation was to present the process they undertook to develop the app/website for Kanga by justifying the decisions made. Providing constructive feedback is essential for students' learning and employability (Archer et al. 2021). Hence, the recorded videos were watched in a synchronous online session with the course director, two professors and the guest from the industry in order to provide a variety of feedback. Then, an online exam, formed by two open questions and multiple-choice questions, followed. The objective of the first open question was to verify their contribution to the group project and further reflection on possible implementations following the final feedback, whereas the second open question provided students the possibility to choose a reading of their choice from the course reading list and identify how it related to the course content. The multiple-choice questions were designed to evaluate the theoretical knowledge.

3.4 Group Project on Kanga

The goal of the group project was to design an app or a website to rise awareness of and spread knowledge about Kanga, a colourful fabric worn by women and occasionally by men throughout the African Great Lakes region (Hamid 1996; Birch and Lutomia 2017; Mahonge 2018). In specific, the project required to conduct a background analysis on Kanga, conduct a benchmark analysis and develop a first business idea, carry out a contextual inquiry, develop personas and design the app or website.

To better understand the relevance of Kanga for fashion students, the next paragraph provides some background information regarding Kanga and frames it as a fashion object, communication media and cultural item.

Fashion Spaces of Kanga Style and Clothing Systems. Kanga is a type of garment, commonly found in Eastern Africa, with a history dating back to at least the mid-nineteen century. It has many uses for the region's various communities including ordinary clothing, cultural and social communication functions (Birch and Lutomia 2017). As such Kanga is a cultural intangible heritage which means that it reflects "the practices, representation, expressions, knowledge, skills - as well as the instruments, objects, artefacts and cultural spaces associated therewith - that communities, groups and, in some cases, individuals recognize as part of their cultural heritage" (Unesco 2003, Art. 2). Intangible cultural heritage is transmitted from generation to generation and is kept alive within communities in accordance with the environment, thus "promoting respect for cultural diversity and human creativity." (Unesco 2003, Art. 2)

East African region and in particular the so-called East African Community (EAC) is a real innovation hotspot, developing products and technical artefacts known and used far beyond the region (e.g., the M-Pesa mobile money app). The fashion industry is one of the mainstays of innovation well poised to lead the way. Jennings and Ude (2011) observed that international designers collaborate with African artisans in order to harness authentic materials and techniques and to bridge the gap between African-born and African-inspired fashion (Jennings and Ude 2011). Suno which is now showcasing in the New York Fashion Week, started its first Kanga vintage collection in 2009 (Jennings and Ude 2011). The point is that Kanga has established spaces across the fashion chain and within a system of meanings.

One of the most evident socio-cultural significance of Kanga is its use as a communication medium by communities in the EAC especially the Swahili. Every Kanga carries a written message, usually a short proverb-like sentence(s) with a meaning. There are several garments in the region similar to kanga, but which do not have this feature. The messaging aspect has been well discussed in Hamid (1996) and Beck (2001, 2005). Kanga is thus often used as a gift to deliver a message in special occasions such as weddings or births. The modern fashion industry needs to find ways of reinventing the use of Kanga by preserving the communication value of Kanga and conform it to modern usages, traditions and taste. It needs to find a balance between maintaining the cultural property of the garment and adapting it to new needs, trends and economical interests. Part of the goal of the OCD group project is also to address this challenge.

Example of a Successful Group Project. With the app "Young Kanga" a group of students[1] wants to build awareness about Kanga's cultural, social and political importance especially among young generations of East African people living in big European cities and allow them to rediscover the meanings of Kanga. The group analyzed existing competitors and their online communication and highlighted both positive and problematic aspects. They then identified the needed personnel resources to successfully manage the app: a Chief Executive Officer, an Artificial Intelligence Programmer for recognizing scanned Kanga motives and sayings, a Chief Financial Officer, a Webmaster, a person responsible for Marketing & Public Relations and Agents who take care of business relations with shops selling Kanga.

Two semi-structured interviews were conducted with young girls originally coming from East Africa and currently living in Lugano. They highlighted that Kanga is used for formal and informal occasions but mainly as esthetic clothing and less because of its cultural meaning. As they are often not aware of the meaning of their Kanga dresses, they liked the idea of a scanning function which allows them to learn more about and engage with Kanga culture and is fun and interactive to use. They also appreciated the option of finding a shop nearby selling Kanga.

Based on the conducted analysis the group decided to include the following main contents and functionalities into their app: a) a general information part about Kanga, its origins, background, and usages in different countries; b) a database of all available Kangas in which each Kanga has a dedicated page including an image, the name, a description, the translation in English of the saying/proverb printed on it, its use and the country of origin and which can be searched by occasion (wedding, funeral, birth) or country of origin; c) a Kanga scanner, which is the main functionality of the app and allows to scan the sayings printed on the Kangas and then visualize the related Kanga page; and d) the find a shop function, which shows nearby shops selling Kangas on a map, and indicates the exact address, contact details and opening hours.

Two different user scenarios illustrate how the app could be used: 1) A girl who is invited to an East African Wedding is looking for a shop where to buy a Kanga. To do so she uses the find a shop function. Inside the shop she then uses the scanner function of the app to understand the meaning of the Kangas she is looking at. 2) A girl who wants to discover more about her origins visits the Kanga exhibition at the British Museum but as not much information about the textiles is displayed, she uses the scanning function to learn more about the exhibited Kangas. She also appreciates the in-depths information about Kanga and its origins presented in the general information part and was happy about her cultural learning experience.

In the future the group would also like to include a forum in their app, where East African people can virtually meet and exchange. This would allow to create a community around the app.

---

[1] The group is composed of four 1st year students of the Master in Digital Fashion Communication: Manon Auriane Baud; Camilla Cospito, Sofia Iannucci, and Larissa Eileen Celia O'Sullivan.

4   Challenges and Opportunities of Teaching the Course Online

The pandemic has forced the adoption of technology enhanced learning and the exposure to different technologies. No one technology will be essential for students' future, whereas a range of experiences with technologies enables to prepare students to constant change (Bolton and Emery 2020). Conducting the course of OCD fully online presented challenges. Yet, opportunities were also derived from the solutions identified when restructuring the course to fit the online needs.

Thi section will discuss the challenges and opportunities of teaching the course online.

Moving the classes online after having started the semester partly in presence represented the first challenge as the course syllabus and the lectures had to be re-designed. In order to make the lessons as interactive as possible, each synchronous lecture was designed with different elements. The first half of the class covered the theoretical aspects with the course professor, whereas the second half was covered by testimonials, a lego session and a final exam explanation. This alternation helped maintain the attention of students through the online classes.

Similarly, for the online classes specific tasks were provided to the students in order to apply their knowledge. Interestingly, it emerged that a higher variety of resources was utilized for the course compared to previous years. In addition to the lecture slides, students were provided access to pre-existing online material. An interesting example is the class on the topic of personas, for which the students were suggested book chapters, articles, and videos. This could be an element to consider implementing also in the next versions of the course.

Another opportunity emerged from the final evaluation. Having students register the presentations beforehand and then having a synchronous moment to share the projects and receive feedback resulted in a very efficient and effective method for conducting group presentations. This also allowed guest professors and an industry expert to participate in the feedback. The video recordings also allow to have a remaining tangible output of the group project rather than having solely a powerpoint presentation and it could be useful to further promote their projects to other interested parties such as the V&A or British Museum.

Despite the challenges, conducting the OCD course online provided opportunities also for the learning development of the students.

Firstly, it enabled to expose students to a variety of online communication experiences through different tools. ICTs are transforming the fashion industry and digital roles are becoming increasingly important in the fashion job market (Nobile and Kalbaska 2020; Ronchetti et al. 2020). Hence, digital fashion students should master digital communication skills as they have been identified amongst the top skills needed by employees (Kalbaska and Cantoni 2017). Students learnt how to utilize a variety of online tools through the course activities, some suggested by the teachers and others chosen by themselves. For example, the LMS iCorsi, was used much more extensively. It did not only serve as the main container of all used learning materials (e.g. recordings of lessons, presentation slides, readings) but was also used as the main communication and interaction tool with the students. It was the instrument that aggregated and linked to all other used tools (e.g. Microsoft Teams, Jamboard, Alexa, etc.) On the other side, students have chosen their own tools for collaborating online on their group project, for recording their presentation and have opted for alternative, collaborative presentation instruments such as Canva, Visme or Zoho. They also practiced important soft skills, such as communication. Additionally, students developed strong collaboration skills from conducting the project fully online which challenged the students to organize the work among themselves. This also reflected in their organization as they had to be fully prepared for every task, not only in the content but also in the small technical aspects, such as agreeing on the person responsible for sharing the screen.

The Lego Serious Play session was a particular challenge. It was planned to do it in-presence and while doing it with a whole class of more than 50 students is already a challenge per se, doing it online raised several other issues. The essence of a LSP is to build models with building bricks using your hands. That was not possible online, as apart one group, students didn't have access to Lego bricks. While in-presence one main facilitator with some assistants was enough, online each group was assigned a facilitator, who before had to be trained about the tasks of a LSP facilitator, the structure of the workshop and the different online tools used. The course instructor did not act as facilitator but coordinated the whole activity. As each group worked inside a dedicated Teams channel, the course instructor could easily move from one group to the other and if needed address problems and questions. Overall, the students considered the LSP session as very useful for their projects but missed the manual experience of building real lego models. The online building tools were much more limited and allowed to work only in 2D instead of 3D.

Offering the OCD course in a fully online mode was challenging but also allowed identifying the potential of online teaching. In future, when back to in-presence lessons, it might be useful to consider including some aspects of online teaching and moving more and more towards a hybrid teaching format.

5   Conclusions

This paper focused on the course of OCD part of the MSc Digital Fashion Communication curriculum at USI. It presents the main theoretical elements which distinguishes it from other design courses and how the course was proactively adapted to respond to the Covid19 pandemic and its restrictions, transitioning from a hybrid modality to a fully online course. Moreover, it introduces some of the challenges and also opportunities derived from the restructuring of the course and highlights some of the skills that the students were able to develop.

This study provides some suggestions that provide to be efficient for students online learning and that could be applied within other courses. Students will enter a fast-moving fashion job market, hence the ability to adapt to new situations will be essential for their future career.

References

Archer, M., Morley, D.A., Souppez, J.B.R.: Real world learning and authentic assessment. In: Applied Pedagogies for Higher Education, pp. 323–341. Palgrave Macmillan, Cham (2021). https://doi.org/10.1007/978-3-030-46951-1

Association of Master Trainers in the Lego Serious Play Method: The Lego Serious Play Method. Serious Play (2019). https://seriousplay.training/lego-serious-play/

Beck, R.M.: Ambiguous Signs: The Role of the Kanga as a Medium of Communication (2001)

Beck, R.M: Texts on textiles: proverbiality as characteristic of equivocal communication at the East African coast (Swahili). J. Afr. Cult. Stud. **17**(2), 131–160 (2005). https://www.jstor.org/stable/4141307

Birch, S., Lutomia, A.N.: Con (Texts): Re-Examining the Social Life of Kanga Cloth (2017)

Bolton, E., Emery, R.: Using educational technology to support students' real world learning. In: Applied Pedagogies for Higher Education, pp. 343–369. Palgrave Macmillan, Cham (2020). https://doi.org/10.1007/978-3-030-46951-1_15

Brindley, J., Sims, S.: The role of professional networks in supporting and developing real world learning. In: Applied Pedagogies for Higher Education, pp. 41–62. Palgrave Macmillan, Cham (2020). https://doi.org/10.1007/978-3-030-46951-1

Cantoni, L., Tardini, S.: Internet. Routledge, New York (2006)

Cantoni, L., Tardini, S.: The internet and the web. The media. An introduction, pp. 220–232 (2010)

Cantoni, L., Cominelli, F., Kalbaska, N., Ornati, M., Sádaba, T., SanMiguel, P.: Fashion communication research: a way ahead. Stud. Commun. Sci. **20**(1), 121–125 (2020). https://www.hope.uzh.ch/scoms/article/view/j.scoms.2020.01.011

Chaeruman, U., Wibawa, B., Syahrial, Z.: Development of an instructional system design model as a guideline for lecturers in creating a course using blended learning approach. IJIM – vol. 14, no. 14, s164–181 (2020). https://doi.org/10.3991/ijim.v14i14.14411

Cheung, W.S., Hew, K.F.: Design and evaluation of two blended learning approaches: lessons learned. Australas. J. Educ. Technol. **27**(8) (2011). https://doi.org/10.14742/ajet.896

Hamid, M.A.: Kanga: it is more than what meets the eye—a medium of communication. Afr. J. Polit. Sci./Revue Africaine de Science Politique **1**(1), 103–109 (1996)

Hanney, R.: Making projects real in a higher education context. In: Applied Pedagogies for Higher Education, pp. 163–185. Palgrave Macmillan, Cham (2020). https://doi.org/10.1007/978-3-030-46951-1

Hartson, R., Pyla, P.S.: The UX Book: Process and Guidelines for Ensuring a Quality User Experience. Elsevier (2012). https://doi.org/10.1145/2347696.2347722

Hein, P.: The road to wisdom?-Well, it's plain and simple to express: err and err and err again but less and less and less. Discrete Math. **101**(1–3), 361 (1992)

Interaction Design Foundation. (n.d.): What is User Experience (UX) Design? Interaction Design Foundation. https://www.interaction-design.org/literature/topics/ux-design

Jakobson, R.: Linguistics and poetics. In: Style in Language, pp. 350–377. MIT Press, MA (1960). https://pure.mpg.de/rest/items/item_2350615/component/file_2350614/content

Jennings, H., Ude, I.: New African Fashion. Prestel, New York (2011). https://prestelpublishing.randomhouse.de/leseprobe/New-African-Fashion-US-Version-/leseprobe_9783791345796.pdf

Kalbaska, N., Cantoni, L.: Digital fashion competences: market practices and needs. In: Workshop on Business Models and ICT Technologies for the Fashion Supply Chain, pp. 125–135. Springer, Cham (2017)https://doi.org/10.1007/978-3-319-98038-6_10

Lunenburg, F.C.: Communication: the process, barriers, and improving effectiveness. Schooling **1**(1), 1–10 (2010). https://www.mcgill.ca/engage/files/engage/communication_lunenburg_2010.pdf

Mahonge, F.R.: The dress that talks: the kanga fabric in contemporary shambaa wedding ceremonies in north-eastern Tanzania. Euro. J. Lit. Lang. Linguist. Stud. **2**(4) (2018). https://doi.org/10.5281/zenodo.1318154

Marques, A.D., Moschatou, A.: Learning process in fashion design students: link with industry and social media. In: IOP Conference Series: Materials Science and Engineering, vol. 254, no. 23, p. 232005. IOP Publishing (2017) https://doi.org/10.1088/1757-899X/254/23/232005

Milner, D.: Fashion Jobs that are in demand now. The Business of Fashion (2020). https://www.businessoffashion.com/articles/workplace-talent/fashion-jobs-future-coronavirus-pandemic-digital-virtual-design-sustainability

Morley, D.A., Jamil, M.G.: Introduction: real world learning—recalibrating the higher education response towards application to lifelong learning and diverse career paths. In: Applied Pedagogies for Higher Education, pp. 1–17. Palgrave Macmillan, Cham (2021). https://doi.org/10.1007/978-3-030-46951-1

Nadiyah, R.S., Faaizah, S.: The development of online project based collaborative learning using ADDIE model. Procedia-Soc. Behav. Sci. **195**, 1803–1812 (2015). https://doi.org/10.1016/j.sbspro.2015.06.392

Norman, D., Nielsen, J. (n.d.). The Definition of User Experience (UX). NN/g Nielson Norman Group. Retrieved from 11 Feb 2021. https://www.nngroup.com/articles/definition-user-experience/

Ressler, P.: The Kanga, A Cloth That Reveals-Co-production of Culture in Africa and the Indian Ocean Region (2012). https://digitalcommons.unl.edu/tsaconf/736/

Rigotti, E., Cigada, S.: La comunicazione verbale. Apogeo Editore (2004). http://hdl.handle.net/10807/15324

Ronchetti, M., Nobile, T.H., Oliveira, N.K., Cantoni, L.: Digital Fashion Competences: Market Practices and Needs during Covid19. Institute of Digital Technologies for Communication of USI – Università della Svizzera italiana, Lugano (Switzerland) (2020)

Su, B., Bonk, C.J., Magjuka, R.J., Liu, X., Lee, S.H.: The importance of interaction in web-based education: a program-level case study of online MBA courses. J. Interact. Online Learn. **4**(1), 1–19 (2005). https://www.ncolr.org/jiol/issues/pdf/4.1.1.pdf

Tardini, S., Cantoni, L.: Hypermedia, internet and the web. Commun. Technol. **5**, 119 (2015). https://doi.org/10.1515/9783110271355-008

Tate, M.A., Alexander, J.E.: Web Wisdom: How to Evaluate and Create Information Quality on the Web. CRC Press (1999). https://doi.org/10.1201/b22397

UNESCO: Convention for the Safeguarding of the Intangible Cultural Heritage (2003). https://ich.unesco.org/en/convention

Van Der Geest, T.: Web Site Design is Communication Design, vol. 2. John Benjamins Publishing (2001). https://doi.org/10.1075/ddcs.2

Visscher-Voerman, I., Gustafson, K.L.: Paradigms in the theory and practice of education and training design. Educ. Technol. Res. Dev. **52**(2), 69–89 (2004). https://doi.org/10.1007/BF02504840

Behavioral Analysis of eSports Spectators: A Research Proposal

Eulerson Rodrigues[1,3] ⓘ, Ernesto Filgueiras[2(✉)] ⓘ, and João Valente[4(✉)] ⓘ

[1] University of Beira Interior, Covilhã, Portugal
[2] CIAUD - Research Centre for Architecture, Urbanism and Design, Lisbon, Portugal
[3] Communication Laboratory – LabCom, University of Beira Interior, Covilhã, Portugal
[4] Polytechnic Institute of Castelo Branco, Castelo Branco, Portugal
valente@ipcb.pt

Abstract. This research aims to discuss the importance of the spectator inside the context of competitive gaming (or eSports) while identifying crucial elements and moments that can influence their behavioral and emotional variation of spectators when watching eSports matches. This investigation is a direct continuation of a recent study conducted by the authors where indie computer game developers were consulted about aspects present in the eSports universe. Among the topics, there were questions about Objectives and Rules, Competitiveness, Interface Information, Visual Identification in Players and Teams, Flow Content and Communication Groups, thus discussing diverse eSports aspects, on how to approach new spectators and improving the experience of those who already watch competitive gaming. The evolution of gaming is due to advances in technology, standing them as special cases in the new media studies, which distinguish interactivity as the main responsible for the gaming scenarios success. When discussing eSports, interaction takes place not only between users (spectators and players) and products (video games), but also with presenters, professional players, coaches, streamers, and content creators, creating a network of fast communication and easy participation. The following study then proposes an analysis of eSports spectators using biosensors to capture indicative data when watching two different clips from Valve's video game Counter Strike: Global Offensive. We specify the use of ECG (electrocardiogram), RESP and EDA/GSR, which are operated and coordinated by the BrainAnswer platform, a system that allows the gathering and storage and analysis of synchronized data in an organized environment.

Keywords: Spectator · eSports · Video games · Competitive gaming

1 Introduction

The eSport's (short for electronic sports) market is growing annually, reaching unthinkable marks in the recent years. With a forecast of 495 million viewers in 2020 and a revenue of 950.6 million dollars in 2019 (Newzoo, n.d.), the figures show us the worldwide reach of the segment. According to Ditmarsch (2013), eSports "is an area of sports activities in which people develop, train and compare mental or physical skills using

M. M. Soares et al. (Eds.): HCII 2021, LNCS 12781, pp. 371–383, 2021.
https://doi.org/10.1007/978-3-030-78227-6_27

information and communication technologies through video games". Two words that are present in this definition draw our attention and support this concept: **sports** and **video games**. By understanding the origin and thus connecting these two areas with eSports, we can define which of the elements present in eSports make this phenomenon, which is relatively a new product, a global success.

2 Literature Review

2.1 Physical Activities and Sport

Sports have been present in humanity since our genesis, and that part of history might be perceived by us through the narrative of activities carried out by our ancestors. Hunting, one of the most necessary activities for human survival, requires both physical preparation and good teamwork. The more skilled a hunter was, the greater the amount of food available and, consequently, the greater the chances of survival. The skills acquired through hunting (and even gathering and crafting activities) also helped to protect tribes and small communities against groups of aggressive invaders. These disputes over territories and resources led to the first conflicts and competitions where the best soldiers stood out, whether for physical or mental abilities (Beck and Bosshart 2003).

Despite all human evolution to the present day, several sports still employ activities like those of the past. For Beck and Bosshart (2003), some examples are: running; boxing; wrestling; horse riding; swimming and dancing. These activities (or exercises) are present in today's society as games and sports competitions, in which individuals with the best performance are awarded. On the other hand, playing (just for fun) and engaging in physical activities (whether through training or competition) have their differences. For McKibbin (2011) play requires greater creativity, freedom, and spontaneity from individuals, as they are rewarded with fun and entertainment, while physical activities require excellence in discipline and organization, in addition to dedication to the competition.

Physical activities, especially those that are practiced in a competitive way, serve as an outlet for boredom and problems that are part of our daily lives. Thus, we might relieve our anger and frustrations in controlled environments, where the people who are present not only know what can happen but are also looking forward to it. It is as if there were a "common agreement" between everyone there, where the exchange of offenses and provocations is allowed for the entire duration of the event. In addition, organized violence in body struggles, combats or physical disputes can serve as a source of physiological, social, and psychological satisfaction for participants and spectators (McKibbin, 2011).

2.2 Games and Video Games

Traditional Games. Humanity has, over time, found playful traces in activities that were exclusively dedicated to survival. Evolving from this scenario, the first games emerged and with them a new activity, as now we know as play, was created. However, according to Caillois (1958), play is not just an activity, but it also involves the symbols, images and pieces that are part of the set. The author highlights some concepts that characterize games, such as the combination of limits, freedom, and invention; the common ground between luck and skill; obtaining advantages through resources; and the choice between patience and audacity.

Still according to Caillois (1958), games have arbitrary rules in their nature, and all players commit themselves to obey and comply with these rules during the duration of the game. Such rules can replace or be grouped with the laws of our daily lives and those of our society, as long as they remain imperative and unappealable, and cannot be violated (although this often occurs through cheating players). According to Huizinga (2020), the rules also serve to protect the participants, guaranteeing the physical and moral integrity of everyone involved.

Games can also be used as tools for exercise and training, improving stamina, flexibility, endurance, vision, touch, and spirit, in addition to bringing pleasure to activities that on another occasion could be monotonous and repetitive. Huizinga (2020) argues that games are older than human culture, being more than mere physiological phenomena or psychological reflexes, and representing more than a physical activity. As a playing activity, the game has a significant function, which gives meaning to the action.

Digital Games. With the evolution of the media, the playing activity underwent through radical changes and gained digital versions, in addition to the creation of new modalities that depend on technology and can only be consumed in a mediatic way. The public in this area, which was made up of spectators and participants, has then become users and players. The interactive nature of digital games (or video games) unites the player and the game in a complex way, expanding the concepts (which already existed in the traditional sense of play) of immersion, simulation and interpretation, transforming all these into what we today call gameplay (Dovey & Kennedy, 2006).

The arrival of new technologies has also changed our ways of consumption. If spectators previously had to travel to be at events, radio and television technologies suppressed this need by taking the content to homes across the entire world. While the radio allowed the transmission of audible content in real time, television adds images to this content, increasing the amount of information that the audience receives (Dovey & Kennedy, 2006). In video games, the addition of interactive elements in streams over the internet, allows spectators to accompany matches in different ways, including personalized content, the selection and placement of preferred cameras, the option of displaying visual elements and information about players, teams, and opponents, in addition to total control of repetitions that are stored in the developers' servers (Ditmarsch, 2013).

The game culture shows the media influence in the contemporary way of life, as shown at Table 1 and discussed by Dovey and Kennedy (2006). The video game industry has proved to be the most established among the new media, being part of a mass market that reaches different social classes. From this, the traditional media tries then to approach this new digital culture by the contact with new aspects, such as systems theory, cyberculture, artificial intelligence and human-computer interaction (HCI) studies.

For Giddings and Kennedy (2006), video games are products developed directly for consumers, and therefore, require new concepts to be studied as media. For this, discussions are needed about the emotional relationship between consumers and products (video games), the origin of games (as they are computer products, unlike other media) and how objects, scenarios and people are represented (in comparison with other media formats).

Table 1. Differences between Media Studies and New Media Studies (Dovey & Kennedy, 2006, p.3).

Media Studies	New Media Studies
The effects of technology are socially determined	The nature of society is technologically determined
Active audiences	Interactive users
Interpretation	Experience
Spectatorship	Immersion
Representation	Simulation
Centralized media	Ubiquitous media
Consumer	Participant/co-creator
Work	Play

The digital games consumption allows a greater engagement between the dominant culture (being the industry, including developers and publishers) and the subculture (being the consumers, including players, spectators, and those who create content for the community), according to Dovey and Kennedy (2006). This engagement hardly occurs in other media, such as cinema or television, for example.

2.3 eSports and Sports

eSports Characteristics. Physical activities have received doses of competition over humanity history and attracted spectators to follow these disputes, thus generating sports practice. Years later, we realize that playful activities led to the creation of games, and that technological expansion generated digital versions of these games, through consoles and computers, creating the products we know as video games. The same sport battles can be found in eSports, which are competitive, regulated, and organized versions of video games. However, this is not the only characteristic that brings the two areas together.

There are several aspects that can be included in this discussion, being some: the use of physical activity (or the lack of it); using (or depending on) technology for the control, regulation and enforcement of rules; organizational differences (who coordinates the sport, or who owns the intellectual property of the video game); the behavioral characteristics of the players (discipline, organization and competition), the careers (of the players, coaches and managers), the tournaments and their respective prizes; the market (values of transfer passes and contracts); the use of other media for the transmission and exchange of information; and the behavioral and consumption habits of the spectators (Beck & Bosshart, 2003; Brenda, 2015; Ditmarsch, 2013; Funk et al., 2018; Hamari & Sjöblom, 2017; Rodrigues, 2019).

According to Funk et al. (2018), in order to a video game become an eSport, it must apply the following concepts: structure, through the creation of standard rules; organization with the monitoring of compliance with the rules; and competition, clearly distinguishing the winners and losers at the end of the contest.

Pizzo et al. (2018) point cycles, rounds, scoring, rules, individual players or teams, managers, leagues, competitions, events, contracts, high values in player transfers and student grants as a common ground between sports and eSports. The negative aspects are also mentioned, with examples of involvement in result manipulation and doping.

When we switch out attention to the main differences between the two areas, Funk et al. (2018) point out the role of the creator / developer of the video game that in organizational terms. While games like Counter Strike: Global Offensive, StarCraft II and League of Legends are products and franchises that belong to private companies, Sports like football, basketball or volleyball do not have a specific owner, but are controlled by an association that manages the rules, licenses, and championships.

As for amateur practice, it is possible and legal to have championships without the approval of a regulatory entity such as the Fédération Internationale de Football Association (FIFA) or the National Basketball Association (NBA), even if these do not count for the global ranking of its participants (e.g., School, neighborhood tournaments and business tournaments), but it is impossible to have any eSports competition without the software provided by the developer and a license granted or acquired to the company that controls all aspects, from the rules to the provision of new content.

Careers and Professionalism. About careers, traditional sport is defined by the constant evolution and overcoming of obstacles throughout the career, according to Wylleman *et al.* (1999). The athletes go then through specific phases that are represented by:

- **Sports specialization:** young athletes are introduced to organized sports, including rules, teammates, co-workers, and coaches.
- **Intensive training:** the athlete needs to dedicate himself to both training and competitions, going through a high risk of muscle fatigue and mental burnout due to excessive activities.
- **Elite competitions:** the adult already needs to stay on top for as long as possible, sometimes embracing the opportunity to change between leagues in search of new challenges.
- **Final transition:** it is the departure of the main teams as a player, for dedication to other activities (which may or may not be related to competitions) and reintegration as an individual in society.

Wylleman and Lavallee (2004) created a model (Fig. 1) that divides athletic levels into four elements, namely: initiation, development, mastery and discontinuity. These levels are based on studies by Wylleman et al. (1999) and adopt a perspective "from beginning to end" when reflecting the nature of development and normative transitions at the athletic, psychological, social, academic, and vocational levels of athletes.

In eSports, on the other hand, these transitions are more complex due the absence of individual monitoring by professionals. This problem is related to the lack of credibility

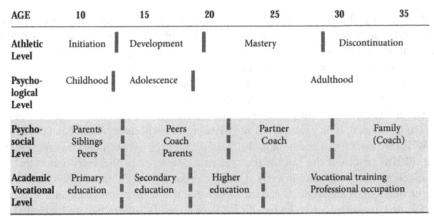

AGE	10	15	20	25	30	35
Athletic Level	Initiation	Development		Mastery		Discontinuation
Psychological Level	Childhood	Adolescence			Adulthood	
Psychosocial Level	Parents Siblings Peers	Peers Coach Parents		Partner Coach		Family (Coach)
Academic Vocational Level	Primary education	Secondary education	Higher education		Vocational training Professional occupation	

Note. A dotted line indicates that the age at which the transition occurs is an approximation.

Fig. 1. A developmental perspective on transitions faced by athletes at athletic, individual, psychosocial, and academic/vocational levels by Wylleman & Lavallee (2004, p.520).

by Olympic and sports committees regarding eSports, in addition to the scarcity of health professionals with specialization focused on cyber athletes.

Salo (2017) proposes the use of a model for the classification of eSports, relating the problems and challenges of the cyberathletes' careers (Fig. 2).

- **Initiation** (up to 13 years old, approximately): it is the stage in which players and spectators are subjected to physical and mental problems due to the excessive time in front of video games and computers.
- **Development** (from 14 to 19 years old, approximately): lack of psychological and professional support, constant changes in the video game industry, lack of interest from organizations.
- **Mastery** (from 20 to 28 years old, approximately): high personal and professional life requirements, dropping out of studies, decisions between dedicating to training or competitions.
- **Discontinuation**: the short duration of eSports careers is a problem present in ex-cyber athletes who have difficulties in entering the job market. It is at this time that studies are lacking, as the skills acquired over the years of competition may not be useful in traditional jobs.

Meantime, three aspects of success can be related to the career of eSports athletes, namely: **performance** (where performance is the key, monitoring and developing skills in order to achieve goals and seek achievements), **discovery** (where learning and having fun is more important than victory) and **relationships** (where the athlete is happy to share moments with friends, family and teammates).

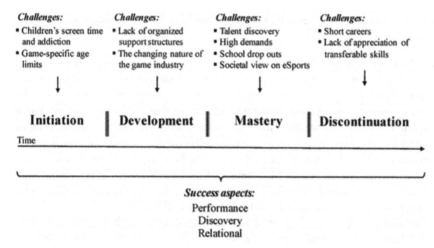

Fig. 2. ESports career framework as proposed by Salo (2017, p.27).

2.4 Spectators' Motivation and Behavior

Recent Literature. Despite all the characteristics that involve the discussion of sport and eSports, the biggest factor of proximity between the two areas becomes that point that is crucial for the existence of the two activities: the spectator. This point is addressed by Rodrigues (2019) where the consumption habits of the spectators and their behavior in events are essential sources of information to the continuation of the research on the relationship between sport and eSports. The study of the spectators is justified by their presence at events, unconditional support for teams and players, dedication of time in streams, and money spent on goods, tickets, and merchandising. Several authors seek to understand what attracts crowds to attend competitive events (Hamari & Sjöblom, 2017; Rodrigues, 2019; Wulf Et Al., 2018. See also: See also: Lee & Schoenstedt, 2011; Pizzo Et Al., 2018;) and how these spectators behave when watching the matches (Brenda, 2015; Rodrigues, 2019; Wulf et al. 2018).

Why Do They Watch. Competitive events attract spectators who get together to follow the course of disputes between the most diverse types of competitors. Among the motivations that lead viewers to follow sporting events, we find regionalism, social environment, and skill level of the participants Rodrigues, 2019). In addition, the pleasure of the activity is related to the escape from problems, anxieties, and personal frustrations, which are common feelings in the daily lives of several people (Zillmann Et Al., 1989). The suspense generated by the unpredictability of a real-time presentation is also appreciated by viewers, and this is due to the difference between, for example, watching a movie, series or video that can be re-watched indefinitely (Wulf et al., 2018).

Hamari and Sjöblom (2017) also cite as motivation the gathering of information about teams and players, where the focus is to understand enough to integrate into a conversation, whether in the work, studies, or leisure environment; that same information can also be used to gain skills within the video game or sport; Or even the communication between supporters of the same player or team that can lead to union through a common liking.

How Do They Behave. Regarding the spectator's behavior, current technological tools allow greater interaction between the spectator and the content generator (a narrator, presenter or even a player). The chat usage in matches broadcasts make it possible for several people to express their opinions in real time, thus facilitating the formation of groups and virtual identities that support the same teams and seek the same goals regarding what they are watching. Aspects related to sociability, status, success, knowledge acquirement and skills, in addition to the emotional connection with unknown individuals are other points present in the streams (Wulf Et Al., 2018). Spectators also show preference for the internet as a platform for monitoring disputes, news, and tournament tables for their favorite sport or eSport (Rodrigues, 2019).

Regarding the behavior in events, according to Rodrigues (2019) observation studies, the public of both traditional and electronic sports may demonstrate high concentration indexes during matches, either through physical posture (e.g., standing still) or the low incidence in using electronic devices (e.g., smartphones and digital cameras). As for verbal activities, eSports' spectators may show a greater interest in supporting / encouraging, while sport's spectators divide the time between talking to each other and protesting against the players.

Fig. 3. Stage and screen at an eSports event (Rodrigues, 2019, p.79).

Brenda (2015) points out that the participation of spectators in eSports events, creates memorable experiences for consumers, thus generating a space where these individuals can participate in temporal and spatial contexts larger than the video game itself, through communities that extend for other media and social groups.

Improving Gaming Streams. Rodrigues and Filgueiras (2020)) conducted a study where computer game developers were consulted about how some specific game aspects should be approached by game designers and if some other aspects may influence the player/spectator experience. All those aspects are common to competitive games, as they are present in the universe of eSports. Among the topics of the conversation, there were questions about how to set objectives and rules, whether to use competitiveness as consume motivation, managing interface information, the use of visual identification in players and teams, flow content and communication groups.

The conversation with the developers brought us new points of view regarding the presentation of the objectives and rules of the game, as noncompetitive games have a different flow, and those aspects may be introduced during prequel or tutorial levels. Also, pointing out goals and objectives at the start of the match can be ineffective in eSports where new spectators may arrive during the match, leaving them without any kind of information.

Another important topic is for games to have a simple, clean and customizable interface, so spectators may choose what and when they want so see statistics and information.

Creating connections between players and their profile also seems to be a good way to keep them interested in the game. This way, famous players are easily recognized by showing their ranks, and even those that are not as renowned may show info about their identification with professional teams or their country.

And finally, the use of communication groups, such as external media may help newcomers to find additional info about the game mechanics, lore or it might be just a good place to socialize and show off skills and cosmetics items.

2.5   Games and Biosensors

Between 2018 and 2020, a study was carried out in Portugal (Dworak et al., 2020) using the BrainAnswer platform, which sought the interaction experience between player-system. According to the study, it is possible to use the physiological changes captured by biosensors along with questionnaires to capture and identify key interaction moments related to gameplay, in order to, afterwards, present those moments to the user for an emotional classification of the system's configuration. subsequently changes are made in the core of the application so that the user experience is increased according to an emotional map.

The use of biosensors in this case is justified to obtain valid and determinant aspects of the subjective states of the players through internal characteristics of the player himself, such as predispositions, expectations, need, motivation and mood, and the system's characteristics, such as specification, objective, usability, and functionality.

The project was then able to increase the interaction experience of the players with a simple gameplay game (Pac-Man), regardless of the skill level of the participants (either novice or experienced). The results of the analyzes were provided to the players who classified as emotions arising from the actions of the game. This personal analysis of each common user then brings answers related to positive and negative/anxiogenic emotions.

3 Study Proposal

From the literature review, an experimental / analytical study emerges, whose object of study is the spectators of competitive video games, where we present two competition situations and observe the effects of each one of them during the test. With this, we seek to identify determining factors that show variations in the physiological behavior of individuals by using biosensors and questionnaires.

For the pilot study, we prepared an experimental protocol that contains questions about the spectators' experience when watching two clips with content from the game Counter Strike: Global Offensive, a game already consolidated in the area of eSports with a high number of tournaments and the second largest total prize pool (among eSports) distributed in tournaments since 2012 (Esports Earnings, n.d.).

The two selected clips for this study were taken from competitive matches, where the first clip shows a professional player streaming a competitive match on the FACEIT[1] platform. The second clip was taken from a semifinal of the Master League Portugal VI with a prize pool of $ 11,746. The game took place on November 7, 2020 and involved a clash between the sAw and Giants teams.

Then, an analysis of eSports spectators is proposed through the use of biosensors to capture indicative data when watching games of a computer game that they are familiar with and usually watch. Regarding biosensors, the use of the ECG (electrocardiogram) stands out, which registers the path of electrical impulses through the cardiac muscle and can be recorded at rest or during exercise to provide information about the heart's response to physical effort, the RESP sensor which comprises a belt that is attached around the chest or abdomen area and is used to measure the user's breathing, and the EDA, also known as GSR, which is a method used to measure the electrical conductance of the skin, which varies according to the user's humidity level. The biosensors are operated and coordinated by the BrainAnswer[2] platform, a system that allows to collect and store synchronized data from several and analyze in an organized environment. These data will be collected through tests carried out in Portugal.

Regarding the protocol, the script follows the following order:

Fig. 4. BrainAnswer protocol (app.brainanswer.pt)

1. Title display and brief presentation of the study, indicating that the spectator should watch the videos and answer the questionnaires.
2. Display of the first video: One of the two clips are played. The order of the clips is random to avoid sequence bias.

---

[1] FACEIT. https://www.faceit.com/pt.

[2] BrainAnswer platform. https://brainanswer.pt/

3. Questionnaire 1 (about the first video) is launched and must be answered by the spectator.
4. Display of the second video: The remaining clip is played. The order of the clips is random to avoid sequence bias.
5. Questionnaire 2 (about the second video) is launched and must be answered by the spectator.
6. Questionnaire 3 (on the viewer's personal gaming profile) is launched and must be answered by the spectator.

Data is collected and stored on the BrainAnswer platform, which has a simple interface and easy access to records.

After data collection, the next step is to identify variations in the physiological behavior of the spectators to find moments and events that may indicate a higher rate of participation of the spectators in relation to the events of the stream. Among the possibilities of physiological behavior, we highlight the tension, attention, stress, relaxation, anxiety, excitement, and concentration that can be demonstrated by the subjects.

By identifying these indicators of emotional participation, it may be possible to map the main moments, actions and events that represent situations of greatest interest to spectators. With the knowledge of these situations, the next step is to try to replicate or emphasize this type of situation so that the stream becomes more interesting, holding the spectator's attention for longer.

4   Conclusion

Humanity is in constant development, as we may notice through the analysis of the tools, activities and concepts that are present in our society. Rudimentary activities such as hunting and fishing, which were previously intended to aid in the struggle for survival, served as inspiration for the creation of sports activities that use competition as a motivation both for the practice by athletes and for consumption by spectators.

With technological advances, new forms of entertainment were created, such as video games, where the actions are digitally mediated and consumption becomes interactive, connecting audiences (who are now users) and consumers (who are participants and content creators). The ease of communication, whether through chat or other social tools, helps participants to express themselves in real time, and all this information reaches those who were previously difficult access figures, such as on television or radio. The real time communication also helps creating groups with similar interests and preferences, making it easier to aim targeted content.

By understanding the role of traditional and electronic sport's (eSports) spectators, it is possible to identify similarities that include (and are not limited to) the consumption motivations (including competitiveness, escapism, drama, and skill appreciation), consumption habits (internet and digital media are preferred) and behavior at events. Despite the difference between the way in which sport and eSports are mediated, the spectators are the common ground between these two areas and it shows that, in the future, eSports competitions might be recognized as sport, incorporating laws, organizations and regulatory committees for the protection of athletes, spectators, organizations, and companies that are part of this universe.

Among the study's field applications, we highlight the opportunity to know how and when during the streams: interact with spectators and players (whether through interviews, chat, or other forms of communication), show physical reactions from spectators and players, inform statistics and data related to this and other games, present information and curiosities, price and target commercial ads and manage scene transitions. In addition, identify spectator profiles to adapt streams according to the preference in the style of play (passive / neutral / aggressive, e.g.) and, finally, to revalidate comparisons with traditional sport, in relation to physiological behaviors (level of dedication, attention and concentration) of spectators while watching competitive matches.

References

Beck, D., & Bosshart, L.: Sports and media. Communication Research Trends, 22(4) (2003).

Brenda, H. K. S.: Spectating the Rift: A study into eSports spectatorship. eSports Yearbook, 16, 9–35 (2015).

Caillois, R.: Les, jeux et les hommes (Man, play, and games). Librairie Gallimard (1958).

Dovey, J., & Kennedy, H. W.: Game cultures: Computer games as new media. McGraw-Hill Education (UK) (2006).

Dworak, W., Filgueiras, E., Valente, J.: Automatic Emotional Balancing in Game Design: Use of Emotional Response to Increase Player Immersion. In: Marcus, A., Rosenzweig, E. (eds.) HCII 2020. LNCS, vol. 12201, pp. 426–438. Springer, Cham (2020). https://doi.org/10.1007/978-3-030-49760-6_30

Esports Earnings :: Prize Money / Results / History / Statistics, https://www.esportsearnings.com/ last accessed 2021/02/10

Funk, D.C., Pizzo, A.D., Baker, B.J.: eSport management: Embracing eSport education and research opportunities. Sport Management Review 21(1), 7–13 (2018)

Giddings, S., & Kennedy, H. W.: Digital games as new media. Understanding digital games, 129–147 (2006).

Hamari, J., & Sjöblom, M.: What is eSports and why do people watch it? Internet research (2017).

Huizinga, J. Homo ludens.: Editora Perspectiva SA (2020).

Lee, D., Schoenstedt, L.J.: Comparison of eSports and traditional sports consumption motives. ICHPER-SD Journal Of Research 6(2), 39–44 (2011)

McKibbin, R.: Sports history: Status, definitions and meanings. Sport in history 31(2), 167–174 (2011)

Newzoo Global Esports Market Report 2020, https://newzoo.com/insights/trend-reports/newzoo-global-esports-market-report-2020-light-version/ last accessed 2020/10/30.

Pizzo, A. D., Na, S., Baker, B. J., Lee, M. A., Kim, D., & Funk, D. C.: eSport vs. Sport: A Comparison of Spectator Motives. Sport Marketing Quarterly, 27(2) (2018).

Rodrigues, E. P. F. Desporto e Videojogos (Master's dissertation) (2019).

Rodrigues, E., Filgueiras, E.: eSports: How Do Video Game Aspects Define Competitive Gaming Streams and Spectatorship. In: Marcus, A., Rosenzweig, E. (eds.) HCII 2020. LNCS, vol. 12201, pp. 506–516. Springer, Cham (2020). https://doi.org/10.1007/978-3-030-49760-6_36

Salo, M.: Career transitions of eSports Athletes: a proposal for a research framework. International Journal of Gaming and Computer-Mediated Simulations (IJGCMS) 9(2), 22–32 (2017)

van Ditmarsch, J. L. Video games as a spectator sport (Master's thesis) (2013).

Wylleman, P., Alfermann, D., Lavallee, D.: Career transitions in sport: European perspectives. Psychol. Sport Exerc. 5(1), 7–20 (2004)

Wylleman, P., Lavallee, D., & Alfermann, D.: Career transitions in competitive sports. Biel: FEPSAC (1999).

Wulf, T., Schneider, F.M., Beckert, S.: Watching players: An exploration of media enjoyment on Twitch. Games and culture **15**(3), 328–346 (2018)

Zillmann, D., Bryant, J., Sapolsky, B.S.: Enjoyment from sports spectatorship. Sports, games, and play: Social and psychological viewpoints **2**, 241–278 (1989)

Exploration of Norms and Policies in Digital Fashion Domain Using Semantic Web Technologies

Soheil Roshankish[(✉)] and Nicoletta Fornara

USI - Università della Svizzera italiana, Via Buffi 13, 6904 Lugano, Switzerland
{soheil.roshankish,nicoletta.fornara}@usi.ch

Abstract. Nowadays, one of the problems in policy notice of fashion companies is that they are not provided in a machine-readable format; therefore, they cannot be searched and monitored by computers. The fact that most of the fashion brands transform their sales into digital format magnifies the importance of automation in policies management for the future of digital business in general and of fashion companies in particular. In this paper, we explore the use of privacy policies of companies in the digital fashion domain not only to protect customer's data but for making it feasible for companies to understand their customer's needs easier and faster. We describe how the Open Digital Rights Language (ODRL), a W3C recommendation for expressing policies using Semantic Web Technologies, can be applied in the field of digital fashion. We then discuss the required components for making it possible to use such a policy language for monitoring and enforcement services.

Keywords: Digital fashion · Policy · Privacy · Semantic Web

1 Introduction

Today, the number of companies using digital technologies for communicating with their customers is increasing expeditiously. After Covid-19 pandemic, traffic to the top 100 fashion brands' owned websites increased up to 45% in Europe in April 2020 [1]. Meanwhile, Human Computer Interaction (HCI) studies are trying to enhance this connection in e-commerce by developing new technologies. Talking about e-commerce, the global fashion industry with the revenue of 606 billion dollars by 2020 has a major role in the economy of every country [2][1]. However, in digital fashion, there are numerous privacy concerns for companies and brands for the digital transformation of their industry [3, 4].

Digital fashion communication embraces communication brands designers and clothes online [5] while using the official media and technological channels such as websites, social media, Augmented Reality applications [6], Haptic Technologies [7] and many others to reach customers [8]. In this paper, we tackle customer's privacy as

---

[1] https://www.shopify.com/enterprise/ecommerce-fashion-industry.

© Springer Nature Switzerland AG 2021
M. M. Soares et al. (Eds.): HCII 2021, LNCS 12781, pp. 384–395, 2021.
https://doi.org/10.1007/978-3-030-78227-6_28

one of the major challenges in digital fashion. Although all the companies are obliged to inform their clients about their policies before using their data, still we face a big gap in this area. For example, if somebody wants to shop on Zalando website, they should create an account and accept terms and conditions provided by Zalando before buying their favourite shoes. It means that they should read over 19,000 words (48 pages in Zalando UK) and consent to practices described in it [9]. That may be the reason why we are not surprised by the result of the survey done by Deloitte in USA showing that 91% of users consent their legal rights without reading them [10].

If we calculate the time to read this policy as 250 words per minute [11], which is a common reading rate for people with the high school education [12], it takes over 75 min to read the policy notes of Zalando. The results show that if Internet users want to read their online privacy polices word by word each time they visit a new website, it costs billions of dollars nationally for the country [11].

In the last decades, discussion about privacy policies have been one of the major subjects in e-commerce applications. In digital fashion, this issue could be crucial since companies could collect rich and accurate personal information about the customers. For example, fashion label Tommy Hilfiger introduced new technology in 2018 using smart chips in its products to collect information about how often the items would be worn by the customers [13]. Though Tommy Hilfiger insured that customers' data is encrypted and cannot be accessed without any permission, it still concerns privacy issues that must be addressed.

Since 2018, all companies must comply with the requirements of the General Data Protection Regulation (GDPR) regarding the collection and handling of customer data. For instance, brands should inform customers about how data will be collected, stored, and used, or whether it will be shared with any third parties. Even having customers' permission to use their data, customers should have the right to access their collected data or even delete them [14].

Although GDPR requires the costumers' consent for fashion brands to collect their data (same for the Tommy Hilfiger case), as mentioned before, most of the people do no read terms and conditions of the websites before registering their information. Therefore, there is not control whether or not companies are violating customer's privacy policies and we believe that transforming this process, thanks to the use of machine-readable formats, helps both parties understand their rights in addition to improving customers' satisfaction.

If we want to solve this problem, we need to address the various issues that cause it. First of all, companies should start expressing their privacy policies in a machine-readable format. It is undoubtedly difficult to take such a measure, and in this paper, we propose to do that by using an existing policy expression language and Semantic Web Technologies. Having done so, we need to create a software infrastructure that can handle the meaning of policies when it is specified in a format that computers can process. To achieve this, the notation used to express privacy policies must have a formal semantics that allows computers to infer conclusions from the data collected on the behaviour of the involved parties and from the policies adopted. Therefore, we will discuss the required components for making it possible to use such a policy language for monitoring and enforcement services and we will briefly present two works that attempt to solve such a problem.

This paper is organized as follows. In Sect. 2 the methodology adopted in this paper is described. In Sect. 3, the Semantic Web Technologies used in this paper are introduced. In Sect. 4 the ODRL policy expression language, which is W3C Recommendation since 2018, is introduced. In Sect. 5, we address the importance of policy monitoring and outline the necessary components that a system should have to accomplish such monitoring automatically, including some references related works proposing solutions to this problem.

2   Methodology

In this paper, we propose an approach for modelling and monitoring policies of brands and companies in digital fashion domain not only to protect customers' data but for making it feasible for companies to understand their customer's needs easier and faster.

In Artificial Intelligence literature, there exist various languages that can be used for the specification of policies using Semantic Web Technologies [15]. One of them is the W3C Recommendation Open Digital Rights Language (ODRL 2.2)[2]. It is a policy expression language that can be used to represent permitted and prohibited actions over a certain asset, and obligations that should be meet by various stakeholders. This language can be used to express the deontic aspect of fashion policies in a machine-readable format.

In addition, in order to be able to unambiguously formalize the actions that should or should not be performed over fashion products, as for example e-commerce actions related to clothes realized with specific materials, it is required to formalize those actions and the properties for describing fashion products using Semantic Web Technologies. In particular, the definition of sharable fashion ontologies and knowledge graphs is fundamental. In literature there are some examples of ontologies used in the fashion domain [2, 16, 17] but it is not yet clear if they are expressive enough to be used for the specification of the actions regulated by policies and for taking advantage of automatic reasoning in the fashion domain.

Finally, in order to provide monitoring services for the evolution in time of deontic policies (e.g. computing the fulfilment or violation of obligations and prohibitions) a formal semantics for the ODRL policy language is required. One attempt to extend the ODRL language and to specify its formal semantics has been proposed in [18]. In this approach different ontologies (such as a domain-specific ontology, the OWL Time Ontology[3] and an Event Ontology [19]) have been used. Therefore, in order to use this model for fashion-related policies, the domain-specific ontology must be a rich and expressive fashion ontology.

3   Semantic Web Technologies in Digital Fashion

Nowadays, norms and policies for regulating the use of personal data and digital assets in digital business in general and in the fashion industry in particular are only expressed

---

[2] https://www.w3.org/TR/odrl-model/.

[3] https://www.w3.org/TR/owl-time/.

in a human-readable format. This means that customers should read the policy terms of the companies before they are able to order their products online and understand all the implications of their actions. In this paper, we propose to use Semantic Web technologies to express those policies and automatically reason about their meaning. This section is a brief introduction to the Semantic Web technologies used in the next sections and explains why the Semantic Web can have a significant impact on the fashion industry today and in the near future.

3.1 Semantic Web and Semantic Web Technologies

There are growing appeals for using Semantic Web in many research areas, since Tim Berners- Lee introduced the Semantic Web (or Web of Data) in 1999. Semantic Web is an extension of current World Wide Web (WWW), in which information is given well-defined meaning that helps computers and people communicate and understand each other's needs [20, 21].

The important goal of the Semantic Web is to help advanced applications improve their search, navigation, and evaluation by making knowledge widely accessible. One of the key benefits of the Semantic Web is enabling computers to read the information in structured format. The strength of Semantic Web lies in modelling the knowledge (our privacy policies) in such a way that computers can draw conclusions from given information.

To have such flexibility we can use Semantic Web Technologies to translate the data to the formal computers' language. All the technologies presented in this paper, have been defined under the lead of the World Wide Web Consortium (W3C).

The eXtensible Markup Language (XML) and the Resource Description Framework (RDF) are the two important technologies for developing the Semantic Web. XML is a text based *Markup Language* which can be used to label structured data by using tags [22]. The meaning of each tag is determined by the mutual agreement of those who are using a specific XML language [23], but XML documents do not have formal semantics. Unfortunately, merging XML data is rather complicated and the result is not always clear.

This limit is exceeded by RDF (Resource Description Framework), which is a formal language for describing structured information. RDF is often considered as the basic representation format for developing Semantic Web. In contrast with XML, the goal of RDF is not only displaying information in a machine-readable format but also exchanging it on the Web while preserving its original meaning.

RDF documents can be used to represent the relation among resources using labelled directed graphs. In this case, the nodes are our *resources* and the *relations* are the edge of the graph. For example, the fact that CompanyX collects customer David's personal information is represented in Fig. 1 graph:

As it is shown in Fig. 1, RDF uses naming system called Universal Resource Identifier (URI). URI is a standard syntax which helps us to simply identify the resources and exchange information on the Web and generally can be assigned to any object that has a clear identity in the privacy policy of the company. In [20], you can find further information about how to create well-formed URIs.

One of the advantages of representing data as RDF graphs is that it is very simple to combine data from multiple sources. This measure is not possible for XML documents

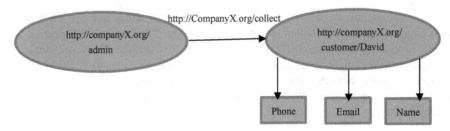

Fig. 1. An RDF graph for describing a customer data.

because they are encoded in tree structure and simple union of two tree structures is not a tree anymore. In the previous example, we represented *phone*, *email*, and *name* as data values or *literals*. *Literals* are reserved names for RDF resources of a certain datatype and their values are usually represented as a string like "+417955555", "david@gmail.com" and "David".

When companies want to express an application independent knowledge on a given domain, it is possible to use RDF Schema. RDF Schema can be used to express schema or terminological knowledge. A well-known example of RDF Schema is *Schema.org* a vocabulary that is used by search engines and web applications to empower their user experience. RDF Schema has a formal semantics; therefore, we can use RDF reasoners for inferring implicit knowledge from the knowledge that is stated explicitly. For example, by using the clothing materials ontology[4] we can infer that a Lycra blouse is done with synthetic fibre.

Now that we know how knowledge can be represented using Semantic Web Technologies, in the next section we present some examples of well-known fashion companies that are currently using Semantic Web technologies to improve their sales and personalization approach.

3.2   Related Works Using Semantic Web Technologies in Digital Fashion

As far as we know, there is no previous research using Semantic Web Technologies (SWT) for monitoring privacy policies in digital fashion. However, SWT have been applied in this domain for other purposes. In [24], they show how in the RISED (Refactoring Imperial[5] Selling Data) project they manage the collected data from customers using Semantic Web Technologies. They created the Imperial Data Ontology (IDO) and developed visualization tools to analyse all the sale data coming from different databases. One practical advantage of their method is that it can be used to answer to many queries that could help the company's sales. For example, the sales department can easily ask to the system "What are the best-selling colours within a certain period of time?".

Offering over 2,000 brands in 15 different countries, Zalando is one of the most successful Europe's leading online platform for fashion. Katariina Kari in Zalando's

---

[4] https://jbarrasa.com/2019/11/25/quickgraph9-the-fashion-knowledge-graph-inferencing-with-ontologies-in-neo4j/.

[5] Imperial Fashion is one of well-known fast-fashion in Italy.

engineering blog [2] explains how they used SWT to improve their customers service and personalization by:

- Suggesting links to the customers for further browsing.
- Implementing business rules. For instance, if customer is browsing a particular brand, the system will not suggest the competing brand.
- Understanding the characteristics of attributes. For example, if the customer search for the vegan coats, then the leather coats will not be in the result list.

More and more companies are going to use Semantic Web Technologies in the next few years. These related works show just few advantages of using Semantic Web in digital fashion domain.

4 The Open Digital Rights Language

All the fashion brands using the Internet as platform to offer their products to their customers must fulfil the General Data Production Regulation (GDPR) since it was introduced in May 2018. There exist some tools such as Microsoft Trust Centre [14] and TrustArc [25] which can be used manually by companies to help in assessing the GDPR regulations. However, as the number of companies in the digital fashion world grows, the automated compliance checking approach can ease these processes [24].

First, we need a formal language for specifying our policies. In this section, we describe the ODRL information model and its core classes. Moreover, we show how it is possible to use the ODRL language for formalizing some examples of privacy policies used in the digital fashion domain.

4.1 The ODRL Information Model

In general, Digital Rights Management (DRM) systems are responsible for describing, layering, analyzing, trading, and monitoring of the rights over digital or physical assets on the Web of Data [26]. Right Expression Languages (REL) is a fundamental part of DRM system, which is machine-readable language, used to express the rights. There are several REL standards such as XrML [27], MPEG 21 [28] and other initiatives, but the most common REL standard is the Open Digital Rights Language (ODRL) [29].

The ODRL Information Model[6] defines a set of core classes and properties for expressing a *Policy*[7]. A *Policy* must contain at least one *Rule* object, that is, one object belonging to one of the *Rule* subclasses that are *Permission*, *Prohibition*, or *Duty*. For example, one policy can describe the permission to use customers' contact details and another one can represent the prohibition of sharing customers' sensitive data.

A *Policy* object must belong to one of the following three policy types: *Set*, *Offer*, or *Agreement*. The *Set* policy is the default type in which any combination of *Rules* can be represented. The *Offer* subclass represents *Rules* that are being offered from an assigner

---

[6] The ODRL Information Model is available at https://www.w3.org/TR/odrl-model/#infoModel.

[7] We use capital letter for referring to ODRL classes.

and normally targets a wider audience. The *Agreement* subclass represents *Rules* that are granted from an assigner to an assignee. Normally in digital fashion when we use terms assigner and assignee, we consider the fashion companies as an assigner who choose the terms of policies and customers as assignee. When there exists an agreement, it means we must have at least one assigner and one assignee. Most of the privacy policies terms are of type *Agreement*. For example, the *Agreement* between a customer and a company about which customer data should be collected by company.

Every *Policy* has a unique identifier. A *Policy* regulates the *Actions* performed on an *Asset*, which is any physical or digital resource or collection of resources. Examples of *Asset* are the email or the telephone number of a customer. The *Actions* are labels that can be specified using *Constraints*, which are Boolean or logical expressions. *Actions* can be for example "*use*", "*share*", '*transfer*", or "*play*". On *Action* can be permitted on a given asset whereas another one can be prohibited. In addition, we can consider some constraints for each *Action*. For example, customers can give permission to the company to collect their contact details, but company can contact the customers only via email. A Policy involves some *Parties*, which can be a person, a collection of people, an organisation, or an agent. For instance, fashion companies are the parties that provide services for other parties like customers.

A *Rule*, which can be a *Permission*, a *Prohibition* or a *Duty*, can be constrained by a condition and, if the condition holds the *Rule* becomes in force. In particular: a *Permission* is used for allowing an *Action*, when all refinements satisfied, to be exercised on an *Asset*. A *Prohibition* disallows an action, with all refinements satisfied, to be exercised on an *Asset* even if all constraints are satisfied. Finally, a *Duty* represents the obligation to exercise an action, with all refinements satisfied. For example, in some fashion websites, customers can be obliged to pay (as a *Duty*) small amount of money if they want to access VIP services. In the next session, we will analyse some existing policies used in the digital fashion and formalize them using the ODRL language in order to express them in a machine-readable format.

4.2   Examples of ODRL Policies for the Fashion Domain

In this Section we will formalize an existing privacy policy, which is taken from Zalando's web site [9] by using ODRL. We want to clarify that Zalando does not use our approach and to the best of our knowledge, neither Zalando nor any fashion company use automated methods for their policy compliance checking processes.

1.2. Contact details

If you contact us, we collect your data. Depending on how you contact us (e.g. by phone or by email), your contact details may include your name, postal addresses, telephone numbers, fax numbers, email addresses, detail on your social network profiles (for example we receive your Facebook ID if you contact us via Facebook), user names and similar contact details.

Fig. 2. Zalando data collection policy when a customer contacts them

Data collection procedure varies in Zalando based on wide range of communication between customers and company. Figure 2 shows the policy of the collection of data while a customer contacts Zalando. As it is shown many personal data can be collected depends on how the company is contacted. Such a permission can be represented in ODRL as illustrated in Fig. 3. To make the formalization of the policy simple, we will formalize only some of the personal information mentioned in the policy reported in Fig. 2 (i.e. phone number and email). More details on the syntax of ODRL policies can be find on ODRL website[8].

```
{    "@context": "http://www.w3.org/ns/odrl.jsonld",
     "@type": "Set",
     "uid": "http://example.com/policy:1001",
     "permission": [{
        "target": "http://example.com/asset:1008.phone",
        "target": "http://example.com/asset:1009.email",
        "action": "archive"    }] }
```

Fig. 3. Representation of the permission to archive customer's contact details such as email and phone number in ODRL

```
{ "@context": "http://www.w3.org/ns/odrl.jsonld",
  "@type": "Agreement",
  "uid": "http://example.com/policy:1002",
  "profile": "http://example.com/odrl:profile:01",
  "permission": [{
  "target": "http://example.com/asset:9898.hometown",
  "assigner": "http://example.com/party:org:CompanyX",
  "assignee": "http://example.com/party:person:CustomerDavid",
  "action": "use"   }]  }}
```

Fig. 4. Representation of permission in ODRL for customer David and CompanyX for the use of David's hometown information. This example highlights an ODRL limitation: it not possible to specify template of policies applicable to a set of agents.

Figure 4 shows an example of agreement between CompanyX and user David to use the hometown of the customer. Such an information could significantly improve the sale of the company by getting information about bestselling article in each city [22]. Figure 5

---

[8] https://www.w3.org/TR/odrl-model/.

represents a policy that includes two rules one permission and one prohibition on the same resource, "phone number". Customer David gives the permission to the company to collect his phone information but on the other hand the company is prohibited to share such data to third parties. In addition, if any conflicts happen between *Prohibition* and *Permission*, the *conflict* property term indicates that which one will take precedence. In this example the *conflict* property is set to *perm* which means that the *Permission* has priority over the *Prohibition*.

```
{   "@context": "http://www.w3.org/ns/odrl.jsonld",
    "@type": "Agreement",
    "uid": "http://example.com/policy:10003",
    "profile": "http://example.com/odrl:profile:08",
    "conflict": "perm",
    "permission": [{
        "target": "http://example.com/phone",
        "action": "collect",
        "assigner": "http://example.com/party:org:CompanyX",
        "assignee": "http://example.com/party:person:CustomerDavid", }],
    "prohibition": [{
        "target": "http://example.com/phone",
        "action": "share",
        "assigner": "http://example.com/party:org:CompanyX",
        "assignee": "http://example.com/party:person:CustomerDavid",   }]
```

Fig. 5. Formalization of one permission and one prohibition in a policy agreement between CompanyX and Customer David. It shows that CompanyX is allowed to collect David's phone number, but it is prohibited to share this information with third-party companies.

5   Monitoring Norms and Policies

In the preceding sections, we outlined the efforts taken to represent and structure the privacy policy of the companies for the sake of ultimately being access and processed by computers. Moreover, in this section we study the role of automated policy monitoring. Firstly, we seek to address the importance of monitoring policies and secondly, we discuss the need of some components for automated monitoring.

Here we describe few useful services that can be provided on a set of machine-readable policies:

- Monitoring the compliance of policies in which a person is involved as debtor. This functionality plays a critical role especially in fashion companies due to their need to collect sensitive customers' data and to their need to monitor their employees' behavior towards customers' privacy inside their organization.

- Giving the flexibility and confidence to customers by providing monitoring platform that they can use to see whether their privacy policies are violated or not. For instance, a customer can attach a prohibition to one picture to be published it on a public platform for advertisement and would like to monitor if the actions performed on the picture are compliant with this prohibition [4].
- Searching accurately the resources and the possible actions that can be performed on them. For instance, we assume that the company offers services to collect some personal data about customer's interest to explore more effective personalization [30].

In order to monitor policies automatically we need the following components:

1. A machine-readable data structure of the actions performed or planned by companies or customers.
2. A mechanism for monitoring the status of policies to check whether there are active or not. For example, as mentioned in the previous section, some policies can contain constrains and as soon as they become satisfied the policies status will be changed.
3. A mechanism for controlling if a given action (realized on given resource by a certain agent) is compliant with the set of active policies.
4. A mechanism for automatically computing if the active policies such as obligations or prohibitions are violated or fulfilled.

In literature there are two interesting proposals of extending ODRL with an operational semantics for monitoring norms and policies automatically. In [16] the model of policies proposed in ODRL has been extended in order to make it possible to express its operational semantics. The authors put in evidence some properties of the policies that are relevant for their life-cycle, in particular the deadline and their activation condition.

In another interesting paper [31] M. De Vos et al. proposes an ODRL profile that can capture the semantics of both business policies and regularity requirement. They use Answer Set Programming for the policy compliance checking with possibility of reporting the problem in case that compliance is not achieved.

6 Conclusion

In this paper we investigated how we can use ODRL and Semantic Web technologies for expressing privacy policies of the fashion brands in the Web of Data. We stressed on the transformation of policies from natural language to the machine-readable format using RDF. We used ODRL as a policy language for expressing the action that should or should not performed on the resources. Finally, we have highlighted the literature for monitoring the policies automatically. Our investigations into this area are still ongoing and, in our future work we plan to investigate the use of the OWL Web Ontology Language for expressing actions performed by the agent and infer their implications by using OWL reasoning.

Acknowledgement. The research reported in this paper has been funded by the SNSF (Swiss National Science Foundation) grant no. 200021 175759/1.

References

1. Gonzalo, A., Harreis, H., Altable, C., Villepelet, C.: The fashion industry's digital transformation: Now or never | McKinsey (2020). https://www.mckinsey.com/industries/retail/our-insights/fashions-digital-transformation-now-or-never. Accessed 12 Feb 2021
2. Kari, K.: The Art of Ontology (2018). https://engineering.zalando.com/posts/2018/03/sem antic-web-technologies.html. Accessed 12 Feb2021
3. Rowshankish, K., Trittipo, A., London, S.: Data privacy: what every manager needs to know. McKinsey Insights, July 2018
4. Oltramari, A., et al.: PrivOnto: a semantic framework for the analysis of privacy policies. Semant. Web **9**(2), 185–203 (2018). https://doi.org/10.3233/SW-170283
5. Garraza, T.S.: Fashion in the digital environment - Ediciones Universidad de Navarra (2015). https://www.eunsa.es/libro/moda-en-el-entorno-digital_102440/. Accessed 12 Feb 2021
6. Sekhavat, Y.A.: Privacy preserving cloth try-on using mobile augmented reality. IEEE Trans. Multimed. **19**(5), 1041–1049 (2017). https://doi.org/10.1109/TMM.2016.2639380
7. Ornati, M., Cantoni, L.: FashionTouch in E-commerce: an exploratory study of surface haptic interaction experiences. In: Nah, F.F.-H., Siau, K. (eds.) HCII 2020. LNCS, vol. 12204, pp. 493–503. Springer, Cham (2020). https://doi.org/10.1007/978-3-030-50341-3_37
8. Kalbaska, N., Cantoni, L.: Digital fashion competences: market practices and needs. In: Rinaldi, R., Bandinelli, R. (eds.) IT4Fashion 2017. LNEE, vol. 525, pp. 125–135. Springer, Cham (2019). https://doi.org/10.1007/978-3-319-98038-6_10
9. Zalando Privacy Notice. https://mosaic01.ztat.net/cnt/privacy-page/pdf/Zalando_Privacy_Notice_(English).pdf. Accessed 12 Feb 2021
10. 2017 Global Mobile Consumer Survey (2017). https://www2.deloitte.com/content/dam/Del oitte/nl/Documents/technology-media-telecommunications/2017%20GMCS%20Dutch%20Edition.pdf. Accessed 12 Feb 2021
11. McDonald, A.M., Cranor, L.F.: The cost of reading privacy policies. I/S: J. Law Policy Inf. Soc., **4**, 543
12. Carver, R.P.: Is reading rate constant or flexible? Read. Res. Q. **18**(2), 190 (1983). https://doi.org/10.2307/747517
13. Tommy Hilfiger introduces Tommy Jeans XPLORE smart clothes. https://www.businessinsi der.com/tommy-hilfiger-smart-clothes-rewards-2018-7?r=US&IR=T. Accessed 12 Feb 2021
14. General Data Protection Regulation, GDPR Overview. https://www.microsoft.com/en-us/trust-center/privacy/gdpr-overview. Accessed 12 Feb 2021
15. Kirrane, S., Villata, S., D'Aquin, M.: Privacy, security and policies: a review of problems and solutions with semantic web technologies. Semant. Web **9**(2), 153–161 (2018). https://doi.org/10.3233/SW-180289
16. Bollacker, K., Díaz-Rodríguez, N., Li, X.: Beyond clothing ontologies: modeling fashion with subjective influence networks. Mach. Learn. Meets Fash. KDD Work, pp. 1–7, August 2016
17. Clothing Product Information Ontology Language Reference. http://www.ebusiness-unibw.org/ontologies/cpi/ns. Accessed 12 Feb 2021
18. Fornara, N., Colombetti, M.: Using Semantic Web Technologies and Production Rules for Reasoning on Obligations, Permissions, and Prohibitions, pp. 319–334. IOS Press, (2019). https://doi.org/10.3233/aic-190617

19. Fornara, N.: Specifying and Monitoring Obligations in Open Multiagent Systems Using Semantic Web Technology. In: Elçi A., Koné M.T., Orgun M.A. (eds.) Semantic Agent Systems. Studies in Computational Intelligence, vol. **344**. Springer, Heidelberg (2011). https://doi.org/10.1007/978-3-642-18308-9_2

20. Hitzler, P., Krötzsch, M., Rudolph, S.: Foundations of Semantic Web Technologies, Chapman & Hall - CRC Press August 2009

21. Berners-Lee, T., Hendler, J., Lassila, O.: The Semantic Web a new form of Web content that is meaningful to computers will unleash a revolution of new possibilities. Accessed 12 Feb 2021. https://www.scientificamerican.com

22. Snyder, R.: A practical introduction to the XML, extensible markup language, by way of some useful examples. In: Proceedings 2004 ASCUE Conference, pp. 239–247 (2004)

23. Alnaqeib, R., Alshammari, F.H., Zaidan, M.A., Zaidan, A.A., Zaidan, B.B., Hazza, Z.M.: An overview: extensible markup language technology, June 2010. http://arxiv.org/abs/1006.4565

24. Peroni, S., Vitali, F.: Interfacing fast-fashion design industries with Semantic Web technologies: the case of imperial fashion. J. Web Semant. **44**, 37–53 (2017). https://doi.org/10.1016/j.websem.2017.06.001

25. Home – TrustArc The Leader in Privacy Management Software. https://trustarc.com/. Accessed 12 Feb 2021

26. Iannella, R.: The open digital rights language: XML for digital rights management. Inf. Secur. Tech. Rep. **9**(3), 47–55 (2004). https://doi.org/10.1016/S1363-4127(04)00031-7

27. XrML Elements | Microsoft Docs. https://docs.microsoft.com/en-us/previous-versions/windows/desktop/adrms_sdk/xrml-elements. Accessed 12 Feb 2021

28. Burnett, I., Van de Walle, R., Hill Rightscom, K., Bormans, U.J., Pereira, F.: MPEG-21: goals and achievements (2003). https://ro.uow.edu.au/infopapers/46. Accessed 12 Feb 2021

29. Guth, S.: Rights expression languages. In: Becker, E., Buhse, W., Günnewig, D., Rump, N. (eds.) Digital Rights Management. LNCS, vol. 2770, pp. 101–112. Springer, Heidelberg (2003). https://doi.org/10.1007/10941270_8

30. Nobile, T.H., Kalbaska, N.: An exploration of personalization in digital communication. insights in fashion. In: Nah, F.F.-H., Siau, K. (eds.) HCII 2020. LNCS, vol. 12204, pp. 456–473. Springer, Cham (2020). https://doi.org/10.1007/978-3-030-50341-3_35

31. De Vos, M., Kirrane, S., Padget, J., Satoh, K.: ODRL policy modelling and compliance checking. In: Fodor, P., Montali, M., Calvanese, D., Roman, D. (eds.) RuleML + RR 2019. LNCS, vol. 11784, pp. 36–51. Springer, Cham (2019). https://doi.org/10.1007/978-3-030-31095-0_3

A Photocomposition Search System to Improve Your Photo Skills

Hiroki Tanaka[✉] and Tatsuo Nakajima

Waseda University, Tokyo, Japan
{h.tanaka,tatsuo}@dcl.cs.waseda.ac.jp

Abstract. With the progress being made in information technology, many photos can be taken and shared. In addition, we have more chances to see evaluated photos and see more photos shared with others on social media. Moreover, there is more information available about how to take better photos. Herein, we create a photocomposition search system called PCSS to develop photography skills. PCSS is created with the idea of "learning by looking". In this research, we evaluated and experimented with PCSS at a university and in a city park. Although the participants did not feel that they were good at photography, they received some photocomposition knowledge from PCSS.

Keywords: Photo compositions · Image search · Web application

1 Introduction

Currently, taking photos is an essential part of our daily lives. However, there was a significant limit to the number of photos taken during the film camera age. Moreover, users had to make photo albums manually. Therefore, it was almost impossible to share with people who were not family and friends. With the progress being made in regards to information technology, especially with the spread of smartphones, people can now take more photos easily [3]. In addition, social networks such as Instagram and Twitter are now widely used, and people are more likely to share the photos they take on social networks. We have had more opportunities to have our photos evaluated, and we have seen more photos that others have shared on social networks. Although there is more information on how to take better photos than in the days of film cameras, there is still no environment or system in place to hone your skills.

A good or bad photo is a personal preference, and there is no absolute, right answer. However, photocomposition is a crucial element of visual effect, as it expresses the photographer's ideas in the process of constructing the photo. Therefore, learning how to compose a photograph is essential to improving our photographic skills. Even though composition plays a vital role in improving photographic skills, few studies aim to support photographic composition. Some systems support photographic composition, such as a smartphone application that can evaluate images being taken instantly [5] and a photo-taking interface that provides real-time feedback on how the subject is positioned

M. M. Soares et al. (Eds.): HCII 2021, LNCS 12781, pp. 396–406, 2021.
https://doi.org/10.1007/978-3-030-78227-6_29

[9]. In those studies, the photographer does not do much to find what he/she wants to take photos of.

This research creates a photocomposition search system called PCSS to develop photography skills. We propose a support system that supports beginners in improving their photographic skills by focusing on "learning by looking" at a photo's composition. Then you can study many compositions about each specific subject.

The rest of the paper is structured as follows. In Sect. 2, we present an overview of PCSS. In Sect. 3, we conduct preliminary experiments using paper prototypes and create research questions. In Sect. 4, we conduct and evaluate experiments compared with and without scenarios. Section 5 shows the experiment results. In Sect. 6, we discuss what is needed to improve photography skills. In Sect. 7, we present some related work. Section 8 concludes the paper.

2 PCSS: A Photocomposition Search System

It is important to "learn by looking" at many good photographs to improve your photographic skills. We have developed a prototype of a system called PCSS, which presents a large number of photos for a specific location (see Fig. 2). In this research, we prepared approximately 170 photos within approximately 100 m × 200 m near Waseda University in Tokyo. PCSS has a field for entering search keywords, similar to a general image search engine such as Google Image Search. You can search by location in the area, the name of the subject in the photo, or the approximate time we took the photo. PCSS has two modes, namely, view mode, which displays all images randomly without entering search keywords, and search mode, which allows you to search by the subject's name in the photo. You can change both view mode and search mode seamlessly.

2.1 View Mode

View mode is a mode that randomly displays a list of images without entering search keywords. When PCSS users want to take a photo in a specific area and cannot find the subject they want, the purpose of this mode is to help them find the subject they want by looking at the list of photos. If they find a subject they want to photograph in view mode, they can enter the subject as a keyword in PCSS and switch to search mode.

2.2 Search Mode

Search mode is a mode that allows PCSS users to enter the subject they want to photograph as a search word and display photos taken from various angles. For example, enter "51" as the search keyword, and we will present you with several photos related to building no. 51. As shown in Fig. 1(b), tapping on an image will display detailed information within the image. For example, the subject, the approximate location, and the approximate time the photo was taken. However, PCSS does not provide each photo's composition information (e.g., rule of thirds). This research's primary purpose is to "learn by looking" at the photos, and we intend to let users learn photocomposition from many photos rather than checking the photo details one by one.

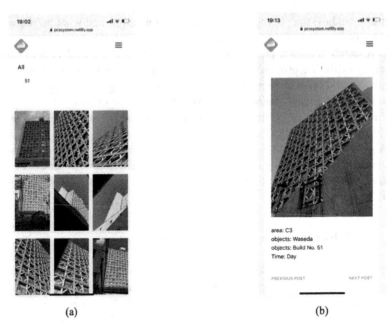

(a)   (b)

Fig. 1. (a) PCSS search mode (b) PCSS image detail

2.3 Implementation

We used Gatsby, a JavaScript library for the PCSS front end. PCSS can search for some words. We implemented PCSS by the Gatsby title search. If an image title contains "51", PCSS can show the image when searching for "51". The PCSS's back end used NetlifyCMS, a headless CMS. If we added some images, NetlifyCMS created new detailed image pages. We also used GraphQL, a query language for API, to connect Gatsby and NetlifyCMS.

3   A Preliminary Experiment

To test this PCSS's effectiveness, we created a paper prototype using Google Forms, and we hired 15 participants (age: m = 23.3, sd = 1.77, 13 males). In this user study, we created the following scenario:

Akira, a college student, has bought a new camera and is trying to learn photography. He chose Tokyo Tower as a well-known object to photograph, but he could not take a good photo. Therefore, he decided to search for pictures of the Tokyo Tower. To find Tokyo Tower photos, he entered the search word "Tokyo Tower" into PCSS. Using PCSS, Akira was able to find the composition of the photo for hints and successfully took the photo.

As shown in Table 1, four questions were prepared using a 5-point Likert score in the preliminary user study. The results are shown in Fig. 3. Additionally, we interviewed the participants about how their photography practices changed before and after using the

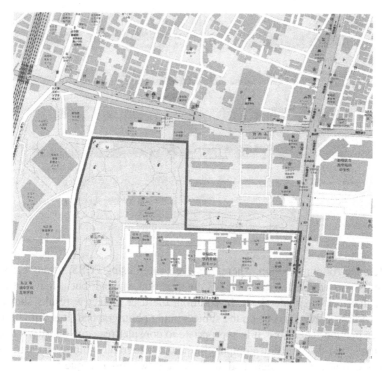

Fig. 2. This is the photo shooting area of PCSS we created.

prototype. One participant noted, *"I think I became more conscious of where to shoot from."* Another participant also mentioned, *"I think I can think of the subject from a new perspective"*.

Table 1. Questions in the preliminary user study

	Questions
Q1	Did the prototype help you with the composition of the Tokyo Tower?
Q2	Did you see any photos of the Tokyo Tower composition in the prototype that you didn't imagine?
Q3	Do you feel that using prototypes can help you improve your own photography skills?
Q4	Do you feel that the prototype can help you to take photos of objects other than Tokyo Tower?

From the results of this user study, 93.3% of the participants agreed that the paper prototype would help them with their composition. Additionally, 60% of the participants felt that the paper prototype would improve their photography skills. However, for subjects other than Tokyo Tower, the participants did not necessarily find it useful

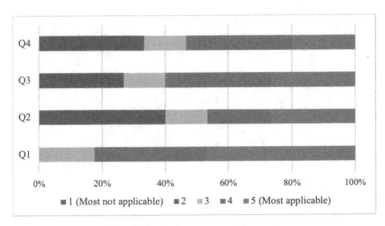

Fig. 3. Preliminary user study result

as a reference for composition. Therefore, even when using PCSS, it may be possible to use it as a reference for the subject's composition at hand, but it may not directly improve their photographic skills. In addition, the user interview results showed that although it is possible to focus on the subject being photographed, it is difficult to gain a new perspective. Therefore, it is appropriate to consider research questions from two perspectives: the discovery of composition and photography improvement. From the preliminary user study, we identified the following two research questions.

- **RQ1: Composition discovery** Can people discover a composition when taking a photo by presenting various photos of a specific subject?
- **RQ2: Improving photo skills** Can people's discovery of composition actually lead to better photos?

4 Experiments

To answer the research questions, we conducted two experiments with subjects using PCSS. One is an experiment where the participants can freely take pictures of a specific area without scenarios (see Fig. 4). In this experiment, we mainly use the view mode of PCSS. In the other experiment, we presented a scenario to photograph a specific subject and asked the participants to take pictures according to the scenario. In this experiment, we mainly used the search mode of PCSS. This experiment's target areas are a city park and a university campus in Tokyo, which are the same areas as the photos stored in PCSS (see Fig. 2).

4.1 An Experiment Without a Scenario

Without the scenarios, an experiment was conducted within the photos' scope in PCSS. The experiment's flow was as follows: First, the participants were asked to freely take pictures of the target area shown in Fig. 2. Next, we explained how to use PCSS. PCSS is

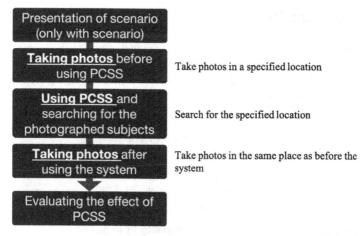

Take photos in a specified location

Search for the specified location

Take photos in the same place as before the system

Fig. 4. Experiment flow

used before taking photos (view mode), and PCSS is used to search for images at the site where pictures are taken (search mode). Then use the system to select photos after taking them (view mode). We explained to the participants that they could use the system in any combination of these modes. After that, we asked the subjects to take photos using PCSS: two of the photos taken before and two of the photos taken after using PCSS, for a total of four photos each. At the end of the study, we conducted a questionnaire and interview to determine how their photography behavior changed before and after the use of PCSS. The number of participants was 9 (age: m = 22.5, sd = 0.86, 7 males).

4.2 An Experiment with a Scenario

We conducted an experiment using the following scenario.

You are a novice college student who has just started taking pictures on your smart-phone. One day, to practice taking photos, you chose Building 51 and Building 63 as your subjects. At first, you took pictures without looking at anything. However, you could not come up with a good composition. Therefore, you decided to use PCSS (the point and shoot system) as a reference for composition. There are many photos in the system, but you find the image you want by searching for "51" and "63". By imitating the photos on the system, I are able to take better pictures.

The experiment's flow was to have the students take photos of Building 51 and Building 63 without using PCSS. Next, we had them use PCSS. In this experiment, we assumed that the participants would search for information at the site where PCSS was used (search mode). The participants took photos of Building 51 and Building 63 using PCSS and submitted four photos: one photo of Building 51 and one photo of Building 63 before using PCSS, and one photo of Building 51 and one photo of Building 63 after using PCSS. Finally, we conducted questionnaires and interviews to see what changes occurred in the participants' photography behavior before and after the use of PCSS. We hired 4 participants (age: m = 23.0, sd = 0.67, 2 males).

5   Evaluation and Results

A questionnaire was administered using a four-question five-point Likert scale and a four-question seven-point Likert scale as a quantitative evaluation. In addition, we conducted some open-ended interviews. Each question is shown in Table 2. Figure 5 and Fig. 6 show the results of the questions.

Table 2. Questions of experiments

	Questions
Q1	Did the search results help you compose your photo?
Q2	Did you find any photos in the search results that you would not have thought of?
Q3	Did you feel that you improved your photography by using PCSS?
Q4	Has PCSS helped you take photos that you are satisfied with?
Q5	Did you move around more after using PCSS than before using PCSS?
Q6	Did you take more photos after using PCSS than before using PCSS?
Q7	Did you take more memorable photos of yourself after using PCSS than before using PCSS?
Q8	Did you have more fun taking photos after using PCSS than before using PCSS?

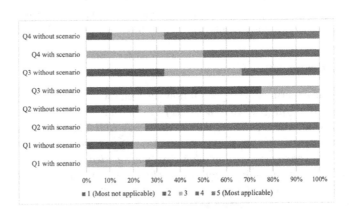

Fig. 5. Experiment results of Q1-Q4

5.1   Composition Guide

(See also Q1 and Q2) Most participants answered that PCSS was helpful for composition regardless of the scenario, but the results showed that it was beneficial for composition when there was a scenario. One participant noted, *"It was hard to think of composition to take a picture with a building in the background."* Some participants commented,

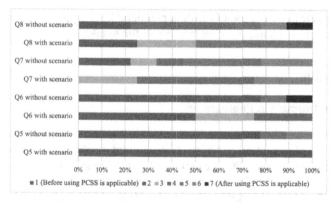

Fig. 6. Experiment results of Q5-Q8

"The direction and distance from which to look at the building was helpful." The reason the results were more helpful in the case with scenarios is that the participants had been focusing on a particular subject before using PCSS, and they may have found something new in what they were paying attention to. Without scenarios, the participants looked at the images in a scattered manner, often using them to find spots to shoot and were not aware of discovering new compositions.

5.2   To Improve Photo Skills

(See also Q3 and Q4) Regardless of the scenario, many participants answered that *"I did not feel that I had improved my photography."* The most common reason was that they could not judge whether they had improved or not. However, they could not think of what to shoot to find a subject to refer to and develop their ideas without scenarios. When there was a scenario, PCSS suggested a composition that they had not thought of, and when they were able to find a new composition by themselves that was similar to the suggested image, they felt they had improved.

5.3   Moving Around

(See also Q5 and Q6) The results show that the participants moved around more before using PCSS, regardless of with or without scenarios. The reason for this, especially noticeable when no scenario was used, was that before using PCSS, the participants freely searched for photos by themselves, but after using PCSS, they tended to go to the same places as the photos on PCSS.

5.4   Memorable Photos

(See also Q7 and Q8) Participants' opinions were mainly divided, regardless of the scenario. Some participants felt that the process of trial and error on their own, regardless of the use of PCSS, was fun, while others enjoyed the result of being able to take a photo that they thought was good. Since there was a large separation in the responses and few participants wrote about the use of PCSS in photography enjoyment, the result was that PCSS does not make photos more memorable or fun to take.

6 Discussion

6.1 What to Improve in Photography

The usage of PCSS can be divided into two main categories. Some participants who do not take any photos at all answered that they did not have any ideas about what kinds of photos to take; thus, PCSS can be used as a reference for ideas. However, other participants who answered that they take photos with their smartphones to some extent said that PCSS makes it difficult for them to search for photos freely and that they could not say that they have become better at taking photos because the subjects they take are fixed.

Since PCSS was developed as a search system, it does not evaluate its images. This may be because novice photographers cannot judge whether the pictures they have taken are right or not, so they do not feel that they have become good at taking pictures, and few people feel that they have improved as a result of PCSS. A third party or a system such as PCSS must evaluate the photos taken. Yeh et al. proposed a personalized ranking system for amateurs [10].

However, several participants answered that they could learn more about their composition. This means that it is easier for them to judge whether they know the composition. When there was a scenario, they said that there were compositions that they had not thought of. Although PCSS has the effect of increasing the number of compositions, it does not increase compositions.

6.2 Usage and Moving Around

Without scenarios, the usage of PCSS differed significantly from person to person. One option is to use view mode to view randomly selected subjects, and the other is to use search mode after arriving at the shooting spot to determine what kind of photos are available for the subject in the shooting spot. One point that is common to both is that before using PCSS, many people walk around in various places, but after using PCSS, the participants are more likely to use both view mode and search mode. In both view mode and search mode, the participants used PCSS to go to the displayed image's location. Thus, it can be said that the distance participants had to travel to take pictures was reduced.

6.3 Enjoyable

Many participants said they enjoyed looking around for interesting subjects to take photos of. Moreover, PCSS has increased the chances of capturing scenery, which can be a source of enjoyment.

7 Related Work

There have been many previous evaluations of photographs in terms of aesthetics; Datta et al. [2] have shown a correlation between the aesthetic information of a photograph and features of the image using machine learning [10]. The rules of composition and basic features of the image (e.g., color histogram) were manually extracted as features. In recent years, aesthetic assessment using deep learning has also existed [7], and some studies have evaluated aesthetic preferences on large image datasets [8].

Even the nonreal-time evaluation of aesthetics has been taken to support photography in evaluating the photo after it has been taken. However, if we can evaluate aesthetics in real time, we will support photography in real time. There are few studies that support photography. Li et al. [5] provide photographic composition support by scoring eight compositions in real time to improve future photography scores. Ma et al. [6] presented a method for suggesting a photo with a better composition than the original one based on the photos taken. Several studies use people as the object of photography, such as one that targets "selfies" [4] and one that targets portraits [9]. From the perspective of "learning by looking" at photos, research [1] looks for photos with good composition on the Web.

8 Conclusion and Future Direction

We have developed PCSS, a photocomposition search system for improving photographic skills, which was designed with the idea of learning composition by looking. We designed PCSS to help users learn about composition by looking at it, so it not only display images randomly but also has a function to display many photos of a specific subject. The results of the experiments in this study show that PCSS can increase the number of compositional options for beginners in photography. Specifically, PCSS was able to find compositions and angles to the subject that the novice had not thought of. However, the number of participants who felt that their photography had improved was small, probably because there was no system in PCSS to visualize their improvement. Several options for ranking personalized photos have been proposed, and it will be essential to combine them.

In this research, we interviewed people about their photography enjoyment when taking pictures. The results showed that it is essential to walk around by oneself to take pictures and that the method of imitating only the images presented by PCSS takes away one of the pleasures of photography. We want to present images that incorporate gamification to make photography more enjoyable in the future.

References

1. Chen, Y.L., Klopp, J., Sun, M., Chien, S.Y., Ma, K.L.: Learning to compose with professional photographs on the web. In: Proceedings of the 25th ACM International Conference on Multimedia, MM 2017, pp. 37–45. Association for Computing Machinery, New York (2017)
2. Datta, R., Joshi, D., Li, J., Wang, James Z.: Studying aesthetics in photographic images using a computational approach. In: Leonardis, A., Bischof, H., Pinz, A. (eds.) ECCV 2006. LNCS, vol. 3953, pp. 288–301. Springer, Heidelberg (2006). https://doi.org/10.1007/11744078_23

3. House, N.A.V.: Personal photography, digital technologies and the uses of the visual. Vis. Stud. **26**(2), 125–134 (2011)

4. Li, Q., Vogel, D.: Guided selfies using models of portrait aesthetics. In: Proceedings of the 2017 Conference on Designing Interactive Systems, DIS 2017, pp. 179–190. Association for Computing Machinery, New York (2017)

5. Li, Y.F., Yang, C.K., Chang, Y.Z.: Photo composition with real-time rating. Sensors **20**(3), 582 (2020)

6. Ma, S., et al.: SmartEye: assisting instant photo taking via integrating user preference with deep view proposal network. In: Proceedings of the 2019 CHI Conference on Human Factors in Computing Systems, CHI 2019, pp. 1–12. Association for Computing Machinery, New York (2019)

7. Mai, L., Jin, H., Liu, F.: Composition-preserving deep photo aesthetics assessment. In: Proceedings of the IEEE Conference on Computer Vision and Pattern Recognition (CVPR), June 2016

8. Murray, N., Marchesotti, L., Perronnin, F.: AVA: a large-scale database for aesthetic visual analysis. In: 2012 IEEE Conference on Computer Vision and Pattern Recognition, pp. 2408–2415 (2012)

9. Xu, Y., Ratcliff, J., Scovell, J., Speiginer, G., Azuma, R.: Real-time guidance camera interface to enhance photo aesthetic quality, CHI 2015, pp. 1183–1186. Association for Computing Machinery, New York (2015)

10. Yeh, C.H., Ho, Y.C., Barsky, B.A., Ouhyoung, M.: Personalized photograph ranking and selection system. In: Proceedings of the 18th ACM International Conference on Multimedia, MM 2010, pp. 211–220. Association for Computing Machinery, New York (2010)

Resonant Irregularities: Sculpture Creation Through Automatic Changes Due to Machine Performance Limits

Masasuke Yasumoto[✉], Daisuke Ichikawa, and Yuichi Ito

Faculty of Information Technology, Kanagawa Institute of Technology,
1030 Shimo-ogino, Atsugi, Kanagawa 243-0292, Japan
{yasumoto,ito}@ic.kanagawa-it.ac.jp,
s1723102@cco.kanagawa-it.ac.jp

Abstract. This research explored a method of creating three-dimensional art based on the concept of creating sculptures that are automatically generated by a machine without human intention. This is similar to glitch art, which is a type of media art. An analog real sculpture is captured as digital data by a 3D scanner, and then a 3D printer is used to produce the output of a 3D sculpture. The result of this process is a sculpture that differs from the original. This is a kind of noise, an irregularity, a limitation of the machine's performance, and a result that is not intended by humans. The data does not just deteriorate, but some information is lost and some new irregular information is added. This is an unintended abstraction and creation. By repeating this series of processes, I create new sculptures and explore the possibility of beauty that exists there. Further, we will reveal the characteristics of each sculpture using a total of four models (two existing sculptures, a Stanford bunny, and a primitive shape created with CAD), four different scanners, and two different 3D printers. We also tried out methods of intentionally adding noise and discussed the sculptures created by each method.

Keywords: Media art · Glitch art · 3D print · 3D scan

1 Introduction

In recent years, 3D printer technology has evolved to the point where it is now possible to produce an almost unlimited number of different shapes and materials. Various types of printers have been developed, allowing for the creation of objects of all sizes, from small parts to houses. This has increased the speed of modern prototyping and product development, thereby contributing to the development of the technology.

3D scanners for scanning three-dimensional objects have also been developed. Various types of scanners have emerged, the most common being turntable and handheld scanners that use infrared depth sensors. Scanners with very high-resolution can also scan the unevenness of a pencil stroke on a piece of paper. Contrarily, if the resolution is low, it is often difficult to obtain accurate 3D data of the shape of the object to be scanned. Recently, smartphones have been equipped with LiDAR sensors, making it easy to scan

© Springer Nature Switzerland AG 2021
M. M. Soares et al. (Eds.): HCII 2021, LNCS 12781, pp. 407–421, 2021.
https://doi.org/10.1007/978-3-030-78227-6_30

objects with high-resolution, and this technology has been applied in various fields. However, these simple scanning devices are not as accurate as the high-resolution 3D scanners mentioned above. There are many examples in which the so-called noise, such as non-existent parts or missing data, works effectively to express art and information media. The value of these works and expressions is often created by examining the reasons why noise is generated and its meaning. This will be introduced in the preceding examples in Sect. 2.

There is an attempt to make use of the noise generated by 3D scanning, Object Resolution by Miyako Atsuro [1]. This aims to repeat the process of scanning a banana, outputting the 3D data on a 3D printer, scanning it again, and printing it out. The purpose of this is to think about the value of the "real" and the "fake." In this experiment by Miyako, the authors conclude that the scanned banana changes its shape and appears to be something else, and they hope to repeat the experiment in the future.

According to the authors' experience, the output shape of the printed 3D object is greatly affected by the output error caused by the performance of the printer, as well as the error and noise of the 3D data caused by the accuracy and error of the scanner. This means that the 3D data generated by each scanner is different, and even if the same 3D object is scanned, different 3D data is generated, and when it is printed, the output shape will be different. The authors consider that the individuality of the scanner is born from this, and by repeating the process, different values may be created from the same 3D object. If the value can be systematically discussed, it will have a novel impact on 3D printer technology and lead to the development of new technology.

Therefore, the authors generated 3D data for the same 3D object using multiple scanners and printed the data. Next, they scanned the printed object, generated 3D data, and printed it again. This indicates repeated copying in 3D. In Miyako's experiment, we have not tried multiple scanners.

2 Related Works

Before carrying out the authors' experiments, we will introduce several categories of similar cases that have been produced and tested before.

2.1 Loops and Feedback

In "I Am Sitting In A Room" by Alvin Lucier, a microphone is used in a reverberant room to read a sentence beginning with "I Am Sitting In A Room....". The voice is recorded and played back from the speakers in the room. The sound from the speakers is recorded again. The sound recorded here includes the reverberation of the space. It was first performed and recorded at the Guggenheim Museum in 1970 [2]. Initially, it was Lucier's voice, but through repeated copying, the voice, words, and even the performers are erased, changing the meaning of the sound and making us aware that sound is a physical phenomenon. This work clearly proves that copying does not produce degradation, but rather a different form of expression.

"I Am Sitting In A Video Room" [3] by Patrick Liddell (ontologist) is an homage to Lucier's "I Am Sitting In A Room." It repeatedly downloads videos uploaded to YouTube and then re-uploads the video files. The original video is compressed and altered to a degree that is generally unnoticeable. The original video is compressed and altered to a degree that is generally unnoticeable due to the compression process used to upload the video to YouTube. The repeated compression process emphasizes the characteristics of the video alteration during the compression process, and the result is a video that differs greatly from the original video, including the audio. The system of video compression, about which we are not usually aware, is brought to our attention. They are also informed that with the advancement of digital technology, various things can be copied.

These works expose the characteristics of the media through repeated copying. This is an important indicator of observing the changes while repeating the copying in the authors' experiment.

2.2 Related About 3D Printer

Object Resolution [3] by Miyako Atsuro is an ongoing project. Inspired by the degradation caused by image compression when a digital image is copied multiple times, Miyako scans a banana in 3D and outputs the 3D data as a 3D print to replicate the banana. This is a banana-shaped with resin, but the shape is exactly copied. We are considering how the shape of the banana will change by scanning the copy and printing it again. However, it is unclear what kind of printer or scanner was used in this project, making it difficult to verify the project. For other writers and researchers to reproduce the experiment, it would be desirable to clarify what kind of environment and equipment were used and how the experiment was conducted. In addition, as mentioned in the previous chapter, it is expected that the output results will differ depending on the environment and equipment; further, a verification is desired.

David Bowen's "growth modeling device (2009)" [4] scans the growth of an onion bud with a laser scanner and prints the growth process of the bud in 3D. This is a record of the time by 3D printing, and it informs us that 3D printing, which has an industrial existence, can also be considered as an artistic expression and a medium.

Debra Thimmesch's web article "3D Printing Glitch Adds Meaning to Art Student's Sculpture" [5] considers the trouble that occurs with 3D printers as a glitch. The article, "3D Printing Glitch Adds Meaning to Art Student's Sculpture," [5] discusses glitching as a form of artistic expression. A glitch is an electronic mistake or error in an industrial product, a momentary malfunction that does not stop the operation. For example, the appearance of block noise when a cartridge is not fully inserted in a cartridge-type game machine, or the noise that occurs when headphones are plugged into a PC or speakers.

We believe that such studies provide a benchmark for the authors to consider the errors and noise of 3D printers and scanners in their experiments.

2.3 Related About 3D Glitches

"Glitch: Designing Imperfection" [6] by Iman Moradi et al. is a book that considers glitching in images as an artistic expression, and was compiled after receiving an open call for submissions. In this book, Moradi states that glitches are diamonds with inclusions. For this reason, he calls unintentional and spontaneous glitches as "pure glitches" and those that are created intentionally "glitches a like." However, Japanese artist ucnv argues in his essay on glitch art [7] that intentional glitching is an artistic expression that can be achieved by taking the viewpoint of a developer of various technologies. Rosa Menkman, in her article "The Glitch Mo-ment(um)" [8], discusses the need to clarify the relationship between the technical and cultural aspects of glitching and examines the cultural value of glitching. For more information on glitching, please refer to this paper, which provides a detailed explanation of glitching.

Thomas Ruff's "jpegs" [9] is a series of works that deal with Jpeg images, the most popular image data format today. Jpeg compresses the image data at the highest compression ratio by reducing the size of the image to a resolution of 128 pixels. Jpegs are photographic files in which the image is enlarged and displayed again, and the block noise characteristic of the Jpeg format is displayed on the photographs in jpegs, resulting in glitchy expressions. In Miyako's "Object Resolution" described in Sect. 2.2, block noise specific to the Jpeg image format is described as image degradation. In Miyako's "Object Resolution" described in Sect. 2.2, the block noise inherent in the Jpeg image format is described as image degradation, but Ruff sees a different value in it.

These studies can be used as a benchmark for handling data containing scanned errors and noise in the authors' experiments.

These cases suggest that the authors' experiment of repeatedly copying objects in 3D and observing the changes in the objects may create novel value, and the experiment should be carried out.

3   Creation Method

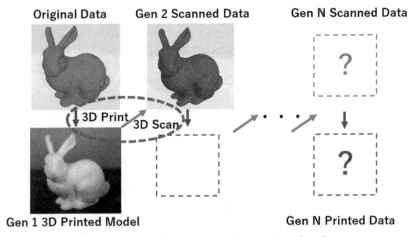

Fig. 1. Creation flow and generation number of works

In this research, 3D printing and 3D scanning will be repeated until the model changes and it converges or becomes impossible to print or scan, as shown in Fig. 1. We will then explore the characteristics of each by changing the model, 3D scan, and 3D printing methods.

Fig. 2. Comparison of the results of the first generation of "Action in Chain" data printed by FDM 3D printer(left) and the SLS 3D printer (right).

3.1 Model Selection

The models to be included are the Stanford Bunny, the complex "Winged Victory of Samothrace," a cube arranged based on primitive shapes, and Aristide Maillol's "Action in Chains," a real sculpture. In selecting the models, we chose several shapes so that the results would vary depending on the shape (Fig. 8).

First, the Stanford bunny is round shaped and is often used in computer graphics demonstrations, so we selected this shape as it is well known and easy to conduct follow-up experiments. "Winged Victory of Samothrace" is highly artistic, and was selected because it is suitable for this project, which is the loss or creation of shapes due to irregular noise, and shapes that already lack arms and heads. Since these two models are based on organic materials, the third model is a primitive figure composed of a set of planes, one of the 3D scanners used is not good at scanning horizontal surfaces, and it is desirable for the model to stand on its own. Given that one of the 3D scanners to be used is not good at scanning horizontal surfaces, and that the model should be able to stand on its own, we created a simple cube base that is partially cut and partially hollow so that it can be placed diagonally. Since these three models were based on digital data, we chose "Action in Chains" from the Hakone Open-Air Museum in Japan as the starting point for the fourth model for comparison.

3.2 About 3D Scanners

A 3D scan with too much accuracy is not desirable, since the goal is to change the shape through noise unintended by the artist by going back and forth between digital and analog. Contrarily, if the accuracy is too low, it is impossible to observe the differences that are created through repeated generations, and the shape will collapse at once. Therefore, the following four 3D scanners were used in this study, hoping that differences would be generated depending on the 3D scanning method and model. In the case of multiple shells separated during scanning, only the largest shell is effective and the other shells are not used.

First, the stationary Matter & Form 3D is a standard 3D scanner with a horizontally mounted camera and laser. Since the camera is mounted horizontally, it is not good at scanning horizontal surfaces. The camera only moves up and down and only the platform on which the 3D model is placed rotates, so some surfaces cannot be scanned depending on the angle.

The Sol 3D Scanner is a stationary scanner as well, but it is slower and more accurate, and less sensitive to outside light since it is covered and scanned. This is designed to improve accuracy by automatically matching the model after multiple scans by rearranging the position and angle of the model, but this does not fit the purpose of this project, so only one scan is performed with the model upright.

Sense is a handheld 3D scanner that uses a built-in depth camera. Because it is a handheld scanner, the results are different for each scan, the photographer's intentions are reflected to some extent, and there are many failures due to lost tracking. For this reason, the most accurate scan will be used after multiple scans.

Trnio is an iPhone application that generates a 3D model from images taken from multiple angles by the built-in camera. When the model moves around, the shutter is automatically released and multiple photos are taken. As with Sense, this method also produces different results depending on how the camera is moved, so after multiple tests, the one with the highest accuracy is adopted.

3.3 About 3D Printers

The process of analog sculpting of the physical world, converting the 3D printed model into digital data using a 3D scanner, and generating the digital data into the physical world by 3D printing are counted as one generation, and the process is repeated. There are glitches due to the digital-to-analog conversion of 3D printing, but due to the nature of 3D printing, if the printing process fails, the original shape will be lost. However, the number of 3D printers that can print is limited, which increases the printing time and cost. Therefore, in this production, the 3D printing process was subcontracted to DMM.Make, a 3D printing service, to achieve high accuracy, eliminate printing errors, and prevent the artist's intentions from entering the process. The equipment used were EOSINT P760 of EOS for FDM(Fused Deposition Modeling) method and PartPro300xT of XYZ Printing for stacking method. As shown in Fig. 2, in the FDM method, which is a common and inexpensive method, the stacked traces are too large relative to the object to be formed, and the print turbulence is large despite the high-performance 3D printer. Therefore, we decided to use only the SLS (Selective Laser Sintering) method for this project, and uncolored nylon was used as the material.

Although this method is highly accurate, it may still be damaged during printing if the thickness is less than 1 mm, and the minimum detail is 0.3 mm. For this reason, some damage due to print failure was already seen in the first generation when the original data was printed. Although it is possible to solve this problem by increasing the size, we decided to set the maximum height at about 137 mm because of the cost. This is 4.5% of the original size of "Winged Victory of Samothrace".

4 Creation

The production was conducted with several categories as shown in the table. The Stanford Bunny was scanned in sol 3d, and the Cube was also scanned in sol 3d. "Winged Victory of Samothrace" was scanned in both sol and Matter & Form 3d for comparison. "Action in Chain" was scanned in both Trnio and Sense. Finally, to deliberately make mistakes in the scans, we took advantage of the fact that Sense is a handheld system and tried to deliberately make noise with the two methods.

4.1 Stanford Bunny

Gen 1 ————————————————————————————→ Gen 5

Fig. 3. Generational changes in the Stanford bunny

Stanford bunnies were tried until the Gen 5 as shown in Fig. 3. The first data was generated by Meshmixer. The changes in weight and volume are shown in Fig. 4. Detail was lost with each generation, but no characteristic changes were observed, probably due to the smoothness of the original shape. As for the bottom surface, it could not be scanned because it was in contact with the scan table, and the software generated it automatically, resulting in a dented shape. Consequently, the weight of the Gen 2 has decreased drastically. Similarly, the part of the body that touches the scan table is not being scanned properly, and the legs are gradually being eroded. The jaggies in the ears that existed at the beginning gradually smoothed out, and the polygonal planes that were visible due to the low polygons smoothed out as well, but since there was no significant change after the Gen 3, we defined it as converged and ended the trial.

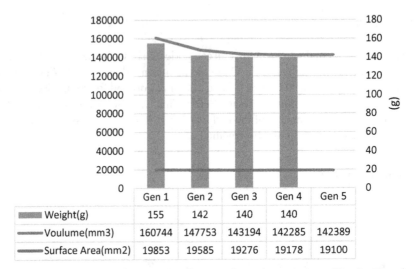

	Gen 1	Gen 2	Gen 3	Gen 4	Gen 5
Weight(g)	155	142	140	140	
Voulume(mm3)	160744	147753	143194	142285	142389
Surface Area(mm2)	19853	19585	19276	19178	19100

Fig. 4. Changes in weight, volume, and surface area for each generation of Stanford bunnies; no weight data for Gen 5 because it was not printed.

4.2 Cube

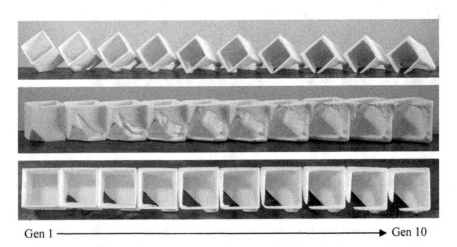

Gen 1 ⎯⎯⎯⎯⎯⎯⎯⎯⎯⎯⎯⎯⎯⎯⎯⎯⎯⎯⎯→ Gen 10

Fig. 5. Generational changes in the Cube

The cubes were tried until the Gen 10 as shown in Fig. 5. The changes in weight and volume are shown in the table. With each generation, as shown in Fig. 6, the thickness of the inner part increases because the inner part is not scanned accurately, and the volume and weight increase because the thickness of the other parts also increase. The bottom part is gradually scraped off, but the weight and volume are on the increase. If the process continues, it is expected to eventually disappear due to gradual erosion from the bottom.

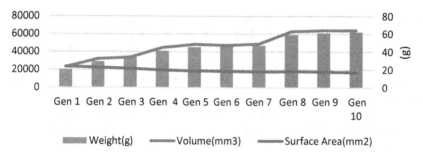

Fig. 6. Changes in weight, volume, and surface area for each generation of the Cube; no weight data for Gen 10 because it was not printed.

In the area close to the bottom, patterns were observed that were formed by erosion due to the insufficient thickness of the material, which could not be formed during the printing process. Since it was predicted that there would be some new changes, we stopped the trial after Gen 10.

4.3 Winged Victory of Samothrace

Fig. 7. Original data on the left, data with reduced polygon count in the middle, and sol 3D Gen 2 data on the right.

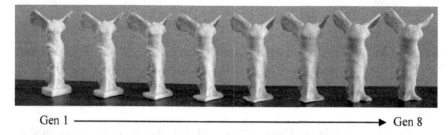

Fig. 8. Generational changes in "Winged Victory of Samothrace" by Sol 3D

"Winged Victory of Samothrace" was compared using two different scanners, Sol 3d and Matter & Form 3d. The original data was taken from the data available on the web (https://www.thingiverse.com/thing:196038). The original data was highly detailed with 2836081 vertices and 3672162 triangles, but the amount of data was too large to be uploaded to a 3D printing service, so the number of vertices was reduced to 213170 and the number of triangles to 426344, as shown in the center of Fig. 7. Trials using Sol 3d were conducted up to Gen 9, and trials using Matter & Form 3d were conducted up to generation 10. Even with the relatively high performance of Sol 3d, most of the detail is already lost and rounded after just one scan, as shown in the right side of Fig. 7. In addition, as with the Cube, the bottom surface was cut away and the overall thickness increased, and the right wing became noticeably thicker. As a result, while the overall length gradually decreased, the volume and weight increased with each generation, as shown in Fig. 9.

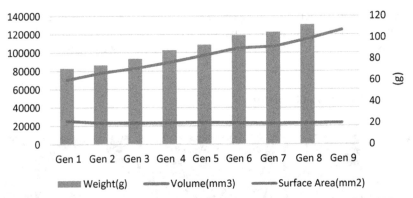

Fig. 9. Changes in weight, volume, and surface area for each generation of "Winged Victory of Samothrace" by Sol 3D; no weight data for Gen 9 because it was not printed.

Fig. 10. Generational changes in "Winged Victory of Samothrace" by Matter & Form 3D

On the other hand, in the Matter & Form 3d scan, the sharp edges remained relatively sharp due to the insufficient accuracy of the scanner and the meshing process, but gradually became thin, as shown in Fig. 10. In particular, the wings, which were thin to begin with, could not be printed because they were below the printable thickness and were gradually chipped away. As shown in Fig. 11, the volume, surface area, and weight

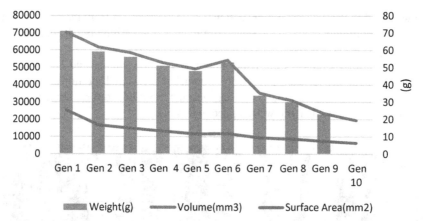

Fig. 11. Changes in weight, volume, and surface area for each generation of "Winged Victory of Samothrace" by Matter & Form 3D; no weight data for Gen 10 because it was not printed.

all showed a decreasing trend. The base of the foot was close to horizontal, so it could not be scanned initially and most of it was chipped off. The reason for the increase in weight and volume in Gen 6 was presumably due to this additional clay. The surface was not smooth, unlike Sol, and noise roughness was observed in all generations. It can be presumed that it will thin out and disappear if the process continues.

4.4 "Action in Chains"

Fig. 12. "Action in Chains" at the Hakone Open-Air Museum, with scanned data and printed models. This is the first generation.

Unlike the previous three, "Action in Chains" by Aristide Maillol was started by scanning an actual sculpture with Trnio, as shown in Fig. 12. The data from the first scan was used as the first generation, and then we branched out from there and scanned with Trnio continuously and with Sense. In this way, we verified the difference in the handheld type scans.

The sculptures scanned with Trnio gradually became thinner and lost details, as Shown in Fig. 13. The surface was close to smooth, but occasional addition of protrusions due to noise was observed. Finally, the legs became too thin and were damaged during printing, so the trial with Trnio was stopped at this point.

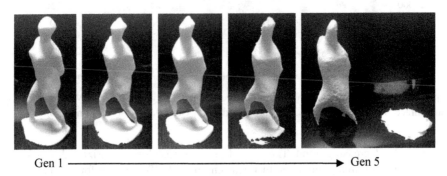

Gen 1 ⟶ Gen 5

Fig. 13. Generational changes in "Action in Chains" by Trnio.

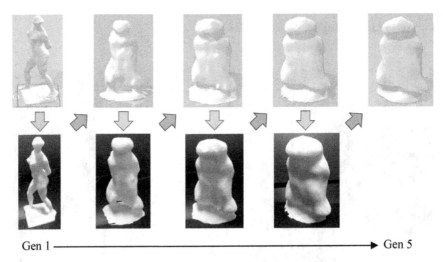

Gen 1 ⟶ Gen 5

Fig. 14. Generational changes in "Action in Chains" by Sense.

Contrarily, as shown in Fig. 14, the Sense scans showed the opposite: gradual rounding and fattening. Perhaps because the resolution of the scan is not very good, there is a noticeable increase in volume on the first scan from the first generation to the second generation, and because Trnio and Sense are hand-reduced type 3d scans, they reflect the manipulation skills and intentions of the scanner user. Therefore, several scans were created and the one with the least visual change and with a shape that can be 3D printed was selected so that human intentions could be avoided as much as possible.

4.5 Intentional Noise Generation

In the case of handheld Sense scanning, the location of the scan can be controlled manually, or the scan can be stopped when it is inadequate, in which case the scanned data is analyzed by software and solidified by estimation. In this case, the software analyzes the scanned data and makes it solid by estimation. Therefore, it is possible to intentionally change the original model significantly. As an experiment, we generated large scan errors using two different methods, as shown in Fig. 14. The resulting changes in volume and surface area are shown in Fig. 15 (Fig. 16).

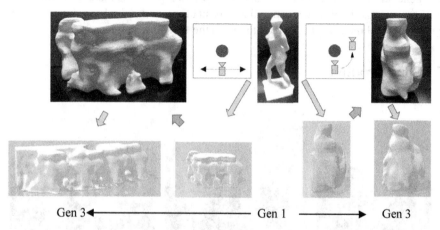

Fig. 15. A model resulting from two types of intentional noise.

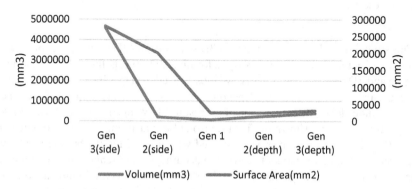

Fig. 16. Changes in volume and surface area per generation with two different methods of intentional noise generation.

In the first method, we placed the scanner in front of the model and moved it back and forth horizontally without changing the direction. In the first method, the scanner was placed in front of the model and moved back and forth horizontally without changing the direction. At this time, the sides and the back of the model were almost impossible to scan, resulting in a distorted solid as shown in the left side of Fig. 14. We repeated this technique for another generation, and the deformation features observed in the first trial were also visible in the second trial. This trial was stopped here because the size of the second trial was already too large.

For the second method, the scanner was placed in front of the model, and the model was rotated a quarter of a turn around the scanner with the angle of the scanner fixed. At this point, the scanner decides that it's tracking is lost and no more scanning is possible. Solidification is performed in this state. The Gen 2 model was scanned in the same way, as shown in the right side of Fig. 14. The second generation was also scanned using the same method, as shown in the right side of Fig. 14. The same characteristics as the first generation were observed here, and as shown in Fig. 15, the increase in volume and surface area was slight, so it was possible to print the second and subsequent generations, but we stopped the trial at this point to match the first generation.

5   Consideration

Fig. 17. Comparison of the last generation model (left and right) and the first-generation model (center) for each scan.

This study utilized the low accuracy of 3D scanners and 3D printers to explore a new method of generating 3D sculptures by deforming 3D objects through alternating 3D scanning and 3D printing. Particularly, we mostly used data loss by 3D scanners, and the differences in deformation results depending on the shape of the model and the type of scanner became clear. The comparison of the results of "Winged Victory of Samothrace" with different scanners, shown in Fig. 17, also helps clarify the process. To reduce the cost of 3D printing, this study was conducted with a small model, but the results will be different with a larger model because the accuracy of the scanner will be relatively higher. In this research, the author's intentions were kept to its minimum, and the main goal was to enjoy the results generated automatically. In this sense, a stationary scanner and outsourced 3D printing are sufficient to achieve the purpose, but in the case of a handheld scanner, it is difficult to sufficiently standardize the way it is moved and the environment in which it is scanned, and the intention inevitably enters at the scanning stage. Although we set a rule to repeat the scan several times and select the one with the least deformation compared with the original data, it is still subject to change due to factors, such as the environment and the scanning operator.

The scan of "Winged Victory" using Matter & Form 3-D showed very interesting results because the original shape of the sculpture could be estimated even though the loss had progressed. In addition, the "Action in Chains" Trnio sculpture gradually lost its characteristics, but became thinner and more Giacometti-like, which was also an interesting feature when viewed side by side. The Stanford bunny, on the other hand, lacked change, and the sol "Winged Victory in Samothrace" was redundant. In the future, I will experiment with other models, sizes, and methods, as well as combine multiple scanners to create a new genre of glitch sculpture.

References

1. Miyako Atsuro: Object Resolution (2020). https://object-resolution.xyz/. Accessed 4 Dec 2020
2. ontologist: VIDEO ROOM 1000 COMPLETE MIX – All 1000 videos seen in sequential order! (2010). https://youtu.be/icruGcSsPp0. Accessed 4 Dec 2020
3. Miller-Keller, A.: Alvin Lucier: A Celebration, p. 43. Wesleyan University Press (2012)
4. Bowen, D.: Growth modeling device (2009). https://www.dwbowen.com/growth-modeling-device. Accessed 4 Dec 2020
5. Thimmesch, D.: 3D Printing Glitch Adds Meaning to Art Student's Sculpture (2015). https://3dprint.com/59131/3d-printing-glitch-sculpture/. Accessed 4 Dec 2020
6. Moradi, I., Scott, A., Gilmore, J., Murphy, C.: Glitch: Designing Imperfection. Mark Batty Publisher (2009)
7. ucnv: "グリッチアート試論". ucnv.stores.jp (2019)
8. Menkman, R.: The Glitch Moment(um), Institute of Network Cultures (2011). https://issuu.com/instituteofnetworkcultures/docs/glitchmomentum. Accessed 4 Dec 2020
9. Ruff, T.: jpegs. Aperture (2009)

Research on Interactive Design of Public Art Landscape at Night

Wenjing Yin[(⊠)]

South China University of Technology, Guangzhou 510006, China
yinwj@scut.edu.cn

Abstract. The construction of public art landscape at night is a direct symbol of the rapid development of modern cities. It has created a grand, integral and interactive field dominated by lighting environment. Moreover, through individualized, artistic and technological forms, it enriches people's cognition of urban public space and strengthens people's perception and experience of urban landscape environment at night. The night public art landscape combines functionality, artistry and culture, endows the city nightlife with symbolic meaning, and constantly expands the boundaries of art, humanities, society, economy and lifestyle. This paper will take the interactive design of night public art landscape as the research object, and through interpreting the typical cases of night public art landscape practice at home and abroad, summarize its interactive features and presentation types, and dig deep into the publicity and humanity contained in this interactive field. The purpose of this paper is to explore the important role of interactive design in promoting the sustainable development of people and cities from the perspective of public art, taking the night landscape as examples. In my opinion, the interactive design of night public art landscape will inevitably return to the core idea of "people-oriented", showing a development trend from the coexistence of technical forms and interactive behaviors to the deep-seated emotional symbiotic interaction.

Keywords: Night public art landscape · Interactive design · Sustainable development

1 Introduction

Before getting down to business, it is necessary to explain the concept of "night public art landscape". It is not difficult to understand that this formulation first defines the specific time category of public art works. Taking the city night as a discussion angle, this is because with the rapid development of modern urbanization, people once described the night as "reaching out and not seeing five fingers", but now the situation has undergone tremendous changes, and there is no longer only a single scene of darkness at night. With the progress of human science and technology, night has become an important window to show the progress of human civilization, science and technology, and to show the vitality of urban development and life style. On the other hand, due to the need of spreading

M. M. Soares et al. (Eds.): HCII 2021, LNCS 12781, pp. 422–436, 2021.
https://doi.org/10.1007/978-3-030-78227-6_31

humanistic spirit and life value, night public art has broken through the practical function of traditional lighting and the formal aesthetics of traditional artistic creation, and has gradually become a social issue that can not be ignore. The particularity of the media carrier of the night public art landscape, as well as the culture and publicity contained in shaping the night city image and guiding the humanistic value, need to be explored.

Secondly, the concepts of "public art" and "landscape" are combined. On the one hand, it breaks through the public's narrow understanding that "public art" is limited to the presentation form of works; on the other hand, based on the macro picture of urban development, public art works are placed in the field, thus connecting works with environment, people, technology and other elements, and placing them in an objective relationship network constructed by each other, thus further expanding the material and spiritual multi-dimensional spatial character. The public art landscape breaks through the environmental category of physical public space, and is no longer constrained by the formal language of public art works. On the possibility of coexistence between individuals and others, it points to the creation and expansion of the relationship between people and urban space, people and things, people and people's interaction, perception and feed-back in the consumption era. Therefore, the public, cultural and interactive value of public art landscape and its characteristics of the times can be further discussed.

The public artistic landscape at night has become one of the explicit expressions of "contemporary urban landscape" proposed by Guy Debo. Professor Weng Jianqing, a Chinese scholar, also regards public art as "art in landscape" in his works. In his book "Art in Landscape", the understanding of "landscape" includes the externality and intuition of the viewer, that is, the "perceived environment" put forward by Appleton; It also contains the built-in nature of the viewer, reflects the interactive and equal relationship between man and the environment, and points to the "environmental perception" put forward by Francis Sppashott and Allen Carlson; At the same time, it also includes the meaning of "scene", which means "including perceptual scenes and related scenes that can be perceived in daily life and social production and power distribution" [1]. From this, it can be known that the consideration of landscape culture in Landscape is carried out from two aspects: materiality and spirituality. The public art landscape is closely related to the construction of urban culture, public life, social morality, ecological ethics and social values in contemporary cities, and is full of profound and rich connotations of anthroposociology. It directly and vividly constitutes the visual culture system of urban space with its tangible materialization form, and its cultural connotation and image aesthetic represent the urban image, which has become the external form of the spirit of the times and the core of the urban spirit, and shows the internal relationship and mutual influence between social structure and individual life in the process of urbanization survival and development.

Thirdly, the interactive technology application of public art landscape at night is more diversified. The creative methods focus on the use of digital technology, acoustic and photoelectric technology, color capture and behavior sensing and other intelligent media. Night public art landscape, that is, through personalized, artistic, aesthetic, scientific and technological multi-media, constructs a grand, holistic, light-based interactive field. It strengthens the vitality of public space perception, as Bruno Adiriani mentioned in the book "The Problem of Sculptors", "The space in art... can be grasped by our feelings."

"It is the sensible scenery of our human experience,' the scope of our activities', and the scope of our relationship with the environment." [2] Public art landscape is a concrete expression of relationship. In the three-dimensional space established by physical means, the interactive system contained in it is in the appearance of dynamic space. In each person's practical experience, it constitutes his unique environment, that is, an objective space centered on individual and having something in common with himself. Night public art landscape enriches people's cognition of urban public space and strengthens people's perception and experience of urban night landscape by creating such a realistic interactive field that can express and spread freely.

2 The Characteristics and Types of Interactive Design of Night Public Art Landscape

2.1 Characteristics of Interactive Design of Night Public Art Landscape

High Technical Characteristics. The interactive design of public art landscape at night benefits from the promotion of high-tech information technology, showing the characteristics of high-tech development. The high-tech features of night public art landscape are mainly reflected in the coordinated application of multi-technical means, the collocation and combination of multi-media carriers, the multi-channel perception and communication channels, and the open interactive process.

Due to the uniqueness of night environment, the technical means of presenting works of art are mainly in the forms of sound, light and electricity, digital control, interface operation, behavior sensing and so on. At the same time, multi-media carriers such as color, material, water environment and other natural elements are comprehensively configured. Various elements, such as the expression form of works of art, geographical environment, crowd behavior and habits, are interrelated and flexibly superimposed, which enlarges the influence range of works themselves, constructs a multi-channel perception transmission path, forms a complete and organic interactive system, and shapes the whole landscape field. This maximizes the interactive effect of public art landscape, realizes the emotional communication between individuals and others, enhances the public's perception and experience, and completes the exchange of certain information, the construction of meaning and the reshaping of spirit. This interactive relationship makes the city more personalized, thus shaping the characteristic aesthetic image of public art landscape at night, which further reflects the humanistic spirit of the city and makes the value of public space excavated.

The Radar, a temporary art installation created by artist Ryoji Ikeda in Rio de Janeiro, Brazil in 2012, is an audio-visual light projection work in a specific place. This work covers many elements such as lights, music, crowds, waves, starry sky, etc. It integrates science and technology, art, man and nature, and creates a complete, poetic and sublime space for people to experience. The greatest success of this work lies in guiding people to participate in the project spontaneously. This is also the moving part of the public art landscape. Radar captures the moment when everything is in harmony. As the producer Marcelo Dantas said, "The Radar produced a poetic immersion into the soul of Rio with lighting, rhythm, beach and sea water" (see Fig. 1).

Fig. 1. The Radar Artist: Ryoji Ikeda Image source: Organizing Committee of IAPA

Tunnel of Light, an installation created by Korean new media artist Yang Minha, is located at the entrance of Le Meridien Seoul Hotel. The artist embeds square panels with colored LED lights into the ground, and creates a visually spiral tunnel by making the difference of embedding angle. When the night comes, the colorful lights change six kinds of geometric figures alternately with the melody of music, which bring people infinite sense of time and space through visual illusion and express the accumulation and extension of time. The creative appearance of the installation works and the comprehensive application of sound, light and electricity technology create a deep feeling like the vast sky, deepen the artistic conception of the works, and make people stop and linger. Nowadays, artistic presentation like this is common in urban public space at night (see Fig. 2).

Fig. 2. Tunnel of Light Artist: Yang Minha

The interactive installation art work Color Domain (Shenzhen, 2018), located in the outdoor public area of Red Cube Science and Technology Museum in Shenzhen, China, was created by British public artist Billy Lee. This work integrates lighting system, music system, sensing technology, network interactive communication technology, color, water mist and other different media into artistic creation. The artist skillfully combines science and technology, artistic imagination and interesting games, takes childhood toy gyroscopes and flying machines as modeling forms, and performs grand performances with dynamic electronic music, combined light show, waterscape fountain, etc. The work also sets a somatosensory interactive mode, which triggers the somatosensory device when people approach the sculpture, and the corresponding sculpture lighting, music and waterscape systems will start. Through participating in the experience, the public and artists have completed the best interpretation of their works. With such artistic expression, artists praise the developed scene brought by science and technology to this era, and also bring people a better imagination of the future (see Fig. 3).

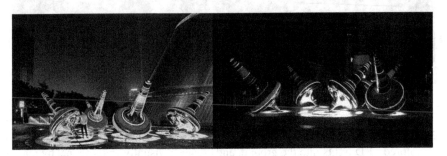

Fig. 3. Color Domain Artist: Billy Lee

As the famous French writer Flaubert wrote: the more Art develops, the more scientific it will be, just as science will become artistic. Separated in their early stages, the two will become one again when both reach their culmination. The wide application of high-tech means further broadens the creative concept and expression form of public art. The space-time created by the night public art landscape has unique styles such as futuristic, fantastic, detached and sublime, which makes the public consciously indulge in it, observe its form, use its function and realize its implication, thus producing multi-level perceptual experience. The promotion of science and technology has greatly enhanced the interactivity and participation of public art landscape, and fully reflected the times, publicity and humanity. Science and technology does bring more possibilities for the development of public art landscape.

High Emotional Characteristics. Lewis Mumford once said, "The main function of a city is to turn force into shape, energy into culture, dead things into living artistic images, and biological reproduction into social creativity." "The main task of the future city is to create a visible regional and urban structure, which is designed to make people familiar with their deeper selves and the bigger world. It has the educational function of human beings and the image of love" [3]. Mum-ford pointed out that the innovation we urgently need is to "apply art and thought to the main human interests of the city, and have a new dedication to the universe and ecological process that contains all life", "because the city should be an organ of love, and the best economic model of the city should be caring for people and cultivating people" [4].

In essence, the night public art landscape provides a reciprocal style for the development of the city and people's life. Art plays a unique advantage and gathers some indispensable functions of the city. People are attracted to meet in such a public space without being restricted or challenged by materials, culture, beliefs, customs, etc. In the space-time network created by the public art landscape, the original intention of urban development is restored to human beings. The emotional expression of people from this also makes the public art landscape no longer a simple functional association of objects, but shows that "individuals and individuals, individuals and communities, and different communities reach coexistence, symbiosis and interaction" [5].

In 2012, the lighting installation work Máximo Silêncio em Paris by artist Giancarlo Neri was presented on the Praça Paris in Rio de Janeiro. The work consists of 9,000 LED star lights of about 10 inches, covering a rolling parkland of nearly 10,000 square feet. The random pulses of colored lights converged into different interesting patterns, and the lights ingeniously changed the urban land-scape and enriched people's sensory experience. The geographical location of Praça Paris was once controversial, which was considered to be unsafe and unattractive for public art. However, the persistence of artists made the originally deserted world glow with splendor, and people from all urban areas flocked to each other. At night, every place in the park becomes crowded, cheerful and safe. The name of the project is Máximo Silêncio em Paris, which attracts people to gather with the warm light source of silent lights, and adds human joy to the quiet night. This public art form has also been widely used for reference and application in many countries and regions, bringing warmth and interest to the city night (see Fig. 4).

Fig. 4. Máximo Silêncio em Paris Artist: Giancarlo Neri Image source: Organizing Committee of IAPA

In 2007, artist Doris Salcedo laid 25,000 candles on Plaza de Bolívar in Bogotá, Colombia, thus creating "The Deputies of the Assembly of Valle del Cauca" to honor 11 Colombian government representatives killed by the FARC (Fuerzas Armadas Revlucionarias de Colombia, or Revolutionary Armed Forces of Colombia). "Memory" has become the main theme of this work. It was an act of mourning that created a space where people could remember. The artist has faced up to the powerlessness of artistic behavior in such events, but has called for dignifying a human life in such an artistic and beautiful way. The flickering of 10,000 candles has created a solemn and sacred space, maintaining dignity for the lost, solemn, magnificent, fragile and memorable life (see Fig. 5).

2.2 Interactive Design Types of Night Public Art Landscape

Presented in the Form of Urban Basic Public Facilities. With the development of urbanization and people's expectation for a better life, the construction of urban basic

Fig. 5. The Deputies of the Assembly of Valle del Cauca Artist: Doris Salcedo Image source: Organizing Committee of IAPA

public facilities no longer meets the need of simply providing convenience in practical functions, but adds more artistic elements, and becomes an emotional form and cultural symbol with distinct artistic meaning in urban development. The night public art landscape is consciously integrated into the construction process of urban upgrading and transformation. On the one hand, it is presented as basic public facilities and becomes a universal existence in people's daily life. On the other hand, as a social artistic expression, it combines artistry, culture and functionality perfectly, which makes people feel the emotion and strength inherent in art form at all times.

A Lamp for Mary, an artistic installation created by Sydney-based artist Mikala Dwyer in 2010, is a unique street lamp, which casts quiet and pink glow on the street named Mary's Place at night, creating a quiet meditation and reminiscence atmosphere for people. As a part of urban street lighting facilities, this work not only provides enough lighting for pedestrians to pass safely, but also bears the functions of memorial, protection, cure and warning. The poems displayed on the plaque show the artist's creative intention to all those who pass by it: "This is a lane with a name and a lamp in memory of the woman who survived being beaten and raped here. She happened to be lesbian. When the sun sets this lamp keeps vigil along with you who reads this in silent meditation." This street lamp not only lights up people's daily living environment, but also builds an artistic bridge of communication with the public in the spirit of humanistic care, which lights up and inspires people's fearless hearts and points to the sense of belonging, identity and pride of individual identity (see Fig. 6).

Donald Lipski's installation art work "F.I.S.H" is located in the riverside space of San Antonio, USA. With the original intention of restoring the "poetic habitat", Lipski chose a familiar fish species in San Antonio River as the prototype, and designed 25 7-inch-long long-eared sunfish made of stained fiberglass, which were hung under the viaduct with cables. They are each filled with around 1000-W LED lights. When the night comes, the fish lamp lights up, reflecting each other with the reflection in the river,

Fig. 6. A Lamp for Mary Artist: Mikala Dwyer Image source: Organizing Committee of IAPA

which makes people have the illusion that the space overlaps and extends, and creates a poetic situation beyond reality. The sound of traffic on the elevated road, the voices of people who play, walk and talk also become the sound of "golden fish schools" swimming in the water, which makes the whole art work more vivid and shows the vitality of the local river. "F.I.S.H" installation transforms the public space with its exuberant scale and colors, and has become a new landmark in San Antonio. This work is full of warmth, care and integration, bearing the hope and yearning of local residents for a better life (see Fig. 7).

Fig. 7. F.I.S.H Artist: Donald Lipski Image source: Organizing Committee of IAPA

The night public art landscape is not only used to decorate the space, but also has practical functions such as route guidance, lighting instruction, pedestrian rest place, environmental atmosphere contrast, emotional output and so on. The original public facilities in the city, such as squares, parks, street corners, etc., have been updated and upgraded because of the intervention of public art, which makes the interactive activities at night more humane. The night public art landscape, which also has the function of social public facilities, has become a perfect model of integrating functionality, artistry, publicity and public welfare.

Presented in the form of Consumer Landscape. As a visual representation of urban nightlife in the consumption era, it is more and more common for public art landscape to intervene in the daily life of the public. The night public art landscape presented in the form of consumption landscape is not pure art in itself, but more for the need and purpose of creating economic value. It has become an important medium of mass culture and commercial information dissemination, and it has also become a direct example of art democratization development. It is an important way to communicate between art, the public and business, so that the three can interact with each other and form a city landscape with contemporary flavor and characteristics of the times. As Bella Dicks said, "Give things and fields a symbolic meaning, point to the way of living of human beings, and place them in the humanistic background, and position them in terms of space, time, narration or theme" [6]. Night public art landscape has practical functions such as consumption promotion and atmosphere creation. To a certain extent, it stimulates people's spiritual demands in the consumption era from both sensory and psychological aspects, promotes the continuous innovation of commercial space, and enhances the recognition and attractiveness of this space to achieve economic goals and benefits. At the same time, however, the design practice of public art landscape remains alert to the influence of secularization of consumer culture. Even if it exists in commercial space as a consumer landscape, it still maintains the independence and cultural meaning of artistic expression, which makes art closer to the daily life of the public and presents a more diverse visual form.

The public art landscape in commercial space is not simply the accumulation of visual images. Guy Debord, a famous French thinker and theorist, thinks that landscape is "a kind of social relationship between people, established through the intermediary of images" in his analysis of "La Société du spectacle", and that "landscape is rooted in the fertile soil of abundant economy, and the result of this economy finally dominates the landscape market" [7]. On the one hand, there is a causal relationship between the economic characteristics of society and the development of public art landscape in the consumption era. The public art landscape and artistic intervention of commercial space is the inevitable result of commercial economic development and multi-level social and cultural needs, and has become one of the landscape phenomena of urban public space and multiculturalism in the consumption era. Its artistic expression forms are various. "The art integrated into the commercial space may be an idea that tends to be aesthetic, stimulates fashion interest or transcends reality, or it may tend to be secular experience, sensual entertainment and directly spread around commerce. This is determined by the basic attributes of commercial space and potential market logic" [8]. The "intervention" of public art landscape at night has shaped a good commercial atmosphere, which has made people form a unique visual memory of urban nightlife, enhanced regional attraction and created new landmarks for urban development. On the other hand, the realistic demand of commercial space also promotes the continuous innovation of the creative idea and expression form of public art landscape. The night public art landscape has become a diversified exploration behavior driven by the wisdom of public groups, which makes art and commerce, artists and the public, art and life form a two-way interactive connection.

The "Very Fun Park" art event, an annual art event in the commercial space of the East District of Taipei, China, is intended to link the unexpected encounter between art and life. Artists and curators jointly uphold the beautiful original intention of "art is everywhere", and explore many possibilities of combining urban commercial space with art, so that public art works can influence people's way of living and thinking and enrich people's spiritual life. Shanghai's "Urban Spectrum Project", which started in 2018, has joined many artists to create a series of lighting public art installations, which have become beautiful light waves to light people's nightlife. Among them, the lighting installation work "Xin Xing" created by artist Shen Linghao is located in the street corner park of the emerging business circle in Xinzhuang, Shanghai, bearing the best wishes for the future development of this area. "Xin Xing" is a star-shaped regular dodecahedron geometry, with 12 three-dimensional surfaces being centrosymmetric, symbolizing 12 months of a year, and the whole work symbolizes the cycle of time. The concept of time and space and the cultural meaning carried by the works are precisely the artists' attempts to arouse the public's thoughts on time, space, emotion, memory and development through artistic presentation. The reason why artists create with "stars" as inspiration is that this area was once a place where "stars" gathered, and surrounding villages, schools, markets, rivers and bridges were all named as "stars" in history. Therefore, the shape of "stars" has become a concentrated symbol of these historical cultures, which is lighted and inherited in the city (see Fig. 8).

Fig. 8. Xin Xing Artist: Shen Linghao

2.3 Internal Logic of Interactive Design of Night Public Art Landscape

The internal logic of interactive design of public art landscape at night includes three levels, which are basically in progressive relationship.

First, interaction takes the original attribute of matter as the basic logic. It mainly highlights the "tangible" existence state, or the composition relationship between materials. It is the design of "material" itself, without deliberately designing the communication between people and substances, and its interaction relationship stays more in the creative experience of creators or artists, and in order to realize some functions. For example, the traditional sculptures or frescoes in urban parks and the night basic lighting of historical buildings in cities all outline the attributes of "tangible" objects. This form of interaction can be regarded as an instinctive interaction, which connects history with reality, objects with objects, and objects with people. It represents a state of "Co-existence".

Second, behavior interaction based on human behavior characteristics. Mainly on the design of "behavior", intentionally creating the occurrence of "behavior". Material is only used as a carrier or medium here, and promoting the generation of "behavior" is the ultimate goal. It makes people and products have more direct dialogue and communication, and creates a field of behavior communication. Through the state of things and people's behavior, a close and mutually beneficial relationship is formed, and the communication between public art landscape and people is dynamic, changing and individual. Behavioral interaction is the mutual projection of the cooperative state between people and things, which makes them map the "Symbiosis" interdependent state in the interaction of sensory behaviors.

Third, emotional interaction based on people's emotional reflection. Night public art landscape carries people's emotional needs and cultural memory, or expresses some social power intention that affects public affairs, which enables people to have deeper emotional association and emotional response in viewing and experiencing. This is a reflective interaction, which is completed in the deep experience of people to objects. As Catherine Grout said: "Meeting with works of art is an opportunity for communication, projecting our common world and the world that we are continuing to develop and construct" [9]. The emotional inter-action and sharing between the public and the public art landscape sublimates the humanistic values and social attributes carried by the public art landscape. With the development and progress of science and technology, the forms of emotional interaction will become more diversified and intelligent. To a certain extent, the public art landscape breaks through the boundaries of materials and is addicted to the "Empathy" connection with people.

3 Sociological Connotation of Interactive Design of Night Public Art Landscape

3.1 Field Holistic Consciousness

Pierre Bourdieu, a famous French sociologist, once defined the concept of "field" accordingly: "Field is a kind of artificial social construction, which is a product gradually formed after a long process of autonomy" [10]. "From an analytical point of view, a field can be defined as a network of objective relationships among various locations. The field can be conceived as a space in which the effect of the field can be brought into play" [11]. It can easily sum up the key words of "field", that is, relational network, artificial social construction and spatial elements. Cities are the main places where social individuals participate in social activities. The cities can be understood as a big field and a big space. Any objects related to this space can be explained with reference to the relationships in the field.

Night public art landscape, in fact, is in such a space, through creative behavior, to create a living field for the public with vitality, strength and potential. By means of artistic innovation, it has designed material media, scene technology and behavior experience in advance, thus building a huge interactive information network in urban public space. This network contains complex elements such as time, space, people, works of art, natural environment, man-made environment and social environment, which are interrelated, superimposed, influenced and interacted to form a complete field. This field has obvious value characteristics such as publicity, artistry, sociality and humanity. In the holistic field consciousness, "on the one hand, it is the restrictive relationship: the field shapes the habit, and the habit becomes the product of a certain field's inherent inevitable attribute embodied in the body. On the other hand, it is a relationship of knowledge, or a relationship of cognitive construction. Habit helps to build the field into a meaningful world, a world that is endowed with feeling and value and worthy of your investment and efforts" [12]. This fully shows the deep interaction between human and specific field.

3.2 Concept of Sustainable Development

Night public art landscape is a realistic representation of contemporary urban development and cultural and artistic prosperity, which has unique value dimension and practical dimension. It includes the interaction between man and city and nature, and the integration of art and life. In the holistic field created by the night public art landscape, there is a profound concept of sustainable development.

Firstly, it contains the sustainable development of human beings. The public, that is, "people", is the most important core element in the process of creation, experience and feedback of night public art landscape. For the night public art landscape, the original intention of its creation always revolves around everything about people. Whether people's emotional value can be stimulated to the maximum extent is also the criterion for judging the success of the work, which depends on people's satisfaction with the function, form, experience and association of public art works. Creator, producer, viewer and experiencer have become a group of molecules connected with each other in the interactive relationship, and their roles are constantly interchanged. In the process of interacting with works, nature and others, people gradually realize the cognition and sublimation of their own values through practice and reflection, and create a better life for human beings. As Joseph Beuys said, all things constructed, developed and created by human beings, as well as all ideological achievements with growing ability and in constant change and development, are mutually beneficial to human life in essence.

An artistic performance named "Speed of Light" was performed in the 2012 Smart Illumination Yokohama Festival. This is a group of temporary artistic intervention projects developed by the Scottish public art organization NVA in cooperation with the Tokyo-based Performance Company, aiming at redefining the city, countryside, energy and green life through people's collective actions. The original intention of the "Speed of Light" project originated from the accident of Fukushima nuclear power plant in Japan in 2011, so it planned such a wake-up action of public participation, advocating public participation, green living and being kind to energy (see Fig. 9).

Fig. 9. Speed of Light Artist: NVA Image source: Organizing Committee of IAPA

Secondly, it pays attention to the sustainable development of cities. The night public art landscape combines functionality, artistry and culture, and becomes a window to show the city image and vitality. It injects new energy into the urban space, brings more attractive urban nightlife to people, and realizes the benign interaction between people and cities. Its creative forms and ideas constantly expand the boundaries of art, humanities, science and technology, society, economy and people's lifestyles.

BLOOMING (2018), a large-scale permanent public art work created by artist Sheng Shanshan, is located in the middle of two buildings in Shenzhen Red Cube. It consists of 416 pieces of German architectural art glass, with a height of 8.8 m, a width of 8.5 m and a length of 7.3 m. The whole work is designed by building information model (BIM), which realizes multi-angle special-shaped modeling and curved surface torsion of sculpture. The works combine traditional Chinese paintings such as flowers, landscapes, oceans and forests with glass art, which brings great visual shock to people. The dazzling artistic modeling symbolizes Shenzhen's urban characteristics of openness and tolerance, and presents the rapid urban development and the blooming trend of regional economy and culture in Shenzhen. In addition, the art work combines many elements such as digital multimedia, music, lighting, etc., and uses the interactive mode of "custom art" to let the public interpret the artistic theme together, bringing "immersive" audio-visual experience to people in urban nightlife (see Fig. 10).

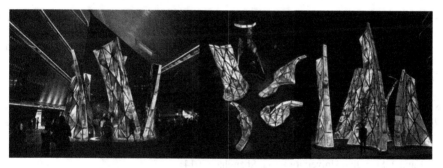

Fig. 10. BLOOMING Artist: Sheng Shanshan

4 Conclusion

Night public art landscape condenses people's current memory and becomes the medium for individuals to meet with cities, others and even the world. It realizes the interaction among various elements, defines the pre-progress of social progress, urban development and human life, and presents the shared and developing world through artistic means. Indeed, there are still many problems to be further discussed about the interactive design of night public art landscape, such as whether the city night public art landscape is a deliberately created standardized aesthetic trap? Will it cause excessive use and waste of energy? Do a large number of public art landscapes at night conform to the objective law of natural environment recuperation? Does the progress of science and technology bring about the convergence of night public art landscape forms? However, in general, the interactive design of night public art landscape in the future will inevitably reflect the true needs of human nature, and the core concepts of "people-oriented" and sustainable development will always carry out the creation and presentation of art works. Although the forms of works are diverse, the emphasis of their interactive relationship will return to the scale of people, paying more attention to the emotional expression and psychological experience of living beings, showing a development trend from the coexistence of technical forms and interactive behaviors to the deep-seated interaction of emotional symbiosis and empathy.

Acknowledgements. This paper is supported by the Youth Fund Project for Humanities and Social Sciences Research of the Education Ministry of China (17YJC760087).

References

1. Weng Jianqing, F.: JINGGUAN ZHONG DE YISHU. Peking University Press, Beijing (2016)
2. Susanne, K., Langer, F.: Feeling and Form. Fu Zhiqiang, Zhou Faxiang, China Social Sciences Press, Beijing (1986). Trans. Liu Daji
3. Lewis Mumford, F.: The City in History, Trans. China Architecture & Building Press, Beijing (2004). Song Junling, Ni Wenyan
4. Wang Yichuan, F.: Art Appreciation. Peking University Press, Beijing (2016)

5. Bella Dicks, F.: Culture on Display: The Production of Contemporary Visitability. Peking University Press, Beijing (2012). Trans. Feng Yue
6. Guy Debord, F.: La Société du spectacle. Nanjing University Press, Nanjing (2007). Trans. Wang Zhaofeng
7. Catherine Grout, F.: Pour de l'art dans notre quotidien: Des æu-vres en milieu urbain. Guangxi Normal University Press, Guilin (2005). Trans. Yao Mengyin
8. Pierre Bourdieu, F.: Logic of Practice. Stanford University Press, California (1990)
9. Pierre Bourdieu, F., Loic Wacquant, S.: Practice and Reflection: Introspection Sociology Guide. Polity Press, London (1992)
10. Jiangbo, J.F., Li Pan, S.: Local Remodeling: Interpretation of International Public Art Awards 1 and 2. Shanghai University Press, Shanghai (2014)

Usability and UX Studies

Usability Testing Experiment Applied to Redesign on Point-of-Sale Software Interfaces Using User-Centered-Design Approach

Patricia Esparza$^{(\boxtimes)}$ (ID), Rony Cueva (ID), and Freddy Paz (ID)

Pontificia Universidad Católica del Perú, Lima 32, San Miguel, Peru
{patricia.esparza,fpaz}@pucp.pe, cueva.r@pucp.edu.pe

Abstract. In this paper, we present a crossover experiment with a remote usability testing to validate a User Centered Design process applied to a point-of-sale user interfaces redesign, in which the original software product interfaces had a low grade of usability. It was developed as a structured usability remote test plan applied with two samples of users through a crossover experiment. Each sample was composed by 6 participants that had close knowledge about information systems features and other personality attributes obtained by the cashier profile designed through the personas technique. Cashiers are a fundamental role, since they use this software many hours per day, and are very rotative employees, that tend to be young people between 18 and 25 years old. We obtained favorable results, as each sample decreased their execution time in completing the 10 given tasks in more than one minute, which is a valuable time in sales, and it reduced their dependency to ask for help or making operational mistakes in the sale's process. They emphasized some improved points such as "more understandable labels", "more striking and pleasant colors", "better visualization of the components", and "much easier process to use".

Keywords: User centered design · Usability testing · Point-of-sale software · Human-computer interaction

1 Introduction

Nowadays usability has become a determinant factor in software development as it grants quality to these products [1]. However, it is still little included in some software development companies, because they have not invested enough in user experience [2], even though they know it can increase productivity and can greatly reduce most of the common operational errors that employees have while using any kind of software [3].

For instance, point of sale software is a particular solution for retail business that should be oriented to be amazingly fast and easy-to use [4], because users that use these points of sale need to avoid large queues and make fast sales as possible to grow the profitability of their retail companies and increase customer satisfaction [5]. In spite of these factors, point of sale software are frequently known for being difficult to learn,

© Springer Nature Switzerland AG 2021
M. M. Soares et al. (Eds.): HCII 2021, LNCS 12781, pp. 439–456, 2021.
https://doi.org/10.1007/978-3-030-78227-6_32

because of the multiple options that it contains, which are not oriented to satisfy user expectations [6, 7].

User centered design is a well-known framework that helps stakeholders, business users, developers, or designers to understand user necessities through the application of some techniques to obtain usable software systems [8]. However, as it is a framework, it does not indicate a particular technique to be applied. Consequently, there is almost no literature related to formal processes applied to the design or redesign of point-of-sale interfaces.

In this paper, we present a crossover experiment with a remote usability testing to validate a User Centered Design process applied to a point-of-sale user interfaces redesign, in which the original software product interfaces had a low grade of usability. It was developed a structured usability remote test plan applied with two samples of users through a crossover experiment. Each sample was composed by 6 participants that had close features about information systems knowledge and other personality attributes obtained by the cashier profile designed through the *personas* technique. Cashiers are a fundamental role, since they use this software many hours per day, and are very rotative employees, that tend to be young people between 18 and 25 years old.

It was presented to the first sample, the initial interfaces and then the new ones, and with the second sample we did the reverse process. Users needed to be novice, so they would not have any prior preference in one or another. Also, they were given a series of questionnaires to perceive their criteria about some usability attributes such as learnability, memorability, satisfaction, and efficiency in each group of interfaces.

The general concepts addressed in the usability experiment will be developed, as well as the design of the usability plan with users, the results obtained from the crossover experiment, and finally, some conclusions.

2   Theoretical Framework

2.1   Usability

Usability is an essential factor to ensure the quality of the software, since it allows to quantify the quality of the user experience when interacting with a software product [1]. ISO 9126 [9] and ISO 25010 [10] define usability as the ability of a software to be easily learned, offer operability and be attractive to users under a certain context. In addition, it is a feature that ensures the quality of the attributes of a software such as user interfaces [11].

2.2   User Centered Design

User-Centered Design, known by its acronym UCD, is a framework that involves a variety of methods that describe the design processes in which end users are a fundamental part of obtaining computerized systems that result in a satisfactory and very usable design [8].

ISO 13407 [12] established a standard focused on offering guidance on a series of User Centered Design activities to apply them during the life cycle of interactive systems at a level of principles and activities, but it does not detail techniques or methods to be used in this framework [13]; this involves four fundamental activities: *understanding and specifying the context of use, specifying the user requirements, producing design solutions* and *evaluating the design.*

2.3 Point of Sale Software

The point-of-sale software, known in its acronym POS, contains vital functions for retail businesses. These software systems allow managing the execution of automatic transactions, such as payment for products or services to be purchased, issuance of receipts, recording of purchase transactions, collection of sales data [14]. These systems allow you to enter the information of the products that a store sells, as well as the information of the customers to facilitate future sales and improve customer satisfaction [15], therefore, these software systems should offer short times to finalize sales in the boxes or sales modules, minimize clerk errors, reduce shortages in stores, reduction of forced or non-promotional sales and possibility of making profitability analysis of the products.

2.4 Crossover Experiment

Crossover experiments consist of a two-period design of two treatments (A and B), in which study participants are randomly assigned to receive treatment A followed by treatment B or B followed by A [16]. The main advantage of applying this type of experiment is that it allows increasing precision, since each participant "has their own control", and the variability within the subject is generally less than the variability between subjects, the sample size for a crossover trial it is less than for a comparable parallel group design [16].

2.5 User Usability Testing

User usability tests are a set of methods, practices and techniques that support the evaluation of the usability of a software product in different environments [17]. These allow to collect empirical and representative information from the end users [18] by observing the users working with the product, executing real and significant tasks. Also, remote usability tests with users can be included thanks to new technologies and the rapid access that users have [17].

3 Design of the Usability Testing Plan

This usability test aimed to evaluate a group of users to validate that the new graphical user interfaces of the point-of-sale software had a higher degree of usability than the interfaces of the current POS software of a retail software development company.

3.1 Products Evaluated

In order to carry out the experiment it was necessary to design each interface so users can follow each task list. In first place, we had the original POS software interfaces, in this sense, we had to make a replica of the original interfaces developed by the retail company. The sale registration user interface of the original product can be seen in Fig. 1. In second place, we had the redesigned POS software interfaces, which were developed under the DCU process for this software category. The sale registration user interface of the redesigned product can be seen inf Fig. 2.

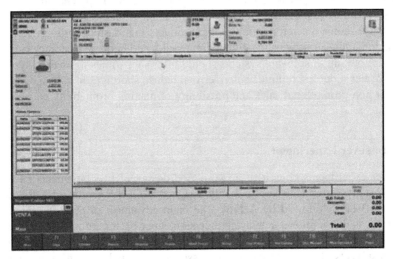

Fig. 1. Sale registration screen of the original point of sale software interfaces.

3.2 Experiment Environment

The test experiments were developed through videoconference in Google Meets, after coordination with each user, to be able to observe their screen in progress while executing the indicated tasks. It was necessary for the participants to have a laptop or PC, as well as an internet connection, to be able to participate in this test.

3.3 List of Participants of the Usability Test

Two samples were selected for this test, since a crossover experiment needed to be run. University students from various careers participated to simulate the profile of the cashier person. The distribution was made equitably with prior knowledge of the age and gender of each participant. The detail is shown below in Table 1.

Fig. 2. Sale registration screen of the redesigned point of sale software interfaces.

Table 1. List of participants of the usability test

User	Age	Gender	Occupation	First interfaces	Second interfaces
User 1	22	Masculine	Informatics Engineering Student	A	B
User 2	22	Feminine	Marketing Student	A	B
User 3	22	Feminine	Management Student	A	B
User 4	23	Feminine	Informatics Engineering Student	A	B
User 5	23	Masculine	Telecommunications Engineering Student	A	B
User 6	22	Masculine	Mechatronics Engineering Student	A	B
User 7	23	Feminine	Informatics Engineering Student	B	A
User 8	23	Masculine	Investment analyst	B	A
User 9	22	Feminine	Telecommunications Engineering Student	B	A
User 10	21	Feminine	Informatics Engineering Student	B	A
User 11	21	Masculine	Civil engineering student	B	A
User 12	22	Masculine	Industrial engineering student	B	A

3.4   Test Execution

Users entered to a Google Meets meeting through a link provided to their emails prior to the day of the evaluation. Each user was monitored, as they shared their screen to observe the actions they were taking. Also is important to mention that we asked to the participants to think-out-loud to detected quickly if they had any problem. It should be noted that the evaluator was present observing from beginning to end each action of the user to solve any inconvenience in the flow task. Help was provided in case the user was in constant difficulty to complete the task, because each task was dependent on completing the above correctly.

The flow followed by the users is described in Fig. 1. The two samples had to complete four phases. We are going to describe each phase.

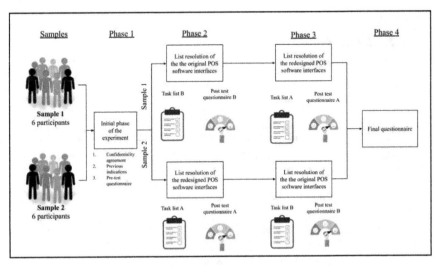

Fig. 3. Crossover experiment

First Phase. In the first phase, they had to read a confidentiality agreement, the previous indications, and the pre-test questionnaire, this one was prepared to be able to know the user, and obtain personal data such as age, occupation, and the experience they have had with information systems and point of sale software products (optionally). This was developed with Google Forms.

Based on the pre-test questionnaire prepared, it was possible to obtain information related to the experience of users with information systems and point of sale software products, which confirms the profile of cashier or store manager *persona* found during the application of the DCU process.

Second Phase. Then, in the second phase, sample 1 had to resolve the task list of the original POS software interfaces, and a post-test questionnaire. On the other hand, sample 2, had to resolve the task list of the redesigned POS software interfaces, and a post-test questionnaire.

The set of interfaces of the original software were called "software A" and the new proposal "software B", since users did not have to know what the result of the redesign was to avoid bias in the test. In this sense, two task lists were prepared: list A and list B.

Task List. The scenarios developed through the DCU process we taken into consideration to develop these lists. This is how those points of improvement in terms of usability were taken into consideration to include them in the tasks that could cause problems for users, whether there were ambiguities in the labels, buttons or the problems identified through the list of usability problems related to product search, customer search or discount application. The task list evaluated were composed by a series of diverse items related to the sale registration such as **task n°1**: login, **task n°2**: customer search, **task n°3**: product search, **task n°4**: remove a product and add another without SKU, **task n°5**: add a promotion, **task n°6**: remove a promotion, **task n°7**: generate the payment receipt and modify the customer information, **task n°8**: process payment and select payment receipt, **task n°9**: generate an electronic bill, and **task n°10**: log out. The following is the scenario to contextualize the user before they initialize each task list:

> *You are a cashier in a store that sells casual clothing for men and women. A customer arrives at the point of sale and wants to buy 1 green jacket and 1 blue jeans. She indicates that she believes they have already registered her previously and provides her ID number: 06799374 and that her name is Patricia Cabanillas, as she would like to accumulate points in the system. Finally, she tells him that she wants an electronic ticket and that she will cancel one part with a VISA card, and the other in cash.*

Task Fulfillment Observation Sheet. In parallel, the evaluator had to fill the observation task sheet for each user, which had a detail description of each task, success criteria, success fulfillment of the task by the user, estimated time required to complete the task and the real time required by the user to complete (with success or not) the task.

Post-Test Questionnaire. Two post-test questionnaires were prepared, one for "software A" and the other for "software B", each questionnaire evaluated the same criteria. Users answered each question after they had taken task list A or B. These questionnaires took into consideration factors as ease of use, complexity of the sale process, user satisfaction, learnability, among others.

Third Phase. In the third phase, sample 2 had to resolve the task list of the original POS software interfaces, and a pos-test questionnaire. On the other hand, sample 1, had to resolve the task list of the redesigned POS software interfaces, and a post-test questionnaire.

Fourth Phase. In the last phase, they were given a brief questionnaire about their general preferences, such as which interface they found the most useful, enjoyable and provide a better experience, which was the most adequate interface in their design, use of colors and labels, and which was the worst in the mentioned aspects.

4   Testing Results: A Comparative Analysis

Below are the results obtained from the usability test on the comparison between the initial product and the new proposal, that is, a comparison between the original product interfaces and the set of interfaces redesigned under the DCU process. The number of tasks executed by each sample of users of the crossover experiment will be presented.

In addition, the execution times to complete the proposed tasks used by each sample will be detailed. Likewise, the results of the applied post-test questionnaire and the final comparison questionnaire will be presented. Finally, a statistical analysis will be shown to compare the average execution times between the new interfaces and the original interfaces.

4.1 Comparison of the Number of Tasks Completed

Original Interfaces. Regarding the original interfaces, it can be observed that the users of both samples had problems to execute the tasks, giving an average ratio of 6.83 of 10 tasks completed without help. The most complex tasks stand out as task n° 1: log in, task n° 6: remove promotion, and task n ° 7: generate the payment receipt and modify the customer, since these tasks did not have direct mechanisms to complete them and were not of easy access, that is why only 7, 4 and 6 users in each task could complete independently those tasks. It is important to mention that successfully completed tasks refer to whether the user followed the expected flow or did not need further external help to complete them. In this sense, it can be observed that the users were only able to successfully complete task n° 5, but the others could not complete by themselves the rest of the tasks, and users required help or were reversed in a difficulty.

Redesigned Interfaces. On the contrary, regarding the interfaces of the new proposal, the total of tasks completed on average was 9.91 of 10 tasks. In this sense, a significant improvement can be observed because of the redesign of the graphical interfaces of the point-of-sale software. Table 2 shows the number of tasks successfully completed by users of each sample between the original interfaces versus the redesigned interfaces.

Table 2. Number of tasks successfully completed by users of each sample on the original interfaces versus the redesigned interfaces.

Sample	Task 1	Task 2	Task 3	Task 4	Task 5	Task 6	Task 7	Task 8	Task 9	Task 10	Average tasks per user
Original interfaces											
Sample 1	2/6	5/6	5/6	4/6	6/6	1/6	2/6	5/6	5/6	5/6	6.67/10
Sample 2	5/6	4/6	3/6	4/6	6/6	3/6	4/6	3/6	5/6	5/6	7/10
Total users per task	**7/12**	**9/12**	**8/12**	**8/12**	**12/12**	**4/12**	**6/12**	**8/12**	**10/12**	**10/12**	**6.83/10**
Redesigned interfaces											
Sample 1	6/6	6/6	6/6	6/6	6/6	6/6	6/6	6/6	6/6	6/6	10/10
Sample 2	6/6	6/6	6/6	5/6	6/6	6/6	6/6	6/6	6/6	6/6	9.83/10
Total users per task	**12/12**	**12/12**	**12/12**	**11/12**	**12/12**	**12/12**	**12/12**	**12/12**	**12/12**	**12/12**	**9.91/10**

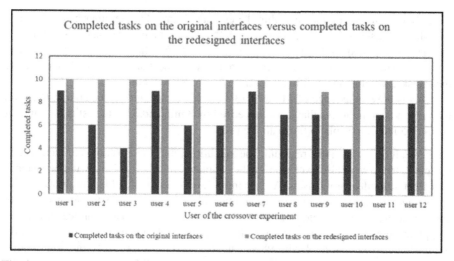

Fig. 4. Completed tasks on the original interfaces versus completed tasks on the redesigned interfaces.

Likewise, Fig. 4 shows the quantitative results: the number tasks fully completed by the 12 users in each user interface. As can be seen, the redesigned interface performs better in every case.

4.2 Comparison of the Execution Times Used to Complete the Tasks

Table 3 shows the comparison of the times spent by the users to complete the first 5 tasks on the original interfaces and the redesigned interfaces. Further, Table 4 shows the comparison of the times spent by the users to complete the last 5 tasks on the original interfaces and the redesigned interfaces. Likewise, Table 5 shows the comparison of the average times to complete the tasks by the samples on the original interfaces and the redesigned interfaces.

Original Interfaces. Regarding the original interfaces, it can be observed that the users of both samples presented problems to execute the tasks, giving an average time of 11.42 min, exceeding the estimated time by 7 min and 42 s (the estimated time to complete the transaction was expected to be 4 min as maximum). They stand out as the longest tasks to complete task n° 1: login with 75.17 s, task n° 4: remove a product and add another without SKU with 81.50 s, and task n ° 7: generate the payment receipt and modify the customer with 146.59 s.

Sample 1. It can be seen that the execution times used to complete each task by sample 1, were largely exceeded by the estimated times, since each task had a maximum estimate between 24 and 40 s. This is how great difficulty is observed on the part of the users of sample 1 to complete these tasks in the original interfaces.

Only task n° 5 stands out as the simplest tasks, adding promotion with 17.83 s and task n° 9, generating electronic bill, with 39 s on average of execution, these two being the only ones to be completed within the estimated time. On the other hand, the most complicated tasks to complete were n° 7 with 143 s, which is the task to generate the payment receipt and modify the customer, and task n° 6 with 126 s, which is the one to remove promotion. This is because there are no direct mechanisms to solve or complete these tasks, which made it difficult for users to complete them.

This is how an average of 811 s or 13.31 min was obtained to be able to finish all the tasks, which indicates that it was exceeded by 8 min and 31 s, the estimated time of 300 s or 5 min to be able to finish all the tasks.

Sample 2. It can be seen that regarding the execution times used to complete each task by sample 2, these were also exceeded by the estimated times. This is how the persistence of a great difficulty for the users. As in sample 1, only task n° 5, adding promotion, with an average execution time of 10.17 s, and task n° 9, generating electronic invoice with 20 s, stand out as the simplest tasks. On the other hand, the most complicated tasks to complete were task n° 7 with 105 s, which is to generate the payment receipt and modify the customer, and task n° 4 with 98 s, which is to remove products and add another product without SKU. This is how an average of 594 s or 9.54 min was obtained to be able to finish all the tasks, which indicates that it almost doubled the estimated time of 300 s or 5 min to be able to finish all the tasks.

Redesigned Interfaces. On the contrary, regarding the interfaces of the new proposal, the average execution time of the tasks was 3.09 s, this time being less than the estimated time of 4 min and 40 s on the redesigned interfaces. In this sense, a significant improvement can be observed as a result of the redesign of the graphical interfaces of the point-of-sale software.

Sample 1. In sample 1, the easiest tasks stand out as n° 6, remove promotion, with an average execution time of 1.67 s, task n° 3: customer search, and task n° 9, generate electronic bill with 9.33 s. On the other hand, the most complex tasks, but still within the estimated intervals, are n° 4 with 24.67 s, which is to remove products and advanced search, and n° 7 with 28 s, which is generate the payment receipt and modify the customer. This is due to the fact that it was developed direct mechanisms to be able to solve or complete these tasks, as well as the use of more understandable labels and buttons, which made it easier for users to complete the flows.

This is how an average of 163 s or 2 min and 43 s was obtained to be able to finish all the tasks, which indicates that the time decreased by 1 min and 57 s compared to the estimated 4 min and 40 s.

Sample 2. The simplest task stand out as n° 6, remove promotion, with an average execution time of 1.33 s, task n° 2: customer search, and task n° 9, generating electronic bill with 11.17 s. On the other hand, the most complex tasks, but which only exceeded the estimated intervals by a very few seconds, are task n° 4 with 41.33 s, which is eliminating products and advanced search, and task n° 7 with 45 s, which is generate the payment receipt and modify the customer.

This is how an average of 214 s or 3 min and 34 s was obtained to be able to finish all the tasks, which indicates that it was less by 1 min and 6 s than the estimated time of 4 min and 40 s.

Table 3. Time spent by the users to complete the first 5 tasks on the original interfaces versus the redesigned interfaces.

Sample	Task 1	Task 2	Task 3	Task 4	Task 5
Original interfaces					
Sample 1	114.33	94.33	49	108	17.83
Sample 2	39.67	90.17	57.83	97.67	10.17
Average time per task	**75.17**	**62.67**	**33.50**	**81.50**	**12.92**
Redesigned interfaces					
Sample 1	22.5	8.67	23.83	24.67	15.67
Sample 2	29.83	17	25.5	41.33	17.83
Average time per task	**26.17**	**12.84**	**24.67**	**33.00**	**16.75**

Table 4. Time to complete the last 5 tasks by users of each sample on the original interfaces versus the redesigned interfaces.

Sample	Task 6	Task 7	Task 8	Task 9	Task 10
Original interfaces					
Sample 1	126.17	143.17	50.67	39	68.33
Sample 2	63.83	105	49.67	20.33	59.5
Average time per task	**74.59**	**146.59**	**51.34**	**30.00**	**44.17**
Redesigned interfaces					
Sample 1	1.67	28	19.33	9.33	9.67
Sample 2	1.33	45	18.5	11.17	6.5
Average time per task	**1.50**	**36.50**	**18.92**	**10.25**	**8.09**

4.3 Post-test Questionnaires

The post-test questionnaires allowed users to analyze a series of criteria related to the list of tasks they performed. Table 6 shows user satisfaction and the facility to complete tasks rated by the users. It is observed that most of the users were able to complete the tasks "very easily" in the new interfaces, as they did not have major difficulties and requested help on a few occasions. While, in the original interfaces, these showed that the tasks were completed in a "neutral" way in average. In addition, the user satisfaction is higher in the redesigned interfaces, being the criteria chosen: "satisfactory" and "very satisfactory". On the other hand, in the original interfaces, it is observed that most users, 9 of 12, opted for "neutral", "unsatisfactory" and "unsatisfactory". That indicates a preference to the redesigned interfaces.

Likewise, 8 criteria were evaluated such as ease of registering a sale, complexity, necessity to receive technical support or help to learn the flows involved, ease in searching

Table 5. Average time to complete all the tasks by users of each sample in the original interfaces versus the redesigned interfaces.

Sample	Total time (in seconds)	Total time (in minutes)
Original interfaces		
Sample 1	810.83	13.31
Sample 2	593.83	9.54
Average time	**702.33**	**11.42**
Redesigned interfaces		
Sample 1	163.33	2.43
Sample 2	214	3.34
Average time	188.67	3.09

Table 6. User satisfaction and facility to complete tasks rated by the users

Facility to complete tasks	Number of users who marked the scales in the new interfaces	Number of users who marked the scales in original interfaces
Very hardly	0	0
Hardly	0	2
Neutral	0	8
Easily	4	2
Very easily	8	0
User satisfaction	**New interfaces**	**Original interfaces**
Unsatisfactory	0	1
Unsatisfying	0	4
Neutral	0	4
Satisfactory	3	2
Very satisfying	9	1

for products and in modifying customer information, ease of learning, if it provided guidance in registering a sale, and if it was consistent in colors, labels, images, buttons, and the other used components. Table 7 shows the results of the comparison of the evaluation criteria of the post-test questionnaire between the redesigned interfaces and the original interfaces.

In this sense, it stands out that the 12 users considered the sale registration as an easy process in the redesigned interfaces, but in the original interfaces, only 4 users considered this to be true. Also, 11 of 12 users contemplated that the redesigned interfaces were not complex, while, in the original interfaces, only 4 of 12 reviewed that they are not complex.

Original Interfaces. In the original interfaces, it stands out that 7 of 12 users considered that they would need technical support or help to learn how to use the software, and that the interfaces do not provide guidance to register a sale. Additionally, 6 of 12 users noted a lot of inconsistency in the interfaces. Likewise, 5 users consider that modifying a client is not an easy task. Finally, 4 users thought that it is not easy to learn to use the software.

Table 7. Comparison of the evaluation criteria of the post-test questionnaire between the redesigned interfaces and the original interfaces.

Criteria	Interfaces	Number of users who marked one of these scales				
		Strongly disagree	In disagree	Neutral	Agree	Totally agree
Register a sale is easy	Redesigned interfaces	0	0	0	2	10
	Original interfaces	0	3	5	3	1
Overly complex	Redesigned interfaces	8	3	1	0	0
	Original interfaces	1	2	5	4	0
Necessity of technical support or help to learn the flow	Redesigned interfaces	6	5	1	0	0
	Original interfaces	0	3	2	5	2
Provides guidance to register a sale	Redesigned interfaces	0	0	0	2	10
	Original interfaces	3	4	2	3	0
Easy of learn (learnability)	Redesigned interfaces	0	0	0	5	7
	Original interfaces	2	2	3	3	2
Product search without a code (SKU) is a simple task	Redesigned interfaces	0	0	0	5	7
	Original interfaces	1	2	3	4	2
Modifying information of a customer is a simple task	Redesigned interfaces	0	0	0	2	10
	Original interfaces	0	5	3	3	1
There is a lot of inconsistency	Redesigned interfaces	9	3	0	0	0
	Original interfaces	2	2	2	4	2

Redesigned Interfaces. Regarding the other criteria evaluated, it stands out that the 12 users considered the sale registration as an easy process, and that the software provided sufficient guidance to register a sale. In addition, all users found it easy to learn, that finding a product without SKU is simple, as well as modifying customers information, and that they would not need technical support or help to learn how to use the software. Finally, all users considered that the product does not present inconsistencies and that it is not complex.

4.4 Final Questionnaire

A final questionnaire was carried out to find out the preferences of the users. It was obtained that the 12 users consider it more useful, pleasant, intuitive, easier to find a product, and that it provides a better experience to the new proposal. Table 8 shows the detail of the criteria presented in this questionnaire.

Table 8. Final questionnaire criteria

Evaluation criteria			
Interface	More useful, enjoyable and provides a better experience	More intuitive	Easier to search for a product
Original interfaces	0	0	0
Redesigned interfaces	12	12	12

Also, users answered to a set of open questions, where they indicate their preference for the new proposal developed, emphasizing the points for improvement such as "more understandable labels", "more striking and pleasant colors", "better visualization of the components", "much simpler and easier to use" and "presents an easier flow".

4.5 Comparison of Averages Execution Time

After we had measured the execution times in both interfaces, we designed an experimental comparison between averages of those variables in each interface. The first step that we applied was a normality test through a Shapiro-Wilk Test, as the entire sample was of $n < 50$, in this case, 12 users. In this sense, we determinate the variable that we needed to compare and the hypothesis.

X1: user execution time on original interfaces.
X2: user execution time on redesigned interfaces.
For both variables we made two hypotheses H_0 and H_1, which are the following:
H_0: The average has a normal distribution.
H_1: The average has not a normal distribution.

```
> original_interface <- c(2.22, 1.56, 3.5, 2.46,
  3.13, 2.13, 3.44, 3.55, 4.04, 3.18, 2.46, 3.37)
> shapiro.test(original_interface)

        Shapiro-Wilk normality test

data:  original_interface
W = 0.94368, p-value = 0.5471
```

Fig. 5. Shapiro-Wilk normality test for user execution time on original interfaces.

```
> redesigned_interface <- c(10.4, 12.31, 15.16, 14.12,
  12.27, 15.59, 12.05, 9.43, 7.41, 11.28, 11.32, 6.54)
> shapiro.test(redesigned_interface)

        Shapiro-Wilk normality test

data:  redesigned_interface
W = 0.95831, p-value = 0.7594
```

Fig. 6. Shapiro-Wil normality test for user execution time on redesigned interfaces.

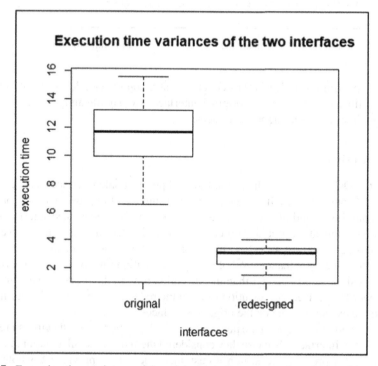

Fig. 7. Execution time variances of the original interfaces versus the redesigned interfaces.

454   P. Esparza et al.

At 95% confidence our alpha is 0.05, our *p_value* in both cases far exceeds 0.05, therefore, we do not have enough evidence to reject H$_0$. So, the distribution in both cases is normal. Figure 5 and Fig. 6 shows the demonstration of both normality tests.

Then we analyzed each user execution time variance to determine which statistical test we needed to apply. In Fig. 7 we can observe that we have different variances for both execution times, so we apply T-Student with different variances.

Finally, we proposed the hypotheses H0 and H1 for compare the average execution time:

H$_0$: The averages of the variables are equal (X1 = X2).
H$_1$: Average(X1)-Average(X2) > 0 = > Average(X1) > Average(X2).

```
> t.test(muestra$time ~ muestra$interface, var.eq = F, conf.int = T)

        Welch Two Sample t-test

data:  muestra$time by muestra$interface
t = 10.299, df = 12.527, p-value = 1.781e-07
alternative hypothesis: true difference in means is not equal to 0
95 percent confidence interval:
  6.765358 10.374642
sample estimates:
  mean in group original mean in group redesigned
                   11.49                     2.92
```

Fig. 8. T-student test to compare the means of the execution times on both interfaces.

After applying T-Student it was concluded at a significance level of 95% that the execution time of a user in the original interface was significantly greater than the execution time in the redesigned interfaces.

4.6   Conclusions

So, was the DCU process applied to redesigned point-of-sale interfaces a success? We can certainly answer a yes. It is concluded that a significant improvement was obtained both in complexity and efficiency to register a sale in the redesigned interfaces, as a result of the application of a DCU process through the design phase. In fact, we could prove it through a statical average comparison in each interface execution times, which indicated that at a significance level of 95%, the execution time of a user in the original interface is significantly greater than the execution time in the proposed new interface, in other words, the average execution time on the redesigned interfaces is significantly less than the execution time on the original interfaces.

Also, we obtained through the post-test and final questionnaires, that users preferred the redesigned interfaces, because they considered them more useful, pleasant, intuitive, easier to find a product and search a customer, and that it provided a whole better experience. In this way, they considered the redesigned interfaces a product easier to learn, that could improve user performance, especially in novice users, as they simulated this kind of user, which is important in this category of software, because in retail business they have very rotative employees that need to learn amazingly fast the point-of-sale software.

We certainly improved task n° 4 and task n° 7, as they were the longest tasks on the original interfaces, and we reduced their time of execution on the redesigned interfaces.

Finally, we could prove a user centered design process can improve usability attributes of the interfaces in many ways that we already had mentioned.

Acknowledgement. This study is highly supported by the Section of Informatics Engineering of the Pontifical Catholic University of Peru (PUCP) – Peru, and the "HCI, Design, User Experience, Accessibility & Innovation Technologies" Research Group (HCI-DUXAIT). HCI-DUXAIT is a research group of PUCP.

References

1. Abdelaziz, T.M., Maatuk, M.A., Rajab, F.: An approach to improvement the usability in software products. Int. J. Softw. Eng. Appl. **7**, 11–18 (2016). https://doi.org/10.5121/ijsea. 2016.7202
2. Ross, J.: The business value of user experience. Infragistics 1–12 (2014)
3. Weinschenk, S.: Usability: a business case (2005). https://humanfactors.com/downloads/whi tepapers/business-case.pdf
4. Sroczynski, Z.: User-centered design case study: ribbon interface development for point of sale software. In: Proceedings 2017 Federated Conference Computer Science Information System FedCSIS 2017. vol. 11, pp. 1257–1262 (2017). https://doi.org/10.15439/2017F273
5. Lenard, D.: Designing point-of-sale systems. https://www.uxmatters.com/mt/archives/2018/ 04/designing-point-of-sale-systems.php. Accessed 09 Aug 2020
6. Finstad, K., Xu, W., Kapoor, S., Canakapalli, S., Gladding, J.: Bridging the gaps between enterprise software and end users. Interactions **16**, 10–14 (2009). https://doi.org/10.1145/148 7632.1487635
7. Kabir, M.A., Han, B.: An improved usability evaluation model for point-of-sale systems. Int. J. Smart Home **10**, 269–282 (2016). https://doi.org/10.14257/ijsh.2016.10.7.27
8. Abras, C., Maloney-Krichmar, D., Preece, J.: User-centered design. W. Encycl. Hum. Comput. Interact. **37**, 445–456 (2004)
9. ISO/IEC: ISO IEC 9126–1:2001 Software Engineering-Product Quality- Part 1-Quality Model (2001)
10. ISO/IEC: ISO - ISO/IEC 25010:2011 - Systems and software engineering — Systems and software Quality Requirements and Evaluation (SQuaRE) — System and software quality models. https://www.iso.org/standard/35733.html. Accessed 16 May 2020
11. Abran, A., Khelifi, A., Suryn, W., Seffah, A.: Consolidating the ISO usability models. In: Proceedings 11th International Software Quality Management Conference, pp. 23–25 (2003)
12. ISO/IEC: Human-centered design processes for interactive systems. Ergon. human-system Interact (1999)
13. Jokela, T., Iivari, N., Matero, J., Karukka, M.: The standard of user-centered design and the standard definition of usability: analyzing ISO 13407 against ISO 9241–11. ACM Int. Conf. Proc. Ser. **46**, 53–60 (2003)
14. Lal, M., Shukla, A., Tarangini, A.: Study of effectiveness of POS data in managing supply chain. Ind. Eng. J. **11** (2018). https://doi.org/10.26488/iej.11.10.1144.
15. Weber, M.M., Kantamneni, S.P.: POS and EDI in retailing: an examination of underlying benefits and barriers. Supply Chain Manag. **7**, 311–317 (2002). https://doi.org/10.1108/135 98540210447755

16. Kotz, S., Read, C.B., Balakrishnan, N., Vidakovic, B., Johnson, N.L., Kenward, M.G.: Crossover design. Encycl. Stat. Sci. 1–9 (2005). https://doi.org/10.1002/0471667196.ess7252
17. Barnum, C.M.: usability testing essentials: ready, Set Test! (2011)
18. Rubin, J., Chisnell, D.: Handbook of Usability Testing. Wiley Publishing, Hoboken (2008)

Research on the Influencing Factors of Users' Satisfaction with the Usability of News App Interface Under the Epidemic

Xi Han, Tao Xi[✉], and Zhiwei Zhou

Shanghai Jiao Tong University, Minhang District, Shanghai, China

Abstract. Under the background of COVID-19 epidemic, starting from the perspective of user satisfaction in the process of user's using news App, the research explores the relevant factors affecting user satisfaction based on the process of user's browsing news. Through user survey and literature research, combined with factor analysis method, the research sums up 13 factors affecting user satisfaction with the interface usability of news App. It uses decision-making experiment method to analyze and research 30 pcs of online and offline questionnaire data and draws cause and effect diagrams. Finally, it concludes that the three key factors affecting the user satisfaction with interface usability of news App are the factors: image, image-text layout, interface clarity; and the factor that affects other factors to a large extent is interface clarity. Finally, it clarifies the relationship among the relevant factors affecting user satisfaction with the interface usability of news App, further analyzes the problems existing in the current news App at the level of human cognition, and puts forward some relevant suggestions for the improvement of user satisfaction with the Interface Usability of news App.

Keywords: News App · Interface usability · Satisfaction · Decision-Making Trial and Evaluation Laboratory (DEMATEL) method · Factor analysis method

1 Introduction

1.1 Research Background

Under the background of the current epidemic of COVID-19, being spread through the tools such as self-media, etc., news information products are also widely favored by people. It covers audiences of different ages, knowledge backgrounds, and classes [1]; and is mainly spread in the forms of text, image, and chart. In the early stage of the development of public health emergencies, especially of this virus with unknown cause, people are more eager to answer their inner confusion through news information products [2], to know their environment and how to protect themselves.

© Springer Nature Switzerland AG 2021
M. M. Soares et al. (Eds.): HCII 2021, LNCS 12781, pp. 457–466, 2021.
https://doi.org/10.1007/978-3-030-78227-6_33

1.2 Research Field

Under the background of the epidemic, this paper studies the interface usability of news App, and finds out the factors that affect the user satisfaction from the angle of interface design. The carrier of communication between users and news information is interface, and the accuracy of information transmission and expression needs to be realized through interface. Among them, the information visualization design plays a vital role. The graphic elements relationship in the interface includes the relationship among color, icon, text and other elements in the information visualization design. Through these elements, the data and text information are transformed into the information intuitively recognized by users to create a clear, smooth and beautiful interface style, and promote the effectiveness and accuracy of information transmission [3].

2 Research Design

2.1 Research Methods

This study uses the method of decision-making trial and evaluation laboratory (DEMA-TEL) to analyze the questionnaire data obtained from survey. DEMATEL method can be used to analyze the correlation among various factors, so as to find out the key decision-making factors of the user satisfaction with the interface usability, and the relationship among the decision-making factors in the process of using the news App. In order to ensure the validity of the questionnaire data, individuals distribute the questionnaire offline and ask the interviewees to fill in the questionnaire on the spot, so as to obtain the data.

DEMATEL method was put forward by scholars A. Gabus and E. Fontela of the Battelle Laboratory in the United States at a meeting in Geneva in 1971. The purpose is to solve the complex and difficult problems in reality by using systematic analysis method of graph theory and matrix tool [4]. The specific operating steps of DEMATEL method are: (1) First determine the factors, design and establish the table for the relationship among various factors, collect data through questionnaire, and establish the direct relationship matrix; (2) obtain the normalized direct influence matrix from the normalized primitive relation matrix; (3) obtain the direct and indirect relationship matrix through the calculation from the normalized direct influence matrix; (4) obtain the influence degree (D), influenced degree (R), and centrality degree (D+R), cause degree (D−R) from the direct and indirect relationship matrix.

2.2 Questionnaire Design

First, through literature research and interview, it discusses the usability of news App products from four dimensions: visual elements, image-text construction, information architecture, and epidemic content respectively. Then it mainly refers to the research content of Tang Peilu, Li Juan [5], Yuan Hao, Hu Shilei, Xu Yan, Xu Xiaoyan [3], Jan Brejcha [6], Carter, AS and CD Hundhausen [7], to divide the decision factors of user satisfaction with the usability of App interface under the epidemic background into 13 items: (1) visual elements in the interface, including text (text- vision hierarchy, font, size, spacing, etc.), image (dynamic, static pictures, short video and their attractiveness), color (monochrome or multicolour, short tone or cool tone), icon (direct meaning-expression clarity degree, style beauty); (2) image-text construction, including the size of the image (size of the picture and video), image-text layout (summarized into four forms: text on the left and image on the right, text on the right and image on the left, text on the top and image on the bottom, image on the top and text on the bottom), methods of content switching (mainly divided into up and down sliding, left and right sliding); (3) Information architecture, including familiarity of the interface (whether the user can start using it easily and flexibly), interface conciseness (concentrated summary of information), interface clarity (whether the information in the interface is clearly visible);(4) content

Table 1. Decision factors of user satisfaction with App interface usability

No.	Dimension	Satisfaction decision factor
1	Visual elements	Text (text content, including text-vision hierarchy, font style, size, spacing, etc.)
2		Image (dynamic, static pictures, short video and their attractiveness)
3		Color (monochrome or multicolor, warm or cool color)
4		Icon (direct meaning-expression clarity degree of the icon in interface, aesthetic degree of the style)
5	Image-text construction	Image size (refers to the size of the banner picture, video window/middle picture, small picture)
6		Image-text layout (mainly studies the layout of banner and text in, summarized into four forms: text on the left and image on the right, text on the right and image on the left, text on the top and image on the bottom, image on the top and text on the bottom)
7		Method of content switching (mainly divided into up and down sliding, left and right sliding)
8	Information architecture	Interface familiarity (whether the user is familiar with the information architecture and can use it easily and flexibly)
9		Interface conciseness (centralized induction of information, can provide more information display space and give users a sense of neatness as a whole)
10		Interface clarity (whether the information in the interface is clearly visible)
11	Content of epidemic news	Freshness of content (closeness of the occurrence of the objective facts, freshness of factual content)
12		Importance of content (relevance to people's interests: objective influence degree of facts on the audience and society)
13		Proximity of content (happening around people)

of the epidemic, including freshness (real-time), importance (relevance to people's interests; objective influence degree of facts on audience and society), proximity (happening around people), see Table 1.

Each factor needs to be compared and scored in pairs for the subjects. The scale of this study is divided into 4 measures: "no influence (0 point)", "low influence (1 point)", and "moderate influence (2 points)", "high influence (3 points)". A total of 30 valid answers are received for this questionnaire.

2.3   Experimental Analysis and Discussion

The questionnaire data is sorted out and normalized to obtain the normalized direct influence matrix of the decision factors of user satisfaction with the usability of App interface is obtained, as shown in Table 2.

Table 2. Normalized direct influence matrix of the decision factors of the user satisfaction with App interface usability

	1	2	3	4	5	6	7	8	9	10	11	12	13
1	0.00	1.37	1.30	1.30	1.57	2.10	1.63	1.62	2.00	2.14	2.03	2.21	1.86
2	1.76	0.00	2.03	1.97	2.07	2.38	1.62	1.59	1.93	2.17	1.83	2.00	2.07
3	1.31	2.10	0.00	2.07	1.14	1.66	1.24	1.55	1.79	2.03	1.41	1.48	1.21
4	1.34	1.72	1.62	0.00	1.48	1.69	1.79	1.93	1.93	2.07	1.31	1.66	1.31
5	1.97	2.21	1.24	1.34	0.00	2.31	1.83	1.55	1.97	2.03	1.66	1.76	1.45
6	2.28	2.28	1.38	1.62	2.17	0.00	2.07	1.90	2.07	2.28	1.34	1.48	1.38
7	1.53	1.72	1.03	1.55	1.83	2.00	0.00	1.79	1.66	1.72	1.31	1.34	1.21
8	1.66	1.37	1.55	1.55	1.72	2.03	1.90	0.00	1.86	1.86	1.24	1.41	1.45
9	2.14	2.28	1.73	1.76	2.03	2.41	1.86	2.14	0.00	2.31	1.41	1.45	1.41
10	2.07	2.17	1.76	1.67	1.97	2.34	1.86	1.93	2.17	0.00	1.72	1.86	1.66
11	1.90	2.03	1.62	1.45	1.47	1.69	1.31	1.34	1.24	1.66	0.00	2.10	1.90
12	2.31	2.14	1.93	1.34	2.10	2.00	1.32	1.41	1.34	1.79	2.21	0.00	1.83
13	1.83	1.79	1.45	1.07	1.52	1.72	1.53	1.52	1.72	1.62	1.86	2.07	0.00

Through matrix operation, the direct and indirect relationship matrix is obtained, as shown in Table 3. The threshold value of 0.74 is obtained through calculation with the method of quartile. The "3": color" and "7: method of content switching" not reaching the threshold value are deleted from the table. In addition, the values of D+R and D−R are calculated, as shown in Table 4.

The centrality degree (D+R) and cause degree (D−R) of the 13 factors are calculated and listed in Table 4.

Table 3. Direct and indirect influence matrix of the decision factors of user satisfaction with App *interface* usability

	1	2	3	4	5	6	7	8	9	10	11	12	13
1	0.67	0.75		0.62	0.70	0.81		0.67	0.73	0.79	0.66	0.71	0.64
2	0.80	0.76		0.70	0.78	0.89		0.73	0.79	0.86	0.71	0.76	0.70
3													
4	0.68	0.72		0.53	0.66	0.75		0.65	0.69	0.75	0.60	0.65	0.59
5	0.75	0.79		0.63	0.65	0.83		0.68	0.74	0.80	0.66	0.70	0.63
6	0.79	0.82		0.66	0.76	0.76		0.72	0.77	0.83	0.67	0.72	0.65
7													
8	0.68	0.70		0.59	0.66	0.76		0.57	0.68	0.73	0.59	0.64	0.59
9	0.80	0.84		0.68	0.77	0.88		0.74	0.71	0.85	0.69	0.73	0.67
10	0.81	0.84		0.68	0.77	0.88		0.74	0.80	0.77	0.70	0.75	0.68
11	0.70	0.73		0.59	0.65	0.75		0.62	0.66	0.73	0.55	0.67	0.61
12	0.77	0.79		0.63	0.73	0.82		0.67	0.72	0.79	0.69	0.64	0.65
13	0.69	0.72		0.57	0.66	0.75		0.63	0.68	0.73	0.62	0.67	0.53

*The bold indicates that the value is greater than the threshold value of 0.74, and the blank indicates that the values in the row and column are not greater than the threshold value of 0.74.

When the D+R value is larger, it indicates the factor is more important in the overall evaluation factors. The factors larger than the average D+R value of 17.94 are selected, so the importance of the decision evaluation factors of user satisfaction with the interface usability of App is in the order of "10": interface clarity, "6" image-text layout, "2" image, "9" interface conciseness, "1" text, "5" image size, "12" importance of content.

When the positive value of D−R is larger, it indicates that this factor directly affects other factors. When the negative value of D−R is larger, it means that this factor is affected by other factors. As the value of factor 7 does not reach the threshold value, it is filtered out. "6: image-text layout" (with the largest positive value of D+R) is the factor mainly affecting other factors. "9: interface conciseness" (with the largest negative value of D−R) is the factor mainly being affected by other factors.

The following table shows the first three items and the last three items of the factor centrality degree and cause degree.

According to the direct and indirect relationship matrix (Table 3). In the causality graph, the factors in different dimensions are distinguished by different colors. Blue represents the visual element dimension, yellow represents the image-text construction dimension, green represents the information architecture dimension, and red represents the epidemic content dimension. The arrow indicates the direction in which one factor affects another factor. The dashed line and the solid line show a strong relationship (value greater than 0.77) and a relative strong relationship (value between the threshold value 0.74 and 0.77). Figure 1 combines with Tables 5 and 6.

Table 4. Centrality Degree and Cause degree

Centrality degree (D+R)		Cause degree (D−R)	
Factor 10	19.90	Factor 6	0.83
Factor 6	19.83	Factor 7	0.51
Factor 2	19.76	Factor 1	0.42
Factor 9	19.04	Factor 8	0.28
Factor 1	18.48	Factor 10	0.20
Factor 5	18.20	Factor 5	−0.09
Factor 12	18.14	Factor 2	−0.09
Factor 8	17.09	Factor 11	−0.15
Factor 11	16.76	Factor 3	−0.18
Factor 7	16.66	Factor 12	−0.38
Factor 4	16.56	Factor 13	−0.39
Factor 13	16.53	Factor 4	−0.48
Factor 3	16.22	Factor 9	−0.50

*The light gray in the table indicates the factor in the row and column of the direct and indirect relationship matrix with value not greater than the threshold value of 0.74 factor; the bold indicates the value greater than the total average value of D+R 17.94

Table 5. The first three items and the last three items of the factor centrality degree

(D+R) The first Three Items	(D+R) The Last Three Items
Factor 10: interface clarity	Factor 4: icon
Factor 6: image-picture layout	Factor 13: proximity of the content
Factor 2: image	Factor 3: color

Table 6. The first three items and the last three items of the factor cause degree

(D−R) > 0 The first Three Items	(D−R) < 0 The Last Three Items
Factor 6: image-picture layout	Factor 13: content proximity
Factor 1: text	Factor 4: Icon
Factor 8: interface familiarity	Factor 9: interface conciseness

I. Because the D+R values of the three factors "10: interface clarity", "6: image-text layout", and "2: image" are ranked the top three items, which are the most important key decision factors of satisfaction. Factor 10 has the largest value of D+R. It can be seen that the clarity of the design of the App interface is the most critical decision-making factor. Therefore, the consideration of the interface clarity should be focused on in design. "2: image" and "6: image-text layout" have a strong influence on it. "2: image" has a strong influence on "6: image-text layout", "6: image-text layout" has a strong influence on "2: image", "10: interface clarity" has a strong influence on "6: image-text layout", 2: "image". Therefore, it is possible to combine other factors to find the design emphasis to improve the clarity of the interface, thereby increasing the user's satisfaction with the interface usability. The improvement of the interface clarity can also assist the improvement and development of other factors. In addition, optimization of image-text layout and matching of reasonable and high-quality image will help improve the overall interface usability, reduce users' troubles in visual cognition and give users a good experience.

II. "13: proximity of content", "4: icon", "9: interface conciseness" has D+R values ranked in the last three items, indicating that these three items have little influence on other factors.

III. With the positive values of D−R ranked the top three items, "6: image-text layout", "1: text", "8: interface familiarity" have a great influence on other factors, and are the cause factors. While with the negative values of D−R ranked the top three items, "13: proximity of news content", "4: icon", "9: interface conciseness" are more easily influenced by other factors and are the result elements. "2: image", "6: image-text layout" and "10: interface clarity" all have a strong influence on "1: text", and the centrality degree of this factor is ranked relatively high. It can be seen that the presentation method of the text content has a great influence on the interface usability of news App.

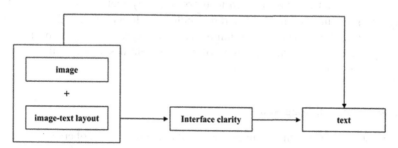

Fig. 1. The secondary association in strong influence

IV. It can be seen from Fig. 1 that among the strong relationships, in addition to the influence of "10: interface clarity" on "1: text", the remaining associated lines can form the secondary association graph, as shown in Fig. 1. 2: image" and "6: image-text layout" can directly affect "1: text", and also can firstly have a strong influence on "10: Interface clarity", and then strongly affect the way of text layout. Thus, the usability of the interface design of news App can be started from two aspects: image selection and image-text layout in the interface, and more consideration should be given to the mutual influence between image and text, so as to optimize the way of text content layout. It can be seen that these four factors are closely related.

3   Conclusions and Recommendations

3.1   Conclusion

I.   Based on the above survey and analysis, "10: Interface clarity" is the most critical factor in the all decisions of user satisfaction Especially under the background of the epidemic, news App is not only a consulting tool for users to spend their free time, but more importantly, it delivers information about the current epidemic situation to users. The data also shows that the factor "10: interface clarity" is closely related to the factors under the dimension of visual elements, indicating that users believe that interface clarity cannot be achieved without the role of visual elements such as text, image, icon, etc.

II. This study explores whether user satisfaction with the usability of the interface will be affected by news content related to the epidemic under the background of the new crown pneumonia epidemic. As can be seen from the results, the proximity of epidemic news content is ranked the first in the cause degree, and it is most affected by other factors. For example, "10: interface clarity" has a strong influence on it, both "2: image" and "6: picture and text layout" have a relatively strong influence on it. This enlightens us from a design perspective that news content should be connected with users in the interface. On the one hand, it lies in its own content, on the other hand, it needs to be dealt with comprehensively from the aspects of visual elements, image-picture construction, information architecture, etc. Only joint collaboration allows it to transmit information to users in a way that users are satisfied with, reflecting the importance of its indirect influence. In addition, "12: importance of news content" is ranked the seventh in centrality degree. Under the background of the epidemic, the priority screening of news content has a great influence on user satisfaction decisions.

3.2   Discussion and Suggestions

I.   The results show that the freshness, proximity of news content of epidemic situation, which was originally estimated to have an influence on the user's decision-making level of satisfaction with the interface usability of News products under the background of the epidemic situation, will not strongly influence other factors. However, as the main content of news consulting products, it does play a role in optimization of interface usability design. Thinking about the reasons: the DEMATEL analysis method studies more about the relationship among various factors, and the freshness and proximity of the epidemic news content is more of a result. It will be presented to the user eventually based on the collaboration of factors on other design levels, so there will be a lack of association with design details. Based on the theory of decision-making laboratory analysis method, it is recommended to strengthen the relationship among "10: interface clarity", "2: image", "6: image-text layout" and

"1: text", and consider the text and image in design. Only coordination of the two can make the interface clear as a whole, and then improve user satisfaction.

II. In the part of the questionnaire design, consideration should be given to reduce the factors as much as possible. Important and representative factors should be screened out for each dimension. In terms of text description, it should be concise and to the point, to reduce the user's memory burden. The combination of image and text is the best presentation form; In the questionnaire collection, the sample size can be still enlarged to get more accurate data, and then get more accurate conclusions.

The National Reading Project aims to promote a wide range of reading behaviors. However, what kind of reading promotion activities can be effective in promoting reading behaviors? According to the behavioral viewpoint, external stimuli often cause psychological changes through acting on the individual's psychology, and then will cause changes in behavior. The act of reading is itself a process of experience [12]. According to the philosophy of experience, experience is the basis for thought changes and also provides a reason for behavior. In other words, a good reading experience is often a precursor to the occurrence and continuation of reading behavior, and it can also become an intermediary factor for reading promotion activities to promote reading behavior. Because of this, in recent years, experience-oriented reading behavior research has become an important field of reading research [13]. The emergence of interaction has brought a turning point in the relationship between the user and the product, and the relationship between the two has gradually returned to nature. This is due to the designer's continuous understanding of the design principle of "people-centered" and perfect. Faced with various challenges in the new technological environment of the data-based, human-computerized, and intelligent era, physical products and virtual products are slowly being integrated with user experience. Designers need to adjust the relationship between people and products according to the needs of users. Accurately grasp and complete the final design goal.

References

1. Mengya, X., Feng, Y.: On the spreading effect of science and technology news in public health emergencies——Taking the "COVID-19" event as an example. Anhui Sci. Technol. **05**, 30–31 (2020)
2. Jijuan, W.: Viewing the plain style of news communication writing from anti-epidemic reports. Drama House **17**, 191–192 (2020)
3. Qin, Y., Renjun, L.: Research on the design of Taobao live broadcast interface based on user characteristics. Packaging Eng. **41**(08), 219–222 (2020)
4. Yuan, H., Hu, S., Xu, Y., Xu, X.: Research on the design of information visualization interface of sports APP[J/OL]. Packaging Eng. 1–7 (2020). http://kns.cnki.net/kcms/detail/50.1094. TB.20200313.1605.019.html
5. Yifan, G.: Research on the design of children's toys based on DEMATEL method. Design **32**(23), 140–142 (2019)
6. Peilu, T., Juan, L.: Research on the design of usability of news APP interface based on eye movement visual tracking technology. Packaging Eng. **40**(14), 247–252 (2019)
7. Brejcha, J., et al.: Chinese UI design guidelines 2.0. design, user experience, and usability: design discourse, pp. 122–129 (2015)

8. Adams, R., et al.: Eye movement desensitization and reprocessing (EMDR) for the treatment of psychosis: a systematic review. Eur. J. Psychotraumatol. **11**(1) (2020)

9. Carter, A.S., Hundhausen, C.D.: How is user interface prototyping really done in practice? A survey of user interface designers. IEEE Symposium on Visual Languages and Human-Centric Computing **2010**, 207–211 (2010)

10. Hurley, W.D.: A method for predicting the impact of user interface design on software design. J. Syst. Softw. **22**(3), 179–190 (1993)

11. Lin, C., Wang, T.: The research of the methods how the brand image design transform scientifically in the digital media era. In: 2016 Nicograph International (NicoInt), pp. 138–138 (2016)

12. Rosenblatt, L.M.: The Reader, the Text, the Poem: The Transactional Theory of the Literary Work. Southern Illinois University Press, Carbondale (1978)

13. Hume, D.: An enquiry concerning the principles of morals . Hume Stud. **26**(2), 344–346 (2000)

User Experience Design Study of Museum Website Based on TRIZ Theory: A Case of Heyuan Dinosaur Museum

Dan Huang, Miao Li$^{(\boxtimes)}$, and Zhen Liu

School of Design, South China University of Technology,
Guangzhou 510006, People's Republic of China
limiao@scut.edu.cn

Abstract. In the Internet age, museums are gradually adopting a combination of online websites and physical museums to serve people. User experience, one of the important criteria to verify the success of a website design, tends to promote the development of the museum itself if applies properly. At present, most museum websites in our country pay insufficient attention to user experience. This paper takes the Heyuan Dinosaur Museum website as an example to redesign the museum website page to improve the user satisfaction of the museum website. This study uses the methods of performance measurement, system usability scale and behavior observation and evaluation to measure user experience, and combines multiple factors to evaluate website user satisfaction. It was found that users of the Heyuan Dinosaur Museum website had low usability score while gaining high satisfaction with the visual and interactive design of the website in the user experience evaluation. Finally, by applying TRIZ theory, this study resulted in a redesigned prototype of the Heyuan Dinosaur Museum website, which received higher user satisfaction and user ratings.

Keywords: User experience · Museums · Website design · TRIZ

1 Introduction

As a platform for the museum's online display and operation, the website is an important part of the museum's operation to provide users with more specific and effective information [1]. The museum website contains a series of promotional functions, from simplifying the user's on-site steps, such as booking tickets, to disseminating museum culture and introducing cultural relics.

User experience design is bound to be targeted at user needs. A user-centered user experience design is a necessary step to create an effective website. The user experience level can be divided into functional design, interaction design and visual design [2]. If something goes wrong with the museum website design, users will encounter many troubles when using the website; a museum website with poor user experience cannot communicate its influence to the outside world, which is not conducive to the long-term

© Springer Nature Switzerland AG 2021
M. M. Soares et al. (Eds.): HCII 2021, LNCS 12781, pp. 467–482, 2021.
https://doi.org/10.1007/978-3-030-78227-6_34

development of the museum. According to researches, it can be found that the main user groups are students, researchers and cultural scholars [3].

Due to the unique and rich dinosaur fossil resources, the special theme of Heyuan Dinosaur Museum is easier to create a museum brand effect. This paper selects the museum website for user experience research and website page redesign. Usability is an important part of user experience indicators. The research on the Heyuan Dinosaur Museum website is mainly to analyze its deficiencies in usability and explore the factors that affect user experience to improve the efficiency of the museum website and user satisfaction.

2   Method

In this study, performance measurement methods were used, and three different groups were set up in typical scenarios and task experiments. The system usability scale is used for usability problems and self-report measurement; behavioral and physiological measurement adopts behavioral observation and evaluation method. In addition, the user testing method used in this study is the Thinking Aloud, which encourages users to express their inner thoughts while performing actions [4].

In this experiment, eight users completed the scenario task and self-report. A video recorder recorded the entire experiment and report process, and recorded some noteworthy points and user feedback. This research analyzes the data such as videos and tables after testing, and proposes improvement directions based on TRIZ theory.

TRIZ (Theory of Intensive Problem Solving), a systematic method of innovative thinking, provides a structured and simple tool for solving problems [5]. TRIZ has been used to solve technical problems in the engineering field [6]. Research in recent years has gradually found that TRIZ theory can also play an important role in other fields. TRIZ can improve usability, and TRIZ's model is the most suitable model to improve usability [7]. This paper summarizes the user experience problems of the Heyuan Dinosaur Museum, introduces the TRIZ model in the improvement stage, combines the TRIZ theory with the website design, puts forward a conceptual idea, and redesign the prototype to give users a better experience.

2.1   Participant Sample Description

The subjects of the study were eight postgraduate students from the School of Design, South China University of Technology. They all had relevant experiences of visiting museums. This is similar to the case of the main natural users of the website. Half of the participants had not used the museum website before, similar to new users of the website. A further half of the participants had used different museum websites in order to complete their research tasks, which could simulate the use of a user with some familiarity with the website.

Additional information about the participants is shown in Fig. 1. Information about the participants. The sample description types are gender, age, whether or not they have visited museums, and whether or not they have visited museum websites.

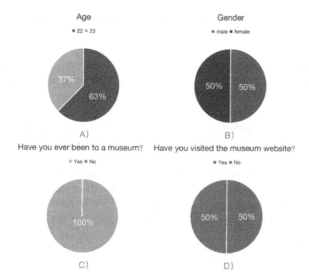

Fig. 1. Information about the participants.

2.2 Performance Metrics

Based on the main user groups and actual usage of the website, three scenarios were set up to test the performance and user satisfaction of the website with three different categories of users. Each scenario contains a different task or tasks that demonstrate the actual use of the basic functionality of the website. As the subjects were postgraduate students from the School of Design, three types of user scenarios were set up as test situations: a university student, a university researcher and a designer. The tasks for three scenarios are shown in Table 1.

Table 1. Tasks of scenarios.

Scenarios	No.	Content
Scenario 1	Task 1-1	Find the exhibition called "Dinosaur Hometown"
	Task 1-2	Find the "Visitor guide"
	Task 1-3	Find the page for booking tickets
Scenario 2	Task 2-1	Find "Cretaceous Huang Heyuan Dragon skeleton"
Scenario 3	Task 3-1	Find the location of cultural and creative products
	Task 3-2	Count the number of cultural and creative products of Heyuan Dinosaur Museum

Scenario 1: After hearing about the "Dinosaur Hometown" exhibition by the Heyuan Dinosaur Museum, a university student is willing to searching the website for information on the exhibition. He plans to visit the museum and wants to find out how to visit and how to book tickets.

This scenario contains basic museum booking functions and enquiry about exhibitions, and is suitable for new website users.

Scenario 2: A university researcher thinks that fossil paleontology is valuable to study. He recently collected information on dinosaur fossils and wants to learn more about the "Cretaceous Huang Heyuan Dragon skeleton" in the museum.

Considering the actual needs of the main user groups, the purpose of researchers differs from the general population. These users are well-experienced in using the site for specific search purposes. Scenario 2 was set to find information on specific collections.

Scenario 3: A designer wants to know the previous cultural and creative products in the Heyuan Dinosaur Museum and counts numbers and kinds in total.

As the last scenario, the design of the creative products requires a deep understanding of the museum's collection and culture, so users will be more familiar with the museum website.

2.3 Usability Issues and Self-reporting Metrics

The use of a quantitative evaluation user perception questionnaire to assist in conducting the experiment would have made the research results more convincing. When eight users completed the experiment, they were asked to complete the System Usability Scale. As the System Usability Scale is a quick measure of the overall usability of a website, it was used for the evaluation.

2.4 Behavioural and Physiological Metrics

In the experiment, video recorder was used to record the whole process of the user's interaction with the website, including the user's steps, the content displayed on the interface and the user's reaction. This article watched and organized the video. In addition, a face-to-face interview was conducted with the users at the end of the task to record their comments on the most and least satisfactory design of the whole website. The above were tallied to produce an analysis report.

3 Results

3.1 Performance Results

Record the time taken by each participant to complete the task and the mistakes they made, as shown in Table 2, Table 3, and Table 4. The average time of the task represents the overall efficiency, and the standard deviation represents the difference between users.

In Task 1, some users chose the wrong navigation bar function. The names of the secondary menus in the exhibition bar are similar, and users do not know what exhibition they are looking for. This will result in a longer completion time and a higher error rate. For Task 2 and Task 3, the access instructions and booking functions can be used on the right and in the navigation bar, but the time spent on these tasks is polarized. It explains

Table 2. The completing time of the tasks in Scenario 1.

No.	User	Total time/s	Total errors	Time of task 1-1/s	Error of task 1-1	Time of task 1-2/s	Error of task 1-2	Time of task 1-3/s	Error of task 1-3
1	Participant 1	80	3	50	3	10	0	20	0
2	Participant 2	48	0	18	0	7	0	23	0
3	Participant 3	32	0	15	0	10	0	7	0
4	Participant 4	153	8	70	4	81	4	2	0
5	Participant 5	42	3	29	3	6	0	7	0
6	Participant 6	175	4	148	4	8	0	19	0
7	Participant 7	104	1	40	1	32	0	32	1
8	Participant 8	85	1	32	1	31	0	22	0
Average		89.88	2.5	50.25	2	23.13	0.5	16.5	0
Standard deviation		48.67	2.5	40.49	1.58	24.02	1.32	9.5	0.33

Table 3. The completing time of the tasks in Scenario 2.

No.	User	Time of task 2-1/s	Error of task 2-1
1	Participant 1	45	1
2	Participant 2	20	0
3	Participant 3	57	1
4	Participant 4	89	1
5	Participant 5	26	2
6	Participant 6	31	0
7	Participant 7	107	1
8	Participant 8	81	3
Average		57	1.13
Standard deviation		30.1	0.93

Table 4. The completing time of the tasks in Scenario 3.

No.	User	Total time/s	Total errors	Time of task 3-1/s	Error of task 3-1	Time of task 3-2/s	Error of task 3-2
1	Participant 1	53	0	24	0	29	0
2	Participant 2	46	0	25	0	21	0
3	Participant 3	56	0	22	0	34	0
4	Participant 4	101	4	55	3	46	1
5	Participant 5	67	2	43	2	24	0
6	Participant 6	81	1	32	0	49	1
7	Participant 7	78	1	41	1	37	0
8	Participant 8	65	0	24	0	41	0
Average		68.38	1	33.25	0.75	35.13	0.25
Standard deviation		16.66	1.32	11.16	1.09	9.43	0.43

the inconspicuous fast-track area on the right, which causes some people to click on it, but others ignore it.

In scenario 2, most testers directly use the search function to find this particular artifact. The search icon is too small to use, and participants can only click on the collection function. Second, there is too much unimportant information in the collection part, which distracts the experimenter.

In scenario 3, a common problem of participants is that they don't know which category the creative product belongs to on the navigation bar, and they think there is no suitable option in the current navigation bar category. Second, the site contains two different museums, but all the products on the "creative products" page are not classified, but mixed together. Third, the naming of some products is very random.

Task Success. All participants were asked to complete the full test, the task success rate was 100%. The three typical scenarios are same in terms of task success rate.

Task Time. The time for each task was obtained by averaging the time spent by the eight subjects. Figure 2 shows that Scenario 2 took the most time, which was caused by the unavailability of the website search function.

Task Error. The number of errors can represent the number of times a user has been misled (see Fig. 3). The number of errors per task is the average of the number of errors made by the eight users.

Task1 in Scenario 1 has the highest mean error value, indicating that the web pages involved in this process are more seriously misleading to users. Scenario 3 requires only one operation to complete each task, while the other two scenarios require multiple steps for each task. However, the average time spent on each task in Scenario 3 is higher (here the result of dividing each task by the number of steps required). As the error rate in scenario 3 is not high, it suggests that the user is in doubt on one page.

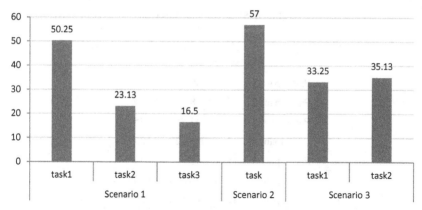

Fig. 2. The average task time of the three scenarios.

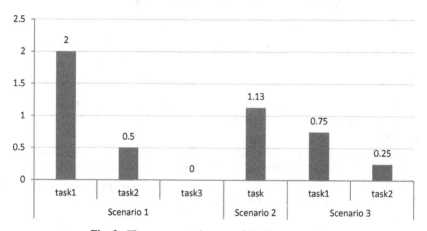

Fig. 3. The average task error of the three scenarios.

3.2 Usability Results

The total the System Usability Scale scores, the scores of the Learn ability and Usability subscales are assessed by the eight subjects recorded in Table 5.

From the scores, it is clear that the overall usability of the Heyuan Dinosaur Museum website is considered poor by the experimenter, with the lowest score for Learnability. The website of the museum has major usability problems, resulting in a poor user experience.

3.3 Behavioural and Physiological Metrics Results

This article summarizes and evaluates the phenomena observed during the experiment, as shown in Table 6.

Through user interviews, the highest satisfaction is the overall beauty of the website, which shows that the visual design of the website is very important to enhance the user

Table 5. SUS data statistics table.

No.	User	SUS score	Usability	Learnability
1	Participant 1	47.5	50	37.5
2	Participant 2	65	68.75	50
3	Participant 3	40	43.75	25
4	Participant 4	47.5	53.125	25
5	Participant 5	45	43.75	50
6	Participant 6	42.5	46.875	25
7	Participant 7	42.5	46.875	25
8	Participant 8	50	53.125	37.5
Average		47.5	50.781	34.375

Table 6. Users' typical behaviors.

No.	Behavior	Analysis
1	Users will browse the navigation bar more than twice before clicking on a specific category	Too much information in the navigation bar and secondary menu
2	Users always close the pop-up window of the home page about recruiting volunteers	The user subconsciously assumes that the pop-up is an online advertisement
3	The banner on the home page takes up a lot of the screen, users do not scroll down the page	The website does not balance aesthetics and usability
4	The banner on the home page takes up a lot of the screen so that users do not scroll down the page	The website does not balance aesthetics and usability, users not know that there is content underneath the banner

experience. The most confusing point is that users cannot understand that cultural and creative products are classified as services. Other evaluations are shown in the Table 7 and Table 8.

4   Website Redesign

4.1   Application of TRIZ

This paper uses the TRIZ Contradiction Matrix method to explore the problems that need to be improved at the Heyuan Dinosaur Museum. The problems are summarised as generic engineering parameters that need to be improved in TRIZ theory, and the corresponding changed deteriorated parameters and improved parameters form a TRIZ

Table 7. The part of the design that users think is most satisfactory.

No.	The most satisfying design	Analysis
1	"The navigation bar is dynamic and the secondary menu appears when the mouse is moved over the corresponding category."	Some of the website's interactive experiences are well designed
2	"The scrolling of the home screen is attractive."	The site is designed with aesthetics in mind
3	"The hover box on the right is very handy. The booking function can be found immediately."	Some users think so, but some don't find it
4	"The 'Collections' section has categories of artefacts, which is convenient."	Some of the site's category features are well done

Table 8. The part of the design that users feel most dissatisfied with.

No.	The most dissatisfied design	Analysis
1	"The right hover box is poorly positioned and easily overlooked."	The site highlights key features, but ignores the user's centre of attention
2	"It is unreasonable to classify cultural and creative products as services."	Users feel that this irrational classification has a serious impact on efficiency of use
3	"There is a confusing overlap in 'information' and 'activity' concepts."	Unclear functional classification of the website
4	"None of the functions listed in the front of the navigation bar are what the user wants."	The website does not order the navigation bars according to the importance of the user's needs
5	"Knew where the target was, but there was so much information that I ignored it."	Too much information conveyed on the page, not enough simplicity
6	"The Search is unobtrusive and the grey font is confusing."	Website design needs to consider the psychological impact of colour on the user

Contradiction Matrix. The vertical columns of the contradiction matrix represent the Improving Parameters, the horizontal rows represent the Worsening Parameters, and the corresponding invention principle numbers are in the cells. The final inventive principle is determined by the cross common numbering of the contradiction matrix. Using these generalised inventive principles, this study has led to specific solutions in the redesign of the website.

This paper identifies the logic, layout and content information issues of the Heyuan Dinosaur Museum, as shown in Table 9.

This study uses the TRIZ Contradiction Matrix to solve the above problem. There are three generic engineering parameters that need to be improved at the Heyuan Dinosaur Museum, which are NO. 25 (Loss of Time), NO. 33 (Ease of Operation), and NO. 36 (Device Complexity). The improvement parameter leads to a deterioration of three

Table 9. Problems of the website.

No.	Logic, layout, content problems
1	Cluttered organizational structure, Error information
2	Disordered information classification
3	Inconsistent functions
4	Incomplete feature priority
5	Dense information elements
6	Regional distribution problem
7	Vaguely similar classification category names
8	Duplicate menu content

parameters: NO. 24 (Loss of Information), NO. 32 (Ease of Manufacture), NO. 26 (Quantity of Substance). The improvement and deterioration parameters were included in the Contradiction Matrix, and the corresponding invention principle numbers were found and analysed in Table 10.

Table 10. TRIZ Contradiction Matrix.

Improving parameter	Worsen parameter		
	No. 24 loss of information	No. 26 quantity of substance	No. 32 ease of manufacture
No. 25 loss of time	24, 26, 28, 32	35, 38, 18, 16	35, 28, 34, 4
No. 33 ease of operation	4, 10, 27, 22	12, 35	2, 5, 12
No. 36 device complexity		13, 3, 27, 10	27, 26, 1, 13

Generally used in the field of engineering innovation, the TRIZ theory is needs to be applied flexibly in the context of website design. In this study, the inventive principle numbers obtained from the matrix are combined with the concepts of website design and the final inventive principles selected are NO. 1 (Segmentation); NO. 2 (Taking Out), NO. 4 (Asymmetry), NO. 5 (Merging), NO. 10 (Preliminary Action) and NO. 12 (Equipotentiality). Based on the above principles, this study proposes conceptual ideas to solve the problem, as shown in Table 11. The specific solutions are described in detail in the next section.

Table 11. Improvement directions of the website.

TRIZ principles	Explanation	Resolutions for website redesign
No. 1 segmentation	Divide the system into independent parts	Disassembling and re-categorising the navigation bar and menu
No. 2 Taking out	Pull out only the necessary parts of the system	Simplify information and avoid too many elements
No. 4 asymmetry	Design the functions differently	Highlight the design of the search function, distinguish it from the layout of other functions
No. 5 merging	Combine similar functions	Ensuring consistency of function
No. 10 preliminary action	Make the changes to the system in advance	Standardise the overall page layout and adjust the typography
No. 12 Equipotentiality	Make similar components are at the same level	Redesign the hierarchy of functions to place functions at the same level in the same menu

4.2 Website Optimization

Based on the directions provided by the TRIZ principles, this paper redesigned the website. The paper divides the improved design into six sections that address some of the logic, page layout and content of the website.

Home Page. The main improvements to the home page are the page layout, the navigation bar categories and the ordering of features (see Fig. 4).

a) the ancient one   b) the redesign one

Fig. 4. Redesign the Home page.

The site was redesigned to increase the size of the navigation bar and pull back the visual focus. The design shortens the width of the rotating image on the home page and the incompleteness of the text suggests that there is content to be viewed below the site pages.

As users subconsciously perceived the hover bar on both sides as advertising in nature, this affected the experience. The optimised design removes the hover bar on both sides and groups the key features under Visit, keeping the site aesthetically pleasing and not affecting the use of key features.

The navigation bar on the home page is the key to guiding users to the target content. By adjusting the content of the columns, the final design of the six first-level columns are Home, Visiting, Exhibitions and Events, Collections, Cultural Creativity and About. Avoiding too many categories and too dense information elements, which makes users browse less efficiently. In accordance with the principle of importance, the functions that users care about are placed in the front.

As the search function is used more frequently, it is placed in a separate section above the navigation bar, adding an outer frame to make the area more obvious and have an emphasising effect.

Visit Page. In the hope that the changes are more intuitive and clear, this paper will be the bottom of the page unchanged intercepted off, leaving only the navigation bar modified places.

Content is the core of building a website, so it is important to pay attention to the rigor of content building. Optimize the design by dividing service functions to maintain functional consistency. The functions of booking and virtual exhibition hall are integrated into the visit pages, as shown in Fig. 5.

a) the ancient one   b) the redesign one

Fig. 5. Redesign the Visit sub-menu.

Exhibition and Event Page. As shown in Fig. 6, titles of exhibitions become more distinctive. Integration of the Virtual Showroom function into the Visit function. A new Event function has been added, with the Exhibition and Event functions are on the same page. The Exhibition is in the top half of the page and the Event are in the bottom half, so that user can slide through them.

Collection Page. As shown in Fig. 7, The Collection News and Protection Reports have been transferred from the Collection to the About category. The only function that remains in Collection is Collection Enjoy.

Cultural and Creativity Page. As the core product of the museum, the cultural and creative product represents the brand image of the museum and a reflection of its external

a) the ancient one of sub-menu　　b) the redesign one of sub-menu

c) the ancient one of specific page　　d) the redesign one of specific page

Fig. 6. Redesign the Exhibition and Event sub-menu and specific page.

a) the ancient one of sub-menu　　b) the redesign one of sub-menu

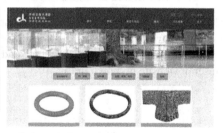

c) the ancient one of specific page　　d) the redesign one of specific page

Fig. 7. Redesign the Collection page.

influence. It is also a category that should be taken seriously, given the needs of design researchers.

As the original website did not have a separate sub-category for culture, it has been designed a new category for Cultural and Creativity. As shown in Fig. 8, the related categories of Cultural Forum, Academic Achievements and Cultural and Creative Products are set as its secondary menu (see Fig. 8).

About Page. The redesign site has set up the less frequently used functions in the About category, and has named the sub-categories carefully. For example, the original page was named 'Information', which could be mistaken for news events instead of the real museum building information (Fig. 9).

Fig. 8. New Cultural and Creativity sub-menu.

Fig. 9. New about sub-menu.

4.3 Satisfaction and Evaluation Results

The original eight participants were conducted the System Usability Scale assessment and interviews of the redesigned websites.

A comparison of the scores before and after the optimisation of the design of the museum website is shown in Fig. 10.

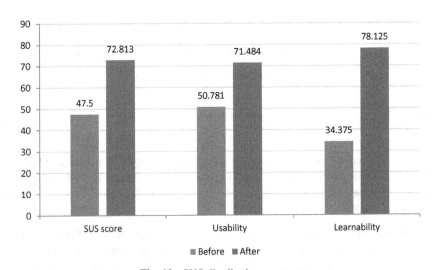

Fig. 10. SUS distribution contrast.

The data shows that the overall satisfaction of the optimised website has improved. The usability score of 71.5 indicates that the changes made to the logic, layout and content design of the website are effective. Secondly, users' scores on Learnability increased significantly, indicating that users felt the website did not require much experience to operate and became easier to operate and master.

User reviews of the prototype shown in Table 12. Comments and analysis of users for the prototype.

Table 12. Comments and analysis of users for the prototype.

No.	Participants' comments	Analysis
1	"Navigation is now clearer and easier than ever before"	Users only look for information they care about
2	"The features I was looking for were in plain sight and easy to find"	Ranking of functions according to user needs is necessary
3	"The pop-up window on the home page disappeared, it looks better"	Visual design is an important element of the user experience
4	"The classification of cultural and creative products has become clear "	Clear categories are very helpful in improving the usability of a website

5 Discussion and Conclusions

This study encountered some problems throughout the process of researching and improving the user experience for the website of the Heyuan Dinosaur Museum, and is also exploring findings and gains. As researchers, it is important to respond to trends and changes, and continuously improve the user experience of the website in design iterations. At the same time, based on the observation and analysis of the results of the experimental process, the following conclusions were harvested.

1. Perceived effect, information content and overall quality will significantly affect user satisfaction with the website. The most important design to improve website usability is the organization and layout of the pages. Only when a website is clearly structured and logically organized, can users easily find what they want. The efficiency of the website has a positive impact on user behavior. This means that high-availability websites are visited more frequently, which is undoubtedly beneficial to the long-term development of the museum.
2. Depending on the main users, the most important design directions differ from one website to another. For museum websites that have a specific primary user, users have their own purpose, the design of navigation and functional categories is very important. The information content needs to be concise and not cause pressure to the user to navigate. The overall design of the museum needs to be a comprehensive balance of user needs and museum needs.

3. Presenting an aesthetically pleasing website is likely to attract the attention of users, thereby increasing the time people spend on the page and the desire to visit the museum. Museum websites that offer aesthetic value are more likely to enhance users' enjoyment of browsing websites. Museum websites need to consider their appearance design, with a logical layout, uniform colour scheme, simple fonts and a selection of quality images.

4. The iteration of the museum website needs to respond to changing times and explore new functions in a user-centric model. The future museum website needs to focus on the interactive experience with users, design online access functions, display dynamic cultural relics and other more interactive functions.

The needs of users determine the development direction of the museum. In feature of user-centric, the design and development of the future museum website needs to analyze the user's functional requirements, design the logic of the website structure, and classify it according to the importance of the function. It is expected that the website design is logical, the structure is clear, the information is concise, the content is clear, the interaction is interesting, and it will bring users a better user experience.

Acknowledgement. The author expresses sincere gratitude to those who provided advice and assistance. The work is supported by Central University project of South China University of Technology [grant number x2sjC2181490 "Research on Product Systematic Innovation for industrial design"].

References

1. Pallud, J., Straub, D.W.: Effective website design for experience-influenced environments: the case of high culture museums. Inf. Manage. **51**(3), 359–373 (2014)
2. Sauro, J., Lewis, J.R.: Quantifying the User Experience: Practical Statistics for User Research, 2nd edn. Morgan Kaufmann, San Francisco (2016)
3. Ji, Q.: Research on the Redesign of Gansu Provincial Museum's Official Website. Lanzhou Jiaotong University, Lanzhou City (2020)
4. Nielsen, J.: Usability Engineering, 1st edn. Morgan Kaufmann, Burlington (1994)
5. Sun, Y., Ikovenko, S.: TRIZ: The Golden Key to Open the Door of Innovation. I. Science Press, Beijing (2015)
6. Al'tshuller, G.S.: The Innovation Algorithm: TRIZ, Systematic Innovation and Technical Creativity. Technical Innovation Center Inc., Worcester (1999)
7. Batemanazan, V., Jaafar, A., Kadir, R.A., Nayan, N.M.: Improving usability with TRIZ: a review. In: Badioze Zaman, H., et al. (ed.) Advances in Visual Informatics. IVIC 2017. LNCS, vol. 10645, pp. 625–635. Springer, Cham (2017). https://doi.org/10.1007/978-3-319-70010-6_58

Understanding Task Differences to Leverage the Usability and Adoption of Voice Assistants (VAs)

Isabela Motta$^{(\boxtimes)}$ (ID) and Manuela Quaresma (ID)

LEUI | Laboratory of Ergodesign and Usability of Interfaces, PUC-Rio, Rio de Janeiro, Brazil
isabelamotta@aluno.puc-rio.br, mquaresma@puc-rio.br

Abstract. Voice Assistants (VAs) are becoming increasingly popular, but evidence shows that users' utilization of features is limited to few tasks. Although the literature has shown that usability impact VA adoption, little is known about how usability varies across VA tasks and its relation to task adoption by users. To address this gap, we conducted usability tests followed by debriefing sessions with Siri and Google Assistant users, assessing usability measures of six features and uncovering reasons for task usage. The results showed that usability varied across tasks regarding task completeness, error number, error types, and user satisfaction. Checking the weather and making phone calls had the best usability measures, followed by playing songs and sending messages, whereas adding appointments to a calendar and searching for information were the most incomplete and frustrating interactions. Furthermore, usability-related factors such as perceived ease of use and the interaction's hands/eyes-free nature influenced task adoption. Nevertheless, we also identified other task-independent factors that affect VA usage, such as use context (i.e., place, task content), VAs' personality, and preferences for settings. Our main contributions are recommendations for VA design, highlighting that attending to tasks separately is paramount to understanding specific usability issues, task requirements, users' perceptions of features, and developing design solutions that leverage VAs' usability and adoption.

Keywords: Voice Assistants · Usability · Technology adoption

1 Introduction

Voice Assistants (VAs), such as Apple Siri and Google Assistant, are artificial intelligence-powered virtual agents that can perform a range of tasks in a system, which users interact through a voice interface that may be supported by a visual display [40]. They run on several devices, such as earphones, smart speakers, and smartphones, and were estimated to be in use in over four billion devices by 2020 [26]. The projections for VAs indicate that interfaces for human-computer interaction (HCI) are in the midst of a paradigm shift from visual interfaces to hands-free, voice-based interactions [40].

Despite the growth in VA adoption, evidence shows that users do not utilize all tasks available in these systems. By 2020, Amazon's Alexa was able to perform over 70.000 skills in the USA [37]. Nevertheless, studies have shown that users' utilization of these

© Springer Nature Switzerland AG 2021
M. M. Soares et al. (Eds.): HCII 2021, LNCS 12781, pp. 483–502, 2021.
https://doi.org/10.1007/978-3-030-78227-6_35

devices is limited to tasks such as checking the weather, adding reminders, listening to music, and controlling home automation [1, 5, 10, 11, 18, 30, 33, 34, 38, 39, 42]. The discrepancy in task availability and feature adoption may suggest that user experience across tasks is heterogeneous, leading to the underutilization of VAs.

The literature indicates varied causes for VA usage and abandonment that may account for such incongruity. Among these motivators, we hypothesize that usability-related factors may be essential for task adoption. While users' attitudes and data privacy concerns are influential [4, 6, 17, 24, 27, 28], these aspects are usually determinant for VA usage as a whole interface rather than for specific features. Conversely, users perceive tasks to have varying levels of difficulty [22] and satisfaction with task types is affected by different factors [14], suggesting inconsistent usability across features.

Although usability issues have been extensively covered in the field of voice interaction, most publications tend to study the VA as a single entity instead of attending to system features separately. Whereas such an approach is useful for understanding users' general impressions and highlighting VAs' major strengths and flaws, it is necessary to regard task specificities to comprehend why users abandon some features. To the extent of our knowledge, no study has examined differences in the usability of VA tasks and their relationship to task adoption.

Thus, this study aimed to assess usability variations in six VA tasks and its relations to VA adoption. Two research questions were developed:

- **RQ1:** How does usability vary across VA tasks?
- **RQ2:** How is usability related to task adoption in VAs?

To answer these questions, we conducted usability tests followed by debriefing sessions with users of Siri and Google Assistant (GA). Participants performed six tasks in both Siri and GA on smartphones: check the weather, make a phone call, search for information, play a song, send a message, and add an appointment to a calendar. In the debriefing sessions, users talked about their perceptions of the tasks and stated reasons for adopting – or not – such VA features in their routines. Our findings showed that task completeness, number and types of errors, and satisfaction varied across tasks, and usability-related factors were mentioned as motivators for feature adoption and abandonment. Moreover, other factors such as customization, VAs' personality, and use context impacted usage. Our main contributions are recommendations for VA design.

2   Related Work

2.1   Task Adoption by VA Users

Although VA adoption has been steadily increasing over the years, several studies have shown that users' utilization of features is limited to a small set of tasks. Commonly used features reported in the literature are playing music, checking the weather, and setting timers, alarms, and reminders [1, 5, 10, 11, 18, 30, 33, 34, 38, 39, 42]. Users also utilize VAs for looking up information [1, 10, 11, 33, 34] such as recommendations on places to eat or visit [20, 42], recipes [21], information about sports and culture [21, 42], and for learning-related activities [12, 21, 33]. Another frequently mentioned task in the literature is controlling Internet of Things (IoT) devices such as lights and thermostats [1, 5, 10, 11, 33, 34, 39, 42], although these features are more commonly performed through smart speakers. Moreover, VAs are used for entertainment purposes: telling jokes, playing games, and exploring the VAs' personality [5, 10, 12, 34, 38, 39]. Other tasks such as creating lists, sending messages, checking the news, and managing calendar appointments are relatively underused, as shown by industry reports on commercially available VAs [25, 29, 41].

2.2 Usability and VA Adoption

As mentioned above, several factors impact VA adoption. Particularly, perceived ease of use has been demonstrated to cause a significant effect on VA usage [27] and may be related to task completeness and effort. On the one hand, due to the use of speech, voice interaction is considered easy and intuitive [31], and the possibility of a hands/eyes-free interaction is valued by users [20] and motivates them to adopt a VA [22, 28, 30]. On the other hand, errors throughout interactions may lead to frustration and underutilization. Purington et al. [35] analyzed Amazon Echos' online reviews and identified that technical issues with the VAs' functioning were associated with decreased user satisfaction levels. As argued by Lopatovska et al. [19], unsatisfactory interactions cause users to lower their VA usage over time.

A central theme around errors in user-VA interaction is VAs' conversational capabilities. While some users expected to have human-like conversations with their VAs, actual system capabilities lead to disappointment and eventual abandonment of the device [5, 22, 30]. Speech recognition problems also impose entry barriers to new users. Motta and Quaresma [28] observed through an online questionnaire that one of the reasons for smartphone users not to adopt a VA was poor query recognition. Likewise, Cowan et al. [6] conducted focus groups with infrequent users and showed that speech recognition problems are a core barrier to VA usage.

Specifically, studies indicated that users consider VAs inefficient to recognize accents and are limited in terms of supported languages [6, 11, 15, 20, 23]. Furthermore, VAs fail to bear contextual references, such as users' physical locations and information provided in past interactions [1, 10, 11, 20–22, 36]. Given these conversational limitations, users often need to adapt their speech to match the VA's capacity, which is an obstacle to VA adoption [28]. Speech adaptations include pronouncing words more accurately [8, 30], removing words, using specific terms, speaking more clearly, changing accents [22], and removing contextual references [1, 22, 30]. Additionally, users have reported needing to check if their commands were understood in a visual interface or provide manual confirmations, making interactions slower [6, 39].

2.3 Differences in Usability Across VA Tasks

The literature provides indications that VA tasks may have different usability. Firstly, Luger and Sellen [22] identified that users judge tasks to be simple (e.g., setting reminders, checking the weather) or complex (e.g., launching a call, writing an email). The authors note that failures such as query misrecognition in complex tasks were more frequent, leading users to feel that the VA could not be trusted for certain activities and limit their usage to simple features. These results echo Oh et al.'s [30] findings, who conducted a 14-day study in which users interacted with a VA, Clova, in a realistic setting (i.e., their homes). The study's participants reported that interaction failures caused them to stop performing complicated and difficult tasks and focus on simple features with reliable results (e.g., weather reports, listen to music).

Further evidence on task differences was provided by Kiseleva et al. [14], who conducted a user study to evaluate variables impacting satisfaction in the use of Cortana for three task types: "control device" (e.g., play a song, set a reminder), "web search," and "structured search dialogue" (tasks that required multiple steps). The authors found that, while user satisfaction was negatively correlated with effort for all task types, the "device control" and "structured search dialogue" tasks were the only ones in which satisfaction was positively correlated with query recognition quality and task completion. That is, for the "web search" activity exclusively, achieving the desired result with good speech recognition did not necessarily guarantee satisfaction. A similar tendency was observed by Lopatovska et al. [19], who collected users' experiences with Alexa through online diaries. The study showed that, even though most participants reported interactions' success to be positively related to satisfaction, there were occasions in which successful interactions were rated as unsatisfactory and vice-versa.

The literature described above provides indications that usability variations across tasks may contribute to discrepancies in task adoption by VA users. As little is known around such a topic, it is necessary to investigate how usability may vary in different VA tasks and how it is related to task adoption in VAs.

3 Method

3.1 Participants and Test's Format

The study's participants were Brazilian smartphone users who used at least one VA on their smartphones – Siri and/or Google Assistant (GA) – at least once a month. The users were recruited by social media and chat apps.

The usability tests had a within-subject design (2 × 6) in which participants had to perform six tasks using Siri and GA on a smartphone. To increase participants' immersion in the test, all tasks revolved around the scenario of a musical concert that was to occur, in which participants were hypothetically interested in attending.

We selected the VAs and tasks based on the literature and a previously conducted survey with Brazilian smartphone users. We chose Siri and GA since these were the most commonly used VAs among our survey's respondents. Tasks with different adoption rates were selected to assess whether usability would vary across tasks and cause discrepancies in task adoption. The tasks selected for this study were: searching for information online, checking the weather, making a phone call, playing a song, adding an appointment to a calendar, and sending a message.

3.2 Apparatus

Two smartphones were used in the usability tests: a Motorola G4 Play running Android 7.1.1. OS for GA and an iPhone XR running iOS 12.4.1. for Siri. We recorded users in video and audio using a webcam placed above their hands, a notebook's camera positioned towards their faces, and apps capturing the smartphones' screens (Fig. 1).

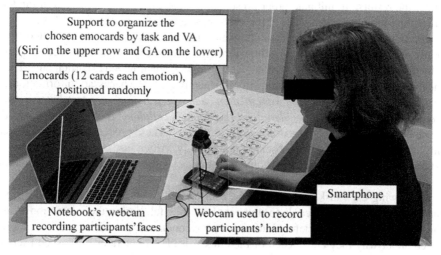

Support to organize the chosen emocards by task and VA (Siri on the upper row and GA on the lower)

Emocards (12 cards each emotion), positioned randomly

Smartphone

Notebook's webcam recording participants' faces

Webcam used to record participants' hands

Fig. 1. Usability test set up.

Moreover, to represent user satisfaction with tasks, we employed the emocards tool [7]. According to Desmet et al. [7], having users describe their emotions towards a product may be challenging since they are difficult to verbalize and users' answers may be affected by cognitive involvement. To tackle this problem, the authors developed the emocards [7]: a set of 16 cards that picture cartoon faces with eight different emotional expressions (eight male faces and eight female faces). The expressions represent emotions that combine levels of two emotional dimensions: Pleasantness and Arousal.

We chose the emocards for this study to help users illustrate their emotional responses and understand how – in terms of pleasantness and arousal – different tasks impact users' satisfaction. We highlight that the emocards were not considered an objective metric for measuring exact levels of satisfaction. Instead, our primary goal in employing this tool was to start a conversation between participants and the moderator [7] during the debriefing sessions to clarify the reasons for users' choice of emotional responses. Each emocard was printed 12 times (for two rounds of six tasks), and a support was developed to help participants registering their preferred emocards.

3.3 Procedure

The usability tests were arranged in three parts: 1) introduction, 2) two rounds of task performance, and 3) debriefing session. In the introduction, participants read and signed a term of consent and filled a digital form to gather profile data. The moderator provided an oral explanation concerning the experiment's goal and procedure.

Users performed tasks through Siri and GA. Independently of participants' previous experience with the VAs, each round started with guidance on how to activate the VA, followed by a training session. Thereafter, all participants performed a trial task (ask for a joke). The initial preparation and training served the purpose of getting participants familiarized with the system and its functioning so that learnability issues would not affect the results. To mitigate order presentation bias, tasks were presented in random order. For the same reason, half of the users started with Siri and half with GA.

Participants were instructed to complete the tasks using the VAs. The moderator orally presented the tasks, one at a time, through a previously scripted instruction. Cards with the information necessary to complete the tasks were provided to participants. Thus, the moderator would give the oral instruction and point to the necessary information, as in the following example: *"You want to attend Sandy and Junior's concert, but you don't want to go alone. So, you decide to call this friend's cellphone* [points to the contact's name on the card] *to ask if he wants to go with you."* These procedures were validated through two pilot studies. We observed that entirely written instructions not only led to confusion but also influenced participants' queries, as they would read the instruction instead of creating their own phrases.

Following each task, participants were instructed to choose one among the eight randomly positioned emocards to illustrate how they felt during the interaction. After the tests' two rounds, debriefing interviews were conducted, in which participants were asked about why they chose each of the emocards. The moderator also asked users if and why they utilized a VA to perform the six tasks in their routines. The tests were conducted from September to November 2019, and sessions lasted around 45 min.

3.4 Data Analysis

For the data analysis, we reviewed the video and audio recordings and analyzed task usability by measuring task completeness, number and types of errors per task, and user satisfaction. We attributed four levels of completeness to measure mean task completeness: *completed* - user completes the task in the first attempt; *completed with effort* - user completes the task but has to try two or more times to do so; *partially completed* - user only completes a part of the task successfully (e.g., schedules an event to the calendar at the correct day but misses the place); *incomplete* - user gives up or achieves a failed result (e.g., plays a song different from what was asked). As for the error types, we described and recorded errors throughout interactions for each task. We considered errors to be any VA output that did not directly answer a request or moved the interaction forwards (e.g., asking the appointment's time). An affinity diagram was made in a bottom-up approach [2] to identify similarities and create categories of errors.

To assess the effects of varied tasks on user satisfaction, the number of emocards chosen by participants for each task was accounted. This analysis was graphically represented to identify patterns in users' preferred emotional responses (regarding pleasantness and arousal) towards the tasks. Moreover, to understand the causes of satisfaction variations, we related the emocards to arguments stated by participants in the debriefing interviews for choosing them. For this cross-checking, we categorized users' claims through an affinity diagram [2].

We employed a similar procedure to analyze users' reasons for adopting tasks in their daily VA usage. Firstly, we transcribed participants' answers and then created affinity diagrams [2] to find categories of reasons to use or not the VA for each task.

4   Results

4.1   Task Usability

In this section, we address RQ1: *"How does usability vary across VA tasks?"*

Task Completeness. Figure 2 shows that the tasks had large variations concerning their completeness. Checking the weather and making a phone call were completed by all participants, and only 8% of the interactions required effort to be successful. Moreover, most participants were able to play a song, but 18% of the trials were ineffective. Sending a message was considered complete for only 30% of the interactions, and most participants had to issue their commands more than once to complete the task. The search task had the greatest number of failed interactions (43%), whereas adding an appointment to the calendar had the highest mean for partially complete outcomes (63%) and the lowest task completeness mean (3%), as only one participant was able to complete the task in his first try.

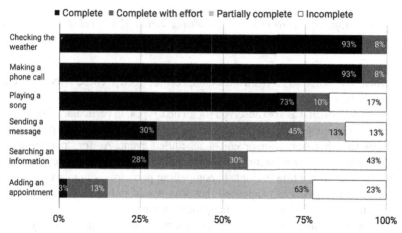

Fig. 2. Task completeness per task (n = 40 interactions per task, i.e., 20 on Siri and 20 on GA).

Number of Errors Per Task. Variations in the number of errors followed similar patterns to task completeness scores (Fig. 3). Few errors happened during weather reports and phone calls, whereas playing a song led to a higher number of errors. Akin to completeness results, in which the calendar task had the lowest completeness rate, "adding an appointment to the calendar" had the largest number of errors. Nevertheless, although "sending a message" had a smaller count of incomplete results when compared to "searching information" (Fig. 2), fewer errors happened during the web search. This difference may mean that participants either gave up the search task sooner or recovered more quickly from errors throughout "sending a message" failures.

Error Types. As completeness and error number, error types varied across tasks. We identified nine error categories: 1) *Query misrecognition*; 2) *Unrequired task;* 3) *System*

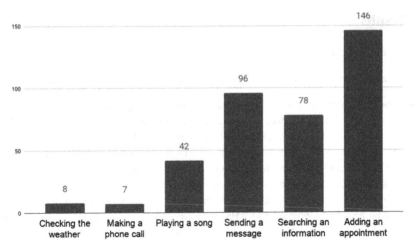

Fig. 3. Number of errors per task (nTotal = 377).

error; 4) *Interruption;* 5) *No capture;* 6) *Editing error;* 7) *Cancellation/confirmation error;* 8) *Request for visual/manual interaction;* 9) *Wrong application.*

Query Misrecognition errors were the most frequent error for all features and happened when VAs failed to recognize users' speech correctly. These issues made users repeat themselves and led to subsequent errors such as Unrequired Task (i.e., performing the wrong task), which was also observed for all task types. In particular, VAs frequently misrecognized appointments' information (i.e., the name, date, time, or place), forcing participants to either start over or edit a scheduled event. As for "playing a song," Query Misrecognition errors were less recurrent than we expected. Since we intentionally chose a song with a title in English, compelling participants to mix two languages (Portuguese and English), we supposed that VAs would fail to understand the song's title. Nevertheless, such an issue only happened six times.

Interruptions occurred when VAs stopped capturing users' inputs midway. No Capture errors were failures from VAs to capture *any* user input (i.e., the assistant did not "hear" participants from the beginning). We observed both issues for all task types, but they were more recurrent for "sending a message" and "adding an appointment."

This tendency might be attributed to the lengthiness of commands issued for these tasks. The message comprised all of the concert's information, resulting in commands with several words. For the same reason, scheduling an event led to long queries when users tried to say all information at once (e.g., "Add to my calendar 'Show Sandy & Junior' on November 9th at 9:30 pm at Parque Olímpico"). No Capture errors were also identified for "step-by-step" interactions (e.g., "What is the appointment's date and time?"), since participants had trouble matching VAs' timing to start input capture.

Contrarily to the issues mentioned above, System Errors were observed mostly during search and sending a message. Systems Errors were bugs or the VAs' inability to fulfill an inquiry. On several occasions, Siri answered search requests by saying, "Sorry, I don't have an answer for that," causing users to give up, especially when the assistant kept repeating the same output after participants adjusted their commands (e.g., changed wording). Likewise, outputs as "Ops, try again" in the message task were frequent and required participants to restate their messages, an effortful work.

Cancellation/Confirmation Errors were problems for confirming or canceling actions and occurred in the calendar and message tasks. Editing Errors were also exclusive for these tasks and happened when users tried to change a message's content or an event's information. We believe that such problems arose exclusively for these features due to their characteristics. Confirmations and cancellations were unnecessary for most tasks as VAs presented outputs without requiring users' permission. Similarly, results for other tasks were not editable and iterations on previous outcomes were unfeasible.

Furthermore, we considered Requests for Manual/Visual interactions as errors since VAs are supposedly a hands/eyes-free interface, and the literature has shown that users deem such requests as failures [22]. On occasions, participants had to read a search result on the screen, complete the appointments' details manually, or press a button to play the song. Finally, Wrong Application errors happened when users explicitly asked the VA to send a message through a specific app (WhatsApp, as requested by the moderator), but it executed the task using a different application.

User Satisfaction. Figure 4 illustrates the number of each emocard chosen by participants for the test's tasks.

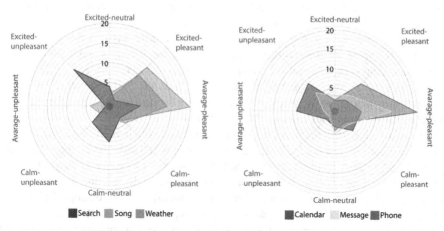

Fig. 4. Distribution of selected emocards for each task.

Except for one participant who chose an unpleasant emotion for the phone task, no other unpleasant emotions were evoked towards making a phone call and checking the weather. A mild preference for neutral emotions was also observed for both tasks. Similarly, playing a song and sending a message elicited mostly pleasant emotions on participants. Nevertheless, users preferred unpleasant emotions on seven occasions for the song task, and we observed two additional points of concentration in participants' emotional preferences for the message task: the "calm-neutral" and "excited-unpleasant" emocards. Participants selected unpleasant emotions towards searching for information and adding an event to the calendar in most cases. We identified a substantial convergence of emotional preferences for the "excited-unpleasant" emocard for both tasks, but the same does not occur for the "excited-pleasant" emocard. A preference for the "calm-neutral" emotion can also be observed for the search task.

Causes for Variations in Satisfaction. The leading causes for variations in user satisfaction were identified in the arguments stated by participants to reason their choices in the debriefing sessions and organized into the following categories: 1) *task completeness,* 2) *perceived ease of use,* 3) *expectations for VAs capabilities and limitations,* 4) *hands/eyes-free aspects of the interaction,* and 5) *individual preferences for settings.*

Firstly, *task completeness* yielded variations in user satisfaction for all tasks. On the one hand, participants who selected pleasant emocards stated that they felt happy and satisfied with completing the tasks. On the other hand, unpleasant emotions were related to unsatisfactory results. As for the neutral emotions, some participants stated that they faced unexpected outcomes but ultimately managed to complete the task.

"Excited-pleasant" emocards were chosen when VAs' answers were perfect or surprising: *"It entered the site and gave me the temperature without any mistakes"* (P10; Weather). Some participants stated that their preference for the "average-pleasant" emocard was due to interactions that were good enough to complete the task: *"It picked a random* [song's] *live version that I didn't really choose, but it handled what I wanted"* (P9; Song). Similarly, "calm-pleasant" emotions were related to incomplete or deficient results: *"It wasn't exactly perfect. Siri put* [the appointment] *as if it was from 9 pm to 9:30 pm, not starting at 9:30 pm"* (P7; Calendar). Contrarily, answers that were insufficient to fulfill requests or too different from users' expectations caused them to choose the "excited-unpleasant" emocard: *"I was upset. Siri didn't even try giving me a result similar to what I asked. It just said 'I didn't understand.'"* (P9; Search). Thus, task completeness may strongly affect users' preferences for pleasantness, and the quality of VAs actions might impact emotions' levels of arousal.

Secondly, the debriefings' results show that interactions' *perceived ease of use* may affect the emotion's levels of pleasantness and arousal for all tasks. Overall, the "excited-pleasant" and "average-pleasant" emocards were related to the quick, easy, objective, and automatic interactions. Unpleasant emocards were selected due to hardships in interactions, illustrating frustration, sadness, anger, annoyance, and disappointment. The perceived ease of use category showed how error types affected satisfaction.

Concerning VAs' communication capacity, the easiness in communicating with the VA was commented by participants in the multi-step calendar task and for playing a song, which required participants to speak in English. Two participants stated that they chose an "excited-pleasant" emotion due to cues given by the VAs that helped them adding the appointment: *"I was happy with Siri because it asked me everything: 'What's the date?' and I answered. (…) It was really easy to set up everything"* (P5; Calendar). Similarly, participants who preferred the "excited-neutral" emotions expressed surprise for playing a song more easily than they expected: *"I was surprised it understood my request in English because I generally try, and it doesn't understand"* (P5; Song). Differently, not being able to communicate with the system led to confusion and frustration: *"I couldn't find the logic that Siri understands. (…) I felt incompetent. Awful. As if I don't know how to communicate"* (P20; Calendar).

Particularly, query misrecognition was related to the "excited-unpleasant" emocard for sending messages, adding events to the calendar, and searching for information. *"Google was kind of dumb. I said everything. All the information was there, and it simply put everything as the* [appointment's] *title."* (P15; Calendar). As mentioned before, such obstacles made users repeat themselves, eliciting unpleasant emotions especially when they could not complete the task even after various interactions: *"Siri kept repeating the same question, and it made me upset because I had already said it several times and it didn't recognize it"* (P12; Calendar). Additionally, interruptions led to the selection of the "excited-unpleasant" emocard: *"It made me anxious. It did not wait for me to end the message. (…). I didn't know how to explain to Siri not to interrupt me after the 'period'"*. (P18; Message).

Furthermore, Editing Errors impacted users' preferred emotions for the message and calendar tasks. A user who chose a "calm-neutral" emocard argued that: *"Although I needed some interactions, I could send the message I wanted"* (P17; Message). Nonetheless, a participant selected the emotion "excited-unpleasant" because: *"Google asked me for the* [appointment's] *end-time. I don't know why, but it set it up for* [the following year]. *I tried to edit it but I couldn't, so I just had to save it as it was."* (P7; Calendar). Therefore, being able to edit outcomes and recover from errors may affect user satisfaction since it determines whether interactions will be successful.

We also identified that users might have had varied *expectations for VAs' capabilities and limitations* for different tasks. Adding an event to the calendar was considered complex due to the number of steps needed to achieve it, as was the recognition of slangs, question intonation, queries that mixed languages, and editing. Contrarily, checking the weather, making a phone call, and searching the internet were considered basic for a VA: *"Checking the weather is a simple request. So, there's a smaller chance of a communication fault."* (P14; Weather).

Participants who selected pleasant emotions despite facing hardships argued that they did not blame the VA. Rather, they believed to have expressed their queries inadequately or considered the task too complicated: *"It got it* [song's name] *wrong, but it was my fault because I said 'fells' instead of 'fails'"* (P6; Song); *"I put a slang, and it didn't recognize the slang. It wasn't perfect, but I was expecting that. It's too hard."* (P8; Message). Differently, errors that happened throughout simple activities evoked unpleasant emotions: *"I couldn't complete the task that is supposed to be banal. It gave me what I wanted, but not in the right way"* (P3; Search). Hence, expectations of VAs' capabilities for each task may affect the interactions' perceived ease of use and perceived quality of the outcomes, impacting satisfaction.

Moreover, the *hands-free and eyes-free aspects of the VAs* impacted users' preferred emotional responses, but such issues affected participants differently. Users who chose "calm-pleasant" and "calm-neutral" emotions argued that they could complete the task despite having to finish it visually or manually: *"If it had read the article's text out loud, I would have been more satisfied, but it showed the results, so I was satisfied."* (P13, Search). However, unpleasant emotions were selected by some users, who argued that this compromises the voice interaction's advantages. *"If I say, 'create an event' and it answers, 'touch the screen,' it's almost an insult. I'm using the assistant because I don't want to touch the screen or because I can't touch the screen"* (P13, Calendar).

Finally, we observed that participants had different *preferences for settings* in checking the weather, making phone calls, and playing songs. For the weather task, participants had different opinions on the amount of information displayed on the interface. While some preferred more detailed weather prevision, others liked an objective answer. *"The interface was interesting because Siri showed me the temperatures for every hour of the day"* (P21, Weather). For making phone calls, Siri's option to call the house's or cellphone's number also divided opinions. Some users positively evaluated this feature, but others considered it an extra step to complete the task and pledged that VAs should know their preferred number and directly call it. *"Siri even gave me the options: 'Cellphone or house?', and I was like: 'Wow! Cellphone!'"* (P15, Phone). For both tasks, participants' individual preferences influenced the levels of arousal of their emotional responses, ranging from the "excited-pleasant" to the "calm-neutral" emocards, indicating a mild influence on user satisfaction.

However, users were more sensitive to their preferred apps to listen to music. The VAs executed users' commands by launching different music apps, evoking variations on both levels of pleasantness and arousal of users' emotional responses. Two participants who chose "excited-pleasant" emocard stated that they were happy because they completed the task, and the VA launched the app in which they usually listen to music. *"This one [emocard] is 'really happy' because I personally listen to music through YouTube much more often."* (P8, Song). On the other hand, three participants who preferred unpleasant emotions stated that despite being able to finish the task, the apps launched by the VAs were not the ones they commonly use: *"iPhone insists on taking me to iTunes or Apple Music"* (P4, Song).

4.2 Task Adoption

During the debriefing sessions, we asked users to state whether they used the test's tasks in their daily VA usage and for which reasons. Figure 5 illustrated users' task adoption. Interestingly, while adoption means for all other tasks are in line with the usability scores, "search for information" was the most frequently employed feature by users. Despite having the largest number of incomplete outcomes (Fig. 2), placing third in the number of errors (Fig. 3), and yielding negative emotions on users for almost half of the interactions (Fig. 4), 17 out of 20 participants reported using a VA to search for information in their routines. Below, we present reasons stated by users to adopt tasks, addressing RQ2 (*"How is usability related to task adoption in VAs?"*).

We identified that usability is influential to task adoption, but other factors also affect tasks differently and impact VA usage. The motivators for feature usage were similar to the causes for variations in satisfaction: 1) *Hands/eyes-free interaction;* 2) *Ease of use;* 3) *Expectations and trust in VAs;* 4) *Preferences for settings and knowledge about VA features;* 5) *Usage context and task content;* and 6) *VAs' personality.*

In the first place, the possibility to interact with their smartphone without requiring their hands or eyes was the most cited reason for using a VA (16 participants). This motivator was mentioned for all tasks. Users argued that voice interaction is beneficial when manual interactions are not safe, practical, or possible. *"I use the assistant a lot when I'm driving, it's safer for me both having it read the message out loud and send the message by voice. So, I can be focused on the road and won't put my life in danger"*

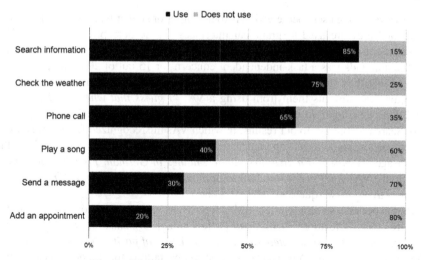

Fig. 5. Adoption rate by task (n = 20 participants).

(P11; Message). Use cases mentioned were cooking, driving, riding a bike, when their hands are dirty or injured, when they are multitasking, or when their smartphone is far away: *"Usually, I use it a lot while cooking. (...) I use it to search lots of things, like, 'I need a recipe for this.'"* (P13, Search).

Notwithstanding, the "eyes-free" characteristic of voice interaction also imposed barriers for some users in specific tasks. Ten users mentioned that activities such as handling a calendar, sending a message, and playing songs naturally require visual attention. Six participants preferred to add appointments manually because they needed to organize their appointments by colors and tags or visualize other scheduled events before adding a new one. *"I do it* [adding events] *by hands because it gives me more options to edit the event, and I like things to be organized"* (P16; Calendar). As for sending a message, five participants said that they preferred to look at unread messages before choosing which ones to answer and that VAs did not support features such as stickers, emojis, and audio messages. *"I don't know if Siri can do this, but I put little hearts and flowers emojis in my messages"* (P21; Message). Besides, five participants mentioned that they usually do not have a specific song in mind, so they need to look at the screen to decide what to play. *"Actually, sometimes I don't know what I want to listen to. I look at the album's list to choose."* (P19; Song).

The second motivator observed in our analysis was the perceived ease of use of performing tasks in VAs. Eleven participants reported that their VA usage was driven by user-VA interaction's easiness and quickness when compared to typing. As with the previous category, easy and quick interactions were a reason to perform all tasks. Specifically, for getting weather reports, three participants mentioned being used to voice interaction. *"I use Google* [Assistant] *a lot to check the weather. I think it's faster. (...) I just got used to it."* (P16; Weather); *"I don't even know where to click* [to check the weather on the smartphone], *so I feel it's easier by voice."* (P8; Weather).

However, some users perceived VAs to be harder or slower than manual interactions or claimed they are used to graphical interfaces. These perceptions did not affect a particular activity specifically. Likewise, the belief that VAs have issues recognizing users' commands was a task-independent concern for 15 out of 20 participants. Users believed that they should speak with VAs in a specific way, which led to a feeling of limitation that prevents them from using a VA. *"I guess that whenever I talk to her [Siri], I set up a logic in my head to communicate with her. It's not natural for me."* (P20, Search). Contrary to our results, in which VAs misrecognized few queries mixing two languages, some users reported having trouble with bilingual commands in their daily usage. *"Words in English, first names, names in German, French. I have to say them [to the VA], but I'm not sure how to pronounce it, so the odds of getting it right are low. So, I avoid these [queries]"* (P9, Message).

Past experiences seem to affect task adoption, as participants showed different trust levels for specific features. *"I say 'call [wife's name]' or something like this, and [the assistant] does it in just one step. (...) I have a history of positive results with it"* (P11; Phone). The trust in the VA determined their expectations for the outcomes of future interactions. Users mentioned that VAs are reliable for making phone calls and checking the weather. *"Checking the weather is the easiest, the most basic [task]. (...) I never had a problem with it"* (P3; Weather). Conversely, negative experiences with sending messages and playing songs led users to lose their trust in VAs. *"When I choose to type, the message is bigger or more elaborated, and I am sure Google [Assistant] will not recognize it."* (P10; Message); *"I don't even try [asking it to play the user's playlist]. I tried once or twice, but it got it all wrong, so I don't even try it."* (P13; Song).

Individual preferences for settings and the lack of knowledge of the VAs' capabilities for some features also caused users to adopt or not specific tasks. Six participants did not know that VAs could send messages, add appointments to a calendar, or play a song. Moreover, five participants said that they did not send messages through a VA because they used WhatsApp, and they were unaware of the VAs integration with this app. Similarly, six users claimed that their preferred applications to play songs and manage a calendar were not supported by their VAs. *"[Siri] goes straight to Apple Music, and I never use it (...) [Nor Apple Music] nor Siri"* (P4; Music).

Our results showed that the usage context and task content might impact users' decisions regarding performing activities through a VA. For example, four users explained that they only listen to music through a VA if they have already chosen which song to play. Moreover, three participants mentioned the complexity of the task's content to search for information (P2) and add appointments to the calendar (P3, P9). *"It depends on the [appointment's] complexity. If it's just 'I have an exam on X day,' then I can do it by voice. But if it's more complex, with a longer description, I'd rather type"* (P3; Calendar). Also, independent of the feature, using the VA was considered inappropriate or embarrassing by six users for situations in which one must be silent (e.g., during class), when there is much background noise, or when other people are listening to interactions. *"If I just got out of the doctor's office and I need to schedule a follow-up appointment (...), and I'm in front of the clerk, I won't open the assistant and speak in front of them. So, I just type"* (P15, Calendar).

Finally, six participants stated that they use a VA because they like its personality. Users mentioned liking voice interaction, enjoying testing and training the VA, and feeling futuristic or "high-tech." *"I feel very smart when I use it. Like, 'Man, I'm a genius! I was able to call by asking the assistant. And I didn't need to use my hands'. It feels magic when these things happen. I feel very clever, technological, and modern"*. (P16; Phone). This factor was also not related to a specific feature.

5 Discussion

Our study aimed to assess variations of usability in six VA tasks and their relations to VA adoption. Below, we provide recommendations for VA design by discussing our results in light of existing literature.

Firstly, **designers should examine VA features separately to assess discrepancies in task usability and motivators for task adoption.** Our findings highlight that VA tasks vary in task completeness, number and types of errors, and user satisfaction. Moreover, users adopt or neglect tasks based on usability-related factors, such as the hands/eyes-free nature of interactions, ease of use, and expectations and trust in VAs. Thus, analyzing tasks individually is essential to uncover a feature's particular usability issues that may otherwise be overlooked in general analysis and understand how it is related to VA adoption. Nonetheless, in line with previous research [6, 11, 15, 20, 22, 23, 39], our findings showed that query misrecognition problems and unrequired task performance were common across all analyzed features. The results also echoed literature indicating that other, more task-independent factors unrelated to usability impacted VA adoption, such as use context [6, 12, 17–19] and the VA's personality [9, 12, 22]. Hence, a comprehensive understanding of user-VA interaction is also vital to designing adequate interactions and leveraging VA adoption.

Secondly, **designers should consider users' perception of task easiness and provide support for complex tasks.** As indicated [22, 30], we observed that participants had varied expectations for how easy and satisfactory interactions with different tasks should be. Likewise, a single activity may vary in perceived complexity depending on its content (e.g., songs with foreign names may be considered more difficult for the VA). Although users are more forgiving of mistakes made in complex tasks [22], expectations and trust impact feature usage, causing users to engage in simple tasks more frequently (e.g., search) than complex activities (e.g., message).

The effects of such perceptions on task adoption may be substantial. As shown in previous studies and this study's results, voice search has a high adoption rate [1, 10, 11, 33, 34] despite the inadequate usability measures observed in this study. We hypothesize that such discrepancy may be due to users considering it an easy activity, among other factors. Notably, we believe users employ voice search in their routines to find other, more straightforward information than the one required on the test (i.e., the name of a band's next tour). Instead of abandoning the search feature when faced with errors, users might adjust their behavior to perform simpler searches that match the VAs' capacity. This possibility is reinforced by Kiseleva et al. [14], who indicated that task completeness and speech recognition are not linked to satisfaction with web searches in VAs, pointing that other advantages may outweigh failures.

Considering users' perceptions of task complexity, designers should understand which tasks users believe to be more challenging and unfold the reasons leading to these beliefs. Thereafter, specific solutions should be employed. As an example, we observed that multi-step activities (i.e., sending messages and adding events to a calendar) are more prone to interruptions or failures in capturing users' inputs. Thus, VAs should provide clear indicators to users about when to speak.

Despite designers' efforts to facilitate interactions, errors are deemed to occur. Therefore, **VAs should facilitate error recovery for users, and such support may vary for different tasks.** Our results converge with previous studies suggesting that task completeness and perceived ease of use strongly affect satisfaction [14, 35] and may shape users' trust and expectations for future interactions with VAs [3, 5, 22, 38]. Therefore, the possibility to recover from mistakes may restore both users' trust and satisfaction with the system. For example, despite having the second-largest number of obstacles, the message task had relatively positive satisfaction scores, as successful editing led to a great number of completed interactions.

To facilitate error recovery, VA responses are essential resources for users to understand trouble sources and handle errors [13, 32] However, as discussed, task characteristics may lead to different types of errors and require specific solutions. On the one hand, tasks in which VAs directly show outcomes are not editable (e.g., search), so it is essential that VAs explicitly present error sources. Responses such as "Sorry, I don't understand" do not display any useful information for error recovery and should be avoided. On the other hand, features that require confirmations or several pieces of information may be challenging for users, and therefore explicit or implicit (i.e., questions) instructions may be presented. Notwithstanding, as subsequential failures may further escalate frustration for editable activities, VAs should avoid repeatedly requesting the same information and allow users to follow other paths.

The hands and eyes-free nature of VA interaction is paramount for VA adoption overall. This interactional characteristic allows users to multitask and cause participants to perceived voice interaction as easier and more manageable than typing on some occasions. We believe that the convenience of a hands/eyes-free interaction may be another factor leveraging the "search" task, as such benefit may counterbalance eventual errors. Conversely, requests for manual interaction (e.g., confirmations) or visual attention (e.g., displaying a search's results on screen) were negatively evaluated by this study's participants, reinforcing previous literature findings [20, 22, 28, 30]. Hence, **VAs should always present interaction outputs auditorily**: the minimum amount of information necessary to fulfill users' commands should be presented out loud, and other complementary elements may be visually displayed if a screen is available (e.g., smartphone, tablet).

Nonetheless, the results indicate that users consider some activities to naturally require visual attention (e.g., scrolling to choose a song, organizing a calendar, or sending emojis on a message). Such statements highlight that, although users value voice-based commands, this characteristic alone may not be enough for users to transition from visual to voice interactions for specific activities. **Designers should understand differences in tasks' requirements to adapt visual tasks to voice interfaces adequately.** Comprehension of how users perform an activity indicates relevant factors and ways to translate features from graphical interfaces to voice interaction. Designers may employ methods such as task analysis to gather such awareness. For example, knowing that users eventually need to visualize a set of options to choose a song, VAs could offer music recommendations features based on user data.

Moreover, **VAs' settings should be customizable.** It was observed that participants' preferences for settings yielded variations in user satisfaction and affected task adoption. As indicated in previous studies [5, 20, 30], users desire to customize their VAs for a personalized experience. However, this study showed that participants were more susceptible to express frustration for undesired settings for music apps than for checking the weather or making phone calls, indicating that users attribute varied values for specific settings on different tasks.

Finally, **VAs' capabilities should be presented to users.** Our findings show that users do not engage in some features because they are unaware of the possibility of performing these activities. Likewise, several studies have indicated that VAs have issues of information transparency, including privacy-related data [1, 6, 16, 39], supported features [30], and system functioning [20]. Such evidence supports the hypothesis that the way information is presented to users is inappropriate, leaving out essential system descriptions, instructions, feedback, and privacy clarifications. Thus, designers must attend to information presentation in voice interaction.

6 Conclusion

Voice Assistant (VA) usage has been shown to be heterogeneous across features. Although the literature indicates that usability affects VA adoption, little was known about how usability varies across VA tasks and its relationship to task adoption. To address this gap, we conducted usability tests followed by debriefing sessions with VA users, assessing usability measures of six features and uncovering reasons for task usage. Our findings showed that task completeness, number and types of errors, and satisfaction varied across tasks, and usability-related factors were mentioned as motivators for feature adoption and abandonment. Moreover, other factors such as customization, VAs' personality, and usage context also impacted VA adoption. Our main contributions are recommendations for the design of VAs. We highlight that, while comprehensive approaches are still vital, attending to tasks separately is paramount to understand specific usability issues, task requirements, and users' perceptions of features, and consequently develop design solutions that leverage VAs' usability and adoption.

Nevertheless, our study had some limitations. Firstly, data privacy, which has been demonstrated to affect VA usage [4, 6, 24, 34], was not mentioned by our participants. This absence may be due to the usability tests' setting - as users were not sharing their own data -, and the debriefing sessions' dynamics, since participants were instructed to talk about each task separately instead of evaluating VAs generally. Furthermore, this study only evaluated six tasks, and therefore further examinations are needed to understand how other tasks' characteristics may impact VA usage. Finally, additional studies are needed to increase our recommendations' significance by indicating specific design solutions (e.g., how to present information about the VA to users appropriately).

Acknowledgements. This study was financed in part by the Coordenação de Aperfeiçoamento de Pessoal de Nível Superior - Brasil (CAPES) - Finance Code 001.

References

1. Ammari, T., Kaye, J., Tsai, J.Y., Bentley, F.: Music, search, and IoT. ACM Trans. Comput. Hum. Interact. **26**, 1–28 (2019). https://doi.org/10.1145/3311956
2. Barnum, C.: Usability Testing Essentials. Ready, Set... Elsevier, Burlington (2011)
3. Beneteau, E., Guan, Y., Richards, O.K., et al.: Assumptions Checked. Proc. ACM Interact. Mob. Wearable Ubiquit. Technol. **4**, 1–23 (2020). https://doi.org/10.1145/3380993
4. Burbach, L., Halbach, P., Plettenberg, N., et al.: "Hey, Siri", "Ok, Google", "Alexa". Acceptance-relevant factors of virtual voice-assistants. In: 2019 IEEE International Professional Communication Conference (ProComm), pp. 101–111. IEEE (2019)
5. Cho, M., Lee, S., Lee, K.-P.: Once a kind friend is now a thing: understanding how conversational agents at home are forgotten. In: Proceedings of the 2019 on Designing Interactive Systems Conference, pp. 1557–1569. Association for Computing Machinery, New York (2019)
6. Cowan, B.R., Pantidi, N., Coyle, D., et al.: What can i help you with? In: Proceedings of the 19th International Conference on Human-Computer Interaction with Mobile Devices and Services, pp. 1–12. ACM, New York (2017)
7. Desmet, P., Overbeeke, K., Tax, S.: Designing products with added emotional value: development and application of an approach for research through design. Des. J. **4**, 32–47 (2001). https://doi.org/10.2752/146069201789378496
8. Doyle, P.R., Edwards, J., Dumbleton, O., et al.: Mapping perceptions of humanness in intelligent personal assistant interaction. In: Proceedings of the 21st International Conference on Human-Computer Interaction with Mobile Devices and Services. Association for Computing Machinery, New York (2019)
9. Festerling, J., Siraj, I.: Alexa, what are you? Exploring primary school children's ontological perceptions of digital voice assistants in open interactions. Hum. Dev. **64**, 26–43 (2020). https://doi.org/10.1159/000508499
10. Garg, R., Sengupta, S.: He is just like me: a study of the long-term use of smart speakers by parents and children. Proc. ACM Interact. Mob. Wearable Ubiquit. Technol. **4** (2020). https://doi.org/10.1145/3381002
11. Huxohl, T., Pohling, M., Carlmeyer, B., et al.: Interaction guidelines for personal voice assistants in smart homes. In: 2019 International Conference on Speech Technology and Human-Computer Dialogue (SpeD), pp. 1–10. IEEE (2019)
12. Kendall, L., Chaudhuri, B., Bhalla, A.: Understanding technology as situated practice: everyday use of voice user interfaces among diverse groups of users in urban India. Inf. Syst. Front. **22**, 585–605 (2020). https://doi.org/10.1007/s10796-020-10015-6
13. Kim, J., Jeong, M., Lee, S.C.: "Why did this voice agent not understand me?": error recovery strategy for in-vehicle voice user interface. In: Adjunct Proceedings - 11th International ACM Conference on Automotive User Interfaces and Interactive Vehicular Applications, AutomotiveUI 2019, pp. 146–150 (2019)
14. Kiseleva, J., Williams, K., Jiang, J., et al.: Understanding user satisfaction with intelligent assistants. In: Proceedings of the 2016 ACM on Conference on Human Information Interaction and Retrieval, pp. 121–130. ACM, New York (2016)
15. Larsen, H.H., Scheel, A.N., Bogers, T., Larsen, B.: Hands-free but not eyes-free. In: Proceedings of the 2020 Conference on Human Information Interaction and Retrieval, pp. 63–72. ACM, New York (2020)

16. Lau, J., Zimmerman, B., Schaub, F.: Alexa, are you listening? Privacy perceptions, concerns and privacy-seeking behaviors with smart speakers. Proc. ACM Hum. Comput. Interact. **2** (2018). https://doi.org/10.1145/3274371

17. Li, Z., Rau, P.-L.P., Huang, D.: Self-disclosure to an IoT conversational agent: effects of space and user context on users' willingness to self-disclose personal information. Appl. Sci. **9**, 1887 (2019). https://doi.org/10.3390/app9091887

18. Lopatovska, I., Oropeza, H.: User interactions with "Alexa" in public academic space. Proc. Assoc. Inf. Sci. Technol. **55**, 309–318 (2018). https://doi.org/10.1002/pra2.2018.145 05501034

19. Lopatovska, I., Rink, K., Knight, I., et al.: Talk to me: exploring user interactions with the Amazon Alexa. J. Librariansh Inf. Sci. **51**, 984–997 (2019). https://doi.org/10.1177/096100 0618759414

20. Lopatovska, I., Griffin, A.L., Gallagher, K., et al.: User recommendations for intelligent personal assistants. J. Librariansh Inf. Sci. **52**, 577–591 (2020). https://doi.org/10.1177/096 1000619841107

21. Lovato, S.B., Piper, A.M., Wartella, E.A.: Hey Google, do unicorns exist? Conversational agents as a path to answers to children's questions. In: Proceedings of the 18th ACM International Conference on Interaction Design and Children, pp. 301–313. Association for Computing Machinery, New York (2019)

22. Luger, E., Sellen, A.: "Like having a really bad PA": the gulf between user expectation and experience of conversational agents. In: Proceedings of the 2016 CHI Conference on Human Factors in Computing Systems, pp. 5286–5297. Association for Computing Machinery, New York (2016)

23. Maués, M.P.: Marcela Pedroso Maués Um olhar sobre os assistentes virtuais personificados e a voz como interface. Dissertation, Pontifical Catholic University of Rio de Janeiro (2019)

24. McLean, G., Osei-Frimpong, K.: Hey Alexa … examine the variables influencing the use of artificial intelligent in-home voice assistants. Comput. Hum. Behav. **99**, 28–37 (2019). https://doi.org/10.1016/j.chb.2019.05.009

25. Meeker, M.: Internet trends 2016. In: Kleiner Perkins (2016). https://www.kleinerperkins.com/perspectives/2016-internet-trends-report/. Accessed 11 Feb 2021

26. Moar, J., Escherich, M.: Hey Siri, how will you make money? In: Juniper Research (2020). https://www.juniperresearch.com/document-library/white-papers/hey-siri-how-will-you-make-money. Accessed 11 Feb 2021

27. Moriuchi, E.: Okay, Google!: an empirical study on voice assistants on consumer engagement and loyalty. Psychol. Mark. **36**, 489–501 (2019). https://doi.org/10.1002/mar.21192

28. Motta, I., Quaresma, M.: Opportunities and issues in the adoption of voice assistants by Brazilian smartphone users. Rev. Ergodes. HCI **7**, 138 (2019). https://doi.org/10.22570/erg odesignhci.v7iEspecial.1312

29. Newman, N.: The future of voice and the implications for news. In: Reuters Institute (2018). https://reutersinstitute.politics.ox.ac.uk/our-research/future-voice-and-implications-news. Accessed 11 Feb 2021

30. Oh, Y.H., Chung, K., Ju, D.Y.: Differences in interactions with a conversational agent. Int. J. Environ. Res. Public Health **17**, 3189 (2020). https://doi.org/10.3390/ijerph17093189

31. Pearl, C.: Designing Voice User Interfaces. O'Reilly (2016)

32. Porcheron, M., Fischer, J.E., Reeves, S., Sharples, S.: Voice interfaces in everyday life. In: Proceedings of the Conference on Human Factors in Computing Systems (2018)

33. Pradhan, A., Mehta, K., Findlater, L.: "Accessibility came by accident": use of voice-controlled intelligent personal assistants by people with disabilities. In: Proceedings of the 2018 CHI Conference on Human Factors in Computing Systems, pp. 1–13. Association for Computing Machinery, New York (2018)

34. Pridmore, J., Zimmer, M., Vitak, J., et al.: Intelligent personal assistants and the intercultural negotiations of dataveillance in platformed households. Surveill. Soc. **17**, 125–131 (2019). https://doi.org/10.24908/ss.v17i1/2.12936

35. Purington, A., Taft, J.G., Sannon, S., et al.: "Alexa is my new BFF": social roles, user satisfaction, and personification of the Amazon Echo. In: Proceedings of the Conference on Human Factors in Computing Systems, pp. 2853–2859 (2017)

36. Rong, X., Fourney, A., Brewer, R.N., et al.: Managing uncertainty in time expressions for virtual assistants. In: Proceedings of the 2017 CHI Conference on Human Factors in Computing Systems, pp. 568–579. Association for Computing Machinery, New York (2017)

37. Statista: Total number of Amazon Alexa skills in selected countries as of January 2020 (2020). https://www.statista.com/statistics/917900/selected-countries-amazon-alexa-skill-count/. Accessed 11 Feb 2021

38. Trajkova, M., Martin-Hammond, A.: "Alexa is a toy": exploring older adults' reasons for using, limiting, and abandoning echo. In: Proceedings of the 2020 CHI Conference on Human Factors in Computing Systems, pp. 1–13. Association for Computing Machinery, New York (2020)

39. Weber, P., Ludwig, T.: (Non-)Interacting with conversational agents: perceptions and motivations of using chatbots and voice assistants. In: Proceedings of the Conference on Mensch Und Computer, pp. 321–331. Association for Computing Machinery, New York (2020)

40. West, M., Kraut, R., Ei Chew, H.: I'd blush if I could. In: UNESCO Digital Library (2019). https://unesdoc.unesco.org/ark:/48223/pf0000367416.page=1. Accessed 11 Feb 2021

41. White-Smith, H., Cunha, S., Koray, E., Keating, P.: Technology tracker - Q1 2019. In: Ipsos MORI Tech Tracker (2019). https://www.ipsos.com/sites/default/files/ct/publication/documents/2019-04/techtracker_report_q12019_final.pdf. Accessed 11 Feb 2021

42. Yang, X., Aurisicchio, M., Baxter, W.: Understanding affective experiences with conversational agents. In: Proceedings of the 2019 CHI Conference on Human Factors in Computing Systems, pp. 1–12. Association for Computing Machinery, New York (2019)

A Case Study of Usability in Virtual Controls

Gunther Paul[1]([email]) [ORCID], Shane Porter[2], and Bruce Thomas[2] [ORCID]

[1] James Cook University, Mackay, QLD 4740, Australia
gunther.paul@jcu.edu.au
[2] University of South Australia, Adelaide, SA, Australia

Abstract. This paper presents the results of a spatial augmented reality (SAR) feasibility study that compares interactions with seven different physical to virtual projected buttons. The virtual 3-D projected buttons in this case act like a touch screen; they are flat, provide no depth feedback when pressed, and activate on touch regardless of how much pressure is used. The study investigated whether these properties impacted on how users interacted with the buttons, and if they influenced the performance of button operation. In the experiment, 13 participants pressed physical and virtual buttons while their movements were recorded with a VICON MX20 motion tracking system. Two types of physical and virtual buttons showed similar performance results, such as how quickly the subjects reacted, or how the hand accelerated to press the button. Physical and virtual buttons were equally rated by the subjects. The study supports usage of SAR technology in Product Development.

Keywords: Spatial augmented reality · Usability · Binary control · Virtual control

1 Background

Virtual projected buttons are of interest in industrial design. During the design process, physical buttons can be reproduced by projecting virtual buttons onto a physical prototype. It is assumed that such virtual buttons will provide a useful tool to help evaluate designs in a similar way to using sketches, viewing 3D models, or building prototypes. The overall goal of virtualization is to provide designers tools to quickly and iteratively develop and test new designs for a final product [1].

Spatial Augmented Reality (SAR) is the technology that was used to present virtual projected buttons. SAR uses calibrated projectors to change the appearance of physical objects. Points on a 3D model of the object are matched to the corresponding points on the physical object. The SAR system can then project a perspectival correct image onto the physical model to give it a different appearance. The projected image matches the geometry of the prototype so that it looks correct to anyone who views the projection. Since the image is computer generated, the design can be modified in real time. This is what makes it useful in the design process since a user can interactively change the design of their product on a virtual prototype. This capability provides the designer the flexibility of virtual designs combined with tangible nature of physical prototypes.

© Springer Nature Switzerland AG 2021
M. M. Soares et al. (Eds.): HCII 2021, LNCS 12781, pp. 503–523, 2021.
https://doi.org/10.1007/978-3-030-78227-6_36

Having interactive virtual prototypes, designers are then able to perform user testing of the functionality of the product.

Of particular interest for the designers is to employ interactive virtual buttons for early ergonomic testing of a final product. Proactively, usability can be tested and fixed quickly by using SAR to change the design.

1.1 Ergonomic Design of Buttons

Ergonomic motion design, as related to operator push-buttons has the goal of reducing mental strain (occupational psychology), reducing physical strain (occupational physiology), reducing task performance time (motion study) and avoiding errors (quality assurance) [2]. Physical push buttons are control actuators [3] that have been extensively researched in the past [2, 4–6] and ergonomic guidelines have been defined to manage and standardize their design and usage [7–9]. Primitive motion elements, which are used to operate such push buttons, have been equally investigated in depth [10].

When designing control actuators, the principles of functions allocation can be met by ensuring the machine does not place unacceptable demands on the operator, as for example, speed and accuracy of response, or the forces required to operate a push-button. To reduce complexity, special consideration shall be given to the type and amount of the information to be processed by the operator, and speed and accuracy are important variables to consider when designing the human-machine interaction. Verification that an operator action has been accepted by the system shall be presented to the operator instantly and simultaneously to an operator's actuation of the push-button. With delays greater than 1 s, the perceived association is reduced, and preliminary feedback becomes necessary. A single visual indicator that changes colour to convey a signal, for example a change from red to green, as present in many conventional push-button actuators, shall not be used. The system shall also be flexible enough to be adapted to differences in personal needs, general physiological and psychological abilities, learning abilities and cultural differences. Additionally, the characteristic of expectation in relation to perception is very important for the design of control actuators, and control actuators that share many shape attributes may be confused because the experienced user may only use some of the attributes for identification. Considering the limits of the short-term memory, and knowledge that the more similar the information units are, the more errors can be expected, not more information than needed should be presented, and the information should be sufficiently discrete to minimize the risk of errors [9]. Currently, virtual actuation is not included in the standards for controls of type "contact actuation with finger". In general, task requirements like speed of setting, the force to apply, need for visual and/or tactile checking of actuator setting, need to avoid inadvertent operation, need to avoid hand slipping from manual control actuator (friction), need for operator to wear gloves, need for easy cleaning, anthropometric and biomechanical conditions, as well as movement characteristics have to be considered when designing a push-button control. To avoid accidental operation, sensors/actors with a touch-sensitive area require protective mechanisms. Actor shape and location on a control panel (e.g., a control activating a valve should be located close to the symbol of a pipe, which is influenced by the valve) influence the understanding of system state and therefore the overall performance of the control [4]. Apart from tactile feedback, all these design requirements can be met by a virtual actuator.

Activation of a push-button control is a predominantly skill-based, reflex driven motion [4], and as such not subject to learning, training or fatigue [10]. The motion is similar to a "reach" motion in the systems of pre-determined times, and the control process is data limited. The measure used to quantify sensomotory skills that relate to the operation of such controls is typically the "task performance time" [5]. While physical push-button controls are representative of a class of haptic controls providing tactile feedback, virtual controls provide no tactile feedback and therefore rely on kinaesthetic feedback only for motion control. Virtual or touch-sensitive actors may use auditory or visual feedback to indicate successful activation. However tactile feedback is preferred over these modes [5]. Physical pushbuttons were in the past recommended for short-cyclic usage, fast and precise control, small space, simultaneous activation, and good protection against unintended use [6]. All of these characteristics do also apply to virtual push-button controls. Moreover, it is specifically recommended for motionless, virtual push-button controls to provide visual feedback upon activation [6]. In summary, virtual push-button controls may have similar qualities as physical pushbuttons, while tactile recognition of the push-button is weak for both the physical [2] and the virtual implementation. However former design guides for physical controls, as for example the recommended control diameter, which were based on control motion distance and the applied force, are not valid and thus have to be newly established for virtual controls.

It should be further noted that ballistic, target oriented reach motion is controlled and corrected towards the end of the motion by the use of visual and tactile signals. The motion velocity until the end phase of the motion depends on reach distance and size of the target, given that the target is visible throughout the motion [2]. Reach motion is further on a planned, velocity-oriented motion, which requires little skill and training. This conclusion is used for the design of this experiment.

Previous research has shown how touch pads compare to other forms of user input such as mice, trackballs, or pointing sticks. Interacting with projected buttons is similar to interacting with a touchpad in that there is no physical button to press, and little 3D feedback is given to the user. Some of the advantages and disadvantages of touch pads also apply to interactive SAR.

A difference between touch pads and mice is that a mouse has buttons that can be clicked to perform actions whereas a touch pad has no buttons and relies on using "lift and tap" techniques for user input. A new form of touch pad was investigated in [11] that could click when pressed down under a certain amount of pressure. The tactile clicking touch pad allowed the user to perform these actions in less time. Measuring pressure to detect a button press is very useful to avoid "lift and tap" input techniques, but it is hard for to implement with SAR as it is desired to place buttons anywhere on the surface of an object.

Placing buttons anywhere on the surface of an object has been investigated in [12] by combining RFID tags with 3D printed models to create a new type of virtual button. Each button had an RFID tag placed on it which could be read by a finger mounted RFID reader. The buttons could be placed and rearranged on the surface of an object and function in a similar manner as momentary push button. Reading the RFID tags determined which button was pressed and this reading action activated the button press event. Due to the simple integration of RFID tags into any shaped button, different shapes of buttons can easily be fabricated, for example by 3D printing. This combination of 3D printed buttons and RFID tags may provide an intuitive solution to test and reconfigure different layouts of buttons on a design.

Button layouts have been used for human factors testing in the past, such as for testing the key layout of push-button telephones. Different arrangements were tested in [13] by measuring the time it took to enter a telephone number as well as the error rate of using the buttons. This study is an example of how a prototype can be effective for testing ergonomic performance and usability.

1.2 Rapid Prototyping and Spatial Augmented Reality

In the area of industrial design, rapid prototyping is the process of iteratively testing a prototype as quickly as possible. This involves developing the form of the prototype as well as how it functions. These two factors are usually developed separately, with the form and function coming together later in the design process. Rapid prototyping is used to make this process quicker, but without sacrificing the quality of the design [14].

A useful design tool for rapid prototyping called BOXES was created in [15]. The researchers used this to make a prototype MP3 player with buttons to control the music coming from the PC. Designers used the system and were able to quickly test and implement their personal designs for an MP3 player. This approach to rapid prototyping allowed the designers to iteratively test the form and function at the same time which was quicker and more useful than testing them separately.

ModelCraft is a rapid prototyping technology that captures annotations made on a paper prototype to iteratively modify the form of that prototype [16]. The annotations modify the 3D model of the object, and when the user finishes annotating, a prototype is printed with an implementation of the changes. A designer can then iteratively work on the model in this way until they find the desired shape for their prototype. Without ModelCraft the designer would make annotations on the prototype and then manually make the changes to the 3D model, whereas using ModelCraft they can save time by having the annotations directly modify the model.

Several other physical tools have been developed for quickly testing prototypes [17–19].

The display of AR information may be performed by one of three major display technologies: projectors, handheld displays, and head mounted displays (HMD). A limitation of handheld displays and HMDs is that the image from an individual display can only be viewed effectively by one person at a time, while SAR information may be conveniently viewed by multiple people. A second advantage of using SAR for design over other forms of AR is that the user does not have to handle any technology to view the projected design. SAR achieves its presentation of information via projectors mounted out of reach of the users, allowing all of the users to view the projections at the same time. This is deemed a large advantage for evaluating designs presented as AR enhanced objects.

Raskar's Shader Lamps is a foundational technology for many SAR investigations [20]. By projecting digital images from projectors onto a physical object, its appearance can be changed. Shader Lamps performs this with calibrated projectors that match the correct perspective view of a 3D virtual graphical model to a physical model. In previous work, studies were conducted that tested the properties of virtual buttons [14]. Several differences to interacting with virtual buttons when compared to interacting with physical buttons were concluded. Firstly, no haptic feedback is provided for pressing the virtual button. The buttons are projected onto simple flat or curved surfaces that do not change when they are pressed. Therefore, when a button is pressed the user does not know if they have correctly pressed the button unless there is some other form of feedback. This can influence how the user interacts with a projected button.

Secondly, blocking the projected light can cast a shadow onto the object. This could cause the button to not appear in the correct spot if something else is occluding it, such as the user's hand. This effect can be minimized by using more than one projector; when one projector is being occluded another can compensate for it and still have the button appear in the correct spot.

Using SAR to assist with rapid prototyping has already been studied in the past. The addition of SAR allows designers to quickly modify their design and iterate over many different design concepts.

How the level of fidelity affected user interaction with a prototype was studied in [21]. The study that they performed showed that interactive prototypes with real-time feedback gave the user a better appreciation of how the device operated, and that using a low fidelity prototype was a fast and low-cost method of getting user feedback.

The use of SAR in the design process has also been looked at in the past. Augmented Foam Sculpting uses SAR to instruct a user on where to cut a piece of foam with a wire cutter [22].

A rapid prototyping platform that used sketch-based interactions and SAR to create interactive prototypes was presented in [23]. This rapid prototyping platform is designed to be used with products that contain integrated hardware and software capabilities such as phones or tablets. When a button was pressed, the SAR system would reflect the change in state by changing the appearance of the prototype.

The use of SAR in design was investigated in [24] by creating "Skin", an augmented reality tool with tangible interaction where designers can test different schemes for a physical model, such as textures to be placed on pottery. Subjects produced prototype pottery shortly after using "Skin", while the process usually involved iterating and evaluating various designs.

2 Aims and Objectives

The results from this feasibility study were to help understand how closely virtual projected buttons emulate physical buttons. Once this is understood, it will be easier to identify how to use virtual projected buttons in the design process.

To enhance an existing SAR prototyping system, a computer vision-based approach to simulate a user pressing a momentary pushbutton was developed [14]. This is shown in Fig. 1 with a subject pressing a projected button. This simulated button press is like a touch screen. For example, a user could press a virtual button and the computer could generate a visual or audible signal to provide feedback that the button has been pressed. To perform this form of prototyping with physical buttons would require custom electronics to be built into the prototype. This process would incur an overhead if the buttons are required to be moved, as the electronic components need to be moved as well. Whereas with the SAR system, the virtual button can be moved very easily and still have interactive capabilities. All that would be required is the designer to drag and drop the virtual button to a different position on the prototype.

Fig. 1. A subject interacting with a projected button.

For example, a user could test how easily they can reach various buttons on the prototype. The virtual button can then be moved to make it easier to reach. It is hypothesized that such an ergonomic test can be done very quickly with SAR.

This hypothesis is tested with a detailed feasibility study in form of a randomized, controlled pairwise comparison experiment by analysis of kinematic parameters as dependent variables. The study supports a vision of using SAR in the design process as well as using it for ergonomic tests. The subjects sat in a rigid chair and interacted with the two buttons in front of them on the table (Fig. 2). Data was captured for a variety of physical and virtual buttons, which allowed deducing the effect of a virtual button on selected variables.

The aim of the study is to investigate in depth the differences in usability between pressing binary momentary physical buttons and binary momentary projected buttons, as a feasibility study for the usage of SAR in ergonomic assessment.

2.1 Experimental Design

To perform this evaluation a small board with two buttons was constructed, a physical and a virtual and had subjects press the buttons in a randomized controlled experiment. The subjects were fitted with 9.5 mm diameter reflective markers to record their movement while performing the task. The VICON® upper limb model (VICON 2007) with 16 markers, as shown in Fig. 3 was chosen for the study.

Fig. 2. A subject performing the experiment.

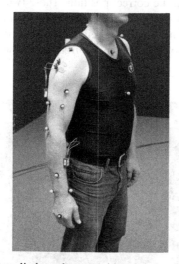

Fig. 3. VICON upper limb marker set, with a right hand-arm system focus.

The layout for the button board used an area of 20 cm × 20 cm, with a button placed on the left and right side of the board. These two buttons were centred vertically, and both buttons were 2.5 cm from the middle line of the board. The whole button area was painted white, along with a 10 cm border around the edge of the area. Figure 4 shows the board for a red rectangular button. The boards were metallic to act as touch sensors.

This layout was repeated for seven different boards, each with a different type of button mounted. A physical button was installed on one side of the board, and the other button was projected to the opposite side of the board. Two additional boards were made with one having two physical buttons, and the other having two projected buttons. These

Fig. 4. Board showing a physical and projected button (left), with alternative positions to control location bias (right). (Color figure online)

were used to measure the right versus left side bias, i.e., how quickly each participant pressed the right button compared to pressing the left button.

The projected visuals were provided by two projectors which augmented the boards to make a button appear in the correct position. These two projectors were placed on either side of the table as shown in Fig. 5. The images from the two projectors overlapped so that it looked like only one image was being displayed. By overlapping the images, it meant that a subject could obstruct the image from one projector, but still see the image from the other projector.

Fig. 5. Working space for the experiment. The subject interacts with the buttons in the white square area on the table.

The experiment was carried out in Ergolab at the University of South Australia. Illuminance in the laboratory at 1 m height was 700–800 lux in the experimental area, which is a level required for tasks with a high precision demand (Fig. 6), and temperature was controlled at 23 °C.

Fig. 6. Experimental *situation*.

2.2 Procedure

Nineteen randomly recruited right-handed, male participants of average age 29.5 (±10.7) yrs, average height 174.9 (±6.3) cm and average weight 78.2 (±11.6) kg participated in the study.

Thirteen subjects were equipped with markers, and six subjects were video tracked at 50 Hz without markers to identify a possible effect of the markers on the experiment. Before each experiment, it took ten minutes to place markers on a subject and measure height and weight. During this time, the subjects were also able to familiarize themselves with the laboratory environment. The experiment lasted approximately 40 s for each of the 9 different buttons and including the change-over of boards between tasks, the overall experimental session lasted approximately 35 min.

The study consisted of nine conditions, one for each button board. The procedure for each condition was identical and consisted of the following:

1. The subject started with their index finger on a green dot on the bottom edge of the centerline to the button area and waited for the task to start.
2. Once the task started, the subject waited for a two second pause. After the pause, one button started flashing.
3. The subject pressed the flashing button with their right index finger and then returned the finger to the green dot.
4. Two seconds after the button had been pressed, another button would randomly flash, and steps one to three would be repeated.

The experiment was repeated ten times for each button board, with five presses of the left button, and five of the right button. The order of the flashing buttons was randomized to prevent participants moving their finger in anticipation of which button would flash next.

This task was repetitive for seven different types of buttons, as well as two more times to measure how quickly subjects pressed the right button compared to pressing the left button. The order of presenting the different button boards was again randomized. The buttons that were used are shown in Fig. 7. As all of the subjects were right-handed, there was a small advantage in the results for pressing the button on the right of the board. This right-hand bias test was done by using two physical buttons at once, and then again using two projected buttons. This way it was determined how quick the subject was to press the button located on the right of the board compared to pressing the button on the left of the board. For each task, the side of the board that the physical and virtual buttons were located on was randomized, and the results were adjusted to account for the right-hand bias.

Fig. 7. The seven buttons used in the experiment, numbered from top left (1) to bottom right (7).

After each experiment, subjects were asked to complete a short subjective comfort evaluation questionnaire (Annex). This simple questionnaire uses a continuous, linear scale ranging from 1…10 to measure subjective comfort of use. As no psychophysical workload is measured, the scale is not based on the law of psychophysics. Marks on the linear scale length of 108 mm were measured with 1 mm precision and converted to a percentage scale with two-digit precision.

All data was statistically analyzed in IBM SPSS® (IBM Corp., Armonk, New York, USA). T-tests (95% CI) and Pearson's Chi-square were computed to test the equality hypothesis of the physical buttons with their virtual counterparts, for subjective evaluations and all kinematic parameters.

2.3 Control System Implementation

The procedure was controlled by one main computer. This computer ran the software for the SAR system, as well as the software that controlled the buttons. A separate micro-board with an MSP430 processor controlled the physical buttons. An Arduino Uno®

board detected pressing on the projected button by means of a capacitive touch sensor. The housing for the button controllers is shown in Fig. 8. with the Arduino® in the bottom left, and the MSP430 board in the bottom right corner.

Fig. 8. Experimental control circuit micro-boards.

The SAR system worked in parallel with the button controlling software, with messages being sent back and forth between the systems to coordinate flashing the projected button. The SAR system did not detect whether the projected button was being pressed or not, as this task was covered by the Arduino board. So, to control the projected button, a "flash button" message was sent from the button controller to the SAR system, and when the button was pressed, a "stop flashing button" message was sent to the SAR system.

For each type of button that was tested, the physical version was connected to the micro-board each time. This board controlled the LED within the button and also detected when the button was being pressed. The board was also connected to the computer via a serial cable connection, which allowed messages to be transferred back and forth between the board and the button controller software. When the board received a "flash button" message, it would make the LED in the physical button flash on and off with the LED going on for 0.5 s and then going off again for another 0.5 s. This was repeated until the user pressed the physical button. When the physical button was pressed, a "button pressed" message was sent to the button controller software.

The Arduino® board sent messages to the button controller software whenever the projected button was pressed. To do this a metal plate was connected to the Arduino® to detect when the plate was being pressed. This plate was placed underneath where the projected button would be, so that when the subject went to press the projected button, they would also press the metal plate. The Arduino® detected that the subject pressed the plate and would then send a "button pressed" message back to the button controller. The VICON® system was not precise enough to determine exactly time and position of the participant's press of the virtual button. In addition, the metal plate was painted white to blend in with the rest of the board, and it was also significantly bigger than the projected button. This design was chosen so that the subjects would not interfere with the detection mechanism.

The button controller software communicated with all three of these parts and coordinated the task for each subject. When the program starts, a list is created that contains the random order that the user must press the buttons in. The list always contains five physical button presses and five projected button presses. The order of these presses was randomized for each task. Since reaction times were recorded, a false start and reaction before the button flashed would have compromised the experiment.

2.4 Kinematic Study Parameters

The movements of thirteen subjects were recorded at 100 Hz using the VICON MX20® 8 camera motion capture system. The motion data was filtered and pre-processed in a VICON Nexus pipeline, recorded into the Nexus database, post-processed in MATLAB® (MathWorks, Natick, Massachusetts, USA) and statistically analyzed in IBM SPSS® after the study was completed. Using this data, the reaction time, average acceleration, peak acceleration, and distance covered of each marker for each button press were determined. However, only the data from the metacarpophalangeal joint marker of the right-hand middle finger was used for analysis in this paper. The following section describes the kinematic parameters used in the analysis.

Distance Travelled. This dimension is defined as the distance that the marker travelled between having the button flash and pressing the button. This was determined by measuring the distance travelled between each frame, and then calculating the total distance covered over all measured frames, for the 13 subjects with markers.

Acceleration. Acceleration is defined as the calculated piecewise linear change over time of the velocity between frames. Average acceleration was calculated as the arithmetic average of all acceleration and deceleration values between the button flashing and the button being pressed. Peak acceleration was determined as the highest acceleration during this time window. Both average and peak acceleration were calculated for the 13 subjects with markers. In Fig. 9 the point of peak acceleration is indicated by a green asterisk.

Reaction Time. Each button press motion is framed by sudden velocity changes of a subject's hand. To identify the instance of reaction, the peak velocity of each button press motion was located, and from there backwards, the time was spotted where that movement started. Once the velocity crossed a threshold of 5% of the peak speed, it was determined that the user reacted to the flashing button. The threshold of 5% was chosen because it was difficult to find a lower velocity starting point of the motion. The fingers were always making small movements, which meant that there was never at a constant resting speed. The 5% threshold was defined as the reaction point, where the finger was not resting but was willingly moving. The time between the flashing of a button and the reaction point is defined as the reaction time. In Fig. 9 the reaction point is indicated by a red asterisk.

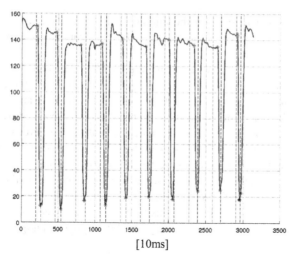

[10ms]

Fig. 9. The ordinate provides a position in millimetres along the X-axis in the Euclidean motion space. Synchronization points marked with blue dotted line. (Color figure online)

Time Synchronization. The motion data captured in VICON Nexus® and the output from the button controller software were not directly synchronized by hardware or software. In the button controller software, a time stamped event was recorded when a button was pressed. VICON Nexus® only captured the kinematic parameters of the motion, with no event recorded for the button press. The two datasets were therefore synchronized ex post. This was done by matching a "button pressed" event in the controller data, with a "button press" movement of the subject's finger in the motion capture data. Figure 9 shows a position along the X-axis of the finger marker on the right hand. The general movement direction was aligned with the X-axis. The motion sequence for the user pressing a button was as follows:

1. The button begins to flash.
2. The subject reacts to the flash and begins to move the hand towards the button.
3. The subject decelerates the hand in anticipation of pressing the button with the finger.
4. The subject presses the button with the finger.
5. The button stops flashing.
6. The subject retracts the hand to the resting point on the green dot.

By comparison with marker movement, it is approximated where each of these events happens along the timeline of each button press. Points on the trajectory were calculated that represented events three and six, which were decelerating the hand as it approached the button and accelerating the hand away from the button. As the exact actuation point of each button press, which makes the 4th event, is not known from the kinematic data, only a time window can be identified. This is due to complications like for example, one type of button may send a signal that it has been activated when the button is only one quarter of its way pressed, whereas another button might need to be pressed all the way down to make it send the activation signal. Due to this problem, it was assumed that the button press happened in the middle of the window of time between events three and six. To synchronize the two datasets, the synchronization points were matched with the button press events. Thus, synchronizing the time base of the two sets of data, the kinematic data was related to experimental events. In the end, the synchronization was calculated once for every task that a subject performed, and the time bases were synchronized using only one of the button presses. This is indicated in Fig. 9 by the two black asterisks. The synchronized button presses are represented by the blue dotted lines (red asterisk = point where subject reacts to button flash; green asterisk = point where peak acceleration is reached; black asterisks = points where events three and six occur). Since the data is time-synchronized on the basis that a button was pressed during a small window of time, there will be a systematic error introduced to the data. This error was minimized by synchronizing on the quickest button press; however, there is intra-subject and inter-subject variation for this timing and subsequent error. Nevertheless, the systematic error value will be kept very small through averaging.

3   Results

There was no influence of age, body stature or body weight on the outcome of any of the experiments. Also, the application of motion tracking markers had no impact on the experiment.

The average distance travelled ranged from 159.8 mm ($\pm$24.9 mm) for physical button five [P5] to 171.5 mm ($\pm$24.6 mm) for physical button two [P2], with no significant difference in distance travelled between any of the physical and virtual combinations ($0.078 \leq p \leq 0.925$). Equally, the average maximum acceleration ranged from 4313 mm/s^2 ($\pm$1678 mm/s^2) [V2] to 5628 mm/s^2 ($\pm$1341 mm/s^2) [P4], with no significant difference in maximum acceleration between any of the physical and virtual combinations ($0.154 \leq p \leq 0.848$).

No differences were found in the ratings of physical versus virtual button perceived ease of use (Table 1) ($0.114 \leq p \leq 0.91$).

Significant differences however were found regarding reaction times (Table 2) and average accelerations (Table 3).

Mean reaction time ranged from 210 ms $\pm$ 94 ms [P6] to 708 ms $\pm$ 139 ms [V5]. Standard error was smaller than 39 ms for any of the button types.

Apparently, there was a large difference in reaction time ($p = 0$) for all button pairs, except pairs two and three where reaction time differed only marginally (P2–V2: −4%; P3–V3: −3.3%), at a non-significant level ($p > 0.3$). For all other pairs, reaction time was roughly three times higher for the virtual buttons. In all cases, reaction time was smaller for a physical button.

Mean average acceleration ranged from 26 mm/s^2 $\pm$ 17 mm/s^2 [V2] to 79 mm/s^2 $\pm$ 36 mm/s^2 [P1]. Standard error was smaller than 18 mm/s^2 for any of the button types.

There was also a significant difference in average acceleration ($0 \leq p \leq 0.038$) for all button pairs, except pair three ($p = 0.076$). Average accelerations differed between the physical and virtual buttons by +36% (P3) up to +57% (P6).

From the equal trajectory distances travelled, while submitted to higher average accelerations, it is apparent that the elapsed time between onset of the motion (reaction point) and button press is higher for all virtual buttons.

Table 1. T-test results for perceived ease of use. Physical vs. virtual buttons one to seven.

		t	df	Sig. (2-tailed)
Pair 1	Rating_B1_P – Rating_B1_V	1.059	18	.304
Pair 2	Rating_B2_P – Rating_B2_V	−1.660	18	.114
Pair 3	Rating_B3_P – Rating_B3_V	−1.420	18	.173
Pair 4	Rating_B4_P – Rating_B4_V	−.803	18	.432
Pair 5	Rating_B5_P – Rating_B5_V	−.412	18	.685
Pair 6	Rating_B6_P – Rating_B6_V	−.115	18	.910
Pair 7	Rating_B7_P – Rating_B7_V	−.477	18	.639

Table 2. Reaction times (simple statistics) for all button types.

		Mean reaction time [ms]	N	SD [ms]	Mean SE [ms]
Pair 1	P1_t	211.35	13	92.156	25.559
	V1_t	629.538	13	79.6716	22.0969
Pair 2	P2_t	624.615	13	67.0790	18.6044
	V2_t	50.462	13	83.3235	23.1098
Pair 3	P3_t	623.654	13	118.6847	32.9172
	V3_t	644.115	13	83.8670	23.2605
Pair 4	P4_t	225.769	13	78.2868	21.7128
	V4_t	638.769	13	66.3252	18.3953
Pair 5	P5_t	270.731	13	115.4821	32.0290
	V5_t	708.769	13	139.9824	38.8241
Pair 6	P6_t	210.462	13	94.0712	26.0907
	V6_t	613.846	13	92.1320	25.5528
Pair 7	P7_t	246.615	13	68.3832	18.9661
	V7_t	639.500	13	101.3135	28.0993

Table 3. Average acceleration (simple statistics) for all button types.

		Mean [mm/s^2]	N	SD [mm/s^2]	Mean SE [mm/s^2]
Pair 1	P1_avg_a	79.536	13	36.5139	10.1271
	V1_avg_a	35.3881	13	24.25486	6.72709
Pair 2	P2_avg_a	42.2834	13	24.79340	6.87645
	V2_avg_a	26.5703	13	17.05023	4.72888
Pair 3	P3_avg_a	44.5485	13	34.12422	9.46435
	V3_avg_a	28.5669	13	19.53238	5.41731
Pair 4	P4_avg_a	60.6647	13	43.89466	12.17419
	V4_avg_a	34.9892	13	31.73456	8.80158
Pair 5	P5_avg_a	69.8868	13	50.99177	14.14257
	V5_avg_a	33.8918	13	26.02902	7.21915
Pair 6	P6_avg_a	75.5180	13	61.33492	17.01125
	V6_avg_a	32.8085	13	20.68028	5.73568
Pair 7	P7_avg_a	64.0891	13	48.76766	13.52572
	V7_avg_a	33.1503	13	26.25541	7.28194

4 Discussion

The experiment shows that sensomotoric task performance in this idealistic setup is independent of the personal anthropometric characteristics age, body height and body weight. Furthermore, the motion trajectory as reflected in the distance travelled, is found to be independent of the variable experimental conditions of the reach task, and the subjects. This is the case for the physical buttons as well as the virtual buttons, with no difference in motion trajectory between the two realizations. As perceived ease of use is not significantly different between a physical and virtual button, the SAR virtual button technology with its many advantages, such as flexibility, ease of change, ease of implementation, maintenance etc., emerges as a time efficient and cost-effective option in the product design domain, where information about human interaction with button-like controls needs experimental testing. Moreover, the study shows that SAR virtual buttons are valid representations of physical buttons in such an environment.

Nevertheless, the tested virtual technology cannot be easily transferred into control panels of production systems. Due to the significant difference in reaction time for most of the combinations tested, and the larger button press time for virtual buttons, any possible implementation of SAR virtual buttons in a production control room environment requires careful planning. It appears that buttons two and three are most suited for such a purpose. Both physical buttons P2 and P3 had a more rounded, lower and slightly concave profile, while buttons P4–P7 were more elevated with a flat profile, and button P1 had a low convex profile. Despite this finding, the relative performance of the physical buttons needs to be considered. Buttons P2 and P3 had much slower reaction times than all other buttons (624 ms vs. 210–270 ms), and much slower average accelerations than the other buttons (42–44 mm/s^2 vs. 60–79 mm/s^2). The similarity between buttons P2/P3 and V2/V3 is therefore due to the relatively poor performance of these physical buttons compared to their peers.

As both reaction time and average acceleration differ between physical and virtual buttons, one possible explanation could be that both the initial visual perception of the trigger condition, which is the button lighting up, and the visual feedback for trajectory planning and execution are distorted for the virtual button. Alternatively, it could be possible that the delayed reaction causes a change in the motion execution. However, this is highly unlikely, as the average acceleration was significantly smaller for virtual buttons, which would not be the case if a delayed motion onset was to be compensated for. It is most likely however that the familiarity with the physical button triggers planned motion execution patterns at a low, autonomous level, whereas the unfamiliar virtual button requires additional higher motion control instances in trajectory planning, slowing down the movement execution.

Given the generally faster reaction times and higher mean accelerations for physical buttons, it is reasonable to conclude that physical buttons get a more succinct perception than SAR virtual buttons at the sensory level and are thus still superior in production systems. This is an area where SAR technology can be further improved, which will likely be the case with the next generation of high-density graphic processors and projectors. Some or all of the discussed effects may also be compensated by training.

5 Conclusion

In summary, despite of the potential of virtual push-button controls to outperform their physical peers, virtual buttons still appear to lack in legibility and visual identification. This deficiency is likely to be eliminated in the course of ongoing technology develop-ment. Until then, only carefully selected SAR virtual buttons can be recommended for control room usage in production systems.

Nevertheless, SAR virtual button technology with its many advantages in usability can be considered a time and cost-efficient alternative in augmented prototyping, given the good performance and high level of user acceptance.

Annex

Participant Questionnaire

Name: _____

Age: _____

Height: _____

Weight: _____

Survey:
- Please mark how comfortable you were pressing the different types of buttons.

Button 1:
How comfortable did you feel when pressing the *physical* button?

1 10
Very Uncomfortable   Very Comfortable

How comfortable did you feel when pressing the *projected* button?

1 10
Very Uncomfortable   Very Comfortable

Button 2:
How comfortable did you feel when pressing the *physical* button?

1 10
Very Uncomfortable   Very Comfortable

How comfortable did you feel when pressing the *projected* button?

1 10
Very Uncomfortable   Very Comfortable

Button 3:
How comfortable did you feel when pressing the *physical* button?

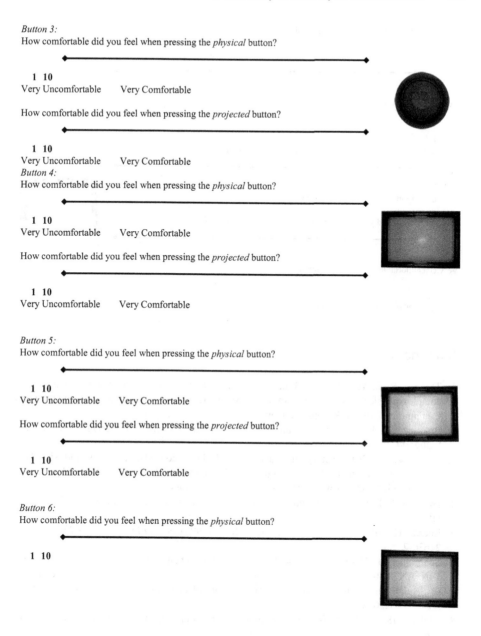

1 10
Very Uncomfortable   Very Comfortable

How comfortable did you feel when pressing the *projected* button?

1 10
Very Uncomfortable   Very Comfortable
Button 4:
How comfortable did you feel when pressing the *physical* button?

1 10
Very Uncomfortable   Very Comfortable

How comfortable did you feel when pressing the *projected* button?

1 10
Very Uncomfortable   Very Comfortable

Button 5:
How comfortable did you feel when pressing the *physical* button?

1 10
Very Uncomfortable   Very Comfortable

How comfortable did you feel when pressing the *projected* button?

1 10
Very Uncomfortable   Very Comfortable

Button 6:
How comfortable did you feel when pressing the *physical* button?

1 10

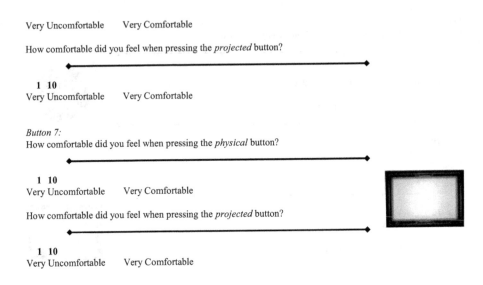

Very Uncomfortable   Very Comfortable

How comfortable did you feel when pressing the *projected* button?

1 10
Very Uncomfortable   Very Comfortable

Button 7:
How comfortable did you feel when pressing the *physical* button?

1 10
Very Uncomfortable   Very Comfortable

How comfortable did you feel when pressing the *projected* button?

1 10
Very Uncomfortable   Very Comfortable

Thank you for your participation in this study

References

1. Thomas, B.H., Von Itzstein, G.S., et al.: Spatial augmented reality support for design of complex physical environments. In: IEEE Annual Conference on Pervasive Computing and Communications Workshops (PerCom), pp. 588–593. IEEE (2011)
2. Bokranz, R., Landau, K.: Einführung in die Arbeitswissenschaft. Verlag Eugen Ulmer, Stuttgart (1991)
3. AS 4024.1901:2014 Safety of Machinery Displays, controls, actuators and signals—Ergonomic requirements for the design of displays and control actuators—General principles for human interactions with displays and control actuators
4. Ivergard, T.: Handbook of Control Room Design and Ergonomics. Taylor & Francis, London (1989)
5. Luczak, H.: Arbeitswissenschaft. Springer, Berlin (1993). https://doi.org/10.1007/978-3-662-21634-7
6. Schmidtke, H. (Hrsg): Ergonomie. Carl Hanser, Muenchen (1993)
7. DIN EN 894-3: 2009 Safety of machinery - Ergonomics requirements for the design of displays and control actuators - Part 3: Control actuators; German version EN 894-3:2000+A1:2008
8. DIN EN ISO 11064-5:2008 Ergonomic design of control centres — Part 5: Displays and controls
9. AS 4024.1906:2014 Safety of Machinery Displays, controls, actuators and signals—Indication, marking and actuation—Requirements for the location and operation of actuators
10. Landau, K., Luczak, H., Laurig, W. (Hrsg): Ergonomie der Sensumotorik. Carl Hanser Verlag, Muenchen (1996)
11. MacKenzie, I.S., Oniszczak, A.: A comparison of three selection techniques for touchpads. In: Proceedings of the SIGCHI conference on Human Factors in computing systems. Los Angeles, CA, USA, pp. 336–343. ACM Press/Addison-Wesley Publishing Co (1998)

12. Simon, T.M., Smith, R.T., et al.: Merging tangible buttons and spatial augmented reality to support ubiquitous prototype designs. In: 13th Australasian User Interface Conference (AUIC 2012), Melbourne, Victoria, Australia (2012)

13. Deininger, R.L.: Desirable push-button characteristics. IRE Trans. Hum. Factors Electron. **HFE-1**(1), 24–30 (1960)

14. Porter, S.R., Marner, M.R., et al.: Spatial augmented reality for interactive rapid prototyping. In: 20th International Conference on Artificial Reality and Telexistence (ICAT2010), Adelaide, South Australia, Australia, VRSJ, pp. 110–117 (2010)

15. Hudson, S.E., Mankoff, J.: Rapid construction of functioning physical interfaces from cardboard, thumbtacks, tin foil and masking tape. In: Proceedings of the 19th Annual ACM Symposium on User Interface Software and Technology, Montreux, Switzerland, pp. 289–298. ACM Press (2006)

16. Song, H., Fran, et al.: ModelCraft: capturing freehand annotations and edits on physical 3D models. In: Proceedings of the 19th Annual ACM Symposium on User Interface Software and Technology, Montreux, Switzerland, pp. 13–22. ACM Press (2006)

17. Greenberg, S., Fitchett, C.: Phidgets: easy development of physical interfaces through physical widgets. In: Proceedings of the 14th Annual ACM Symposium on User Interface Software and Technology (UIST 2001), Orlando, Florida, pp. 209–218. ACM Press (2001)

18. Lee, J.C., Avrahami, D., et al.: The calder toolkit: wired and wireless components for rapidly prototyping interactive devices. In: Proceedings of the 5th Conference on Designing Interactive Systems (DIS 2004), Cambridge, MA, USA, pp. 141–146. ACM Press (2004)

19. Lifton, J., Broxton, M., et al.: Experiences and directions in pushpin computing. In: Proceedings of the Information Processing in Sensor Networks Conference (IPSN 2005), pp. 416–421. IEEE (2005)

20. Raskar, R., Welch, G., Low, K.-L., Bandyopadhyay, D.: Shader lamps: animating real objects with image-based illumination. In: Gortler, S.J., Myszkowski, K. (eds.) EGSR 2001. E, pp. 89–102. Springer, Vienna (2001). https://doi.org/10.1007/978-3-7091-6242-2_9

21. Hare, J., Gill, S., Loudon, G., Ramduny-Ellis, D., Dix, A.: Physical fidelity: exploring the importance of physicality on physical-digital conceptual prototyping. In: Gross, T., Gulliksen, J., Kotzé, P., Oestreicher, L., Palanque, P., Prates, R.O., Winckler, M. (eds.) INTERACT 2009. LNCS, vol. 5726, pp. 217–230. Springer, Heidelberg (2009). https://doi.org/10.1007/978-3-642-03655-2_26

22. Marner, M.R., Thomas, B.H.: Augmented foam sculpting for capturing 3D models. In: IEEE Symposium on 3D User Interfaces (3DUI), Waltham, MA, USA, pp. 63–70. IEEE (2010)

23. Nam, T.-J.: Sketch-based rapid prototyping platform for hardware-software integrated interactive products. In: CHI '05 Extended Abstracts on Human Factors in Computing Systems, Portland, OR, USA, pp. 1689–1692. ACM Press (2005)

24. Saakes, D., Stappers, P.J.: A tangible design tool for sketching materials in products. Artif. Intell. Eng. Des. Anal. Manuf. **23**(03), 275–287 (2009)

Heuristic Evaluation of Android-Based Applications with Multiple Screen Sizes Support: A Case Study

Juan-Carlos Romaina[✉] [ID]

Pontificia Universidad Católica del Perú, Lima 32, San Miguel, Peru
jromaina@pucp.pe

Abstract. In recent years, mobile devices have become one of the main tools for communication and now represent a unique opportunity to reach great numbers of users. Also, Google's Android OS is the one that has grown into a first choice for developing applications. This situation has a diversity of challenges, one of them being ensuring a rich and engaging user experience. One of the most restrictive and unique aspects of mobile development is the diversity in support for screen sizes and/or resolutions. This characteristic can mean different user experiences for users with the same application and has become increasingly important to consider when evaluating usability. In view of this, a proposal was made of an adaptation for the Heuristic Evaluation method, targeting applications that could be used in a range of devices with multiple screen sizes. To validate the proposal, a case study was conducted, evaluating a well-known banking application in Peru, using the proposed adaptation of the method described by Nielsen. This validation consisted of two groups of evaluators, one using traditional Nielsen heuristics, and a second group using context specific heuristics. As a result of the validation, the second group found more issues related with screen size. The proposed adaptation showed positive results, especially if a predefined set of devices, representative of the most common sizes sub-groups is used. As conclusion to the study, the evaluation conducted is an indication that careful consideration should be taken when building applications for a broad range of users, and devices.

Keywords: Heuristic evaluation · Mobile application · Usability · Human-computer interaction

1 Introduction

Software usability testing has been long used in the evaluation of user interfaces and Nielsen heuristics are the most well-known and the most applied. Different studies have been conducted to determine the effectiveness of such testing in mobile applications [1]. With the increased availability and diversity of mobile devices sharing software, it has become apparent that testing an application built to work in all kinds of hardware configurations represents a challenge [2]. One of the most significant of these characteristics is the screen size [3].

© Springer Nature Switzerland AG 2021
M. M. Soares et al. (Eds.): HCII 2021, LNCS 12781, pp. 524–534, 2021.
https://doi.org/10.1007/978-3-030-78227-6_37

In the present work, a revision of current studies has been conducted, and using heuristics found to be effective in the evaluation of applications for mobile devices, a proposal was made for an adaptation to the traditional heuristic evaluation method, taking into consideration groups of different screen sizes, as supported by the Android platform.

To validate the proposal, a case study was conducted, using a popular banking application in Peru. Here we present a detailed description of the work, how it was conducted, and the results.

2 Related Work

2.1 Mobile Application Usability

Depending on the context, it can be necessary to develop heuristics that cover specific requirements, as is the case with videogames or smartphones [4]. For mobile applications in particular, the traditional Nielsen heuristics can result overly generic. This is the main reason why diverse studies have been conducted with the objective to determine their effectiveness or to come up with new heuristics, better suited for the situation [5, 7–9]. A study in 2006, used an empiric approach to develop new heuristics, although the number of problems found was smaller and took double the time to complete. This study proposed 2 heuristics less than Nielsen's [10]. In 2012, another study was conducted about heuristics based on human factor combined with years of empiric studies about situations that stress the user while interacting with mobile devices [6]. In 2012, Nielsen et al., presented results of research on mobile usability, showing design problems, and highlighting a distinction between mobile devices with limited sizes, predicting the eventual preference to develop apps independent of the web sites (and their mobile counterparts), and making a particular distinction that larger screen sizes (as done with iPads or the Kindle Fire) reflect better usability results. As a side note, these were presented as results of the studies conducted and not as guides on how to conduct the usability evaluations, but they do offer details on how they were handled [11].

A different study in 2012 evaluated touchscreen devices and applications made for them, proposing new heuristics and a methodology for their development [3]. This work remarks that these kinds of heuristics are necessary, but they cannot be too specific, or they will become difficult to use. The comparison with a control group showed that the proposed heuristics can help find a higher number of usability issues.

In 2013, the work of Machado N. et al., used a comparison between their proposed heuristics for mobile devices and Nielsen's, finding higher effectiveness in the proposed heuristics. This study included a heuristic specific for the utilization of screen space and screen size [5].

2.2 Use of Screen Size

Research on screen sizes and their effects on usability are abundant, although through the years most of them have focused on small screen sizes [12–14]. Even during the first years of the new century, many studies have continued to focus their efforts in small screen sizes, which could have been considered common for the time, as the size of the screen for a PDA [15]. More recent research, as with Nielsen in 2011, included devices with bigger screens, as the first-generation iPad, or the Kindle Fire, showing differences in usability with the variety of devices available to the public [11].

As with usability, heuristic evaluation and screen sizes, several authors highlight the latter as a particular restriction when designing mobile applications [1, 12–14].

A laboratory study from 2004 found that information structure and the screen size can affect significatively the behavior and perception of the user. This research focused on web sites with mobile versions [12].

Some other research conducted found the importance with some specific tasks, like video learning [15], or the navigation of large images [17].

2.3 Conclusions

The literature reviewed highlighted the importance of the continued use and development of methods for the design of mobile applications. Of all the limitations and restrictions found by different authors with mobile devices (ex: difficulty of data input, storage capacity, bandwidth, processing power, battery life, compatibility, among others), many highlight the screen size as one of the main restrictions to be considered.

On the side of mobile usability and heuristic evaluations, recent studies have focused on the screen size as a factor to be considered during evaluations, and while developing new heuristics.

3 A Proposal for Heuristic Evaluations of Application with Multiple Screen Sizes Support

In this section, we will discuss the proposed adaptation of the traditional method of Heuristic Evaluations, considering the context of mobile applications and the characteristic of multiple screen-sizes support.

3.1 Considerations

This section describes the considerations and concepts used during the development of the present work.

Case Study Methodology. We followed the case study methodology as described by Hernández Sampieri [21], which comprises the following components: *case context, case propositions, results, case analysis* and *conclusions.*

Heuristics Selection. Nielsen heuristics were used for the control groups. To validate the proposal, heuristics that aim to help in the evaluation of mobile applications and identify issues related with the screen size were needed. Different works were considered [3, 5–7] and 2 were pre-selected. The heuristics developed by Rusu et al. [3] cover important aspects of evaluations of mobile devices with touchscreens, while the heuristics developed by Machado et al. [5] have one heuristic related with the use of screen size. The latter were selected for this reason.

Evaluator Selection. The "5 users are enough" principle was used. The evaluators were selected from a software consultancy company based in Lima (Peru).

Selecting Devices. The Android platform groups screen sizes in 4 generalized categories: small, normal, large, and xlarge [18]. Described below:

- *xlarge*: devices with a resolution of at least 960 dp × 720 dp, from 7 to 10 in.
- *large*: devices with a resolution of at least 640 dp × 480 dp, from 4 to 7 in.
- *normal*: devices with a resolution of at least 470 dp × 320 dp, from 3 to 5 in.
- *small*: devices with a resolution of at least 426 dp × 320 dp, from 2 to 3 in.

3.2 Preliminary Evaluation

A preliminary evaluation was prepared for the development of the proposal [19]. This was a first step into what would eventually be the proposed adaptation. A case study was conducted that consisted on the selection of an application and 5 different heuristic evaluations: 3 control evaluations using Nielsen heuristics [20], and 2 evaluations using heuristics for mobile devices [5], each evaluation with a different device, with different screen size.

The application chosen to be object of the study is a popular fast-food restaurant application in the city of Lima (Peru). It was available for Android smartphones with version 4.0 or higher, which made the software work with devices without any hardware restrictions. For each evaluator, it was required for them to complete the following tasks: Login into the application, add and remove items from the shopping cart, add a new address, complete an order, verify old purchases.

The groups of evaluators were divided as follows:

- Group 1 (G1), control group, used Nielsen heuristics (NH), in a device with a standard screen size (*Normal*).
- Group 2 (G2), used Nielsen heuristics (NH) in a device with a small screen size (*Small*).
- Group 3 (G3), used Nielsen heuristics (NH) in a device with a large screen size (*Xlarge*)
- Group 4 (G4), used heuristics by Machado (MH), in a device with a small screen size (*Small*).
- Group 5 (G5), used heuristics by Machado (MH), in a device with a large screen size (*Xlarge*).

The main objective of doing this set of evaluations is to compare control groups (G1, G2, G3) in a normal environment, using devices representative of extreme ranges (G2, small device and G3 with a large device), with groups G4 and G5, using MH heuristics. Figure 1 shows issues found related with the screen size, aggregated by group.

G1 group found a total of 17 usability issues, of which none was related with the screen size. We considered the closest heuristics to this metric were Nielsen heuristics *Aesthetic and Minimalist Design* and *Consistency and Standards*. For the first heuristic, no issues were reported, for the latter, no issue was related with the screen size.

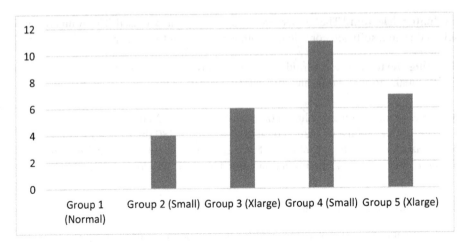

Fig. 1. Issues related with the screen size, found by group (aggregated).

G2 group found 4 issues related with the screen size, while G3 found 5. The first conclusion with these evaluations is that doing them only on devices considered in the normal category of screen sizes (*Normal*), as G1 did, we would have not been able to find issues that affect users with devices in the other groups.

Groups G4 and G5 found the most issues, in respect to groups G1, G2, G3. The issues were diverse as well. As shown in Fig. 2, this is an indication that heuristic evaluations of mobile applications can benefit from using heuristic designed for their context.

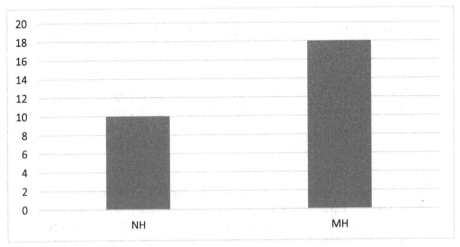

Fig. 2. Issues found by set of heuristics, NH (Nielsen Heuristics) and MH (Machado Heuristics).

From the analysis of this first part, one question emerges: Is it valid (or a good approach) to do an adaptation of the traditional Heuristic Evaluation, to cover as many user groups as possible? Using the traditional method has limits in finding this type of issues, and the context-appropriate heuristics used by groups G4 and G5, did show better results.

In conclusion: It is important to consider this characteristic while doing heuristic evaluations.

3.3 Proposal

According to Wiberg C. et al. (2003), even though there are many inspection methods described in usability, and their uses and descriptions are well-known, the development process of such methods has mostly not been accurately described [22]. It was not the intent of the work discussed here to do a deconstruction or complete revamp of the known heuristic evaluation method, but to do an adaptation based on the literature review, a preliminary evaluation and the objectives we want to achieve. Based on the work by Wiberg C. [23].

The proposal adapts the traditional method of Heuristic Evaluations [20], considering:

- The results obtained by the case study described above, which gave indications that issues related with the screen size can be found using the appropriate heuristics and selecting devices from the different size groups in existence.
- Selecting appropriate devices, representative of the most common size groups.
- The method used by Nielsen [11] for evaluations in mobile devices, in which one evaluator was used with different sets of devices.

Otherwise noted, the process for conducting the heuristic evaluation follows the method proposed by Nielsen [20], the traditional and most well-known.

In conclusion, the proposal consists of taking into consideration the following aspects when conducting heuristic evaluations of Android mobile applications with support for multiple screen sizes:

1. Selection of 4 devices, representative of the 4 screen size groups as defined by Google [18].
2. Each selected evaluator will use the 4 devices for each evaluation. To avoid a prolonged session (considering it should not take more than 2 h) and that preferences may interfere with the process, each evaluator will have a main device. This device will be used to run the totality of tests, while other devices should be used to verify (on a second run).
3. All issues are discussed by evaluators and a level of severity is applied (median). In Table 1, the "Device" column shows the affected devices (can be one or several), in a sample report with severity levels.

Table 1. Example of issue report with severity levels

Id	Issue description	Heuristic	Device(s)	Level
1	Message is now shown	MH1	ABC	3
2	Image is cut	MH1	D	1
3	"Next" button is cut	MH1	CD	3
4	Too much space is left unused	MH1	A	1

4 A Validation of the Proposal

To validate the proposed adaptation, a case study was conducted. We used a variation of the methodology of the heuristic evaluation described by Rusu [8], in which different groups are tasked to work with the same case, and the method of case study research as described by Hernandes Sampieri [21].

4.1 Context of the Case Study: A Banking Application

For the case study we used the mobile application for a bank with the higher number of users in Peru. This is pertinent since the application belongs to a large and recognized private institution, for which transactions are of high value for the users. Since it is available for Android from version 4.0 on-ward, the application is usable in devices without hardware restrictions like the size of the screen, which allows us to use it as a subject in the study.

The application allows the user to see account balance, credit card usage and state, payment of services, money transfers, in-between several other functionalities. The present study only considered transfers and payment of services.

Each evaluator was asked to complete the following tasks:

- Account affiliation
- Transfer
- Save transfer as favorite
- Use a favorite transfer
- Payment of a service

4.2 Prepositions of the Case Study

From the case study we expected to find the following:

- Issues related with screen size.
- Conclude if the issues could have been found by the control group.

4.3 Results

For the validation of the proposal, 2 groups were used: a control group (G1) which used the Nielsen heuristics, and the group using the heuristics from the proposal (G2). The control group (G1) conducted an evaluation following the traditional method and using a device from the "Normal" category. As a result, G1 could not find any issues directly related with the screen size of the device. The results from G2 are shown in Table 2.

Table 2. Summary of issues found by Group 2.

Id	Heuristic	No.	Perc.
MH1	Use of screen size	11	44%
MH2	Standards and Consistency	5	20%
MH3	Visibility and easy Access to all information	1	4%
MH4	Adequacy of the component and functionality	1	4%
MH5	Adequacy of the message and communication to the user	0	0%
MH6	Error prevention and rapid recovery to last stable state	1	4%
MH7	Ease of input	1	4%
MH8	Ease of access to all functionalities	2	8%
MH9	Immediate and observable feedback	0	0%
MH10	Help and documentation	1	4%
MH11	Reduction of the user's memory load	2	8%
	Total:	25	100%

Most problems found belong to heuristic MH1, "Use of Screen Size". The second group with issues belongs to heuristic MH2 (Standard and consistency). Issues related with the screen size; each letter represents a device:

In Table 3 we show the issues found by device. The device with the most issues is the Small model. The screen size resolution puts the device used in the small category, but the screen size is considered standard (4 in.). This is important to note since it can

Table 3. Issues found related with screen size, by device (A: Small, B: XLarge, C: Normal, D: Large)

Device	Issues
A	5
A D	1
B	3
B D	2

help find issues that would otherwise be missed and could affect the performance for some users.

Figure 3 also helps see the device with most issues is A (Small) followed by B (Xlarge). Next is the combination of B (Xlarge) and D (Large), and last is the combination of A (Small) and D (Large). As mentioned before, no issues were found for device C (Normal).

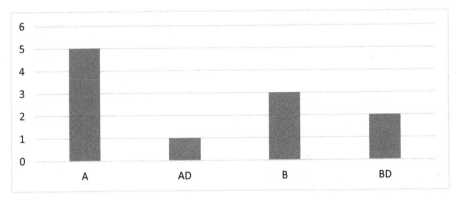

Fig. 3. Issues related with screen size, per device.

Of the obtained results, we can conclude that the used method has helped to uncover specific issues related with the use of screen size, which would not have been found without the use of the proposed adaptation. Group 1, or the control group, could not find issues related with the screen size, most likely because a standard device was used. To be able to know if the traditional use of the Nielsen heuristics can help even in these cases, devices with different screen sizes can be used. The present work does not include additional studies in such regard.

5 Final Remarks

- Usability and heuristic evaluations, in all aspects, have been and continue to be focus for research, and the use of mobile applications is in continued growth. Several authors remark the user interface and the screen size as limitations and/or characteristics that need to be considered before doing evaluations. As such, the necessity to continue studying these aspects persist, and their impact on the implementation of software.
- Nielsen heuristics can be used on mobile device applications with support for different screen devices, but with limitations. It is a necessity to specify the objective users and conduct tests with different devices, to find issues that otherwise could be overlooked and reach the final user.
- It is important to have available technical specifications that allows for the discovery of issues, such as the adaptation of the present work.
- The conducted validation of the proposed adaptation allowed us to find issues in an application currently in used for production environment. These issues do not appear

when a device considered standard is used, but on others, with different screen sizes. The conducted validation of the proposal is not enough to confirm its usefulness as a final or definitive tool, but it is an indication that these issues do exist and can occur. This is an intrinsic characteristic of mobile applications, and should be taken into consideration during development, especially if the intent is to reach a great number of final users.

6 Future Work

- Depending on costs and available resources, an evaluation consisting of groups of evaluators per device could be considered, instead of having one evaluator doing the tests with all devices. Keeping in mind that heuristic evaluations should come at a reasonable cost.
- Simulating evaluations in a controlled environment, using emulators instead of physical devices. This will allow for greater variety but would have different requirements, and costs.
- Evaluating other type of applications, with high number of users.

Acknowledgment. This study is highly supported by the *Pontifical Catholic University of Peru* "HCI, Design, User Experience, Accessibility & Innovation Technologies" Research Group.

References

1. Nayebi, F., Desharnais, J., Abran, A.: The state of the art of mobile application usability evaluation. In: 2012 25th IEEE Canadian Conference on Electrical and Computer Engineering (CCECE), Montreal, QC, pp. 1–4 (2012). https://doi.org/10.1109/ccece.2012.6334930
2. Higginbotham, J.: The future of the android operating system for augmentative and alternative communication, SIG 12. Persp. Augment. Alternat. Commun. 20(2), 52–56 (2012)
3. Inostroza, R., Rusu, C., Roncagliolo, S., Jiménez, C., Rusu, V.: Usability heuristics for touchscreen-based mobile devices. In: 2012 Ninth International Conference on Information Technology – New Generations. IEEE (2012)
4. Korhonen, H., Koivisto, E.: Playability heuristics for mobile games, mobile. In: HCI 2006 Proceedings of the 8th Conference on Human-Computer Interaction with Mobile Devices and Services, pp. 9–16 (2006)
5. Machado Neto, O., Da Graca Pimentel, M.: Heuristics for the assessment of interfaces of mobile devices. In: Proceedings of the 19th Brazilian symposium on Multimedia and the web. (WebMedia 2013). ACM (2013)
6. Moraveji, N., Soesanto, C.: Towards stress-less user interfaces: 10 design heuristics based on the psychophysiology of stress. In: CHI 2012 Extended Abstracts. ACM (2012)
7. Bertini, E., Gabrielli, S., Kimani, S.: Appropriating and assessing heuristics for mobile computing. In: Proceedings of the Working Conference on Advanced Visual Interfaces, AVI 2006. ACM (2006)
8. Rusu, C.: A methodology to establish usability heuristics. In: ACHI 2011: The Fourth International Conference on Advances in Computer-Human Interactions (2011)

9. Coursaris, C., Kim, D.: A meta-analytical review of empirical mobile usability studies. J. Usabil. Stud. **6**(3), 117–171 (2011)
10. Raptis, D., Tselios, N., Kjeldskov, J., Skov, M.: Does size matter? Investigating the impact of mobile phone screen size on users' perceived usability, effectiveness and efficiency. In: Proceedings of the 15th International Conference on Human-Computer Interaction with Mobile Devices and Services, pp. 127–136 (2013)
11. Nielsen, J., Budiu, R.: Mobile Usability, Pearson Education (2012)
12. Chae, M., Kim, J.: Size and structure matter to mobile users: an empirical study of the effects of screen size, information structure, and task complexity on user activities with standard web phones. J. Behav. Inf. Technol. **23**(3), 165–181 (2004)
13. Buchanan, G., Farrant, S., Jones, M., Thimbleby, H.: Improving mobile internet usability. In: Proceedings of the 10th International Conference on World Wide Web, pp. 673–680. ACM (2003)
14. Chittaro, L.: Visualizing information on mobile devices. J. Comput. **39**(3), 40–45 (2006)
15. Maniar, N., Bennett, E., Hand, S., Allan, G.: The effect of mobile phone screen size on video-based learning. J. Softw. 3(4), 51–61 (2008)
16. Mobile Usability 2nd research update (2011). https://www.nngroup.com/articles/mobile-usability-2nd-study/. Accessed 27 Jan 2021
17. Liu, H., Xie, X., Ma, W.Y., Zhang, H.J.: Automatic browsing of large pictures on mobile devices. In: MULTIMEDIA 2003 Proceedings of the Eleventh ACM International Conference on Multimedia, pp. 148–155 (2003)
18. Android Developer's Guid., https://developer.android.com/guide/index.html. Accessed 27 Sep 2017
19. Romaina, J.: Heuristic evaluation of android applications with multiple screen-size support: a case study. Master thesis, Pontificia Universidad Catolica del Peru (2018)
20. Nielsen, J.: Usability Engineering, Academic Press Inc, (1994)
21. Hernández Sampieri, R., Fernández Collado, C., Baptista Lucio, P.: Metodología de la Investigación – 6ª. Ed. – México D.F., MacGraw-Hill (2014)
22. Wiberg, C., Jegers, K., Desurvire, H.: How applicable is your evaluation methods – really? Analysis and Redesign of evaluation methods for fun and entertainment. In: Advances in Computer-Human Interactions. ACHI 2009 (2009)
23. Wiberg, C.: A Measure of Fun, Department of Informatics, Umea University. Print & Media AB, Umea (2003)

UX Aspects of AI Principles: The Recommender System of VoD Platforms

Cinthia Ruiz$^{(\boxtimes)}$ ⓘ and Manuela Quaresma ⓘ

LEUI | Laboratory of Ergodesign and Usability of Interfaces - PUC-Rio, Rio de Janeiro, Brazil
cinthiaruiz@aluno.puc-rio.br, mquaresma@puc-rio.br

Abstract. This paper aims to investigate the user experience with recommender systems of Video on Demand (VoD) platforms based in Machine Learning (ML), focusing on the Artificial Intelligence (AI) principles. We start from the hypothesis that the inclusion of AI algorithms has the potential to improve the user experience in digital systems, but they are still developed with a greater focus on technology, however, they should also consider more aspects regarding human factors. Nine principles on AI related to UX were selected from a compilation of seven lists of government and industry entities to understand the bases that every AI system should respect to ensure a good user experience. In sequence, we discuss their effects on the user experience of VoD platforms. To finish, the experience with these platforms were explored in a directed storytelling method involving thirty-one participants. Some behaviors and patterns found were analyzed and discussed to suggest guidelines to be applied to ML algorithms of VoD Platforms.

Keywords: User Experience (UX) · Artificial Intelligence (AI) · Recommender system

1 Introduction

We live in an era of great value for data. Data in the 21st century is like oil in the 18th century, as data drives the digital economy with new opportunities [1]. As technological advances arise, several digital products use the storage and processing of large volumes of data at high speed, such as those based on Artificial Intelligence.

Artificial intelligence (AI) is intelligence similar to humans, manifested by machines. AI is the ability of machines to use algorithms to learn from data and use what has been learned to make decisions as a human being would [2]. Without the need for rest, machines can analyze large volumes of information at once and with much more assertiveness than humans. Machine Learning (ML), is one of the main approaches to artificial intelligence, with which machines have the ability to learn from data without being explicitly programmed [2]. The result is suggestions or predictions for a specific situation, which allows a personalized experience for each user /individual.

ML application is already present in many of the innovative interfaces with which we interact, such as search engines, recommended links in e-commerce, audio or video

© Springer Nature Switzerland AG 2021
M. M. Soares et al. (Eds.): HCII 2021, LNCS 12781, pp. 535–552, 2021.
https://doi.org/10.1007/978-3-030-78227-6_38

streaming systems, facial detection, tax fraud detection, information technology security, car automation, medical applications, etc.

ML algorithms are dramatically changing the way we interact and how we develop systems. Before, we needed to invest a lot of time planning the best information architecture. Thus, the users could orient themselves through the entire volume of content and reach their choices, taking into account their mental model. Now, we have recommender systems with ML algorithms filtering the content and selecting the most appropriate for each profile, according to the machine standards.

In theory, this operation seems ideal for human-centered design, as it saves the user's cognitive effort and time in making decisions, presenting personalized navigation for each individual. In practice, some possible issues are already studied by researchers, such as bubble formation [3], loss of control [3, 4], weak mental model [4], and lack of transparency, among others.

Technologically, a lot has evolved and there is still a lot to evolve, mainly in the human factors of these human-computer systems. Currently, the evolution of ML /AI is still very much focused on the technology itself, driven by the technology's capacity and not the need for its users. Design methods can be employed to improve the users' experience with AI-based digital systems.

This paper aims to present a study that investigates the user experience with the ML of VoD platforms, focusing on AI principles on human interaction. Therefore, we seek to understand the user experience with AI-based recommender systems, so we choose VoD platforms for their popularity and wide audience. First, we selected nine principles described in available lists [5–13], related to interaction with AI, to understand the bases that every AI system must respect. To demonstrate the principles' relevance, we listed how each of these principles could affect the user experience with VoD platforms.

Subsequently, principles were explored in a directed storytelling method [4], an exploratory and qualitative approach that allows the researcher, through a conversation guided by some questions, to gather stories from the participants, related to their real experiences. Our goal with this method was to understand and document the participants' experiences with AI-based VoD platforms. We describe and analyze the behaviors and patterns found, to suggest guidelines to be applied to ML algorithms.

2 Recommender System of VoD Platform

Hidden algorithms increasingly govern our lives, making decisions for us every day, as those decisions made in our favor directly influence our behavior [14]. AI-based VoD platforms (e.g., Netflix, YouTube Premium, and Amazon Prime Video) recommend movies /series/videos we should watch. In reality, the final decision is up to the user, but the degree of influence is directly related to the degree of trust the user places in the system.

Recommender systems that use ML exploit contextual user behaviors and data. The recommendation functionality seeks to offer the user a direct path to the content appropriate to their profile. The ML algorithm aims to know the user, learn from him/her and make increasingly accurate predictions of the type of content he/she would choose, based on analysis of behavioral data and comparisons.

Recommender systems gained importance in the 90', due to the use of the Web for commercial and e-commerce transactions [15]. Innovation is personalization based on data collection, not viable in other media. The basic idea here is to infer the interests of users based on various data sources. In the case of VoD platforms, it can be explicit feedback, when the user marks the "like" or implicit, when the user watches a movie and the system interprets that he/she likes that type of content, or similar. Therefore, the analysis considers the interaction between users and content, as they assume that past choices and trends are good indicators of future choices. For their operation, recommender systems use collaborative filtering methods, content-based methods, and knowledge-based methods. There is also an exception in which the recommender system suggests based on the requirements specified by the user, and not on their history.

In order to maintain user engagement, the recommender system needs to be assertive. To accomplish this goal, it must select relevant content to the user, in addition, to presenting news, that is, content not yet watched by the user but adhering to his/her interest. Another important factor is the novelty, with content that surprises you positively. It occurs when content is not obvious according to his/her profile, but that captures his/her interest. Finally, the diversity in the types of content presented increases the chances of being chosen and avoids the tedium of a selection with items very similar to each other.

Although ML systems appear to be autonomous in making decisions, they are made for humans and by humans. These are human decisions that drive data processing and mining, the selection of optimization goals, and the dialogue designed with end-users with their implicit and explicit feedback mechanisms. In this way, they are totally influenced by humans, from design decisions to interaction. Human decisions affect the results of ML systems in practically all stages of the process [16]. The authors also point out that the ecosystem that surrounds any machine learning system is a completely human issue, whether consciously designed or not. Therefore, there is already much recent research investigating the problems in user interaction with AI-based systems.

Bodegraven [3] makes a connection with what Eli Pariser described as "the filter bubble" in 2011, about how the personalized web influenced people's reading and thinking, with predictive systems. He believes that the same risk applies when devices anticipate our needs and act accordingly. An experience bubble is formed in which the user is caught in a cycle of interaction with the content. "When everything is foreseen and anticipated without the opportunity to change this pattern, it violates the concept of free will." [3]. There are many situations in which people prefer AI to just expand their skills rather than completely automating a task [6]. Bodegraven [3] concludes that the design principles from renowned usability researchers (such 10 usability heuristics or usability golden rules) are insufficient for automation, as they disregard the principles of transparency, control, loops, and privacy, but reinforces that the UX Design is fundamental to offer the user an unprecedented and predictive experience with technology.

The lack of transparency of the algorithms hinders users to understand the operation of the system, as they do not know how random the recommendations are or influenced by their interaction [4]. This fact is aggravated because the user's actions do not immediately impact the result of the recommendations. The recommender systems of the ML-based VoD platforms are considered black boxes, which therefore impairs the formation of the users' mental model of functioning.

3 AI Principles

With so many issues mainly involving ethics and the possibilities for the future with the use of AI in digital systems increasingly present in society, several entities, such as groups of researchers, government agencies and private institutions, have dedicated themselves to defining AI principles. The intention of these lists is to provide recommended practices to protect society and its individuals, ensuring the best use of the potential of AI.

None of these lists are focused on the user experience from the UX Design point of view, but we can make relationships because they deal with issues that impact the way people relate to these systems. After raising and studying several lists, we selected the ones that we think are most suitable for our study: Beijing AI Principles [5]; Google AI Principles [6]; Statement on Artificial Intelligence, Robotics and 'Autonomous' Systems [7]; Asilomar AI Principles [8]; Microsoft AI principles [9]; AI R&D Principles [10]; OECD Principles on AI [11]; Harmonious Artificial Intelligence Principles [12]; Montreal Declaration Responsible AI [13].

We extract the arguments that impact the user experience and compile them in the following table (Table 1), discussing the effects on the user experience of VoD platforms:

Table 1. AI Principles and their impacts in User Experience with VoD Platforms

1 - Transparency	
It must be clear to users the inputs and outputs of the interaction with the AI system, as well as the rationale of the system's decision making, so that people can understand and trust the predictions	The absence of tranparency generates fragility in the users' mental model, hindering the interaction with VoD platforms, as users do not understand how the content is organized, to orient themselves. Furthermore, it undermines the rationale and confidence in the system's predictions, as they do not understand the logic of the selection offered to it. Users must be able to apply their own judgments to make their choices
2 - Controllability	
Users should feel in control of the AI system and not the other way around, that is, controlled by it. People must choose how and when to delegate decisions to the system, in order to expand their own skills. People cannot be deceived or manipulated by AI	The lack of user control risks the dosage of the automation of the VoD platform and consequent disrespect to the decision-making power of the user. When users feel manipulated, they do not trust the content offered to them
3 - Safety and Well-being	
Users should be safe and feel comfortable using the AI system. The systems must be designed to improve people's personal and professional life conditions, without increasing stress and anxiety, respecting their choices, as long as they do not cause harm to other individuals	Failure to respect this principle can generate psychological damage to users, leading to the abandonment of the VoD platform

(continued)

Table 1. (continued)

4 - Privacy	
Users must have the right to consent or not to the collection, distribution and analysis of their data, as well as to access, manage and control the data they generate	Failure to comply with this principle violates ethics and exposes users of the VoD platform. When users feel their privacy violated, they lose confidence in using the system
5 - Human Dignity	
Users should be aware of when they are interacting with a machine or another human being. AI systems must respect international human rights law	A VoD platform that did not respect human rights, would be hurting ethics and would lose the trust of its users
6 - User Assistance	
AI systems should guide users in their choices, with a view to good information architecture and usability. Users should have technical information, support and an open dialogue channel available to send feedback	The absence of assistance directly impacts the interaction with the VoD platform. If the system does not have a good usability and/or is not organized according to the users' expectation, it requires a lot of cognitive effort. In addition, users may feel lost without access to technical information and without being able to use a direct communication channel
7 - Fairness	
AI systems should not practice injustice, prejudice and stigmatization. They must balance competing interests and objectives, considering means and ends	When not followed, it can make users feel excluded or prejudged by the VoD platform
8 - Solidarity	
AI systems should encourage the interpersonal relationships of their users, as well as collaboration between people	The lack of solidarity can increase the loneliness and individuality of the users of the VoD platform
9 - Diversity	
Users should not have their choices restricted to certain standards. AI systems must consider the diversity of society, respecting different behaviors and opinions. AI systems must prevent the formation of filter bubbles, which trap users in restricted profiles	Failure to comply with this principle may result in personalization not being effective, since they would not consider diversity. In addition, it would always offer the same content cycle, capturing the user to his/her history, without novelty. These factors create monotony and decrease user engagement

4 Methodology

Directed Storytelling is an exploratory and qualitative research method that allows the researcher, through a conversation guided by some questions, to gather participants' stories from the past, related to their real experiences [17]. Our goal with this method was to understand and document the participants' experiences with AI-based VoD platforms.

We created a screening questionnaire with a consent form for participation in Directed Storytelling session, with some essential explanations pertaining to the method and questions to define the volunteers' profile. We use the snowball method to expand our recruitment. We applied the pilot tests with five volunteers, and after adjustments to the form and script, we continued the study with thirty-one participants, users of AI-based VoD platforms.

The selected participants were residents in Brazil, aged 18 to over 65, users of VoD platforms. We seek to cover different levels of experience, considering when they became a user and the frequency of use, regardless of the devices used for interaction. The vast majority of participants (25) interact with VoD platforms through SmartTV or Television with an device that allows streaming of content. Only one of the participants has contact with only one VoD platform present in Brazil and the vast majority (29) preferentially use Netflix over other platforms such as Globo Play, YouTube Premium, Amazon Prime Video, HBO Go, Telecine, Fox Play, Apple TV+, Now NET Claro, Looke, Mubi, Disney+, Stremio and Stan. As participants were asked to focus their responses on the platform of their choice, most of the comments referred to Netflix, which did not prevent them from making comparisons with other platforms that used it.

The sessions were carried out during the period of social isolation caused by COVID-19, in July 2020, an opportune moment to encourage the consumption of content from VoD platforms, although only slightly less than half of the participants (14) have declared having increased its frequency. There was already the movement of VoD platforms to replace cable and open TV subscriptions, so some participants spontaneously commented on their migration. The data released by Anatel [18] – the Brazilian agency of telecommunication, also show a constant drop in access to pay-TV since 2017. The fact that users can access a vast catalog of content at a very accessible value and available at any time, through different devices is certainly a great attraction of VoD platforms.

The sessions were held remotely, using the Zoom platform, with video - audio and image recording. We started from a guide of questions to be addressed, not necessarily in the same order, and added what we deemed necessary, according to what each participant told us. Although not foreseen in a Directed Storytelling session, we have included some moments of observation through the computer screen. The observation was essential to confront people's perception of reality, in addition to motivating people to give more details about the interaction.

All the stories reported by the participants were transcribed in a table, with which we organized the comments by topics. The narratives of experiences that emerged from the stories were grouped together in an affinity diagram to identify common patterns. We performed a top-down analysis, relating the comments to the nine principles proposed in our list, to identify which ones are served.

5   Results

We identified several issues to be considered when designing AI-based VoD platforms. As this system is used primarily for entertainment, using it is a free choice for people and contributing to their well-being. They do not seem to bring problems related to human dignity and fairness since their predictions do not affect equity or harm people.

The principle of transparency of the system decision-making is not used by VoD platforms. It was clear that people understand that there is an automated mechanism making recommendations for content in a personalized way for them, based on their browsing history, but the rules are not explicit. In this way, many users are suspicious of the system's recommendations and resort to external recommendations, such as tips from others or searches on the Internet through specialized channels. VoD platforms could take advantage of the strength of the recommendations that exist between people, to encourage solidarity and collaboration between them, increasing the engagement of users on the platform and improving the experience. Explainable AI literature addresses the importance of transparency in scenarios in which decision making, aided by ML predictions, involves high risks, especially in life [19, 20]. Transparency should also be valued for entertainment in order to increase trust in the recommendation system.

Directly impacted by the lack of transparency, there is the principle of controllability, because the rules of operation of the system are not clear, in order to be able to control it. Most people know that there is a mechanism that they need to learn from, but they do not know how to teach it. When users feel manipulated or want more control, they turn to the search engine, a resource also used to escape the filter bubble, treated in the principle of diversity. To improve control over the system, the profile preference information could be configurable. The privacy principle has also been widely discussed in the market and academia [21]. However, users still do not seem to understand all the issues involved and are unaware of the policies applied by VoD platforms.

Related to user assistance and diversity principles, we identified divergent behaviors, leading us to question whether the interfaces could be even more personalized, with customization of the operating rules of the VoD platforms. The solidarity principle could also be explored, considering that users use external references to assist in their decision. We realized that gender, age or education were not determinants for certain types of behavior. The most relevant was the familiarity with the technology, because people with more knowledge, feel more secure in criticizing what they think is wrong with the systems, while people with less knowledge in technology, are more permissive with the problems that hinder the interaction.

Although problems with interaction with AI have been raised, the mechanism is useful for most users, who are already accustomed to its model and take these expectations as a reference for other similar systems. Below, we present the result and analysis of the findings organized by the principles.

5.1 Transparency

The system must make clear to the user the rules of its operation, for this, users need to understand which aspects of their interaction generate which reactions of the system. It is essential that the system makes the rational of its decisions transparent to the user, so that people understand and have confidence in the recommendation system.

More transparency and control are needed for users to know the basic decisions and interpretation made by the predictive system, so implementing feedback loops can offer users the opportunity to express themselves during interaction [3]. "Explainability" and trust are inherently linked, although it warns that it is not always possible for an AI system to exhibit a high degree of self-explanation [6]. Unfortunately, the models with the best performance are the least transparent [20]. The perfect time to show explanations is in response to user action [6]. It is important to provide meaningful explanations for the user to understand why he/she may find a particular movie interesting. This approach increases the likelihood that the user will accept the recommendation, improve the user experience, loyalty and retention [15].

Normally, VoD platforms have a help area, but they do not explain all the operation and rules of the built-in ML algorithms. We tried to understand the participants' perceptions according to their presentations regarding the use of the platforms and we found some issues.

It is not clear to users the rationale of the recommendations, therefore, they do not form an adequate mental model for the functioning of the system:

Twenty-six participants declare that the recommender system is based on their consumption habit, as they identify that the content offered is related to what they watch, but they are not clear about the level of customization versus randomness, influence of content popularity or promotional disclosure. It is also unclear how the system learns, as some believe that the recommendations are based on the types of content they watch most often, but others believe that only the most recent ones are taken into account.

Users are not clear about the level of customization of platform:

Many doubts arise regarding which categories are personalized or common to all users, as well as, if the customization would be by account or by profile. They also do not know that the images of the contents, the names and order of the categories are personalized.

Users do not know how to influence the recommendations, to improve the assertiveness of the system:

As the participants are not clear about the rules of the recommender system, they differ in their beliefs about the factors that can influence it. A feature that goes unnoticed is the "like" content, as only one of the participants demonstrated to perceive their influence for the recommendations. Three participants believe that the fact of using the search tool already influences the recommendation, while two believe that the system considers the trailers watched by them. Three believe that navigation data on other systems connected to the internet are also collected to contribute to the platform's content recommender system. Three understand that there is a relationship of profiles influencing the recommendations.

The lack of transparency reduces users' confidence in the system:

More issues arose, mainly involving the lack of confidence in the recommender system. Seven participants commented that they enjoyed watching content indicated by other people, the same ones that did not arouse interest while being offered by the platform. Also, twenty participants demonstrate that they trust other people's opinions more than the recommender system, since they prioritize the choice of content by referral from other people, searches on social media or categories clearly influenced by other users such as those that take into account the popularity and ranking of views. We believe that if there were more transparency in the recommendations, users would trust the results of the system's predictions. Five participants even comment that the platforms make recommendations for commercial interests, which reduces the credibility of the recommender system.

The delay in the system's learning process makes it difficult for users to perceive the result of their actions:

A perceived problem with the report of three participants was that as the ML algorithm needs time to learn from the use of people, the first interactions still do not bring recommendations that are so aligned with the user's profile and some people get used to not browse categories. Greater transparency could increase the tolerance of these people and motivate them to continue investing in the recommender system. It occurred to one of these participants, during the sessions, to navigate through the interface and be surprised how the recommendations were appropriate to their profile, but he did not explore it, based on his first experiences.

Working with AI transparency is essential to gain trust and improve users' experience with the recommender system. We found that most of the participants are aware that there is an automatic mechanism, but it is not clear how it works and the level of customization to make the most of its capacity. Despite this, we understand that a limit must be found for the algorithm's explainability, which does not interfere with the business model of the platforms, and does not reveal important secrets for its competition.

5.2 Controllability

AI systems must not induce humans, on the contrary, they must expand their capabilities with the human in control. Therefore, the final decision must always be made by the human.

We want to understand how people feel about the fact that ML algorithms make a selection of content to present to users, according to what the machines identify are most appropriate for each profile. Do people feel they have control over the system or do they feel controlled by it?

Platform recommendations benefit most users:

Seven participants demonstrated that they liked the guidance given to them by the recommendations, as they believe that it facilitates the work of choice, although one has declared the feeling of persecution and another two has said that they feel restricted by the AI, because they always think they are losing good content that are not offered to them.

Users are not able to configure their profiles to help the recommendation:

Eighteen participants would like to be able to indicate their tastes to help the recommender system, not least because their interests may change and the automated system would still take a while to reflect the change. For five participants, more important than even indicating their tastes, would be to indicate what should never be suggested to them. The platforms could be flexible to the level of configuration that the user was willing to do. People have different preferences in using the system and different levels of error tolerance. Some people prefer to spend more time entering data to have full control over the system, while others prefer to start using the system right away, accepting corrections during the interaction with the system [22].

Users do not know how to help the recommendater system:

Regardless of the feeling of control, in general, participants are not clear how to influence the recommender system, a theme that also touches on the principle of transparency, because if users do not know the rules of the system, they cannot have control over it. The greatest perception is that the system recommends based on the browsing history, so eight believe that increasing the frequency of interaction with the platform, would be the best way to influence the recommender system. Only one demonstrated a more active attitude, such as marking "like", and three suggested the inclusion of this functionality, showing the lack of knowledge.

Users should have more control over some features:

Three participants complained about being offered abandoned content in the "keep watching" category, since they did not like the content, they would like to be able to withdraw it. Two participants are uncomfortable with the automatic trailers and would like to be able to disable them.

The search engine is interpreted by users as the best way to take control of the system:

Ten were satisfied with the level of control they currently have over the platforms, as they claim that when they need more control, they resort to the search engine. However, some somewhat controversial arguments emerged, such as one who said he did not want to have more control over the recommender system, so that the platform does not know more about his profile. Four others who believe that the more the recommender system gets the choices right for their profiles, it leads to more content restrictions, hiding some that might interest them. Three still declare themselves satisfied claiming they do not consider themselves demanding in relation to technology.

Eighteen participants would like to be able to indicate their tastes to help the recommender system, not least because their interests may change and the automated system would still take a while to reflect the change. For five participants, more important than even indicating their tastes, would be to indicate what should never be suggested to them.

Although innovation is in the recommender system, people prefer to use search:

Only six participants navigate the interface before resorting to the search tool, as they are uncomfortable with typing letters using a remote control. It is worth mentioning that this limitation is inherent to the input device, the remote control, not to AI. In contrast, twenty-five use the search engine directly, believing that they will spend less time, despite the fact that most of the content recommended by external sources is available in categories based on news or popularity.

The control principle is also very important to ensure a good experience. We note that although the recommender system can be improved with more conscious interference from users, VoD platforms are not interpreted as manipulative, since the final option of choice is the user's and the search tool allows the expansion of the options offered. The point of concern is the fact that the search is more used than personalized recommendations, highlighting the need for investment in improvements to increase user engagement.

5.3 Safety and Well-Being

An AI system should allow its users to make their choices, as long as they do not harm others, promoting well-being. VoD platforms offer content - series and movies - very much focused on people's entertainment. We try to verify with what objectives the participants use VoD platforms.

VoD platforms provide leisure for users:
All participants claimed to watch the content for entertainment, leisure, distraction, relaxation, with two also watching documentaries for knowledge and two also for work. Twenty-five declare that they use the platforms preferably at night, alone or accompanied. On weekends, the frequency also increases.

We conclude that the principle of safety and well-being is well attended by the AI of the platforms, since no participant was irritated by its use, on the contrary, they use it to relieve the stress of daily life, exercising their freedom of choice.

5.4 Privacy

Ideally, AI systems should allow people to have knowledge and management about the use of their data, as well as the right not to be tracked, ensuring protection and respect for their data. Bodegraven [3] warns about data privacy. According to the author, users tend to think that they "have nothing to hide", and companies are increasingly sharing user data without their knowing and being aware of the consequences. Automation will ask for much more data from its users to correctly estimate needs. Google PAIR [6] suggests that the system explain to users the origin of the data and how it is used by the AI system, so as not to damage trust. This is because users can be surprised by their own information when they see it in a new context, usually in a way that does not appear to be private or that they did not know the system had access to.

AI systems need to collect user data to make their predictions, but they must comply with the privacy principle. Platforms generally make their privacy policy available on their interfaces. We seek to understand the users' knowledge of the use of their data.

Users do not know which, how many and how their data is stored and used by the platforms:
Five participants claimed not to know which of their data would be stored by the platforms. In contrast, nineteen point out the registration and billing data, two already look at the platforms to store their navigation data. The remaining five declare that the platforms do not have any data, since the account would not be in his/her name.

It is evident that most people are unaware of the amount of data they generate, data that is stored and used for some purpose unknown to them.

The privacy policies of the platforms are extensive and not very objective, making it difficult for users to understand it:
One participant claimed to have authorized the system to store and use their data, the others do not remember, but imagine having accepted the contract, which they do not read. The vast majority are not concerned with the use of their data or claim to feel obligated to use the service. The scenario is already different when it is for your data to

be marketed or provided to partners. Nineteen say they do not accept and twelve accept. Since this authorization is already included in the platform policy and to be using it, they were accepted.

Few users feel a lack of privacy when using the platforms:

Along the sessions, more questions related to privacy appeared. Two participants highlighted the lack of privacy between the profiles of the same Netflix account, which does not require authentication to switch. Three other participants reported that they feel their privacy invaded by the necessary screening for the recommender system, but that they recognize its benefit.

Data privacy is a topic that is being discussed a lot, as data is a rich source to reach knowledge, giving a lot of power to those who hold it. Privacy policies make information available, but not accessible to people, who are unaware of the dangers to which they are exposed. Platforms make it difficult for users to have access to their own data, as they can even request it, but the process implies a long wait. They also do not allow data management and do not make tracking optional, therefore, they infringe the privacy principle.

5.5 Human Dignity

Basically, this principle implies respecting human rights and not deceiving users into believing that they are interacting with a person, when they are interacting with a machine.

The human rights of users are respected by the platforms:

It is evident to all participants that there is an automated content selection mechanism, as there was no reference to humans making this choice. No disrespect for human rights was raised. Only one said he was offended by the recommendations he receives by email, as he considers them of questionable quality and would not like them to be related to his profile.

We believe that VoD platforms do not pose problems related to the principle of human dignity.

5.6 User Assistance

The principle of user assistance relates to the usability and information architecture of the system, to assist the user in making appropriate choices. It should provide information about the system and collect feedback from users, seeking improvement. We seek to raise user behaviors to understand details of the interaction with the system, check the assertiveness of ML algorithms incorporated into the platforms and confirm whether there is a feedback collection channel.

The content information provided by the platforms helps users' choices:

Fourteen participants comment that to choose content, they use titles, images, synopses, casts and/or genres, with five still adding trailers. All are useful information to help guide your choice. Two participants pointed out the duration of the content as a decisive factor for choosing the content, which needs to fit in the time they have available, however there is no way to search for the duration and it seems that the AI does not take this into account for the recommendations. The titles of the categories themselves already have the function of guiding the choice, although two participants comment not to notice them, being attracted more by the mosaic of images, although the same content is repeated on the screen, it can already appear in more than one category.

The platform recommender system disregards the users' state of mind:
One factor that can influence the choice of users, but that is overlooked by ML is the people's mood. Thirteen participants believe that humor does not influence their choice of content. Some justify that when they are following a series, they follow the sequence. In contrast, thirteen declare that humor influences and comment on examples. Five did not know how to answer. Some AI-based streaming audio platforms do a good job of offering different playlists considering possible moods of their users.

The search result presents recommendations in addition to those requested by the user:
The search tool is a widely used resource when users access the platform to watch predefined content, in this case, the most common is to write the title already known. However, the search tool can also assist in the exploration of the catalog, in case the user wanted to escape the selection made by ML. We then raised some ways of using it. It is possible to search for actor, director, genre and even year on Netflix. One participant complained that when looking for the actor in the search, movie with the actor appear and movies of only the similar genre, without the actor. He feels uncomfortable because although he has already searched for the specific actor, he still needs to check the list of each content offered. This is because the search never reports that it did not find what was sought and, in addition, it always takes the opportunity to include recommendations mixed with the expected result. Although only one participant spoke about the result of the search, we believe that the issue deserves to be explored to better understand users' expectations.

Some features present in the platforms help users:
Depending on the platform, there are some features that also help in choosing the content. Eight participants create lists of content, selecting their interests to watch later. Seven participants like to filter the contents in series or movies, so as not to get confused when choosing. Two participants who are unaware of this functionality, complain that they waste a lot of time identifying the type. Even with all these features to help choose the content, four participants complain that it takes too long to reach their goal.

The same platform has different features according to the device, frustrating users' expectations:
There have been some complaints regarding Netflix, from users who use more than one device to access the platform. The functionality that presents the contents that will be released soon is available in the mobile app, but not in the TV interface. The functionality to access the history is available on the computer interface, but not on the TV. That way, users need to access their account on more than one device, to have the full experience. We understand that VoD platforms are cross-device and interfaces must respect their context of use, but also meet users' expectations.

The organization of the content and ease of use of the platforms are satisfactory for users:

VoD platforms seek to leave the traditional gender classification to bring new forms of groupings, which can be useful and interesting to users. We concluded that they are on the right path, as twenty-four participants showed satisfaction with these personalized categories, against only seven who prefer the traditional ones. In spite of pointing out some problems, in general, the participants consider the platforms to be easy to use. AI brings a new way of organizing content, less hierarchical than the traditional and more varied, as it allows for more combinations and specifics. We understand that this change is being well accepted. If, on the one hand, the user loses track of the whole and of the levels to go to a certain content, on the other hand, he/she is already one step away from each category pre-selected by the system.

There is no open channel for user feedback:

Regarding maintaining an open channel for feedback, we have not identified a great incentive on the part of VoD platforms. Although there is a "like", no participant claimed to be aware of how to give feedback. In the current development scenario, digital products are launched from the market and are constantly evolving. For this continuous improvement and adaptation to the new needs of users, it would be of great value that all VoD platforms maximize this direct and spontaneous contact from users, made possible by the feedback channels.

Shared profiles impair the assertiveness of the recommendations made to users:

Another key issue to ensure a good use experience with ML is its assertiveness. In order for ML to be able to correctly target recommendations, people with different tastes cannot use the same profile. We noticed that some users are not aware of this issue. We found that of the thirty-one participants, seventeen use individual profiles and fourteen share a profile, although seven of them claim that people who share the profile with them, watch together or have the same taste. Although our sample is small because it is a qualitative approach, we have indications that a large number of users of VoD platforms share a profile. This factor compromises the success of the recommendations and, consequently, damages the experience of these users. VoD platforms could seek ways to raise awareness among users to avoid this problem.

Platforms can improve ML algorithms to increase assertiveness for users:

Nine participants claim that the suggestions do not match their taste. Twelve have the perception that sometimes they get it right and sometimes they don't, and four say that generally the categories are in accordance with their profile, but the contents are not interesting. Seven claim that the recommendations match your profile. Three were unable to locate the recommendations. In addition, nine say they are not bothered by the errors of the recommender system, taking the blame for watching content that is too varied or that they judge outside their profile. To make a choice, ten participants focus on the first categories and the first contents that appear on the lines. These users claim that some categories that they don't like, appear at the end, probably used to the ordering by relevance, typical of the search engines present in web interfaces. Four participants comment that they like the content related to the selected content. One even looks for something he has watched just to choose a similar one in the recommendations. Eighteen claim that already watched content is offered.

The principle of user assistance involves many important issues that need to be studied very carefully by the platforms, in order to target ML algorithms according to the expectations of their users.

5.7 Fairness

AI systems must be fair and free from prejudice. VoD platforms make inferences relating to user profiles, but we have not identified any results that violate this principle.

5.8 Solidarity

AI systems should encourage relationships and collaboration between people. We try to understand how the platforms meet or could meet this principle. We know that platforms use a relationship between the profiles of users, to assist in the recommender system, in addition to guiding new productions, but this is not explicit in the interface.

Platforms do not exploit exchanges between users:
Generally, the recommender system uses a relationship between the profiles of users, to assist in suggestions, but is not explicit for the end-user. Twenty-six participants exchange tips with others or collect posts on social networks. Twelve participants said that usually search for tips in the media: internet, social networks, youtubers, feeds or newspaper. We believe that the system could better exploit these interactions between users.

5.9 Diversity

AI systems should not impose a standardization of society, as well as trap people in a filtering bubble. We try to understand whether this principle is respected by platforms.

Users behave differently when choosing content, but platforms apply the same recommendation rules to everyone:
People explore the interface in different ways to choose content. Twelve participants are attracted by the novelty, since they showed a preference for choosing highlighted content such as launches, news or recently added. While eleven prefer to choose in categories where there is evidence of the opinion of other people, such as "popular", "on the rise" or "Top10". In contrast, four participants claim to be prejudiced against this type of category by popularity, as they believe that their tastes do not coincide with that of the masses or are bothered by a wide variety of topics within the same category. One is attracted when there is a warning that it is the last days that the content will be available on the platform. Seven participants already explore the interface browsing all kinds of categories. Although the platforms work with several features to personalize the recommendations, the same rules apply to all users, even if they behave differently. There is a lot of talk about a single interface for each user, made possible by ML. Indeed, the final result can be unique when we consider the composition of the content selection

and some elements of the interface, such as categories and images. However, there is room for systems to go deeper into the types of behaviors and relevant choice factors, to adapt their recommendations and enrich the use experiences.

Some categories/features are common to all users:

Some platforms, in addition to the categories based on genre, releases and popular, have custom categories. We found divergent behavior also in its use. Eight participants comment that they like the category that recommends content similar to a recently watched one, while six complain that the related content does not maintain the same quality or that they do not want to watch something similar afterwards. Another divergence was in relation to the category that suggests for the user to watch content again, while three aimed to use it a lot, as they keep repeating a content they liked, four say that I will never or rarely review a content already seen, as they prefer to invest their time in new contents. Considering these differences in use, it would be good to customize the interface to go beyond the type of content chosen and suppress categories that seem fixed, when not used by users.

The search engine helps users not feel trapped in a filtering bubble:

We found that people understand that the recommender system filters content for them, according to what they define for their profile, but they know that they can access the catalog through the search tool. Only two report discomfort in having to resort to searching to access the complete catalog, although one believes that not even the search has access to the total.

When it comes to diversity, platforms could be more flexible to different behavior profiles, going beyond the customizations already practiced for content recommendations. In addition, as the ML algorithm tends towards a filtering bubble, the search tool is seen by users as best way out when they want to expand the diversity of content options. Like Makatos et al. [23] suggested a way to maximize the diversity of exposure on social networks, there may be ways for VoD platforms to evolve their ML algorithms, without losing the adherence of the recommendations to each user profile.

6   Conclusion

Several types of data are being generated by our interactions and stored without even being aware of the volume and purpose. Artificial Intelligence takes advantage of this data to provide us with amenities. Machine Learning algorithms are present in several digital systems, processing data at high speed to guide us with their predictions, but are they really working according to our expectations and meeting our needs?

We believe that systems with AI are still designed with a greater focus on the possibilities of technology, but we need to analyze the interaction with AI from the point of view of human factors. Although AI is not a new area, its spread across so many innovative digital products is relatively recent. We are still getting used to the new model of interaction brought by it. In the same way, we are still getting used to designing systems with this technology.

Our intention was to investigate the users' experience with the AI-based VoD platforms. We understand that respecting the AI principles proposed here is a key factor in improving the users' experience with ML-based VoD platforms. With the Directed Storytelling method applied, we concluded that some requirements of the principles are being met, but many still need to be improved, as we pointed out in their respective analyzes.

As a next step, we would explore in a quantitative way the behaviors found in this study, to expand the sample and dimension the findings, so that prioritization is possible.

Acknowledgments. This study was financed in part by the Coordenação de Aperfeiçoamento de Pessoal de Nível Superior – Brasil (CAPES) – Finance Code 001.

References

1. Tsihrintzis, G.A., Sotiropoulos, D.N., Jain, L.C.: Machine learning paradigms: advances in data analytics. In: Tsihrintzis, G.A., Sotiropoulos, D.N., Jain, L.C. (eds.) Machine Learning Paradigms. ISRL, vol. 149, pp. 1–4. Springer, Cham (2019). https://doi.org/10.1007/978-3-319-94030-4_1
2. Rouhiainen, L.: Artificial intelligence: 101 things you must know today about our future (2018)
3. Van Bodegraven, J.: How anticipatory design will challenge our relationship with technology. In: AAAI Spring Symposium - Technical report SS-17-01-:435–438 (2017)
4. Budiu, R.: Can users control and understand a ui driven by machine learning? (2018) https://www.nngroup.com/articles/machine-learning-ux/. Accessed 22 Nov 2020
5. BAAI: Beijing AI Principles (2019). https://www.baai.ac.cn/news/beijing-ai-principles-en.html. Accessed 07 May 2020
6. Google PAIR: People + AI Guidebook (2020). https://research.google/teams/brain/pair/. Accessed 07 May 2020
7. European Group on Ethics in Science and New Technologies (EGE), European Commission Statement on artificial intelligence, robotics and "autonomous" systems. Brussels (2018)
8. Future of Life Institute (FLI): Asilomar AI Principles (2017). https://futureoflife.org/ai-principles/. Accessed 07 May 2020
9. Microsoft: Microsoft AI Principles (2018). https://www.microsoft.com/en-us/ai/our-approach-to-ai. Accessed 07 May 2020
10. Ministry of Internal Affairs and Communications (MIC) the Government of Japan: AI R&D Principles (2017)
11. OECD Council Recommendation on Artificial Intelligence: OECD Principles on AI (2019). https://www.oecd.org/going-digital/ai/principles/. Accessed 07 May 2020
12. Research Center For Brain-Inspired Intelligence, Institute of Automation CA of S Harmonious Artificial Intelligence Principles (2018). http://bii.ia.ac.cn/hai/index.php. Accessed 07 May 2020
13. Université de Montréal: Montreal Declaration Responsible AI (2017). https://www.montrealdeclaration-responsibleai.com/the-declaration. Accessed 09 Jul 2020
14. Springer, A., Hollis, V., Whittaker, S.: Dice in the black box: user experiences with an inscrutable algorithm. In: AAAI Spring Symposium - Technical report SS-17-01-:427–430 (2017)
15. Aggarwal, C.C.: Recommender Systems: The Textbook. Springer International Publishing, Yorktown Heights (2016). https://doi.org/10.1007/978-3-319-29659-3
16. Cramer, H., Thorn, J.: Not-so-autonomous, very human decisions in machine learning: Questions when designing for ML. In: AAAI Spring Symposium - Technical report SS-17-01-:412–414 (2017)

552 C. Ruiz and M. Quaresma

17. Evenson, S.: Directed storytelling: interpreting experience for design. In: Bennett, A. (ed.) Design Studies, pp. 231–240. Princeton Architectural Press, New York (2006)
18. Agência Nacional de Telecomunicações (Anatel), Painéis de Dados Homepage. https://www.anatel.gov.br/paineis/acessos/tv-por-assinatura. Accessed 10 Sep 2020
19. Ribera, M., Lapedriza, A.: Can we do better explanations? A proposal of user-centered explainable AI. In: Joint Proceedings of the ACM IUI 2019 Workshops, Los Angeles, USA, March 20. ACM, New York, p. 7 (2019)
20. Samek, W., Wiegand, T., Müller, K-R.: Explainable artificial intelligence: understanding, visualizing and interpreting deep learning models (2017)
21. Holzinger, A.: From machine learning to explainable AI. In: DISA 2018 - IEEE World Symposium Digital Intelligence for Systems and Machines Proceedings, pp. 55–66 (2018)
22. Setlur, V., Tory, M.: Exploring synergies between visual analytical flow and language pragmatics. In: AAAI Spring Symposium - Technical report SS-17-01-:423–426 (2017)
23. Matakos, A., Aslay, C., Galbrun, E., Gionis, A.: Maximizing the diversity of exposure in a social network. IEEE Trans. Knowl. Data Eng. 1 (2020)

A Usability Evaluation Process Proposal for ATM Interfaces

Joe Sahua$^{(\boxtimes)}$, Arturo Moquillaza , and Freddy Paz

Pontificia Universidad Católica Del Perú, Avenida Universitaria 1801, Lima 32,
San Miguel, Peru
{jsahuad,amoquillaza,fpaz}@pucp.pe

Abstract. Usability evaluations are relevant to know the Usability of a software product. However, it is becoming increasingly important to obtain quantitative information that can be measured, and therefore be compared and be classified. In the ATM domain, not only there is very little literature on proposed methods, but in general very little information on usability benchmarking between ATM applications. In that sense, we propose a Usability Evaluation Process for ATM interfaces. This process allows, through an ordered set of stages, a set of artifacts, techniques and a checklist, to carry out a Usability Evaluation and to obtain both qualitative and quantitative information on the usability level of the interfaces of an ATM application, and to be able to make comparisons and benchmarking. Likewise, one of the proposed artifacts is a questionnaire of relevant aspects in the ATM domain. This process has been validated by usability experts and ATM domain experts. Finally, further validations are expected by applying this proposal in real measurement cases.

Keywords: Usability · Automated teller machine · Usability evaluation · Banking systems · Human-computer interaction

1 Introduction

Nowadays, usability is an important factor for the success of any software product, including automated teller machines or ATMs [1]. Usability offers several benefits, those are: (1) Increased user productivity, (2) Decrease in user errors, (3) Decrease in software training costs, (4) Lesser design changes in early stages of the project and (5) Reduction of user support [2].

ATM system functionalities have been increasing over the years, however, this growth has not kept pace with the improvement of the interface that usually shows usability defects, which could cause a frustrating user experience [3]. The poor consideration of user needs on the design of ATM interfaces have produced some severe Usability and Accessibility issues, causing discomfort and operational errors.

This may be because, despite the existence of some principles and guides for web and mobile devices interfaces; there is few evidence about how to apply these principles and guidelines on the ATM domain [4].

© Springer Nature Switzerland AG 2021
M. M. Soares et al. (Eds.): HCII 2021, LNCS 12781, pp. 553–562, 2021.
https://doi.org/10.1007/978-3-030-78227-6_39

The importance of Usability and know if a software possesses this characteristic has led some Usability Evaluations for ATM interfaces. However, some of these Usability Evaluations were developed using adapted heuristics and guidelines due to the lack of standards and criteria for the ATM domain.

Having few guidelines and heuristics for ATM Usability Evaluation generate insufficient information about usability level of ATM applications and errors that may cause some problems to the users. Perform evaluations helps to know if the software fulfills the guidelines and heuristics that the evaluation method exposes, it also helps to find out the errors and problems on interfaces.

The main objective of this paper is to propose a Usability Evaluation Process for ATM interfaces, to provide information about Usability Evaluation methods that can be used for ATM, taking as a source of information interviews with ATM experts and studies found in various databases. A usability evaluation process that allows quantitative and qualitative data to be obtained allows for a more detailed understanding and a better vision of the product being evaluated, and allows sharing and benchmarking with other similar ATM software products.

This paper is organized as follows: Sect. 2 defines some important terms for this study, Sect. 3 shows the information used to define the process, Sect. 4 defines the evaluation process through the steps that must be followed to carry it out correctly, and, finally, Sect. 4 shows some conclusions and future works.

2 Background

This section describes the main concepts used in this research.

2.1 Self-service

Self-service is called to any activity that does not require interaction with human beings. This scenario is not necessarily an operation carried out only on the Internet, it can also be done through a telephone (for example: interactive voice response) or physically (for example: ATM). In addition, the searches made on websites such as Google or Wikipedia are also considered self-services, although, care must be taken with these as they could provide erroneous information [5].

2.2 Automated Teller Machine (ATM)

An ATM, also called Cash Dispenser or Automated Teller Machine, is an electronic computerized telecommunications device that allows clients of financial institutions to access their bank accounts securely. An ATM is a self-service banking terminal that accepts deposits, cash withdrawals or other functionalities. ATMs are commonly activated by inserting a card into the card reader slot. For example, when a customer is trying to withdraw cash, the ATM first connects the bank's system to verify the balance, then dispenses the cash and sends a completed transaction notice [6].

2.3 Usability Evaluation Method

A Usability Evaluation Method is a procedure composed of a set of well-defined activities to obtain data related to the interaction between the end-user and the software, and how the specific properties of this software contribute to its own usability. These methods were initially developed to evaluate the WIMP interfaces (Window, icon, menu, pointing device), which are the most representative of desktop applications. One of the most representative examples is the heuristic evaluation method, proposed by Nielsen. Usability evaluation methods can be broadly classified into two different types [7]:

- Empirical methods: They are based on capturing and analyzing the usage data of a real end user. Real end users use the software or a prototype to complete a set of predefined tasks, while the evaluator records the results of their work. Analyses of these results can provide useful information to detect usability problems.
- Inspection methods: They are carried out by expert evaluators or designers and are based on the review of the usability aspects of Web artifacts, which are commonly user interfaces according to their set of guidelines.

3 Research and Previous Studies

This section shows the information obtained during research and interviews with ATM experts. Through a questionnaire and a systematic review, information was obtained to define an evaluation process for ATMs.

3.1 ATM Relevant Aspects

A list of the most relevant aspects of ATM applications was obtained from and interview made to experts in the ATM domain. Experts were interviewed individually in a remote way by using a structured interview.

The information consolidated from those interviews constitutes the expert judgment about the following aspects:

- The importance of usability in ATMs,
- Deficiencies in their graphic interfaces,
- Relevant aspects on ATM applications, and
- How important they are.

Questions used in the interview were the following:

- Describe your experience working with ATMs.
- How would you describe your current job in relation to ATMs?
- How important is that ATMs are easy to use for users?
- Do you consider that the graphical interfaces of ATMs are usable?
- According to you, what are the deficiencies or points to improve in the ATM graphic interfaces?

- Do banks care that ATM graphic interfaces are attractive and user-friendly?
- What measures do banks take or should take to have usable graphical interfaces?
- What aspects of ATMs (security, speed, etc.) are the most important when making graphical interfaces?
- How do these aspects influence on the design of ATM graphic interfaces?

From the interviews with four experts in the ATM domain, an analysis of the results was carried out and the following list of relevant aspects of the ATM applications was obtained.

1. **Information Security and Protection:** The system must be safe and easy to use. It must avoid displaying sensitive information with large letters and prevent users located in the queue from viewing.
2. **Approved Screens (Design Consistency):** Make use of the same standard of screens (position of buttons, type of notices, etc.), both in tactile ATMs and those with buttons, to avoid confusion of users who use both types of ATM.
3. **Minimize User Memory Load:** Prevent the user from becoming saturated with a lot of information on the screens, reducing the time of this in front of an ATM. Have a shorter flow of screens. Give preference on the screen (place them first in the menu) the most used operations by the user.
4. **Simplicity and Speed:** Decrease the number of screens and make their use easier, reducing the time of use of the ATM.
5. **Feedback and Transaction Status:** Constantly provide the user with information about the transaction being carried out by the ATM.

3.2 Related Studies

From the usability evaluation studies reported in a Systematic Literature Review previously carried out [14], evaluations and tools used by each one to carry out the evaluation process were listed. Several features and tools were identified, so from these a comparative chart was made that allows you to observe the differences that exist. Usability Evaluation studies analyzed are the following:

- Skill Specific Spoken Dialogues Based Personalized ATM Design to Maximize Effective Interaction for Visually Impaired Persona [8]
- Token Access: Improving Accessibility of Automatic Teller Machine (ATMs) by Transferring the Interface and Interaction to Personal Accessible Devices [9]
- Usability Evaluation of Model-Driven Cross-Device Web User Interfaces [10]
- Usability Evaluation of Ticketing System of Metro Manila Train Network [11]
- User-centered design approach for interactive kiosks: Evaluation and redesign of an automatic teller machine [12]
- Improving comparisons of seven main functions for automated teller machine (ATM) banking service of five banks in Thailand [13]

Table 1. Comparative table of usability evaluation studies and tools.

Evaluation tools	Study					
	1	2	3	4	5	6
Questionnaires	N	N	Y	N	Y	Y
Video cameras/Screen Recorder Software	N	N	N	Y	Y	N
Event Logging Software	Y	N	N	N	N	Y
ATM's own system	N	N	Y	Y	Y	N
Prototypes/simulators	Y	Y	N	N	N	Y
Heuristic evaluation	N	Y	N	N	N	Y
User evaluation	Y	N	Y	Y	Y	Y

Table 1 shows a list of principal tools reported by usability evaluation studies founded in the systematic review (Y: The study used the evaluation tool, N: The study did not use the evaluation tool).

As the previous table shows, the tools that were be found were the following:

- Questionnaires
- Video cameras/Screen Recorder Software
- Event Logging Software
- ATM's own system
- Prototypes/simulators
- Heuristic evaluation
- User evaluation

From this, the most used tools were selected, these are:

- Questionnaire
- ATM's own system
- Prototypes/simulators
- Evaluation with users

Table 2 shows the rate of occurrence of each tool.

As we can see, there are two types of evaluations that depend on the tool to be used, either one focused on experts or users of the system evaluated, the choice of heuristic evaluation or user evaluation will depend on each study and its objective.

Besides, depending on the specific techniques, we can obtain quantitative or qualitative data.

Table 2. Frequency of use of the tools in the selected studies.

Evaluation tools	Times used	Percentage
Questionnaires	5	83.3%
Video cameras/Screen Recorder Software	3	50%
Event Logging Software	3	50%
ATM's own system	3	50%
Prototypes/simulators	2	33.33%
Heuristic evaluation	2	33.33%
User evaluation	2	33.33%

4   Usability Evaluation Process

This section details the proposed evaluation process, which consists of six main steps or stages, which are shown in Fig. 1, and are detailed as follows.

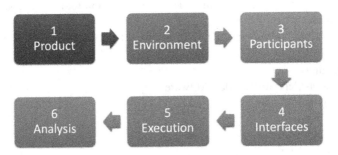

Fig. 1. Usability evaluation process with stages

4.1   Selection of ATM Systems to Evaluate

The first stage to be carried out is the selection of the ATM product (software or application) that will be the subject of evaluation for the study. At this point, it must be defined which banks will be part of the process and what characteristics they have in common to be evaluated and compared without problems.

It must be defined what will be evaluated of each system, that is, what features and screens will be evaluated.

4.2   Evaluation Environment

In this stage, we must define the place and date where the Usability Evaluation will be carried out. This will allow a safe environment for evaluations and will provide a closer experience that users are used to. We recommend that the environment try to be the closest thing to the real environment of using an ATM. Documents and artifacts must be identified and updated (if necessary): Surveys, Observation Guides, Questionnaires, Pre-test, Post-test, etc. Finally, we start with the checklist filling.

4.3 Selection of Participants

This stage defines the requirements that participants must have in order to be part of the evaluation. In addition, the reasons why a participant profile will have to be established must be defined.

Having a pre-defined participant profile will facilitate the search for these and will allow us to assign the systems that will be evaluated and the tasks the participants will perform.

Once the participants have been chosen, they will be notified of the place, the date and time where the evaluation will take place.

4.4 Prototypes/Interfaces from the ATM System

The next stage consists in selecting the tool that will represent the system to evaluate. In case the selected tool is the ATM proper system, the availability of it must be secured for the selected dates of the evaluation. If the selected tools are the use of prototypes, real screens of the system to be evaluated must be obtained and the software that will allow replicating these screens as close as possible to the real ones must be selected.

4.5 Execution

At this stage, the evaluation must be carried out. On the indicated day and time, each participant is invited. The experience in which they will participate is presented, at that time, the participant is explained what the study is about, and what he will face during the evaluation. All in a clear and concise manner, they are asked to complete the informed consent form, pre-test is applied, the usability evaluation is applied with an observation guide, and finally a post-test with relevant aspects of the ATM domain and a SUS questionnaire are applied. Figure 2 shows the steps corresponding to this stage of the evaluation.

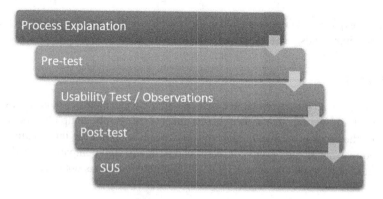

Fig. 2. Steps of the execution stage

A brief explanation of each step can be found below.

Process Explanation. Before the process properly starts, some important points should be explained to the participants:

- Purpose of the study
- Object of study
- Confidentiality agreement (if necessary)

Pre-test. A test is taken before the participant starts to use the interfaces prepared. This pre-test consists of a list of questions and options to know more about the participant. It also allows determining which banks the participant will test. A participant cannot test an ATM bank interface that he or she has already used.

Usability Test/Observations. While the participants are testing the interface prototypes, some notes will be taken about how the participant reacts while using the interface, as well as errors or problems that could take place during the process.

These observations will allow us to obtain specific errors that may arise during the testing of the interfaces by the participants and will support the identification of common errors.

Post-test. Once the test with the prototypes is completed, the participants will fill a post-test questionnaire, a set of questions about the relevant aspects previously mentioned, which were obtained from interviews with experts.

SUS Questionnaire. Finally, SUS questionnaire is carried out. It is explained to participants that this questionnaire is quantitative, exclusively for usability evaluation and can be applied to multiple systems.

Once the explanation is completed, participants continue to complete the questionnaire.
Once the questionnaire is completed, the evaluation process of the interface assigned to the participant ends.

4.6 Analysis

In this last stage, all the data obtained, both quantitative and qualitative, is processed and analyzed. It also verifies that a checklist has been successfully completed to ensure the quality of the process followed. After this last stage, and with the information already processed, we can already point out that it is possible to start comparisons and analysis of the quantitative type that complement the qualitative findings obtained.

5 Validation

For this proposal, we consider two type of validations: A first one, by experts on the ATM domain, and by experts in Usability. This first validation has been reached. The experts in the ATM domain were professionals working in the ATM development team of BBVA Peru. Usability experts were members of the HCI-DUXAIT research group of the Pontifical Catholic University of Peru. In both cases, the experts interviewed agreed with the present proposal.

As a second validation, we expect to apply this proposal on the interfaces of several ATM applications on Peru. This validation is still in process.

6 Conclusions and Future Works

Experts in Usability and experts in the ATM domain have validated this proposal. In that sense, the proposal is ready to use. We are currently applying the proposal in order to obtain the second validation.

On the importance of qualitative and quantitative information obtained from the application of various usability evaluation methods, we conclude that both are complementary and allow us to have a more comprehensive view of what is evaluated and of the problems encountered.

This method will allow usability evaluations that generate quantitative and qualitative data on interfaces of different ATM applications, and, in that sense, will allow classification, comparison and benchmarking between different applications.

One of the artefacts developed has been a questionnaire of relevant aspects of ATM, which is complemented very well with the SUS and which has been validated by the aforementioned experts.

A future work, for the second validation, we will carry out Usability Evaluations for users of different profiles using this method. Since our own questionnaire of relevant aspects of ATM is applied and SUS is applied, its results will be compared. Likewise, we plan to interview to the professionals who will apply this process to get their feedback about how they developed with the method compared to not using it.

Another future work seeks to explore this extension of the SUS to the ATM domain through this questionnaire generated as part of this research.

Acknowledgments. We want to thank the participants from BBVA Peru, especially its ATM team. Also, we thank the "HCI, Design, User Experience, Accessibility & Innovation Technologies (HCI DUXAIT)" for its support throughout the whole work. HCI-DUXAIT is a research group from the Pontificia Universidad Católica del Perú (PUCP).

References

1. Aguirre, J., Moquillaza, A., Paz, F.: Methodologies for the design of ATM interfaces: a systematic review. In: Advances in Intelligent Systems and Computing, pp. 256–262 (2019). https://doi.org/10.1007/978-3-030-02053-8_39

2. Bias, R.G., Mayhew, D.J.: Cost-Justifying Usability: An Update for an Internet Age. Elsevier, New York (2005). eBook ISBN: 9780080455457

3. Curran, K., King, D.: Investigating the human computer interaction problems with automated teller machine navigation menus. Interact. Technol. Smart Educ. (2008). https://doi.org/10.1108/17415650810871583

4. Moquillaza, A., et al.: Developing an ATM interface using user-centered design techniques. In: Marcus, A., Wang, W. (eds.) DUXU 2017. LNCS, vol. 10290, pp. 690–701. Springer, Cham (2017). https://doi.org/10.1007/978-3-319-58640-3_49

5. Rosenbaum, S.: Creating usable self-service interaction. In: 2010 IEEE International Professional Communication Conference (IPCC), pp. 344–349 (2010). https://doi.org/10.1109/IPCC.2010.5530033

6. Zhang, M., Wang, F., Deng, H., Yin, J.: A survey on human computer interaction technology for ATM. Int. J. Intell. Eng. Syst., 20–29 (2013). https://doi.org/10.22266/ijies2013.0331.03

7. Fernandez, A., Insfran, E., Abrahão, S.: Usability evaluation methods for the web: a systematic mapping study. Inf. Softw. Technol. (2011). https://doi.org/10.1016/j.infsof.2011.02.007

8. Shafiq, M., et al.: Skill specific spoken dialogues based personalized ATM design to maximize effective interaction for visually impaired persona. In: Marcus, A. (ed.) DUXU 2014. LNCS, vol. 8520, pp. 446–457. Springer, Cham (2014). https://doi.org/10.1007/978-3-319-07638-6_43

9. Zaim, E., Miesenberge, K.: Token access: improving accessibility of automatic teller machines (ATMs) by transferring the interface and interaction to personal accessible devices. In: LNCS (including subseries LNAI and LNB), pp. 335–342 (2018). https://doi.org/10.1007/978-3-319-94277-3_53

10. Yigitbas, E., Anjorin, A., Jovanovikj, I., Kern, T., Sauer, S., Engels, G.: Usability evaluation of model-driven cross-device web user interfaces. In: Bogdan, C., Kuusinen, K., Lárusdóttir, M.K., Palanque, P., Winckler, M. (eds.) HCSE 2018. LNCS, vol. 11262, pp. 231–247. Springer, Cham (2019). https://doi.org/10.1007/978-3-030-05909-5_14

11. Canicosa, T., Medina, J., Guzman, B., Custodio, B., Portus, A.: Usability evaluation of ticketing system of metro manila train network. In: Advances in Intelligent Systems and Computing, pp. 591–602 (2018). https://doi.org/10.1007/978-3-319-60492-3_56

12. Camilli, M., Dibitonto, M., Vona, A., Medaglia, C., Di Nocera, F.: User-centered design approach for interactive kiosks: Evaluation and redesign of an automatic teller machine. In: ACM International Conference Proceeding Series, pp. 85–91 (2011). https://doi.org/10.1145/2037296.2037319

13. Taohai, K., Phimoltares, S., Cooharojananone, N.: Usability comparisons of seven main functions for automated teller machine (ATM) banking service of five banks in Thailand. In: Proceedings - 2010 10th International Conference on Computational Science and Its Applications, ICCSA 2010 (2010). https://doi.org/10.1109/ICCSA.2010.5

14. Sahua, J., Moquillaza, A.: A systematic review of usability evaluation methods and tools for ATM interfaces. In: Marcus, A., Rosenzweig, E. (eds.) HCII 2020. LNCS, vol. 12202, pp. 130–141. Springer, Cham (2020). https://doi.org/10.1007/978-3-030-49757-6_9

Usability Study of a Public Culture Website for Improvement: A Case of Guangzhou Museum of Art

Cihui Wu and Zhen Liu[(✉)]

School of Design, South China University of Technology, Guangzhou
510006, People's Republic of China
liuzjames@scut.edu.cn

Abstract. Museum websites usually possess a large number of high-quality content and their information is relatively objective and authoritative. So these websites are often used by researchers, visitors and other external users. The usability of museum website has a great impact on user's experience, which determines whether users can quickly obtain information and services in the easiest way especially for public culture site such as museum, which few have been done. In this paper, Guangzhou Museum of Art is selected as the experimental object of usability evaluation museum website. Through the methods of observation, discussion, thinking aloud protocol, questionnaire and mouse tracking, the usability of the website is evaluated by 10 university researchers in terms of efficiency, effectiveness and satisfaction. The results show that there are some problems in the usability of the website, such as content service form, overall structure, navigation design and so on. The lack of attention to user habits causes users' cognitive pressure. Suggestions are provided in the study to enhance the usability of these websites.

Keywords: Usability testing · Museum website · Mouse tracking · Usability improvement · Usability scale

1 Introduction

Museums are ideal web content providers because they usually have a large amount of high-quality content, owning the intellectual property rights of these content, and their information is relatively objective and authoritative [1]. Therefore, more and more people tend to search for information on museum websites. However, many museum developers treat web development as a visual design and creative issue rather than an application development issue [2]. Many developers are not aware of the real problems and challenges involved in major web development, and fail to recognize their main key visitors, leading to an unprincipled development process and ignoring the needs of visitors [3]. The sites have not been evaluated to find out whether they match the users' needs and wishes. However, more and more researchers are conducting museum

© Springer Nature Switzerland AG 2021
M. M. Soares et al. (Eds.): HCII 2021, LNCS 12781, pp. 563–583, 2021.
https://doi.org/10.1007/978-3-030-78227-6_40

usability research, focusing on what users expect to find on the website and the experience of accessing this information [4].

Usability evaluation is crucial to determine whether a website can successfully meet the needs of its users. Usability refers to the degree to which a system, product or service can be effectively, efficiently and satisfactorily achieved by a specific user in a specific environment [5]. Usability indicators commonly used by people are shown in Table 1.

Table 1. Usability analysis index.

Usability standard	Index	Define
International standard ISO9214	Efficiency	The degree of correctness and completeness of users when they complete a specific task and achieve a specific goal
	Effectiveness	The ratio between the accuracy and completeness of tasks completed by users and the resources (such as time) used
	Satisfaction	The subjective satisfaction and acceptance of users in the process of using products
Nielsen (1994)	Learn-ability	The system should be easy to learn, so that users can start to do something with the system in a short time
	Memorability	The system should be easy to remember, so that those users who use the system frequently can use the system after they haven't used it for a period of time, instead of learning everything from scratch
	Efficiency	The use of the system should be efficient, so when users learn to use the system, they may have a high level of productivity
	Errors	The system should have a low error rate, so that users can make fewer errors in the process of using the system and recover quickly after errors
	Satisfaction	The system should be pleasant to use, so that users feel satisfied subjectively and like to use the system

In order to study and improve the usability of the museum website, this paper selects Guangzhou Art Museum as the experimental website for usability research. This paper combines traditional usability testing with usability questionnaires, mouse tracking and other research methods to explore the problems of users in the usability testing process, collecting and evaluating the user's operation target data, and finally propose methods to solve the problems.

2 Method

2.1 Research Framework

The research framework of this paper is shown in Fig. 1, which is divided into five parts.

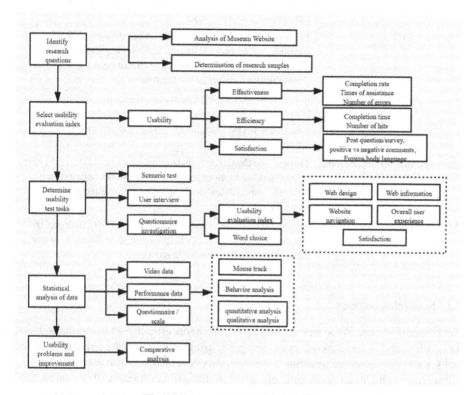

Fig. 1. Research framework flow chart.

2.2 Research Method

The usability research methods adopted in this paper are shown in Table 2:

There are three parts of testing: scenario test, user interview and questionnaire filling. In this study, ten subjects were tested in three scenarios. Throughout the test, subjects were encouraged to "think aloud", the usability test recorded the whole process by using screen recording software Debut. After the test, SPSS 24 and excel were used for quantitative analysis of the data, and mouse tracking, behavior analysis and other methods were used for quantitative analysis. The results of the analysis will put forward the improvement direction for the website.

Table 2. Research method.

Methods	Content
Scenario test	The task test based on scene and role enables users to complete tasks according to the requirements of different roles in the scene environment, instead of completing task instructions mechanically
Think-aloud	Thinking aloud is a way for the subjects to operate while speaking. In the process of testing, users are allowed to express their ideas while operating. It can be used to analyze the usability of scripts in the later stage
User interview	In the early, middle and late stages of usability testing, interview users with questions set in advance, and then understand users' thoughts and experience deeply after users' answers
Questionnaire survey method	Through the design and distribution of a unified questionnaire, researchers learn about the situation from the respondents. After the scenario test, users need to select adjectives and score the scale
Mouse tracking	The trajectory of the mouse can indicate how to interpret the information. Mouse tracks help us to collect data sets of users and analyze their cognitive behaviors

2.3 Scenarios Settings

According to the use of the website in real life, three scenarios are set to test the website, and each scenario has several tasks. The participants are all college students, and the test scenario is set as the academic research process. Three scenarios are presented as a time flow, which can approximately simulate the growth process of website users' proficiency. These scenarios was determined after a pre-test, consisted of 8 tasks that represented potential usability problems.

Scenario 1. As a researcher in the school of design of South China University of technology, who have a course on Chinese calligraphy and painting works in the past dynasties recently. He wants to go to Guangzhou Art Museum to learn about the relevant content. He need to know the opening information and the latest exhibition of Guangzhou Art Museum, and hope that someone can provide explanation service during the visit.

The first scenario task is the operation that university researchers need to find some information through the museum website in the early stage of academic research. The tasks of Scenario 1 are shown in Table 3.

Table 3. Tasks of scenario 1.

Task	Content	Task type
1-1	Find Museum opening hours and transportation information	Free browsing
1-2	Find out the latest exhibition information about calligraphy and painting in the museum	Exploratory search
1-3	Book a guide service in advance	Targeted search

Scenario 2. A student from the school of design, South China University of technology, through his understanding of Chinese painting and calligraphy, now needs to conduct academic research on the local Lingnan Painting School in Guangdong. He wants to know about the painters of Lingnan Painting School through the website, such as Gao Jianfu (painter of Guangdong Modern Lingnan Painting School), and obtain some relevant research materials. In addition, he need to interview museum experts (such as pan he).

Scenario 2 is set for researchers who need to use the website to find academic research materials. These tasks can find the main problems of the website and make the evaluation more practical. The tasks of Scenario 2 are shown in Table 4.

Table 4. Tasks of scenario 2.

Task	Content	Task type
2-1	Learn about works and information of Gao Jianfu	Exploratory search
2-2	Find relevant academic materials of Lingnan art school, such as articles and lectures on Lingnan regional art research	Targeted search
2-3	Find the contact information of Pan he, the art consultant	Targeted search

Scenario 3. A graduate student of design in South China University of technology is eager to leave some memories in Guangzhou and wonder if there are any handicrafts activities in the museum. And because he has done research on painting and calligraphy before, he is very interested in painting and calligraphy, so he want to find a job in the museum (Table 5).

Table 5. Tasks of scenario 3.

Task	Content	Task type
3-1	Find the museum's latest handicrafts activities, such as traditional Chinese painting experience	Free browsing
3-2	Learn about Museum job recruitment information	Exploratory search

2.4 Participant Sample Description

According to the Nielsen Curve [6], 9 to 12 test users can reflect 90% of the usability problems, so 10 University researchers are selected to do the test. The participants were ten postgraduates from School of Design, South China University of Technology. Six of the participants were male and four were female, with an average age of 22 years.

All subjects have not used the website of Guangzhou Museum of Art before the test. The statistical information of subjects is shown in Table 6.

Table 6. Statistical information of subjects.

Statistical attributes	Frequency	Percentage
Gender		
Male	4	40%
Female	6	60%
Major		
Industrial Design Engineering	6	60%
Information interaction design	1	10%
Science of Design	3	30%
Educational background		
Undergraduate	2	20%
Postgraduate	8	80%
Have you ever used the museum website		
Yes	8	80%
No	2	20%

3 Result

3.1 Performance Results

The data of the Scenario-task test is shown in Tables 7, 8 and 9.

Completion rate, times of assistance, number of errors reflect the effectiveness of users using the website, while completion time, number of hits reflect the overall efficiency of users. In order to get the overall performance, the participants' task completion time, the number of errors, and the number of assistance times in each task are accumulated and averaged. With the development of scenario testing, users go from the initial understanding stage to the stage of searching for academic materials. As the tasks progress, it also makes users encounter more difficulties. Among the tasks 1-1, 1-2, and 3-1 (Figs. 2, 3 and 4), the number of users who complete these tasks at one time is the most, and the important information contents such as museum opening hours, exhibitions and activities are well designed; Users need to try multiple times when completing

Table 7. The completing time of the tasks in scenario 1.

User	Total time/s	Task 1-1			Task 1-2			Task 1-3		
		Time/s	Error	Assist	Time/s	Error	Assist	Time/s	Error	Assist
1	353	55	0	0	18	0	0	280	8	0
2	207	95	3	0	14	0	0	90 + 8	4	1
3	132	16	0	0	13	0	0	103	8	0
4	330	33	0	0	18	0	0	279	14	0
5	175	49	1	0	34	0	0	80 + 12	5	1
6	118	28	0	0	27	1	0	63	3	0
7	196	26	0	0	58+51	5	1	35 + 26	2	1
8	124	17	0	0	23	0	0	62 + 22	2	1
9	236	52	0	0	22	1	0	144 + 18	8	1
10	143	18	1	0	15	0	0	87+23	7	1
Total	2014	389	5	0	293	7	1	1332	61	6
Average	201.4	38.9	0.5	0	29.3	0.7	0.1	133.2	6.1	0.6

The number added in the table means: the number before the plus sign represents the time to test before asking for assistance, and the number after the plus sign represents the time to find the expected task result after the prompt.

Table 8. The completing time of the tasks in scenario 2.

User	Total time/s	Task 2-1			Task 2-2			Task 2-3		
		Time/s	Error	Assist	Time/s	Error	Assist	Time/s	Error	Assist
1	326	38	0	0	189 + 5	4	1	94	3	0
2	314	103 + 18	3	1	98 + 65 + 5	2	2	21	0	0
3	374	55	2	0	157 + 35	4	1	118 + 9	7	1
4	207	37	2	0	155	6	0	15	0	0
5	422	98 + 7	4	1	199 + 22	5	1	96	6	0
6	326	48	1	0	88 + 41	5	1	98 + 51	6	1
7	213	46 + 20	3	1	54	5	0	86 + 7	5	1
8	235	50	2	0	73 + 37	3	1	61 + 14	2	1
9	219	79	0	0	113+11	8	1	16	0	0
10	266	34	0	0	63	1	0	134 + 35	9	1
Total	2902	637	17	3	1410	43	8	855	38	5
Average	290.2	63.7	1.7	0.3	141	4.3	0.8	85.5	3.8	0.5

Table 9. The completing time of the tasks in scenario 3.

User	Total time/s	Task3-1			Task3-2		
		Time/s	Error	Assist	Time/s	Error	Assist
1	116	21	0	0	95	2	0
2	104	69	1	0	35	1	0
3	92	30	0	0	55+7	1	1
4	80	43	0	0	37	1	0
5	96	13	1	0	83	3	0
6	122	37	0	0	85	3	0
7	63	19	0	0	44	2	0
8	87	14	0	0	54+19	3	1
9	100	26	0	0	74	4	0
10	135	16	1	0	119	3	0
Total	995	288	3	0	707	23	2
Average	99.5	28.8	0.3	0	70.7	2.3	0.2

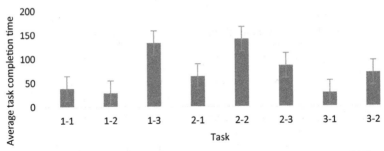

Fig. 2. Average completion time of different tasks (The error bars represent a 90% confidence interval).

task 3-2, because there is a big problem with the placement of the information module in the museum, which does not match the user's cognition, making users continue to search on the website; Tasks 1-3 and 2-2 have the most assistance, which indicates that it is difficult for users to find these information without external guidance, and the content location structure and hierarchical relationship need to be improved.

3.2 Satisfaction Results

From the Fig. 5, it can be seen that the task satisfaction score is negatively correlated with the task completion time. The longer the task completion time is, the lower the task satisfaction score is. The satisfaction of task 1-1 and task 1-2 is high, which indicates that the important information presentation of museum website is very important to

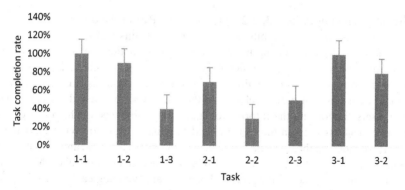

Fig. 3. Different task completion rates (the error bars represent a 90% confidence interval).

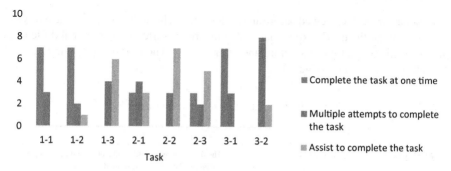

Fig. 4. Completion of each task.

user experience. It is very necessary that the important information presented in the home page can greatly improve user satisfaction. Task 2-1, 3-1 satisfaction is also high, mainly because the user's familiarity with the website is gradually increasing, which can quickly guide users into the correct page. At the same time, the logic and layout of the exhibition activity page is relatively clear, so that users can quickly complete the task. The satisfaction of these tasks mainly comes from their fluency.

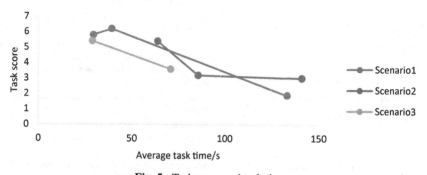

Fig. 5. Task score and task time.

The satisfaction of tasks 1-3, 2-2 and 2-3 is low. Part of the original reason is that some participants' browsing habits are not reflected in this website, and the website does not do a good job in sorting information, the information are scattered. Another important problem is the logic and hierarchy of the website, which leads users to get a variety of different results through different paths, making users easily confused and not clear about their position in the website. At the same time, because there is no search function, users cannot find the information and content they need, which causes users to look like headless flies on the website, and eventually leads to giving up using the website. If we redesign the museum website, we can refer to the logic and layout of other large museums, such as the Guangdong Provincial Museum and the Palace Museum, in order to meet the user's cognitive level and behavioral psychological habits.

3.3 User Interview Results

Ten students were interviewed before and after the test. The main purpose of the interview is to understand the user's experience and compare the different operational difficulties and problems found by users before and after the test. The following are the results of this interview shown in Table 10.

Table 10. User interview response and analysis.

Question	Analysis
1. What's your first impression of the website?	The design of the website looks old-fashioned, simple and unsightly, 70% of people think that the design style is consistent with the main content of the website
	The size of the web page is not responsive and adaptive to the computer screen
2. Do you use other similar websites?	Many people rarely use similar website, this led to the neglect of the management of the website by museum managers, which makes the website very difficult to use
3. What did you do when you last used?	Check the exhibition information, exhibition location and time. Such information should be clearly displayed on the homepage of the website
4. Will you use these websites to assist in academic research?	90% of users willing to use the museum website to assist academic research. Museums usually have higher quality and authoritative materials
	Directly use document retrieval websites such as WOS and Google Scholar
5. What are the best aspects of the site?	40% of users think the layout design and visual style of this website are unified. The unified design style gives users a more comfortable visual experience, reducing users' cognitive pressure
6. What are the worst aspects of the site?	There are serious navigation problems, the classification is not clear
	The division of information structure and the level is too complicated. The complex information structure of the website will cause users to abandon use
7. What do you want to change on the site	Add search bar60% of people think that search bar can improve the usability of this website

Through the interview results, we can analyze points that should be paid attention to in website design as follows: 1. Correct navigation and classification can better guide users. 2. The content of the website needs to be more professional and time-efficient, and meet the needs of the core users of the website. 3. The search function is very important and can improve the efficiency of the website. 4. When designing, the visual design of the webpage should be consistent. 5. The title and buttons should be simpler and clearer. 6. General introduction and important information should be placed on the homepage. It can be seen that high-quality content will attract users to use the website, but poor website usability makes users give up using it.

3.4 Questionnaire Analysis

Word Choice. As shown in Fig. 6, 7, from the statistical analysis of the questionnaire, it can be seen that 'useful', 'straightforward', 'reliable' and 'clean' are the most people chose to represent this museum website, while most people chose negative words such as "old", "time consuming" and "illogical" to describe this museum website. Even though the website information is more direct and reliable, it is obvious that the website content has not been updated for a long time, and the design style is old. There are many problems in the information structure, which makes it very difficult to use.

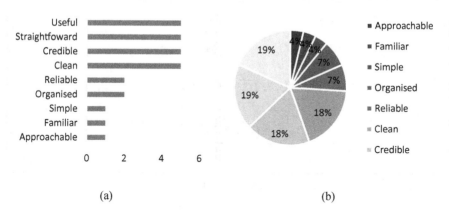

(a)   (b)

Fig. 6. Statistics of positive adjective selected by testers in word choice.

Usability Scale. While fully learning from the evaluation indicators of usability proposed in the existing research, combined with the characteristics of the museum website, this paper constructs the usability evaluation index system, and carries out the scoring after the users complete the scene task test.

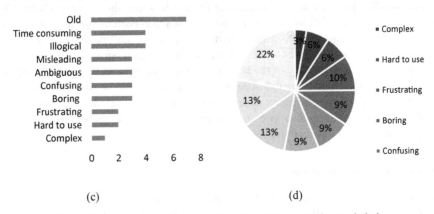

(c)   (d)

Fig. 7. Statistics of negative adjective selected by testers in word choice.

The whole evaluation system includes five dimensions, each dimension contains m evaluation indexes. For each index, users will be given a 1–7 grade score according to their satisfaction. In each dimension, the contribution weight of an indicator to user satisfaction can be calculated, which is recorded as the importance coefficient I. The calculation formula is as follows:

$$I = \frac{\overline{M_r}}{\sum_{i=1}^{m} \overline{M_i}} \tag{1}$$

$$U_r = (\overline{C_r} - 1) \times I \times 7 \tag{2}$$

$$D_i = \sum_{i=1}^{m} U_r \tag{3}$$

$$S = \sum_{i=1}^{5} D_i \tag{4}$$

In formula (1)–(4): r: Index serial number of a dimension, r = 1, 2, ..., m; m: The number of indicators of a dimension; i: Dimension number, i = 1, 2, 3, 4, 5; $\overline{C_r}$:Average score of index r; Ir: Importance coefficient of index r, r = 1, 2, ..., m; Ur: Usability evaluation value of index r; Di: Usability evaluation value of dimension i; S: The overall usability evaluation value of the existing museum website.

Add the usability evaluation value of each dimension, that is, the overall usability evaluation value of all users to the existing website. The value can be changed from 0 to 210. Setting 0–42 points indicates that the usability evaluation of the website is very poor, 43–84 points indicates poor, 85–126 points indicates average, 127–168 points indicates good, and 169–210 points indicates that the user's evaluation is excellent.

Table 11. Usability scale calculation.

Evaluating indicator	Average	Importance coefficient	Usability evaluation value (Ur/Dr/S)
Website design (dimension1)	5		28.294(D1)
The site image is clear and loading speed is appropriate	5.5	0.18	5.78
The website structure is simple, the content layout is reasonable	4.4	0.15	3.49
All pages on the site have the same style	5	0.17	4.67
The text on the site is appropriate and legible	4.4	0.15	3.49
Not too much interference	5.2	0.17	5.10
The links in the page are valid and uncorrupted	5.5	0.18	5.78
Website information (dimension2)	4		24.79(D2)
The information provided is valuable and is what the user needs	5.1	0.21	6.10
The information provided is clear and correct	5.2	0.22	6.37
The information provided is up to date and updated frequently	3.3	0.14	2.21
The information provided is abundant	3.8	0.16	3.10
Provides effective retrieval capabilities	1.2	0.05	0.07
Provide contact information for the museum	5.4	0.23	6.93
Website navigation (dimension3)	4.52		25.41(D3)
The navigation position is obvious	4.6	0.20	5.13

(*continued*)

Table 11. (*continued*)

Evaluating indicator	Average	Importance coefficient	Usability evaluation value (Ur/Dr/S)
Navigation tabs are clear and consistent with the content	3.9	0.17	3.50
Navigation menu classification clear, reasonable level	3.7	0.16	3.09
Home page logo is obvious, you can return to the home page at any time	5.7	0.25	8.30
Can be executed backwards or forwards at any time	4.7	0.21	5.39
Overall user experience (dimension4)	4.45		24.48(D4)
Language description is accurate, in line with the user's understanding and habits	3.9	0.22	4.45
Users know where they are on the site	4.1	0.23	5.00
The site responds quickly to user actions	4.9	0.28	7.52
Easy to use and easy to learn	4.9	0.28	7.52
User satisfaction (dimension5)			D5
Rate your overall satisfaction with the usability of your site	3.95	1.00	20.65
Total	4.384		123.62(S)

As shown in Table 11, the final result is: the overall usability evaluation value s of Guangzhou Art Museum is 123.62. The value is between 85 and 126, which means that the user's rating of the museum website is average. It can be seen that users have a low evaluation of the information content and navigation design of the Guangzhou Art Museum website, and believe that the information content provided by the website is old and infrequently updated, and there are also big problems with the navigation label content and classification.

3.5 Mouse Tracking

Eye tracking can closely monitor and observe the user's behavior. It helps to quantify which parts of a web page are read, viewed, or skipped/ignored. But eye tracking also has its disadvantages, calibration operation is more complex, and the equipment will make the test unable to be in a relaxed normal state, which is usually time-consuming, expensive and not easy to obtain.

Studies have shown that Internet users move their mouse according to their focus of attention. Most people use the mouse pointer as a reading aid when browsing web pages [7]. Existing studies have explored mouse trajectory as an alternative method for user behavioral cognitive research. For example, the movement track of the mouse can indicate how to interpret the information. When the user moves the mouse, the track of the mouse movement will show a state of mind [8]. The advantage of mouse tracking is that it is transparent and common to the user, so it does not introduce the psychological bias of the experimenter to cause the user to do the test differently from usual. This study uses mouse tracking to assist usability test analysis and improvement.

Fig. 8. Mouse tracking.

The blue circle represents the sliding track of the mouse on the page. The larger the circle is, the longer it stays, indicating that the user is reading and viewing information at this time. As you can see, users tend to browse the navigation bar first, rather than other content parts of the web page, as shown in Fig. 8. The results show that good navigation bar button settings can effectively improve the efficiency of web pages. When users stay on the navigation bar for a long time, the key content can be listed on the navigation bar as the title, because longer stay means more consideration and more attention (Table 12).

According to the track record of the mouse, we can see that the main stop is in the navigation and the left module of the page. This is because when users search for information, they mainly filter through the header field of the information line, which is the area on the left side of the module. The mouse slide path is scattered, searching almost all parts of the navigation bar. It shows that the content classification of the navigation bar is not appropriate, the navigation bar words are too small to adapt to the screen.

3.6 Concept for Improvement

After testing and result analysis, the statistics of usability problems are as follows (Table 12):

Table 12. Usability problems.

No.	Problem description	Proportion	Usability problem
1	The page size of the website is too small, and the page will not adapt to different device sizes	60%	Interface design and layout
2	Museum services are too hard to find	70%	Functional rationality
3	Disordered information classification, unreasonable arrangement of some information points	80%	User perception
4	Lack of retrieval function	100%	Element/control design
5	The navigation position is not obvious	30%	Functional rationality
6	The classification of navigation tags is not clear, the tags are inconsistent with the content, and even there are problems with the definition of navigation words.	70%	User perception
7	There are problems in the division of information structure, and the level is too complex	20%	User perception
8	Users don't know where they are on the site	30%	User perception
9	The display content of the activity page is incomplete, and the page content design is not standardized	60%	Interface design and layout

The problems to be solved are listed in Table 13.
The newly added functional modules are shown in the Table 14.

3.7 Redesign of the Website

From the above analysis, according to the usability of the website test to improve the design. The redesigned web pages are shown as below, which partially solve the problems (Fig. 9).

Table 13. Improvement directions.

No.	Improvement directions
1	Different operations can achieve the same result,multiple entries and routes should be directed to the same result page
2	Increased the area of the navigation bar and changed it to horizontal version
3	Navigation content is classified according to people's cognitive habits, make more obvious clues about classification
4	Make good use of labels for navigation to prompt the contents and improve their usability of searching
5	Adjust web fonts and size to fit people's viewing
6	Simplify the website information structure, reasonable layout of website content
7	For university researchers, the provision of information should be more professional and the data division should be more precise
8	Standardized and standardized website information content design
9	After clicking to navigate each module, delete the banner part

Table 14. New features.

No.	New features
1	Increased the area of the navigation bar and changed it to horizontal version
2	Add a new service module in the navigation
3	The home navigation bar is fixed when scrolling
4	New search function
5	The content of the activity is redesigned, so users don't need to click inside the information bar to know the general content
6	Make the banner smaller and delete the unimportant information
7	Add a brief introduction to the museum, visit routes to the exhibition hall, consultation, activity booking, explanation services, etc

Adding search module and adjusting web fonts and web size to fit people's viewing. In terms of navigation, the area of the navigation bar has been increased and changed to a horizontal version. The navigation classification has also been redesigned, and information is sorted according to human perception. In addition, the redesign simplifies the information structure of the website and rationally lays out the content of the website, also simplify the information displayed on the web page.

To make it easier for users to find service modules on the website, adding activity booking, explanation service, online consultation and other modules on the museum website home page.

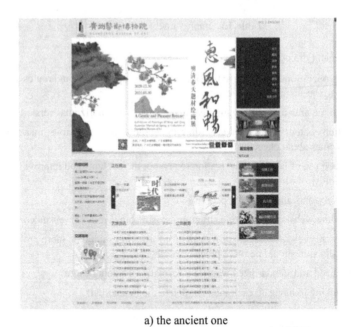

a) the ancient one

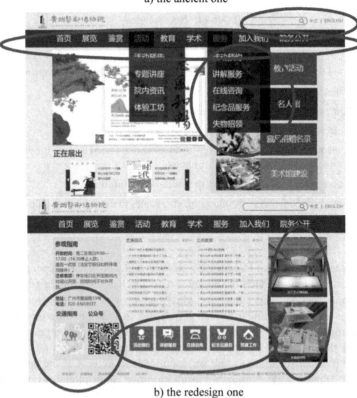

b) the redesign one

Fig. 9. The redesign of Guangzhou Art Museum website.

3.8 Comparative Anaylsis

Aiming at several serious problems, we improve the usability of the website, and test the usability of the improved website again, repeating the steps of the first experiment, collecting data again and analyzing the results.

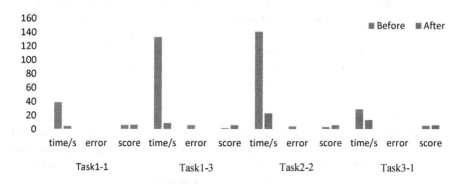

Fig. 10. Comparison of before and after

The data obtained after the test were compared and analyzed by t-test, as shown in Fig. 10, after the improvement, the completion time of the four tasks is reduced by 34.4 s, 124.9 s, 117.8 s and 15.4 s respectively. After importing the task completion time data before and after the improvement into SPSS for paired sample t-test, it is found that the sig value of the first three tasks is less than 0.01, and the sig value of the fourth task is less than 0.05, which proves that the improvement result is very significant and the task completion time is greatly reduced. In terms of task error frequency, the first two tasks almost have no error frequency, while the latter two tasks have less than one error frequency. After importing the task completion time data before and after the improvement into SPSS for paired sample t-test (Table 15), it is found that the sig value of the first three tasks is less than 0.01.

Table 15. Paired sample t test of completion time before and after four tasks

T test		t	df	Sig. (2-tailed)
Pair 1	Time before improvement (Task1-1) - Time after improvement (Task1-1)	4.383	9	.002
Pair 2	Time before improvement (Task1-3) - Time after improvement (Task1-3)	4.824	9	.001
Pair 3	Time before improvement (Task2-2) - Time after improvement (Task2-2)	6.826	9	.000
Pair 4	Time before improvement (Task3-1) - Time after improvement (Task3-1)	2.888	9	.018

4   Discussion and Conclusion

As a module for providing online content services for museums, the museum website needs to allow visitors to quickly and accurately understand various information about the museum. This research takes university staff as the research object and uses the website of Guangzhou Museum of art as an example to conduct usability testing. From the analysis results of the test, it can be seen that the tester takes a long time to complete the set task, the error rate is high, and the satisfaction is generally low. This shows that improving the usability of the museum website is of great significance.

According to the observation and results analysis of the testing process, several opinions and conclusions are obtained as follows:

1. Focus on core users, provide corresponding services and reduce user pressure: For museum websites, important information should be prominently displayed, and can quickly and accurately allow users to find the information they need. The path of website information structure, efficient navigation and content layout need to be more professional, easy to use, and improve use efficiency.
2. Pay attention to user cognition and habits: For the same type of websites, users' past experience and knowledge enable them to have their own usage and reading habits. The website should be adjusted according to user habits. Pay attention to the user's "obvious habit." These can greatly improve the usability of the website.
3. Uniform and beautiful design: When designing a webpage, a uniform and beautiful image can improve the authority and professionalism of the website. A well-designed web page can improve the impression of the museum, pleased the user's mood, and enhance user's experience. Website developers should do a good job in the visual design of the website on the basis of ensuring usability.

This study has the following shortcomings: the characteristics of the participant sample are relatively single, and the test website only selects the website of Guangzhou Art Museum, which is less representative. There is a certain difference between the improved prototype and the real web page during testing. In the future research will continue to improve the test.

However, this article summarizes the various problems in the use of the website by museum users by combining traditional usability testing methods, usability scale calculations and mouse tracking testing methods. According to the comparative analysis, the improved prototype is obviously better to use than the original website. It provides guidelines for the usability improvement of the museum and has certain value. This article also proposes a variety of methods for usability testing.

Acknowledgements. The authors wish to thank all the people who provided their time and efforts for the investigation. The author, Cihui Wu, is also officially known as TZU-HUI WU as her name. This research is supported by "South China University of Technology Central University Basic Scientific Research Operating Expenses Subsidy, project approval no. XYZD201928, (x2sjC2191370)".

References

1. Cunliffe, D., Kritou, E., Tudhope, D.: Usability evaluation for museum web sites. Mus. Manage. Curatorsh. **19**(3), 229–252 (2001)
2. Murugesan, S., Deshpande, Y., Hansen, S., Ginige, A.: Web engineering: a new discipline for development of Web-based systems, pp. 3–13 (2001)
3. Hertzum, M.: A review of museum Web sites: in search of user-centred design. Arch. Mus. Informat. **12**(2), 127–138 (1998)
4. Hale, L.A., Smith, C., Mulligan, H., Treharne, G.J.: "Tell me what you want, what you really really want....": asking people with multiple sclerosis about enhancing their participation in physical activity. Disabil. Rehabil. **34**(22), 1887–1893 (2012)
5. Hu, F.: The studies of eye tracking and usability test. p. 5 (2006)
6. Nielsen, J.: Usability Engineering. Elsevier, New York (1994)
7. Arroyo, E., Selker, T., Wei, W.: Usability tool for analysis of web designs using mouse tracks. In: CHI 2006 Extended Abstracts on Human Factors in Computing Systems, Association for Computing Machinery, Montréal, Québec, Canada, pp. 484–489 (2006)
8. Hong, J.I., Heer, J., Waterson, S., Landay, J.A.: WebQuilt: a proxy-based approach to remote web usability testing. ACM Trans. Inf. Syst. **19**(3), 263–285 (2001)

Author Index

Printed in the United States
by Baker & Taylor Publisher Services